Company Law

THIRD EDITION

by

THE HON MR JUSTICE RONAN KEANE
CHIEF JUSTICE OF IRELAND

Members of the LexisNexis Group worldwide:

Ireland	Lexis Nexis, DUBLIN
Argentina	LexisNexis Argentina, BUENOS AIRES
Australia	LexisNexis Butterworths, CHATSWOOD, New South Wales
Austria	LexisNexis Verlag ARD Orac GmbH & Co KG, VIENNA
Canada	LexisNexis Butterworths, MARKHAM, Ontario
Chile	LexisNexis Chile Ltda, SANTIAGO DE CHILE
Czech Republic	Nakladatelství Orac sro, PRAGUE
France	Editions du Juris-Classeur SA, PARIS
Germany	LexisNexis, Deutschland GmbH, FRANKFURT, MUNSTER
Hong Kong	LexisNexis Butterworths, HONG KONG
Hungary	HVG-Orac, BUDAPEST
India	LexisNexis Butterworths, NEW DELHI
Italy	Giuffrè Editore, MILAN
Malaysia	Malayan Law Journal Sdn Bhd, KUALA LUMPUR
New Zealand	LexisNexis Butterworths, WELLINGTON
Poland	Wydawnictwo Prawnicze LexisNexis, WARSAW
Singapore	LexisNexis Butterworths, SINGAPORE
South Africa	LexisNexis Butterworths, DURBAN
Switzerland	Stämpfli Verlag AG, BERNE
United Kingdom	LexisNexis UK, a Division of Reed Elsevier (UK) Ltd, Halsbury House, 35 Chancery Lane, LONDON, WC2A 1EL, and 4 Hill Street, EDINBURGH EH2 3JZ
USA	LexisNexis, DAYTON, Ohio

© Ronan Keane 2000

First edition printed 1985
Second edition printed 1991
Third edition 2000
First reprint 2001
Second reprint 2003
ISBN 1 85475 8756

Typeset by Marlex Editorial Services Ltd, Dublin
Printed and bound in Great Britain by Antony Rowe, Chippenham, Wiltshire
Visit us at our website: http//www.lexisnexis.ie

Preface

There have been many significant developments in the area of Irish company law since the publication of the second edition in 1991, some of them, as it happens, in comparatively recent times. The Companies (Amendment) (No 2) Act 1999 has effected major changes to the institution of the examiner and has introduced new and stringent requirements to ensure compliance by companies with their obligations as to the filing of returns. It also freed some small businesses from the obligation to have their accounts audited. In addition, concern that Ireland is being used as a convenient base by enterprises of dubious legality operating in other countries led to provisions in the same Act requiring companies registered in this jurisdiction to have at least one resident director and to be carrying on an activity in this country. With a view to ensuring that the new controls are not circumvented by the appointment of nominal Irish directors to the boards of such companies, there is an interesting new prohibition on a person being a director of more than 25 companies. It remains to be seen to what extent the elaborate exemptions allowed for directors in the financial sector dilute its efficacy.

There have also been important changes in other areas, such as the complex regulations concerning group accounts emanating from the European Union, which are certainly not for the faint hearted. The torrent of case law in Ireland continues undiminished, with important developments in such areas as investigations by inspectors appointed by the Minister of the High Court, the constitutional and legal dimensions of fraudulent and reckless trading and the seemingly never-ending ramifications of *Salomon v Salomon* [1897] AC 22, particularly reflected in the much discussed Supreme Court decision in *Re Frederick Inns* [1994] ILRM 387.

I am grateful to Mr John Donnelly FCA, Ms Roseanne Kelly ACA, Mr Daniel O'Keeffe SC and Mr Pat McCourt of the Companies Registration Office for their assistance and to Dr Nuala Corcoran, Barrister-at-Law, for helpful research which she carried out. I am also grateful to the staffs of the Judges' Library in the Four Courts, the Bar library, King's Inns Library and Lincoln's Inn Library for their courtesy at all times. I am also grateful to my publishers, in particular Louise Leavy, for their patience and consideration.

Since the publication of this edition brings to an end my career as an author of text books on the law, I would like to take the opportunity of thanking all those who helped me from the beginning. Judge John Buckley and Mr Michael O'Mahony as members of the publications committee of the Law Society gave me invaluable encouragement when I first embarked on that career and I also gratefully recall the support and friendship over the years of David Millett, Finola O'Sullivan and Gerard Coakley of Butterworths. When another old friend, Mr Gerard O'Keefe, solicitor, of Kanturk, Co Cork, enthusiastically urged me to produce a book on local government for the benefit of the legal profession, the number of Irish textbooks was so pitifully small that the collection resembled Major Petkoff's 'library' in Shaw's *Arms and the Man*, a single shelf containing a few much-thumbed volumes. I have been happy to have played a part, along with many others, in the development, from those modest beginnings of an Irish law library which, in its range and quality, is cause for justifiable pride for all of us who work in the law.

The law is stated as of 1 May 2000.

Ronan Keane
Chief Justice
The Four Courts
Dublin

1 May 2000

ɔa

fir
rt
'erd

___

Company Law

THIRD EDITION

To the memory of the Hon Mr Justice Kenny
Judge of the High Court and of the Supreme Court

Contents

Part I: Introduction

Chapter 1   Companies and Other Forms of Business Organisations

Chapter 2   The Development of Company Law in Ireland

Chapter 3   Irish Company Law and European Community Law

Part II: Formation of a Company

Chapter 4   How a Company is Formed

Part III: Corporate Personality of the Company

Chapter 11   Separate Legal Personality of the Company

Chapter 12   Contracts

Chapter 13   Tort and Crime

Part IV: The Capital of the Company

Chapter 14   Types of Capital

Chapter 15   The Maintenance of Capital

Part V: Borrowing by the Company

Part VI: Membership of the Company

Chapter 31   Dividends and Distribution of Profits

Chapter 32   Mergers, Arrangements, Reconstructions and Takeovers

Chapter 33   Fraudulent and Reckless Trading

Chapter 34   Insider Dealing in Shares

Chapter 35   Investigation of a Company's Affairs

Part VIII: Winding up of Companies and Protection Orders

Chapter 36   Winding up by the Court

Chapter 38   Voluntary Winding up

Table of Cases

B

H

I

L

M

N

O

P

Q

R

S

Y

Table of Statutes

Pre-1922 and United Kingdom Statutes

Statutory Instruments

Part I
Introduction

Chapter 1

Companies and Other Forms Of Business Organisations

What is a company?

[1.01] The word company has no strictly technical meaning in law[1]. In everyday language, it is normally taken to mean a number of people combined for some common object. But many people, when they use the expression, are referring specifically to a form of business enterprise the members of which enjoy limited liability. In simple language, if the company runs out of money, the members are not responsible for its debts. That is probably the feature which comes to mind at once when the word company is used to-day, although, as we shall see, it is not unknown for companies to be formed without limited liability.

[1.02] The characteristic, however, which unites the companies with which this book is concerned is that they are registered under a series of Acts known as the Companies Acts 1963 to 1999 (referred to in this book as the 'Acts')[2]. Where the object is gain, no such group consisting of more than 20 members can be lawfully formed unless it is registered under the Acts or is formed pursuant to some other statute[3]. It should be borne in mind, however, at the outset that, in the context of the Acts, a company historically did not have to consist of a significant number of members. It was common to find companies registered under the Acts which consisted of as few as two people and frequently the second member was there simply to comply with the legal requirement that a company have at least two members. Since 1994, it has been legally possible to form a company under the Acts with only one member[4].

---

1   *Re Stanley* [1906] 1 Ch 131 at 134 per Buckley J.
2   Eight Acts have been passed amending the Companies Act 1963 (which is the Principal Act) in 1977, 1982, 1983, 1986, two in 1990 and two in 1999. In this book, references to the Principal Act are to the Companies Act 1963. References to the 1990 (No 1) Act are to the Companies (Amendment) Act 1990 and the 1990 Act to the Companies Act 1990. References to the 1999 (No 1) Act and 1999 (No 2) Act are to the Companies (Amendment) (No 1) Act 1999 and the Companies (Amendment) (No 2) Act 1999.
3   Companies Act 1963, s 376. For banking groups, see para **[1.32]** below.
4   European Communities (Single-Member Private Limited Companies) Regulations 1994, SI 1994/275. See para **[4.05]** below.

Corporate bodies in Irish law

[1.03] The companies formed and registered under the Acts are all corporate bodies, ie they are regarded in law as having a legal personality separate and distinct from the individual members. Our law enables such corporate bodies to be formed for a variety of reasons, endows them with certain rights and provides a general legal framework within which they are required to operate. Corporate bodies can be formed for many objects other than the business activities which are the normal object of companies formed under the Acts: trade unions and building societies are two important examples.

[1.04] The concept of corporate personality was familiar for centuries to the English statutory and common law which also prevailed in Ireland. It is also well known in civil law jurisdictions. Although there is no reference to corporate bodies as such in the Constitution, the existing statute and common law remained part of our law except to the extent that it was inconsistent with the Constitution and there had been a similar 'carry over' provision in the Constitution of the Irish Free State. The existence of such corporate bodies and the conferring on them by the law of certain privileges was in harmony with the guarantee in Article 40.6.1°(iii) of the Constitution of the 'right of the citizens to form associations and unions'.

[1.05] Considerably more difficulty, however, was experienced in determining whether the provisions of the Constitution guaranteeing or acknowledging the personal rights of the citizens extended to corporate bodies, such as companies formed under the Acts. Thus, it was held by the Supreme Court in *Quinn's Supermarkets Ltd v Attorney General*[5] that they could not avail themselves of the guarantee of equality of treatment contained in Article 40.1, since it is confined to citizens 'as human persons'. Moreover, in *Private Motorists' Provident Society v Attorney General*[6] Carroll J held that they could not successfully invoke the provisions of Article 43.1, which recognise the general right of private property, since the article describes it as a 'natural right' inherent in man 'by virtue of his rational being'. However, one of the shareholders was joined as a plaintiff in those proceedings and Carroll J found that his interest as a shareholder (including his contractual rights) was a property right capable of being harmed by an injury to the company. Hence such a shareholder could rely on the provisions of Article 40.3 which protect the property rights of the citizen against 'unjust attack'.

[1.06] On appeal, the Supreme Court expressed no opinion on whether a corporate body was precluded from relying on the property rights guaranteed by

---

[5]   [1972] IR 1.
[6]   [1983] IR 339.

4

the Constitution, since they agreed that the shareholder was entitled to invoke them.

[1.07] When the matter next came before the High Court in *Chestvale Properties Ltd v Glackin*[7], Murphy J took the same view as Carroll J. However, a different approach was adopted by Keane J in *Iarnród Éireann v Ireland*[8]. In that case, the plaintiffs claimed that certain provisions of the Civil Liability Act 1961 were unconstitutional. The defendants contended that they had no *locus standi*. However, Keane J declined to follow the decision in *Private Motorists' Provident Society v Attorney General*[9]. He pointed out that in *Blake v Attorney General*[10], the Supreme Court had rejected the view that the property rights guaranteed by the Constitution were to be found in Article 43 and not elsewhere and had said that the right to individual items of property was protected by Article 40.3.2°. The rights protected by that article were not defined as rights of human persons only. As to whether the guarantee was sufficiently broad in its terms to extend to bodies corporate, he said:

> 'There would ... be a spectacular deficiency in the guarantee to *every* citizen that his or her property rights will be protected against "unjust attack", if such bodies were incapable in law of being regarded as "citizens", at least for the purposes of this article, and it was essential for the shareholders to abandon the protection of limited liability to which they are entitled by law in order to protect, not merely their own rights as shareholders, but also the property rights of the corporate entity itself, which are in law distinct from the rights of its members'.

He accordingly held that the plaintiffs had *locus standi*. The decision was appealed to the Supreme Court, but that court expressed no opinion on the *locus standi* issue. In the result, the question as to the capacity of companies formed under the Acts to rely on the constitutional guarantees as to private property still awaits authoritative resolution.

[1.08] As we shall see, the provisions of the Constitution are also frequently of significance when the relations between the company and its members, its creditors and the public in general are being considered.

[1.09] Although the Constitution does not protect corporate, as distinct from individual, rights, save in the oblique manner just mentioned, it should not be thought that its provisions are of no significance when the relations between the company and its members, its creditors or the public in general are being considered.

---

7   [1993] 3 IR 35.
8   [1996] 3 IR 321.
9   [1983] IR 339.
10 [1982] IR 117.

Companies, single traders and partnerships

[1.10] The most popular form of business organisation in Ireland is the limited liability company formed and registered under the Acts. While there are still many people who carry on business as single traders or in partnership with others, the benefits of forming a limited liability company are so overwhelming that businesses of any size almost inevitably take advantage of them.

[1.11] Partnerships closely resemble companies and the modern company can indeed be seen as having evolved from the idea of a partnership. Both are essentially groups of people combined for business and professional purposes. The peculiar advantages of the company can, however, be summarised as follows:

(1) A company can be incorporated with limited liability

The liability of the members for the debts and wrongs of the company can be limited to the amount unpaid on the shares which they own in the company (in which case it is known as a company limited by shares) or to the amount which they undertake to pay in the event of the company ceasing to exist (in which case it is known as a company limited by guarantee). In the case of a partnership or an unlimited company, there is no such limitation on the liability of the partners or members.

(2) A company is a legal entity distinct from its members

Partnerships in contrast are not legal entities: there may be a name attached to the firm, but the partnership consists solely of the individual partners and the firm has no independent legal existence. When one partner dies, the partnership comes to an end. A company, on the other hand, enjoys perpetual succession as a corporate body and continues to exist despite changes in its membership. It can own property and sue and be sued in the company name.

The company is, as a result, afforded a flexibility in its operations denied to other organisations. For example, when the shares in a company change hands, its property does not have to be transferred to the new members. Since it is vested in the company and not in the individual members, it remains vested in the company and this is the case even when the majority of the shares change hands. By contrast, when one partner assigns his rights to another, the property remains vested in the original partners. This flexibility may also provide certain tax advantages.

6

(3) The shares in a company are freely transferable unless the constitution provides otherwise and a person who acquires shares becomes a member with all the rights of the person who transferred the shares to him

When a partner assigns his share, the assignee does not become a partner, unless the original partner agrees[11].

(4) The affairs of a company are managed by its directors and not by the members

By contrast each partner is entitled to participate in all the partnership activities. Management by directors on behalf of the members is generally regarded by businessmen as preferable to the partnership system.

(5) The structure of a company facilitates the raising of capital

Prospective investors can be given a stake in the company by being allotted shares. So too can financial institutions who lend the company money: in this case the shares will usually be preference shares entitling the lender to be paid a dividend and/or the return of his money before the other ordinary shareholders[12]. Today, it is more usual for such lenders to secure their loans by a debenture which covers not merely the fixed assets of the company but also the other assets used in the business by the form of security known as floating charge[13]. The legal structure of the company is particularly well adapted to the creation of such charges.

Reasons for not forming a company

[1.12] The advantages for business organisations of forming a company are so clear that it may well be asked why people still carry on business as single traders or in partnerships. In the case of very small businesses, the cost of incorporation, though not great, sometimes acts as a deterrent. Some activities of their nature - and this applies particularly to certain professions such as the law and accountancy - can only be carried on individually or in partnership[14].

[1.13] As we have seen, there cannot be more than 20 members in a partnership and each partner is the agent of the others. It provides, accordingly, a suitable legal basis for an association of a small body of persons having trust and confidence in each other[15]. It should be noted, however, that the limitation on the

---

[11] Partnership Act 1890, s 24(7).
[12] See Ch 17 below.
[13] See Ch 20 below.
[14] In the case of barristers, not even partnerships are allowed.
[15] Gower, *Modern Company Law* (6th edn), p 3.

number of members in a partnership was removed in the case of accountants and solicitors by the Companies (Amendment) Act 1982[16].

Companies not formed under the Acts

[1.14] While this book is principally concerned with companies formed and registered under the Acts, there are other forms of companies in existence which will be referred to from time to time. The three principal types of such companies are now considered in more detail.

(1) Chartered companies or corporations

[1.15] There are many such bodies in Ireland, but very few of them carry on business for gain. They include learned and professional bodies, such as the Incorporated Law Society, the universities, the Royal Irish Academy, the Royal Colleges of Surgeons and Physicians, voluntary hospitals etc[17]. They were incorporated by charters or grants of letters patent from the British Crown and preserve their corporate existence by virtue of the transitional provisions of the Constitution and the relevant adapting legislation[18]. Although they have many of the features of companies registered under the Acts, they lie outside the scope of this book.

(2) Companies incorporated by statute

In the Victorian era when railways and similar undertakings were being promoted by private enterprise, parliament passed a number of special Acts, some of them applicable to Ireland, providing for the incorporation of such undertakings as companies. Since 1921, most of the companies so formed have been dissolved and their assets and functions transferred to other bodies[19]. Thus, railways and canals were transferred to Coras Iompair Éireann which is not a company but a board established by statute. Its assets are now vested in three subsidiary companies, Iarnród Éireann, Bus Éireann and Bus Atha Cliath. It has also been a frequent practice since 1921 for the Oireachtas to provide for the establishment of companies intended to carry out certain functions considered to

---

[16] Companies (Amendment) Act 1982, s 13. The Minister for Enterprise, Trade and Employment may add to the categories of such partnerships by order.

[17] The inclusion of the Honourable Society of the King's Inns in this list in previous editions was erroneous. This body was granted a royal charter in 1792, but it was revoked by statute in 1793, following protests by junior barristers and it remains an unincorporated body to this day. See Colum Kenny, *King's Inns and the Kingdom of Ireland*, pp 240-253.

[18] Constitution of Saorstát Eireann, Article 73; Constitution of Ireland, Article 50.1; Adaptation of Charters Act 1926. Cf *Re Commercial Buildings Company of Dublin* [1938] IR 472.

[19] But some survive, eg the Alliance and Dublin Consumers Gas Company incorporated under 37 & 38 Vict cxxxv.

be of national importance. The companies concerned include Aer Rianta Teoranta, Aer Lingus Teoranta and An Post. While such companies are often referred to as semi-state bodies, they should be carefully distinguished from other bodies also so described, such as Coras Iompair Éireann and the Electricity Supply Board, which are not companies. The Act usually empowers the relevant Minister to obtain the incorporation of a company under the Acts with appropriate objects. The enabling Act and the subsequent amending legislation generally contain special provisions relating to the Minister's shareholding in the company, the composition of the board of directors, its authorised capital and borrowing powers etc.

Companies of this nature play a major role in the Irish economy, accounting for a significant proportion of business activity and employment. It should always be borne in mind that, while they are normally incorporated under the Acts and many of the legal principles explained in this book are accordingly applicable to them, the Acts providing for their establishment contain many special provisions relating exclusively to them. In considering the legal powers and duties of such companies, therefore, it is not sufficient to have regard to the constitution of the company under the Acts (the memorandum and articles of association): the special provisions of the enabling Act and any amending legislation must also be taken into account.

(3) Bodies with special objects

There are certain corporate bodies with special objects which can be formed under statutes other than the Acts. While in some respects they resemble companies registered under the Acts, their primary objects are not normally the making of profits for their members. They include friendly societies, industrial and provident societies, building societies, trade unions and trustee savings banks. The cooperatives, which play a large part in the agricultural and food industries, are usually industrial and provident societies, but in some cases are formed as limited companies. While they are occasionally referred to, they lie outside the scope of this book.

Semi-state bodies which are not companies

[1.16] As has been pointed out in the preceding paragraph, many semi-state bodies in Ireland take the form of companies established under other statutes but incorporated under the Acts. There are, however, a number of semi-state bodies which are not companies of this type. They take the form of bodies corporate with all the usual features of corporations, such as perpetual succession, the capacity to sue and be sued, the power to hold property etc. They do not, however, have any share capital or shareholders: all their funds are provided by the State or by borrowing guaranteed by the State. They are usually described as a board or authority. Examples of such bodies in Ireland are:

(i)   The Electricity Supply Board;

(ii)   The Central Bank

(iii)   Coras Iompair Éireann;

(iv)   Bord na Móna;

(v)   Radio Telefís Éireann;

(vi)   Bord Fáilte;

(vii) Udarás na Gaeltachta.

While the list could be extended further, it is to be borne in mind that a number of these bodies have been or may privatised, eg, Telecom Éireann.

Partnerships

[1.17] Partnerships, which do not have a separate legal personality, are an important feature of Irish life, particularly in the field of the professions. As they are wholly different in their legal nature, any extended discussion of them would be outside the scope of this book. It may be noted, however, that it is still possible to form a partnership which extends to one or more of the partners the privilege of limited liability. This can be done under the Limited Partnerships Act 1907 but there are severe restrictions on the application of limited liability. In addition to the partners whose liability is limited, there must be one or more general partners whose liability is unlimited. Moreover, a limited partner cannot take part in the management of the business without losing his immunity from liability. In practice, very few such limited partnerships are formed in Ireland[20].

[1.18] As we have seen[21], any association with more than 20 members whose object is gain must be incorporated under the Acts: if this does not happen, the association in the eyes of the law does not exist. There are, of course quite a number of groups in Ireland which do not have gain as their object. Some of them find it convenient to become companies under the Acts, usually in the form of a company limited by guarantee. Others remain unincorporated, in which case the individual members are regarded in law as having entered into a contract with each other, the terms of which are usually to be found in the rules. The many clubs, social, educational and recreational, which flourish in Ireland are

---

[20] Their numbers have increased in recent years, perhaps because of certain tax advantages. Where such a partnership is formed for the purpose of investing its funds in property, it must now obtain a certificate of authorisation from the Central Bank: see Investment Limited Partnerships Act 1994.

[21] Para **[1.02]** above.

examples of groups not established for gain, some of them being incorporated under the acts as companies limited by guarantee, others remaining unincorporated.

Companies formed and registered under the Acts

[1.19] It is with such companies that this book is principally concerned. As we have seen[22], companies can be registered under the Acts either with or without limited liability; and where liability is limited, it may be limited either by shares or by guarantee.

[1.20] When a company is limited by shares, the liability of the members for the debts and wrongs of the company is limited to the amount which they have agreed to pay for the shares which they own in the company. These shares collectively represent the share capital of the company. The members, or shareholders, as they are more often called, effectively own the company by virtue of their ownership of the share capital, although the property and assets of the company are vested in the company itself and not in the members. Their ownership of shares usually gives certain important rights to the shareholders, ie

 (i)   the right to receive a share at fixed intervals of the companys profits in the form of a money payment called a dividend;

 (ii) the right to attend meetings of the company and, in the case of those holding voting shares, to vote at the meetings[23];

 (iii) the right to receive copies of certain important documents, ie the balance sheet, profit and loss account and directors' and auditors' reports;

 (iv) the right to participate in the surplus assets of the company in the event of its ceasing to exist or being wound up, as the process is generally called.

[1.21] A further distinction of great importance among companies registered under the Acts exists. They can be either public or private companies. In practice, the most important distinction between the two forms of company is that the shares in a public company are offered for subscription to the public: those in a private company are not. Accordingly, there is in general terms no restriction on the right to transfer shares in a public company. By contrast, shares in a private company cannot be sold to the public and, in particular, cannot be quoted or dealt in on a stock exchange. Moreover, while there is no limit on the

---

[22] Para **[1.01]** above.
[23] But note that these rights may be altogether abolished by the company's constitution.

number of members in a public company, a private company cannot have more than fifty[24].

[1.22] Companies are also now classified for certain purposes according to the scale of their activities. Before the enactment of the Companies Act 1986, private companies were exempted from the general requirement that companies publish their accounts. This complete exemption was ended by that Act, but the disclosure requirements were significantly modified in the case of small companies and, to a lesser extent, medium-sized companies. The classification is by reference to the assets, turnover and number of employees of the company concerned[25].

[1.23] One of the major differences between a company and a partnership is that in the case of a company there is a separation between the ownership of the company, which is vested in the shareholders, and the day to day management of the company, which is carried on by the directors. In the case of a partnership, each of the partners is usually concerned in the management of the business in addition to owning it in part. But the shareholders - or in the case of a company not limited by shares its members - may remove the directors at any time, so that the ultimate control of the company is in their hands. In the apt analogy of Gower, the members are the legislature of the company and the board of directors is the government[26].

[1.24] Any decision of the members at a general meeting of the company is accordingly regarded as the act of the company itself. Similarly, any decision of the board of directors acting within the powers vested in them under the companys constitution is regarded as the act of the company. For this reason, the members in general meeting and the board of directors are frequently referred to as the organs of the company. By contrast, an officer or employee is at best no more than an agent of the company and his actions are not the actions of the company itself, although they may involve the company in legal liability where he is acting within the scope of his authority as such agent.

[1.25] The procedure for forming companies is relatively straightforward and is explained in greater detail in Chapter 4. It is sufficient to say at this point that the persons wishing to form the company - the promoters, as they are usually called - lodge with a government official called the Registrar of Companies[27] a document setting out the name and objects of the company (the memorandum) and its rules (the articles of association). If the Registrar is satisfied that the

---

[24] Companies Act 1963, s 33(1)(b).
[25] See further Ch 29 below.
[26] Gower, *Modern Company Law* (6th edn), p 15.
[27] Referred to in this book as 'the Registrar'.

documents are in order, he issues a certificate of incorporation. It is then in general terms entitled to avail of the various privileges conferred by the law on such companies but must also comply with the requirements of the Acts and any other applicable law.

[1.26] The law governing such companies is to be found principally in the Acts and the regulations made by the relevant authorities under the Acts. These authorities are 'the Minister for Enterprise, Trade and Employment' (usually referred to in this book as 'the Minister') who has a general supervisory jurisdiction over companies and the Superior Courts Rules Committee which is the rule making authority for the High Court and the Supreme Court.

[1.27] The interpretation of the Acts and the regulations is the exclusive province of the courts established under the Constitution. In some areas, such as the winding up of companies, the High Court alone has jurisdiction, but its decisions are subject to an appeal to the Supreme Court whose decisions are final. This is subject to one important qualification: the ultimate authority on the interpretation of any of the provisions of the Treaties under which the European Communities were established are the Courts of Justice of the EC. T hose courts are also the ultimate authority on the interpretation of any regulations or directives issued by the Council established under the Treaties[28]. Any reference to the court, however, in this book, unless there is an indication to the contrary, is a reference to the High Court.

[1.28] It is accordingly essential for the student of company law to be familiar with the more important decisions of the courts on the Acts, since this body of case law is as much part of company law as the Acts themselves. Moreover, the decisions applied by the Irish courts include many cases decided by the courts before the enactment of the Principal Act and by the Irish and English courts before the establishment of the Irish Free State. Decisions of English courts since 1921 are not, of course, part of Irish law unless they have been expressly adopted by an Irish court, but they are referred to in this book where they throw light on provisions in the English legislation which correspond to ours.

[1.29] In the case of public companies. one must also be familiar with the Rules of the Stock Exchange. Those rules set out the requirements that must be met before shares in a company will be admitted to that body's list of securities. Until 1985, they did not form part of the law of the State. In that year, however, the exchange's minimum requirements in this area were given the force of law by the European Communities (Stock Exchange) Regulations 1984[29]. Take-overs of

---

[28]   See Ch 3 below.
[29]   S1 1984/1989.

public companies are now affected by the provisions of the Irish Take-Over Panel Act 1997.

[1.30] Two other Acts of special significance in the context of company law should be mentioned. The Mergers Take-overs and Monopolies (Control) Act 1978 contains important provisions designed to ensure, among other things, that mergers and take-overs do not take place which are inimical to the public interest. That Act was amended in some important respects by the Competition Act 1991.

Banks and insurance companies

[1.31] No company, association or partnership consisting of more than ten members may be formed for a purpose of carrying on the business of banking unless it is registered as a company under the Acts or is formed in pursuance of some other statute[30].

[1.32] There is no definition of banking in the Acts, but it is generally recognised that the usual features of a banking business are:

    (i)   the collection of cheques for customers;

    (ii)   the payment of cheques drawn on the bank by customers;

    (iii)   the keeping of current accounts[31].

In addition, banking business is defined by s 2 of the Central Bank Act 1971 (which requires the obtaining of licences from the Central Bank by all persons carrying on banking business) as including, subject to certain exceptions, the business of accepting deposits payable on demand or on notice or at a fixed or determinable future date.

[1.33] Section 15 of the Central Bank Act 1971 requires the Registrar to notify the Central Bank of the delivery to him of any memorandum and articles of any company which would, in his opinion, be holding itself out as a banker or have as one of its objects the carrying on of banking business. A certificate of incorporation may not be granted by the Registrar in respect of such a company unless and until the Bank indicates its willingness to grant a licence to the company or to exempt it from the requirements as to a licence. The Registrar must also notify the Bank of the delivery to him of any documents by a foreign company establishing a place of business in Ireland which would have a similar

---

[30] Companies Act 1963, s 372.

[31] But note that a person may be in law a 'banker', although he does not keep current accounts or issue cheque books: per Fitzgibbon LJ in *Re Sheilds* [1901] 1 IR 172 at 199. It will comfort some to know that the learned judge virtually equated the terms 'banker' and 'gombeen man'.

effect. There is a similar provision where the constitution of a company is being altered to the same effect.

[1.34] Insurance companies, in addition to being subject to the provisions of the Acts, are also subject to the provisions of the Insurance Acts 1908 to 1989 which deal with such matters as the granting of licences to insurance companies by the Minister, the maintaining of deposits in the High Court by such companies, the monitoring by the Minister of their accounts (and, in particular, the ratio between their reserves and their actual and contingent liabilities) and the appointment of an administrator by the court where such a company gets into difficulties.

Chapter 2

The Development of Company Law in Ireland[1]

[2.01] The general structure of Irish company law is closely modelled on that of England. The reason is obvious: the two countries had a common legal tradition and, after the Act of Union in 1800 and until 1921, all statute law affecting Ireland was enacted at Westminster. While there have been substantial changes in Irish company law since 1921, it was thought better to preserve the general structure inherited from the English, and such changes as have been made since 1921 have in many instances been based on changes in the neighbouring jurisdiction. Since the accession of Ireland to the European Economic Community in 1973, however, many changes have resulted from compliance with directives of the community, now the European Union, requiring the harmonisation of company law in the member states.

The joint stock company

[2.02] The modern Irish companies with which this book is concerned are descended from the joint stock companies which first became a feature of English commercial life in the seventeenth century. Legal historians have seen shadowy prototypes of such companies in the gilds of the middle ages, but the medieval institution with which they had more in common was the *commenda*[2]. This had its origins partly in the medieval dislike of usury: the *commendatores* advanced money to the *commendatarii* so that the latter might use it in their trade, but no interest was charged. Instead the commendatores were entitled to participate in the profit of the venture. Since they took no part in the management, leaving that to the *commendatarii*, one can discern in the commenda the development of the division, familiar to us in company law today,

---

[1] For readable accounts of the history of English company law see Gower, *Modern Company Law* (6th edn), Chs 2 and 3 and Hahlo, *Cases in Company Law* (2nd edn), Ch 1. A more detailed account will be found in Holdsworth, *History of English Law*, Vol 8, pp 192-222, Vol 13, pp 365-370 and Vol 15, pp 44 61. There is no Irish work dealing specifically with the topic of which I am aware but useful background information will be found in Lyons, *Ireland since the Famine*, pp 42-61; Lynch & Vaisey, *Guinness's Brewery in the Irish Economy 1759-1876*, Ch 1; *The Formation of the Irish Economy* (ed LM Cullen), particularly the chapter by Lee on *Capital in the Irish Economy*; Robinson, *A History of Accountants in Ireland*; Meenan, *The Irish Economy since 1922* and Lee, *Ireland 1912-1985*.

[2] Holdsworth, *History of English Law*, Vol 10, pp 193-7.

between ownership and management. The interest of the commendatores was confined to their financial investment, as was their liability.

[2.03] From this institution there evolved in turn the structure, familiar on the continent, of the *société en commandite*, whose nearest equivalent in our law was the limited partnership. But the limited partnership concept never really became established in England or Ireland, although it is of interest to note that the first statute which recognised its existence was the Irish Anonymous Partnership Act of 1781.

[2.04] English commercial development initially took the form of the 'regulated companies', the individual members of which traded with their own stock. Since each member was responsible for his own trade, it might have been thought that there were no advantages to be derived from forming any sort of corporation. In fact there were: the benefits which the members of such companies derived from the charters under which they were incorporated consisted of monopolies and similar privileges then in the gift of the crown. This was particularly the case with the great overseas companies, of which the most celebrated was the East India Company[3].

[2.05] The merchant adventurers, who were the members of such companies, developed the practice during the seventeenth century of forming a 'joint stock' for a particular venture. At the end of the venture, the stock and the profits were divided between the members. From this it was a short step to having a permanent joint stock which was the property of all the members and hence the name 'joint stock company', still sometimes used to describe the limited liability company of today.

[2.06] Although the concept that the members were not responsible for the debts of the company developed at an early stage in the history of the joint stock companies (the concept of limited liability)[4], it did not have the practical significance that it does today, since the company could exact from the members *leviations* (calls to meet the liability), at least where it was authorised so to do by its charter.

[2.07] There also developed during the seventeenth century the practice of raising funds from the public for such ventures and in the early decades of the eighteenth century such *flotations*, as they came to be called, became extremely common. Many of the new ventures came to grief and ultimately parliament felt obliged to intervene when the speculative frenzy which accompanied the launching of such schemes reached fever pitch with the remarkable project of the South Sea Company to acquire virtually the whole of the English national

---

[3]   Holdsworth, *History of English Law*, Vol 10, p 209.

[4]   *Edmunds v Brown & Tillard* (1668) 1 Lev 237, Hahlo, *Cases in Company Law* (2nd edn), p 11.

debt. The resultant legislation, passed in 1720 and known as the 'Bubble Act', prohibited the formation of joint stock companies in the future except under Act of Parliament or by the grant of a royal charter. The Bubble Act, although well intentioned, has been generally regarded as having seriously impeded the development of a proper framework of company law in the United Kingdom.

[2.08] The passing of the Bubble Act did not mean that joint stock companies ceased to be formed. It was still possible to obtain a royal charter for that purpose; but this was a difficult and expensive process. If the project was thought to be of sufficient importance, parliament was prepared to permit the incorporation of a company by a special Private Act and this was the statutory framework for the establishment by private enterprise of the various railway and canal undertakings in both England and Ireland. The many smaller traders, however, who could not make use of such elaborate machinery were driven to form a new sort of association to obtain some at least of the advantages of carrying on business in combination. This was the 'deed of settlement' company and in it we can see many of the features of the private commercial company of our own time. It was not an incorporated body like our modern companies: instead the individual members entered into a deed of settlement with one or more trustees which declared that the individuals constituted a company with a specified name, in the capital of which they all held shares. The deed also provided that the affairs of the company should be managed by a committee of directors and that the property of the company should be vested in them. This arrangement secured to traders one of the great advantages of incorporation, continuity of existence, but the members continued to be liable for the debts of the company.

[2.09] The Bubble Act was repealed in 1825 but it continued to be difficult to obtain the necessary charters and the case for radical reform was strengthened by the confusion and uncertainty surrounding the formation and composition of the numerous incorporated and unincorporated bodies seeking funds from the public for a wide range of enterprises. Investors found it extremely difficult to discover who the real promoters and managers of fraudulent schemes were and to bring home legal responsibility for the losses they sustained against anyone[5]. Dickens pilloried the dubious enterprises that flourished in those days in *Nicholas Nickleby*.

> 'It's the finest idea that was ever started. 'United Metropolitan Improved Hot Muffin and Crumpet Baking and Punctual Delivery Company'. Capital, five million in five hundred thousand shares of £10 each. Why, the very name will get the shares up to a premium in ten days.'

---

5   Holdsworth, *History of English Law*, Vol 15, pp 45-60.

"And when they are at a premium", said Mr Ralph Nickleby smiling.

"When they are, you know what to do about them as well as any other man alive, and how to back quietly out at the right time", said Mr Bonney, slapping the capitalist familiarly on the shoulder.'

[2.10] It was against this background that the first modern companies legislation appeared on the statute book in 1844. The Joint Stock Companies Act 1844, the enactment of which owed much to the energy of the young Gladstone as President of the Board of Trade, was primarily designed to curb fraudulent enterprises and introduce some degree of order into the affairs of joint stock companies. With this object in view, it established the requirements as to publicity in the formation and management of such enterprises which have been a feature of company law since then.

[2.11] The office of Registrar of Companies was established in both England and Ireland, provision was made for the registration of the names of the promoters, for the execution of a deed by the shareholders and the appointment of named directors before the company commenced business and for defining the rights of shareholders and powers of directors. The company could now own property and sue and be sued itself. In the same year legislation was introduced, which again applied to Ireland, providing a machinery for the winding up of insolvent companies, in many respects similar to the well established bankruptcy procedures applicable to individuals. The advantage of limited liability was still withheld but was ultimately granted by the Limited Liability Act 1855, which also introduced the requirement that the names of companies availing of such a privilege had to end with the word 'limited'.

[2.12] The 1855 Act was replaced in less than a year by the Joint Stock Companies Act 1856, which has generally been seen as representing the highwater mark of the Victorian *laissez faire* philosophy as applied to company law. The principle that the company's name had to end in the word 'limited' when limited liability was availed of was maintained. But a much simpler process of registration was introduced, the deed of settlement was replaced by the now familiar memorandum and articles as the constitution of the company, and many of the restrictions imposed by the earlier legislation on those seeking the benefits of incorporation and limited liability were swept away.

Other legislation followed the 1856 Act and ultimately the Acts were consolidated in the Companies Act 1862, the first statute to bear that short title.

Economic development in Ireland

[2.13] The new companies legislation was also applicable in Ireland. Conditions were, however, very different in the neighbouring island. Ireland had enjoyed a significant degree of economic development in the seventeenth and eighteenth centuries, characterised by the emergence of a number of crafts and industries and the growth in size and prestige of some of the cities and towns, most notably Dublin. But its history in the nineteenth century was overshadowed by the catastrophe of the great famine and there was no real counterpart to the massive expansion of trade and industry in England.

[2.14] Such significant commercial developments as there were tended to be confined to the north-east of Ulster and certain major ports, cities and towns[6]. In this period the most important expansion was in the north-east with the development of ship building and linen, while in other areas such industry as there was tended to be dominated by brewing and distilling. Ironically, Ireland was also the scene at this period of a rapid expansion of two services which would have been an important asset to industrial development on the English scale, if it had ever occurred: with the end of the monopoly of the Bank of Ireland, other banks began to flourish, and an extensive railway network was built throughout the country.

[2.15] Thus, while the new legislation undoubtedly had its effect in Ireland, one of its by-products being a substantial growth in the numbers and respectability of the relatively new profession of accountancy[7], there was no equivalent in Ireland to the vast number of public flotations in England.

The private company

[2.16] The new legislation had obviously been framed with relatively large public companies in mind. But it did not take lawyers long to realise that it could also be used to give the ordinary trader, who did not wish to seek funds from the public, the benefits of incorporation and limited liability. This paved the way for the development of the 'private company', as it came to be called, which was to be the central institution of Irish company law. It was only a short step from this to the formation of 'one man companies', in which virtually all the shares were held by one trader who also nominated the directors. Their validity was recognised by the House of Lords in 1897 in the great case of *Salomon v Salomon & Co*[8] in which the Court of Appeal had reacted with shocked disbelief

---

[6] Lynch & Vaisey, *Guinness's Brewery in the Irish Economy 1759-1876*, Ch 1.

[7] Thus shortly after the enactment of 7 and 8 Vic c III providing for the winding up of insolvent companies, a Mr Henry Brown became the first of a long and illustrious line of official liquidators appointed by the Irish courts. The firm of which he was a member subsequently became the well known firm of Craig Gardner & Co. See Robinson, *A History of Accountancy in Ireland*, pp 17-21.

[8] [1897] AC 22.

to the proposition that such bodies were perfectly lawful. No less a judge than Lindley LJ thundered that companies of this nature:

> 'do infinite mischief; they bring into disrepute one of the most useful statutes of modern times by perverting its legitimate use and by making it an instrument for cheating honest creditors.'[9]

The House of Lords, however, made it clear that the benefits of the Acts were no less available to the small businessman than to the large public enterprises and, when the Companies Act 1907 became law, it did not merely give statutory recognition to private companies, but also exempted them from the requirements of the Acts as to the filing with the Registrar of accounts. This exemption, which effectively removed from public scrutiny the financial affairs of such companies, remained a feature of Irish company law until the 1986 Act.

The 1907 Act was followed by the second great consolidating measure, the Companies (Consolidation) Act 1908 which was to be for Irish lawyers the bedrock of company law for over half a century.

Company law in Ireland after 1921

[2.17] The pattern had been established in the United Kingdom during the nineteenth century of setting up committees at intervals of approximately twenty years to consider what changes might be required in the legislation dealing with companies. Due in part perhaps to the lesser role played by industry and business in a predominantly agricultural economy, this pattern was not reflected in the legislation of the new Irish State after 1921. A committee was appointed in 1927 to investigate the law and procedure relating to bankruptcy and winding up of companies and duly reported, but no legislation was introduced as a result of its recommendations. There was no Irish equivalent to the English Acts of 1929 and 1948.

[2.18] In 1951, a committee was appointed to report on the reform of company law. The first chairman of the committee was Mr H Vaughan Wilson SC who was replaced on his death in 1956 by Mr Arthur Cox. The secretary of the committee was Mr John Kenny, subsequently a Judge of the High Court and of the Supreme Court, with whom much of the development of modern Irish company law is associated.

[2.19] The most significant feature of Irish companies since the enactment of the first companies' legislation in the nineteenth century was the vast number of private companies formed as opposed to the relatively small number of public companies. This obviously raised the question, with which Cox dealt, as to whether the continued exemption of such companies from the requirement to

---

9   [1895] 2 Ch 323 at 339.

file accounts was justified. In England, following the recommendation to that effect of the Cohen Committee. the 1948 Act had confined the privilege to exempt private companies. There was the further problem in this context presented by the growth of subsidiary companies: the requirement that a public company should file accounts was rendered almost meaningless by the fact that its wholly owned private subsidiaries were under no such obligation.

[2.20] The Cox Committee, whose report[10] was presented in 1958, recommended that the exemption of private companies in this area should continue. They considered that any harm that might result for creditors and investors was more than outweighed by the difficulties which would be caused to small businesses if they were compelled to disclose their trading situation to competitors. They also considered that the legislation required to define the type of private companies which should file accounts would be of necessity highly technical and complex and that in the Irish context this sort of legislation should be avoided where possible. To deal with the problem of public companies which owned private subsidiaries, they recommended the adoption of the practice which had existed in England since the 1929 Act of requiring holding companies to file the group accounts which would show the financial position of both the parent company and its subsidiaries taken as a whole. In the case of a private company owning subsidiaries, however, they recommended that the obligation to file group accounts should not be imposed: it would be sufficient if the private subsidiaries had the right to obtain a copy of the accounts of all the subsidiaries in the group. All of the committee's recommendations in this area were embodied in the Principal Act.

[2.21] Another major change recommended by Cox related to the keeping and publication of accounts generally. It is a remarkable fact that, until the committee's recommendations in this area were implemented by the Principal Act, there was no general obligation on companies to keep proper accounts or to present their shareholders with a picture of the financial situation of the company in which they had invested their money. The only requirement of the 1908 Act was that public companies should include in their annual report to the shareholders a statement in the form of a balance sheet. The Principal Act gave effect to Cox's recommendation that all companies, public and private, should be required to keep proper accounts and should be obliged to present the shareholders each year with an audited balance sheet and profit and loss account.

[2.22] Another development which had given rise to concern since the enactment of the 1908 Act related to the position of minority shareholders. Short of putting an end to the company's existence by obtaining a winding up order from the court, no remedy was available to such shareholders and their interests

---

[10] *Report of the Company Law Reform Committee,* 1958 (pl 4523).

could be disregarded almost with impunity by the majority. The English 1929 Act had enabled shareholders who found themselves in this position to obtain relief from the court, and the Cox recommendation that a similar reform should be introduced in Ireland was implemented by the Principal Act. Recommendations intended to ensure that the practice of giving loans to directors was not abused were also implemented, but Cox advised against any general prohibition on such loans and this advice was also accepted by the legislature.

[2.23] In the area of winding up, two of the most important recommendations of Cox were not implemented. Although the committee was not unanimous on the matter, some at least of the members were in favour of the proposal that in the case of the winding up of companies, there should be an official receiver attached to the High Court who would perform functions roughly analogous to those of the official assignee in bankruptcy. They thought that the delays associated with the existing system, under which a winding up by the court was carried out by a liquidator (almost invariably an accountant) under the control of the court, would be reduced by the adoption of this system which had been in existence in England since 1890. Other members of the committee, however, were opposed to this suggestion which had also been considered by the committee established in 1927 and rejected by them[11].

[2.24] Cox also recommended (and here there was no indication of any dissent) that the priority given to debts due to the State in a winding up should be abolished. That priority is, of course, of far greater significance in modern conditions than it was when the committee reported: the huge increase in the volume of taxation and the introduction of PAYE and Value Added Tax means that in the vast majority of winding ups conducted by the court the Revenue Commissioners are the largest single creditor.

[2.25] On another topic, however, which has also become of critical importance in modern conditions, Cox's recommendation was adopted in the Principal Act. The committee was seriously concerned by the abuses which had developed of the protection of limited liability. The report recommended that where in the course of a winding up it appeared that the business of the company had been carried on with intent to defraud creditors or for any fraudulent or dishonest purpose, the court should have power to declare that any persons who were knowingly concerned in the carrying on of the business in that manner should be personally responsible for the debts of the company. The relatively more

---

[11] *Report of the Company Law Reform Committee,* 1958 (pl 4523), paras 197-8. An attempt in 1893 to extend the British system to Ireland in the form of the Official Liquidators (Ireland) Bill had also foundered, largely, it would seem, because of the well organised opposition to the proposal in the accountants' profession. See Robinson, *A History of Accountants in Ireland,* pp 115-9.

frequent use of this power - which was significantly strengthened by the 1990 Act - by the High Court has been a feature of company law in recent times[12].

[2.26] Cox also recommended that the power given to the relevant Minister under the 1908 Act to investigate the affairs of a company should be less restricted and this recommendation was implemented. But such investigations continued to be extremely rare, principally, it would seem, because of the reluctance of Ministers to order an investigation. Now, under the 1990 Act, the order for an investigation can be made by the High Court[13].

[2.27] Cox was also concerned with the injustices and inconveniences which had resulted from the strict application by the courts of the rule that a transaction entered into by a company which was not authorised by its constitution (in legal language 'ultra vires') could not be enforced against the company even where the other party did not know that it was ultra vires. Although the committee confined themselves to recommending a simpler and less expensive method of altering the objects of a company as set out in the memorandum of association, the legislature went further. The Principal Act provides that the rule is not to apply where the other contracting party was actually unaware of the *ultra vires* character of the transaction[14].

[2.28] The functions of auditors had become of increasing importance since the 1908 Act. As the number of companies increased, so did the desirability of ensuring that their accounts were checked by independent experts. It was not until the Principal Act, however, that, following a recommendation by Cox, a requirement was introduced that such auditors be professionally qualified.

[2.29] Another area which also gave rise to concern was the practice of registering nominee shareholdings. Since the 1908 Act expressly prohibited the entry of trusts on the register of shareholders, it was possible for the real owners of shares to be concealed from the public gaze, the registered shareholders being merely their nominees. This was seriously at odds with the great principle of publicity established in the Gladstone legislation, but Cox considered that the only modification of the law which was practicable was the introduction of a requirement that there should be a register of directors' shareholdings. The recommendation was implemented in the Principal Act. The requirements as to disclosure of interests in shares were substantially increased by the 1990 Act.

[2.30] Between the presentation of the report of the Cox Committee in 1958 and the enactment of the Principal Act in 1963, the report of the Jenkins Committee in Britain was published, and the Principal Act embodies some of their recommendations in addition to Cox's recommendations. A shorter Act in 1959 had also made some useful changes.

---

12 See further paras **[35.01]** et seq below.
13 See Ch 35 below.
14 For a more detailed discussion of this topic see para **[12.09]** below.

[2.31] The Principal Act, which remains the charter of Irish company law, is one of the largest on the statute book, containing as it does, 399 sections and 13 schedules. Although its structure closely resembles that of the English 1948 Act and many of the sections are taken word for word from that Act or with only the most minor variations, there are also important differences between the two Acts. Some of them, such as the contrasting treatment of private companies, have already been mentioned, and others will be referred to in other parts of this book. The corpus of Irish company law has more recently been significantly increased by the enactment of the 1990 Act containing 262 sections. Again, although many of the provisions are modelled on English legislation, there are significant divergencies. The differences between Irish and English legislation are sufficiently numerous and striking to make it a somewhat hazardous exercise for Irish practitioners and students to rely uncritically on the leading English textbooks.

[2.32] The appearance on the statute book of the Principal Act coincided with the beginning of a period of considerable growth in the Irish economy. The industrial expansion of the decade which followed and the increase in agricultural incomes with the country's entry into the EEC in 1973 was accompanied by an unprecedented property boom. This new economic climate also led to the formation of a number of so-called 'secondary banks', a phenomenon which ultimately led to stricter government control of banking with the enactment of the Central Bank Act 1971.

[2.33] All of this increased economic activity, however, did not alter the predominance of the private company in Irish company law. The number of public companies had remained virtually static between 1925 and 1956. as the following table demonstrates.

As at 31st December	Public Companies	Private Companies
1925	368	1,088
1930	361	1,380
1935	359	2,000
1940	362	2,567
1945	336	3,513
1950	357	5,377
1955	375	7,111
1956	372	7,385[15]

---

[15] *Report of the Company Law Reform Committee,* 1958 (pl 4523), para 41. It should he pointed out, however, that there was a considerable growth in the number of public industrial companies during the period. In 1933 there were only 24 such companies whose shares were quoted on the Dublin Stock Exchange with a total issued capital of £4.8 million. By 1957 the number had risen to 80 with a total issued capital of £19.5 million. a reflection ot the incentive to development resulting from protectionism. (See Meenan, *The Irish Economy since 1922,* pp 14-7).

By contrast, as the table demonstrates, there had been a considerable increase in the number of private companies. These trends were not significantly reversed during the decades of comparative affluence which followed.

As at 31st December	Public Companies	Private Companies
1994	484	133,521
1995	557	134,769
1996	661	139,012
1997	749	149,522
1998	844	161,864[16]

While the rise in the number of public limited companies is striking, the disproportion with the number of private limited companies is still enormous.

[2.34] As the economy moved into a deepening depression during the nineteen eighties, the problems presented by the growing number of insolvencies among companies began to receive more attention. The collapse of major firms in the building and retail shopping areas and of two insurance companies focused the minds of commentators and legislators alike on the deficiencies of existing company law. In particular, there was increasing anxiety at what seemed to be fairly widespread abuse of the protection of limited liability. Eventually, the response came in the form of the 1990 (No 1) Act and the 1990 Act which did not reach the statute book until that year, although introduced in 1987.

[2.35] The 1990 Act sought to combat the abuse of limited liability in a number of ways. In addition it was intended to bring under tighter legislative supervision generally the operations of those controlling companies. The power to order the investigation of a company's affairs was now vested in the High Court and the range of circumstances in which such an investigation could be ordered broadened. With some important exceptions, the making of loans by companies to their own directors was prohibited and the shareholders were given greater control over substantial property transactions in which they were involved. These controls were extended to cases in which the loans or transactions were entered into with members of the directors' families, and 'shadow directors' ie people who controlled companies through nominees while not being directors themselves. There were stricter requirements as to disclosing such matters in the annual accounts. The range of circumstances in which people could be disqualified from acting as directors or placed under restrictions was also greatly increased. 'Fraudulent trading', which was first introduced by the Principal Act, was now expanded into 'fraudulent and reckless trading' and it was no longer necessary in every case to wind the company up before making its controllers personally liable. Where the company was wound up, other 'related companies'

---

16 *Companies Report* 1998, published by the Department of Enterprise, Trade and Employment.

could be required to contribute to the payment of its debts and the assets of related companies could be pooled.

[2.36] Some of the features of the 1990 Act in this area were clearly influenced by the report in England of the Cork Committee on Insolvency Law. So also was the establishment of the new institution of an 'Examiner' by a shorter act, the 1990 (No 1) Act which was hurriedly enacted earlier that year. This was in response to a crisis in the meat processing industry and, in particular, the difficulties being experienced by the largest firm in the industry, the Goodman Group of companies. There were, however, also major points of difference from the corresponding legislation which implemented the Cork report in England. The concept, which ultimately derives from the Chapter 11 procedure in the US, is designed to enable ailing companies which may have prospects of survival to avoid liquidation. An examiner appointed by the court investigates the company's affairs and, if possible, works out a scheme for its survival: in the meantime, the company remains under court protection.

[2.37] While there was general agreement as to the desirability of the new examiner procedure, particularly since it could ensure the preservation of jobs in companies threatened with liquidation, there were also criticisms of the legislation, which appeared to have been borne out in practice. In 1994, the Company Law Review Group was established by the Minister to consider these and other areas of the law which appeared to be in need of reform. The company in its first report published in that year recommended a number of important changes in the examiner procedure, most of which were implemented by the 1999 (No 2) Act.

[2.38] As the twentieth century came to an end, Ireland had not merely moved out of the depression which overshadowed the previous decade: the pace of economic development had quickened remarkably with a major increase in new business and employment. This has been particularly marked in the new field of information technology and, with the successful establishment of the International Financial Services Centre in Dublin, there has also been a notable expansion of the financial services sector.

[2.39] The decade, however, was also marked by a succession of business scandals, including the exposure of dubious practices of banks in facilitating tax evasion and exploiting their privileged position to the detriment of the customers. This led to the invocation by the Minister on a number of occasions of the power of the High Court to appoint inspectors into a company's affairs.

[2.40] The continuing concern as to the abuses of limited liability and frequent failures to comply with the requirements of company law led to the establishment, by the Minister, of a working group on company law compliance and enforcement under the chairmanship of Mr Michael McDowell, SC. Their report, published in November 1998, made a number of important recommendations which were, in general, accepted by the Government. At the time of writing, legislation is understood to be in preparation to give effect to the principal recommendations in the report. These include:

(i)   The establishment of the Office of Director of Corporate Enforcement to take over the powers of the Minister to initiate summary proceedings for company law offences.

(ii)   The conferring on the director of power to apply to the High Court for various orders, such as restriction and disqualification orders in relation to directors under the Companies Act 1990 and orders calling to account company officers responsible for companies ceasing to trade and leaving substantial debts without putting the company into liquidation.

(iii)   The conferring on the director of further powers to apply to the Court for orders such as the examination of officers and other persons, the requirement of payment of money or delivery of property and the arrest of contributories, directors and other officers.

(iv)   New obligations on liquidators of insolvent companies to report on various aspects of liquidations to the director, including an obligation to make a 'company law compliance report' on the company being liquidated to the director within six months of their appointment.

(v)   Substantial increases in the penalties for summary and indictable offences under the Companies Acts.

(vi)   Strengthening the powers of the Companies Registration Office so as to ensure greater compliance with the requirements of the Companies Acts.

[2.41] Another feature of business activities in the 1980s had been the scale and ferocity of corporate take-over battles in London and New York. The manner in which they were sometimes conducted led to much adverse comment; manoeuvres such as 'concert parties' and 'dawn raids' were the subject of particular criticism. So too was the activity labelled 'insider trading', ie dealings in shares by people armed with information not available to the public generally. It must be doubtful whether in the far smaller Irish stock market such problems were really acute and the elaborate measures taken to counteract them in the 1990 Act probably owed more to a desire to bring our law into harmony with our European partners and to prevent Ireland being used as a base for such activities, than to any major domestic concerns. The problem of how to counteract attempts to manipulate the stock market, while at the same time not unduly restricting legitimate interventions in the market, led to the enactment of the 1999 (No 1) Act, permitting what are called 'stabilising' activities in relation to the issue or sale of stocks and shares, provided the rules laid down in the Act are complied with.

[2.42] The 1990 Act also facilitated the disclosure by auditors of matters which may require further investigation and also strengthened the requirements as to the keeping of accounts. In this, as in other areas, the Act allowed for the imposition of significantly increased penalties.

[2.43] The major event in Irish company law, however, since the Principal Act has been the accession by Ireland to the European Union – then called the European Economic Communities – in 1973. This has already led to important changes in our domestic law and more may be expected. The effect of our membership of the European Union on our company law will be explained in detail in the next chapter. It is sufficient to note here that it has already involved substantial legislation. Coupled with the 1990 Act – much of which was neither prompted by nor required by our membership of the European Union – it means that Irish commercial activity, which is principally carried out through the medium of companies, is now regulated to a quite staggering degree. The Principal Act and the 1990 Act contain between them nearly 700 sections and this is in addition to the other shorter Acts, the regulations and the ever growing mountain of case law.

[2.44] One can readily understand the pressures, both domestic and European, which have driven the executive and the legislature to weigh down Irish business with this stupefying burden. The object is, of course, the common good: the reality, unhappily, is that people who actually conduct commercial life are enmeshed in webs of unnecessarily complex legislation from which, in some instances, only lawyers and accountants ultimately benefit and which helps to foster a climate on non-compliance. This cannot be a desirable state of affairs and the McDowell report also recommended that a reforming bill should be laid before the Oireachtas at least every two years and that a company law review group, composed along similar lines to the group which recommended the changes in the examiner procedure, should be established on a statutory basis to develop proposals to provide the basis, at least in part, for this new legislative programme. It also recommended the codification and consolidation of existing company law so that all the relevant law would be contained in one single comprehensible companies code.

[2.45] It must also, however, be recognised that, as the rest of this book abundantly demonstrates, our company law is resolutely set in an antique mould: the structure of the public company anxious to trap the unwary investor in its maw. The reality of Irish business life is utterly different. If at some stage we are afforded a breathing space and the insistent pressures from Brussels and the constraints of domestic crises are for the time at least relaxed, could we not contemplate an even more radical review of our company law than that contemplated by McDowell? Such a reassessment would have to acknowledge that the concept of the Victorian company, with its 'annual general meeting', 'reports to the members', and so on is wholly at odds with what actually happens in day-to-day life in Ireland. We might then begin to forge a system of company law which would accommodate both the imperatives of our European commitment and the commercial realities of a small island on the periphery of that great economic power.

Chapter 3

Irish Company Law and European Community Law[1]

[3.01] Ireland joined the European Economic Communities, as the European Union was then called, on 1 January 1973. As a result, the Oireachtas was no longer the only body capable of making laws for the country, since the treaties which established them entrusted legislative functions to two of the institutions created by the treaties, ie the Council of Ministers and the Commission. The treaties, moreover, also provided for the establishment of a Court of Justice whose decisions on matters within its remit were binding on Irish courts. Thus, justice could now be administered by a body other than the courts established under the Constitution and the Supreme Court in such matters ceased to be the final court of appeal in Ireland. In these areas, Ireland's accession to the EU was clearly in conflict with the Constitution and, consequently, an amendment by referendum of the Constitution was a necessary precondition to our accession.

[3.02] The amendment[2] provided that the State could become a member of the three communities. This enabled the State to cede legislative power in the relevant areas to the EU and to abridge the exclusive judicial role of the courts to the extent required by membership. But a further provision was thought necessary, since either acts by the State itself or the EU required by membership might conflict with other articles of the Constitution. Hence, the amendment also provides that laws, acts or measures necessitated by membership, whether they emanate from the State or the EU are not to be invalidated by the Constitution. Such laws, acts or measures are in the result effectively shielded from constitutional challenge in the Irish courts[3].

[3.03] The European Communities Act 1972 gave legislative effect to the amendment by providing that both the treaties and the existing and future acts adopted by its institutions should be binding on the State and part of our domestic law. It also empowered Ministers to make regulations for the purpose of enabling this provision to have full effect.

---

[1] See further McMahon and Murphy, *European Community Law in Ireland*; Temple Lang, *Three EEC Draft Directives on Company Law, Capital, Mergers and Management*, Ir Jur (ns) Vol VII; Quinn, *Company Law - the European Dimension*, ILT, November/December 1989.
[2] The Third Amendment of the Constitution contained in Article 29.4.
[3] *Crotty v An Taoiseach* [1987] IR 713.

[3.04] European Union Law (or 'EU Law', as we shall call it) is divided into four major sections. First, there are the treaties themselves which became part of our law by virtue of the 1972 Act and of which by far the most important in practice is the Treaty of Rome which established the economic community. Second, there are the regulations made by the Council of Ministers. These represent in essence the legislation of the EU and take effect directly in the member states: no implementing legislation is required. They are thus the most importance source of EU law. Third, there are the directives also made by the Council. These in general do not take effect directly but the member states are required to implement their provisions by appropriate legislation. Fourth, there are the decisions of the Courts of Justice of the EU. Because the civil law tradition espoused by countries in continental Europe has been a more powerful influence on the jurisprudence of those courts than the common law, these decisions in strict theory are of no effect save in the case with which they deal: our system of judicial precedent or *stare decisis* was not in general recognised by that tradition. In practice, however, such decisions are persuasive precedents of the first importance and, while the EU courts do not regard themselves as bound by their previous decisions, the extent to which they refer to them specifically in their judgments is an interesting reflection of the influence of the common law judges and advocates-general in the court and of the common law advocates who appear before them.

Impact of EU law on Irish company law

[3.05] The objectives of the Treaty of Rome and the manner in which the EU has sought to achieve them have had a major influence on Irish business which will be of even greater significance in the future. In particular, the introduction of an unrestricted market in goods and services, of freedom of movement and establishment of workers throughout the community, of a common agricultural policy and of measures intended to eliminate distortions in competition have had a profound effect on our economy and hence on our businesses. So too have the measures in the social sphere, such as those ensuring equal pay for women and outlawing sexually discriminatory employment practices. More recently, Irish membership of the single European currency has clearly profound implications for our economy, made more significant, in the short term at least, by continued uncertainty as to the future participation in the currency of our largest single trading partner, the United Kingdom. But these broader effects of EU membership are outside the scope of this book: we confine ourselves in this chapter to examining the extent to which EU law has affected business structures in general and those of companies, public and private, in particular.

[3.06] Article 100 of the Treaty of Rome empowers the Council to issue directives for the approximation or harmonisation of such provisions laid down by law, regulation or administrative action in the member states as directly affect the establishment and functioning of the common market created by the treaty. Article 54(3)(g) deals specifically with companies: it requires institutions of the community to co-ordinate national measures so as to provide equivalent (but not necessarily identical) safeguards for shareholders, creditors and others in the member states dealing with companies.

[3.07] In pursuance of these objectives, the Council have issued a number of directives and further directives have been drafted but not issued. Some of the directives have been implemented in Irish law: of these the most important in practice have been those dealing with the formation, maintenance and alteration of the capital of companies, the contents and publication of accounts and the legalisation of 'one man' companies. These directives are considered in more detail below. One directive embodies a long standing proposal of a wide ranging nature dealing with the structures of companies, which envisages among other things greater employee participation in the management of companies. So far this proposal has failed to make progress because of opposition from business interests, notably in the UK. In recent times, attention has tended to focus instead on a proposal for a 'European Company', ie a company which would owe its existence and legal structure to EU rather than national law. Effect has already been given in Ireland to a measure establishing 'European Economic Interest Groupings', intended to facilitate co-operation between undertakings in different member states in areas such as research and development and the marketing and sale of products[4].

[3.08] The European Company Statute, if adopted, could provide the framework for a genuinely comprehensive harmonisation of the company laws of the different member states. In the meantime, as one commentator[5] has pungently remarked, the EU have been adopting 'salami tactics' in a slice-by-slice approach. He adds with justification: 'the cumulative effect is a patchwork sewn on to basic fabrics of national laws which are often threadbare and uneven'. The ad hoc tinkering with 'domestic' company law referred to in the last chapter without any serious attempt to identify an underlying philosophy suitable to both Irish and EU conditions has exacerbated the problem for practitioners.

---

4   See para **[3.23]** below.
5   Quinn, *Company Law-- the European Dimension*, ILT, November/December 1989.

The Directives

[3.09] There are eleven directives in force. The numbering of them is somewhat confusing, since directives are not necessarily numbered according to the time at which they are adopted: thus the Fourth Directive was in fact adopted before the Third.

[3.10] Two further points about them should be noted. Although they are not in general of direct effect in the member states, the EU Commission, (the executive arm of the Council) can bring proceedings against a member state for failure to implement the directive by appropriate legislation. (The Second Directive was only implemented in Ireland following a finding by the EU Court of Justice that the State was in default. It is, however, fair to add that in recent years our record of compliance with directives in the company law area has significantly improved.) Moreover, although not in general of direct effect, it has been held that individuals can rely on the provisions of a directive in national courts even though it has not been implemented, at least so far as actions against the State itself are concerned[6]. This might be of importance at some stage in this country: as we have already seen, a considerable number of Irish semi-state bodies take the form of companies incorporated by special Acts. It has also been held that the right of individuals to rely on directives in proceedings against the State applies to such bodies[7]. Hence, an individual aggrieved by non-compliance by such a body with the terms of a directive could institute proceedings in an Irish court, even though the directive had not been implemented by legislation.

[3.11] The First Directive, which dates from 1968, contained two requirements which were relevant to Ireland. The first which sought protection for third parties dealing with a company so far as *ultra vires* transactions are concerned had been broadly anticipated by the Principal Act[8]. The second was intended to provide for the publication of certain information concerning the company throughout the community[9]. Both requirements were implemented by the European Communities (Companies) Regulations 1973[10].

[3.12] The Second Directive was implemented by the 1983 Act. It introduced the new designation of 'public limited company' and its abbreviation 'plc' for all public companies with limited liability. It contained detailed provisions as to the minimum authorised share capital of such companies, the payment for such share capital, the obligation to offer newly issued shares in such companies to

---

[6] *Van Duyn v Home Office* 41/74,(1974) ECR 1337.
[7] *Marshall v Southampton and SW Hampshire Area Health Authority* [1986] QB 401.
[8] See paras **[12.14]**, **[12.15]** below.
[9] See para **[4.20]** below.
[10] SI 1973/163.

the existing shareholders and the maintenance of the capital of such companies[11].

[3.13] The Third Directive is concerned with mergers of public companies. This directive, and the complementary Sixth Directive which deals with divisions of such companies (or 'scissions' as they are sometimes called on the continent), were implemented by the European Communities (Mergers and Divisions of Companies) Regulations 1987[12]. They are confined to mergers of such companies within member states. There is, however, a draft Tenth Directive which applies to trans-national mergers. These directives are of limited importance in Ireland, however, since companies here usually become associated as a result of a take-over (of which there are in any event relatively few) rather than a merger.

[3.14] The Fourth Directive concerns the contents and publication of accounts of companies, both public and private. It was implemented in Ireland by the 1986 Act and effected a significant change in Irish company law. Until then private companies were entirely exempted from the requirement of the Acts that the company's accounts be annexed to the annual return filed with the Registrar and thus be available for public inspection. The State, however, availed of the greater latitude which could still be enjoyed by small and medium-sized private companies, such companies, although they must now publish their accounts, can present them in significantly abbreviated form. The requirements of the 1986 Act are discussed in detail in Chapters 29 and 30.

[3.15] The Seventh Directive dealing with consolidated accounts complements the Fourth Directive and was implemented by the European Communities (Companies) (Group Accounts) Regulations 1992[13]. The Eighth Directive deals with the qualifications, professional integrity and independence of auditors and was implemented by Part X of the 1990 Act.

[3.16] The Eleventh Directive deals with disclosure of the accounts of branches of companies opened in the State by companies governed by the law of another state. It was implemented by the European Communities (Branch Disclosure) Regulations 1993[14].

[3.17] The Twelfth Directive on 'one man companies' was intended to remove what were regarded as unnecessary obstacles to the development of small and medium sized enterprises. As we have seen, companies which in practice, if not

---

11 See Chs 9 and 15 below.

12 SI 1987/137.

13 SI 1992/201. As to these regulations which should be read in conjunction with the European Communities (Accounts) Regulations 1993, SI 1993/396, see Ch 30.

14 SI 1993/395.

in theory, are 'one man' companies are common in Ireland. Under our company law, however, until 1994 a company had to have at least two shareholders and two directors and hence one frequently finds that the second share holder and director are nominees of the real proprietor.

[3.18] The Directive was implemented in Ireland by the European Communities (Single-Member Private Limited Companies) Regulations 1994[15]. Regulation 3(1) provides that, notwithstanding any enactment or rule of law to the contrary, a private company limited by shares or by guarantee may be formed by one person, and may have only one member, to the extent permitted by the Acts and the Regulations. Enactments and rules of law which apply to private companies limited by shares or guarantee are, in the absence of any express provision to the contrary, to apply with any necessary modifications in relation to a single member company as these apply in relation to such a company when formed by two or more persons.

[3.19] The Regulations also provide that certain provisions of the Acts, such as the holding of annual general meetings and the presentation of accounts to such meetings are not to apply to single member companies. These modifications of the Acts, as they apply to such companies, are dealt with in the appropriate parts of this book[16].

[3.20] Surprisingly, no change has been made in the law as to the number of directors: there still must be at least two, even in the case of single member private companies.

[3.21] The Fifth Directive is the controversial proposal dealing with the structure and management of public limited companies, including a provision for participation by the employees in a two-tier board. The draft Ninth Directive deals with the structure and framework of groups which contain public limited companies as subsidiaries.

[3.22] There are also other directives which have been implemented in Ireland and which are of interest to company lawyers. Those dealing with the co-ordination of the regulations as to stock exchanges in the member states were given effect to in the European Communities (Stock Exchange) Regulations 1984[17]. Those concerned with information which must be published when major holdings in public companies are sold were implemented by Part V of the 1990 Act which deals with 'insider dealing' generally[18]. A directive requiring the co-ordination of laws relating to unit trusts was implemented by the European

---

[15] SI 1994/275.
[16] See Ch 25 (Meetings); Ch 29 (The Annual Return); and Ch 30 (Accounts and Audit).
[17] SI 1984/282.
[18] See Ch 34 below.

Communities (Undertakings for Collective Investment in Transferable Securities) Regulations 1989[19] and by Part XIII of the 1990 Act.

European Economic Interest Groupings

[3.23] The EU has also given birth to a new form of business entity called the European Economic Interest Grouping, abbreviated to EEIG. This is in essence an association of businesses in different member states formed with a view to pooling knowledge and resources in areas where they have a common interest. Thus firms in a number of countries in the community could combine to maximise their expertise in marketing their particular products or in stimulating research and development. The primary object is not to make profits for the group, although that is not excluded, but to benefit the individual members by making the greatest use of their combined skills in areas where otherwise there might be wasteful duplication of effort and resources. The activities of the grouping are, in other words, ancillary to the main activities of the individual members.

[3.24] The EEIG was initially established by an EU regulation which was implemented by the European Community (European Economic Interest Grouping) Regulations 1989[20]. While it constitutes a form of partnership between firms in different member states, unlike partnerships in our law it is a corporate entity which can sue or be sued. The members of an EEIG can be individuals, partnerships, companies and public bodies or scientific organisations. There must be at least two members and one at least must be based in a different EU state: it is essentially a trans-national form of business organisation.

[3.25] The structure of an EEIG is not unlike that of a company registered under the Acts. Corresponding to the memorandum and articles, there is a contract forming the grouping which must be registered with the appropriate registry, in the member state, in this country the Registrar. The name must include the words 'European Economic Interest Grouping' or the initials 'EEIG' or their Irish equivalents. There are also provisions similar to those as to companies, requiring the publication of relevant information in *Iris Oifigiúil* and the furnishing of an annual return to the Registrar.

---

[19] SI 1989/78.
[20] SI 1989/191.

Part II
Formation of a Company

Chapter 4

How a Company is Formed

Distinction between public and private companies

[4.01] A distinction of fundamental importance is drawn in the Acts between public and private companies. It is accordingly essential at the outset to understand the nature of the distinction.

[4.02] A private company to be such must have a share capital and include three provisions in its articles:

(i) the right to transfer shares must be restricted;

(ii) the number of members must not exceed 50; and

(iii) there must be a prohibition on any invitation to the public to subscribe for shares or debentures of the company[1].

A public company is defined by s 2 of the 1983 Act as being 'a company which is not a private company'. This is the first time that the Acts have defined a public company. The theory which has always been present in companies' legislation is preserved, ie that the public company is the basic form of company and that private companies are variants from the norm. In practice, the reverse is the case: there are far more private companies in Ireland than public.

[4.03] In England, the 1980 Act brought theory into line with practice: it is no longer necessary in that jurisdiction for a private company to include the three provisions just referred to in its articles. The basic form of company is the private company, the public limited company being treated by statute as the exception rather than the rule. It was apparently not thought necessary to go so far in Ireland.

[4.04] Public companies are almost invariably registered with limited liability. Where they are so registered, they must now be described as 'public limited companies' and the abbreviation 'plc' used instead of the familiar 'Ltd'.

[4.05] A public company must have at least seven members[2]. Since the enactment of the European Communities (Single-Member Private Limited

---

[1] Companies Act 1963, s 33. A private company is also expressly prohibited by the Companies (Amendment) Act 1983, s 21 from offering its shares or debentures to the public. The company and any officer in default is liable on summary conviction to a fine not exceeding £500 in the event of a breach of the section.

[2] Companies Act 1963, s 5.

Companies) Regulations 1994[3], a private company limited by shares or by guarantee may be formed by one person only. Where a company becomes such a single-member company by a reduction in the number of its members, the Registrar must be so informed within 28 days. Conversely, where the number of members of a single member company is increased to two or more, the Registrar must be similarly informed.

[4.06] Where a private company is in breach of one of the relevant provisions, in its articles - eg where its membership exceeds 50 - it does not cease to be a private company. It does, however, forfeit certain of the privileges and exemptions available to a private company[4].

[4.07] Where public companies are formed, the company is almost invariably in existence already as a private company. The Acts contain machinery enabling private companies to re-register as public companies.

[4.08] A public company will usually invite the public to subscribe for shares by means of a document called a prospectus. This must comply with the strict requirements of the Acts. Moreover, before the company's shares can be quoted or dealt in on the stock exchange, those responsible for the formation of the company must comply with the requirements of that body as set out in the Rules of the Stock Exchange on the *Admission of Securities to Listing*. It is only when those requirements are met that the Council will give permission for the shares to be quoted or dealt in.

[4.09] In the case of all companies, public or private, certain steps must be taken before the company comes into being as a legal entity. These are explained in this Chapter. In the case of private companies, the steps to be taken - principally the preparation of the memorandum and articles - are relatively straightforward. But where a private company is re-registered as a public limited company, there are additional requirements to be met. At one time it was sufficient simply to delete the three provisions, already referred to, which are necessary in the case of a private company. Now it is also necessary to ensure that it has the minimum nominal capital required of such companies, that its shares are paid up to a specified extent and that its net assets and share capital are in balance.

It is also possible for a public company to re-register as a private company.

---

[3] See para **[3.18]** above.

[4] Under the Companies Act 1963, s 34, the company is treated as though its minimum membership was seven. It also loses the privilege (now somewhat abridged: see Ch 29 below) of not having to file its balance sheet and auditor's and director's reports with its annual return to the Registrar. The court has power under s 34(2) to relieve the company from such consequences if it is satisfied that the non-compliance with the relevant condition was accidental or due to 'some other sufficient cause'.

[4.10] In the case of all companies, public or private, formed after the coming into force of the 1999 (No 2) Act, there is now an additional important step that must be taken before they can be registered. In the case of such companies, it must be demonstrated to the Minister that, when registered, it will carry on an activity in the State. How this requirement may be met is explained in more detail below[5]. At this point, it is sufficient to note that the change in the law was prompted by the realisation that a large number of companies with no Irish connections were being registered in this country and that, in the case of some of them, there were good grounds for suspecting that their Irish registration was being availed of to conceal their activities from regulatory authorities in other countries and thus shield money laundering, tax evasion and criminal activities generally.

Essential steps in forming a company

[4.11] Persons who wish to form a company to be registered under the Acts - the 'promoters' - must first prepare the documents which provide the company with its constitution. These are the memorandum of association and the articles of association. These documents - together with certain others set out in para **[4.14]** below - are then lodged with the Registrar with the registration fee[6]. He issues a certificate of incorporation when he is satisfied that the documents are in order and that the name chosen for the company is acceptable. The company is thenceforth in existence.

[4.12] The amount of the registration fee is fixed by s 369 of the Principal Act and Part I of the Eighth Schedule to that Act. The Schedule may, however, be altered at any time by the Minister by order[7] and, as so altered, now provides that the fee for the registration of any company is £50[8].

[4.13] There must also be paid before the certificate of incorporation is issued the appropriate amount of capital duty. The rate of this duty - which replaced the stamp duty formerly payable on the formation of a company - is fixed by ss 69, 70 and 71 of the Finance Act 1973. Broadly speaking, it is 1% of the actual value of assets of any kind contributed in connection with the subscription for the shares less any liabilities which have been assumed or discharged by the company in consideration of the contribution.

---

[5] See para **[4.19]** below. The relevant provisions of the Companies (Amendment) (No 2) Act 1999 came into force on 18 April 2000.

[6] The Office of the Registrar is at Parnell House, 14 Parnell Square, Dublin 1.

[7] Companies Act 1963, s 395(2).

[8] Companies (Fees) Order 1997.

Documents to be delivered to the Registrar

[4.14] At one time, the only documents which had to be delivered to the Registrar when a company was being formed were the memorandum, the articles (if there were any)[9] and a statutory declaration of compliance with the requirements of the Acts as to registration[10]. Since the enactment of the 1982 Act, the Registrar must also be furnished with particulars of the directors' names, addresses, nationalities and occupations, the names and addresses of the secretary or joint secretaries and the location of the registered office of the company[11].

[4.15] The following documents must accordingly be delivered when the company is being formed:

(1)   the memorandum;

(2)   the articles (if any);

(3)   a statutory declaration by the solicitor engaged in the formation of the company or by a person named in the articles as a director or secretary of the company of compliance with the requirements of the Acts in respect of registration.[12]

(4)   a statement in the prescribed form[13] containing particulars of
        (i) in the case of the first directors

            (a)   their present and former Christian names and surnames;
            (b)   their usual residential addresses;
            (c)   their nationality, if not Irish;
            (d)   their business occupation, if any; and
            (e)   particulars of any other directorships of bodies incorporated in Ireland held by them.

        (ii) in the case of the secretary or joint secretaries

            (a)   where he is an individual, his present and former Christian names and surnames and his usual residential address; and
            (b)   where it is a body corporate, the corporate name and registered office.

        (iii) the situation of the registered office of the company.

---

9   In the case of companies limited by shares and companies limited by guarantee and not having a share capital, it is not necessary to register articles: see para **[4.26]** below.
10 Companies Act 1963, s 19(2).
11 Companies (Amendment) Act 1982, s 3.
12 The appropriate form for such a declaration is Form A2 of the Companies (Forms) Order 1987, SI 1987/147.
13 Form A2 of the Companies (Forms) Order 1987, SI 1987/147.

In addition, since the coming into force of s 42 of the 1999 (No 2) Act, it has been necessary to furnish the Registrar with sufficient evidence that the company (when registered) will carry on an activity (mentioned in its memorandum) in the State. This evidence may be contained in a statutory declaration in the prescribed form.

[4.16] The statement required by the 1982 Act must be signed by or on behalf of the subscribers to the memorandum and it must be accompanied by a consent signed by each of the persons named in it as a director, secretary or joint secretary to act in that capacity. If the memorandum is delivered to the Registrar by a person as agent for the subscribers, the statement must so specify and it must also contain the name and address of the person in question.

[4.17] As soon as the company is incorporated, the persons specified in the statement as directors, secretaries or joint secretaries are deemed to have been appointed to those offices. Any indication in the articles specifying a person as director or secretary is void unless that person is specified as a director or secretary in the statement[14].

[4.18] The Registrar is expressly precluded from registering a memorandum unless there is delivered with it the statement required by the 1982 Act[15].

[4.19] The statutory declaration verifying that the company will carry on an activity in the State must contain either a precise description of the activity or, where it belongs to a division, group or class in the relevant European Community classification system[16], a description of the general nature of the activity and the division, group or class to which it belongs. In every case, there must be stated the place or places in the State where it is proposed to carry on the activity and the place, whether in the State or not, where the central administration of the company will normally be carried on. If it is proposed to carry on two or more activities in the State, the particulars in question must relate to whichever activities the person making the declaration considers to be the principal activity which will be carried on in the State.

The statutory declaration must be made by one of the persons named in the statement required by the 1982 Act as a director or secretary of the company or the solicitor, if any, engaged in the formation of the company.

---

14 Companies (Amendment) Act 1982, s 3.
15 Companies (Amendment) Act 1982, s 3(6).
16 Set out in the Annex to Council Regulation (EEC) 3037/90 of 9 October 1990 on the Statistical Classification of Activities in the European Community (OJ L293 24.10.90 p 1).

Official notification

[4.20] When a company is incorporated, the company must publish in *Iris Oifigiúil* notice of certain matters. These are specified in Article 4 of the European Communities (Companies) Regulations 1973[17]. These requirements were introduced in compliance with the Second EU Directive which requires the member states to take steps to ensure that certain essential information concerning companies is easily accessible throughout the EU.

[4.21] The article obliges the company to publish in *Iris Oifigiúil* among other matters notice of the delivery to the Registrar by the company and the issuing by him of the following documents and particulars:

(1)   the certificate of incorporation;

(2)   the memorandum and articles;

(3)   any document making or evidencing an alteration in the memorandum or articles;

(4)   every amended text of the memorandum and articles; and

(5)   notice of the situation of the registered office and any change therein.

The notice must be published within six weeks of the relevant delivery or issue.

[4.22] Two important features of this requirement should be noticed. In the first place, the company is not required to publish the contents of the various documents in *Iris Oifigiúil:* simply the fact of their having been delivered or issued. In the second place, the failure of the company to publish the relevant notice will not preclude the company from carrying on business. It will, however, mean (under Article 10) that the company will be unable to rely on the relevant documents or particulars as against any other person unless the company proves that the person had knowledge of them.

[4.23] There is also a curious provision in Article 10 that in the case of transactions taking place within 16 days of the date of publication, the documents and particulars cannot be relied on against a person who proves that it was impossible for him to have knowledge of them. It is far from clear how such a burden of proof could be discharged, since once the publication takes place, it is obviously possible for anyone who reads *Iris Oifigiúil* to have knowledge of the documents. It may be that the provision would only be applicable where the person was abroad at the relevant time or for some other reason unable to obtain a copy of *Iris Oifigiúil*.

---

[17] SI 1973/163.

[4.24] It is obviously important for those concerned in the formation of new companies and the alteration of the memorandum and articles of existing companies to ensure that the company has complied with the requirements.

Distinction between memorandum and articles

[4.25] At one time the constitution of a company was contained in one document, ie the deed of settlement. The Joint Stock Companies Act 1856, however, provided for the division of the constitution into two documents, one containing the conditions upon which the company is granted incorporation - the memorandum - and the other setting out the rules under which the company proposes to regulate its affairs (the articles). The distinction has been retained in all subsequent legislation. Because the memorandum contained the fundamental law applicable to the company, the manner in which it could be altered was subject to strict statutory control, which was, however, relaxed with the passage of years, most notably by the Principal Act[18].

[4.26] In the case of a company limited by guarantee and having a share capital and an unlimited company, articles of association must be registered with the memorandum[19]. This is not necessary in the case of a company limited by shares or a company limited by guarantee and not having a share capital; but where no articles are registered in the case of such companies, the model articles contained in Tables A and C of the First Schedule to the Principal Act will be applicable[20]. In practice, articles are almost invariably registered in the case of such companies, although they frequently do no more than adopt the relevant model articles with appropriate amendments. Unlike the memorandum, it has always been possible to amend the articles with comparative ease[21].

Articles are controlled by the memorandum

[4.27] As we have seen, the memorandum contains the conditions upon which the company is granted incorporation. It must contain provisions dealing with certain matters - eg the name and objects of the company - known as the obligatory clauses[22]. While the company may adopt such articles as it thinks appropriate and amend them from time to time, the articles cannot extend the area of the company's activities as they are defined and circumscribed by the memorandum. The law was thus stated by Carroll J in *Roper v Ward*[23]:

---

[18] See paras **[5.35]** and **[5.46]**.
[19] Companies Act 1963, s 11 as amended by the Companies (Amendment) Act 1982, s 2.
[20] Companies Act 1963, s 13(2) as amended by the Companies (Amendment) Act 1982, s 14.
[21] See para **[6.14]** below.
[22] See para **[5.02]** below.
[23] [1981] ILRM 408.

'In construing the articles, I am guided by the principle that they are subordinate to and controlled by the memorandum of association which is the dominant instrument. While the articles cannot alter or control the memorandum or be used to expand the objects of the company, they can be used to explain it generally or to explain an ambiguity in its terms.'

[4.28] While, as Carroll J indicated, the articles may be used to explain ambiguities in the memorandum or to explain it generally, they cannot be used to interpret any of the obligatory clauses. As Bowen LJ put it in *Guinness v Land Corpn of Ireland*[24]:

'It is ... certain that for anything which the Act of Parliament says shall be in the memorandum you must look to the memorandum alone. If the legislature has said that one instrument is to be dominant you cannot turn to another instrument and read it in order to modify the provisions of the dominant instrument.'

Memorandum and articles are public documents

[4.29] The memorandum and articles of association of a company are public documents. Any person is entitled to inspect them in the Registrar's office on payment of a small fee[25]. This at one stage could have serious consequences for persons dealing with the company, since it meant that they were assumed to be aware of the powers which the company enjoyed and the objects for which it was created. If the company entered into a contract which was beyond its powers or outside its objects- in legal terms *ultra vires* - the company was frequently in a position to repudiate its obligations because the other party was presumed to be aware of its invalidity. This principle has, however, been substantially modified in recent times[26].

What kind of company?

[4.30] Once it has been decided to form a company, public or private, the next question for the promoters is whether they will avail of the benefits of limited liability and, if they do, whether the company should be limited by shares or guarantee. The advantages of forming a company limited by shares have already been explained[27]; we now proceed to consider the other types of company which may be formed.

---

[24] (1882) 22 Ch D 349 at 281.
[25] Companies Act 1963, s 370.
[26] See Ch 12 below.
[27] See para **[1.11]** above.

Companies limited by guarantee

[4.31] In the case of a company limited by guarantee, the liability of the members is limited by the memorandum to the amount which they each undertake to contribute to the assets of the company in the event of its being wound up. While the amount which each member undertakes to pay is normally the same, there is nothing to prevent the memorandum from stipulating different amounts for different members[28].

[4.32] It will be seen that in the case of such companies the members will not be required to provide the company with any cash either on its formation or during the course of its active life. It is accordingly a suitable vehicle for associations which wish to secure the benefits of a separate legal personality and of limited liability but do not require to raise funds from the members. Many charitable and professional bodies find this form of company suitable to their special needs. The management of such companies is normally entrusted by the articles to a council or committee elected by the members rather than a board of directors.

[4.33] A company limited by guarantee may also have a share capital. This, however, is not particularly common. The formation of public companies limited by guarantee and having a share capital is now prohibited by s 7 of the 1983 Act.

Unlimited companies

[4.34] A company may be formed and registered under the Act which is limited neither by shares nor by guarantee. In such a case, it is known as an unlimited company. Such companies are frequently formed where it is intended that the company will not carry on business. They have proved particularly popular as vehicles for the avoidance of tax, since such schemes frequently involve the transfer of assets from individuals to companies. The company usually holds the property on behalf of the individual whose tax burden is being lightened, with no expectation that it will carry on any business. In such circumstances, the protection of limited liability is not required and is usually not availed of since no capital duty is payable in respect of the formation of such a company[29].

[4.35] Unlimited companies also have the advantage of being exempted from the requirement of the 1986 Act that the accounts be annexed to the annual return.

Formation of a public limited company

[4.36] A public limited company may be formed as an entirely new company. It is, however, far more common for such companies to be formed by converting

---

[28] Cf *Palmer's Company Law* (25th edn), Vol 1 para 2.009.
[29] Finance Act 1973, s 67.

an existing private company into a public company. At one stage, it was possible to do this by simply passing a special resolution deleting the three provisions which, as we have seen, must be contained in the articles in order to constitute it a private company. The 1983 Act, implementing the Second EU Directive, imposed additional requirements intended to ensure that a public limited company has a minimum nominal share capital, that its shares are paid up in money or money's worth to a specified extent and - in the case of a private company being converted into such a company -that its net assets at least equal the total of its called up share capital and undistributable reserves[30].

[4.37] Accordingly, where a public limited company is being formed, the amount of the share capital as stated in the memorandum must be not less than the authorised minimum. This is fixed by s 19 of the 1983 Act at £30,000, but the Minister has power to increase the amount by order. As we shall see in more detail in Chapter Eight, its allotted share capital must also be paid up in money or money's worth to at least 25% of the nominal value.

Re-registration of private company as public limited company

[4.38] Before a private company can re-register as a public limited company, it must meet the following conditions:

    (1)   the amount of the nominal share capital must be not less than the authorised minimum;

    (2)   the allotted share capital must be paid up in money or money's worth to at least 25% of the nominal value; and

    (3)   its net assets as shown by the balance sheet must at least equal the total of its called up share capital and undistributable reserves[31].

[4.39] As we shall also see in more detail in Chapter 9, while shares may be paid up other than in cash, the 1983 Act requires that such non-cash considerations be properly valued by qualified experts and - where they take the form of undertakings - further requires that the undertaking has been performed or must as a matter of contract be performed within five years. Accordingly, the Act also requires that before a private company is re-registered as a public limited company, such undertakings should have either been performed or their performance be required by contract within five years.

[4.40] We can now consider in detail the steps which must be taken when a private company wishes to re-register as a public limited company.

---

[30] For the meaning of the expressions 'called up share capital' and 'undistributable reserves' see paras **[14.07]** and **[31.24]** below.

[31] Companies (Amendment) Act 1983, ss 10(1) and 9(3)(e).

(1)   A special resolution[32] must be passed

(a) that the company be re-registered as a public limited company;

(b) that the company's memorandum be altered so that it states that the company is a public limited company and so that it complies with the appropriate form for such a company[33]; and

(c) that the three provisions in the articles which are necessary to constitute it a private company be deleted[34].

(2)   An application in the prescribed form[35] signed by a director or secretary of the company must be delivered to the Registrar together with the following documents;

(a) a printed copy of the memorandum and articles as altered in pursuance of the resolution;

(b) a copy of a written statement by the auditors of the company that in their opinion its balance sheet - which must have been prepared not more than seven months before the date of the application - shows that at its date the amount of the net assets were not less than the aggregate of the called up share capital and undistributable reserves;

(c) a copy of the balance sheet together with a copy of an unqualified report[36] by the auditor in relation to the balance sheet;

(d) a statutory declaration in the prescribed form[37] by a director or secretary of the company, stating

(i)   that the special resolution has been passed;

(ii)   that between the balance sheet date and the application there has been no change in the financial position that has resulted in the net assets becoming less than the aggregate of the called up share capital and the undistributable reserves;

(iii)   that the valuation and report mentioned at (3) below have been made and obtained (where they are required) and that the conditions referred to in para **[4.38]** above have been complied with[38]

---

[32] For special resolutions see para **[25.28]** below.

[33] Set out in the Companies (Amendment) Act 1983, Sch 2 Pt I.

[34] Companies (Amendment) Act 1983, s 9(2).

[35] Companies (Forms) Order 1983, SI 1983/289, Form 71.

[36] An unqualified report is one which states 'without material qualification' that the balance sheet complies with the Acts (see Ch 32 below) and presents a 'true and fair view' of the company's affairs. A qualification is not 'material' if the auditors state in writing that it is not material for the purpose of determining whether the net assets and share capital are in balance.

[37] Companies (Forms) Order 1983, SI 1983/289, Form 72.

[38] Companies (Amendment) Act 1983, s 9(3)(e).

(3) Where shares are allotted by the company between the balance sheet date and the date of the special resolution as fully or partly paid up otherwise than in cash, the consideration must be valued in accordance with s 30 of the 1983 Act[39], a report with respect to the value must be obtained during the six months preceding the allotment and a copy of the report must accompany the application[40].

Formation of unlimited public company

[4.41] It is still possible to form an unlimited public company. It is also possible to re-register a limited private company as an unlimited public company. This can be achieved by deleting the three provisions in the articles constituting it a private company and following the procedures outlined in para **[4.50]** below for the conversion of limited into unlimited companies. There must also be delivered with the application for re-registration a document called a statement in lieu of a prospectus[41].

[4.42] It is not possible to re-register an unlimited private company as an unlimited public company. If such a company deletes the three provisions in its articles already referred to, it can only re-register as a public limited company. There seems no reason why an unlimited private company should be denied the facility available to limited private companies and it must be assumed that the lacuna is simply due to inadvertence on the part of the draftsman.

Re-registration of 'old public limited companies'

[4.43] The 1983 Act also contained transitional provisions enabling public companies already in existence and limited by shares or guarantee to re-register as public limited companies under the new legislation. Such companies (referred to in the legislation as 'old public limited companies',) where given a period of three years commencing on 13 October 1983 to bring their share capital into conformity with the requirements of the Act. If they did not meet those requirements within that period, which has now expired, re-register as another form of company or wind up voluntarily, they could be wound up by the court. The Act also contained provisions for the imposition of penalties on such companies and their officers who failed to re-register within 15 months as public limited companies, with a saver for companies who had applied to be re-registered as another form of company.

---

[39] See para **[9.27]** below.

[40] Companies (Amendment) Act 1983, s 9(5).

[41] The only occasion on which such a document is required. It was dispensed with in England by the 1948 Act.

[4.44] It should be noted that failure of the company to re-register within the three year period did not affect its status as a company, so that all transactions entered into it remained valid notwithstanding its failure to re-register.

Conversion of public company into private company

[4.45] A public company may be converted into a private company by altering its articles so as to add the three restrictions already referred to to the articles. These alterations may be made by special resolution of the company in general meeting. In the case of public limited companies the 1983 Act contains additional provisions.

[4.46] Under s 14 of the 1983 Act, the resolution in such a case must alter the memorandum so that it no longer states that the company is to be a public limited company and must make other such alterations in the memorandum as are requisite in the circumstances. There is provision under s 15 for an application to the court for the cancellation of such a resolution. It may be made by the holders of not less than five per cent in nominal value of the company's issued share capital or any class thereof, by not less than five per cent of the members (in the case of a company not limited by shares) or by not less than 50 of the members. No person may make the application who has consented or voted in favour of the resolution. It must be made to the court within 28 days after the resolution; and the company must give notice of any such application and any order made thereon to the Registrar. The court has power to make an order either cancelling or confirming the resolution and, in addition, may adjourn the proceedings to enable the interests of the dissentient members to be purchased. It may also provide for the purchase by the company of shares of the members, the reduction of the company's capital accordingly and consequential alterations in the memorandum or articles.

Conversion of unlimited company into limited company and vice versa

[4.47] An unlimited company may be converted into a company limited by shares or guarantee or both. This is provided for by s 20 of the Principal Act as amended by s 53 of the 1983 Act. A special resolution must first be passed by the company in general meeting that the company should be re-registered as a limited company. The resolution must state:

(1)   whether the company is to be limited by shares or guarantee; and

(2)   if it is to be limited by shares, what the share capital is to be;

and must provide for the making of such alterations in the memorandum and articles as are necessary to bring those documents into conformity with the requirements of the Acts relating to the type of company in question.

[4.48] An application in writing must then be made to the Registrar[42], signed by a director or secretary of the company and accompanied by a printed copy of the altered memorandum and articles. The re-registration of a company under the section is not to affect any existing rights or obligations of the company.

[4.49] A limited company may re-register as an unlimited company, an innovation in our company law which was introduced by s 52 of the 1983 Act. The assent of all the members of the company is, however, required.

[4.50] Section 52 of the 1983 Act (which is taken almost word for word from the corresponding s 43 of the English Act of 1967) requires an application in the prescribed form[43] signed by a director or secretary to be made to the Registrar. This must set out such alterations in the memorandum as are required in the case of an unlimited company and the necessary alterations of the articles. It must be accompanied by the following:

(1)   an assent in the prescribed form[44] signed by or on behalf of all members;

(2)   a statutory declaration by the directors that the persons who have signed the assent constitute the whole membership of the company and that the directors have taken all reasonable steps to satisfy themselves that any person who signed on behalf of a member was empowered to do so;

(3)   a printed copy of the altered memorandum, and

(4)   a printed copy of the altered articles.

[4.51] Section 52(6) provides that past members who are not members at the time of the application for re-registration and who do not become members again are not to be liable to contribute anything more in the event of a winding up than they would have been liable to contribute had the company not been re-registered.

[4.52] There is no provision in the Acts for the conversion of companies limited by shares into companies limited by guarantee or vice versa; nor for the conversion of companies limited by guarantee and not having a share capital into companies limited by guarantee and having a share capital or vice versa.

---

[42]   The appropriate form is the Companies (Forms) Order 1983, SI 1983/289, Form 86.
[43]   Companies (Forms) Order 1987, SI 1987/147, Form D6.
[44]   Companies (Forms) Order 1987, SI 1987/147, Form D6.

Companies incorporated outside Ireland

[4.53] The Principal Act also contains certain requirements applicable to companies incorporated outside Ireland which have established places of business within Ireland. All such companies are required to deliver to the Registrar within one month of the establishment of the place of business the following documents:

(1) A certified copy of the charter, statutes or memorandum and articles of the company or other instrument containing its constitution and, if it is not in English or Irish, a certified translation.

(2) A list of directors, containing (in the case of individuals) the Christian names and addresses, nationality (if not Irish), business occupations, particulars of other directorships held in bodies corporate incorporated in Ireland and (in the case of bodies corporate) the corporate name and registered or principal office.

(3) Where an individual is the secretary, his Christian name and surname, any former name or surname and his usual residential address and, where a body corporate is the secretary, its corporate name and registered or principal office.

(4) The names and addresses of one or more persons resident in Ireland authorised to accept service of process on behalf of the company and the address of the company's principal place of business in Ireland[45].

[4.54] The Act also requires the delivery within a prescribed time to the Registrar of particulars of alterations in any of the above[46]. There is also provision for the delivery to the Registrar of copies of the balance sheet and profit and loss account and (in the case of a holding company) group accounts in the form in which, if it were a company within the meaning of the Acts, it would have had to lay such documents before the company in general meeting[47].

[4.55] Such a company must also state in any prospectus inviting subscriptions for shares and debentures within Ireland the country in which it is incorporated, and must exhibit conspicuously on every place in Ireland where it carries on business and in a legible manner on its various bill heads, letter headings etc the name of the company and the country in which it is incorporated. If the liability of the members is limited, a statement to that effect must appear in legible characters in any such prospectus, in all such bill heads etc and on every place where it carries on business[48].

---

[45] Companies Act 1963, s 352. As of 31 December 1998, there were 2,953 such companies registered under the Companies Act 1963 or Regulations.

[46] Companies Act 1963, s 353.

[47] Companies Act 1963, s 354.

[48] Companies Act 1963, s 355.

[4.56] There is provision for the service of any process or notice on any person whose name has been delivered to the Registrar in compliance with the requirements just mentioned. Where there is no such person in existence or the company has made default in delivering to the Registrar the relevant particulars, any such process or notice may be served by leaving it or sending it by post to any place of business established by the company in Ireland[49]. Where the company has not established a place of business in the State within the meaning of the Principal Act, but has a 'branch' in the State within the meaning of the European Community (Branch Disclosures) Regulations 1993, similar particulars are required to be filed.

[4.57] There are also provisions in Part XII of the Principal Act setting out certain requirements as to the contents of prospectuses relating to companies incorporated outside Ireland.

Companies not formed under the Acts

[4.58] Companies formed under the legislation which was replaced by the Principal Act continue to exist despite the repeal of that legislation, and the relevant provisions of the Acts apply to such companies[50]. In addition, the Principal Act enables joint stock companies incorporated before 1862 and companies incorporated under royal charters, letters patent and statute, subject to certain qualifications, to be registered under the Acts[51].

---

[49] Companies Act 1963, s 356.
[50] Companies Act 1963, Pt VIII.
[51] Companies Act 1963, Pt IX.

Chapter 5

The Memorandum of Association

Essential features of the memorandum

[5.01] The memorandum is the fundamental document of the company's constitution and contains the conditions upon which the company is granted incorporation. The name and objects of the company must be stated and, if it is to be a company with limited liability, that fact must also be stated[1].

[5.02] The Principal Act provides that in the case of each category of company which may be registered under the Acts the memorandum must be in the form set out in the appropriate table in the First Schedule 'or as near thereto as circumstances admit'. In the case of a company limited by shares, the type most frequently formed, the appropriate form is set out in Table B[2]. (In the case of public limited companies, the appropriate forms are contained in the Second Schedule to the 1983 Act). In the case of such a company, the memorandum must contain the following clauses, sometimes referred to as 'the obligatory clauses':

    (1)   the name clause,

    (2)   the objects clause;

    (3)   the limited liability clause;

    (4)   the capital clause, and

    (5)   the association clause.

[5.03] In contrast to English law, there is no requirement that the location of the registered office be stated in the memorandum. But it is essential to give particulars of its location to the Registrar before the company can be incorporated[3].

Each of the obligatory clauses is considered in detail below.

[5.04] The memorandum of a public company must be subscribed to by at least seven persons[4]. In the case of a private company, only one person's subscription has been required since 1994[5]. The signature of each subscriber must be attested

---

[1] Companies Act 1963, s 6(1) and (2).
[2] Companies Act 1963, s 16.
[3] See para **[4.15]** above.
[4] Companies Act 1963, s 5(1).
[5] European Communities (Single-Member Private Limited Companies) Regulation 1994, SI 1994/275, reg 4.

by at least one witness. The entire memorandum other than the signatures, must be printed[6].

The name clause

[5.05] This clause must state the company's name. In the case of a company limited by shares or by guarantee, the last word of the name must be 'limited' or its Irish equivalent 'teoranta'[7].

[5.06] There are important restrictions on the choice of a name for a new company. Under s 21 of the Principal Act, no company may be registered by a name which, in the opinion of the Minister, is undesirable. This will most frequently arise where the name submitted for registration is too like the name of a company already registered.

[5.07] It should be noted that the power to refuse registration is, in effect, vested in the Minister and not in the Registrar. The latter is not obliged, however, to submit every name proferred for registration to the Minister for approval. It is, accordingly, only where the Registrar himself considers that there is a possibility of the name being undesirable that the Minister's powers come into play. It is therefore important for persons forming a new company to ascertain from the Registrar whether a particular name appears to be available for registration before going through the time-consuming and expensive process of preparing and printing the memorandum and articles.

[5.08] The Registrar of Companies has issued a leaflet giving guidance as to the names that may be refused registration. Generally speaking, a name will not be registered if:

(a)   it is identical to a name already appearing on the register of companies;

(b)   in the opinion of the Minister, it is offensive;

(c)   it would suggest State sponsorship;

(d)   the name includes 'bank' or cognate words, unless an appropriate licence or exemption has been granted by the Central Bank[8]

(e)   the name includes the word 'insurance' or cognate words unless an appropriate licence has been granted by the Minister[9]

(f)   the name includes the words 'society', 'co-op' or 'co-operative'.

---

[6]   Companies Act 1963, s 7.
[7]   Companies Act 1963, s 6(1).
[8]   See para **[1.33]** above.
[9]   See para **[1.34]** above.

It should be borne in mind that these are informal guidelines. This is in contrast to the position in England: there, ss 26 and 29 of the Companies Act 1985 give the Secretary of State discretion to refuse registration on a variety of grounds or to permit registration of specified names only with his consent or after objections (if any) from an appropriate government department or public body have been considered. If criteria used in England were applied, it would mean that names implying multi-national status, business pre-eminence or charitable status would be refused registration. Thus, expressions such as 'Chartered', 'Charitable' and 'European' would be refused registration.

[5.09] It must be remembered that while it is a sensible precaution to ascertain from the Registrar whether a particular name is available for registration, the Registrar cannot give any binding assurance that the company will be registered under the suggested name. It may happen, for example, that by the time the memorandum and articles are prepared and printed, another company will have been registered under the same name or a similar name. To avoid this difficulty, Jenkins recommended that the English legislation should be amended to enable company promoters to reserve a particular name for a short period on payment of a fee. Unfortunately, this practical suggestion has not been adopted here so far.

[5.10] Section 21 provides for an appeal to the court against a refusal to register a company by a particular name. This right (which is not conferred by the equivalent English legislation) is rarely availed of in practice, but is a useful safeguard against the use by the Minister of his power in an arbitrary or unreasonable manner.

[5.11] It may happen that through inadvertence a name may be accepted for registration which is in fact identical with or similar to that of a company already registered. Accordingly, the Principal Act provides that the Minister may within six months after registration compel the company to change its name if the name is too like that by which a company has already been registered. Where a direction is given to this effect by the Minister, the company must comply with it within six weeks from the date of the direction or such longer period as the Minister may allow[10].

[5.12] The mere fact that a company has been registered under a particular name without objection from the Minister will not necessarily protect the company if the name in fact closely resembles that of an existing company or business. The company registering under such a name may be liable in proceedings for the tort or civil wrong of 'passing off', ie representing a business which is being carried on by another as being carried on by oneself. Similarly, if a company is

---

[10] Companies Act 1963, s 23(2).

precluded by contract from using that name, it will in an appropriate case be restrained by injunction from so doing, despite its having been duly registered.

[5.13] A company may change its name at any time by passing a special resolution to that effect and obtaining the approval in writing of the Minister[11].

[5.14] A company may carry on business under a name other than its corporate name but must register the name under the Registration of Business Names Act 1963. The following particulars must be registered:

    (1)   the business name;

    (2)   the general nature of the business;

    (3)   the principal place of business;

    (4)   the name and registered or principal office of the company;

    (5)   the date of the adoption of the business name.

[5.15] As in the case of the registration of the company's name, a name cannot be registered which in the opinion of the Minister is undesirable and there is again a right of appeal to the court from the Minister's decision.

[5.16] We have seen that the name of a company limited by shares or by guarantee must end with the word 'limited' or 'teoranta'. This reflects a principle of company law which dates from the middle of the nineteenth century that persons who obtain the statutory protection of limited liability must bring the fact that their liability is so limited to the notice of the public. The Principal Act contains provisions intended to ensure that this rule is observed.

[5.17] In particular the name must be painted up or affixed to the outside of every office or place in which the business of the company is carried on in a conspicuous position in easily legible letters. It must also be engraved in legible characters on the company's seal. It must be mentioned in legible characters in all business letters of the company, all notices and other official publications, all bills of exchange, promissory notes, endorsements, cheques and orders for money or goods purporting to be signed by or on behalf of the company and in all invoices, receipts and letters of credit of the company. In the event of breaches of this requirement, the company and any officer of the company (or any other person acting on its behalf) who is responsible for the breach is liable to fines ranging from £125 to £150[12].

[5.18] In the case of public limited companies, the 1983 Act contains special provision as to the name. It must end with the words 'public limited company' or 'cuideachta phoibli teoranta' or with their respective abbreviations 'plc' or 'cpt'.

---

[11] Companies Act 1963, s 23(1).

[12] Companies Act 1963, s 114 as amended by the Companies (Amendment) Act 1982, s 15.

Neither the words nor the abbreviations may be preceded by the word 'limited' or 'teoranta' or their respective abbreviations 'ltd' or 'teo'[13].

[5.19] Section 56 of the Act makes it an offence for any person who is not a public limited company to carry on any trade, profession or business under a name which includes as its last part the words 'public limited company' or their Irish equivalent or the respective abbreviations. It is also an offence for a public limited company to use a name which may reasonably be expected to give the impression that it is a company other than a public limited company, in circumstances in which the fact that it is a public limited company is likely to be material to any person.

[5.20] A person guilty of an offence under the section and, in the case of a company any officer in default, is liable on summary conviction to a fine not exceeding £500 and, in the case of a continuing offence a fine not exceeding £50 for every day on which the offence is committed, and not exceeding £1,000 in total.

[5.21] In addition to exposing the company and its directors to penalties, the use of the company's name in an incorrect form may also render the director or officer concerned personally liable for a debt of the company.

[5.22] Section 114(4) of the Principal Act provides that any officer of a company or other person acting on its behalf who signs, or authorises to be signed, on behalf of the company any bill of exchange, promissory note, endorsement, cheque or order for money or goods in which the name of the company is not mentioned as required by the Acts is personally liable to the holder of the bill or cheque or whatever it may be for the amount involved, unless it is paid by the company. The effect of the provision is to make the officer concerned liable as a surety, ie he has to pay only if the company defaults.

[5.23] It is clear that the officer concerned will be liable even though the holder of bill or cheque was not in any way misled by the error[14]. It is also clear that even a minor error may have these consequences. Thus in *Durham Fancy Goods Ltd v Michael Jackson (Fancy Goods) Ltd*[15] the plaintiffs in drawing a bill of exchange on the defendant company described it as 'M Jackson (Fancy Goods) Ltd'. A director of the defendant company accepted the bill on behalf of the company in this form by signing his name to it. It was held that he was prima facie personally liable on the bill under the corresponding English section. Since, however, the plaintiffs had expressly or impliedly represented that they would accept the incorrect form of name, it was also held that they could not rely

---

13 Companies (Amendment) Act 1983, s 4.
14 *Atkins v Wardle* (1899) 58 LJ QB 377; on appeal 5 TLR 734.
15 [1968] 2 QB 839.

on the section, an application of the legal doctrine of estoppel. But it should be noted that the plaintiffs' position in that case was particularly unmeritorious: they themselves had inscribed the incorrect name of the company on the bill. Absent facts of that nature, the director is unlikely to escape personal liability, as recent English decisions have demonstrated[16].

[5.24] A private company limited by shares or by guarantee may be granted a licence by the Minister to omit the word 'limited' or 'teoranta' from its name. It must, however, comply with certain requirements before such a licence can be granted ie:

(1)   its objects must be the promotion of commerce, art, science, religion, charity or any other useful object and the application of its profits or income must be confined to the promotion of its objects;

(2)   it must be precluded from distributing any dividend to its members.[17]

Such a licence may be subject to such conditions as the Minister thinks fit. It may also be revoked at any time by the Minister, but he must give notice to the company in advance of his intention to revoke the licence and the company is entitled to be heard in opposition to the revocation.

The objects clause

[5.25] The memorandum must state the objects of the company. The objects are entirely a matter for the promoters: provided they are not unlawful (eg the running of illegal lotteries), they may adopt whatever objects they wish[18].

[5.26] Once the objects are stated in the memorandum, the company is strictly confined to them. The law confers on the company the power to attain them; but it also restrains the company from travelling beyond them. The statement of objects, in other words, has a positive and a negative effect defined as follows by Lord Cairns LC in the leading case of *Ashbury Railway Carriage and Iron Co Ltd v Riche*[19]:

> 'It states affirmatively the ambit and extent of vitality and power which by law are given to the corporation, and it states, if it is necessary so to state, negatively, that nothing shall be done beyond that ambit, and that no attempt shall be made to use the corporate life for any other purpose than that which is so specified'

---

[16] *Blum v OCP Repartition USA* (1988) BCLC 170; *Rafsanjan Pistachio Producers Co-operative v Reiss* (1990) BCLC 352. In the former case, May LJ expressly reserved the question as to whether *Durham Fancy Goods Ltd* was correctly decided. In both cases, an attempt by the director to escape liability by seeking 'rectification' of the cheque failed. See also *Scottish & Newcastle Breweries Ltd v Blair* 1967 SLT 72.

[17] Companies Act 1963, s 24 as amended by the Companies (Amendment) Act 1983, s 58.

[18] *R v Registrar of Companies, ex p Moore* [1931] 2 KB 197.

[19] (1875) LR 7 HL 653 at 670.

[5.27] At common law, a corporation, unless expressly precluded by its charter or other constitution from doing so, could do any act of which an individual was capable. The reason for confining a company incorporated under the Acts to its stated objects was to protect creditors and investors against the adverse consequences which might result to them from an unauthorised use of the company's assets. The rule caused considerable hardship to persons who dealt with companies, since they were deemed to be aware of the stated objects of the company, the memorandum, as we have seen, being a document open to public inspection. If the transaction was ultra vires - or outside the powers of - a company, the other contracting party was frequently unable to enforce any rights he would otherwise have against the company. Ultimately, the ultra vires rule was modified in its application to such persons by s 8 of the Principal Act and Article 6 of the European Communities (Companies) Regulations 1973[20]. Its effect on such transactions is considered further in Chapter 12 below.

[5.28] There is one important qualification to the strict canon of construction referred to in the para **[5.26]**. It was held in *Attorney General v Great Eastern Rly*[21] that whatever may fairly be regarded as incidental to or consequential upon those things specified in the memorandum as objects ought not, unless expressly prohibited, to be held by judicial construction to be ultra vires. Thus in the case of companies whose objects entitle them to carry out a particular trade or trades certain powers would normally be implied as incidental or consequential to the stated objects, ie power

- (1)   to employ labour;
- (2)   to draw and accept bills of exchange (including cheques);
- (3)   to borrow and give security;
- (4)   to make contracts for the purchase of supplies;
- (5)   to open a bank account;
- (6)   to take and defend legal proceedings and settle them;
- (7)   to employ agents;
- (8)   to pay bonuses and pensions to employees.

[5.29] While the modification of the strict rule of construction just referred to eased the position of directors and managers of companies, it has nonetheless been standard practice since the rule first evolved for draftsmen of memoranda to state the objects of the company in huge detail in order to avoid the pitfalls of the rule. Many directors of small newsagency or confectionery businesses would be staggered to find that as a result their solicitors had found it necessary to give

---

[20]   SI 1973/163.
[21]   (1880) 5 App Cas 473.

them power to construct docks and harbours and promote private acts of parliament.

[5.30] A further difficulty for the draftsman was the so-called 'main objects' rule. Where the objects are expressed in a series of numbered paragraphs (as is usually the case) and the first object appears to represent the main object of the company, all the other paragraphs are to be treated as merely ancillary o the main object and as limited and controlled thereby[22]. In order to avoid this rule, it became common practice to insert a paragraph stating that the objects specified in each paragraph of the clause were, except where otherwise expressed in such paragraph, to be 'in nowise limited or restricted by reference to or inference from the terms of any other paragraph or by the name of the company'. It was held by the House of Lords in *Cotman v Brougham*[23] that these words effectively excluded the 'main objects' rule of construction.

[5.31] It also became common for the objects clause to conclude with the words

'to do all such things as are incidental or conducive to the attainment of the above objects of any of them.'

Such words did no more than declare what the law already was, but a refinement was introduced empowering the company to do anything which 'in the opinion of the directors' could be carried on advantageously in connection with its other objects or incidentally thereto. It has been held in England that these words envisage a subjective test: if the directors honestly believe that a particular act can be advantageously combined with the other objects, it will be authorised by such a clause even if their view proves to be mistaken[24]. Such clauses are now almost invariably used, since they significantly reduce the risk that a transaction will be deemed to be ultra vires.

Distinction between powers and objects

[5.32] The powers of a company must be carefully distinguished from its objects. The objects clause, for example, will frequently authorise the company to borrow money; but in the case of most companies this is not an object of the company properly speaking but rather a power which it requires to achieve its objects. As we have seen, in addition to powers expressly conferred, a company may also enjoy implied powers which it may require to attain its stated objects. But such powers, whether conferred expressly or by implication, may not be used for purposes which are themselves ultra vires or for an object not stated in the memorandum[25].

---

[22] *Re German Date Coffee Co* (1882) 20 Ch D 169 at 188.
[23] [1918] AC 514. See also *Anglo-Overseas Agencies v Green* [1961] 1 QB 1.
[24] *Bell Houses Ltd v City Wall Properties Ltd* [1966] 2 QB 656.
[25] *Introductions Ltd v National Provincial Bank Ltd* [1970] Ch 199. See further Ch 12 below.

General principles of law applicable in construing objects clauses

[5.33] Whether any act is within the objects and powers of a company is a question of law which depends on the construction to be placed on a relevant clause. In ascertaining the meaning of the clause, the court will seek to discover the intention of the parties, and in so doing will usually be guided by certain well established rules of construction.

[5.34] These rules may be briefly summarised. The whole document must be read and considered and the court must give effect to the expressed intention. The grammatical and ordinary sense of the words is to be adhered to, unless that would lead to absurdity or inconsistency with the rest of the instrument in which case the grammatical and ordinary sense of the words may be modified so as to avoid that absurdity or inconsistency but no further[26]. Popular words are to be used in their popular sense and technical words in their technical sense, but in each case the prima facie meaning may be modified by the context The words used must be read with reference to their subject matter. The *ejusdem generis* rule and the maxim *expressio unius est exclusio alterius* may also be applicable[27].

Alteration of objects

[5.35] As we have seen, the company's memorandum, unlike its articles, was at one stage extremely difficult to alter, and prior to the enactment of the Principal Act any alteration invariably required the sanction of the court. Section 10 of the Principal Act, however, enabled a company by special resolution to alter its objects by abandoning, restricting or amending any object or adopting a new object or objects. Unlike the corresponding section in the English Act of 1948, it does not confine the exercise of the power to specific purposes stated in the section.

[5.36] There is provision in the section for a dissenting minority to apply to the court to have any such alteration cancelled. The application must be made by the holders of at least 15% of the issued share capital. It must be made within 21 days of the passing of the special resolution, and no member who voted in favour

---

[26] The so-called 'golden rule' of construction laid down in *Grey v Pearson* (1857) 6 HL Cas 61 at 106.

[27] *Palmer's Company Law* (25th edn), Vol 1, para 2.607. The *ejusdem generis* rule means that where one has a list of things which can constitute a *genus* or category (ie have certain features in common) followed by general words (eg 'and other activities'), the general words should normally be construed as referring to other things in the same genus. The *expressio unius* rule means that where the draftsman has expressly prescribed a particular mode of dealing with a matter, this excludes any other mode unless it is expressly authorised. See further *Craies on Statute Law* (7th edn) pp 178-186 and 259-260.

of the resolution can be counted as part of the 15%. On the hearing of the application (which is made by petition) the court may

(1)   confirm the alteration and dismiss the petition;

(2)   cancel the alteration;

(3)   confirm the alteration, subject to conditions; or

(4)   adjourn the petition in order that an arrangement may be made to the satisfaction of the court for the purchase of the interests of the dissenting members.

As amended by the 1983 Act, the section enables the court to make an order permitting the purchase of the dissenting members' shares by the company and the consequent reduction of the company capital[28].

[5.37] A special resolution for the alteration of the objects must be registered with the Registrar within 36 days of its having been passed by the company. If there is no dissenting minority, the company may deliver a printed copy of the memorandum to the Registrar at once. If there is a dissenting minority of the required size but no application is made within the specified time (21 days), the company must deliver the printed copy as altered within 15 days, making in all 36 days. If there is an application by a dissenting minority, the company must at once give notice of the application to the Registrar. It must deliver to the Registrar an office copy of the court order confirming or cancelling the alteration within 15 days of the date of the order. Where the court confirms the alteration with or without conditions, the company must deliver a printed copy of the memorandum as altered within the same period, ie 15 days from the date of the court order. The company and its officers are liable to penalties for failure to give these notices or to deliver these documents.

[5.38] The passing of such a resolution does not render valid a transaction which was *ultra vires* when it was entered into by the company. Thus, in *Northern Bank Finance Corporation v Quinn*[29], a company entered into a guarantee which was *ultra vires*. A resolution was subsequently passed giving it such a power, but it was held that the defect could not be cured retrospectively in this manner.

The limited liability clause

[5.39] In the case of a company limited by shares or by guarantee. the memorandum must contain a statement that the liability of the members is limited. The appropriate clause is

'the liability of the members is limited'.

---

[28] Companies (Amendment) Act 1983, Sch 1 para 3(b). It would seem that this procedure is not available in the case of a company limited by guarantee and not having a share capital.

[29] [1979] ILRM 221.

The capital clause

[5.40] In the case of a company limited by shares, the memorandum must contain a clause stating the amount of the nominal capital[30], the number of shares into which it is divided and the amount of each share.

[5.41] The shares in the capital can be, and frequently are, divided into different classes. The most common divisions are between preference and ordinary shares and voting and non-voting shares. These will be discussed in more detail in later chapters: for the moment, it is sufficient to note that preference shares confer on the holders certain rights to be paid dividends in priority to other shareholders and certain rights on the winding up of the company. Voting and non-voting shares are usually distinguished by letters, eg 'A Ordinary Shares' and 'B Ordinary Shares'. There are additional categories such as deferred shares and founders' shares.

[5.42] It is not necessary to specify the division of the share capital into classes in the memorandum (it can be dealt with in the articles) but it is usual to do so. The rights attached to the classes are, however, usually dealt with in the articles.

[5.43] The amount of the nominal capital in the case of a private company is entirely a matter for the promoters: it can be as large or as small as they wish. In fixing the amount of the capital, they have to bear in mind the funds the company will require and the possible necessity to keep some shares in reserve in case the company requires further capital in the future. In the case of a public limited company, the nominal value of the share capital must be at least the authorised minimum (at present £30,000)[31].

The association clause

[5.44] The memorandum concludes with a clause in which the subscribers declare that they desire to be formed into a company and agree to take shares. The names and addresses of the subscribers are appended to this in one column, while a corresponding column states the number of shares taken by each of them.

[5.45] Each subscriber must sign the memorandum in the presence of at least one witness who must attest the signature. He must write opposite his name the number of shares, which he agrees to take, and he must take at least one. In addition to his address, his occupation should also be stated and if he has none there should be a statement to that effect. The witnesses should also state their

---

[30] The nominal capital is the value in money of the shares which the company is authorised to issue. See further Ch 14 below. For relaxations of these requirements in the case of unit trusts, see the Companies Act 1990, s 253.

[31] Companies (Amendment) Act 1983, s 5(2).

addresses and occupations. Subscribers cannot attest each other's signatures, but one witness can attest all the signatures.

Alteration of other clauses

[5.46] The memorandum, as we have seen, may contain other clauses in addition to the obligatory clauses. Such clauses may be altered in the same manner as the objects of the company, ie by special resolution subject to the right of holders of at least 15% of the issued share capital or any class thereof to object to the alteration within 21 days from the date of the resolution by applying to the court to have the alteration cancelled. This procedure will not, however be applicable if the memorandum itself prohibits the alteration or provides its own procedure for the alteration. Nor can such an alteration take the form of a variation or abrogation of the special rights of any class of members.

As to the alteration of the *name* of the company, see para **[5.11]** above[32]; and as to the alteration of the capital clause see Chapter 16 below.

Requirements to be observed when memorandum is altered

[5.47] Any alteration of the memorandum, whether of the obligatory or additional clauses, must be embodied in the memorandum and the company and its officers are liable to a fine if they issue a copy which does not contain the alterations[33]. All alterations must be notified to the Registrar, and the company is required by virtue of Clause 4 of the European Communities (Companies) Regulations 1973[34] to publish the alteration in *Iris Oifigiúil.*

Effect of the memorandum

[5.48] Section 25(1) of the Principal Act provides that the memorandum and articles are to have the same effect as if they had been a deed duly signed and sealed by each member and containing covenants on the part of each member to observe all the provisions of the memorandum and articles. The effect of this section is considered in more detail in Chapter 6.

[5.49] No member of the company is, however, bound by an alteration in the memorandum or articles after the date on which he becomes a member which requires him to take more shares than the number held by him or increases his liability to contribute to the share capital of, or otherwise to pay money to, the company[35].

---

[32] Companies Act 1963, s 28.
[33] Companies Act 1963, s 30.
[34] SI 1973/163.
[35] Companies Act 1963, s 27.

Chapter 6

The Articles of Association

[6.01] The articles of association set out the rules for the management of the company's affairs. They deal with such matters as the appointment and removal of directors, the powers to be exercised by them, the holding of meetings of the members and the transfer and transmission of shares. It is also usual to specify in the articles the rights to be attached to the different classes of shares, eg ordinary and preference shares.

[6.02] A company limited by shares or limited by guarantee and not having share capital need not register articles of association[1]. Where it does not do so, the model forms set out in Table A or Table C will apply[2]. As we have seen[3], in the case of a private company limited by shares, the articles must contain certain provisions. These provisions are included in Part II of Table A and accordingly that part of the Table will automatically apply in the case of a private company limited by shares which does not register articles. If a company limited by shares does register articles, the Table A regulations will be applicable, except insofar as they are modified or excluded by the articles. This also applies to a company limited by guarantee and not having a share capital, save that the applicable table is Table C[4]. In practice, it is usual for both types of companies to register articles adopting the relevant table with such amendments as are thought appropriate.

[6.03] In the case of a company limited by shares whose memorandum is in Irish, the appropriate regulations are set out in that language in Tábla A[5].

[6.04] In the case of companies limited by guarantee and having a share capital and unlimited companies, the articles must be in accordance with Tables D and E respectively 'or as near thereto as circumstances admit'[6].

[6.05] The articles must be printed, divided into consecutive numbered paragraphs and stamped as if they were a deed. They must be signed by each subscriber to the memorandum in the presence of at least one attesting witness[7].

---

[1] Companies Act 1963, s 11 as amended by the Companies (Amendment) Act 1982, s 2.
[2] Companies Act 1963, s 13(2) as amended by the Companies (Amendment) Act 1982, s 14. Tables A and C are set out in the Companies Act 1963, First Schedule.
[3] See para **[3.01]** above.
[4] Companies Act 1963, s 13(2) as amended by the Companies (Amendment) Act 1982, s 14.
[5] Companies Act 1963, s 13(3).
[6] Companies Act 1963, s 16.
[7] Companies Act 1963, s 14.

Interpretation and enforcement of articles

[6.06] The articles of association are regarded by the courts as commercial documents and are to be construed so as to give them 'reasonable business efficacy'. They are not to be interpreted as meticulously as conveyances and other documents of title to property[8].

[6.07] Section 25(1) of the Principal Act provides that the articles, when registered, are to bind the company and the members to the same extent as if they had been signed and sealed by each member and contained covenants by each member to observe all the provisions which they contain. The same applies to the memorandum.

[6.08] The articles, accordingly, constitute a contract between each member and the company. The company is entitled to secure the enforcement of the articles by proceedings against the members and to restrain them from committing breaches of the articles. The members also have a corresponding right to sue the company on foot of the articles[9].

[6.09] Section 25(1) of the Principal Act also enables members of the company to enforce the rights conferred by the articles on them, as such members, against other members of the company. The authorities differ as to whether this is because the articles constitute a contract between the individual members, but the entitlement of the members to enforce the rights conferred by the articles *inter se* is beyond doubt, at all events when the company is joined as a party[10].

[6.10] It must be borne in mind, however, that the rights and duties which can be enforced by or against the members in this manner are those conferred or imposed on them in their capacity as members. Rights and duties conferred or imposed on members in some other capacity - eg as directors - cannot be so enforced.

[6.11] Thus, in the leading case of *Eley v Positive Government Security Life Assurance Co*[11], the company's solicitor sought to enforce against the company a clause in the articles which restricted the company's right to terminate his employment as their solicitor. Although he was a member of the company, it was held that the proceedings could not be maintained by him, since the clause relied on by him did not confer any rights on him as a member.

---

[8] *Holmes v Keyes* [1959] Ch 199 at 215; *Roper v Ward* [1981] ILRM 408.
[9] *Imperial Hydropathic Hotels Co Blackpool v Hampson* [1882] 23 Ch D 1 at 13.
[10] *Wood v Odessa Waterworks Co* (1889) 42 Ch D 636 at 642; *Welton v Saffrey* [1897] AC 299 at 315.
[11] (1876) 1 Ex D 20 at 28.

[6.12] But although the articles cannot constitute a contract in respect of such 'outsider rights', as they are sometimes called, the relevant clauses can be treated as having been incorporated, either expressly or by implication, into some other contract. In this manner, the courts have succeeded in modifying what might seem to be a somewhat harsh rule. Thus, where the articles provide that a director is to receive certain remuneration and a person acts in that capacity without any express contract, he will be regarded as having been employed by the company on the terms set out in the articles, this being the presumed intention of the parties[12]. This will be the case whether or not the director is also a member[13].

[6.13] It should also be remembered that any contract which can be spelled out from the articles between the company and its members differs significantly from other contracts, since it is always open to the company unilaterally to alter the terms of the contract by amending the articles in the manner permitted by law.

Alteration of articles

[6.14] The articles of association may be altered or added to by means of a special resolution[14] 'subject to the provisions of (the Acts) and to the conditions contained in (the) memorandum'. Any alteration or addition so made is (subject again to the provisions of the Acts) as valid as if it had been contained in the articles and is subject to alteration in the same way[15].

[6.15] Accordingly, provided the alteration or addition is not rendered invalid by some provisions in the Acts or in its own memorandum, the company is at liberty to alter or add to its articles as it thinks fit by means of a special resolution. But this general principle is subject to one important qualification: the power thus given must be exercised by the members *in good faith for the benefit of the company as a whole*[16].

[6.16] While the words italicised represent the law on this matter, some difficulty has been encountered by the courts in defining the criteria by which the validity of an impugned alteration should be determined. The words 'in good faith' indicate that the test is a subjective one: in other words, if a sufficient

---

[12] *Swabey v Port Darwin Cold Mining Co* (1889) 1 Meg 385.

[13] *Isaac's Case* [1892] 2 Ch 158.

[14] A special resolution must be carried by a majority of three fourths of the members entitled to vote who vote at a meeting. At least twenty one days' notice of the intention to propose it must he given. See para **[25.28]** below.

[15] Companies Act 1963, s 15.

[16] *Allen v Gold Reefs of West Africa Ltd* [1900] 1 Ch 656 at 671.

majority of the members honestly believe that a particular alteration is in the interests of the company as a whole, it does not matter whether the court takes the same view. In the words of Scrutton LJ in *Shuttleworth v Cox Bros & Co*: 'it is not the business of the court to manage the affairs of the company. That is a matter for the shareholders and directors'[17]. If, however, there is no reasonable ground for deciding that the proposed alteration is for the benefit of the company, this of itself may be sufficient evidence of a lack of good faith[18].

[6.17] Applying these principles, alterations of articles have been upheld although their effect was detrimental to individual members of the company. Thus in *Greenhalgh v Arderne Cinemas Ltd*[19] a minority shareholder claimed that an alteration which enabled the majority to sell their shares to outsiders without first offering them to existing shareholders (which they were obliged to do under the original articles) was invalid. The interests of the minority were, it was said, being sacrificed to those of the majority. The Court of Appeal agreed with the trial judge that the plaintiff's case could not succeed. However, Lord Evershed MR seems to have regarded the test as more in the nature of an objective one. Observing that the phrase 'for the benefit of the company as a whole' did not refer to the company 'as a commercial entity' but to the members as a general body, he went on:

> 'the case may be taken of an individual hypothetical member and it may be asked whether what is proposed is, in the honest opinion of those who voted in its favour, for that person's benefit.'[20]

Applying that test, it was held that the alteration was valid.

[6.18] Lord Evershed's test may be criticised as begging the question. Whether the alteration is seen as being for the benefit of the 'individual hypothetical member' may depend on whether that member is one of the majority who approve the alteration and presumably see it as for their benefit or the minority who see it as to their detriment.

[6.19] While the cases are not easy to reconcile, it would seem that the mere fact that the alteration is to the detriment of the minority is not enough to justify the intervention of the court: there must be something in the conduct of the majority which can be described as unfairly discriminatory or inequitable. These were the criteria invoked by Henchy J in *G & S Doherty Ltd v Doherty*[21], which was not a

---

[17] [1927] 2 KB 9 at 23.
[18] [1927] 2 KB 9 at 23.
[19] [1951] Ch 286.
[20] [1951] Ch 286 at 291.
[21] High Court unrep, 4 April 1968 and 19 June 1968; Supreme Court unrep, 19 December 1969. This case resurfaced, so to speak, with two others when it was the subject of a note by TJ O'Dowd in 1989 DULJ Vol 11, p 120.

case where any alteration of the articles was involved: the conduct complained of was, *inter alia,* the use by a majority of the directors of their powers to allot shares in order to wrest control of the company from the person who was effectively running the enterprise. But Henchy J cited the English authorities on amending articles in reaching the conclusion that the court should intervene where the majority were acting 'for the ulterior purposes of benefiting themselves to the detriment of other shareholders' and his judgment was upheld on appeal.

[6.20] A somewhat similar but even broader approach was adopted in the later English decision of *Clemens v Clemens Bros Ltd*[22]. In that case, it was held that the decision of the majority could be set aside where it was detrimental to the minority if such a result could be considered 'equitable'; and that although the decision was taken in good faith in what were thought by the majority to be the interests of the company as a whole, including the minority. It must be doubtful, however, whether as a general principle, that can be supported: the language used by Henchy J in *Doherty* suggests that he would have reached a different conclusion had he thought that the majority of the directors were acting in good faith in what they believed to be the interests of the company as a whole.

[6.21] It must also be remembered that a proposal by the majority to alter the articles, although valid in law, may nonetheless enable the minority to obtain relief from the courts under s 205 of the Principal Act on the ground that the affairs of the company are being conducted in disregard of their interests[23]. In addition, when the alteration involves the variation of rights attached to classes of shares, an application may be made to the court under s 78 of the Principal Act by not less than 10% of the holders of the issued shares in that class for the variation to be cancelled[24].

Company cannot bind itself not to alter articles

[6.22] Subject to the principles explained in the preceding paragraphs, a company has an unfettered right to alter its articles conferred by statute, and it cannot deprive itself by contract of that right[25]. If by altering its articles it commits a breach of contract, that will clearly render the company liable to damages. It is thought, however, that the company cannot be restrained by injunction from committing a breach of contract by altering its articles and that the remedy of the injured party is in damages only. The decision to the contrary in *British Murac Syndicate Ltd v Alperton Rubber Co Ltd*[26] proceeds on the

---

[22] [1976] 2 All ER 268.
[23] See para **[26.43]** et seq below.
[24] See para **[17.22]** below.
[25] *Allen v Gold Reefs of West Africa* [1900] 1 Ch 656 at 673.
[26] [1915] 2 Ch 186.

assumption that an earlier decision of *Punt v Symons & Co Ltd*[27] (where it was held that no action for a declaration lay in such circumstances) had been overruled by the Court of Appeal in *Baily v British Equitable Assurance Co*[28]. That assumption, however, may not be correct. But it would seem that the company may be restrained from acting on foot of the articles as so altered, if to do so would constitute a breach of contract. An *obiter dictum* to the contrary of Lord Porter in *Southern Foundries (1926) Ltd v Shirlaw*[29] is not supported by authority[30].

Other features of alterations

[6.23] An alteration may be lawful, although it affects members' rights retrospectively, eg by giving the company a lien on the shares of members for debts incurred before the alteration[31].

[6.24] The articles may include a provision that they can only be altered or added to with the consent of a named person. This is a somewhat meaningless provision, however, since the article giving such a veto can itself be removed by means of a special resolution.

---

[27] [1903] 2 Ch 506.
[28] [1904] 1 Ch 374.
[29] [1940] AC 701 at 740.
[30] See also Gower, *Modern Company Law* (6th edn), pp 729-30.
[31] *Allen v Gold Reefs of West Africa* [1900] 1 Ch 656.

Chapter 7

The Promoters

[7.01] Those who bring about the formation of a company are known as 'the promoters'. It is important to appreciate that the expression has this wide significance for lawyers, because to the layman the expression 'company promoter' probably suggests a professional financier of some sort (not infrequently with unsavoury overtones). But although it applies to those who organise a massive public flotation, it equally applies to the small shopkeeper who decides to convert his business into a limited liability company. The relatively wide meaning given by the law to the expression must be stressed, because the law treats promoters as having certain obligations to the companies which they bring into being and gives corresponding rights to the companies.

[7.02] A promoter is, therefore:

'one who undertakes to form a company with reference to a given project, and to set it going and who takes the necessary steps to accomplish that purpose.'[1]

Thus, to take the commonest form of company promotion in Ireland, a person running a business may decide at some stage to convert it into a limited liability company. With this in mind he will normally instruct an accountant or solicitor to take the steps set out in the succeeding chapters. One of the objects of the company, as set out in the memorandum, will be:

'to acquire the business now being carried on by A B as a going concern and for that purpose to enter into an agreement in the terms of a draft already prepared and for the purpose of identification signed by the said A B.'

[7.03] A B is the promoter of the company and so also is any person who assists him in the operation. But it should be noted that the accountant or solicitor will not be treated as a promoter simply because he has prepared the necessary documents or valuations[2]. If, however, he goes further than this as, for example, by finding someone else to invest in the company, he may well be treated as a promoter[3].

---

[1] Per Cockburn CJ in *Twycross v Grant* (1877) 2 CPD 469 at 541. This passage was approved by Costello P in *Re Greendale Ltd* (unreported, 12 March 1996).
[2] *Re Great Wheel Poolgooth Ltd* (1883) 53 LJ Ch 42.
[3] *Bagnall v Carlton* (1877) 6 Ch D 371.

Duties of promoters

[7.04] Where the company is formed as a 'one man company', ie where all the shares are owned by the promoter and he also nominates the directors, the duties owed by the promoter are of little importance. Where there are other investors - and most importantly of all where the public is invited to subscribe - his duties are of more significance. It cannot be said that in Ireland the topic is of great practical importance, however, and its treatment here is correspondingly abridged.

[7.05] The promoters of the company stand in a fiduciary position towards the company[4]. This means that the law regards promoters as being bound by certain obligations of trust which are not applicable to persons engaged in ordinary commercial dealings. It means that they may have to disclose certain matters which in an ordinary business context they would be free to keep secret; and it also means that they may have to account to the company for certain profits which in such a context they would be free to retain[5].

[7.06] One of the most obvious examples of this fiduciary position of promoters arises in the purchase and sale of property by a promoter. The promoter may buy a property expressly as a trustee for the company which he is forming or helping to form: in that case, he must disclose any profit he is making on the sale to the company and, if required, pay over the profit to the company. Even where the purchase is not made expressly as trustee for the company, he will still be under a duty to disclose any profit on the resale, if he originally bought the property with the formation of the company in mind[6]. It would seem, however, that he cannot be required to pay over the profit to the company unless his intention was to buy on behalf of the company, rather than on his own behalf with the object of reselling to the company[7].

[7.07] The duty of disclosure is not fulfilled by telling the facts to people who are in theory in positions of control in the company, such as directors, but who are merely the instruments of the promoters. The disclosure must be made either to a board of directors which is genuinely independent or to all the members of the company.

[7.08] This principle was laid down by the House of Lords in the well known case of *Gluckstein v Barnes*[8]. There the promoters had formed a syndicate for

---

[4] *Erlanger v New Sombrero Phosphate Co* (1878) 3 App Cas 1218 at 1236 per Lord Cairns LC, *Hopkins v Shannon Transport Systems Ltd* High Court, unrep, 10 January 1972.

[5] *Emma Silver Mining Co v Grant* (1878) 11 Ch D 918.

[6] *Gluckstein v Barnes* [1900] AC 240.

[7] *Omnium Electric Co v Baines* [1914] 1 Ch 332 at 347.

[8] [1900] AC 240. It had been previously held in *Erlanger v New Sombrero Phosphate Co* (1878) 3 App Cas 1218 that the disclosure had to be to an independent board of directors. *Gluckstein's* case made it clear, however, that disclosure to all the members of the company would suffice.

the purpose of buying and reselling Olympia, the exhibition centre in London. They bought the freehold of the property for £140,000 and then promoted a company to whom they agreed to sell the freehold for £180,000. They disclosed the profit of £40,000 to the public who were invited to subscribe: what they did not disclose was that they had also bought debentures in the company which originally owned the property at prices below par and that these were being paid off by the liquidator of that company at par out of the £140,000. As a result they were making an additional profit of £20,000 but this was disclosed only to the initial members of the company who were all part of the original syndicate. It was held that this could not possibly be regarded as a genuine disclosure to the company.

The case also illustrates another proposition: that a partial disclosure of the facts can sometimes be worse than no disclosure.

[7.09] The principles outlined in the preceding paragraphs were applied by Pringle J in one of the few modern Irish cases dealing with the duties of promoters, *Hopkins v Shannon Transport Systems Ltd*[9]. The plaintiff launched a project for a ferry service across the River Shannon. He was aware of the availability of suitable vessels and secured the interest of JG, the chairman of a hotel group, in the venture. It was hoped to raise the necessary capital in the form of grants from a government department and subscriptions for shares in a public company, which was duly formed and of which the plaintiff and JG were directors. Some of the money paid for the shares was used, unknown to at least some of the investors, to fund the purchase by the plaintiff and JG in partnership of the vessels and some other assets needed for the venture. They were then resold by the partnership to the company. Ultimately the Department of Finance refused to provide the grants unless the plaintiff severed his connection with the company. He subsequently issued proceedings against the company claiming his share of the sums due to the partnership in respect of the sale of the assets. Pringle J held that the plaintiff and JG were in the position of promoters and that accordingly they were under a duty to make full disclosure to the subscribers of the fact that they were making a profit on the transaction. He further held that this obligation could only be discharged by a disclosure to the subscribers themselves, since there was no independent board of directors. As there had not been such a disclosure, the contract was voidable at the instance of the company.

Remedies for breach of duty by promoters

[7.10] Where the breach of duty on the part of the promoters has resulted in a secret profit, the remedy of the company will normally be an action for

---

9   High Court, unrep, 10 January 1972. The judgment is the subject of a helpful note by O'Dowd in 1989 DULJ Vol 11 p 120.

damages. In some circumstances, however, the company will be entitled to rescission of the contract. This is the remedy provided by the law to put the parties to the contract back in the same position as they would have been in if no contract had been entered into. But a contract will not be rescinded by the court unless the parties can be restored to that position. In the words of Lord Blackburn in *Erlanger v New Sombrero Phosphate Co*:

> 'It is, I think, clear on principles of general justice, that as a condition of a rescission there must be a *restitutio in integrum*. The parties must be put in *status quo* ...'[10]

[7.11] Even where the parties cannot be restored precisely to the state they were in before the contract, however, rescission may be possible if the result can be regarded as 'practically just'[11]. For example, rescission may require the return of the property by one contracting party to another and the fact that the property has deteriorated in value may not be an obstacle to rescission where the result could be regarded as equitable in the circumstances. This will be particularly the case where the party who will suffer the consequences of the depreciation in value has been guilty of fraud.

[7.12] The principle is well illustrated by the decision in *Armstrong v Jackson*[12], which was not a case involving company promoters, but indicates the approach the courts have tended to adopt in such cases. The plaintiff engaged the defendant stockbroker to buy 600 shares in a company. The defendant fraudulently concealed from the plaintiff the fact that he was the owner of the shares[13]. Even though the shares had dropped substantially in value, rescission was ordered of the contract.

[7.13] But such a result will not be possible where the rights of innocent third parties will be affected or where no 'practically just' result can be achieved by rescission. The difficulties which may flow from rescission, even in the case of fraud, are clearly illustrated by a celebrated Irish case.

[7.14] In *Northern Bank Finance Corporation v Charlton*[14] the defendants, GC, HC and GS and two parties who were not defendants, PQ and VD, wished to acquire control of a public company named J & G Mooney & Co Ltd which owned a well known chain of public houses. The plaintiff bank, who were their

---

[10] (1873) 3 App Cas 1218 at 1278.

[11] *Erlanger v New Sombrero Phosphate Co* (1878) 3 App Cas 1218; *Spence v Crawford* [1939] 3 All ER 271.

[12] [1917] 2 KB 822.

[13] Fraudulently because as the plaintiff's agent he owed him a duty to disclose any interest he had in the shares.

[14] [1979] IR 149.

advisers, recommended that for this purpose they should form a holding company, PQ Holdings Ltd. The bank agreed to act as the agents of the promoters and to advance the major portion of the money required for the purchase of the shares. They stipulated, however, that the promoters were to provide £500,000 which was to be used before the money advanced by the bank was used. The sum to be provided by each promoter was agreed and it was also agreed that each contribution was to be deposited in the bank and maintained at the agreed figure until the bid for the shares in Mooney's either succeeded or failed.

The promoters duly formed PQ Holdings Ltd and its issued share capital was allotted to them. The bank advanced £1.3 million to PQ Holdings Ltd on security provided by the promoters and the company. The defendants deposited their agreed contribution with the bank and the purchase of the Mooney shares began. Unknown to the defendants, however, PQ had withdrawn three-quarters of his contribution. During the course of the acquisition the other promoters and the bank decided that it would be desirable that PQ should cease to be associated with PQ Holdings Ltd and the defendants purchased his share with the aid of £50,000 advanced by the bank. The trial judge (Finlay P) found as a fact that the defendants were informed, by one of the bank's officials before this advance was made, that PQ was not substantially indebted to the bank, contrary to the fact. The whole venture collapsed when the stock exchange refused a re-quotation of the Mooney shares; and the bank ultimately sued the defendants for interest on the money advanced. The defendants, who had become aware for the first time that PQ had withdrawn three-quarters of his contribution without their having been informed, counter-claimed for fraudulent misrepresentation and this was treated as a claim for rescission.

In the High Court, Finlay P held that the bank had been guilty of fraudulent misrepresentation through one of their officials and ordered the rescission of the agreement between the bank and the defendants by the repayment to the defendants of the various sums deposited with the bank and the transfer to the bank of the shares in Mooney and PQ Holdings Ltd. On an appeal to the Supreme Court, that court declined to interfere with the trial judge's findings of fact. By a majority of three to two, however, they also decided that rescission should not have been granted, since *restitutio in integrum* was not possible, and ordered a retrial on the issue of damages. The majority took the view that the transfer of the shares in Mooney and PQ Holdings to the bank, far from effecting *restitutio in integrum*, radically altered the *status quo ante*, since the bank had never owned the shares.

The defendants relied on the decision in *Armstrong v Jackson* but this was distinguished by Henchy J on the ground that in that case the broker had been the owner of the shares and accordingly *restitutio in integrum* was possible. In

Northern Bank Finance Corporation v Charlton the bank had never been the owner of the shares and had never acted other than as agent for the promoters. Accordingly, the only remedy available to the defendants was damages for fraudulent misrepresentation by the bank as agent-advisers.

Northern Bank Finance Corporation v Charlton was, of course, a case in which the fraud relied on was not that of the promoters, but of agents and advisers on whom the promoters relied. But it is thought that the principles referred to by the majority, which are derived from the law of contract generally and are not peculiar to company law, would also apply in a case where the fraud was that of the promoters.

[7.15] It should be noted that where the promoters fail to make a full disclosure of the fact that they are making a profit on the sale of assets to the company, the contract is voidable only. Hence, where the company adopt the benefit of the contract knowing that the promoters have made a profit, it will not necessarily be set aside in its entirety. Thus, in *Hopkins v Shannon Transport Systems Ltd*[15], Pringle J held that the plaintiff was entitled to recover certain sums in respect of the relevant assets from the company, since the contract had been subsequently approbated by them.

Remuneration of promoters: pre-incorporation contracts

[7.16] A company cannot enter into a contract before it is formed. Accordingly, a promoter who expects to obtain a reward for his services has to take the risk that the company will not pay him when it does come into existence.

[7.17] It was also the law at one time that a company could not even ratify a contract entered into on its behalf before it was formed. Thus, even if the promoter could obtain the assent of the company to the agreement to pay him for his services, the agreement was still unenforceable. The law was, however, amended in Ireland by s 37 of the Principal Act, which implemented a recommendation to that effect by Jenkins. The recommendation has never been implemented in England. The section provides:

(1) Any contract or other transaction purporting to be entered into by a company prior to its formation or by any person on behalf of the company prior to its formation may be ratified by the company after its formation and thereupon the company shall become bound by it and entitled to the benefit thereof as if it had been in existence at the date of such contract or other transaction and had been a party thereto.

(2) Prior to ratification by the company, the person or persons who purported to act in the name or on behalf of the company shall in the absence of express

---

[15] See para **[7.09]** above.

agreement to the contrary be personally bound by the contract or other transaction and entitled to the benefit thereof.

(3) This section shall not apply to a company incorporated before [1 April 1964].

[7.18] It will be seen that in addition to enabling the company to ratify contracts entered into before its formation (sometimes called 'pre-incorporation contracts') the section also makes it clear that unless and until such a contract is so ratified, the contracting parties remain personally liable. It is, accordingly, open to the promoter to sue the person who promised him remuneration where that person has acted on behalf of the company and has not expressly stipulated that he is not to be personally liable.

[7.19] The remuneration of the promoter may take various forms. He may simply sell on a business or a particular property to the company at a profit. Or the business or property may be sold directly by its owners to the new company and the promoter may receive a commission from the owners. Another method is for the promoters to ensure that part of the share capital takes the form of founders' shares entitling the holders to be paid dividends in priority to other shareholders. The promoters may also be relieved of their liability to pay for such shares in cash: they can be credited as having been fully paid up in consideration of the rendering of services by the promoter to the company. Lastly, the promoters may be given an option to subscribe for unissued shares at par, ie at their nominal value, within a specified time, such as a year, from the formation of the company. Since the shares may well rise in value during that time, this will often represent a valuable option to a promoter.

Chapter 8

Flotation of a Company

[8.01] A company is said to be 'floated' when its shares are offered for sale either to the public at large or to clients of an 'issuing house'; ie a merchant bank or similar financial institution specialising in this business. The operation is described as the 'flotation' of the company. As we have seen, a private company cannot invite the public to subscribe for shares or debentures in the company. Accordingly, a flotation will usually take place only when a company is formed as a public company or an existing private company is re-registered as a public company.

[8.02] As has been frequently stressed in this book, the majority of companies formed in Ireland are private companies. The total number of public companies on the register has never exceeded 844[1], a relatively small figure compared to the number of public companies in the United Kingdom at the corresponding times. Traditionally, the businesses that were floated tended to start life as family concerns. They were generally formed as private companies and the decision to float them was normally taken when the family was no longer able to provide the capital needed for expansion from its own resources or were advised that it was imprudent so to do for tax reasons.

[8.03] In recent years, the picture has changed somewhat. The marketing of shares and debentures is normally done by securing a quotation for them on a recognised stock exchange. The Irish Stock Exchange operates four markets, the main market - the official list - and three secondary markets, the Development Companies Market, the Exploration Securities Market and Finex, a market for securities and options. The nature of these markets is explained later.

[8.04] A knowledge of the basic legal requirements of flotations is essential for both the student and the practitioner. Both should remember, however, that because of the lesser significance of the topic in Ireland, the treatment of it in this book is substantially less detailed than in the leading English text books.

Types of flotation

[8.05] A company can be floated in a number of different ways:

---

[1] See para **[2.33]** above.

(1)   The company may make an offer for sale to the public. This is done by selling all the new shares to an issuing house who then offer the shares to the public by the publication of a prospectus. The issuing house are thus committed to taking up the whole issue even though it may not be fully subscribed: in other words, they underwrite the issue. (It is still possible in theory to make a direct offer to the public without any underwriting, but this rarely happens in practice.)

(2)   The company may decide not to offer the shares for sale to the public at large either directly or by an offer for sale through an issuing house. Instead they may allot the shares to an issuing house who place them with their clients. The placing is usually done in large blocks and the issuing house may either purchase the shares themselves and then sell them to individual clients or simply arrange beforehand to place the shares with the clients. Placing of shares in this manner has become particularly common in modern conditions, where potential sources of new capital will often be 'institutional investors' such as insurance companies, pension funds etc. A company wishing to raise new capital other than by borrowing may be advised to seek the necessary finance from such large investors rather than adopt the more hazardous procedure of inviting the public at large to subscribe.

(3)   The company may decide to offer the shares by tender. If any of the methods already mentioned are employed, the shares will all be offered at the same price. This may enable speculators to make an easy profit by 'stagging', ie applying for shares and disposing of them immediately if they rise in value. To avoid this, shares are sometimes offered by tender: a minimum price is fixed below which the shares will not be allotted and bids are invited. The shares will then normally be allotted to the highest bidders.

(4)   The company may make a rights issue. This only arises where there has already been a flotation. The company may wish to raise fresh capital and rather than make a new offer of shares, either to the public at large or by means of a placing, it may decide to raise the necessary funds by allotting shares to the existing shareholders. They are given the right to apply for a given number of new shares in proportion to their existing holdings.

[8.06] A rights issue should be carefully distinguished from an issue of *bonus shares* which is essentially a method of distributing profits which have hitherto been undistributed by increasing the nominal amount of the issued share capital. In the case of an issue of bonus shares, no new funds are raised for the company. By contrast, the whole purpose of a rights issue is to raise new funds. In order to make the issue more attractive to the shareholders, the shares are offered to them on better terms than would be the case if they were being offered to the public, and there is consequently an element of 'bonus' in a rights issue, which leads to the shares being sometimes rather misleadingly described as bonus shares.

Legal controls on flotations

[8.07] Although one of the major objects of the new companies' legislation in mid-nineteenth century England was to protect the public against unscrupulous promoters, it soon became apparent that it was not adequate for that purpose. The celebrated and much criticised decision of the House of Lords in *Derry v Peek*[2] that directors were not liable for misleading statements in company prospectus unless they were shown to be fraudulent seemed to place a premium on careless and irresponsible publicity. It led to the enactment of the Directors' Liability Act 1890 which was ultimately replaced by s 49 of the Principal Act. This entitles persons who have suffered loss and damage as a result of any untrue statement in a prospectus to recover compensation from persons connected with the issue, such as the directors at the time the prospectus is issued and the promoters.

[8.08] The Principal Act also contains detailed provisions designed to ensure that prospectuses of companies offering shares for subscription by the public contain adequate information about the company's business and are not misleading. In particular, there are requirements as to the publication of information relating to the company's financial commitments, 'material' contracts entered into by the company within the period of five years before the issue of the prospectus and reports by the company's auditors. There are also requirements as to statements by experts - such as geologists in the case of a mining company or valuers in the case of property - which may be included in the prospectus. These provisions are contained in ss 44 to 52 inclusive and in the Third Schedule.

[8.09] The prospectus must also comply with the requirements of the EU Prospectus Directive, implemented in Ireland by the European Communities (Transferable Securities and Stock Exchange) Regulations 1992.

[8.10] As we have noted, traditionally the marketing of shares and debentures in public companies has been done by securing a 'quotation' for them on a recognised stock exchange. The largest and most celebrated such exchange in these islands is the London Stock Exchange, but stock exchanges were also established in Dublin, Cork and Belfast. That in Dublin was established in 1799 by 39 Geo III c 40 (An Act for the Better Regulation of Stockbrokers). In 1965,

---

[2]   (1889) 14 App Cas 337.

a federation of stock exchanges in the United Kingdom and the Republic of Ireland was formed and ultimately all the stock exchanges in the two islands were merged in 1973 in the International Stock Exchange of the United Kingdom and the Republic of Ireland.

[8.11] That body was, however, destined to have a relatively short life. In 1995, the Stock Exchange Act was enacted under which the Irish Stock Exchange became an autonomous entity. This was as a result of the European Community Investment Services Directive. That Directive sought to facilitate the provision of services by investment firms in the various member states of the EU and other states. Where such a firm complied with the minimum standards applicable under the Directive, it was authorised to provide services in other member states. It was, however, regarded as essential that the firms in question should have been authorised to operate by the supervisory body of the member state in which it carried out business. Hence, a supervision and authorisation body was required in each member state.

[8.12] Since, under the arrangements put in place in 1973, the supervisory body in the case of Ireland was located in the United Kingdom, it was clearly essential to separate the two exchanges so that, in the case of Ireland, there would be an independent supervisory authority for the Irish Stock Exchange.

[8.13] Under the Stock Exchange Act 1995 the regulatory authority for the Irish Stock Exchange is the Central Bank. It is required by the Act to administer the system of regulation and supervision of stock exchanges and their member firms. No one may operate or establish a stock exchange in the State unless it is approved of as an exchange by the Central Bank. The Irish Stock Exchange was deemed to be an approved exchange on the coming into force of the 1995 Act. The Act contains provisions enabling the Central Bank to extend approval to 'member firms', ie those who are members of an approved stock exchange and whose regular occupation or business is the provision of investment services on a professional basis on or off the floor of the exchange. In order to be approved as a member firm, the firm must be a company incorporated by statute or under the Companies Act, a company formed under royal charter or a formally constituted partnership.

[8.14] In addition to complying with the requirements of the Acts, a flotation must also comply in practice with the requirements of the stock exchange. It is in theory possible to invite the public to subscribe for shares and debentures without seeking stock exchange approval, but in practice this is not feasible. Unless the shares are admitted to listing or are dealt with on one of the secondary markets already mentioned, they will have little attraction for the investor. Moreover, where an offer is made or a placing effected with the assistance of an issuing house, they will insist on the exchange's requirements being met so far as they are applicable. These requirements have become progressively more stringent in recent years: and ultimately the stock exchange's minimum requirements were given the force of law by the European Communities (Stock Exchange) Regulations 1984[3] which implemented in Ireland three of the EEC Directives[4].

[8.15] The first of the three directives (the Admissions Directive) sets out he conditions. which must be met before shares or debentures may be admitted to the official stock exchange listing. The Irish Stock Exchange is established as the 'competent authority' for deciding on the admission of securities to listing.

[8.16] The second directive (the Listing Particulars Directive) requires the member states to ensure that the admission of shares or debentures to the official listing is conditional upon the publication of an information sheet, called in the directive and the Regulations the Listing Particulars. The Directive sets out detailed requirements as to the information which must be given in the listing particulars and again the Irish Stock Exchange is designated as the competent authority for ensuring that these requirements are met and for permitting exemptions from the requirements in certain areas.

[8.17] The third directive (the Interim Reports Directive) requires information to be published on a regular basis by companies the shares of which have been admitted to an official stock exchange listing. Again the competent authority for ensuring that these requirements are met or for adapting them to the circumstances of particular companies is the Irish Stock Exchange.

[8.18] Article 12(3) of the Regulations provides that where the application form for shares in or debentures of a company contains the listing particulars approved of by the stock exchange or indicates where they can be obtained or inspected, most of the provisions of the Principal Act already referred to as to the information which must be contained in a prospectus are not to apply.

[8.19] The Admissions Directive stipulates that companies must be of a specified minimum size before they are admitted to official listing. It also permits the member states, however, to provide for admission to listing when that condition is not fulfilled, if the competent authorities are satisfied that there will be an adequate market for the shares concerned. In Ireland, the relevant rules are the listing rules used by the London Stock Exchange and known as the 'yellow book' rules, together with a supplement adapted to Irish conditions, generally known as the 'green pages'. These rules include requirements that the

---

3   SI 1984/282. The Regulations which were made by the Minister under the European Communities Act 1972, s 3, came into force on 1 January 1985.

4   See para **[3.22]** above.

company should have a minimum market value of £700,000 and that at least 25% of the equity capital should already be in the hands of the public.

[8.20] Article 4.1 of the Listing Particulars Directive requires the particulars to contain

'the information which, according to the particular nature of the issuer and of the securities for the admission of which application is being made, is necessary to enable investors and their investment advisers to make an informed assessment of the assets and liabilities, financial position, profits and losses, and prospects of the issuer and of the rights attaching to such securities.'

[8.21] By virtue of Article 4(1) of the 1984 Regulations, this obligation is imposed on the persons responsible for preparing the particulars and their solicitors. In addition to this general requirement, there are detailed provisions (contained in the Schedules to the Directive) as to the specific information which the particulars must give. Apart from full details as to the issue of shares and the manner in which it is being financed or underwritten, information must also be given as to the ownership of the company, its borrowings and the activities which it carries on.

[8.22] It should also be noted that under Article 5.1 of the Admissions Directive, the Irish Stock Exchange may make the admission of securities to official listing subject to more stringent conditions than those set out in the Directive. Accordingly, the current regulations of the stock exchange for the admission of securities to listing must always be consulted when a flotation is being contemplated.

[8.23] It will be seen that the Listing Particulars Directive and the stock exchange regulations are now the instruments which must be referred to when a company is being floated, rather than the Third Schedule to the Principal Act. One provision of the Act, however, remains applicable: where the listing particulars contain a statement by an expert - eg a geologist's report in the case of a mining company - the particulars must not be issued unless the expert has given his consent to their issue with the statement included in the form and context in which it is included. The expert must not have withdrawn his consent before a copy of the particulars is delivered for registration.

[8.24] A copy of the listing particulars must be delivered for registration with the Registrar before the date of publication. The issuer and every person who is knowingly party to their publication without their having been so registered is guilty of an offence and liable on summary conviction to a fine not exceeding £1,000.

[8.25] The 1984 Regulations provide for an appeal to the High Court from a decision of the Irish Stock Exchange to reject an application for admission to official listing or the discontinuance by the exchange of a listing. The High Court may set aside the decision of the stock exchange where it is satisfied that the procedures laid down by the Regulations and the directives have not been complied with by that body in any material respect and the matter is then remitted to them for reconsideration. Where the stock exchange in dealing with the application or in discontinuing a listing have complied with the procedures in all material respects, the court must confirm their decision.

The secondary markets

[8.26] With a view to encouraging small businesses to seek capital from the public, the stock exchange has created a special market called the Development Companies Market (the 'DCM'). This has several advantages for a company whose capital requirements are small when compared with those which normally seek a Stock Exchange quotation and hence has proved particularly attractive to some Irish entrepreneurs. The DCM is not subject to the strict requirements of the 1984 regulations and the directives, and separate admission rules therefore apply which are not as rigorous as the full listing 'yellow book' rules.

[8.27] In order for a company to be admitted to the DCM market, it must normally have a minimum of one year's trading record, although this may be waived in exceptional circumstances. Applicants must be supported by a sponsor who must ensure their suitability, the adequacy of the board of directors and the carrying out by the directors of their various responsibilities. There must be a minimum amount of securities in public hands at the time of listing in order to ensure a sufficient market will exist once listing takes place.

[8.28] There is also an Exploration Securities Market (the 'ESM'). At the time of writing this consists of less than twenty mineral, oil and gas exploration companies. Again, the rules require at least one year's trading accounts to be produced prior to application for admission and that a report be produced demonstrating that the company is engaged in some exploration activity. At least 10% of the shares of each class must be in public hands at the time of admission unless the exchange otherwise agrees. It should also be noted that an exploration company's listing must contain a report by a competent person so that the exchange can be satisfied that there are mineral resources existing on the site of the proposed extraction of minerals.

[8.29] Finally, mention should be made of FINEX, a market for futures and options which is independently regulated by the Central Bank pursuant to the Central Bank Act 1989.

Civil liability for misleading statements made in connection with flotations

[8.30] As we have seen, s 49 of the Principal Act entitled persons who suffer loss and damage as result of any untrue statement in a prospectus to recover compensation from persons connected with the issue. This section remains in force and applies to untrue statements in listing particulars (which are deemed to be a prospectus by Article 12 of the 1984 Regulations) made by the following:

(a) every person who is a director of the company at the time of the issue of the prospectus;

(b) every person who has authorised himself to be named and is named in the prospectus as a director or as having agreed to become a director either immediately or after an interval of time;

(c) every person being a promoter of the company;

(d) every person who has authorised the issue of the prospectus.

They are relieved of liability in certain specified circumstances. Section 49(3) provides that if the person concerned can prove:

(a) that, having consented to become a director of the company, he withdrew his consent before the issue of the prospectus, and that it was issued without his authority or consent; or

(b) that the prospectus was issued without his knowledge or consent, and that on becoming aware of its issue he forthwith gave reasonable public notice that it was issued without his knowledge or consent; or

(c) that after the issue of the prospectus and before allotment thereunder, he, on becoming aware of any untrue statement therein, withdrew his consent thereto and gave reasonable public notice of the withdrawal and of the reason therefor;

he will not be liable in damages.

[8.31] The person concerned will also be relieved of liability where he can prove that he had reasonable grounds for believing the statement to be true and did in fact believe it to be true up to the time of allotment. In the case of a statement by an expert or a copy or extract from a report or valuation of an expert[5], he must be able to prove that what was in the particulars fairly represented the statement or was a correct and fair copy of an extract from the report or valuation; and that he had reasonable grounds for believing and did in fact believe up to the issue of the particulars that the person making the statement was competent to make it. He must also be able to prove that the expert had given the consent required by the Act and had not withdrawn it before delivery of the particulars for registration or (to his knowledge) before allotment. Where the statement

---

[5]   See para **[8.11]** above.

purports to be a statement made by an official person or contained in what purports to be a copy or extract from the public official document, he must prove that the statement was a correct and fair representation of the statement or copy or extract from the document.

[8.32] It will be seen that the section places the onus of proof on the directors or promoters where the statement is shown to be untrue. In general terms, they must be able to establish that they did not authorise the misstatement or that they had reasonable grounds for believing it to be true.

[8.33] The measure of compensation is the difference between the actual value of the shares (not exceeding the price paid) and the value they would have had if the statement in question had been true. The limitation period for issuing proceedings making a claim under the section is six years from the date on which the cause of action arises, ie the date on which the shares were allotted to the plaintiff[6]. In the case of fraud the period begins to run from the time when the fraud was, or might with reasonable diligence, have been discovered[7].

[8.34] In addition to the statutory remedy under s 49, an action for damages for a negligent misstatement in a prospectus has been maintainable since the decision of the House of Lords in *Hedley Byrne & Co Ltd v Heller & Partners Ltd* in 1964[8], which has also been applied in Ireland[9].

[8.35] A person entitled to compensation under the Principal Act or damages at common law in respect of untrue statements in listing particulars is not necessarily entitled to rescission of the contract of allotment, ie he may not be entitled to have his name removed from the register and be repaid the money which he had subscribed for his shares. Where the misstatement is not material and is not made negligently, he will not be entitled to rescission[10]. Moreover, even in the case of a negligent misstatement, the remedy for rescission will only be available to the original subscriber for the shares and not to a subsequent purchaser[11]. The right of rescission, where it is applicable, may be lost if the allottee of the shares fails to repudiate the allotment as soon as he discovers that the statement on the faith of which he subscribes is true[12]. He may also lose the right to rescind where he takes some step which in effect ratifies the contract, eg endeavouring to sell the shares to someone else, accepting dividends or attending meetings of the company[13].

---

6   Statute of Limitations 1957, s 11.
7   Statute of Limitations 1957, s 71(1).
8   [1964] AC 465.
9   *Securities Trust Ltd v Hugh Moore & Alexander Ltd* [1964] IR 417.
10 *Re Wimbledon Olympia Ltd* [1910] 1 Ch 630.
11 *Peek v Gurney* (1873) LR 6 HL 377.
12 See para **[23.23]** below.
13 *Hop and Malt Exchange and Warehouse Co, ex parte Biggs* (1866) LR 1 Eq 483.

Criminal liability in respect of misstatements in connection with flotations

[8.36] The Principal Act also imposes criminal liability in respect to misstatements in a prospectus. Section 50 provides that where a prospectus includes an untrue statement any person who authorised the issue of the prospectus is liable on conviction on indictment to imprisonment for a term not exceeding two years or a fine not exceeding £2,500 or both[14]. The section also provides, however, that the person is not to be liable if he proves either that the statement was immaterial or that he had reasonable grounds to believe and did in fact believe up to the time of publication that the statement was true.

---

[14] Companies Act 1963, s 50 as amended by the Companies (Amendment) Act 1982, s 15.

Chapter 9

Application for and Allotment of Shares

[9.01] One of the first steps to be taken in the formation of a company limited by shares is the giving of the shares to the members of the company. This process is known as the allotment of shares and is effectively set in train as soon as the memorandum is signed by one or more subscribers as required by the Principal Act. These persons agree to take a specified number of shares in the company and, when the company is incorporated, it proceeds to allot that number of shares to the subscribers and to allot further shares to other persons who may apply.

[9.02] The procedure of allotment is governed by a number of rules which are somewhat similar to the rules relating to the formation of contracts: understandably so, because an allotment of shares in response to an application is a form of contract. In addition, however, there are a number of statutory restrictions to be observed, some of them applicable only in the case of public companies.

[9.03] In the case of a company limited by shares, every shareholder is normally a member of the company. In addition to the allotment of shares to him, however, there is another step which must be taken before he becomes in law a member: his name must be placed on the register of members. But in the case of the subscribers to the memorandum, this is not necessary: s 31(1) of the Principal Act provides that:

> 'the subscribers of the memorandum of a company shall be deemed to have agreed to become members of the company, and, on its registration, shall be entered as members in the register of members.'

[9.04] It has been held in England that the effect of the corresponding section is that a subscriber automatically becomes a member and a shareholder as soon as he signs the memorandum, even though the company fails to allot the shares to him[1].

The application

[9.05] The application for shares may be made orally or in writing. Like any other offer, it may, under the general law of contract, be revoked before acceptance[2]. Under that law, to constitute a valid contract there must be an offer

---

[1] *Evans' Case* (1867) 2 Ch App 427.
[2] For statutory restrictions on the revocability of an application in the case of an allotment in a public company, see para **[9.49]** below.

which has been accepted. The application may also be conditional, in which case an allotment which does not comply with the condition may be repudiated[3].

The allotment

[9.06] The allotment of the shares in response to the application does not constitute the acceptance of an offer. The acceptance only takes place when the applicant is notified that he has been allotted the shares for which he applied. At that stage, a valid and enforceable contract comes into being. As we have seen, however, the applicant does not become a member of the company until his name has been placed on the register. But where there is such a valid contract, both parties, the company and the allottee, are entitled to secure its performance by a decree of specific performance[4].

[9.07] The notification to the applicant, which is necessary to constitute a valid contract of allotment, may be in writing, verbal or by conduct[5]. Notice may be given either to the applicant or his agent duly authorised to receive such notice[6]. The notice must be given within a reasonable time from the application. The applicant is entitled to revoke his application at any time before the notice of the allotment (subject to certain statutory restrictions in the case of an allotment of a public company), but the revocation must also be made within a reasonable timed[7].

[9.08] It was held in *Household Fire Insurance Co v Grant*[8] that the notice of allotment was given to the allottee as soon as the notice was posted. This has repeatedly been stated to be the law in the leading English text books. The learned editors of Palmer, however, suggest that it may need reconsideration in the light of the decision of the Court of Appeal in *Holwell Securities v Hughes*[9]. It was held in that case that, where notice of acceptance of an offer is communicated by post, the notice must actually reach the offeror before a contract comes into existence, save in exceptional circumstances where it is clear that the parties intended that the posting of the notice was sufficient to make the acceptance effective. However, that was a case of an option which had to be exercised by 'notice in writing to the intended vendor' and it is thought that

---

[3] *Ex parte Wood, Sunken Vessel Recovery Co* (1859) 3 de G & J 85.
[4] *New Brunswick etc Land Co v Muggeridge* (1860) 1 Dr & Sn 363.
[5] *Gunn's Case* (1867) 3 Ch App 40.
[6] *Levita's Case* (1870) 5 Ch App 489.
[7] *Crawley's Case* (1869) 4 Ch App 322.
[8] (1879) 4 Ex D 216.
[9] [1974] 1 All ER 161; *Palmer's Company Law* (25th edn), Vol I, para 9.035. See also *Re Thundercrest Ltd* (1995) 1 BCLC 117.

the reasoning would not necessarily be applicable to a notice of allotment of shares in a company.

Renounceable letters of allotment

[9.09] As we have seen, a person to whom shares have been allotted does not by virtue of that fact alone become a member. For this to happen, his name must be entered on the register of members. Sometimes, however, the letter of allotment is 'renounceable', ie the allottee is entitled to renounce his rights to become a member in favour of another person. Where such renounceable letters of allotment are issued, they incorporate two forms: a form of renunciation to be signed by the original allottee and a form of acceptance to be signed by the acceptor of the renunciation.

[9.10] Where the letters are renounceable, any person in effect may become a shareholder in whose favour the letters are renounced. Accordingly, the issue of such letters may result in an issue being construed to be an offer of shares to the public which will be governed by the rules relating to such offers. In the case of a private company, letters of allotment as such are usually not required at all: it is sufficient to issue the allottee with a share certificate which both indicates that his offer has been accepted and constitutes his title to the shares.

Authority required for allotment of shares by directors

[9.11] The articles normally provided that the allotment of shares was entirely a matter for the directors (article 5). By virtue of s 20 of the 1983 Act, the directors must be authorised to make the particular allotment by:

(a)   the company in general meeting, or

(b)   the articles of association.

[9.12] It is also provided that the authority to allot shares may be general and not limited to a particular allotment. It may also be unconditional or subject to conditions. Presumably, draftsmen of articles will take care to include a general authority which is unconditional. The authority must state the maximum amount of shares which may be allotted and the date on which the authority will expire, which cannot be more than five years from the date of incorporation (where the authority is contained in the articles of the company on its incorporation) or from the date of the resolution (in any other case). The authority may be revoked or varied by the company in general meeting, whether or not it is contained in the articles.

[9.13] The authority may be given, varied, revoked or renewed by an ordinary resolution of the company, even where an alteration of the articles is involved. (Normally a special resolution is required for the alteration of the articles[10].)

---

[10] For special resolutions, see para **[25.28]** below.

Notice of the delivery of a copy of the resolution to the Registrar must be published in *Iris Oifigiúil* by the company, if it is a public limited company, within six weeks of its delivery[11].

[9.14] The authority may be renewed for a further period not exceeding five years, whether or not it has already been renewed. This must be done, however, by the company in general meeting and must again specify the amount of shares which may be allotted and the date on which the authority will expire. The directors are allowed to allot shares even though the authority has expired, where the allotment is in pursuance of an offer or agreement by the company before the authority expired and the authority allowed it to make such an offer or agreement which might require shares to be allotted after the expiration of the authority.

[9.15] The section does not apply to shares taken by the subscribers to the memorandum or to shares allotted in pursuance of an employees' share scheme. Nor does it apply to a right to subscribe for, or to convert any security into, shares other than the allotted shares.

[9.16] An allotment of shares made in contravention of the section remains valid. But a director who knowingly and wilfully contravenes or authorises or permits a contravention of the relevant provisions is guilty of an offence and liable on conviction to a fine not exceeding £2,500.

[9.17] It is thought that these provisions (which implement requirements of the Second EU Directive and are virtually the same as corresponding provisions of the English 1985 Act) have made little difference in practice to the operations of most companies. The articles of new companies will probably include a provision authorising the directors to allot shares up to the limit of the nominal share capital of the company. In the case of existing companies, the articles have doubtless been amended to give such an authority in respect of unallotted share capital. It is true that the authority cannot be for longer than five years and can then be renewed only by the company in general meeting. But this would be of importance only where a majority of the company was unwilling to extend the authority of the directors any further; and since the majority in any event has power to remove the directors (except life directors) the change is not of any great practical significance.

Rights of pre-emption in the allotment of shares

[9.18] A 'right of pre-emption' might be broadly described as a right of 'first refusal'. We have seen that articles of a private company must include provisions restricting the right of the members to transfer their shares[12]; and it has long

---

[11] Companies (Amendment) Act 1983, s 55(1)(b).

been common in such articles to provide that a member wishing to dispose of his shares must first offer them to the other members of the company. The 1983 Act (again implementing the relevant requirements of the Second Directive in language virtually indistinguishable from the English 1980 Act) gives members of all companies, public and private, such a right on the allotment of new shares in the company. This in effect obliges the company when making a new issue of shares, to give an existing shareholder a right of first refusal in respect of shares in the new issue equal in proportion to his existing holding. In the case of a private company, however, the right of pre-emption may be excluded by a provision to that effect in the memorandum or articles.

[9.19] This right of pre-emption is not given to the holders of preference shares. Moreover, where the new issue takes the form of shares allotted, or to be allotted, under an employees' share scheme, the general body of shareholders has no right of pre-emption in respect of such an issue. But the holders of employees' shares themselves enjoy the right of pre-emption in respect of any new issue of shares to the general body.

[9.20] In addition to being generally authorised to allot shares under s 20, the directors may also be authorised to allot shares pursuant to the authority as if the statutory pre-emption rights did not apply to the allotment or applied only in a modified manner. Such a power must be given either by the articles a special resolution of the company. The company is also given power (where the directors have a general authority to allot) to exclude the application of the right of pre-emption to a specified allotment where such a course recommended by the directors. The notice of the meeting at which the necessary resolution is to be proposed must be accompanied by a written statement from the directors giving their reasons for the recommendation, the amount to be paid to the company in respect of the shares allotted and the directors' justification of that amount.

[9.21] Section 23 confers the pre-emption right. It precludes the company from allotting 'equity securities' unless it has made an offer to the holders of 'relevant shares', or 'relevant employee shares' to allot to them on the same - or more favourable - terms a proportion of the securities as nearly as practicable equal to the proportion in nominal value held by them of the aggregate of relevant shares and relevant employee shares.

[9.22] 'Equity securities' are defined by s 23(13). They do not include shares taken by the subscribers or bonus shares. With these exceptions they include all relevant shares and the right to subscribe for, or convert securities into, relevant shares. 'Relevant shares' are defined as meaning all shares other than:

---

[12] See para **[4.02]** above.

(a) shares which as respects dividends and capital carry a right to participate only up to a specified amount in a distribution; and

(b) shares which are held by a person who acquired them in pursuance of an employees' share scheme, or, in the case of shares which have not been allotted, are to be allotted in pursuance of such a scheme.

The offer must be open for a period of at least 21 days, and must not be withdrawn before the end of that period.

[9.23] The statutory right of pre-emption does not apply where the allotment of equity securities is made in accordance with a provision in the memorandum or articles which confers a right equivalent to the statutory right. It is also excluded where the shares to be allotted are to be wholly or partly paid up otherwise then in cash.

[9.24] By virtue of s 23(12), the definition of shareholders entitled to pre-emption rights is extended to include those who held appropriate shares at any time during the period of 28 days ending on the day before the date of the offer.

[9.25] While these complex provisions are of importance in the case of public limited companies, obliging such companies to turn to their existing shareholders first if they wish to raise fresh capital, their practical significance is much reduced in Ireland by the fact that private companies may exclude the pre-emption rights by amending the memorandum or articles. It will not even be necessary to effect such an amendment where the memorandum or articles already contain a requirement or authority inconsistent with the statutory pre-emption rights. As we have seen, however, the form of pre-emption right most frequently to be found in memoranda and articles is one which obliges the shareholders to offer the shares to the existing shareholders before selling to an outsider, and such a provision would not appear to be inconsistent with s 23.

Directors' duty of good faith in relation to allotments

[9.26] In exercising powers to allot shares, the directors are bound to act in good faith in the best interests of the company[13]. It is important to bear in mind that this limitation on their powers may invalidate an allotment even where the complex requirements of the 1983 Act as to allotments have all been observed or where they have succeeded in derogating from those requirements by procuring the necessary alterations of the memorandum or articles.

---

[13] *Nash v Lancegaye (Ireland) Ltd* (1958) 92 ILTR 11; *G & S Doherty Ltd v Doherty* (unreported, (High Court) 4 April 1968 and 19 June 1968, (Supreme Court) 19 December 1969). See para **[27.89]** below.

Paying for shares

[9.27] Shares may be issued either for cash or some other consideration equivalent to cash, such as the rendering of services or the transfer of property. Where the issue is for cash, the allottee becomes liable to pay the full nominal value of the shares allotted to him either upon allotment or at some time in the future. Any person who subsequently becomes the owner of the shares is liable to pay the full amount remaining unpaid on the shares. The person whose name appears on the register as the owner of the shares is liable to pay the unpaid amount, even where he holds the shares in trust for someone else: under s 123 of the Principal Act no notice of any trust may be entered on the register or be receivable by the Registrar.

[9.28] The principle that shares could be issued for a consideration other than cash has been accepted since the last century. It was implicitly acknowledged by the legislature when it required, in the case of an allotment, the registration of the contract under which the shares were allotted. It was given express statutory recognition for the first time, however, in s 26 of the 1983 Act which provides that:

> shares allotted by a company and any premium payable on them may be paid up in money or money's worth (including goodwill and expertise).[14]

That Act, however, also contains elaborate provisions, applicable only to public limited companies, as to the valuation of such 'non-cash consideration'.

[9.29] Where shares are allotted for a consideration other than cash, the company must under s 58(1)(b) of the Principal Act deliver to the Registrar for registration, within one month of the allotment, the contract in writing constituting the title of the allottee to the shares. If the contract is not in writing, particulars of it must be registered.

[9.30] Where shares are allotted on foot of such a contract, the court cannot enquire into the adequacy of the consideration[15]. But, in the case of a public limited company, there is now a statutory requirement that the non-cash consideration be valued by an independent expert; and since a company may not issue shares at a discount[16], the creditors and investors may reasonably assume that the capital described as 'paid up' is, in real terms, paid up.

[9.31] These provisions do not apply to private companies, and in the case of such companies the rule that the adequacy of the consideration cannot be

---

[14] The draftsman has rightly avoided the ugly expression employed by the draftsman of the English 1980 Act, 'know how'.

[15] *Pell's Case* (1869) 5 Ch App 11.

[16] See para **[9.56]** below.

enquired into represents a significant erosion of the supposed protection afforded to creditors by the existence of a paid up capital. The only exceptions to the rule are where the contract itself can be set aside - as in the case of fraud - or where the consideration, on the face of the transaction itself, is clearly inadequate or illusory[17]. There must be, of course, what the law regards as consideration and thus shares allotted by way of gift or in consideration of services freely rendered in the past cannot be regarded as paid up[18].

[9.32] Where the shares are allotted in consideration of the release of a debt due by the company to the allottee, this is treated as an issue for cash and no contract need be registered[19]. But where the shares are allotted by way of accord and satisfaction, ie as part of a compromise or settlement, they are not treated as having been paid for in cash and a contract must be registered[20].

[9.33] In the case of a public limited company, s 26(2) of the 1983 Act prohibits the company from accepting in payment for its shares or any premium payable on them an undertaking to do work or perform services for the company or any other person. If the company allots shares in consideration of such an undertaking, the shareholder becomes liable to pay the company their nominal value and the whole of any premium, or a proportionate part where the shares are treated as partly paid up, together with interest at the appropriate rate. A subsequent purchaser is similarly liable unless he is a purchaser for value who did not know of the contravention of the section.

[9.34] A public limited liability company is also prohibited from allotting shares as fully or partly paid up otherwise than in cash if the consideration is, or includes, an undertaking which is to be or may be performed more than five years after the date of the allotment. This would apply to a case where, for example, the company accepted an undertaking to transfer property to the company in payment for shares at some date in the future. Such a deferred payment is permissible but only if it is to be made within the five year period. There are similar provisions rendering the allottee liable for the amount involved in the event of a contravention of the section or where the undertaking is not performed.

[9.35] In the case of a public limited company, where shares are allotted as fully or partly paid up otherwise than in cash, the consideration must be valued in accordance with s 30 of the 1983 Act, a report obtained from the valuer and a

---

[17] *Re Wragg Ltd* [1897] 1 Ch 796 at 836; *Hong Kong & China Gas Co v Glen* [1914] 1 Ch 527.
[18] *Re Eddystone Marine Insurance Co* [1893] 3 Ch 9.
[19] *Re Harmony and Montague Tin and Copper Mining Co, Spargo's Case* (1873) 8 Ch App 407; *Larocque v Beauchemin* [1897] AC 358.
[20] *Re Johannesburg Hotel Co* [1891] 1 Ch 119.

copy of the report sent to the proposed allottee. The report must be made within the period of six months immediately preceding the allotment.

[9.36] The valuation and report must be made by an independent person, who is defined as a person qualified at the time to be appointed as auditor of the company. That would normally be a qualified accountant; but the section also enables him to obtain a further report from another expert, eg a valuer in the case of property, where he thinks it reasonable to do so. That expert must not himself be an officer or servant of the company or an associated company.

[9.37] The report must state the nominal value of the shares and any premium, describe the consideration and the date and method of valuation and state the extent to which the shares are to be treated as paid up. It must include, or be accompanied by, a note to the effect that the consideration as valued (together with any cash paid) is not less than the nominal value of the capital to be treated as paid up and any premium. The note must also state, where another expert has been employed, that it appeared reasonable to employ such an expert, that any method of valuation employed was reasonable and that there appears to have been no material change in the value of the consideration since the valuation.

[9.38] The section provides that, where the allotee has not received the report or there has been some other contravention of the section of which he knows or ought to have known, he is to be personally liable to the company for so much of the nominal capital as was to be treated as paid up by the consideration together with interest. There are also supplementary provisions in s 31:

(a) enabling the person making a report or valuation for the purposes of s 31 to obtain information necessary for the report or valuation from any officer of the company;

(b) requiring the company to deliver a copy of any such report with the return of allotments; and

(c) making it an offence to make a false or misleading statement to a person making a report or valuation.

[9.39] Arrangements involving an allotment in consideration of the transfer of shares in another company, and mergers which involve an allotment, are exempted from the requirements of s 30. This exemption applies to an arrangement only where it is open to all the shareholders in the other company or to all the shareholders in the class affected.

[9.40] Companies have often been formed on the basis of an agreement by the promoters to transfer particular assets to the company in consideration of the allotment to them of shares in the company. The interests of the creditors can be adversely affected if such assets are transferred at an artificially inflated value and in the case of public limited companies the 1983 Act also contains provisions designed to prevent this. As in the case of ss 30 and 31, there are requirements as to the obtaining of an expert's valuation and report where the company acquires non-cash assets from the subscribers for a consideration equal in value to one-tenth of the nominal capital within two years from the date when it is issued with a certificate that it is entitled to do business[21].

Minimum payment for shares in public limited company

[9.41] In the case of a public limited company, a share may not be allotted unless it is paid up as to at least 25% of the nominal value of the shares together with the whole of any premium on it. The proportion which had to be paid up on allotment was 5% under the Principal Act but was increased to 25% by s 28 of the 1983 Act. That section also renders the allottee liable to the company for so much of the 25% as is not paid, together with interest. This does not apply, however, to the allotment of a bonus share in contravention of the section, unless the allottee knew or ought to have known that the allotment was a contravention.

The section does not apply to shares allotted in pursuance of an employees' share scheme.

Additional statutory restrictions on allotments by public companies

[9.42] In addition to the restrictions already referred to, there are three specific limitations on the power of a public company to make an allotment. In the first place, there must have been a minimum response to the invitation to the public to subscribe. In the second place, the company must allow a short period to elapse from the issuing of the prospectus before it makes an allotment. In the third place, if it has been stated that a stock exchange quotation will be sought, that quotation must be obtained.

[9.43] The first restriction is imposed by s 53 of the Principal Act. It prohibits the making of an allotment of any share capital offered to the public for subscription unless an amount described in the section as the minimum subscription has been subscribed. This is defined as the amount which, in the opinion of the directors, must be raised by the issue of share capital in order to provide for certain specified matters, such as working capital, the purchase of property, the payment of preliminary expenses, etc. These requirements - which must be carefully distinguished from the obligation to fix the nominal share capital at not less than the authorised minimum[22] - are intended to ensure that the company does not proceed with the flotation until the funds and assets which it has told the public it will require have in fact been provided.

---

[21] Companies (Amendment) Act 1983, s 31. Note that the requirements of the section are not confined to cases where the consideration is an allotment of shares.

[22] See para **[4.37]** above.

[9.44] If the minimum subscription is not raised at the expiration of 40 days from the issue of the prospectus, any money received from applicants for shares must be repaid forthwith. If it is not repaid within 48 days after the issue of the prospectus, the directors are jointly and severally liable to repay it with interest at the rate of 5% per annum from the expiration of the 48th day. A director is not liable, however, if he proves that the default was not due to any misconduct or negligence on his part.

[9.45] This restriction is supplemented by s 22 of the 1983 Act. It prohibits a public limited company from making any allotment of any share capital offered for subscription unless:

(a)   the capital is subscribed in full; or

(b)   the offer states that even if it is not subscribed in full, the amount of the capital subscribed may be allotted in any event or in the event of specified conditions being satisfied.

[9.46] Where conditions are specified, they must be satisfied before any allotment is made. In the event of an allotment being made contrary to the provisions of the section, the same consequences follow as in the case of a contravention of s 53 of the Principal Act.

[9.47] The second restriction is imposed by s 56 of the Principal Act. It provides that no allotment may be made of any shares in pursuance of a prospectus issued generally, ie to persons who are not existing members, until the beginning of the fourth day after the date of issue of the prospectus. This is to enable prospective investors to consider the flotation carefully before committing themselves. The prospectus may fix a longer period; and whichever day is chosen, whether the statutory minimum of the fourth day or some later day, is known as 'the time of the opening of the subscription lists'.

[9.48] The third restriction is imposed by s 57 of the Principal Act. This provides that where a prospectus, whether issued generally or not, states that application has been made or will be made for permission for the shares to be dealt in on any stock exchange, any allotment of the shares will be void if the permission is not applied for before the third day after the issue of the prospectus or, if the permission has not been granted, within six months of the closing of the subscription lists. There is provision for the repayment forthwith by the company without interest of all money received from applicants where the permission has not been so applied for or has been refused. If the money is not repaid within eight days, the directors are liable to repay it with interest at 5% from the expiration of the eighth day, except where a director proves that the default in repayment was not due to any misconduct or neglect on his part.

Consequences of irregular allotments

[9.49] An allotment made in contravention of the statutory requirements set t in para **[9.47]** above, ie before the fourth day, is valid, but the company and its officers are liable to a fine not exceeding £500. Where the statutory requirement as to the minimum subscription is not complied with, the allotment is voidable, ie may be set aside at the instance of the applicant for shares. There is a time limit, however: the allotment may only be set aside within one month of the allotment. Any director who knowingly contravenes or permits the contravention of the requirement is liable to compensate the company and the allottees for any loss, damages and costs which they may have sustained as a result. The claim must be made, however, within two years of the date of the allotment.

Revocability of application for shares in public company

[9.50] An application for shares is, as we have seen, usually revocable by the applicant until the shares have been allotted to him. In order to discourage 'stagging' - applications for shares by speculators hoping to make a quick profit instead of a long term investment- the Principal Act imposes a restriction on this power of revocation in the case of an application made in pursuance of a prospectus issued generally. Such an application is irrevocable until after the expiration of nine days after the day on which the prospectus is issued[23]. (The period is longer than the period provided for in the English 1948 Act and than the period recommended by Jenkins, which was seven days.) The effect of the statutory restriction is that 'stags' can no longer apply for shares and withdraw their application as soon as it becomes apparent that the shares are not going to rise significantly.

[9.51] There is an exception to the restriction on revocability: the application is revocable within the statutory period where a promoter, director or other person who has authorised the issue of the prospectus gives public notice under s 49 which relieves him of responsibility for mis-statements in the prospectus.

Return of allotments

[9.52] Whenever a company limited by shares or a company limited by guarantee and having a share capital makes any allotment of its shares, the company must, within one month thereafter, deliver to the Registrar for registration a return of the allotments stating:
  (a)   the number and nominal value of the shares allotted;
  (b)   the names, addresses and occupations of the allottees; and
  (c)   the amount, if any, paid or due and payable on each share.

---

[23] Companies Act 1963, s 56(5).

[9.53] If the return is not made in accordance with these requirements (or if the contract referred to in para **[9.28]** is not delivered for registration) every officer of the company who is in default is liable to a fine not exceeding £500. Where the court is satisfied that the failure to comply with any of these requirements was accidental or due to inadvertence or that it is just and equitable to do so, it may extend the time for delivering the document in question for such period as it thinks proper[24].

Issue of shares at a premium

[9.54] There is nothing to prevent the company from issuing shares at a premium, ie at a nominal value which is lower than the cash or its equivalent which it receives for them. This frequently happens in the case of private companies, because in that case, as we have seen, the company very often begins life when a person operating a business decides to convert it into a limited company. Since he will own virtually all the shares himself, there will be little point - and some additional expense - in allotting shares which are equivalent in nominal value to the value of the business which he is transferring to the company. The shares allotted to him in such a case will frequently be substantially less in nominal value than the actual value of the business transferred to the company and consequently will be regarded as having been issued at a premium.

[9.55] But, while the company is perfectly entitled to get more from the shareholders in cash or kind than the nominal value of the shares on allotment, such a premium is not part of the trading profits of the company and may not be treated as such. It must accordingly be transferred to a separate account known as the share premium account[25]. The provisions of the Principal Act which ensure that a company's capital can only be reduced in specified circumstances apply equally to the share premium account[26]. It may, however, be applied for the following purposes.

(1)   paying up unissued shares (other than redeemable shares[27]) as fully paid bonus shares to the members;

(2)   writing off the preliminary expenses of the company;

(3)   writing off the expenses of, or the commission paid on, any issue of shares or debentures in the company;

---

[24]   Companies Act 1963, s 58 as amended by the Companies (Amendment) Act 1982, s 15.

[25]   Companies Act 1963, s 62.

[26]   See para **[14.17]** below.

[27]   See para **[15.05]** below.

(4)   providing for the payment of the premium payable by the company on
the redemption of redeemable preference shares pursuant to s 220 of
the 1990 Act[28] or debentures.

[9.56] It was held in England that the corresponding section in the 1948 Act
applied in a takeover where the company making the allotment was a newly
formed company which had no assets other than those which it acquired from
the company being taken over as consideration for the allotment of its shares[29]. It
accordingly received substantially more than the nominal value of the shares
allotted and this sum had to be transferred to the share premium account,
although in fact it represented pre-acquisition profits made by the company
being taken over. Such sums should normally have been available for
distribution to the shareholders in the form of a dividend, but the section did not
make any provision for this. The law was altered in England[30] to provide for an
exemption in these circumstances from the obligation to transfer the premium on
such an issue to capital account, but the law has not been changed in Ireland[31].

Issue of shares at a discount

[9.57] A company may not issue shares at a discount, ie at a price which is lower
than the nominal value of the shares. This rule was laid down almost a century
ago by the House of Lords in *Ooregum Cold Mining Co of India v Roper*[32] and
was given statutory force by s 27 of the 1983 Act. This also provides that where
shares are allotted at a discount, the allottee is liable to pay the amount of the
discount to the company together with interest. The same liability attaches to a
subsequent purchaser of the shares, unless he purchases for value without notice
of the contravention.

---

[28] See para **[15.05]** below.
[29] *Henry Head & Co v Ropner Holdings Ltd* [1952] Ch 124; *Shearer v Bercain Ltd* [1980] 3 All
ER 295.
[30] Companies (Amendment) Act 1982, s 37.
[31] Ussher, *Company Law in Ireland* suggests (p 37) that the distribution of the profits does not
necessarily involve the diminution of the share premium account, since the lack of physical
correspondence between profit items on the liabilities side of the balance sheet which have
been reduced to pay a dividend and the assets actually used to pay it is immaterial. But the
return of the premium to the shareholders in any form other than one authorised by the section
would seem to be in the teeth of the section itself and not merely of the two English decisions.
In this context, Ussher points out that such profits may in Ireland be distributed to the
shareholders in the holding company where the auditors are satisfied that it is fair and
reasonable to do so and no one's rights or interests are prejudiced. (See the Companies Act
1963, s 149(5).) But although this means that such a distribution is not of itself unlawful, it
would seem to leave unaffected the question of whether it is prohibited by s 62(2) where the
holding company has no other assets and the allotment is accordingly at a premium.
[32] [1892] AC 125.

[9.58] It had been possible to issue shares at a discount with the sanction of the court but this provision in the Principal Act was repealed by the 1983 Act. It is still lawful, however, to pay a commission not exceeding 10% of the price at which the shares were issued to any person in consideration of his agreeing to take shares or procure others to take shares. This exception, which is provided for by s 59 of the Principal Act, is intended to facilitate the payment of commission for underwriting or other services. The wording of the section is sufficiently wide to cover a commission for simply subscribing for the shares; but such an arrangement will usually be viewed with suspicion by the courts.

[9.59] The rule is simply one against issuing shares at a discount; there is no obligation on a company, as we have seen, to issue shares for cash[33].

---

33 Para **[9.27]** above.

Chapter 10

Commencement of Business

[10.01] The company comes into being when the Registrar issues a certificate to the effect that it has been incorporated. In the case of a private company, it may thereupon commence business and exercise any power it may have to borrow money. In the case of a public company, however, there are certain requirements which must be met before the company commences business or exercises its borrowing powers. And in every case, the company must have a registered office in Ireland.

Certificate of incorporation

[10.02] When the memorandum of a company is delivered to the Registrar for registration, he must first satisfy himself that all the requirements of the Acts in respect to the registration and connected matters have been met. He then certifies under his hand that the company is incorporated; in the case of a limited company, that the company is limited; and in the case of a public limited company, that it is such a company. This document is called the certificate of incorporation.

[10.03] From the date mentioned in the certificate as the date of incorporation the subscribers to the memorandum become in law a body corporate with the name mentioned in the memorandum[1]. Usually the date of incorporation specified in the certificate is the date on which the Registrar actually signs the certificate, but if the Registrar specifies an earlier date as the date of incorporation, it is from that date and not the date of actual signature that the legal existence of the company dates.

[10.04] The certificate is conclusive evidence that:

    (1)   all the requirements of the Acts in respect of registration and of matters precedent and incidental thereto have been complied with;

    (2)   the association is a company entitled to be registered and duly registered under the Principal Act; and

    (3)   the company is a public limited company, if the certificate contains a statement to that effect[2]

---

[1]   Companies Act 1963, s 18(2).

[2]   Companies Act 1963, s 19; the Companies (Amendment) Act 1983, s 5(4).

[10.05] It follows that in no circumstances may the courts look behind the certificate to ascertain whether the company has in fact been lawfully incorporated, eg by having the requisite number of subscribers (seven) in the case of a public company[3].

Restrictions on the commencement of business

[10.06] A private company is entitled to commence business as soon as the certificate of incorporation is issued. Public companies are, however, precluded from commencing business or exercising borrowing powers until a number of requirements imposed by the Acts have been met. In the case of public limited companies formed as such, these requirements are set out in s 6 of the 1983 Act.

[10.07] Such a company may not commence business or exercise any of its borrowing powers until the Registrar has issued it with a certificate under the section or the company is registered as another form of company. The Registrar must issue the certificate where:

(a) an application is made in the prescribed form[4];

(b) he is satisfied that the nominal value of the allotted share capital is not less than the authorised minimum[5]; and

(c) there is delivered to him a statutory declaration complying with the section.

[10.08] The statutory declaration must be in the prescribed form and must state:

(a) that the nominal value of the allotted share capital is not less than the authorised minimum;

(b) the amount paid up, at the time of the application, on the allotted share capital;

(c) the amount, or estimated amount, of the preliminary expenses of the company and the persons by whom any of those expenses have been paid or are payable; and

(d) the amount of benefit paid or given or intended to be paid or given to any promoter of the company, and the consideration for the payment or benefit[6]

---

[3] *Oakes v Turquand* (1867) 2 HL Cas 325.
[4] Companies (Forms) Order 1983, SI 1983/289, Form 70.
[5] See para **[4.37]** above.
[6] The company must publish notice in *Iris Oifigiúil* of the delivery of the declaration within six weeks of its delivery.

[10.09] The section applies only to public limited companies which are formed as such. A private company does not require such a certificate.

[10.10] A certificate under the section is conclusive evidence that the company is entitled to do business and exercise any of its borrowing cowers.

[10.11] Where a public limited company does business or exercises any borrowing powers in contravention of s 6, the company and any officer in default are guilty of an offence and liable on summary conviction to a fine not exceeding £500. A transaction entered into by a public limited company which has not complied with the section remains valid, but if the company fails to comply with its obligations under the transaction, the directors are jointly and severally liable to indemnify the other party for any resulting loss or damage.

[10.12] The restrictions on public companies commencing to carry on business were formerly contained in s 115 of the Principal Act. That section remains in force, but since it is confined in its application to public unlimited companies, its significance is greatly reduced. Companies affected by the section who have a share capital and issue a prospectus inviting the public to subscribe for their shares may not commence business or exercise any borrowing powers until the requirements set out in sub-s (1) have been met. These include a requirement that shares to the amount of the 'minimum subscription'[7] have been allotted, being shares subject to the payment of the whole amount thereof in cash. This requirement need not be met where the company does not issue a prospectus, but in that case the company must deliver to the Registrar for registration a statement in lieu of a prospectus[8].

The registered office of the company

[10.13] Every company registered under the Acts must at all times have a registered office in Ireland to which communications and notices may be addressed. Notice of its situation must be given to the Registrar prior to incorporation[9]. The situation of the office need not be stated, however, in the memorandum. A company and every officer in default which carries on business without having such an office or omits to notify the Registrar of its situation is liable on summary conviction to a fine not exceeding £500[10].

[10.14] The situation of the office within Ireland can be altered from time to time. Notice of any such change must be given to the Registrar within fourteen

---

7   For the meaning of the 'minimum subscription' see para **[9.42]** above.
8   See para **[4.41]** above.
9   Companies Act 1963, s 113 as substituted by the Companies (Amendment) Act 1982, s 4.
10   Companies Act 1963, s 113 as substituted by the Companies (Amendment) Act 1982, s 4.

days from the change. It is not sufficient to include the change in the annual return.

[10.15] The fact that the registered office of every company registered under the Acts must be in Ireland means that all such companies are Irish in nationality and have an Irish domicile. It does not necessarily follow, however, that such companies reside in Ireland. Whether a company is properly regarded as resident in Ireland can be important when questions of tax arise and it can also be material in determining whether a company can be served with legal process.

[10.16] For taxation purposes, a company is normally regarded as residing where the actual management of the company is carried on[11], even though it ought to be managed elsewhere according to its constitution[12]. The application of this principle may mean that a company is resident in more than one jurisdiction at the same time[13]. Some at least of the superior and directing authority of the company must, however, be present in the jurisdiction in which it is sought to establish such residence[14].

[10.17] The following documents must be kept at the registered office:

  (1)   The register of members;[15]

  (2)   The register of debenture holders (where such a register is kept);[16]

  (3)   The register of directors and secretaries;[17]

  (4)   The register of directors' and secretaries' interests in shares;[18]

  (5)   The register of interests in shares in public limited companies;[19]

  (6)   Copies of instruments creating charges;[20]

  (7)   The book containing minutes of general meetings;[21]

  (8)   The books of account[22].

---

[11] *De Beers Consolidated Mines Ltd v Howe* [1906] AC 455.
[12] *Unit Construction Ltd v Bullock* [1960] AC 351.
[13] *Swedish Central Rly v Thompson* [1925] AC 495.
[14] *Union Corporation Ltd v MC* [1953] AC 482.
[15] Companies Act 1963, s 116(5).
[16] Companies Act 1963, s 91.
[17] Companies Act 1963, s 195(1).
[18] Companies Act 1990, s 59.
[19] Companies Act 1990, s 80.
[20] Companies Act 1963, s 109.
[21] Companies Act 1963, s 146(1).
[22] Companies Act 1963, s 147(3).

Part III

Corporate Personality of the Company

Chapter 11

Separate Legal Personality of the Company

The rule in Salomon's case

[11.01] A company registered under the Acts is an artificial legal entity separate and distinct from the members of which it is composed. This central principle of company law has several important consequences, not least that where the liability of the members is limited, they cannot, save in exceptional circumstances, be required to pay the company's debts. The principle was first laid down in unequivocal terms by the House of Lords in the celebrated case of *Salomon v Salomon & Company Ltd*[1].

[11.02] Aaron Salomon was a leather merchant and boot manufacturer carrying on a small but profitable business in Whitechapel. When his sons who worked with him in the business pressed him to give them some form of stake in it, he went to his solicitors. They advised him to follow the course taken by several businessmen before him and thousands since then: to sell his business in its entirety to a newly formed company, make his family directors and give them nominal shareholdings and take the purchase price in the form of fully paid up shares. The essential control of the business would thus remain in his hands, his family at the same time would be formally recognised as having an interest in the business and he would in addition, and as a bonus, enjoy the protection of limited liability. He accordingly sold the business to the company for £39,000 and took his payment in the form of 20,000 £1 shares, his wife and five children getting one share each. The payment of the balance of the purchase price was secured by the issue in his favour of a mortgage debenture.

[11.03] The company encountered unexpected trading difficulties and in an effort to keep it afloat, Salomon arranged for a loan to the company secured by a further mortgage. When the mortgage interest fell into arrears, the mortgagee put the company into liquidation and Salomon claimed to be entitled to what little was left in priority to the ordinary creditors on the strength of his mortgage debenture. The liquidator contested his claim and was upheld by Vaughan Williams J at first instance. In the Court of Appeal, Salomon again failed, all three judges treating the formation of the company as a wholly unwarranted perversion of the companies' legislation[2]. They said that the company was a

---

[1]   [1897] AC 22.
[2]   Reported *sub nom Broderip v Salomon* [1895] 2 Ch 323.

117

sham, that Salomon was simply carrying on the same business as before through its agency and that he could not be paid his debt at the expense of the ordinary creditors.

[11.04] Salomon appealed to the House of Lords which made it clear that there was nothing whatever to prevent the formation of what were in effect 'one man companies'. While he has been regarded admiringly by some commentators - including in previous editions the present writer - as a heroic figure battling his way up through the legal hierarchy to ultimate victory, it must be admitted that the unfortunate creditors whom he outwitted might be forgiven for taking a different view. However that may be, the case undoubtedly marked a critical turning point in the evolution of modern company law. As the great Irish judge, Lord MacNaghten succinctly put it:

> 'The company is at law a different person altogether from the subscribers to the memorandum; and though it may be that after incorporation the business is precisely the same as it was before, and the same persons are managers and the same hands receive the profits, the company is not in law the agent for the subscribers or trustees for them. Nor are the subscribers as members liable in any shape or form, except to the extent and in the manner provided by the Act.'[3]

The decision of the Court of Appeal was unanimously reversed.

[11.05] The principle laid down in *Salomon's* case has been applied over a wide range of cases in England and Ireland. But, as we shall see, it has also been restricted in its operation to an increasing extent by legislation, principally designed to prevent the protection of limited liability from being abused and to ensure that liability for tax has not been avoided. In addition, in a number of cases, the courts have been prepared to treat the principle as inapplicable. However, while the legislative restrictions have increased, there has also been a tendency in recent years on the part of judges both here and in England to resist further dilution of the principle. We consider first the diverse circumstances in which it has been applied.

[11.06] A good example is *Lee v Lee's Air Farming*[4]. A pilot in New Zealand had formed a company for the purpose of carrying on his soil spraying business. He was the controlling shareholder and governing director. When he was killed in a flying accident, it was sought to resist a claim by his widow under the relevant workmen's compensation provisions on the basis that he was not a 'worker', ie a servant of the company. The court in New Zealand upheld this contention, but it was rejected on appeal by the Judicial Committee of the Privy Council. Since the pilot and the company were separate legal entities, they were

---

3   [1897] AC 22 at 51.
4   [1961] AC 12.

capable in law of entering into a contract of service despite the extent of the control exercised by the pilot over the company.

[11.07] There is a curious feature of the decision, however: Lord Morris of Borth-y-Gest, giving the advice of the Judicial Committee, appears to suggest that the result might have been different had the company been 'a sham or a simulacrum'. Whatever about being a sham, the company was clearly a 'simulacrum': no one had any real control over it except the pilot. But the essence of the decision in *Salomon's* case is that it is entirely immaterial that the company is in effect a 'one man company': it remains a separate legal entity. A company may well be described as the 'alter ego', 'simulacrum', 'puppet' or whatever expression one may wish to employ, of the person who promotes it, but of itself this does not prevent it from being a separate legal entity with all the consequences that follow in law. As we shall see, there have been other judicial dicta which have been similarly unclear[5], but it is believed that the fundamental principle, in Ireland as in England, is as stated.

[11.08] The principle worked to the advantage of the shareholder's dependants in *Lee's* case; in *Turnstall v Steigman*[6], it operated to the shareholder's detriment. There a landlord of property sought to resist the grant of a new tenancy on the ground that she required the property for the purposes of a business carried on in an adjoining premises. It transpired, however, that the business was in fact being carried on by a company in which the landlord was a majority shareholder. It was held that she could not rely on the company's business requirements to defeat the tenant's claim: it was a different legal entity and was not the landlord[7]. It also defeated a claim by a shareholder in *Roberts v Coventry Corporation*[8]. There the defendants compulsorily acquired premises the freehold of which was vested in the plaintiff. She had granted a yearly tenancy of the premises to a company which carried on business in them and of which she was a majority shareholder. In addition to the value of her freehold interest, she claimed a further sum in respect of the loss she would suffer when the defendants terminated the company's yearly tenancy. It was held that this was the company's loss and not hers and that she could not recover compensation in respect of it.

---

5   See para **[11.33]** below.
6   [1962] 2 QB 593.
7   The reverse situation occurred in *Pegler v Craven* [1952] 2 QB 69, when the tenant failed to obtain a new tenancy, where the premises had been occupied by a company in which he was the majority shareholder. This decision is not applicable in Ireland, however the Landlord and Tenant (Amendment) Act 1980: s 5(3) provides that a tenant's rights are not to be affected where the occupation is that of a company controlled by him and occupying the premises under a licence from him.
8   [1947] 1 All ER 308.

[11.09] In Ireland, the principle also worked to the shareholder's disadvantage in *Battle v Irish Art Promotion Centre Ltd*[9], where the majority shareholder in, and managing director of, a company was refused leave by the High Court and the Supreme Court to conduct the defence of an action against the company. The company had not enough money to retain solicitor or counsel and the applicant wished to defend the case so as to protect his own business reputation. He was, of course, entitled to appear for himself, but the company was a separate legal entity and accordingly could only be represented by solicitor or counsel

[11.10] The principle was also applied by Barrington J in *Irish Permanent Building Society v Registrar of Building Societies and Irish Life Building Society*[10]. In that case, the plaintiffs sought to prevent the registration of the second defendants, the Irish Life Building Society, as a building society on the grounds *inter alia* that it was not an autonomous body but was the subsidiary of another, ie the Irish Life Assurance Company. It was accepted by Barrington J that the building society was the 'creature' (in no pejorative sense) of the insurance company: its directors were all nominees of the latter which also provided all the funds. He held, however, applying the principle in *Salomon*'s case, that this did not mean that the society was not a separate legal entity: it was such an entity and was accordingly registerable.

[11.11] Again, in *Gresham's Industries Ltd (in liquidation) v Cannon*[11], the liquidator of the plaintiff company brought proceedings against the majority shareholder claiming the repayment of sums said to have been lent by the company to him. The defendant, while admitting that the payments had been made, claimed that they were intended for, and used for, the purposes of other companies of which he was the majority shareholder and that in effect the money was being used for the benefit of a group of companies of which he was the owner. Rejecting the contention that this afforded any defence, Finlay P said:

> 'It seems to be a fundamental principle of the law that if a person decides to obtain and use the benefit of trading through limited liability companies and if for any purpose, whether the limitation of his liability, tax purposes or otherwise he transfers assets from one company to another or makes drawings from one company and invests them in his own name in another company, he cannot subsequently be heard to ignore the existence of the legal entities consisting of the different companies and to look upon the entire transaction as a personal one.'

---

[9]   [1968] IR 252.
[10] [1981] ILRM 242.
[11] Unreported, 2 July 1980. See also *Rex Foods Ltd v Lamb Brothers (Ireland) Ltd* (unreported, 5 December 1985) (Costello J).

[11.12] In *Taylor v Smyth*[12], McCarthy J, speaking for the Supreme Court, reaffirmed the principle and said that it followed that a director of a company which was wholly controlled by him was capable in law of entering into an actionable conspiracy with the company, since they were separate legal entities.

[11.13] It also follows logically from *Salomon's* case that a shareholder cannot sue, or be sued, on foot of contracts entered into by the company. Similarly, he can neither sue or be sued in respect of torts committed against or by the company[13]. It follows that a shareholder does not have an insurable interest in the assets or business of the company[14]. By contrast, a debenture holder has such an interest because, unlike a shareholder, he has an interest in the property and business of the company. Consistently with the general principle, a shareholder can be convicted of stealing from a company, even though it is effectively controlled by him[15].

[11.14] The continuing vitality of the *Salomon* principle was demonstrated in England in *Maclaine Watson & Company Ltd v Department of Trade and Industry*[16]. That case arose out of the collapse of the world price of tin in the nineteen eighties. A body called the International Tin Council ('ITC') had been established by a treaty between a number of countries to control fluctuations in the price of tin. All the relevant states were members of ITC which under the relevant UK legislation was to have 'the legal capacities of a body corporate'.

[11.15] When ITC ran out of money, its creditors sought to hold the individual member states liable for its debts. The attempt failed and in the House of Lords, Lord Oliver remarked

> 'It was to the ITC and not to its members that credit was extended and it is elementary that the only persons liable and entitled under a contract in the absence of trust or agency are the parties to the contract. The decision of this House in *Salomon v Salomon & Co Ltd* is as much the law today as it was in 1896.'

Yet, as we shall now see, contrary to what this might suggest, there have in fact been substantial inroads on the principle of the decision by the legislature and the courts since its was first pronounced.

---

[12] [1991] 1 IR 142. It had been held in England that a prosecution for conspiracy could not be brought in such circumstances since the nature of the crime required that there be two minds at work (*R v McDonnell* [1956] 1 QB 233). McCarthy J considered that this principle did not apply in the case of a civil conspiracy, but the validity of the distinction has been questioned: see McCann, *Companies and Conspiracy*, ILT Vol 8 197.

[13] *British Thompson-Houston Company v Sterling Accessories Ltd* [1924] 2 Ch 33.

[14] *MacCaura v Northern Assurance Company* [1925] AC 619.

[15] *Attorney General's Reference (No 2 of 1982)* [1984] QB 624.

[16] [1989] 3 All ER 1056.

[11.16] The legislature has provided that, in certain circumstances, the normal consequences of the rule in *Salomon*'s case are not to follow. That case established that a company is not in law the agent of a shareholder simply because of the degree of control enjoyed by that shareholder. It follows that such a shareholder, whatever the extent of his shareholding or of the control exercised by him over the board of directors, cannot normally be made liable for the debts of the company. In certain instances, however, considered in more detail below, the legislature has provided that shareholders or directors may be liable for the debts of the company despite the fact that the company is not their agent.

[11.17] *Salomon*'s case also established the general principle that control of a company, however extensive, cannot justify the inference that the company and the shareholder are to be treated as one legal entity. In a steadily widening range of cases, this principle has also been drastically modified by legislation. Commercial realities today make it essential for the law to recognise that businesses are frequently carried on by groups of connected companies. The first major step in this direction in Irish law was taken by the Principal Act in relation to the accounts of companies. In the case of a company which is a shareholder, where the extent of the control by that company is sufficient to render one or more of the companies the subsidiary or subsidiaries of that company, the latter - the parent or holding company - may be required to present its own shareholders with group accounts, showing the state of affairs in the group of companies as a whole. This result should not logically follow if each of the companies is to be treated for all purposes as a separate and distinct legal entity. As we shall see, there have been many other examples of the same approach.

[11.18] There have also been a number of cases in which the courts in England and Ireland have refused to apply the fundamental principle established by *Salomon*'s case or have at least declined to apply it in its full rigour. Commentators have wrestled bravely with the task of extracting general rules underlying these cases, but have usually found it an impossible one.

[11.19] These modifications in special circumstances by the legislature and the courts of the principle in *Salomon*'s case have been frequently described as occasions on which 'the veil of corporate personality is lifted': so frequently, indeed, that it is almost impossible to dislodge the phrase in any discussion of the topic. Yet it is a singularly unhelpful and confusing metaphor: there is no veil, as Gower points out[17], which prevents the law from seeing who owns a company. On the contrary, the great principle underlying all modern companies' legislation is the requirement that the identity of those who control the company

---

[17] Gower, *Modern Company Law* (6th edn), p 148.

should be ascertainable by the public. There is nothing to prevent a court in any case from ascertaining who the persons in control of a company are, if that is relevant to any issue which the court has to resolve[18]. What it cannot do (without modifying the rule in *Salomon*'s case) is draw the inference from the mere fact of that control that the company is the agent or trustee of the shareholders or treat the controlling shareholders and the company as one legal entity.

We now examine in detail the cases in which the legislature and the courts have modified the rule in *Salomon*'s case.

Modifications of the rule in Salomon's case

The legislature

[11.20] A reduction in the number of members of a company below the legal minimum - seven in the case of a public company - may expose the surviving member or members to liability for the debts of the company. In such a case, the company continues to exist as a legal entity. To that extent, the principle in *Salomon*'s case is respected, but is modified so as to render the surviving member or members liable for the company's debts. They are, however, given a breathing space of six months. Where the company carries on business for longer than that period, every person who is a member during that time and is aware that it is so operating is to be liable for the debts of the company contracted during that period[19]. Since a private limited company may now consist of one member only, the provision is applicable only to public companies and in any event was rarely used in practice.

[11.21] The Principal Act, substantially amended by the 1990 Act, provides that an officer of a company such as a director can be declared to be personally responsible, without limitation of liability, for all or part of the debts of the company, where it appears that, while he was an officer, he was knowingly party to the carrying on of the business of the company in a reckless manner. Moreover, any person, whether an officer or not, can be made similarly liable, if he was knowingly a party to the carrying on of any business of the company with intent to defraud its creditors or for any fraudulent purpose.

[11.22] These provisions, which are a significantly more elaborate version of the 'fraudulent trading' provisions originally contained in the Principal Act, are a far more important erosion of the rule that control of a company's affairs does not make the controller responsible for its debts. The 1990 Act contains similar provisions empowering the court to impose responsibility for the debts on

---

[18] Subject to the qualification that the shares may be held by nominees on behalf of persons whose identity is not ascertainable from an inspection of the register. See Chs 23 and 24 below.
[19] Companies Act 1963, s 36.

directors and others when proper books of account have not been kept and when an improper declaration of solvency has been made in a voluntary winding up. These provisions are discussed in more detail in Chapters 32, 35 and 40 below.

[11.23] Where a company is a 'subsidiary' of another - ie where a majority of its shares are held by that company or it is effectively controlled by it - it remains in law a separate legal entity and the central principle established by *Salomon*'s case is preserved. There has, however, been a growing tendency for the legislature to modify this principle in a number of areas. One which has already been mentioned is the requirement that holding companies publish group accounts. This topic is considered in more detail in Chapter 31. Other examples are to be found in the 1990 Act, such as the provisions enabling the court to require one company in a group to pay the debts of another company in the same group and requiring the assets of companies in the same group to be pooled for the benefit of the creditors and contributories. Another is the provision enabling the court to order that an examiner appointed to deal with a particular company's affairs be appointed examiner of other 'related companies'.

[11.24] The concept of the separate legal personality of the company has obvious possibilities for people seeking to reduce the burden of taxation. This led the legislature in England to introduce further modifications of the *Salomon* principle by permitting tax liability to depend on the degree of actual control exercised by people over the affairs of companies. For that purpose, it developed the concept of the 'close company' and thus sought to ensure that individuals do not ease the burden of taxation on their business profits by retaining them in such companies and obtaining the benefit of them without taxation through such stratagems as loans and interest payments from the companies. The Oireachtas has again followed the English example. The relevant provisions, which will be found in Pt X of the Corporation Tax Act 1976, are of great complexity and lie outside the scope of this book. It is sufficient to note that 'close companies' are, generally speaking, companies under the control of five or fewer 'participators' and that the Act brings within the taxation net various 'distributions' of their profits made, or deemed to be made, by such companies to the participators. Similar provisions are to be found in the Capital Gains Tax Act 1975.

[11.25] The Oireachtas has also had regard to the extent of the control enjoyed by shareholders in order to regulate mergers and takeovers. For the purposes of the relevant legislation - the Mergers Takeovers and Monopolies (Control) Act 1978 - a merger or takeover is defined as existing when two or more enterprises come under 'common control'. In the case of a company, common control is deemed to exist when the right to appoint a majority of the board of directors or a specified proportion of voting shares is acquired by another enterprise. These provisions are considered further in Chapter 34.

[11.26] The foregoing are all cases where the legislature has modified the consequences of *Salomon*'s case in clear and unequivocal language. It has been held by the House of Lords[20] that such language must be used before the courts will treat the principle of the case as having been dislodged. Lord Diplock, acknowledged, however, the possibility that even in the absence of express words, a purposive construction of a statute might lead to the conclusion that it must have been the intention of parliament to modify the rule.

The courts

[11.27] As we have noted, while there have been a number of cases in which the courts have modified the rule in *Salomon*'s case, it is not easy to extract any general principle underlying the cases. One qualification is clearly established beyond doubt, however: the courts will not permit the statutory privilege of corporation to be used for a fraudulent purpose. This is entirely consistent with the general approach adopted by the House of Lords in *Salomon*'s case: in that court the view which found favour with the Court of Appeal that the Act was being used for a fraudulent purpose was emphatically rejected. Had the law lords been dealing with a case in which the company was formed for a fraudulent object, the result might have been different. There has also been, however, a further refinement of this qualification: in a number of cases, it has been held that the courts will not allow the Acts to be used for the purpose of evading contractual or other legal obligations.

[11.28] Thus, in *Cummins v Stewart*[21], the defendant attempted to escape from his liability to pay royalties to the plaintiff under a licence agreement which had proved commercially unattractive by transferring a licence to a company formed for that purpose. Meredith MR held that *Salomon*'s case was no answer to the plaintiff's claim, saying:

> 'It would be strange indeed if (the Companies Act) could be turned into an engine of destruction of legal obligations and the overthrow of legitimate and enforceable claims. The most casual reader of the speeches of the law lords in *Salomon v Salomon and Company* cannot fail to observe that there is nothing in any of those speeches contrary to the view I have just expressed.'

[11.29] Again, in *Gilford Motor Company v Horne*[22], the defendant had entered into an agreement with the company which employed him not to canvass their customers for business in the event of his leaving. He sought to evade this agreement on leaving the company by forming a company and using it as a

---

[20] *Dimbleby & Sons Ltd v NUJ* [1984] 1 All ER 751.

[21] [1911] 1 IR 236.

[22] [1933] Ch 935.

vehicle for such canvassing. It was held that he could be restrained from so doing. Similarly, in *Jones v Lipman*[23], the defendant who had contracted to sell his house to the plaintiff tried to avoid a decree of specific performance being given against him by conveying the house to a company formed by him. Russell J rejected a defence based on the company being a separate entity, describing the company as:

> 'the creature of the defendant, a device and a sham, a mask which he holds before his face in attempt to avoid recognition by the eye of equity.'[24]

[11.30] A similar form of reasoning has been applied in cases where a court has a discretion to grant or withhold a particular remedy. In *Re Bugle Press*[25], for example, the holders of 90% of the shares in a company wished to buy out the holder of the remaining 10%. For that purpose, they formed a company, and transferred their shares to it. They then attempted to acquire the remaining 10% under the statutory procedure provided for buying out compulsorily a minority shareholding when a company is being taken over[26]. There had, of course, been no real takeover of the company: the new company had been formed solely with a view to expropriating the minority. An application by the minority shareholder to set aside the expropriation succeeded in the Court of Appeal: the granting of such relief was a matter of discretion and a court in exercising that discretion should have regard to the fact that the so-called take-over was a sham.

[11.31] In *Merchandise Transport Ltd v British Transport Commission*[27], the decision of a licensing authority not to grant a haulage licence to a subsidiary company where it was proposing to carry the goods of its parent company was upheld as valid by the Court of Appeal. The relevant provision was intended to prevent traders using their vehicles to carry their own goods and employing any surplus capacity to carry outsiders' goods, which was regarded as unfair competition. The object would have been frustrated by granting the licence in that case and it was held that the authority in exercising its discretion was entitled to have regard to the relationship between the two companies[28].

[11.32] In these cases, the company was variously described as 'a cloak', 'a sham', 'a device' and 'a mask'. One should not be misled, however, by the use of such metaphors. The more pejorative their overtones, the more seductive is the

---

[23] [1962] 1 All ER 442.

[24] [1962] 1 All ER 442 at 445.

[25] [1961] Ch 270. See also *Duggan v Stoneworth Investment Ltd* (unreported, 21 December 1999).

[26] See para **[32.26]** below.

[27] [1962] 2 QB 173.

[28] A similar approach seems to have been adopted by the Supreme Court in *The State v District Justice Donnelly* (unreported, 5 November 1977). No written judgments are available but the case is noted in Ussher, *Company Law in Ireland*, p 33.

conclusion that the court is justified in ignoring the separate personality of the company. Yet the formation of a company which has no genuinely separate existence, which may be in truth no more than a nameplate on an office building, and is all part of an elaborate legal stratagem is not of itself unlawful and the court is not entitled to disregard its separate existence.

[11.33] An interesting example of how these rhetorical expressions may lead to such a conclusion is the following passage from the judgment of Lord Denning in *Wallersteiner v Moir*[29], where he described the relationship between the plaintiff and certain companies in these terms:

> 'He controlled their every movement. Each danced to his bidding. He pulled the strings ... I am of the opinion that the court should pull aside the corporate veil and treat these concerns as his creatures, for whose doings he should be, and is, responsible ...'[30]

[11.34] All these expressions could have been applied with equal force to the relationship between Salomon and the company (or between the insurance company and the building society in the *Irish Permanent* case.) Not surprisingly, Lord Denning's brethren on the Court of Appeal in *Wallersteiner v Moir* did not find it necessary to go as far as he did. It is submitted that such a relationship of itself does not justify the court in disregarding the separate personality of the company. It is only where, in addition, the company has been formed for some fraudulent, illegal or improper purpose that the court may do so.

[11.35] Thus, in *Roundabout Ltd v Beirne*[31], Dixon J described a plan of action adopted (in part at least) with a view to preventing the picketing of a licensed premises as a 'legal subterfuge'. But he also held that it was an effective subterfuge. A company controlled by a family owned the licensed premises which they were anxious to preserve as a 'non-union' house. When all the members of the staff joined the union, they were dismissed. The defendants, who were officers of the relevant trade union, threatened to picket the premises, if the family persisted in their efforts to keep it a non-union house. The family then formed the plaintiff company which was also effectively controlled by them. In addition, however, three new barmen who were working in the premises were made directors. The licensed premises were leased to the plaintiff company, the defendants began to picket and the plaintiff company thereupon sought an injunction to restrain the picketing, claiming that it was not protected by the Trade Disputes Act 1906 since it was not being carried on 'in contemplation or in furtherance of a trade dispute'. The staff who had been

---

[29]   [1974] 3 All ER 217.
[30]   [1974] 3 All ER 217 at 238.
[31]   [1959] IR 423.

dismissed had never been employed by the plaintiff company and the three new barmen were directors and not employees. Hence, it was argued, there was no trade dispute as defined by Act, ie 'a dispute between employers and employees'. The defendants urged the court to look behind the formal legal structures to the reality, namely, the continuing control of the business and effective ownership of the premises by the same family. Dixon J found for the plaintiff company: the two companies were separate and distinct legal entities and, although the scheme could be described as a subterfuge designed to circumvent the statutory protection of peaceful picketing, it was legally unassailable[32].

[11.36] The same approach was adopted by the Court of Appeal in England more recently in *Adams v Cape Industries plc*[33]. The defendant company presided over a group of companies involved in mining asbestos in South Africa and marketing it in, among other places, the US. Separate companies were formed for the purpose of marketing the asbestos in the US which were either controlled by the defendants or their business associates. A large number of employees in a US factory brought actions in a court in Texas claiming that their health had been damaged as a result of exposure to asbestos dust, the defendants' asbestos being used by the factory in question. The defendants were joined in two sets of proceedings, but having been a party to a settlement in one set, did not enter an appearance to the second set. It was sought to enforce judgments in the second set of actions against them on the ground *inter alia* that they were resident in the jurisdiction of the US court at the relevant time, it being urged on the plaintiffs' behalf that the activities of the US companies should be treated as those of the defendants. The Court of Appeal held that the companies had been established with the twofold object of minimising the appearance of any involvement of the defendants in the sale of the asbestos and reducing by any lawful means the risk of the defendants or any subsidiary being held liable to US taxation or subject to the jurisdiction of the US courts. But the court declined to treat this as a sufficient ground for lifting the corporate veil. Slade LJ said:

> 'We do not accept as a matter of law that the court is entitled to lift the corporate veil as against a defendant company which is the member of a corporate group merely because the corporate structure has been used so as to ensure that the

---

[32] The decision may be questionable in another context: it appears to assume that a premises cannot be picketed where the persons carrying on the business are all self-employed. even though the picketing is in furtherance of a trade dispute (in this instance, the dispute between the original company and their dismissed employees as to the company's policy of employing only non-union labour). Dixon J remarked that 'the object of the picketing must be to act by influence or persuasion on employees', but this is surely doubtful: the object may be, for example, to dissuade suppliers or customers from entering the premises.
[33] (1990) BCLC 479.

legal liability (if any) in respect of particular future activities of the group (and correspondingly the risk of enforcement of that liability) will fall on another member of the group rather than the defendant company. Whether or not this is desirable, the right to use a corporate structure in this manner is inherent in our corporate law.'

It should be noted that the defendants in that case were not attempting to evade existing legal obligations, as in *Cummins v Stewart* and *Jones v Lipman*.

It should also be noted that the Irish courts have also been circumspect in 'lifting the veil' in applications which seek to make directors personally liable for the failure of the company to comply with planning permission: see *Dun Laoghaire Corpn v Parkhill Developments Ltd*[34].

[11.37] The cases mentioned in the previous paragraph are readily enough reconcilable with a general legal principle that the courts will not permit a statutory privilege to be used for fraudulent purposes, using the word 'fraudulent' in its more generous equitable sense as including attempts to evade contractual or other legal obligations or the use of such statutory privileges for improper purposes. We next come to a series of cases in which the courts have been prepared, in apparent conflict with *Salomon*'s case, to infer the existence of a relationship of agency or trust between companies in the same group. These are less easy to explain on the basis of any general principle. In *Smith Stone & Knight v Birmingham Corpn*[35], a holding company was the owner of property in which one of its subsidiaries was carrying on business. When it was compulsorily acquired by the defendants, the holding company was held entitled to compensation for disturbance arising from the relocating of the business, Atkinson J taking the view that the subsidiary was carrying on business as the agent of the holding company. This decision suggested a number of criteria for determining whether such an agency should be inferred, ie:

(1) were the profits of the subsidiary treated as the profits of the holding company?

(2) were the persons running the business of the subsidiary appointed by the holding company?

(3) was the holding company the 'head and brain' of the trading venture?

(4) did the holding company govern the adventure, decide what should be done and what capital should be employed in it?

(5) were the profits from the business the result of the 'skill and direction' of the holding company?

(6) was the holding company in 'effectual and constant control'?

---

[34] [1989] IR 447.
[35] [1939] 4 All ER 116.

[11.38] It is doubtful whether these criteria are capable of general application: if an agency were to be inferred in every case where they were met, a significant number of subsidiaries would have to be treated as the agents of their holding companies. It would then be difficult to avoid the logical corollary that the holding company was in each case liable for the debts of the subsidiary, opening up a huge breach, not merely in the principle of separate corporate existence, but in the principle of limited liability as well.

[11.39] It can safely be said that the courts have been more willing to draw the inference of agency where the controlling shareholder is another company (as in *Smith Stone & Knight v Birmingham Corpn*) and particularly where there is no other shareholder. There has also been a tendency to draw this inference with greater readiness in cases where any other result might lead to avoidance of tax liability. Thus in *Firestone Tyre & Public Company v Llewellin*[36], an American company formed a wholly owned subsidiary in England for the purpose of manufacturing tyres and supplying them to the European market. The English company received the payments for the tyres and, after deducting the costs of the manufacture and a figure of 5% transmitted the balance to the American market. Although the English company was independent in its day-to-day operations and only one of the directors was a director of the American company as well, it was held to be carrying on the business as the agent of the American company and the latter was accordingly liable to pay tax in respect of the profits of the business. It is virtually impossible to reconcile this decision with the earlier decision of *Ebbw Vale UDC v South Wales Traffic Area Licensing Authority*[37] where the Court of Appeal refused to treat the plaintiff transport company as the agent of the British Transport Commission, although that body held all the shares except two in the company. The defendants had argued that they had no jurisdiction to deal with an application by the plaintiff company to increase their fares, since the service was being 'provided' in effect by the commission and hence, under the relevant legislation, a fare increase had to be approved by another body. The court held on the authority of *Salomon*'s case that as the company was a separate legal entity it was providing the service itself and not as the agent of the commission.

[11.40] The desire to avoid apparent injustice or illogicality or to frustrate the ingenuity of tax lawyers has also led the courts to flirt on occasions with the heresy of treating the company as trustee for its shareholders. As we have seen, one of the fundamental differences between the company and other forms of business organisations, such as partnerships, is that the property of the business

---

[36] [1957] 1 All ER 561.
[37] [1951] 2 KB 366.

is vested in the company and not in its proprietors. For that reason, a shareholder has no insurable interest in the assets of the company and the suggestion that he had was rejected by Devlin J in one case as being 'beyond the reach of sustained argument'[38]. Yet in *Littlewood Mail Order Stores Ltd v IRC*[39], the Court of Appeal was not deterred by these well established principles from treating property vested in a subsidiary as being held on behalf of a parent company where a contrary conclusion would have enabled the parent company to avoid tax liability.

[11.41] This decision is in stark contrast to *William Cory & Son Ltd v Dorman Long & Company Ltd*[40] where a parent company claimed that barges registered in the name of a subsidiary were held in trust for them. Had this argument proved successful, they would have been entitled as owners to the benefit of a statutory limit on liability for the negligence of the master of one of the barges. It was held that the barges were not held in trust for them and that they were not the owners within the meaning of the relevant section.

[11.42] A similar inconsistency can be seen in what may be called the 'club cases'. Many clubs formed for social reasons find it convenient to incorporate themselves as companies, usually limited by guarantee. Such clubs are frequently registered under the Registration of Clubs (Ireland) Act 1904 in order to avail of the provisions of that Act enabling clubs to supply their members with drink without a licence. In the case of an unincorporated club, no difficulty arises: the assets of the club, including the stock of drink, are vested in trustees or a committee on behalf of the members and the sale of drink to the members is clearly a distribution of the members' common property to individual members, which under the Act does not require a licence. But where it is vested in a company, it cannot be said to be held in trust for the members, if the principles already stated are applicable. Accordingly, a sale to an individual member would seem to be a transaction between two legal entities - the company and the member - rather than a distribution of the common stock of the association among the members. This was the view taken in *Wurzel v Houghton Main Home Services Ltd*[41], disapproving of an earlier decision to the contrary of *Newell v Hemingway*[42]. Yet in a later case of *Trebanog Working Men's Club v Macdonald*[43], where the same view was taken as in *Newell v Hemingway*, Lord

---

38 *Bank voor Handel en Scheepvart NV v Slatford* [1953] 1 QB 248 at 269.
39 [1969] 3 All ER 855.
40 [1936] 2 All ER 386.
41 [1937] 1 KB 380.
42 (1888) 60 LT 544.
43 [1940] 1 KB 576.

Hewart CJ swept aside the argument based on *Salomon's* case as applied to such clubs, saying:

> 'once it is conceded that a member's club does not necessarily require a licence to serve its members with intoxicating liquor because the legal property in the liquor is not in the members themselves, it is difficult to draw any legal distinction between the various legal entities which may be entrusted with the duty of holding the property on behalf of the members, be it an individual, or a body of trustees, or a company formed for the purpose, so long as the real interest in the liquor remains, as it clearly does, in the members of the club. In this connection, there is no magic in the expression 'trustee' or 'agent'. What is essential is that a holding of property by the agent or trustee must be a holding for and on behalf of, and not a holding antagonistic to, the members of the club.'

This passage was cited by McWilliams J in *Re Parnell GAA Club Ltd*[44], where he rejected as not well founded an objection to the renewal of a company's registration under the 1904 Act on the ground that the assets, including the drink, were vested in the company.

[11.43] Accordingly, in this area also, the courts have declined to apply in its full vigour the principle in *Salomon's* case and it would seem to be the law in both Ireland and England that a member's club is not debarred from selling drinks to members merely by reason of the fact that it is a company.

[11.44] There were also a number of English cases which reflected a tendency to ignore the separate legal entities of various companies within a group and to look instead at the economic entity of the whole group. But that tendency received something of a setback with the Court of Appeal decision in *Adams v Cape Industries plc*[45].

[11.45] The leading example of the 'economic entity' approach was *Holdsworths & Co v Caddies*[46]. Mr Caddies was employed by the plaintiff company as its managing director under a written contract. He claimed damages for breach of contract on the ground that the company had confined him to performing duties as managing director of one of their subsidiaries. The company relied successfully on a clause in the contract which provided that:

> 'as such managing director he shall perform the duties and exercise the powers in relation to the business of the company and the businesses ... of its existing subsidiary companies ... which may at any time be assigned to or vested in him by the board ...'

---

[44] [1984] ILRM 246.
[45] See para **[11.36]** above.
[46] [1955] 1 All ER 725.

One of the arguments advanced on behalf of Mr Caddies was that the subsidiaries were separate legal entities under the control of their own boards. But even applying *Salomon's* case in its full rigour, this fact did not seem to assist his case, since the clause expressly envisaged that the company could assign him duties in relation to the subsidiaries. It appeared to follow that if the parent company could procure the assignment to him of such duties by virtue of their control of the subsidiaries, they would not be in breach of their contract. This scarcely involved any watering down of the *Salomon* principle and the opinions of the law lords appear for the most part to be based on the actual words of the clause itself. Lord Reid, however, did observe that the argument based on the separate legal personalities was 'too technical since an agreement in *re mercatoria* ... must be construed in the light of the facts and realities of the situation ...'[47].

[11.46] A somewhat similar observation was made by Viscount Simonds in *Scottish Co-operative Wholesale Society Ltd v Mever*[48], where a number of minority shareholders in a company claimed relief under the relevant section of the companies legislation which entitles the court to grant relief where shareholders are being treated oppressively[49]. The oppressive conduct in that case was passive rather than active: the majority shareholding was held by another company which was prepared to let the subsidiary go to the wall since that suited their interests. Again the law lords were in general content to decide the case on the ground that culpable inaction of this nature on the part of the majority could constitute oppression just as much as active oppression. Viscount Simonds, however, thought that the court could have regard to the positively detrimental actions of the parent company, remarking that:

> 'the section warrants the courts in looking at the business realities of a situation and does not confine them to a narrow legalistic view.'[50]

[11.47] A similar approach was adopted by Lord Denning MR in *DHN Food Distributors Ltd v Tower Hamlet London Borough Council*[51]. As in some of the earlier decisions, this case arose out of a compulsory acquisition of property. The acquiring authority sought to resist a claim for compensation for disturbance on the ground that the company which owned the property was one of a group of three companies in common ownership, one of which carried on business in the property. Lord Denning held that the court could look to the

---

[47] [1955] 1 All ER 725 at 738.
[48] [1959] AC 324.
[49] See Ch 28 below.
[50] [1959] AC 324 at 342.
[51] [1976] 3 All ER 462.

economic entity of the whole group and treat the business as being carried on by that group. It is a noteworthy feature of the decision, however, that his brethren, Goff LJ and Shaw LJ, were of the view that the case could, in any event, have been decided against the acquiring authority on two other grounds, ie that the company actually in occupation and carrying on the business was the owner in equity of the property and was further entitled to occupy the property in perpetuity under an irrevocable licence. On either basis, they said, the company could be regarded as entitled to be compensated as the true owner[52].

[11.48] Reservations as to the correctness of Lord Denning's view were expressed in the House of Lords in *Woolfson v Strathclyde Regional Council* where Lord Keith of Kinkel said:

> 'I have some doubts ... whether the Court of Appeal properly applied the principle that it is appropriate to pierce the corporate veil only where special circumstances exist indicating that (it) is a mere facade concealing the true facts.'[53]

And, one might add, as has been suggested already, where the reason for concealing the facts is itself improper. It would appear from *Adams v Cape Industries plc* that in England the view is taken that the fact that a company, by the use of separate corporate structures, may intentionally create the impression, contrary to the fact, that businesses are operating independently is not, of itself, an improper misuse of the corporate structure.

[11.49] Lord Denning's view was, however, adopted in Ireland by Costello J in *Power Supermarkets Ltd v Crumlin Investments Ltd*[54]. This is the most important modern Irish decision in the area and the facts must be set out in some detail.

[11.50] The first defendants entered into an agreement with the plaintiffs, who controlled the Quinnsworth chain of supermarkets, to grant them a lease of a large unit in a shopping centre. In the agreement, the first defendants covenanted:

> 'not during the term to grant a lease for or to sell or permit or suffer the sale by any of its tenants or so far as within (the first defendant's) control any sub or under tenants of groceries or food products in or over an area exceeding 3000 square feet in any one unit ... forming part of the shopping centre ...'

The shopping centre was not initially a financial success and was sold to a company called Cornelscourt Shopping Centre Limited, the sale of them being carried out by way of a transfer of shares in the first named defendants. This company was one of the Dunnes Stores group of companies who operated a rival

---

[52]   See also *Dublin Corpn v Underwood* [1997] 1 IR 69.
[53]   (1978) SC (HL) 90.
[54]   (Unreported, 22 June 1981).

chain of supermarkets. It was important, indeed essential, from their point of view that they themselves should have a retail outlet in the shopping centre. Since it was the policy of the group that each of its retail units should be operated by a separate company, a new company - Dunnes Stores (Crumlin) Ltd - was formed and the freehold in one of the units conveyed to it by the first named defendants. When the company began to trade, the plaintiffs sought to restrain them from so doing.

[11.51] It was established in evidence that the individual companies - approximately 150 - which made up the Dunnes Stores group were only notionally separate companies. All the affairs of the group were managed by members of the Dunne family and, in the case of Dunnes Stores (Crumlin) Ltd, there had been no further meetings of the directors after the first meeting. In the case of the purchase of shares, the unit was conveyed by the first named defendants to Dunnes Stores (Crumlin) Limited for a nominal consideration and without any of the covenants which would normally have accompanied the transaction, if carried out at arms' length.

[11.52] Costello J held that Dunnes Stores (Crumlin) Ltd were bound by the covenant, although not a party to it. Having cited the views of Lord Denning and Shaw LJ in *DHN Ltd v Tower Hamlets London Borough Council*, he went on:

> 'It seems to me to be well established from these as well as from other authorities (see *Holdsworth & Company v Caddies*; *Scottish Co-operative Wholesale Society Ltd v Meyer*) that a court may, if the justice of the case so requires, treat two or more related companies as a single entity so that the business notionally carried on by one will be regarded as the business of the group, if this conforms to the economic and commercial realities of the situation ... It would, in my view, be very hard to find a clearer case than the present one for the application of this principle.'[55]

[11.53] This passage was subsequently approved of by the Supreme Court[56] and may be treated as representing the law in Ireland. But it may be thought that it states the law too widely. The 'justice of the case' is a somewhat elusive concept and it is extremely difficult to predict with anything approaching certainty how it might or should be applied in specific cases. Thus in the case under discussion it was perhaps open to question whether justice required the reading of the covenant in the sense favoured by Costello J. It was after all a stipulation which restricted the covenantor's freedom to trade and as such hardly merited any

---

[55] He also decided in favour of the plaintiff on another ground, ie that the covenant in question was a restrictive covenant which ran with the land.

[56] *Re Bray Travel Limited and Bray Travel (Holdings) Ltd* (unreported, 13 July 1981), HC. As this was a decision on an interlocutory application in which no written judgments were delivered, it may be of somewhat doubtful value as an authority.

particular benevolent or purposive construction. It is an important feature of the case that Dunnes Stores (Crumlin) Ltd, although a company without any real independent existence, was not formed with a view to evading the covenant but simply in pursuance of the general policy of the group to have their outlets operated by separate companies. Hence there was no room for the application of the principles underlying cases such as *Gilford Motor Company v Horne* that the courts will not countenance the formation of companies for illegal or improper purposes. Nor was it suggested that it and the other companies were 'a mere facade to conceal the true facts', so that even if, contrary to what has already been suggested, that of itself justifies piercing the corporate veil, that stage was not reached in *Power Supermarket Ltd v Crumlin Investments*.

[11.54] The decision does, however, reflect another important tendency in this field: the courts will be more inclined to disregard the separate corporate personalities of the companies in a group if to do so will avert the possibility of injustice to outside parties. It will be less inclined to do so where the companies themselves seek to avoid the disadvantages of incorporation while clinging to the advantages[57].

[11.55] This approach was to a limited extent endorsed in *The State (McInerney & Co Ltd) v Dublin County Council*[58]. In that case, a subsidiary company served a purchase notice under s 29 of the Local Government (Planning and Development) Act 1963 in respect of land of which its holding company was the registered owner. The local authority on whom the purchase notice was served disputed its validity on the ground that the subsidiary was not the 'owner' within the meaning of the section. The subsidiary relied on both *Smith Stone & Knight* and *DHN Ltd*, but the court rejected the contention that on the basis of these decisions the subsidiary could be treated as the owner. Carroll J said:

> 'in my opinion, the corporate veil is not a device to be raised or lowered at the option of the parent company or group. The arm which lifts the corporate veil must always be that of justice. If justice requires (as it did in the *DHN* case) the courts will not be slow to treat a group of subsidiary companies and their parent companies as one. But can it be said that justice requires it in this case?'

She went on to answer the question in the negative.

---

57 A point made in an interesting article on this topic by Mr Gerard McCormack, *Judicial Application of Salomon's case in Ireland*, Incorporated Law Society of Ireland Gazette, May 1984.
58 [1985] ILRM 513.

[11.56] In England, the 'justice of the case' approach has been recently rejected in *Adams v Cape Industries plc*[59]. Slade LJ speaking for the Court of Appeal, said:

> 'As counsel for the defendants submitted, save in cases which turn on the wording of particular statutes or contracts, the court is not free to disregard the principles of *Salomon v Salomon* merely because it considers that justice so requires. Our law, for better or worse, recognises the creation of subsidiary companies which though in one sense the creatures of their parent companies, will nevertheless under the general law fall to be treated as separate legal entities with all the rights and liabilities which would normally attach to separate legal entities.'

[11.57] An attempt to invoke the decision in *Power Supermarket Ltd v Crumlin Investments* to justify the joining of a parent company in an action against a wholly owned subsidiary failed in *Allied Irish Coal Supplies Ltd v Powell Duffryn International Fuels Ltd*[60]. In that case, the plaintiff alleged that the subsidiary company was in breach of a commercial contract to supply industrial coal and, because it was apprehensive that the parent company was in the process of selling the subsidiary and endeavouring to distance itself from it, sought to join the parent company as a co-defendant in the proceedings. It was claimed that the subsidiary was not financially or otherwise independent of the parent company as regard control, finance or operations. In the High Court, Laffoy J rejected the application on the ground that the proposition advanced by the plaintiff was fundamentally at variance with the principle of separate corporate legal personality laid down in *Salomon v Salomon & Co*. That conclusion was upheld by the Supreme Court, Murphy J pointing out that the case was distinguishable from *Power Supermarkets Ltd v Crumlin Investments Ltd* since there was a very substantial business carried on by the subsidiary, and that, in any event, there was nothing in the judgment of Costello J to suggest that the principle in *Salomon v Salomon & Co* was being eroded.

[11.58] Similarly, the application of the rule in *Salomon v Salomon & Co* was held in *Re Frederick Inns Ltd (in liquidation)*[61] to render *ultra vires* the payment of sums in respect of tax arrears owed by a parent company and its subsidiaries to the Revenue Commissioners. In the case of the parent company, the sum paid greatly exceeded the company's tax liability, but insufficient money was credited to that company by the Commissioners to completely discharge its liability. The remainder of the sum paid was appropriated to the credit of other companies in

---

[59] The facts of this case are set out at para **[11.36]** above.
[60] [1998] 2 IR 519.
[61] [1991] ILRM 582; [1994] 1 ILRM 387.

the group and this was held to be contrary to the principle laid down in *Salomon*'s case.

[11.59] Finally, it should be noted that it has been suggested that the 'corporate veil' approach should not be followed in determining questions of EU competition law. Thus, a parent company and its subsidiary could be properly regarded, on this view, as a single undertaking for the purposes of Articles 81 [85] and 82 [86] of the Treaty of Rome[62].

[11.60] While, as we have noted, the courts in England, following the lead of the legislature, have been willing on some occasions to raise the veil where keeping it in place would facilitate tax avoidance schemes, it cannot be said with certainty that a similar pattern will emerge in Ireland.

[11.61] In this context, the decision of the Supreme Court in *McDermott v McGrath*[63] is worth noting in passing. That was not a case in which the *Salomon* principle arose directly: what was at issue was the so called 'fiscal nullity' doctrine which had emerged in a number of English decisions. They had established in that jurisdiction that the courts were entitled to have regard to the fact that a series of interlocking transactions had no purpose, business or otherwise, save the avoidance of tax and hence could be treated as sham or illusory transactions in the context of fiscal legislation. That doctrine was unanimously rejected by the Supreme Court: it remains to be seen whether a similar approach would be adopted in the area now being considered.

[11.62] A company, being an artificial personality, can only act through human agency. For certain purposes, it is accordingly necessary to ascertain the conduct and status of those who control its activities, whether they be shareholders, the directors or the managers. We have already seen that it is only in this manner that the residence of the company can be ascertained: a company which is wholly owned by French shareholders and carries on its activities in France through a staff resident in that country does not reside in Ireland, simply because its registered office is in Ireland[64]. Similarly, as we shall see in Chapter 13, a company is capable of committing crimes, but can only do so through the agency of human beings. In order to determine whether the company had the criminal intent necessary in the case of serious crime, it may be necessary to examine the conduct of those who control the company. Similarly, in deciding whether a company should be granted a particular statutory privilege, such as a licence under the Intoxicating Liquor Acts, it may be necessary to consider its

---

[62] Cf opinion of Advocate-General Warner in *Commercial Solvents Corp v EC Commission* Nos 6 7/74, (1974) ECR 223 at 263

[63] [1988] IR 258.

[64] See para **[10.15]** above.

character, and this may involve an examination of the conduct of its controllers and employees[65].

[11.63] While these are sometimes referred to as instances of 'lifting the veil' it is thought that this is not an accurate statement of the legal position. These cases do not involve any modification of the rule in *Salomon*'s case, since they do not erode in any sense the separate legal personality of the company. This was made clear by the House of Lords in the leading case of *Daimler Company Ltd v Continental Tyre (Great Britain) Company Ltd*[66], where the issue was whether the famous motor car company should be treated as an enemy alien during the First World War because it was owned by German shareholders and controlled from Germany, although its registered office was in England. In his speech, Lord Parker disposed of the fallacy that *Salomon*'s case prevented the courts from looking at the individual members in order to determine the character of the company. The company was held to be an enemy alien. It is thought that this also justifies the later decision of Danckwerts J in *The Abbey Malvern Wells Ltd v Minister of Local Government and Planning*[67]. In that case, the plaintiff company claimed to be a charitable body and hence exempt from certain development charges. The company managed a school on a profit making basis, but the shares were all held on charitable trusts so that the proprietors made no private profit. It was held that the court was entitled to take this into account in deciding whether the company was a charitable body and their claim succeeded on this basis.

[11.64] From this welter of conflicting decisions, the following principles may be extracted with some hesitation:

(1)   The rule in *Salomon*'s case is still the law. The company and its shareholders are separate legal entities and the courts normally cannot infer from the degree of control exercised by the shareholder a relationship of principal and agent or beneficiary and trustee between the shareholders and the company.

(2)   The courts, however, will not permit the statutory privilege of incorporation to be used for a fraudulent, illegal or improper purpose. Where it is so misused, the court may treat the company thus incorporated as identical with its promoters.

(3)   In certain cases, where no actual misuse of the privilege of incorporation is involved, the courts may nonetheless infer the

---

[65] See *Rex (Cottingham) v The Justices of County Cork* [1906] 2 IR 415.
[66] [1916] 2 AC 307.
[67] [1951] Ch 728.

existence of an agency or a trust if to do otherwise would lead to injustice or facilitate the avoidance of tax liability.

(4)   In the case of a group of companies, the court may sometimes treat the group as one entity, particularly where to do otherwise would have unjust consequences for outsiders dealing with companies in the group.

(5)   The rule in *Salomon*'s case does not prevent the court from looking at the individual members of the company in order to determine its *character* and *status* and where it legally resides.

Chapter 12

Contracts

[12.01] A company, being a legal entity, can enter into contracts as an individual can. It is, however. subject to one major limitation from which the individual is free: it cannot enter into a contract which is *ultra vires*, ie beyond its powers. As we have seen, any act which is not authorised, either expressly or by implication, by the memorandum is *ultra vires* the company. This rule renders such contracts void, not merely as between the company and its members, but also as between the company and the other party to the contract (referred to in this chapter as 'the outsider'). Coupled with the principle that persons dealing with the company are presumed to be aware of the contents of its public documents, including the memorandum, (an application of the legal doctrine known as *constructive notice*) this rule was capable of causing serious injustice and has been significantly modified by the Oireachtas in favour of outsiders dealing with the company[1].

Pre-incorporation contracts

[12.02] A company cannot enter into any contract until it has been incorporated, since until that time it does not exist in law. Nor until the enactment of the Principal Act 1963 could the company ratify the contract after its incorporation. Section 37(1) of the Act, however, provides that:

> Any contract or other transaction purporting to be entered into by a company prior to its formation or by any person on behalf of the company prior to its formation may be ratified by the company after its formation and thereupon the company shall become bound by it and entitled to the benefit thereof as if it had been in existence at the date of such contract or other transaction and had been a party thereto.[2]

[12.03] If the company does not ratify the pre-incorporation contract, it can neither sue nor be sued on foot of it. But if the other party to the contract can prove that the company has benefited under the contract - if, for example, it has received goods and refused to pay for them - he may be entitled to recover the money in a quasi-contractual action. And, even without ratification, the contract is binding on those who purported to contract on the company's behalf.

---

[1]   Para **[12.11]** below.

[2]   This was one of the Irish innovations in the Act. The English Acts contain no such provision.

[12.04] A company may ratify a pre-incorporation contract by a resolution of the members in general meeting. A resolution of the board of directors will also be sufficient for this purpose when the articles of association provide that the powers of management of the company are to be vested in the directors. But even an informal rectification by conduct may also be sufficient. Thus in *HKN Invest OY v Incotrade PVT Ltd*[3], Costello J held that where a controlling shareholder implemented the contract without any formal resolution having been passed, the contract had been effectively ratified for the purpose of s 37.

[12.05] Until a pre-incorporation contract is ratified, the persons who entered into it in the name or on behalf of the company are personally bound by it and entitled to the benefit of it in the absence of an express agreement to the contrary[4].

Form of contracts

[12.06] Provided the contract is not *ultra vires*, it can be entered into by the company in the same form as a similar contract entered into by an individual. Section 38 of the Principal Act provides that a contract which if made between private persons would be required to be in writing and under seal may be made on behalf of the company in writing under the common seal of the company. Where if made between private persons, it would have to be in writing and signed by the parties to be charged therewith, it may be made on behalf of the company in writing, signed by any person acting under its authority, express or implied. It may be varied or discharged in the same manner in which it is authorised to be made. It should be noted that this last provision of the Principal Act is permissive and not mandatory. Consequently, where a contract can be validly varied or discharged in some other manner under the general law, it can be so varied or discharged in the case of a company. Thus, a contract under seal can lawfully be varied or discharged by a simple contract and this also applies to contracts executed under the seal of a company.

[12.07] The number of instances in which a company must contract under seal are rare. A conveyance or assignment of freehold or leasehold land must, however, be by deed, and an agreement made without consideration will not normally be enforceable unless it is under seal. In both of these cases, accordingly, the document must be under the common seal of the company.

[12.08] The most important examples of contracts which must be evidenced in writing to be enforceable are those specified in the Irish Statute of Frauds and, of such contracts, the most important in practice are contracts for the sale of land.

---

3 [1993] 3 IR 152 at 160.
4 Companies Act 1963, s 37(2).

Where a company is party to such a contract, it will accordingly not be enforceable against the company unless it is evidenced in writing signed by a person acting under the authority of the company, express or implied.

The ultra vires rule and the doctrine of constructive notice

[12.09] The rule that a company had no power to enter into a contract which was not expressly or impliedly authorised by its constitution - the 'ultra vires' rule - was firmly established in the early days of the Companies Acts in England. Moreover, persons dealing with the company were presumed to be aware of the contents of the company's public documents, including the memorandum. This latter principle - an application of the doctrine of constructive notice - meant that a trader who entered into a contract with a company which was *ultra vires* the company's memorandum could not seek to uphold the contract by pleading that he was unaware of the company's incapacity.

[12.10] The injustice which the rule was capable of producing was vividly illustrated in *Re Jon Beauforte (London) Ltd*[5]. In that case, the company was engaged in manufacturing veneer panels, an object which was not authorised by the memorandum. They ordered coke from a fuel merchant for use in the factory where the panels were being manufactured. Since the company's notepaper indicated that they were in the business of manufacturing veneer panels, the fuel merchant was held to be actually aware that the coke would be used for that purpose; and although he was wholly unaware that the company was not entitled to carry on that business, he was assumed to be so aware under the doctrine of constructive notice. In the event, he was unable to recover the price of the coke.

[12.11] The doctrine was modified in Ireland by s 8(1) of the Principal Act which provides that:

> Any act or thing done by a company which if the company had been empowered to do the same would have been lawfully and effectively done, shall, notwithstanding that the company had no power to do such act or thing, be effective in favour of any person relying on such act or thing who is not shown to have been actually aware, at the time when he so relied thereon, that such act or thing was not within the powers of the company, but any director or officer of the company who was responsible for the doing by the company of such act or thing shall be liable to the company for any loss or damage suffered by the company in consequence thereof.

[12.12] Accordingly, an outsider who entered into a transaction unaware of the contents of the memorandum and articles was now able to enforce the transaction against the company, even though it was *ultra vires*. To that extent,

---

[5]   [1953] Ch 131.

the section implemented the recommendations of Jenkins in this area. Jenkins has also recommended, however, that the transaction should be enforceable even where the memorandum and articles had been read, provided that the person reading them had 'honestly and reasonably failed to appreciate that they had the effect of precluding the company from entering into the transaction'. It appeared that the draftsman of the Principal Act had refrained from following this recommendation and this was also decided in *Northern Bank Finance Corpn v Quinn and Achates Investment Company*[6].

[12.13] In that case, Q borrowed £145,000 from the plaintiff bank. The loan was secured by a guarantee of the defendant company supported by a mortgage of certain property. When Q defaulted on the repayment instalments, the plaintiff bank issued proceedings against Q and the company. The evidence established that the memorandum and articles of the company had been furnished to be read by the solicitor for the plaintiff bank. Keane J held that the transaction was *ultra vires* since it was not authorised by the memorandum and articles and s 3(1) of the Principal Act did not assist the plaintiff bank since their solicitor had read the memorandum and articles, although he failed to appreciate that they precluded the company from entering into the transaction.

[12.14] The First EU Companies Directive required the abolition of the *ultra vires* rule as it affected outsiders. But in an important proviso, it permitted member states to maintain the rule, where the company proved that the outsider knew that the act was beyond the objects of the company 'or could not, in view of the circumstances, have been unaware of it'. Disclosure of the statutes (ie the memorandum and articles) was not to be sufficient for this purpose.

[12.15] The Directive was implemented in Ireland by the European Communities (Companies) Regulations 1973[7], article 6 of which provides that:

(1) In favour of a person dealing with a company in good faith, any transaction entered into by an organ of the company, being its board of directors or any person registered under these regulations as a person authorised to bind the company, shall be deemed to be within the capacity of the company and any limitation of the powers of that board or person whether imposed by the memorandum or articles of association or otherwise may not be relied upon as against any person so dealing with the company.

(2) Any such person shall be presumed to have acted in good faith unless the contrary is proved.

---

6   [1979] ILRM 221.
7   SI 163/1973.

(3) For the purposes of this Regulation, the registration of a person authorised to bind the company shall be effected by delivering to the Registrar of Companies a notice giving the name and designation of the person concerned.

[12.16] The scope of this regulation and its relationship to s 8 of the Principal Act is not clear. It is certainly more limited in its application than s 8, since it is confined to contracts entered into by the board of directors and registered agents and does not apply to unlimited companies. Such contracts are enforceable by outsiders under the terms of article 6 even though *ultra vires*, provided the outsiders entered into them in 'good faith'. Where the person is not aware of the lack of capacity of the company - as in the case where he has not read the memorandum and articles - it seems clear that he should be treated as having acted in good faith. Insofar as the directive can be used as a guide to the construction of the Regulations, its terms would appear to confirm this, stating as it does that disclosure of the statutes is not to be treated as putting the outsider on notice of the company's lack of capacity. To that extent, the Article goes no further than s 8 of the Principal Act. It is thought, however, that it would also protect the outsider who read the memorandum and articles but - to use again the language of Jenkins - 'honestly and reasonably failed to appreciate that they had the effect of precluding the company from entering into the transaction'[8].

[12.17] We have seen that the powers of a company cannot be used for purposes which are *ultra vires*. We shall see at a later stage that the directors must use their powers in good faith for the benefit of the company as a whole[9]. If, for example, the company borrows money for an object not stated in the memorandum, the act of borrowing, while within the capacity of the company, is nonetheless unlawful. Similarly, if the directors enter into a contract which is authorised by the memorandum but is solely for their own financial advantage, their action is unlawful. In either of these cases, the transaction, although not *ultra vires*, may be set aside as an improper use of the company's powers.

[12.18] Where, however, an outsider is not aware of the fact that the transaction is an improper exercise of the company's powers and there are no circumstances which should have caused him to inquire whether it was improper, it will be binding on the company. The English decisions in *Re David Payne*[10] and *Rolled Steel Products (Holdings) Ltd v British Steel Corpn & Co Ltd*[11] make it clear that an outsider will be able to enforce such a contract, unless he has actual or

---

[8] The article was not relied on in *Northern Bank Finance Corpn Ltd v Quinn and Achates Investment Company*, presumably because the company was not a limited company.

[9] See para **[27.29]** below.

[10] [1904] 2 Ch 608.

[11] (1984) BCLC 464.

constrictive notice of its unlawful nature. That principle was applied by Blayney J in *Parkes & Son Ltd v Hong Kong and Shanghai Banking Corpn*[12].

[12.19] Such transactions, it should be emphasised, are within the powers of the company. They must be distinguished from transactions affected by s 8 of the Principal Act. The latter are unenforceable by the outsider only when he has actual notice of their *ultra vires* character, ie when he has read the memorandum and articles. Even though he has constructive notice of the memorandum and articles, in the sense that he is deemed to be aware of their existence and could ascertain their contents if he wished, he will not be precluded by such constructive notice from enforcing the contract. As we have seen, it would seem that the same considerations apply to a transaction within the scope of Article 6 of the 1973 Regulations.

[12.20] It would seem logical that an *ultra vires* contract, being a legal nullity, should be incapable of enforcement by the company. This was so held at first instance in *Bell Houses Ltd v City Wall Properties Ltd*[13]: the decision was reversed in the Court of Appeal, but on the ground that the contract was not ultra vires. While doubts have been expressed as to the correctness of this view[14], it would seem a logical corollary to the general ultra vires rule which remains the law notwithstanding its statutory modification in favour of outsiders seeking to enforce such contracts.

Liability of company in respect of unauthorised or irregular transactions

[12.21] A contract may be fully within the capacity of a company and hence not affected by the *ultra vires* rule. But the outsider may still be unable to enforce the contract against the company because the person who entered into it on behalf of the company was not authorised to do so. Again a contract may be within the capacity of the company and yet be unenforceable because some condition as to its validity has not been complied with. Thus it may be fully within the powers of the company to borrow money but only with the sanction of a resolution of the members. If such a resolution is not passed, the contract may be unenforceable.

[12.22] It must be emphasised that these two categories of contract are not instances of contracts which are *ultra vires*: they are within the capacity of the company but are either unauthorised, or irregular because of non-compliance

---

[12] [1994] ILRM 341. See also *Re MJ Cummins Ltd, Barton v Bank of Ireland* [1939] IR 60.

[13] [1966] 1 QB 207; [1966] 2 QB 656.

[14] See Gower, *Modern Company Law* (4th edn), p 204.

with some legal requirement whether contained in the memorandum and articles or elsewhere.

[12.23] In the case of each of these categories, however, the contract may still be enforceable. In the case of the unauthorised contract, it may be enforceable because the person who entered into it was acting under an apparent or ostensible authority as an agent of the company. In the case of an irregular contract, it may be enforceable because the outsider did not know of the irregularity and cannot be presumed to have been aware of it. He may be actually aware, to take the example already given, that the memorandum and articles require the sanction of a resolution to borrowing, because he has read these documents, but he is not presumed to be aware whether the resolution has actually been passed or not. In the case of such matters of 'indoor management', as they are called, the rule in the leading case of *Royal British Bank Ltd v Turquand*[15] applies and the outsider is not affected by an irregularity of which he has no notice.

[12.24] Although these two categories of contract are different, they may on occasions overlap. Thus the articles of association may require certain formalities to be complied with when the company appoints a managing director. The company may permit someone to act as managing director without complying with those formalities. If he then enters into a contract of a type normally within the authority of a managing director, it will be binding on the company, although never authorised by them, in favour of an outsider who was unaware of the irregularity. It will be so binding for two reasons: first, because it was within the person's ostensible authority and secondly because under the rule in *Turquand*'s case the outsider is not affected by a non-compliance with the articles of which he had no knowledge.

Each of the categories will now be considered in turn.

Unauthorised contracts: the doctrine of ostensible or apparent authority

[12.25] There is a general principle of law which may be stated as follows. Where one person (known as an agent) enters into a transaction purportedly on behalf of another (known as a principal) the transaction will be binding on the principal only if the agent acts either within the scope of an authority conferred on him prior to the transaction or subsequently by ratification or within the scope of an ostensible or apparent authority not actually conferred on him[16].

[12.26] As applied to companies, cases of actual authority present no difficulty. If a person is expressly authorised by one of the 'organs' of the company - the

---

[15] (1856) 6 E & B 327.
[16] *Bowstead on Agency* (15th edn) 4,29.

board of directors or the members in general meeting - to enter into a contract which is within the powers of the company, it will be binding on the company. Similarly, if a person duly appointed to a particular office in the company enters into a contract which is normally within the scope of the relevant officer's authority, it will also be binding on the company.

[12.27] The majority of trading companies employs a managing director whose function is to carry on the business of the company in the usual way and do all acts necessary for that purpose. Such acts normally include signing cheques, borrowing money, giving security for the company's indebtedness, receiving the payment of debts on behalf of the company and giving guarantees. A managing director, accordingly, has actual authority to bind the company in the case of such transactions[17]. But his authority is generally limited to commercial transactions: he would not normally be entitled, for example, to approve a transfer of shares or to sell the property of the company. Again, it must be emphasised that there is nothing to prevent the company from expressly authorising the managing director to enter into such a transaction, in which event it will be binding on the company. In the case of ordinary commercial transactions, however, express authorisation is not required: the managing director has authority by virtue of his appointment to enter into such transactions and this is an example of actual authority[18]. His authority may, of course, be limited by the terms of his contract with the company or the articles, but unless the outsider is actually aware of the limitation, he will not be affected by it. In this case, the authority is ostensible rather than actual.

[12.28] The position of the chairman of a company may be contrasted with that of the managing director. The former will not usually be regarded as having authority to enter into everyday commercial contracts in the same manner as the managing director: his functions are limited, as his title suggests, to presiding at meetings of the board of directors and the members.

[12.29] In most cases, of course, an outsider dealing with the company will not know whether the agent was in fact actually authorised to carry out the transaction in question or whether he was actually appointed to the office in question. He may still be protected in such cases, however, even if it should transpire that the agent was not so authorised or was not actually appointed to the particular office. This will arise when the agent is acting under an ostensible or apparent authority.

---

[17] *Hely-Hutchinson v Brayhead Ltd* [1968] 1 QB 549; *Thomas Williamson Ltd v Bailieborough Co-operative Agricultural Society Ltd* (unreported, 31 July 1986) (Costello J).
[18] *Hely-Hutchinson v Brayhead Ltd* [1968] 1 QB 549.

[12.30] In the leading modern case on the topic, *Freeman and Lockyer v Buckhurst Park Properties (Mangal) Ltd*[19] Diplock LJ laid down four conditions which must be satisfied before the doctrine can be successfully invoked.

(1)   There must be a representation made to the outsider that the agent had authority to enter on behalf of the company into a contract of the kind sought to be enforced. Such a representation can be either positive or tacit. If the company have acquiesced in the agent's entering into such contracts on previous occasions, they may be regarded as having tacitly represented that he had authority to do so.

(2)   Such a representation must be made by a person or persons who themselves had actual authority to manage the business of the company either generally or in respect of the matters to which the contract relates.

(3)   The outsider must have been induced by the representation to enter into the contract, ie he must have actually relied on it.

(4)   The memorandum or articles of association must not deprive the company of the capacity to enter into the kind of contract sought to be enforced or to delegate the authority to enter into a contract of that kind to the agent.

In that case, the plaintiffs were a firm of architects who sued the defendant company for fees due to them in respect of plans prepared by them at the request of one of the directors. The evidence established that, although the director in question had never been formally appointed managing director of the company, he had acted for some time as if he were managing director without objection from the only other director. It was held that the company was bound by the contract entered into by him, since they tacitly represented that he was entitled to act as managing director and such a contract was within the normal scope of the authority of such an agent. There was no question of the company being unable to delegate that authority, since the appointment of a managing director was expressly authorised by the articles. These principles were expressly approved by the Supreme Court in *Kett v Shanon & English*[20].

[12.31] The doctrine of ostensible authority was also applied by Hamilton J in *Kilgobbin Mink and Stud Farms Ltd v National Credit Co Ltd*[21]. In that case, the plaintiff company was the lessee of premises in Suffolk Street, Dublin. When the rent fell into arrears, they came to an arrangement with the lessors, the

[19]   [1964] 2 QB 480.

[20]   [1987] ILRM 364 at 366 *per* Henchy J. See also *EES-Food ES v Crown Shipping (Ireland) Ltd* [1991] ILRM 97.

[21]   [1980] IR 175.

defendant company, under which they agreed to surrender the premises in consideration of being forgiven the arrears and being paid a sum of £8,500. The plaintiff company passed a resolution authorising the chairman, BL, to surrender the premises. BL (who owned all except one of the shares in the plaintiff company) wrote to the lessors requesting them to pay the sum of £8,500 by direct debit into the bank account of another company of which he was the controlling shareholder, which they did. The plaintiff company having got into financial difficulties, a receiver was appointed and he instituted proceedings in their name claiming the sum of £8,500 from the lessors. Hamilton J dismissed the claim, holding that BL in requesting the payment to be made into the bank account of another company (which was trading in the same premises) was acting with the ostensible authority of the plaintiff company and that the lessors were entitled to rely on that authority.

[12.32] It is thought that the decision is not free from difficulty. This was not a case of actual authority: the resolution did no more than authorise BL to surrender the premises and did not entitle him to divert the £8,500 to another company. The transaction was not within the normal scope of a chairman's authority. There are moreover clearly difficulties in treating it as a case of ostensible authority. There was no express representation that BL was entitled to write the letter in question and there had been no tacit acceptance by the company of his acting in a similar manner in the past and hence no 'holding out' of BL as having authority. The transaction was obviously a somewhat unusual one and the facts were wholly unlike those in *Freeman and Lockyer*'s case. It is, of course, the case that in strict logic the position in law should have been the same if no receiver had been appointed and, as Hamilton J pointed out, it is inconceivable that the plaintiff company could have recovered the £8,500 if the receiver had not been appointed. But if the plaintiff company had had the temerity to sue for the £8,500 at the instance of BL rather than the receiver, the court might have been able to dismiss the claim on the basis that the recovery of the money by BL, when it had already been paid, would be a fraudulent misuse of corporate personality and hence within one of the established exceptions to the rule in *Salomon*'s case[22].

[12.33] It is respectfully submitted that *Kilgobbin Mink and Stud Farms Ltd v National Credit Company Ltd* is not a sufficient authority for extending the doctrine of ostensible authority as laid down in earlier decisions and may properly be regarded as capable of distinction having regard to the unusual nature of the facts.

---

[22] See para **[11.27]** above.

The rule in Royal British Bank v Turquand

[12.34] The rule in its original form may be stated as follows. While persons dealing with a company are assumed to have read the public documents of the company (ie the memorandum and articles) and to have ascertained that the proposed transaction is not inconsistent therewith, they are not required to do more: they need not inquire into the regularity of the internal proceedings - the indoor management - of the company and may assume that all is being done regularly.

[12.35] A characteristic example of the rule in operation relates to meetings of the board of directors of a company. The articles may stipulate that certain acts may only be done with the authority of the board. A person dealing with the company may be aware of the provision because the articles are sent to him or someone acting on his behalf such as a solicitor. He may also be aware that the articles contain requirements as to a quorum for such meetings. But he may not know - and cannot be presumed to know - whether a quorum was present when the particular act was authorised or indeed whether the board ever authorised the act at all.

[12.36] Since the abolition of the doctrine of constructive notice in relation to ultra vires by s 8 of the Principal Act, the rule in *Turquand*'s case is not of such significance as before. An outsider who has not actually read the memorandum and articles need not rely on the rule: he is protected by s 8. But where the company establish that the outsider was aware of the relevant provisions, the rule can still be of importance. In *Ulster Investment Bank Ltd v Euro Estates Ltd*[23], for example, the liquidator of the first defendant company challenged the validity of a mortgage executed by the company in favour of the plaintiff bank on the ground *inter alia* that a quorum was not present at a meeting of the directors which authorised the affixing of the seal to the deed. The memorandum and articles had been furnished to the bank and s 8 was not relied on; but Carroll J rejected the liquidator's claim, holding that the rule in *Turquand*'s case applied.

[12.37] The exceptions to the rule in *Turquand*'s case should be noted. Clearly it can have no application where the outsider is shown to have been aware of the irregularity. Equally it does not apply where the circumstances were such as to put the outsider on enquiry as to whether the transaction was irregular. Thus in *Underwood v Bank of Liverpool*[24], it was held that the fact that a director was lodging company cheques to his own personal account was sufficiently unusual to have put the outsider on enquiry; and accordingly that he was not entitled to rely on his lack of knowledge as bringing him within the rule.

---

[23] [1982] ILRM 57. See also *Allied Irish Banks Ltd v Ardmore Studios International (1972) Ltd* (unreported, 30 May 1973), HC (Finlay J).
[24] [1924] 1 KB 775.

[12.38] The rule applies only to outsiders. Consequently, a director of the company who enters into a particular transaction in his capacity as a director will not be able to make the case that he was unaware of the internal management of the company which rendered the transaction irregular. But this is only so where he enters into the transaction as a director: if he contracts as an outsider, the fact that he happens to be a director of the company with whom he is contracting is not necessarily a ground for attributing to him knowledge of the 'indoor management' of that company which he does not actually possess[25].

[12.39] It should, however, be born in mind that even directors who contract as outsiders are not in the same position as complete outsiders: they have, for example, means of knowledge denied to the latter. such as access to the minutes and accounts of the company. In an appropriate case, this may be a relevant factor in determining whether knowledge of an irregularity should he attributed to them.

[12.40] It is usually said that the rule does not apply where a document is forged so as to purport to be the company's document. This view has, however, been strongly challenged by one leading English commentator[26]. It is based upon a dictum by Lord Loreburn LC in *Ruben v Great Fingall Consolidated*[27]. In that case, the forged document - a share certificate - was both forged and issued by the company secretary in return for an advance of money. Quite clearly, such a transaction was not merely unauthorised: it was also incapable of attracting the protection either of the rule in *Turquand's* case or of the doctrine of ostensible authority. Even if the document had been genuine, it would still have been a patently irregular transaction, since a secretary would not normally be empowered to enter into such a transaction; and the case could have been decided on that basis without regard to the forgery. It is thought that even in the case of a forged document, the rule should still apply where

(a)   the transaction was within the ostensible authority of the company's agent and was not *patently* irregular,

(b)   the outsider was unaware of the forgery, and

(c) ·   there were no circumstances to excite suspicion.

[12.41] Finally, it should be borne in mind that the rule is for the protection of outsiders and not of the company. The outsider who enters into a transaction which he subsequently discovers to be invalid because of some defect in indoor management is entitled to rely on the invalidity if sued on foot of the transaction, unless he can be shown to have waived the invalidity.

---

[25] *Hely-Hutchinson v Brayhead Ltd* [1968] 1 QB 549.

[26] Gower, *Modern Company Law* (6th edn), p 228. See *Uxbridge Building Society v Pickard* [1939] 2 KB 248.

[27] [1906] AC 439 at 443.

Chapter 13

Tort and Crime

Capacity to sue in tort and liability for torts

[13.01] A tort is a wrongful act, other than a breach of contract, in respect of which the remedy in law is an action for unliquidated damages[1]. Although historically the specific tort or wrong of negligence was of limited importance only, it has in modern times become by far the most common of torts. A wide range of other torts, however, still comes before the courts, such as defamation, assault, trespass, passing off of goods and false imprisonment.

[13.02] A company is entitled to sue in respect of torts committed against it. Clearly, however, there are some torts which, of their nature, cannot be committed against a company, such as assault and false imprisonment. It has been held, however, that a trading company can sue for defamation where its business reputation - as distinct from the individual reputation of a shareholder, director or employee - has been damaged[2].

[13.03] This has been widely criticised on the ground that defamation of character is a purely personal tort and that there is no ground for extending it to corporate bodies. However, the Law Reform Commission in their report on the *Civil Law of Defamation* (1991) recommended that there should be no change in the law.

[13.04] While the company is entitled to recover damages for negligence, it does not follow that the shareholders are also entitled to recover in respect of loss sustained by them as a result of the allegedly negligent act or omission. That will depend on whether the defendant owed a distinct duty of care to the shareholders as well as to the company. Thus, in *McSweeney v Burke*[3], where a consultant was sued by shareholders in a company in respect of financial advice given by him to the company on which they relied to their detriment, Carroll J, while holding on the facts that there had been no negligence on the consultant's part, was also of the view that he owed no duty of care to the shareholders. That approach, which is a logical consequence of the rule in *Salomon v Salomon & Co Ltd*[4] was also

---

[1] *Salmond and Heuston on Tort* (21st edn), p 13.
[2] 28 *Halsbury's Laws of England* (4th edn) para 25.
[3] (Unreported, 24 November 1980).
[4] [1897] AC 22; see Ch 11 above.

taken by the Court of Appeal in England in *Verderame v Commercial Union Assurance Company plc*[5].

[13.05] A company may also be sued in respect of torts committed by it. As we have seen, a company, being an artificial entity, can only act through its organs and agents and accordingly is liable in tort only where the tort in question is committed by one of its organs or agents.

[13.06] It follows that if one of the organs of the company, such as the board of directors or the members in general meeting, authorise the commission of a tort, the company will be liable. Similarly, if the company expressly authorises an agent to commit a tort on its behalf, the company will be liable.

[13.07] It is submitted that the company will be so liable even where the tort is committed in the course of pursuing an object which is *ultra vires* the company[6]. But, while agents of the company have on occasions an implied authority to commit acts on behalf of the company without being expressly authorised to do so, it is submitted that they can never enjoy an implied authority to commit a tort in pursuance of an *ultra vires* object. Thus an employee of the company has implied authority to do any act which is necessary for the performance of the work he is employed to do; and this implied authority may render the company liable for a tort, such as a negligent act committed in the course of his work. But this does not extend to such an act where it is *ultra vires* the company[7].

Criminal liability

[13.08] A company is capable in law of committing a crime and of suffering the punishment prescribed by law for the crime in question. To this general rule, however, there are certain exceptions which again flow from the fact that the company is an artificial legal entity different in its nature from a human being.

[13.09] Certain crimes, ie bigamy and perjury, can only be committed by the person actually charged with them: they cannot be committed by someone else acting on the accused's behalf. Accordingly, a company is incapable of committing such crimes. Moreover, there are certain punishments which can be

---

[5] (1992) BCLC 793.

[6] *Campbell v Paddington Corpn* [1911] 1 KB 869. It has been suggested that the case is not an entirely satisfactory authority for the statement in the text, since the act in question - the erection of stands in the street by the defendant local authority - may have been within their powers. (See A I Goodhart, 'Corporate Liability in Tort and the Doctrine of Ultra Vires', *Essays in Jurisprudence and the Common Law* (1931), and an essay under the same title by Dafydd Jenkins in Ir Jur (New Series) Vol 5, p 11.) The view of the law in the text is, however, also supported by *National Telephone Co Ltd v Constables of St Peters Port* [1900] AC 317 and *Batson v School Board for London* (1903) 67 JP 457.

[7] *Poulson v London & SW Rly* (1867) LR 2 QB 534.

inflicted only on human beings, ie forms of custody. (The celebrated question asked by counsel in the reign of James II, 'can you hang its common seal?'[8] retains its validity in the era of the limited company.) A company can, of course, suffer other punishments, such as a fine and sequestration of its assets.

[13.10] In general, a person cannot be found guilty of a criminal offence unless he intended - or can be presumed to have intended - to commit that offence. In the language of the criminal law, there must not only be *actus reus,* ie the actual commission of the offence, there must also be *mens rea,* ie an intention to commit the offence.

[13.11] In the case of a company, proof of the *mens rea* presents no difficulty where an organ of the company - such as the board of directors or the company in general meeting - has authorised the commission of the offence either by itself or an agent. But express authority of that nature is rare enough and problems can arise in determining whether a particular officer or employee plays a sufficiently crucial role in the company's affairs to justify the court in treating his guilty mind as that of the company itself. In the frequently quoted words of Lord Haldane LC in *Lennard's Carrying Co v Asiatic Petroleum Co Ltd*[9]:

> 'My lords, a corporation is an abstraction. It has no mind of its own any more than it has a body of its own; its active and directing will must consequently be sought in the person of somebody who for some purposes may be called an agent, but who is really the directing mind and will of the corporation, the very ego and centre of the personality of the corporation ...'[10]

So, in the case of a 'one man company', there is no difficulty in imputing the criminal intent of the controlling shareholder to the company and courts have not seen the 'corporate veil' doctrine as an obstacle to so doing. In larger companies, of course, it may not be so easy to treat the company as criminally responsible for the actions of employees at a lower level of the hierarchy. Thus, in England recently a prosecution of a ferry company for manslaughter arising out of the *Herald of Free Enterprise* disaster off Zeebrugge proved abortive. But it should not be assumed that we have seen the end of attempts to bring home charges of 'corporate manslaughter', particularly in cases where a jury might be entitled to conclude that the board had culpably failed to keep itself informed of possible serious lapses in safety standards. There is certainly a strong and understandable public concern that an individual employee should be found

---

8   In *R v City of London* 8 State Trials 1087 at 1138.
9   [1915] AC 705.
10   [1915] AC 705 at 713. This passage was cited with approval by McCarthy J speaking for the Supreme Court, in *Taylor v Smyth* [1991] 1 IR 142. See also *The State (John Hennessy and Chariot Inns Ltd) v Commons* [1978] IR 238 and *McMahon v Murtagh Properties Ltd* [1982] ILRM 342.

guilty of manslaughter, while the management which allowed lapses in safety standards goes free[11].

[13.12] Sometimes the effect of a particular statute may be to impose criminal liability on the company where the offence is committed by one of its employees and in such cases it will be unnecessary to prove *mens rea* against the company. Whether the statute imposes such a liability will depend on the language used. In the absence of express language to that effect, the company will be held criminally liable only where there is active participation in the commission of the crime by those who are managing its affairs: the court, in other words, will apply the criteria laid down by Lord Haldane LC in the speech already cited[12].

[13.13] While there is no authority on the point, it seems clear in principle that the fact that a criminal act is *ultra vires* the company or committed in the course of pursuing an *ultra vires* object is no defence to a criminal charge.

---

[11] In this connection, a recent English decision is worth noting. In *Jones v DPP* a divisional court ordered the DPP to reconsider a decision that a prosecution for manslaughter would not be brought against an allegedly negligent employer: see (2000) *The Guardian*, 24 March.

[12] *Tesco Supermarkets v Nattrass Ltd* [1972] AC 153.

Part IV
The Capital of the Company

Chapter 14

Types of Capital

Meaning of capital

[14.01] The word capital suggests to the layman that part of an enterprise, be it commercial, social or even domestic, which is permanent in its nature and not used up in the day-to-day operations. In this sense, when one thinks of the capital of a business, one usually has in mind the factory or office premises, the machinery and furniture, its investments etc. By contrast, the actual cash receipts from its trading operations one thinks of as its 'income' to be applied in paying day-to-day debts, with any surplus going to the owners as representing the profits. Similarly, a family may regard their house and furniture, together with any savings and investments they may have, as their 'capital'.

[14.02] This is not, however, what the term 'capital' necessarily means to lawyers and accountants. For them it may have a different significance which it is important to appreciate.

[14.03] It is normal in the case of a well run business of any size to prepare at regular intervals a statement of all the property of the business- its assets -and what it owes - its *liabilities*. This document - the balance sheet - is one with which every student of company law should be familiar. In its traditional form, it shows on the right hand side of the page, the assets, ie the buildings, plant, machinery, stock in trade, debts owing to the business, cash in the bank, etc. On the left hand side are shown the liabilities. Where the assets are not cash, such non-cash assets in modern accountancy are carried at certain valuations, the basis of the valuations being shown either on the face of the balance sheet or indicated by accounting policies. The total of the liabilities will appear on the left in cash and the balance, where they are less than the assets, is the value in money terms of the business to its owners as it appears from the balance sheet. As we shall see, when we come to deal with company accounts in more detail, because of the valuation methods employed it is not necessarily an accurate guide to that value at the time when the balance sheet is available for scrutiny. This balance in the case of a company is referred to by accountants as 'the shareholders' equity'.

[14.04] The description just given of the essential features of a balance sheet is deliberately simplified. A moment's consideration will show that even the simplest balance sheet will have further refinements. Thus some assets, of their nature, will not be disposed of in the day-to-day operations. These assets, which include buildings, machinery, etc, are called fixed assets to distinguish them from those assets which are regularly disposed of, such as the stock in trade. The latter are called current assets or working capital.

[14.05] We now come to the meaning of the word 'capital' in company law. Here again it has a precise significance and one that is different from the meanings we have been discussing. Generally speaking, it refers to the share capital of the company.

[14.06] We have seen that in the case of a company limited by shares the company is owned by its members - the shareholders - in shares having a specified money value. The shareholders either pay for their shares in money or by means of some other consideration or agree to pay for them when called upon to do so. The individual shares will generally have the same cash value - £1, £5, £10 or as the case may be - and a shareholder will be allotted one or more such shares. The value of the units is set, in the case of a public company, at a level which will create the most attractive market for the shares by making them more easily traded on the stock exchange. The total value of the shares thus issued and allotted is usually called the issued share capital of the company and it is this that is normally meant when the 'capital' of the company is referred to. It must be distinguished from the authorised or nominal share capital, ie the amount of the capital as stated in the memorandum which represents the limit of the capital which the company is authorised to issue.

[14.07] We can now return to our balance sheet: and we find that, in the case of a company having a share capital, an item appears on the liabilities side which is unique to such enterprises. This is the issued share capital of the company. It is not in the strict sense a liability of the company: the members will have no legal grievance if it is all lost in the course of the company's operations. But, as the fund contributed by the members, it appears logically along with the liabilities in order, again, to give an indication of the worth of the company to the people who own it, ie the members. If the assets on the right hand side exceed the total liabilities including the share capital, the surplus represents that value as it appears from the balance sheet. It might seem logical that where the balance sheet shows such a surplus the issued share capital should simply be increased to bring the two sides into balance, but this is not the way a company's accounts are treated. Instead, the balancing figure is separately shown, usually with the description reserves.

[14.08] We have seen that the issued share capital must never exceed the nominal share capital. Both figures should always appear in the balance sheet of a company limited by shares; and with this in mind, we can now construct a typical balance sheet of a company limited by shares.

[14.09] We will use the modern vertical layout rather than the old fashioned right/left layout.

Leinster Industrial Processes Ltd
Balance Sheet As At 31st December 1999

	Notes	1999	1998
		£	£
FIXED ASSETS	1	170,000	160,000
CURRENT ASSETS			
Stocks		20,000	18,000
Debtors		12,000	15,000
Cash		8,000	5,000
	Total	40,000	38,000
CURRENT LIABILITIES			
Creditors		15,000	17,000
Overdraft (secured)	2	6,000	7,000
	Total	21,000	24,000
NET CURRENT ASSETS		19,000	14,000
		189,000	174,000
Financed by:			
Share Capital	3	100,000	100,000
Reserves		65,000	44,000
Shareholders' Funds		165,000	144,000
Loans (secured)		24,000	30,000
		189,000	174,000

Notes:
1. A separate note will be attached showing fixed assets and depreciation analysed over major categories of assets.
2. That part of the loans payable within twelve months of the balance sheet will be shown as a current liability. The balance will be included as a long term loan.
3. A separate note will be given showing the authorised, issued and paid up position for each class of capital[1]

[14.10] One further feature of the balance sheet should be noted. As we have seen, the issued share capital of the company consists of the shares which have been allotted to the shareholders and for which they have paid or agreed to pay. The issued share capital must accordingly be divided in the balance sheet between the amount which has actually been paid - the paid up capital - and the amount which shareholders have agreed to pay if called upon to do so - the uncalled capital. Accountants treat the paid up share capital as part of 'the

---

[1] This is a simplified version of what is now required under the Companies Act 1986: see Ch 32 below.

shareholders' equity' and it appears in the balance sheet proper. The amount unpaid appears by way of a note, because accountants treat it as more in the nature of a contingent asset.

[14.11] Clearly the actual value of the shares will fluctuate with the fortunes of the company; and one of the major factors in determining their value will be the net asset value of the company. Whatever their actual value may be, however, the nominal value of the shares - £1, £5, £10 - will remain the same. In the case of a public limited company, the shares may rise and fall in value on the stock exchange from day to day, but the nominal value is always the same.

[14.12] It is obviously somewhat anomalous that the nominal value of the shares should bear no relationship to their actual value in the market and this has led to calls from time to time for the introduction of 'no par value' shares. Such shares have been permitted in some states in the USA since 1912 and in Canada since 1918. Their introduction was recommended by Cox and there have been frequent suggestions to the same effect in England. As yet, however, no attempt has been made in either jurisdiction to give statutory effect to these proposals.

Reserve capital

[14.13] A company may resolve by special resolution that a specified portion of its uncalled capital is not to be capable of being called up, except in the event, and for the purposes of, its being wound up. The amount in question is called the reserve capital of the company. Where this power is availed of, the company is in a position not unlike that of a company limited by guarantee and having a share capital. The members may each have to contribute in the event of a winding up; but it differs from the case of a company limited by guarantee, since in the latter case each member, or class of members, normally undertakes to pay the same amount in the event of a winding up. In the case of a company with a share capital, the amount which each member has to pay in respect of the reserve capital will vary depending on the number of shares which he owns.

Importance of capital

[14.14] The courts have from the earliest days of modern company law attached great importance to the capital of the company; and they have been particularly concerned to see that it is not reduced save with proper safeguards and subject to specified conditions. The limitations on a company's power to reduce its capital will be considered in detail in the next two chapters, but it is sufficient to note at this point that the courts' concern springs from an anxiety to see that creditors of the company are not prejudiced by an unwarranted reduction of the capital on the faith of which they may have extended credit to the company.

[14.15] It must be said, however, that in many instances the protection supposedly afforded to creditors by the maintenance of this legal principle is largely illusory. As we have seen, the huge preponderance of companies formed under the Acts are private companies. The amount of the paid up capital of such a company can be as small as the promoters wish. (In this context, its position is markedly different from that of a public limited company.) Moreover, even where the paid up capital is substantial, it may still be no real guide to the financial strength of the company. That can only be ascertained from the balance sheet and even that is not a wholly reliable guide.

[14.16] Because of the importance of the principle referred to in the preceding paragraph, the law requires certain items which are not strictly part of the capital of the company to be dealt with as though they were.

Share premium account

[14.17] The first of these items arises when the company issues shares at a premium, ie receives more in cash or kind than the nominal value of the shares. The amount by which the cash or other consideration exceeds the nominal value must be transferred to a separate account known as the share premium account. It would not be regarded as a proper business practice to pay any part of this as a dividend, since it is not really a profit. It may, however, be paid out in the form of bonus shares[2] because no reduction in the capital in real terms is thereby effected[3].

Capital redemption reserve fund

[14.18] The importance attached to ensuring that a company did not reduce its capital to the supposed disadvantage of its creditors meant that, in general, companies were prohibited from returning any part of the capital to the shareholders. Thus, a company could not redeem the shares by returning the amount paid up on them to the shareholders and cancelling the shares. Similarly, a company could not purchase any of its own shares from the shareholders. These restrictions have been progressively dismantled to a significant extent, as will be explained in detail in the next chapter. At this point, it is sufficient to note that a power to issue redeemable shares was first given to Irish companies in 1959, but until the enactment of the 1990 Act, such shares could only take the form of redeemable preference shares, ie shares which gave their holders rights to the payment of a dividend or the return of their capital in priority to other shareholders. This was a method sometimes employed by companies of raising

---

[2] See para **[8.06]** above.
[3] For other circumstances in which the company may apply the share premium account, see para **[9.54]**.

additional funds: the lenders had some guarantee that their investment would yield an income while the company retained the option of paying off its liability at any stage. Now the power to issue redeemable shares is no longer confined to the issue of preference shares.

[14.19] One of the ways in which shares may be redeemed is out of profits, but since it is not regarded as good commercial practice to utilise profits for the reduction of capital, the company is required in that event to form a capital redemption reserve fund, which appears as a liability in the balance sheet. The company may, if it wishes, use this fund to issue bonus shares which are treated as fully paid up. Thus the shareholders get the profits, but the capital of the company remains the same in real terms, since the capital redemption reserve fund is simply replaced by the bonus shares.

Equity share capital

[14.20] The phrase 'equity capital' is sometimes used by accountants to describe the net asset value of a company limited by shares. In company law, however, it has a different meaning: it refers to the total issued share capital of the company, excluding only those shares which do not confer on the holders participating rights or which limit the rights of the holders in relation to dividends or capital.

Loan capital

[14.21] Many companies raise money for their operations in other ways beside the issuing of shares. The money thus borrowed will normally be secured by a debenture or series of debentures or debenture stock. While, generally speaking, any document issued by the company which acknowledges a debt due by it may be called a debenture, in modern usage it invariably refers to such an acknowledgement when supported by a security of some sort. That security may take the form of a fixed charge of one of the company's assets or a floating charge over the assets and undertakings of the company or of both. Debentures are frequently referred to as loan capital; but it will readily be seen that it is not an appropriate description, since a debenture does not confer on its holder the status of a shareholder. Nor has the debenture holder any of the rights of a shareholder in relation to such matters as dividends, the right to attend at meetings and vote, etc.

Chapter 15

The Maintenance of Capital

[15.01] The law has always attached great importance to the maintenance by a company of its issued share capital. It is regarded as a basic protection to creditors since, whether it is paid up in whole or in part, it constitutes a fund to which the creditors may have recourse in the event of the company being unable to pay its debts as they fall due.

[15.02] This protection is, as we have seen, somewhat illusory, since there is nothing to prevent a private company from fixing its share capital at a token figure of £10; and many people deal with limited companies on a day-to-day basis without troubling to enquire what the issued share capital of the company is. Moreover, the requirement that a company should maintain its capital intact is subject to the important qualification that losses of capital suffered in the ordinary course of business are recognised as legitimate.

[15.03] In the case of public limited companies, however, the requirements of the law in this area are more stringent. We have already seen that, under the 1983 Act, such a company cannot commence business until the Registrar has certified that the nominal value of its allotted share capital is not less than the authorised minimum, ie £30,000. In addition it must be paid up in money or money's worth to at least 25% of the nominal value[1]. That Act, which implemented in Ireland the Second EU Directive, also contains provisions, which must now be examined in detail, designed to ensure the maintenance of a company's capital. Some of these are confined in their application to public limited companies: others, including s 40 which imposes on companies the obligation to convene an extraordinary meeting in the event of a serious loss of capital, are of general application.

[15.04] The importance attached by courts to the maintenance intact by a company of its capital in the interests of its creditors was in part responsible for the settled rule that a company could not purchase its own shares. Nor could a company redeem the shares, ie return the money paid up on them to the shareholders and treat the liability represented by the shares as cancelled. As we have seen[2], the only relaxation of the latter prohibition was the power of the company to issue redeemable preference shares. Both of these restrictions have

---

[1] Para **[10.07]** above.
[2] Para **[14.18]** above.

given rise to concern that private companies, whose shares are not marketable, may be starved of funds since investors will be unwilling to lock their capital into companies whose shares cannot be traded. As a result, the restrictions have been progressively dismantled, a process which culminated in Part XI of the 1990 Act. This extends the power to issue redeemable shares to all shares and also enables companies to buy their own shares provided the company has armed itself with the necessary authority. In these areas, the Oireachtas has in some respects adopted similar measures to those contained in the English 1985 Act, but the provisions are by no means identical. They also to some extent reflect the requirements of the Second EU Directive on Company Law.

Redemption of shares

[15.05] A company, public or private, may issue redeemable shares at any time and redeem them in due course, provided that at least one-tenth in nominal value of the issued share capital is non-redeemable[3]. Section 207 of the 1990 Act enables a company to issue such shares where it is authorised by its articles so to do. A company wishing to avail of the power must, accordingly, amend its articles by special resolution. The terms of the issue must provide for payment on redemption. Where the company redeems shares in exercise of these powers, it may then cancel the shares, thus reducing the amount of its issued share capital by the nominal value of the cancelled shares[4]. Alternatively, it may retain the shares as treasury shares in which case the issued share capital remains the same, but the treasury shares carry no voting rights and do not entitle the company to a dividend[5]. They may, however, subsequently be re-issued by the company.

[15.06] Redeemable shares may only be redeemed where they are fully paid up. There is no reason why a shareholder should be released from his liability to pay the balance owing to the shares to the detriment of creditors in a winding up. The shares, moreover, may only be redeemed out of profits which are available for distribution. In this way, while the actual amount of the issued share capital is ultimately reduced when the shares are cancelled, the physical assets corresponding to that liability remain intact. But where the company intends to cancel the shares, it may, instead of redeeming the shares out of profits, do so

---

[3] The corresponding English legislation requires only that some shares remain non-redeemable in order to ensure that the company has at least two members as was then required by law. This was also the position when the Companies Act 1990 was introduced: the change was made at the Report Stage in the Dáil and seems to be based on the mistaken view that there should be a correspondence between this ratio and the ratio between treasury shares and the remaining issued share capital.

[4] Companies Act 1990, s 208.

[5] Companies Act 1990, s 209.

out of the proceeds of a fresh issue made for the purposes of the redemption. In this way, the amount of the issued share capital remains intact.

[15.07] If the company pays a premium on the redemption, ie if it pays the shareholder more than the nominal value, this can in general be paid only out of profits. It should be noted that this is more restrictive than the procedure formerly applicable for the redemption of preference shares, where the premium could be paid out of the share premium account. The latter fund, as we have seen already, is essentially part of the capital of the company[6]. But where the shares were issued at a premium, the company may pay a premium on redemption out of the proceeds of a fresh issue made for the purposes of the redemption. It may only do so, however, up to the aggregate of all the premiums received on the original issue or the amount of the share premium account, whichever is the less. Where it does so, the amount of the share premium account must be reduced accordingly.

[15.08] The company may cancel the redeemed shares under the provisions of s 208. Where it is proposing to redeem the shares out of a fresh issue, the company must cancel the redeemed shares or retain them as 'treasury shares', ie without voting rights or entitlement to dividend. Where the shares are redeemed and cancelled, the company must transfer a specified amount to the fund called the *Capital Redemption Reserve Fund*[7]. The intention is to ensure that the capital structure of the company remains essentially the same. Consequently, the fund is treated in the same way as the paid up capital of the company and can only be reduced in the same manner. If the shares have been redeemed out of profits, an amount equal to the nominal value of the shares must be transferred. If they have been redeemed out of the proceeds of a fresh issue and the proceeds are less than the nominal value of the redeemed shares, the amount of the deficiency must be transferred. Where the redeemed shares are cancelled, the nominal value of the issued share capital is correspondingly reduced, but the amount of the authorised share capital remains the same.

[15.9] Where shares have been redeemed, the company, instead of cancelling them, may retain them as 'treasury shares'. They will then be in effect 'frozen', since the company, which is of course the owner, can neither vote nor pay itself a dividend in respect of the shares. They may, however, be re-issued and, unless the re-issue is being effected by a public company on a recognised stock exchange, the price at which they are to be re-issued is governed by s 209(6) of the 1990 Act. This requires the company to fix a 'price range', ie stipulating a maximum and minimum price before any contract for the re-issue is entered

---

[6]   Para [9.24] above.
[7]   See para [14.18] above.

into[8]. Where the treasury shares are derived in whole or in part from shares purchased by the company, as distinct from having been redeemed, the price range is to be fixed by the company at the time when the contract for the purchase is being entered into.

[15.10] The nominal value of treasury shares so held by the company may not, at any one time, exceed ten per cent of the nominal value of the issued share capital. This corresponds to the proportion of issued shares that must remain redeemable.

[15.11] These provisions are derived ultimately from US law and there is no equivalent in the English legislation. The object would seem to be to enable the company to keep in reserve unissued share capital which can be re-issued if, for example, an employees' share-owning scheme were envisaged. They would seem to be of little practical utility: under the present law, there is nothing to prevent a company from making a new issue, even where its authorised share capital will be exceeded, by passing the necessary special resolutions.

[15.12] The company may at any time convert shares which have been already issued into redeemable shares provided the requirements of the Acts relating to the variation of shareholders' rights are met[9]. A shareholder may also object to the conversion of his shares and, if he does so, the conversion is not to take effect with respect to his shares. The 10% ratio between redeemable and non-redeemable shares must also be preserved[10].

[15.13] The provisions of the Principal Act dealing with redeemable preference shares were repealed by the 1990 Act, but where such shares had already been issued they are now redeemable in accordance with the new provisions. To this there is one qualification: the less stringent requirement of the Principal Act that any premium payable on redemption may be paid out of the share premium account is retained[11].

Acquisition by a company of its own shares

[15.14] The traditional view of the law, laid down by the House of Lords in *Trevor v Whitworth*[12], was that a company could not acquire its own shares. The practice was considered objectionable for two reasons. The rights of creditors

---

[8] It is not clear what is meant by a 'contract for re-issue'. The draftsman seems to have overlooked the fact that the issuing of shares is a unilateral act and to have confused it with the process of allotment.

[9] See para **[17.10]** below.

[10] See para **[15.04]** above.

[11] Companies Act 1990, s 220.

[12] [1887] 12 AC 409.

and of the shareholders themselves could be eroded if a company were allowed to acquire control over its own capital. In addition, the directors could manipulate the price of the company's shares with possibly adverse results for others. With the passage of time, however, the law was seen as unduly restrictive in this area and, in particular, as discouraging investment in private companies. It was substantially modified in England in 1981, reflecting the recognition by the Second EU Directive that such a provision in national law was unobjectionable, provided certain conditions were met. The 1990 Act effected a similar relaxation in Ireland and the relevant provisions are closely modelled on those in the UK. In particular, a distinction is drawn between 'market' and 'off market' purchases. The former - which broadly encompass acquisitions by public companies of their own shares which are listed or traded on the stock exchange - can be effected on foot of a general authority from the members. The latter - which mainly affect acquisitions by private companies of their own shares - can also be effected, but only on foot of a specific contract to purchase the shares in question.

[15.15] In one important respect, the provisions of the 1990 Act differ from the corresponding provisions in England. In both jurisdictions, such acquisitions, like redemptions, can only be funded out of distributable profits or the proceeds of a fresh issue. In the case of private companies, however, payment may be made out of capital in England. This cannot be done in Ireland and, whatever the reason may have been, we have at least been spared further provisions of tortuous complexity.

[15.16] The general prohibition of an acquisition by a company of its own shares, first stated in statutory form by s 72 of the Principal Act and elaborated in s 41 of the 1983 Act remains, as do the express exemptions from the prohibition stated in the latter section, viz:

(1)   where the shares are acquired otherwise than for valuable consideration, eg where the company is acting as an executor or trustee;

(2)   the redemption of shares in pursuance of the articles;

(3)   the purchase of any shares in pursuance of orders of the court made under s 15 of the 1983 Act and ss 10 and 205 of the Principal Act;

(4)   the forfeiture of any shares, or the acceptance of any shares surrendered in lieu, in pursuance of the articles for failure to pay any sum payable in respect of the shares.

To these are now added the wide-ranging exceptions for purchases authorised by the company, divided into 'market' and 'off market' purchases.

[15.17] A 'market' purchase takes place where the shares are purchased on a recognised stock exchange and are subject to a 'marketing arrangement'[13]. The latter phrase means that they are either listed on the exchange or the company has been afforded unconditional facilities for dealing in the shares on the exchange. An 'off market purchase' is one that does not take place on a recognised stock exchange or, if it does, is not subject to a market arrangement[14]. Hence an off market purchase means in effect a purchase by a private company or by a public company whose shares are not listed or which does not have unrestricted access to a recognised stock exchange.

[15.18] A market purchase of its own shares by a company must be authorised by the company in general meeting[15]. But this does not mean that a particular contract must be entered into in respect of each purchase: the company may give a general authority for the entering into of such transactions. In the case of a public limited company - which will almost invariably be the purchaser in market purchases - the authority must specify the maximum number of shares which may be purchased and the maximum and minimum price which may be paid for the shares. The authority must specify a date - not later than 18 months after it has been granted - on which it is to expire[16].

[15.19] An off-market purchase of its own shares by a company must be authorised by a contract entered into in advance of the purchase[17]. The terms of the contract must be authorised by a special resolution but the authority may be varied, revoked or renewed, also by special resolution. The resolution authorising the purchase will be ineffective if a member holding shares affected by the resolution exercises his voting rights in respect of the shares in favour of the resolution and it would not have been carried without his vote. It will also be ineffective unless a copy of the proposed contract, or a written memorandum of its terms, is available both at the registered office of the company (for a period of at least 21 days from the date of the relevant meeting) or at the meeting itself. Any variation of the contract must be approved by special resolution.

[15.20] All the provisions of ss 207(2), 208 and 209 of the 1990 Act applicable to the redemption of shares apply also to an acquisition by a company of its own shares[18]. The shares must be fully paid up and the payment must be out of distributable profits or the proceeds of a fresh issue. They may also be cancelled when purchased and this does not effect a reduction in the nominal value of the

---

[13] Companies Act 1990, s 212(1)(b).
[14] Companies Act 1990, s 212(1)(a).
[15] Companies Act 1990, s 215.
[16] Companies Act 1990, s 216.
[17] Companies Act 1990, s 213.
[18] Companies Act 1990, s 211(2).

issued share capital. If paid for out of the proceeds of a fresh issue, they must be cancelled or retained as treasury shares. The appropriate amounts must be transferred to the capital redemption reserve fund.

[15.21] A company may also purchase its own shares under a 'contingent purchase contract' provided it is authorised so to do by a special resolution[19]. Under such a contract, the company becomes entitled or obliged to buy the shares at some stage in the future, ie the company effectively acquires an option to buy the shares. The price of the option must be provided out of profits available for distribution. So also must payments in consideration of the variation of a contract by a company to purchase its own shares or the release of any of its obligations with respect to the purchase of its own shares[20].

[15.22] A company cannot assign its rights under a contract to purchase its own shares, whether it is an authorised market purchase or a specific off market purchase. It may, however, release its rights under such a contract, but in the case of off market purchases the release must be authorised by a special resolution[21].

[15.23] Copies of contracts for the purchase of its own shares by a company, whether they are market or off market purchases, must be kept at the registered office for at least 10 years after the contract has been fully performed. They must be available for inspection to any member and (in the case of a public limited company) the public generally during business hours, subject to such reasonable restrictions as the company may in general meeting impose, but so that they are available for inspection for at least two hours in each day. The company and every officer in default are guilty of an offence on failure to comply with these provisions and liable on summary conviction to a fine not exceeding £1,000 or imprisonment for a term not exceeding 12 months or both or, on conviction on indictment, to a fine not exceeding £10,000 or imprisonment for a term not exceeding three years or both. The court may also order an inspection of a contract where it is refused[22].

[15.24] A company which has purchased any of its own shares under the relevant provisions of the 1990 Act must also deliver to the Registrar a return in the prescribed form giving certain particulars. In the case of all companies, the return must state the number and nominal value of the shares purchased and the date on which they were delivered to the company. In addition in the case of a public limited company, it must state the aggregate amount paid by the company for the shares and the maximum and minimum price in respect of each class

---

[19] Companies Act 1990, s 214.
[20] Companies Act 1990, s 218.
[21] Companies Act 1990, s 217.
[22] Companies Act 1990, s 222.

purchased. The penalties for non-compliance are the same as for the offence referred to in the preceding paragraph and the offence in this case may be prosecuted summarily by the Registrar[23].

[15.25] In the case of a market purchase where dealing facilities in the shares on a recognised stock exchange are provided, the company purchasing the shares must notify the stock exchange of the purchase and the stock exchange may publish the information in question. The penalties for non-compliance are the same as for the offences referred to in the two preceding paragraphs. There are also provisions requiring the stock exchange authorities to report apparent breaches of this requirement to the Director of Public Prosecutions which are virtually identical to those requiring the same authorities similarly to report apparent cases of insider dealing[24].

Other provisions dealing with redemption and purchase of its shares by a company

[15.26] Section 219 of the 1990 Act protects companies from consequences which might ensue if the company, for any reason, finds itself unable to fulfil a contract for the redemption or purchase of any of its shares. They are not liable in damages for such a failure and the contract may not be enforced against them by an order for specific performance where they can show that they are unable to meet the cost of purchase or redemption out of distributable profits.

[15.27] However, where a company is wound up, such a contract may be enforced against the company. There are two exceptions:

(1)   where the contract provided that the redemption or purchase was to take place at a date later than the commencement of the winding up and

(2)   where the company could not lawfully have made a distribution equal to the cost of redemption or purchase at any time between the date fixed for completion and the commencement of the winding-up.

In any other case, the contract may be enforced against the company in liquidation and the shares will then be treated as cancelled. The cost of the shares cannot be paid, however, until the creditors and the preferential shareholders have been paid what they are owed.

[15.28] Section 228 of the 1990 Act empowers the Minister to make regulations governing the purchase by companies of their own shares and the sale by

---

23   Companies Act 1990, s 226.
24   Companies Act 1990, ss 229 and 230. For the provisions as to insider dealing. see para **[34.21]** below.

companies of shares held by them as treasury shares. These regulations may deal with the class or description of shares which may he purchased or sold, the price, the timing, the method of purchase or sale and the volume of trading in the shares which may be carried out by companies. At the time of writing, no regulations have been made.

[15.29] The 1983 Act also contains in s 42 provisions designed to ensure that the provisions restricting the acquisition by a company of its own shares are not circumvented by means of an acquisition of the company's shares made by a nominee of the company. Where shares in a company affected by s 41 are issued to a nominee of the company, they are to be treated as held by the nominee on his own account and the company are to be regarded as having no beneficial interest in them. The same result follows where they are acquired by the nominee from a third party as partly paid up.

[15.30] The section further provides that if a person who acquired shares or to whom shares were issued as a nominee fails to pay what is due on them within 21 days from being called on to do so, the directors of the company at the time of the issue or acquisition are to be jointly or severally liable to pay that amount. (The same result follows where the shares were issued to him as a subscriber save that in such a case it is the other subscribers who are so liable). If, however, the director or subscriber appears to the court to have acted honestly and reasonably and the court is of the view that, having regard to all the circumstances of the case, he ought fairly to be excused from liability, the court may relieve him either wholly or partly from his liability on such terms as it thinks fit. Where a director or subscriber has reason to apprehend that such a claim will or might be made against him, he may apply to the court for relief and the court has then the same power of granting relief as if the proceedings had been brought.

[15.31] The section does not apply where the company has no beneficial interest in the shares or to shares issued in consequence of an application before 13 October 1983 or transferred in pursuance of an agreement made before that day.

Meeting to consider serious loss of capital

[15.32] 'Paid up capital may be diminished or lost in the course of the company's trading; that is a result which no legislation can prevent ...'. This observation of Lord Watson in *Trevor v Whitworth*[25] reflects the acknowledgement by the law that losses of capital suffered in the ordinary course of business are legitimate. The object of s 40 of the 1983 Act is to ensure that the directors and

---

[25] (1887) 12 App Cas 409 at 423.

shareholders are given an opportunity of at least considering what steps, if any, should be taken in the event of the capital falling below a defined level.

[15.33] The section, which applies to all companies having a share capital, provides that where the net assets of the company are half or less of the amount of the company's called-up share capital[26] the directors must convene an extraordinary general meeting of the company for the purpose of considering whether any, and if so what, measures should be taken to deal with the situation. The meeting must be convened not later than 28 days from the earliest day on which the fact of the loss becomes known to any director and must be for a date not later than 56 days from that day.

[15.34] The 1983 Act provides for stringent penalties where there is a failure to convene a meeting in accordance with s 40[27]. Each of the directors who knowingly and wilfully authorises or permits that failure to continue, is guilty of an offence. He is liable on indictment to a fine not exceeding £2,500 or, at the discretion of the court, to imprisonment for a term not exceeding two years or to both the fine and the imprisonment. The District Court is given jurisdiction to try these offences summarily, where the justice is of opinion that the facts proved or alleged against the director constitute a minor offence fit to be tried summarily, the Director of Public Prosecutions consents and the defendant, having had his right to be tried by jury explained to him, does not object. In that event, the defendant is liable on conviction to a fine not exceeding £500 or, at the discretion of the court, to a term of imprisonment not exceeding six months or to both.

[15.35] The section is intended to provide some sort of safeguard for shareholders in a company in the event of a serious worsening in the net asset position of the company. It may be of some limited benefit to creditors, since directing the minds of the shareholders to the company's real financial position may also alert them to the dangers of becoming involved in fraudulent trading. There is, however, no obligation on the shareholders to take any steps to bring the company's net assets into line with the paid up capital. It would appear, moreover, that the section, although not expressly so confined, will in practice be of most relevance to public limited companies. There is still nothing to prevent private companies from having token share capitals only and accordingly being outside the ambit of the section.

[15.36] What was thought to be the undesirable practice of a company trafficking in its own shares could be carried on indirectly, if a subsidiary were permitted to own shares in its parent company. Hence, s 32 of the Principal Act

---

[26] For the meaning of these expressions, see paras **[14.02]**, **[14.03]**, **[14.04]** and **[14.07]** above.
[27] Companies (Amendment) Act 1983, s 57(2).

provides that, with certain limited exceptions, a body corporate cannot be a member of a company which is its holding company. In line with the general policy of the 1990 Act, this prohibition was substantially lifted by s 224. A company may now acquire shares in its holding company, provided the payment is made out of its distributable profits and its distributable profits are subsequently restricted by the amount of the purchase price. The subsidiary is also prohibited from exercising the voting rights attached to the shares. The purchase must be authorised in advance by both the subsidiary and the holding company and the provisions already discussed in relation to the acquisition by a company of its own shares (including the distinction between market and off market purchases) are in general applicable[28].

Financing by a company of an acquisition of its shares

[15.37] The belief that the financing by a company of a purchase of its own shares was open to the same objections as the direct purchase of its shares by the company prompted the enactment of s 60 of the Principal Act. This prohibits the giving of financial assistance by a company for the purchase of its shares. This prohibition remains in force, despite the wide ranging exemptions from the restriction on a company directly purchasing its own shares effected by the 1990 Act. In the case of public limited companies, this is in conformity with the requirements of Article 23 of the Second EU Directive. In the case of private companies, however, it is subject to a most important proviso: such a transaction is valid if it has been authorised by a special resolution passed within the preceding 12 months and certain other conditions are fulfilled[29]. A modification of the strict prohibition on such transactions contained in the English Act of 1948 was recommended by Jenkins but not implemented in that jurisdiction until 1981.

[15.38] In addition to the passing of the special resolution just referred to, a statutory declaration of a specified nature must also be made if the proviso is being availed of. The declaration must be made by two directors of the company (or, where there are more than two, by the majority of them) and must state

(1)   the form such assistance is to take;

(2)   the persons to whom it is to be given;

(3)   the purpose for which it is intended to be used; and

(4)   that the declarants have made a full enquiry into the affairs of the company and have formed the opinion that the company, having

---

[28]   See para **[15.14]** above.

[29]   Companies Act 1963, s 60.

carried out the transactions in question, will be able to pay its debts as they fall due.

[15.39] The declaration must be made at a meeting of the directors held no more than 24 days before the meeting of the company at which the resolution is to be considered. Copies of the declaration must be forwarded with each notice of the meeting and must be delivered on the same day as the notices are issued to the Registrar.

[15.40] Any director who makes such a declaration without having reasonable grounds for his opinion as to the capacity of the company to pay its debts is liable to imprisonment for a term not exceeding six months or a fine not exceeding £500 or to both[30]. Where the company is wound up within the period of 12 months after the making of the statutory declaration and its debts are not paid in full within the period of 12 months after the commencement of the winding up, there is a presumption until the contrary is shown that the director did not have reasonable grounds for his opinion.

[15.41] Every member of the company has the right to receive notice of and attend the meeting at which the resolution is to be proposed and any provision to the contrary in the articles is of no effect.

[15.42] Unless all the members of the company entitled to vote at general meetings of the company vote in favour of the resolution, the transaction authorised by the resolution cannot be carried out until a period of 30 days has elapsed after the passing of the resolution. During that period, an application may be made to the court by the holders of not less in the aggregate than 10% of the nominal value of the issued share capital or any class thereof for the cancellation of the resolution. If such an application is made, the resolution is of no effect except to the extent that it is confirmed by the court. The application must be made within 28 days after the date on which the resolution is passed; and once made the transaction cannot be carried out until the application has been disposed of by the court. The application cannot be made by anyone who has consented to, or voted in favour of, the resolution.

[15.43] Where no such resolution is passed, the prohibition will apply except in five specified cases dealt with below. It is in extremely wide terms: it is unlawful for a company:

> 'to give, whether directly or indirectly, and whether by means of a loan, guarantee, the provision of security or otherwise, any financial assistance for the purpose of or in connection with a purchase or subscription ... of or for any shares in the company.'

---

[30] Companies Act 1963, s 60(5) as amended by the Companies (Amendment) Act 1982, s 15.

It has been held in England that this invalidates a purchase by the company where the purpose of the transaction is to put the vendor in funds and thereby enable him to buy shares in the company[31].

[15.44] The prohibition against giving the assistance in the form of a guarantee may have serious consequences for lending institutions; an Irish example is *Re Northside Motor Co Ltd, Eddison v Allied Irish Banks Ltd*[32]. The facts are somewhat complicated and it is sufficient to say that, in the course of a winding up, the liquidator challenged the validity of a payment made to the defendant bank by the company out of the proceeds of the sale of part of its premises. The payment was in part discharge of a debt owed by a subsidiary of the company to the bank which the company had guaranteed. In turn, that debt had been incurred and the guarantee given in order to enable the holder of 50% of the shares in the company to buy out his fellow shareholder. The bank advanced the money and obtained the guarantee before the procedures required by s 60 had been complied with. Costello J held that the transaction was within the ambit of s 60 and that since it had been entered into without the passing of the special resolution and making of the statutory declaration required by the section, it was invalid and could not be retrospectively validated. It should also be noted that the learned judge held that even if it had been possible for the company to validate the transaction retrospectively, he would have concluded that the resolution and statutory declaration were ineffectual. since they referred to the shares as being still in the ownership of the original shareholder whereas they had in fact long since been transferred. Costello J said that a 'materially inaccurate and misleading' resolution and/or declaration would not be a sufficient compliance with s 60(2) and (3).

[15.45] The importance of meticulous compliance with the requirements of the section was again stressed by Costello J in *Lombard and Ulster Banking Ltd v Bank of Ireland*[33]. In that case, a number of people sought to acquire a school by purchasing most of the shares in the company which owned it. Since they had not the necessary funds, it was agreed that they should get a bank loan which the company would procure by executing a charge over the school buildings and executing a guarantee. This was manifestly affected by s 60 and a special resolution was passed and a statutory declaration furnished. However, when the company went into liquidation and the liquidator challenged the validity of the bank's guarantee and charge, the bank were not in position to adduce satisfactory evidence that the resolution and declaration had been passed at the appropriate times, the burden of proving which, as Costello J held, rested on the person

---

[31] *Belmont Finance v Williams Furniture Ltd (No 2)* [1980] 1 All ER 393.
[32] (Unreported, 24 July 1985) (Costello J).
[33] (Unreported, 2 June 1987) (Costello J).

seeking to uphold the transaction. The cases illustrates the importance from the lender's point of view of obtaining copies of all the relevant documents, including minutes of the relevant meetings of the directors and the company, before the money is advanced. However, in the circumstances of that case, Costello J held that the bank were not actually on notice of the invalidity and hence the transaction was upheld[34].

[15.46] It has been held in England[35] that, while the assigning by a subsidiary of its tax losses to the parent as part of a transaction under which the parent acquired shares in the subsidiary could be regarded as the giving of financial assistance for the purchase of the shares, the court was entitled to look at the whole of the transaction in deciding whether it offended against the corresponding section. Since in that case the subsidiary was also afforded substantial benefits by the parent, the court held that the transaction did not violate the spirits of the section. Hoffman J observed:

> 'One must examine the commercial realities of the transaction and decide whether it can properly be described as the giving of financial assistance by the company, bearing in mind that the sanction is a penal one and should not be strained to cover transactions which are not fairly within it ...'

[15.47] Where a company acts in contravention of the section, every officer who is in default is liable on conviction on indictment to imprisonment for a term not exceeding two years or a fine not exceeding £2,500 or to both; or, on summary conviction, to imprisonment for a term not exceeding six months or to a fine not exceeding £500 or to both[36]. The section also provides that any transaction which is in breach of it is to be voidable at the instance of the company against any person (whether a party to the transaction or not) who had notice of the facts which constitute the breach.

[15.48] A security given by the company (such as a mortgage) which assists the purchase of its shares is also voidable in such circumstances.

[15.49] It will be noted that a transaction in breach of the section is only voidable as against another party where that party had notice of the facts constituting such a breach. It was held by the Supreme Court in *Bank of Ireland Finance Ltd v Rockfield Ltd*[37] that 'notice' in the section means *actual* as distinct from *constructive* notice. The fact that if appropriate enquiries had been made the illegality would have come to light will not be sufficient to invalidate the transaction. In that case the plaintiffs had advanced money to a company on the

---

34   See para **[15.49]** below.
35   *Charterhouse Investment Trust Ltd v Tempest Diesels Ltd* (1986) BCLC 1.
36   Companies Act 1963, s 60(15) as amended by the Companies (Amendment) Act 1982, s 15.
37   [1979] IR 21.

security of a mortgage of the company's property. The advance was in fact being used to finance the acquisition by a third party of shares in the company, but the plaintiffs were not aware of this, although had enquiries been made it would have come to light. When the plaintiffs sought to enforce their security against the company, their claim was resisted on the ground *inter alia* that s 60 of the Principal Act had not been complied with. This defence succeeded in the High Court but on appeal the Supreme Court held that as the plaintiffs had taken the security without actual notice of the irregularity it should not be set aside as against them.

[15.50] The decision was applied by Costello J in *Lombard and Ulster Banking Co v Bank of Ireland*, the facts of which have been referred to above. In that case, the learned judge held that neither the plaintiffs nor their agent were aware of the invalidity of the transaction.

[15.51] There are five exceptions to the prohibition in the section (apart from cases where the transaction is authorised by a resolution). They are:

(1)   the payment of a dividend properly declared by a company;

(2)   the discharge of a liability lawfully incurred by the company;

(3)   the lending of money by the company in the ordinary course of its business, where the lending of money is part of its ordinary business;

(4)   the provision by the company of money in accordance with a scheme intended to assist employees or former employees (including directors holding salaried offices) to acquire shares in the company;

(5)   the making of loans to persons other than directors *bona fide* in the employment of the company with a view to enabling them to acquire shares in the company.

[15.52] The power to validate a transaction prohibited by s 60 of the Principal Act has not been available to public limited companies since the 1983 Act. Such a company may only provide financial assistance for the purchase of its own shares where the case falls within one of the permitted exceptions set out in the preceding paragraph. Moreover, even in such cases, the company may only give such assistance if:

(1)   the company's net assets are not thereby reduced or

(2)   to the extent that they are so reduced, the assistance is provided out of profits available for dividend.

The prohibition extends to companies registered or re-registered under the 1983 Act as public limited companies in addition to public limited companies formed as such. In the case of the former, there is a saver for transactions in breach of the section which were authorised by a special resolution passed before the application for registration or re-registration[38].

Other provisions

[15.53] Another general principle which reflected the law's concern that capital should be maintained intact was the prohibition on paying dividends out of capital. This is dealt with in detail in Chapter 33 below.

[15.54] The law does permit the reduction of a company's capital where the reduction is sanctioned by the court. The circumstances in which this may be done are discussed in the next chapter.

---

[38] Companies (Amendment) Act 1983, First Schedule, para 10.

Chapter 16

Alteration (Including Reduction) of Capital

[16.01] A company may wish to alter its capital for a variety of reasons. Before considering the various alterations that it may wish to make and how such alterations may be lawfully made, it is well to remind ourselves of the different types of capital. There is first the authorised share capital, ie the amount of the share capital which the company is authorised to issue. There is secondly the issued share capital, ie the shares which the company has allotted or agreed to allot to the members or shareholders for cash or some other valuable consideration[1].

[16.02] If a company wishes to raise more money by increasing its issued share capital, there is no difficulty in doing so even where the resolution will exceed the authorised share capital. By simply passing a resolution, the company may increase its authorised share capital to the required amount and the new shares can then be issued, provided only that this machinery is authorised by the articles of association. By contrast, where a company wishes to reduce its issued share capital, the procedure is more complex. In particular, the reduction must be confirmed by the court before it becomes effective. This again reflects the concern of the law with ensuring that the company's capital remains intact[2]. Where, however, the company simply wishes to reduce the capital by cancelling shares which have not been taken or agreed to be taken by anyone, it may do so by a resolution. This is called a diminution of the capital and is deemed by the Principal Act not to be a reduction[3].

[16.03] Finally, the company may wish to consolidate shares (eg convert every block of five £1 shares into one £5 share) or sub-divide shares (the reverse operation) or convert shares into stock or *vice versa*. The difference between shares and stock is that (a) shares may have to be numbered while stock need not be and (b) stock need not be divided into equal parts.

The various ways in which a company's capital may be altered are now considered in greater detail.

---

[1] There is, technically, a difference between the issued and allotted share capital. A company making a new issue must first issue the capital and then proceed to allot it. In practice, the issued and allotted share capital are invariably the same.

[2] See para **[14.14]** above.

[3] Companies Act 1963, s 68(1)(e) and (2).

Increase in capital

[16.04] When a company wishes to increase its share capital and for that purpose to alter its memorandum, it can do so by a resolution passed at a general meeting of the company, provided it is authorised to do so by the articles of association. This is provided for by s 68 of the Principal Act and s 70 requires notice of the increase to be given to the Registrar within 15 days after the passing of the necessary resolution. If such notice is not given, the company and every officer who is in default is liable to a fine not exceeding £250[4].

[16.05] If the articles do not authorise an increase, it is, of course, possible to amend the articles so as to confer such a power on the company. Where the Table A regulations apply, the increase may be effected under Article 44 by an ordinary resolution of the company.

Consolidation and sub-division of shares

[16.06] Section 68 of the Principal Act also empowers a company by a resolution passed at a general meeting to consolidate and divide all or any of its share capital into shares of larger amount than the existing shares; and to sub-divide its shares, or any of them, into shares of smaller amount than is fixed by the memorandum. Where a sub-division is effected, the proportion between the amount paid and the amount, if any, unpaid on each share is to be the same in the case of the reduced share as it was in the case of the original share. Notice must be given to the Registrar within one month of the consolidation or sub-division; and again there is provision for a fine not exceeding £250 on the company and every officer in default[5].

[16.07] If the articles do not authorise consolidation or sub-division, they can be altered to give the necessary power. Where the Table A regulations apply, the consolidation or sub-division may be effected under Article 45 by an ordinary resolution of the company. The articles may properly contain a provision enabling the company on a sub-division to attach a preference to some of the shares resulting from the sub-division[6].

Conversion of shares into stock and reconversion of stock into shares

[16.08] Section 68 of the Principal Act also empowers a company by resolution passed at a general meeting to convert all or any of its paid up shares into stock and reconvert that stock into paid up shares of any denomination, provided it is authorised by its articles so to do.

---

[4]   Companies Act 1963, s 70(3) as amended by the Companies (Amendment) Act 1982, s 15.
[5]   Companies Act 1963, s 69(2) as amended by the Companies (Amendment) Act 1982, s 15.
[6]   *Andrews v Gas Meter Co* [1897] 1 Ch 361.

[16.09] At one time shares had to be numbered. This was not necessary, however, in the case of stock. It was, accordingly, possible to transfer, say, £25,000 of stock in a company: if shares to the equivalent amount were being transferred, it was necessary to transfer, say, 25,000 shares of £1 each numbered 1 to 25,000. The advantages of converting shares into stock were therefore significantly reduced when it became possible to have shares without numbers. Section 80(2) of the Principal Act provides that if at any time all the issued shares in a company (or all of the issued shares of a particular class) are fully paid up and rank *pari passu* for all purposes (ie are on the same footing with regard to rights to dividends, etc), they need not have a distinguishing number, so long as those conditions still obtain.

[16.10] As in the case of the other powers conferred by s 68, it is always possible to amend the articles so as to confer the power to convert shares into stock and vice versa if the articles do not contain such a power. If the Table A regulations apply to the company, the conversion or reconversion may be effected under Article 40 by an ordinary resolution of the company. Under Article 41, the directors have power to fix the minimum amount of stock transferable. This must not exceed the nominal value of the share from which the stock arose. Thus if the shares are £5 each in nominal value, the directors can fix the minimum amount of stock transferable at £5 or less. The units thus created are called stock units.

Stock cannot be issued directly by the company.

Reduction of capital

[16.11] Where a company proposes to reduce its share capital, it can usually do so only with the confirmation of the court. As we have seen, importance has always been attached to the maintenance intact by the company of its capital, but there are circumstances where it has been thought legitimate for a reduction to be effected.

[16.12] A reduction of capital can take two forms. First, the amount involved may be returned to the shareholders in the form either of cash or assets or their liability for the uncalled capital reduced or extinguished. Secondly, there may be no actual return of cash or assets, the reduction in this case taking the form of an adjustment to the balance sheet to bring the capital into line with the assets.

[16.13] A reduction of the first type may be considered desirable because the company is over-capitalised, ie has more capital than it requires, or because it is paying too much interest on its capital and wishes to raise alternative capital more cheaply. Section 72(2) of the Principal Act provides that, subject to confirmation by the court, a company may by special resolution reduce its share capital by:

(1) extinguished or reducing the liability of the shareholders in respect of uncalled capital, or

(2) paying off any paid up capital which is in excess of the wants of the company.

Where (2) is adopted, the company may pay off capital on the basis that it may be called up again in whole or in part.

[16.14] A reduction of the second type is appropriate where the company has lost a significant part of its capital. The original capital may have been used to purchase assets to be used in the course of the company's business. In time, because of trading losses, the assets may be significantly reduced. A reduction of the capital to allow for such losses will mean that the balance sheet accurately reflects the true situation of the company. Moreover, one of the items on the assets side in such circumstances - the profit and loss account -will probably be in debit, thereby precluding the company from distributing dividends until the losses have been cleared off out of subsequent profits. By writing down its capital, the company can write off this debit balance and put itself in a position to distribute future profits in the form of dividends.

[16.15] Section 72(2), accordingly, further provides that a company may, subject to confirmation by the court, by special resolution cancel any paid up share capital which is lost or unrepresented by available assets.

Reduction must be fair and equitable

[16.16] The reduction of capital must be fair and equitable. Shareholders who belong to the same class and have the same rights must be treated in the same way: the same percentage must be paid off or cancelled or reduced in respect of each share[7]. But the fact that the reduction means that one class of shareholders will benefit at the expense of another will not of itself be a sufficient ground for the court to refuse to confirm the reduction. Thus, a rateable reduction of ordinary and preference shares was permitted where the latter had no priority as to capital, even though the dividend payable on the preference shares was inevitably reduced as being paid on a smaller amount[8].

[16.17] The leading Irish case on the matters to which the court should have regard when it is asked to confirm a reduction of capital is *Re John Power & Son Ltd*[9]. Fitzgibbon J, in the Supreme Court, said that the court must be satisfied

---

[7] *Bannatyne v Direct Spanish Telegraph Co* (1886) 34 Ch D 287.

[8] *Re McKenzie & Co* [1916] 2 Ch 450, followed by Costello J in *Re Credit Finance Bank plc* (unreported, 19 June 1989), HC.

that the statutory requirements have been met and that the majority in favour of the reduction are using their powers in a *bona fide* manner. If the majority were seeking to coerce the minority in order to promote interests of their own which conflicted with those of the minority, the scheme would not be approved. The court, moreover, should satisfy itself that the scheme is a reasonable one or whether there is any objection to it which a reasonable person could take.

Procedure on a reduction of capital

[16.18] As in the case of any other alteration of the share capital, a reduction must be authorised by the articles before any reduction can be effected. Once the alteration is authorised by the articles - which can always be amended if necessary for this purpose - a special resolution can then be passed. The application for confirmation to the court is then made by petition[10], which states that the company is incorporated, its business, its subsequent history, the facts on which the application for a reduction is grounded and the passing of the special resolution[11].

[16.19] The subsequent procedure depends on whether the reduction is being effected simply because the capital has been lost or is not represented by assets; or because the company is over capitalised and it is desired to pay off capital or reduce the liability of the shareholders. In the former case, the procedure is relatively straightforward: the court fixes a day for the hearing of the petition and directs the publication of advertisements in *Iris Oifigiúil*. Creditors are usually not entitled to be heard[12].

[16.20] In the latter case, the rights of creditors are carefully protected by s 73 of the Principal Act. Any creditor who is entitled to any debts which would be admissible against the company in a winding up is entitled to object to the reduction[13]. A list of creditors must be settled by the court; and the court may only dispense with the consent of the creditor in any particular case if the company secures the payment of the debt by appropriating the full amount of the debt. Where the company is disputing the amount of the debt or it is not ascertained, it must secure or appropriate so much of it as the court fixes after an inquiry and adjudication similar to that in a winding up[14].

---

9   [1934] IR 412.
10 Rules of the Superior Courts 1986, Order 75 r 4.
11 Form No 1, Appendix N.
12 *Re Meux's Brewery Ltd* [1919] 1 Ch 28.
13 Companies Act 1963, s 73(2)(a).
14 Companies Act 1963, s 73(2)(c).

Forfeiture of shares not a reduction requiring confirmation

[16.21] As we shall see in Chapter 17, shares in a company can always be forfeited for non-payment of calls or failure to pay an instalment due in respect of a call[15]. This does not constitute a reduction of capital requiring confirmation by the court[16]. Where, however, the shares are surrendered, different considerations will apply, even though they are surrendered by the shareholder in anticipation of their being forfeited. Generally speaking, a surrender of shares is regarded as a reduction of capital requiring confirmation by the court before it can be effective[17].

---

[15] See para [17.59] et seq below.

[16] It is expressly envisaged by Articles 33 to 39 of Table A. See also *Bellerby v Rowland and Marwoods' SS Co Ltd* [1902] 2 Ch 14 at 32.

[17] *Trevor v Whitworth* (1887) 12 App Cas 409 at 438; *Bellerby v Rowland and Marwoods's SS Co Ltd* [1902] 2 Ch 14 at 22.

Chapter 17

Shares

General

Nature of a share

[17.01] Where a company has a share capital, each of the members owns at least one share of that capital and is consequently a shareholder in the company. This does not mean that he is the owner of any part of the company's assets or that he owns them jointly with his fellow shareholders[1]. But he is along with them the owner of the company itself and the controller of its destinies.

[17.02] While there has been much debate as to the precise nature of a share, it is clear that its most important practical feature is that it confers certain rights on the shareholder. These rights are essentially contractual since, as we have seen, the articles of association constitute a contract between the shareholders and the company[2]. But a share is also more than a mere contractual right: its ownership gives the shareholder an interest recognised by the law in the company itself. The importance of this interest of the shareholder in the company is reflected by the opinion of the Supreme Court in *Private Motorists' Provident Society v Attorney General*[3] that it constitutes a right of property protected by Article 43 of the Constitution.

[17.03] Since the shareholders are in effect the owners of the company, and not merely persons with contractual rights against the company, they are clearly distinguishable in law from debenture holders. The latter have no proprietary interest in the company itself, although they normally have an interest in its assets.

Rights of the shareholder

[17.04] The principal rights of the shareholder are threefold:

    (1)   to receive a share of the company's distributable income in the form of dividend[4];

---

[1] This statement of the law was cited with approval by Costello J in *Kerry Co-operative Creamery Ltd v An Bord Bainne Co-op Ltd* [1990] ILRM 664.

[2] Para **[6.08]** above. See *Attorney General v Jameson* [1904] 2 IR 644 at 669-70.

[3] [1984] ILRM 88.

[4] But note that the articles may lawfully provide - and usually do - that a dividend to be payable must first be declared, either by the company or the directors.

(2)   to attend at and (normally) to vote at meetings of the company, and

(3)   to participate in the distribution of the assets of the company where it is wound up and its creditors have been paid.

[17.05] Any of these rights may, however, be abridged, or excluded completely, by the memorandum and articles. In addition, the shareholders have other rights conferred on them by the Acts such as rights in relation to seeing the accounts of the company, inspecting its books, petitioning the court in relation to its affairs, etc which are dealt with in the appropriate sections of this book.

Duties of the shareholder

[17.06] The shareholder's principal duty is to pay the amount which he has agreed to pay for his shares in the company. Sometimes that amount is payable in full when the shares are allotted to him. Alternatively, part or the whole of the amount may only become payable when a call is made by the company on the shareholder; or the terms of the allotment may provide for the payment of the amount by instalments at fixed times. In the case of a public limited company, one-quarter at least of the agreed amount must be paid on allotment[5].

Amount and numbering of shares

[17.07] An essential feature of a share is that the extent of the shareholder's interest in the company is measured by a money sum. Accordingly, each share has a specific monetary value, known as its nominal value. This is provided for by s 6(4)(a) of the Principal Act which requires the memorandum in the case of a company having a share capital to state 'the division thereof into shares of a fixed amount'. Thus the memorandum may provide that:

'the capital of the company is £250,000 divided into 50,000 shares of £5 each.'

[17.08] Since the coming into force of the Decimal Currency Act 1969, it has been necessary to state the value of the share in terms of decimal currency. Although companies have been registered with share capitals expressed in foreign currency, the better view appears to be that the capital must be expressed in terms of Irish pounds or pence.

[17.09] Section 80 of the Principal Act requires each share in a company having a share capital to be distinguished by its appropriate number. This requirement may, however, be dispensed with where all the issued shares (or all the issued shares of a particular class) are fully paid up and rank *pari passu* (ie stand on the same footing) for all purposes, so long as those conditions continue to exist.

[17.10] Shares - or any other interest of a member in a company - are personal estate. They are not of the nature of real estate. This distinction was formerly of

---

5   Companies (Amendment) Act 1983, s 28.

importance in determining succession to property on death, but has ceased to be of any significance since the abolition of the different rules governing the devolution of real and personal property which was initiated by the Administration of Estates Act 1959 and completed by the Succession Act 1965.

Different classes of shares

[17.11] *Prima facie* all shares are presumed to be of equal status. The rights of all the shareholders are the same in regard to the payment of dividends, voting at meetings and participation in the assets on a winding up. Obviously, the amount of cash to which each shareholder is entitled by way of dividends or on a winding up will depend on the number of shares held by him; but the shares themselves all stand on an equal footing.

[17.12] At an early stage in the development of modern company law, however, it became common for the constitutions of companies to provide for the division of the shares into different classes and for the giving of preferential rights, as they were called, to classes of shares. The shares to which such rights were attached were known as preference shares.

[17.13] The provision for the division of the shares is usually contained in the memorandum. If, however, the memorandum expressly provides that all the shares are to be equal, that provision cannot be modified by the articles. And if the memorandum provides for the division of the shares into classes and the rights to be attached to such classes, the articles cannot be subsequently altered by special resolution so as to alter those provisions[6]. In practice, the rights attached to the different classes are usually dealt with in the articles.

[17.14] A preference share normally gave its holder the right to a dividend of fixed amount - 5%, 10% or as the case might be - in priority to the holders of other shares. It could also give its holder the right to participate in the capital available for distribution on a winding up in priority to other shareholders. Or it could give the preference shareholder both rights. It became an accepted method of giving someone prepared to fund the operations of the company a form of security; but the advantages from the investor's point of view of taking a debenture led to the latter replacing the preference share as the more attractive security. (As we have seen, a debenture holder, unlike a shareholder, almost invariably has an interest in the assets of the company.) Preference shares are, however, still frequently encountered in practice in Ireland in both private and public companies. They are dealt with in detail later in this chapter[7].

[17.15] Another division of shares sometimes encountered is between voting and non-voting shares. It is permissible for a company to divide its shares into

---

[6] *Campbell v Rofe* [1933] AC 91 at 98.
[7] See para **[17.38]** et seq below.

such categories (usually distinguished by letters, eg 'A' shares and 'B' shares) but the practice is not approved of by the Stock Exchange, since it can mean in practice that those who own the company - the shareholders - do not necessarily control its activities.

[17.16] A category of shares which has virtually ceased to exist today is founders' or deferred shares. These entitled their holders to various rights, such as the right to a fixed percentage of the profits in any year after a specified dividend - also expressed in percentage terms - had been paid on the other shares. They were usually allotted to the persons with whom the enterprise had begun, eg the vendors of a business sold to the company on its formation.

[17.17] Any shares which do not have preferential rights attached to them are known as ordinary shares. Their holders reap the principal benefit when the company is doing well, since they will receive all the distributed profits that remain after the payment of any fixed preferential dividend. Similarly, when the company is doing badly, they will be the principal victims, since the preference shareholders will cream off what profit there is. It is for this reason that in the case of a company whose shares are dealt in on the Stock Exchange it is the value of the ordinary shares which really reflect the value placed by the market on the company itself. The holders of the ordinary shares are regarded as the owners of the equitable interest in the company as contrasted with the secured lenders, whether they be debenture holders or preference shareholders; and hence the reference frequently encountered to the ordinary shares of such companies as 'equities'.

Variations of rights of classes of shareholders

[17.18] As we have seen, the rights attached to the different classes of shares are usually specified in the articles. We have also seen that the articles can be amended at any time by a special resolution of the company. Can the company alter the special rights attached to a particular class of shares, eg the right of the preference shareholder to a fixed dividend in priority to the other shareholders?

[17.19] It was held in *Andrews v Gas Meter Co*[8] that where the rights were dealt with by the articles, they could be so altered by special resolution. However, the practice continued of providing in articles a special procedure for altering the rights, generally with the consent of three-fourths of the effected shareholders[9].

[17.20] Section 78 of the Principal Act made it clear that where the memorandum or articles themselves contained a procedure for the variation of such special rights with the consent of a specified proportion of that class or the sanction of a resolution passed at a separate meeting of the class, the rights could

---

[8] [1897] 1 Ch 361.
[9] Cf Article 3.

be lawfully varied by complying with the procedure. This, however, was subject to the right of a dissenting minority of the class to apply to the court for an order cancelling the variation. What was not clear was whether the rights could be varied if no such procedure was contained in the memorandum or articles. The position has now been clarified by s 38 of the 1983 Act.

[17.21] Where the rights are attached to the class otherwise than by the memorandum (eg by the articles) and the articles do not contain any procedure for the variation of the rights, they may be varied, but only where the following requirements are met:

(1)　the holders of three-quarters in nominal value of the issued shares of the class consent in writing, or

(2)　the variation is sanctioned by a special resolution passed at a separate general meeting of the holders of that class.

Any other requirements imposed by the articles or otherwise must also be met.

[17.22] Where the rights are so varied, the holders of not less in the aggregate than 10% of the issued shares of that class (not being persons who consented or voted in favour) may apply to the court to have the variation cancelled. Where such an application is made, the variation is not to have effect unless and until it is confirmed by the court.

[17.23] The application must be made within 28 days after the consent has been given or the resolution passed. It may be made by such one or more of the dissenting shareholders on behalf of them all as they may appoint in writing for that purpose. The court, after hearing the applicant and any other person who applies to be heard and appears to the court to be interested, may disallow the variation if it is satisfied that, having regard to all the circumstances of the case, the variation would unfairly prejudice the affected shareholders. If it is not so satisfied, it must confirm the variation. The decision of the court is final, but there is provision for an appeal to the Supreme Court on a question of law.

[17.24] The company must forward a copy of the court's order to the Registrar within 21 days after it has been made. If default is made in complying with this provision, the company and every officer in default is liable to a fine not exceeding £250.

[17.25] Where the rights are attached to the class by the memorandum or otherwise and the memorandum or articles contain a procedure for the variation of the rights, they may be varied in accordance with that procedure. But if the variation of the rights is connected with:

(1)　the giving, variation, revocation or renewal of an authority to the directors to allot shares[10], or

(2)　a reduction of capital under s 72 of the Principal Act,

the two requirements mentioned in para **[17.21]** must also be met, ie the variation must receive the consent of the holders of three-quarters in nominal value of the issued shares of the class or the sanction of a special resolution passed at a general meeting of the class.

[17.26] Where the procedure for the variation provides for obtaining the consent of a specified proportion of the holders of the issued share capital or the sanction of a special resolution passed at a general meeting of the class, the holders of not less than 10% of the issued shares of the class who do not consent or vote in favour may apply to the court for an order cancelling the variation under the procedure explained in para **[17.23]**.

[17.27] Where the rights are attached to the shares by the memorandum and the memorandum and articles do not contain any procedure for their variation, they may be varied if all the members agree to the variation. The rights may also be varied if all the members agree to the variation. The rights may also be varied if this is required by an order of the court made under ss 10, 203, or 205 of the Principal Act or s 15 of the 1983 Act.

[17.28] The English courts have adopted a somewhat restrictive approach in defining what constitutes a variation or abrogation of a special right attached to a class of shares. It might be thought, for example, that to make a new issue of shares ranking *pari passu* (ie on an equal footing so far as rights to dividends, capital on winding up, etc are concerned) with existing shares would be to vary the rights of the existing shareholders. Article 4 of Table A, indeed, expressly provides that the rights conferred upon the holders of any shares are not to be deemed to be varied by the issue of new shares ranking *pari passu* with them. But even without such a provision in the articles, it would appear that such an issue does not constitute a variation of the rights of existing shareholders[11].

[17.29] Again, in *Greenhalgh Cinemas v Arderne Cinemas (No 2)*[12], the Court of Appeal held that a subdivision of ordinary shares of 10s each into shares of 2s each did not constitute a variation of the rights of the holders of another class of ordinary shares of 2s each, although the result was to change the control of the company. Even more surprisingly in *White v Bristol Aeroplane Co Ltd*[13], where the articles provided that the rights attached to any class of shares might be affected in any manner with the sanction of a resolution at a separate meeting, it was held that the rights of existing preference shareholders were not 'affected' within the meaning of the articles by the issue of new preference stock to the

---

[10] See para **[9.12]** above and the Companies (Amendment) Act 1983, s 20.
[11] *Re Schweppes Ltd* [1914] 1 Ch 322.
[12] [1945] 2 All ER 719, [1946] 1 All ER 512.
[13] [1953] Ch 65.

ordinary shareholders giving them a majority over the existing preference stock. Lord Evershed MR drew a distinction between being 'affected as a matter of business' (which the rights clearly were) and 'varied as a matter of law' (which they were not). It was the enjoyment of the rights, and not the rights themselves, which in the view of the court was affected.

There must be some doubt as to whether the last two decisions, which have been criticised by English commentators[14], will be followed in Ireland.

Shares certificates

[17.30] Each shareholder in a company is furnished with a document called a share certificate. This is the evidence of the shareholder's title to the shares. It is issued under the common seal of the company and s 87(1) of the Principal Act provides that as so issued it is to be *prima facie* evidence of the member's title to the shares. It enables dealings with the shares to be accomplished more expeditiously, since it can be produced on any sale or mortgage of the shares by the owner and may be safely accepted by the purchaser or mortgagee as evidence of his title.

[17.31] The articles of association sometimes provides (Article 8) for the issue by the company of split certificates. Persons or bodies who hold shares on trust for a number of people avail of split certificates in order to enable the different holdings to be disposed of individually.

[17.32] The fact that the share certificate is *prima facie* evidence of the title of the shareholder to the shares may mean that the company will be liable to those who suffer damages as a result of an incorrect share certificate being issued. This may happen in two ways: first, the certificate may be issued in the name of a person who was not entitled to be a member and, second, the certificate may incorrectly state the amount paid up on the shares.

[17.33] In each case, the company may be liable to a person who suffers damage as a result of the issue of the incorrect certificate because of the legal doctrine of estoppel. In the first case, if the company issues a certificate to a person who is not entitled to be registered as a member - because, for example, he had lodged a forged transfer of the share - the company will be liable to a person who purchases the shares on the faith of the certificate[15]. The purchaser will not be entitled to be registered as a member in such circumstances - the original shareholder whose name was forged on the transfer will remain the member- but he will be entitled to damages. Although the company cannot register him as a member they must compensate him for the damage he thereby suffers: they are precluded or estopped from asserting that the facts set out in the certificate are

---

[14] *Palmer's Company Law* (25th edn), Vol 1, 6.038.
[15] *Re Bahia and San Francisco Railway Co* (1868) LR 3 QB 584.

incorrect. In the second case, where the certificate wrongly states that the shares are fully paid up, the company cannot make a call upon the shareholder for the amount unpaid: again, they are estopped from asserting that the certificate is incorrect[16].

[17.34] The company will not be liable where the certificate itself is forged by a person who had no authority to issue such a certificate[17]. Nor will the company be liable where the transferee is aware of the incorrect nature of the certificate[18]. But where the shares have been transferred to a purchaser who takes them in good faith without notice of the irregularity, a subsequent purchaser who takes them with notice will get a good title. The application of the estoppel principle would be frustrated if the purchaser in whose favour it operates could not freely transfer the shares without regard to the state of knowledge of subsequent transferees[19].

[17.35] Normally the estoppel operates only in favour of a purchaser of the shares: it is seldom available to the person to whom the certificate was issued. But there are exceptional cases where the person to whom the certificate was issued may hold the company liable. Thus where the company issued a certificate to a person who was lending money to the company on the security of an allotment of shares and the certificate incorrectly stated that the shares were fully paid up, the company were held to be estopped from asserting the contrary[20].

Share warrants

[17.36] A company may issue a document called a share warrant instead of a certificate. This entitles the bearer of the warrant to the shares, with the result that they can be transferred to other persons simply by delivery of the warrant. They are treated in the result in the same manner as other negotiable instruments, such as cheques, which do not require the execution of an instrument of transfer. Section 88 of the Principal Act entitles a company to issue such share warrants where it is authorised so to do by its articles.

[17.37] Private companies may not issue share warrants. They are, in fact, extremely rare in practice today in the case of public companies.

---

16 *Burkinshaw v Nicholls* (1878) 3 App Cas 1004.
17 *Ruben v Great Fingall Consolidated Co* [1906] AC 439.
18 *Re Caribbean Co Crickmer's Case* (1875) 10 Ch App 614.
19 *Barrow's Case* (1880) 14 Ch D 432.
20 *Bloomenthal v Ford* [1897] AC 156.

Preference Shares

[17.38] As its name indicates, a preference share is one that gives the shareholder certain preferential rights not enjoyed by the other shareholders. Invariably it confers on the holder the right to the payment of a dividend representing a fixed percentage of the distributable profits in priority to the payment of the dividend to the other shareholders. In addition, it may confer on him the right to be repaid his capital in priority to the other shareholders in the event of a winding up.

Cumulative and non-cumulative preference shares

[17.39] No problem arises if the distributable profits of the company are sufficient to pay the fixed dividend (of 5% or whatever it may be) on the preference shares. But what if the profits are insufficient? Is the shareholder then entitled to be paid the arrears the following year or whenever the profits are sufficient to pay him? This depends on whether the shares are cumulative or non-cumulative. Where they are cumulative, the arrears[21] must be paid off as soon as the profits permit. Where they are non-cumulative, the preference shareholder is not entitled to be paid arrears of dividend. If the clause defining the rights simply declares that the preference shareholders are to be entitled to a preferential dividend of a specified percentage, that is enough to make the shares cumulative[22]. Where it is desired to make them non-cumulative, this must be made clear in the relevant clause. The clause should state that the dividend is to be paid 'out of the profits made by the company in each year' or words to the same effect. Such words will be enough to make the shares non-cumulative preference shares[23].

Preferential dividends payable only out of profits

[17.40] As can be gathered from the last paragraph, and as common sense would suggest, a preferential dividend can only be paid where distributable profits are available from which it can be paid. Moreover, even where such profits are available, the terms on which the shares were issued may make it plain that the preferential dividend is only to be paid when it is declared; and this is indeed usually the position. The terms of issue sometimes, however, provide that the profits shall be distributed by way of preferential dividend where the directors declare a dividend, in contrast to the usual position where such a dividend is declared by the company in general meeting. But even in such a case, the

---

[21] 'Arrears' is a convenient but imprecise description. Where the profits are not sufficient to pay a preferential dividend, the company need not pay it and hence does not owe any arrears.
[22] *Webb v Earle* (1875) LR 20 Eq 556.
[23] *Staples v Eastman Photographic Materials Co* [1896] 2 Ch 303.

directors will retain a discretion as to whether the dividend should be declared or not[24].

[17.41] It follows from the foregoing that, unless the articles otherwise provide, a preferential dividend can normally only be paid when the company or directors declare a dividend. There is nothing to prevent the company continuing to put profits to reserve and declining to pay any dividend. Moreover, even where the articles expressly confer a right to a preferential dividend in the event of sufficient profits being earned, a question may still arise as to the fund out of which it is to be paid. Thus, where the directors were authorised by the articles to set aside sums to reserve before recommending any dividend, and the preferential dividend was payable out of 'profits available for dividend' it was held that any sums transferred by the directors to reserve had to be deducted before the profits available for dividend could be ascertained[25].

[17.42] If there are arrears of preferential dividend, must they be paid out of the reserves (assuming that there are distributable reserves) in priority to the ordinary dividend? As always when the rights of shareholders are being considered, the answer will ultimately depend on the wording of the particular articles or the terms of issue of the shares. Unless the articles or the terms of issue indicate otherwise, however, it would seem that arrears of preferential dividend should be paid out of reserves, where the reserves are created by transferring profits to reserve which would otherwise have been available for the preferential dividend.

[17.43] In *Re Lafeyette Ltd, Lafeyette v Nolan*[26], the relevant article provided that

'such dividend shall be cumulative and arrears thereof shall be a first charge on the *subsequent profits* of the company.'

[17.44] Kingsmill Moore J held that the effect of this article was that a preferential dividend in arrears could not be paid out of profits which had been earned before the dividend was payable and placed to reserves: such a dividend could only be paid out of profits earned subsequently. This is an example of how the general principle referred to may be displaced by the actual wording used in the articles. It should be said, however, that the authority of the decision is somewhat weakened by the fact that the point appears to have been conceded in argument by counsel for the preference shareholders. It has been criticised by Pennington as being unduly restrictive in its construction of the rights of preference shareholders[27]. It does, however, illustrate the important general

---

[24] *Bond v Barrow Haematite Steel Co* [1902] 1 Ch 353 at 362.
[25] *Fisher v Black & White Publishing Co* [1901] 1 Ch 174.
[26] [1950] IR 100 at 230.
[27] *Company Law* (7th edn), p 262.

principle that the undoubted right of the preference shareholders to be paid arrears of dividend out of profits placed to reserves which would otherwise have been available to pay their dividend may be excluded by the articles or the terms of issue.

Preferential rights as to capital

[17.45] Where a preference share confers a preferential right to a dividend, it does not follow that the shareholder is also entitled to the return of his capital in priority to the other shareholders in the event of a winding up. On the contrary, it is clear that, unless such a right is expressly conferred by the articles all shareholders stand on the same footing so far as their right to payment of capital is concerned, because the presumption of equality between shareholders has not been displaced[28].

Right to participate further in profits and capital

[17.46] Once the preference shareholder has been paid his fixed dividend, he is not entitled to participate further in the division of the profits, unless an express right to do so is conferred on him by the memorandum or articles. So much was made clear by the decision of the House of Lords in *Will v United Lankat Plantations*[29]. It also appeared from the earlier House of Lords decision in *Birch v Cropper*[30], however, that the preference shareholder was entitled to participate in the distribution of the surplus assets of the company on winding up after the debts had been paid and the capital returned. It also appeared that this result followed whether or not the preference shareholder was entitled to the return of his capital in priority to the ordinary shareholders. If the preference shareholder was entitled to the return of his capital in priority to the other shareholders, this did not necessarily exhaust his rights.

[17.47] This is still the law in Ireland, as is made clear by the decision of the former Supreme Court in *Cork Electric Supply Co Ltd v Concannon*[31]. That case (which arose out of the establishment of the Electric Supply Board and the consequent compulsory acquisition of the Cork company's assets and undertakings by the Board) came before the High Court in the form of a construction summons in which the company sought the directions of the court as to whether, in the event of the company being wound up, the rights of the preference shareholders should be treated as exhausted by the existence of a clause in the articles entitling them to a fixed cumulative preferential dividend of

---

[28] *Re Driffield Gas Light Co* [1898] 1 Ch 451; *Birch v Cropper, Re Bridgewater Navigation Co Ltd* (1889) 14 App Cas 525.

[29] [1914] AC 11.

[30] (1889) 14 App Cas 525.

[31] [1932] IR 314.

5% per annum and also the right in a winding up to the return of their capital in priority to the ordinary shareholders. If they were to be treated as exhausted, it followed that the preference shareholders would not be entitled to participate in the distribution of the surplus assets which were expected to be available as a result of the anticipated winding up. Johnson J was of the opinion that the rights were exhausted by the existence of such a clause, but his decision was unanimously reversed on appeal. Kennedy CJ, having referred to a number of English decisions, went on as follows:

> 'Out of all these cases, after consideration, what we derive is only this, that the right to participate in a distribution of surplus assets on a winding up will be taken from preference shareholders by a clause in the Articles of Association delimiting their rights exhaustively to the exclusion of any other rights and that the question whether a particular clause does so exhaust the rights attached to the preference shares exhaustively and exclusively is a question of the construction of the particular Articles of Association in each case ...'[32]

He went on to hold, in common with the other members of the court (Fitzgibbon and Murnaghan JJ) that the particular clause in that case did not exhaust the rights.

[17.48] It does not appear that the question was ever reopened in the Irish courts. In England the Court of Appeal came to a similar conclusion not long afterwards in *Re William Metcalfe & Son Ltd*[33]. But in a series of later decisions in the House of Lords and the Court of Appeal, the view of the law which had found favour in *Concannon*'s case and *Re William Metcalf & Son Ltd* was rejected. It is now clear from *Scottish Insurance Corpn v Wilsons and Clyde Coal Company*[34], *Prudential Assurance Co v Chatterly-Whitfield Collieries Co Ltd*[35] and *Re Isle of Thanet Electricity Supply Co Ltd*[36] that in that jurisdiction the law now is that where the articles set out the rights attached to a class of shares to participate in the profits while the company is a going concern or to share in the property of the company in liquidation, *prima facie* the rights so set out in each case are exhaustive.

[17.49] *Concannon*'s case remains the law in Ireland unless and until it is overruled by the Supreme Court, which is not, of course, bound rigidly by *stare decisis*[37]. The later English decisions reflect the growing tendency among businessmen to treat preference shares as more in the nature of securities akin to

---

[32] [1932] IR 314 at 328.
[33] [1933] Ch 142.
[34] [1949] AC 462.
[35] [1949] AC 512.
[36] [1950] Ch 161.
[37] *Attorney General v Ryan's Car Hire Ltd* [1965] IR 642.

debentures rather than as shares in the ordinary sense. It would follow logically from such a view that, in the absence of an express provision in the articles indicating an agreement to the contrary, a preference shareholder should not normally expect to receive more than the preferential rights actually given to him.

[17.50] It should be noted that, although a preference shareholder may not be entitled to share in the profits remaining after the payment of a fixed dividend, this does not exclude his right to share in the profits which remain undistributed when the company is wound up. This is because the profits at that stage ceases to be profits and became assets of the company[38].

Arrears of preference dividends in a winding up

[17.51] We have seen that in the case of cumulative preference shares, the shareholder will normally be entitled to be paid his dividend out of the profits of succeeding years where the particular year's profits are insufficient. This right to be paid arrears of dividend does not necessarily apply in a winding up, however; whether such arrears are payable in those circumstances will depend on the wording of the articles. If the article makes it clear that the priority afforded to dividends extends to a winding up, the shareholder will be entitled to such arrears. Where the articles are silent, the courts have in some cases been able from the words used to infer such an intention[39]. But if the dividends are not merely in arrears, but are actually *owed* by the company (as where they have been declared), they are payable as a preferential debt[40].

Redeemable preference shares

[17.52] The power to issue redeemable shares was formerly confined to redeemable preference shares. As we have seen, the 1990 Act now provides for the issue of redeemable shares, generally, but preserves the rights of existing holders of redeemable preference shares and of companies in relation to them[41].

Calls

Nature of a call

[17.53] When the entire amount due to be paid by a shareholder for his shares is not paid on allotment, the company is generally entitled to require the unpaid balance to be paid at any time thereafter. The liability continues until the company is dissolved or struck off the register, so that in the event of the

---

[38] *Wilson (Inspector of Taxes) v Dunnes Stores (Cork) Ltd* (unreported, 22 January 1976) (Kenny J).

[39] *Re de Jong (F) & Co Ltd* [1946] Ch 211; *Re E W Savory Ltd* [1951] 2 All ER 1036.

[40] *Re Imperial Hotel (Cork) Ltd* [1950] IR 115.

[41] Para **[15.03]** and **[15.69]** above.

company being wound up each shareholder remains liable including those who have ceased to be shareholders. The process of collecting the unpaid balance is known as a call; and hence the totality of the balances unpaid on the shares is known as the uncalled capital.

[17.54] The amount due may also be payable by fixed instalments payable at specified times: strictly speaking, a demand for the payment of such an instalment is not a call. In the case of public limited companies, the terms of issue very rarely, if ever, leave any part of the capital to be called. The normal provision is to require the payment of the entire amount by instalments within a relatively short time.

How a call is enforced

[17.55] The articles usually contain a procedure for the making of calls. That contained in Table A is to be found in Articles 15 to 21 inclusive. They provide that the directors may from time to time make calls, provided that no call exceeds one-fourth of the nominal value of the share and that at least one month elapses between successive calls. They also provide that the shareholder is to receive at least 14 days' notice of the making of a call. The directors are also given power to revoke or postpone calls.

[17.56] Where a call is properly made in accordance with the articles and the amount is not paid by the shareholder, the necessary proceedings should be by way of summary summons. The articles usually contain a provision providing for the payment of interest at a rate to be determined by the directors but not to exceed a specified sum.

[17.57] While the directors have a discretion as to when they will exercise a power to make calls, it is a discretion that must be exercised in good faith and for the benefit of the company. The calls should be made *pari passu* unless the articles otherwise provide: ie each of the shareholders should be asked to pay the same amount and the call should be made at the same time on each of them. The articles sometimes provide (Article 20) that the directors may, on the issue of shares, differentiate between holders as to the amount of the calls to be paid and the times of payment. While the articles may be amended to include such a provision, the amendment cannot impose liability on shareholders who were allotted shares before the amendment. Even where the articles permit such a differentiation between shareholders, it would require special grounds to justify it[42].

---

[42] *Galloway v Halle Concerts Society Ltd* [1915] 2 Ch 233.

Payment in advance of calls

[17.58] The articles sometimes include a provision enabling the directors, if they think fit, to receive from shareholders money uncalled and unpaid on any shares. Where they exercise this power, they may pay interest at such rate not exceeding a specified sum as may be agreed between themselves and the shareholders in question on the money advanced until such time as the money would have become payable. Clearly, this is a power capable of being abused by the directors and it has been held that it must be exercised by them in good faith and for the benefit of the company[43]. The rate of interest must not be excessive.

Forfeiture of shares

General

[17.59] The articles almost invariably contain a provision enabling the company to forfeit the shares in the event of the failure of a member to pay any call or instalment of a call on the day appointed for payment (Articles 33 to 39 inclusive). In the Table A form, they empower the directors in such an event to serve a notice on the defaulting shareholder requiring payment of so much of the call or instalment as remains unpaid together with interest on or before the expiration of 14 days from the date of service of the notice. The notice must state that, in the event of the amount not being paid on or before that date, the shares will be liable to be forfeited. If the requirements of the notice are not complied with, the shares may then be forfeited by resolution of the directors.

[17.60] The forfeiture of a share means, of course, that the capital of the company is to that extent reduced. Where the forfeiture is in respect of non-payment of a call, however, it is a valid reduction of the capital which does not require the sanction of the court under s 72 of the Principal Act. Forfeiture of shares for any other cause constitutes a reduction of capital and is accordingly not lawful[44].

[17.61] Where shares in a public limited company are forfeited, the result may be to bring the nominal value of allotted shares of the company below the authorised minimum under s 19 of the 1983 Act. Section 43 of the 1983 Act, accordingly, provides that, where shares in such a company are forfeited and not disposed of by the company within three years of the date of forfeiture, the company must cancel the shares and reduce the amount of its share capital by the nominal value of the shares. If this has the effect of bringing the nominal

---

[43] *Sykes' Case* (1872) LR 13 Eq 255. In that case, the directors made a call in advance when the company was insolvent and used the amount collected to pay their own fees. It was held that this was an improper use of the power.

[44] See Ch 15.

value of the company's allotted share capital below the authorised minimum, the company must apply for re-registration as another form of company, stating the effect of the cancellation. The directors are then dispensed from complying with ss 72 and 73 of the Principal Act - dealing with reduction of capital with the confirmation of the court - but must pass a resolution altering the company's memorandum so that it no longer states the company is a public limited company and making any other alterations in the memorandum and articles as are requisite in the circumstances. The application for re-registration must be in the prescribed form[45] and signed by a director and secretary of the company. It must be delivered to the Registrar together with a printed company of the memorandum and articles as altered by the resolution.

[17.62] If a company required to register under the section fails to do so, s 21 of the 1983 Act is to apply to it as if it were a private company, ie the company or its officers commit an offence if they offer its shares or debentures to the public either directly or through an offer for sale or placing. Except for that purpose, however, the company in the event of failure to re-register continues to be a public limited company. If the company fails to cancel any share or to re-register when required to do so by the section, the company and any officer in default is guilty of an offence and liable on summary conviction to a fine not exceeding £25 for every day on which the offence continues, but not exceeding £500 in total[46].

[17.63] If the Registrar is satisfied that a company may be re-registered in accordance with s 43 of the 1983 Act he is required to retain the application and other documents delivered to him and issue the company with an appropriate certificate of incorporation. The company by virtue of its issue becomes the form of company stated in the certificate and the alteration in the memorandum and articles takes effect accordingly. Such a certificate is to be conclusive evidence that the requirements of s 43 in respect of re-registration and matters precedent and incidental thereto have been complied with.

[17.64] The procedure described in the immediately preceding paragraph is also applicable in the following circumstances:

(1)   where shares in the company are surrendered in lieu of forfeiture;

(2)   where a company acquires its own shares in a manner not permitted by s 41 of the 1983 Act or Part XI of the 1990 Act;

(3)   where a person acquires shares in a company with financial assistance from the company and the company has a beneficial interest in the shares; and

---

[45]   Companies (Forms) Order 1983, SI 289/1983, Form 83.
[46]   Sub-s (8).

(4)   where a nominee of the company acquires the shares from a third party without financial assistance from the company and the company has a beneficial interest in the shares.

[17.65] If in any of these instances the shares (or the company's interest in them) are not disposed of by the company within the period of three years from their surrender or acquisition, they must be cancelled and, if the cancellation brings the nominal value of the allotted share capital below the authorised minimum, there must be an application for re-registration.

Cessation of membership on forfeiture

[17.66] Article 37 provides that a person whose shares have been forfeited ceases to be a member of the company. It should follow from this that he would also cease to be liable for calls, including calls made while he was a member. However, the article goes on to provide that he is to remain liable to pay all moneys which were payable by him to the company at the date of the forfeiture.

Relief against forfeiture

[17.67] Since a court applying principles of equity 'leans against' forfeiture, it will be essential for a company seeking to rely on a forfeiture of shares to be in a position to establish that it has complied strictly with all the relevant requirements of the Articles. Provided, however, those requirements have been met in full, there is no room for the application of the equitable doctrine of relief against forfeiture such as would be available, for example, if a lease of land were being forfeited[47].

[17.68] Article 36 empowers the directors to sell the forfeited shares or otherwise dispose of them on such terms and in such manner as the directors think fit. The share certificate will still be in the possession of the shareholder and since he may not return it to the company upon his shares being forfeited, Article 38 provides that a statutory declaration that the declarant is a director or secretary and that a share in the company has been duly forfeited on a date stated is to be conclusive evidence of the facts therein stated against all persons claiming to be entitled to the shares.

Surrender of shares

[17.69] Shares in a company may be surrendered in order to avoid all the formalities of a forfeiture, provided that the articles authorise such a procedure. They cannot be validly surrendered, however, unless circumstances justifying their forfeiture have arisen. A surrender in any other circumstances would constitute an unlawful reduction of the company's capital[48].

---

47   *Ward v Dublin North City Milling Co* (1919) 1 IR 5.
48   *Bellerby v Rowland & Marwood's SS Co Ltd* [1902] 2 Ch 14.

[17.70] Where a valid surrender of shares in a public limited company brings the allotted share capital below the authorised minimum fixed under s 19 of the 1983 Act, the requirements of s 43 of the same Act which oblige the company to re-register as another form of company in such circumstances, must be complied with.

Lien on shares

General

[17.71] A lien is, in essence, the legal right of a person to keep possession of another's property until a claim he has against that person has been met. A lien can also arise, however, where the claimant is not in possession of the property in question: it is then known as a non-possessory lien.

[17.72] A company has no lien over its shares either for amounts outstanding in respect of the shares themselves or for any other debts owing to the company by the shareholders, unless such a lien is expressly conferred by the articles. In practice the articles invariably confer such a lien, usually described as:

> 'a first and paramount lien on every share (not being a fully paid share) for all moneys (whether immediately payable or not) called or payable at a fixed time in respect of that share ... and a first and paramount lien on all shares (other than fully paid shares) standing in the name of a single person for all moneys immediately payable by him or his estate to the company ...' (Article 11)

[17.73] A lien of this nature is of no practical significance so far as money unpaid on the shares is concerned, since the company will normally have available to it the far more effective remedy of forfeiture. Where it is sought to enforce the lien in respect of other debts owing by the shareholder to the company, questions may arise as to the priority of the lien over other charges to which the shares may be subject. It is clear that the company's lien will be enforceable where it has no notice of such other charges. Where the company has notice, however, the other charges will normally prevail. It is true that under s 123 of the Principal Act no notice of any trust is to be entered on the register or is receivable by the company, but it was decided by the House of Lords in *Bradford Banking Co v Briggs*[49] that this did not mean that the company was entitled to disregard notice of other charges or interests and that they retained their priority. The principle of the decision was applied by the Irish Court of Appeal in *Rearden v Provincial Bank of Ireland*[50].

---

[49] (1886) 12 App Cas 29.
[50] [1896] 1 IR 532, 571.

[17.74] It would appear that the same considerations apply even where the articles provide, as they frequently do, that the company is not to be bound to recognise any equitable claim to or interest in the shares. But where the company has no notice of the equitable interest or charge, it will be able to rely on a clause of this nature. It was held in *New London and Brazilian Bank v Brocklebank*[51] that a person who acquired an equitable interest in shares could not assert his title to the shares and at the same time repudiate the terms upon which the shares were allotted, including such a clause.

[17.75] The lien will normally be enforced by a sale. (See para **[17.76]** below). However, in *G & S Doherty Ltd v Doherty*, (para **[6.19]** above), the lien was enforced by the directors' attaching a term to a new allotment of shares that the amount owed by the shareholder should be paid first. Henchy J seems to have accepted the legitimacy of this procedure.

[17.76] Article 12 provides that the company may enforce a lien conferred by the articles by a sale of the shares. The sale cannot be effected, however, until after the expiration of 14 days after notice in writing has been given to the registered holder demanding payment of the amount then due. To provide for the possibility that the registered holder will not execute a transfer of the shares, article 13 empowers the directors to authorise some person to transfer the shares to the purchaser. The purchaser is not bound to see to the application of the purchase money and his title to the shares is not to be affected by any irregularity in the proceedings in reference to the sale.

Public limited company cannot create charges over its own shares

[17.77] A public limited company is precluded by s 44 of the 1983 Act from creating a lien or other charge over its own shares, except in respect of amounts unpaid on the shares. The section makes void all other charges over its own shares except:

(1)   charges entered into by banking and hire purchase companies in connection with transactions entered into by them in the ordinary course of their business;

(2)   charges which were in existence before the registration or re-registration of the company as a public limited company; and

(3)   charges by a public company which did not apply to be re-registered in the period prescribed by s 12 of the 1983 Act which were in existence during that period.

---

[51] (1882) 21 Ch D 302.

Chapter 18

Transfer and Transmission of Shares

General

[18.01] A share is a chose in action, ie a thing recoverable only by action and not by taking possession of it. The most obvious example of a chose in action is a debt: a person who claims to be owed money by another can only enforce such a claim by recovering judgment for the amount owed and then executing the judgment. By contrast, if he claims to be entitled to land, for example, he can bring proceedings claiming recovery of the land itself. A share is in essence a bundle of rights and duties to which the shareholder is entitled or subject; and the rights, as in the case of a debt, can only be enforced by action against the company.

[18.02] A share, like any other chose in action, can be assigned to a third party. It has, however, one peculiar feature which is of importance when one is considering the requirements for an effective assignment. In order to make the person to whom the share is being assigned the successor to all the rights and duties of the original shareholder, a transfer of the share itself is not enough; the transferee must also be entered on the register as a member of the company. It follows, as Johnston J held in *Tangney v Clarence Hotels Ltd*[1], that the transferee has a legal right to be registered (subject to any restrictions in the articles) which he can enforce against the directors.

[18.03] An assignment of shares can be of two kinds: voluntary or involuntary. A voluntary assignment occurs when the shareholder transfers his shares to another either by way of a sale or gift. An involuntary assignment occurs when the shares are vested in another person because of the insolvency or death of the shareholder. A vesting of the shares on the insolvency or death of the shareholder is usually referred to as a transmission.

Transfer of shares

Transferability of shares

[18.04] It is an essential feature of a share that it is freely transferable, unless the articles provide otherwise. In this it differs, as we have seen, from an interest in a partnership: the succession of one partner by another requires the consent of the

---

[1]   [1933] IR 51.

ongoing partners. But we have also seen that in the case of private company, the right to transfer shares must be restricted by the articles. Such a restriction can take a variety of forms, but the most common are provisions:

(1)   giving the directors a discretion to refuse to register the transfer of a share to a person of whom they do not approve;

(2)   requiring the shareholder to offer any shares which he proposes to sell to the existing shareholders first, ie what is sometimes called a right of pre-emption.

A provision of the first type is to be found in Article 24 and is invariable in private companies in Ireland. A provision of the second type is also extremely common. In both instances, the objective (apart from ensuring that the company is a private company and, accordingly, enjoys the various privileges accorded to such companies) is to preserve the relatively closed nature of the enterprise. In some cases, this will mean confining it to members of the family originally associated with the enterprise or their friends and business connections.

[18.05] Where the directors are given an unqualified discretion as to registering transfers, the courts will not interfere with the exercise of that discretion, provided they exercise it in good faith and for the benefit of the company[2]. As in the case of other such powers conferred on them by the acts or the articles, it is for them, and not the court, to decide what is in he best interests of the company[3]. Sometimes the articles provide that the directors may only decline registration on prescribed grounds, and in that event the court can enquire as to whether they did in fact decline on one of the specified grounds[4]. Thus, in the case of the article which entitles the directors to refuse to register a transfer to any person of whom they do not approve, the court can enquire as to whether the refusal was on grounds personal to the proposed transferee. In one case, it was held that such an article gave no power to the directors to decline registration of a transferee to whom they had no personal objection but who was the nominee of a person of whom they disapproved[5].

[18.06] Frequently, the language used in such a provision enables the directors to refuse registration of a transfer to a person whom they consider it would be undesirable to admit to membership. It was held in *Tangney v Clarence Hotel Ltd*[6] that this did not entitle the directors to refuse registration of a transfer to an existing shareholder. The articles may provide that the directors may refuse

---

[2]   *Re Dublin North City Milling Co* [1909] 1 IR 179; *Re Smith & Fawcett Ltd* [1942] Ch 304.
[3]   See para **[27.80]** below
[4]   *Re Bede Steam Shipping Co Ltd* [1917] 1 Ch 123.
[5]   *Re Bede Steam Shipping Co Ltd* [1917] 1 Ch 123.
[6]   [1933] IR 51.

without assigning any reasons for their refusal. If, however, they elect to give reasons, the court may consider whether they were legitimate or not, ie whether they have applied the correct principles in exercising their discretion[7].

[18.07] As we have just seen, where the articles empower the directors to decline to register a transfer and no grounds are specified on which the refusal to register must be based, their decision will only be set aside on proof of lack of good faith; and the burden of proof rests on the person who alleges bad faith[8]. It is not an easy onus to discharge since the directors may simply decline without specifying reasons; but an example of a case in which the onus was discharged is *Re Hafner, Olhausen v Powderly*[9]. In that case, the plaintiff's uncle left him by his will 500 shares in a private company which carried on a long established and highly regarded business as pork butchers. The personal representatives having transferred the shares to the plaintiff, the directors refused to register the transfers. The articles entitled them to decline to register

'in their absolute and uncontrolled discretion without assigning any reasons.'

The plaintiff claimed that the directors had refused to register the transfers because they had voted themselves excessive remuneration which would have the effect of starving the shareholders of dividends and they realised that, if the plaintiff became a shareholder, he would be in a position to challenge this behaviour. The directors had in fact adamantly refused to give any reasons for their refusal to register the transfers. Black J held that, while the directors were within their legal rights in not giving any reasons, he was also entitled to infer from their refusal that the plaintiff's apprehensions were well founded. It followed that the plaintiff had discharged the onus of proving that the directors were not exercising their discretion in good faith for the benefit of the company as a whole. The Supreme Court on appeal held that he was entitled to come to this conclusion on the evidence.

[18.08] The company must have ready for delivery to the transferee the certificate of any shares transferred within two months after the lodgment of the transfers for registration. This is provided in s 86 of the Principal Act which also provides that if the company fails to issue the certificate within 10 days after the service on it of a notice requiring its issue, it can be directed to do so by the court. Where the directors refuse to register a transfer, the company must notify the transferee of their refusal before the expiration of the two months' period.

---

7   *Re Bell Bros ex parte Hodgson* (1891) 65 LT 245.
8   *Re Dublin North City Milling Co* [1909] 1 IR 179 at 183-4; *Re Smith & Fawcett Ltd* [1942] Ch 304.
9   [1943] IR 426.

[18.09] An article giving a right of pre-emption usually takes the form of a provision that a share shall not be transferred to any person who is not a member of the company so long as any member is willing to buy the share at a fair price[10]. Where the articles contain such a provision, there is no restriction on transfers of shares between members; but should the member wish to sell his shares to an outsider, the pre-emption clause comes into effect. The articles usually provide that the 'fair price' is to be determined in the absence of agreement by the auditor of the company.

[18.10] While the articles must be phrased in clear and unambiguous language in order to give such a right of pre-emption to the existing shareholders, the courts will not allow the obvious purpose of such a provision to be defeated by too literal a construction of the articles. This was made clear by the House of Lords in *Lyle & Scott Ltd v Scotts' Trustees*[11], where the articles provided that the existing shareholders were entitled to a right of pre-emption where any of their number was 'desirous of transferring his ordinary shares'. A takeover bid was made for the company and the shareholders who were in favour of accepting the offer were paid the full price without executing any transfers of the shares. They gave the purchaser irrevocable proxies to vote on their behalf, thus avoiding any necessity for the purchaser to be registered as a shareholder. When the transaction was challenged on behalf of the company, the shareholders in question argued that it was not invalidated by the articles: they were not obliged to offer the shares to the other shareholders, since they were no longer 'desirous' of transferring their shares, they having been paid their money and the purchaser being in effective control. Not surprisingly, this bold argument was rejected, the House of Lords holding that it was not open to shareholders who had agreed to transfer shares and had been paid for them to contend that they were not 'desirous' of transferring their shares.

[18.11] It has been held in England that the right of pre-emption may be defeated by a mortgage of the shares or even by an outright sale, since the mortgagee or transferee will be entitled to the beneficial or equitable interest; see *Safeguard Industrial Investments Ltd v National Westminster Bank Ltd*[12] and *Hawks v McArthur*[13]. As to the readiness of the Courts to uphold pre-emption

---

[10] For an example of such a clause see *Lee & Co (Dublin) Ltd v Egan (Wholesale) Ltd* (unreported, 24 April 1978) where Kenny J ordered the procedure to be complied with. See also *McCauliffe v Lithographic Group Ltd* (unreported, 2 November 1993).
[11] [1959] AC 763.
[12] [1982] 1 All ER 449.
[13] [1951] 1 All ER 22.

agreements, see *Re Champion Publications Ltd*[14] and *Tett v Phoenix Property and Investment Co Ltd*[15].

[18.12] It was said by Denning LJ in *Dean v Prince*[16] that the auditor of the company in determining the fair price of the shares for the purpose of a pre-emption clause is acting as an expert and not as an arbitrator. The practical consequence is that he may be liable to a party who suffers loss as a result of a negligent valuation carried out by him. While *Dean v Prince* is accepted in both England and Ireland as correctly stating the law, it is usual to provide expressly in articles that the auditor in carrying out such a valuation shall be deemed to be acting as an expert and not as an arbitrator.

Form of transfer

[18.13] At one time, the formalities for transferring shares were regulated by the articles. Since the Stock Transfer Act 1963, however, the procedure has been simplified in the case of fully paid shares. They can now be validly transferred by an instrument under hand in the form set out in Schedule I of the Act. In the case of unpaid shares, the mode of transfer is still in theory regulated by the articles; but these usually require no more than that the transfer should be in 'the usual or common form'. It is thought that in the case of partly paid shares this requirement would be met by a transfer complying with the Stock Transfer Act 1963.

[18.14] Section 81 of the Principal Act provides that, notwithstanding anything in the articles of a company, it shall not be lawful for the company to register a transfer of shares or debentures unless a proper instrument of transfer has been delivered to the company. This ensures that the stamp duty payable on the transfer is not avoided by the company's dispensing with a transfer when the parties have agreed to the transfer and the price has been paid. In the case of a fully paid share, this requirement is met by an instrument which complies with the Stock Transfer Act 1963; and, as has been pointed out above, such an instrument will also usually be sufficient in the case of a partly paid up share.

[18.15] It should be noted that in the case of fully paid shares the transfer need not specify the name of the transferee, having regard to the provisions of the Stock Transfer Act 1963. It is thought, however, that in a case to which the Act does not apply, eg a partly paid share, the name of the transferee must still be specified to render the instrument a 'proper instrument of transfer' for the purpose of s 81 of the Principal Act.

---

[14] (Unreported, 4 June 1991), HC (Blaney J).
[15] (1986) BCLC 149.
[16] [1954] Ch 409 at 426.

Certification of transfers

[18.16] We have seen that it is an essential feature of a transfer of shares that the transferee should become registered as a shareholder in succession to the transferor. No difficulty arises where the transferor is parting with all his shares in the company: on completion of the transaction, he hands over his share certificate to the transferee who can thereupon be registered. Where, however, the transferor is retaining some of his shares or where he is selling the shares to a number of transferees, such a course is not practicable. In such circumstances the appropriate procedure is for the company to certificate the transfer of shares. The company should not do this unless the transferor lodges the certificate with the company. Where the company certificates the transfer of shares, s 85 of the Principal Act provides that the certification shall be taken as a representation by the company to any person acting on the faith of the certification that there have been produced to the company such documents as on the face of them show a *prima facie* title to the shares in the transferor.

Capacity to transfer

[18.17] A minor is capable of transferring his shares in the company. In the case of a person of unsound mind so found, the transfer must be authorised by the President of the High Court.

Transmission of shares

Death of shareholder

[18.18] Where a shareholder dies, his shares in common with his other property vest in his personal representatives, ie his executors or administrators. This takes place automatically by operation of law: no transfer will have been executed in favour of the personal representative. We have seen that the company cannot in general register a transfer of shares unless a proper instrument of transfer has been delivered to the company. This does not mean, however, that the personal representative cannot be registered as a member: s 81(2) of the Principal Act provides that the company may have power to register as shareholder or debenture holder any person to whom the right to any shares in or debentures of the company has been transmitted by operation of law.

[18.19] The articles usually contain a provision (Article 30) enabling the personal representative to elect either to be registered himself as shareholder or to have his nominee registered as shareholder. Where he elects to be registered himself, he must notify the company in writing to that effect. Where he elects to have his nominee registered, he must execute a transfer to the nominee. Any restrictions imposed by the articles on the transfer of the shares, such as a power vested in the directors to refuse to register a transfer or a right of pre-emption given to the other shareholders, are usually made applicable to such a notice of transfer (Article 31). The article also usually enables the directors to require the personal representative to elect either to be registered himself or transfer the shares within 90 days and, until he so elects, to withhold the payment of dividends, bonuses or other moneys payable in respect of the shares (Article 32).

[18.20] Although the company can, accordingly, register a personal representative as a member, he cannot be placed upon the register without his consent. If he is lawfully registered as a member, he may become personally liable for the amounts unpaid (if any) on the shares. Section 82, however, enables the personal representative to transfer the shares before he is registered as a member of the company. Moreover, s 87 provides that the production of the grant of probate or letters of administration must be accepted by the company as sufficient evidence of the personal representative's title. The appropriate procedure for a personal representative to adopt who does not wish to be registered as a member is to transfer the shares to the persons beneficially entitled or to sell them in exercise of his powers as personal representative.

Bankruptcy of shareholder

[18.21] As in the case of the death of the shareholder, so also on his bankruptcy there may be a transmission of shares by operation of law, in this case to the official assignee in bankruptcy. Section 44(1) of the Bankruptcy Act 1988 provides that on his being adjudicated a bankrupt, all the bankrupt's property vests in the official assignee. Articles 30, 31 and 32 referred to above apply to a vesting of shares in the official assignee in the same manner as in the case of a transmission on death.

[18.22] If the shares are onerous, the official assignee may, with the leave of the court, within 12 months of the vesting of the shares in him, disclaim the shares[17]. Such a disclaimer does not affect the rights of any third parties in respect of the shares: it simply relieves the estate of the bankrupt from the obligations of membership, such as the liability to pay uncalled capital.

---

[17] Bankruptcy Act 1988, s 56(1).

Part V
Borrowing by the Company

Chapter 19

Borrowing Powers of Companies

General

[19.01] The memorandum almost invariably authorises the company to borrow money. But even where such a power is not given in express terms, the company may still be entitled to borrow, if the borrowing can fairly be regarded as incidental to the objects of the company[1]. In the case of non-trading companies, however, it will only be implied if there is something in the memorandum or articles to indicate, either expressly or by implication, that it was intended to give such a power[2]. If the memorandum or articles do not confer such a power, either expressly or by implication, they can be altered by special resolution to provide the company with the necessary powers[3].

[19.02] If the memorandum or articles restrict the amount which the company may borrow, such a limitation must be observed or the necessary amendment effected. It is, however, most unusual for a modern memorandum or articles to contain such a restriction. In the case of a public unlimited company, the borrowing powers cannot be exercised until a certificate has been issued by the Registrar under s 115 of the Principal Act[4]; and in the case of a public limited company, until a certificate has been issued by him under s 6 of the 1983 Act[5].

Security for borrowing

[19.03] A company has, as incidental to a power of borrowing, the power to give such security as is necessary for the purpose of obtaining the required advance[6]. In the case of a company which has borrowing powers, accordingly, it is not necessary to confer such a power in express terms, but again it is usual to do so. Such a power includes a power to mortgage the uncalled capital of the company[7].

---

[1] See para **[5.28]** above.
[2] *R v Reed* (1880) 5 QBD 483 at 488, 489.
[3] See paras **[5.35]** and **[6.14]** above.
[4] See paras **[10.07]** and **[10.08]** above.
[5] See para **[10.07]** above.
[6] *Australian, etc, Company v Mounsey* (1858) 4 K & J 733.
[7] *Re Phoenix Bessemer Co* (1876) 4 CH D 108.

[19.04] The advance may be secured by a mortgage of the company's real or leasehold property, which can be either legal or equitable. In the former case, the mortgage will be by deed, in the latter by deposit of title deeds. Or it may be secured by an issue of debentures or debenture stock, secured in turn by a floating charge over the company's assets and undertaking or a fixed charge or both. The nature of debentures and the meaning of a floating charge are fully discussed in the following chapter.

Ultra vires borrowing

[19.05] If the company borrows money without having power to do so, the transaction is *ultra vires* and void. Where, however, the borrower can show that he was not aware that the transaction was *ultra vires* the company, it may be enforceable by him against the company. This modification of the *ultra vires* rule has been fully discussed in Chapter 12.

Chapter 20

Debentures and Floating Charges

[20.01] The simplest definition of a debenture is that it is a document which provides evidence of a debt. In practice, however, for businessmen, lawyers and accountants it has assumed a more complex significance. It is now normally taken as meaning an instrument by which a company acknowledges its indebtedness and which is secured by a charge on the company's assets and/or undertaking. The charge can be either a fixed or specific charge of a particular asset - eg a mortgage of land - or a 'floating' charge over the assets and undertakings which is not attached to any specific asset.

[20.02] A debenture can be either one instrument standing by itself and entered into between the company and a single lender or it can be one of a series of similar instruments issued to a number of lenders. The person to whom the debenture is issued - the debenture holder - does not become a member of the company and therefore is legally in a category distinct from a shareholder. He might be regarded as being in a position inferior to the shareholder in that he cannot attend meetings of the company or vote or inspect the company's accounts. He is in a position superior to the shareholder, however, in that he has the right to payment of a fixed rate of interest on his investment which is payable irrespective of whether the company has made profits or not. In addition, where the debenture is secured by a charge, he has a direct interest in the company's assets which a shareholder has not.

[20.03] When a company issues debentures to the public, it can do so by issuing a series of debentures in identical terms but for different amounts to individual lenders. In practice, however, it is more common to issue debenture stock. Where this is done, the company creates a loan fund and issues stock certificates to each of the debenture holders stating the share of the fund to which he is entitled. The advantage of so doing is that the debenture holder can then sell as much of his investment as he pleases, whereas otherwise he would have to sell the whole debenture or nothing at all. The debenture stock certificate will declare him entitled to, for example, £500 debenture stock divided into £1 units. He may then transfer, say, 100 stock units and go through the same process of transfer and certification as if he were selling 100 £1 shares in the company[1].

---

[1] See para **[18.16]** above

[20.04] Where a debenture is secured by a charge on specific property of the company, the charge thus created has the characteristics of an ordinary mortgage of property, with one important exception. It is a fundamental principle of the law applicable to mortgages generally that the person whose property is mortgaged must have the right to get it back upon repayment of the advance, and whatever interest is due, either at any time or at a specified time. This right of the mortgagor - the 'equity of redemption' - may not be curtailed: there cannot be a 'clog' upon the equity of redemption, as the courts of equity put it. In the case of a debenture, however, it may be redeemable at a fixed time or at the option of the company; or it may be irredeemable. The creation of irredeemable debentures - or 'perpetual debentures' as they are sometimes called - is expressly authorised by s 94 of the Principal Act. This provides that a condition in a debenture or any deed securing a debenture is not to be invalid by reason only that the debentures are thereby made irredeemable or redeemable only on the happening of a contingency, however remote, or on the expiration of a period, however long.

[20.05] Where a debenture is secured by a fixed or floating charge, and the borrower defaults, the lender has the normal remedies available to a mortgagee including an order for sale. Usually, however, the first remedy invoked by a debenture holder in the event of a default is the appointment of a receiver, who takes possession of the company's assets and normally has power to sell them.

[20.06] Debentures issued by public companies are not unknown in Ireland and, in addition, semi-state bodies, such as the ESB, from time to time make issues of 'loan stock' which in its essential features is not very different from debenture stock. But by far the most common form of debenture in Ireland is the single debenture secured by a floating charge (and frequently by a fixed charge as well) issued by a private company to a bank or other lending institution to obtain the finance necessary for the company's operations which cannot be provided by the promoters.

Debenture stock

[20.07] Where debenture stock is issued by a company, it is usual for a trust deed to be executed by the company. When trustees are appointed, the company covenants with the trustees (who are expressly appointed to represent the interests of the debenture holders) to pay the capital sum secured by the debenture either at a fixed date or in the event of a particular contingency, such as the winding up of the company, and to pay the agreed interest on the advance. The deed usually provides for the securing of the repayment of the capital by a fixed and floating charge.

[20.08] The trustees are expected to protect the interest of the debenture holders. To that end, s 93 of the Principal Act provides that any provision in the trust deed or any contract with the debenture holders secured by such a deed which relieves the trustees of liability for breach of trust where they fail to show the 'degree of care and diligence' required of them as trustees is to be void.

Series of debentures

[20.09] Where a series of debentures is issued by the company, they incorporate standard conditions endorsed on the back of each debenture. One of the standard conditions provides that each debenture is to rank *pari passu*, ie on an equal footing, in point of time, without priority or preference one over another. This is necessary because all the debentures are not issued at the same time and it would affect their marketability as securities if one debenture holder were to secure priority over another simply by the accident of his debenture being issued first.

[20.10] The 'pari passu' condition referred to in the preceding paragraph also incorporates a prohibition on the company's creating any mortgage or charge on its assets so as to rank *pari passu* with the series of debentures. There is generally an exception for specific charges for securing temporary loans or bank overdrafts in the ordinary course of business. The standard conditions also include provisions for the immediate repayment of the monies advanced in the following circumstances:

(1)   if the company makes default in the payment of interest for a period of six months and the debenture holder calls in the principal;

(2)   if a winding up order is made or a valid winding up resolution passed;

(3)   if a distress or execution is levied against any of the chattels or property of the company and not discharged within five days;

(4)   if a receiver is appointed over the undertaking and/or assets of the company; or

(5)   if the company ceases or threatens to cease to carry on business.

Similar conditions are also invariably included in a single debenture. In addition, the conditions endorsed on a series of debentures include provisions requiring a register of debenture holders to be kept by the company and enabling the company to regard the registered debenture holders as entitled to the benefit of the debenture to the exclusion of persons equitably entitled.

Transferability of debentures

[20.11] A debenture is transferable in the manner provided by the debenture itself. Section 81 of the Principal Act is applicable, however, and the company accordingly may not register a transfer of debentures unless a proper instrument of transfer has been delivered to the company. But it is possible to issue bearer debentures which can be transferred by delivery in the same manner as share warrants[2]. Such bearer debentures are in law negotiable instruments.

[20.12] The transferee of a debenture takes it subject to the same equitable rights of the company as the debenture holder, even where he acquired the interest of the debenture holder in good faith for valuable consideration and without notice of any such equitable rights. However, in the case of a series of debentures the standard conditions usually provide that the capital and interest are to be payable by the company without regard to any such equities.

Requirements as to prospectus, allotment, etc in the case of debentures

[20.13] The requirements of the Acts in the case of public companies as to the prospectus or statement in lieu thereof are generally speaking the same in the case of debentures as in the case of shares. Similarly, where the debentures are listed on a stock exchange, the regulations of that exchange will be applicable.

Convertible debentures

[20.14] A company may issue convertible debentures, ie debentures which may be converted into shares in the company at a stated rate of exchange.

Remedies of debenture holders

[20.15] Where there is a default in the payment of capital or interest by the company, the debenture holder may in every case bring proceedings for the recovery of the money which he is owed and prosecute them to judgment and execution in the ordinary way. He may also petition for the winding up of the company in such circumstances. Indeed where the debenture is unsecured - an extremely rare circumstance in Ireland today - these are his only remedies.

[20.16] Where, however, the debenture is secured by a fixed charge, a floating charge or both, the debenture holder has a remedy which is frequently more attractive to him and, in many instances, the company itself. This is the appointment of a *receiver*. He can be appointed either by the debenture holder in exercise of a power granted for that purpose by the debenture or by the court on the application of the debenture holder. On his appointment the powers of the company and the directors' authority in relation to the property charged are suspended and may only be exercised with the consent of the receiver. Moreover,

---

[2]   See para **[17.36]** above.

since he is usually appointed as a manager in addition to being a receiver, he can conduct the business of the company for as long as he deems appropriate in the interests of the debenture holder.

Action by individual debenture holders where series issued

[20.17] Where a series of debentures is issued, an individual debenture holder can bring an action to enforce his debenture against the company. Such an action can be grounded either on an actual default by the company or on the fact that the company is in jeopardy. The debenture holder brings the proceedings on behalf of all the debenture holders[3] and the terms of the debenture usually require him to obtain the consent of a specified majority of his fellow debenture holders before proceedings are issued. Normally, the first step taken in such an action is the appointment of a receiver. Where a number of different actions are brought by the debenture holders, the court has power to consolidate them[4].

Proof by debenture holders in winding up

[20.18] A debenture holder who wants to prove for his debt in the winding up of an insolvent company may either realise his security or value it and in either case prove for the balance. For the purpose of ascertaining the balance for which he can prove, the debenture holder must apply the proceeds of his security in the payment of interest accrued due up to the commencement of the winding up. He may then prove as an unsecured creditor for the balance of the principal and interest due at the commencement of the winding up after deducting the amount realised from the security[5].

Floating charges in general

[20.19] A floating charge is a form of charge particularly associated with companies. The conventional *fixed* or *specific* charge invariably involves the vesting of the legal interest in the property in the lender at the time of the transaction. Thereupon the lender has all the usual remedies in the event of the borrower's default, such as sale, possession, a receiver, etc. The charge, in other words, attaches immediately to the specific property being offered as security.

[20.20] By contrast the floating charge does not attach to any specific asset at the time of its creation. There is no vesting of the legal estate in any property at that point: the charge floats above the entire assembly of assets to which it relates and which frequently consists of all the assets and undertaking of the

---

[3] Rules of the Superior Courts, Ord 15, r 9
[4] Rules of the Superior Courts, Ord 49, r 6.
[5] See para **[36.144]** below.

company. It does not descend, as it were, and attach itself to any specific asset until certain specified events occur. At that stage, the floating charge is said to crystallise.

[20.21] Floating charges became a popular form of security with joint stock companies at an early stage[6]. Such companies often wished to raise finance on the strength of assets other than real or leasehold property, such as their stock-in-trade, book debts, etc. It was difficult, however, to create fixed charges over such items, since they were constantly being disposed of in the course of the company's business, and it might have been necessary in theory to create a fresh security every time a new item was acquired by the company while releasing the charge on those which were being disposed of. The floating charge, which enabled the borrower to go on using the charged assets in the ordinary course of his business, provided a solution to this problem.

[20.22] Floating charges also created their own problems. Precisely because they were attached to no specific asset and were usually taken by banks and similar institutions to secure both present and future borrowing, it was peculiarly difficult for an unsecured creditor of the company to estimate the availability of assets to meet the debt owing to him by the company. If the company was wound up, such a creditor could find that all the assets had been captured by a floating charge. Quite often such charges were created by the company in the knowledge that the company was in serious financial straits and in response to pressure from one of its creditors. Sometimes directors of the company, who would be in the best position to know that the company was tottering, tried to protect their own position by taking floating charges to secure advances previously made by them.

[20.23] To deal with such problems, the 1908 Act provided that such charges were to be invalid if created within three months from the commencement of the winding up except in relation to any money paid to the company at the time of or subsequently to the creation of the charge, together with interest thereon. Cox recommended the extension of the period to 12 months in the case of a floating charge in favour of a director and six months in any other case. In the event, the draftsman of the Principal Act provided that the charge was to be invalid if made within the 12 months' period, without distinguishing between charges in favour of directors and others, thus following the example of the English 1948 Act. Section 288 as originally enacted provides that a floating charge created within 12 months before the winding up shall, unless it is proved that the company

---

[6] Their validity was first recognised in *Re Panama, New Zealand and Australian Royal Mail Co* (1870) 5 Ch 318. It should be remembered, incidentally, that while they are normally created by companies rather than individuals, there is nothing to prevent an individual creating one: see Gough, *Company Charges* Part II.

immediately after the creation of the charge was solvent, be invalid, except to the amount of any cash paid to the company at the time of or subsequently to the charge, together with interest at the rate of 5% per annum[7]. It was amended by s 136 of the 1990 Act so as to provide that in the case of a charge in favour of a director, a 'connected person', or a 'related company'[8] the period is two years.

[20.24] The Principal Act also provides that a receiver appointed under a floating charge must pay preferential creditors (such as the Revenue) out of assets coming into his hands before paying over any sums due to the holder of the charge[9].

[20.25] In *United Bars v Revenue Commissioners*[10] where assets were subject to both fixed and floating charges and the receiver was left with a surplus after the sale of some of the assets, Murphy J held that s 98 did not apply and that the surplus was payable to the company and not to the Revenue Commissioners as preferential creditors[11].

[20.26] It should also be noted that this provision does not apply where the company is in liquidation. However, in *Re Eisc Teo*[12], a company went into liquidation after a receiver had received a surplus from the sale of assets subject to a floating charge. It was held by Lardner J that the receiver could not be required to pay them over to the liquidator: he remained under a statutory duty, notwithstanding the commencement of the winding up, to apply the surplus first in payment of the preferential creditors.

[20.27] Where a receiver is appointed under a floating charge, it is frequently the case that the property is already subject to a fixed charge. In that event, the floating charge, which usually crystallises only upon the receiver's appointment, must yield priority to the fixed charge and, as a result, the receiver will be unable to sell the property without the consent and co-operation of the holder of the fixed charge.

[20.28] It may accordingly be important to ascertain whether a particular charge is properly described as a 'floating charge'. It was defined as follows by Lord Macnaghten in *Illingworth v Houldsworth*[13]:

---

[7]   See para **[20.69]** below.
[8]   For the meaning of 'connected person', see para **[27.57]** below. In this context, it also includes 'shadow directors', as to which see para **[27.05]**.
[9]   Companies Act 1963, s 98.
[10] [1991] 1 IR 396.
[11] Following the English decisions of *Re GL Saunders Ltd* (1986) BCLC and *Re Lewis* [1939] 1 Ch 232.
[12] [1991] ILRM 760.
[13] [1904] AC 355 at 358.

'I should have thought there was not much difficulty in defining what a floating charge is in contrast to what is called a specific charge. A specific charge, I think, is one that without more fastens on ascertained and definite property or property capable of being ascertained and defined; a floating charge, on the other hand, is ambulatory and shifting in its nature, hovering over and so to speak floating with the property which it is intended to affect until some event occurs or some act is done which causes it to settle and fasten on the subject of the charge within its grasp and reach.'

[20.29] In another frequently quoted passage, Romer LJ in *Re Yorkshire Woolcombers' Association*[14] said that if a floating charge had three characteristics, it was a floating charge, viz:

'(1) If it is a charge on a class of assets of a company present and future;

(2) if that class is one which, in the ordinary course of the business of the company, would be changing from time to time; and

(3) if you find that by the charge it is contemplated that, until some future step is taken by or on behalf of those interested in the charge, the company may carry on its business in the ordinary way so far as concerns the particular class of assets I am dealing with.'[15]

[20.30] It is important to note, however, that Romer LJ also made it clear that a charge could still be a floating charge without having all three of these characteristics. An interesting example is afforded by the Supreme Court decision in *Welch v Bowmaker (Ireland) Ltd and the Bank of Ireland*[16].

In that case the company had issued a debenture in favour of the first defendant, clause 3 of which charged the undertaking and assets of the company, present and future, with the payment of moneys owed to that defendant and also charged 'as a specific charge' the lands 'specified in the schedule hereto'. The schedule described three of the four parcels of land owned by the company. The first condition endorsed on the debenture stated that the charge thereby effected was to be 'as regards the company's lands and premises for the time being' a specific charge and as regards the other assets of the company a floating charge and stated that the company was not at liberty to create any mortgage or charge on its property for the time being in priority to the debenture.

One month after the execution of the debenture, the company deposited with the defendant bank the title deeds of the fourth parcel of land by way of equitable mortgage to secure the repayment of moneys owed by the company to the bank. At the time of the deposit, the bank was aware of the existence of the debenture

---

[14] [1903] 2 Ch 284 at 295. *Illingworth v Houldsworth* [1904] AC 355 is in fact the same case, as decided on appeal in the House of Lords.

[15] Cited by Costello J in *Re Lakeglen Construction Co Ltd* [1980] IR 347.

[16] [1980] IR 251.

but not of its terms. The company became insolvent and its assets were insufficient to pay both defendants. In the course of the winding up of the company, the first defendant claimed that a specific charge had been created over the fourth parcel which took priority over the bank's equitable mortgage. The bank claimed that a floating charge only had been created over which its mortgage took priority. The floating charge, if it were one, did not crystallise until the commencement of the winding up and consequently would be postponed to any legal or equitable mortgage created before the winding up. The High Court upheld the first defendant's claim, but the Supreme Court (Henchy and Parke JJ, Kenny J *dissentiente*) allowed the bank's appeal, holding that the terms of the first condition endorsed on the debenture when read with clause 3 made it clear that the intention of the parties was to create a floating charge only. It seems a reasonable inference from the judgments that the majority, although accepting that the asset in dispute was not of a class which in the ordinary course of business would change from time to time, did not consider that fact sufficient to prevent the charge from being a floating charge.

[20.31] There has been considerable discussion as to whether the floating charge is a form of security which takes immediate effect but allows the borrower to continue using the assets captured by it until crystallisation; or whether it is a mortgage of future assets which is of no legal effect until crystallisation. In *Evans v Rival Granite Quarries Ltd*[17], Buckley J said emphatically that it was 'a present security which immediately affects all the assets expressed to be included in it' and his view was adopted by Blayney J in *Re Tullow Engineering (Holdings) Ltd*[18]. It has been pointed out that this is also consistent with the requirement of registration under s 99(1) of the Principal Act[19].

[20.32] It was clear from an early stage that there was no difficulty in creating a floating charge over the book debts of the company. The subject matter presented the three characteristics referred to by Romer LJ, and even prior to his judgment in the *Yorkshire Woolcombers' Case*, it had been held by the House of Lords in *Tailby v Official Receiver*[20] that a floating charge could be created over book debts, even though the debts had not yet come into existence.

[20.33] A fixed charge over book debts had, of course, the attraction for the lender that it would retain its validity even if the winding up took place within 12 months and would not be postponed to any preferential debts. Lending institutions were naturally attracted to schemes under which charges over book

---

[17] [1910] 2 KB 976 at 999.

[18] [1990] 1 IR 452.

[19] Courtney, *The Law of Private Companies*, para 124.044. For a different view, see Gough, *Company Charges*, pp 135-7.

[20] (1883) 13 App Cas 523.

debts combined the advantages of both the fixed and the floating charge. It was sought to achieve this by allowing the borrower to continue collecting the book debts but requiring him to keep the proceeds in a special bank account which would then be frozen at a particular level. The validity of such devices was upheld in England by Slade J in *Siebe Gorman v Barclays Bank Ltd*[21] and their efficacy in Ireland was established in *Re Keenan Brothers Ltd*[22] in which the Supreme Court reversed the decision of Keane J in which he declined to follow the English authority.

[20.34] It appears not to have been generally appreciated that the decisions in both *Siebe Gorman Ltd* and *Re Keenan Brothers Ltd* turned on the specific wording of the debentures in each case. The consequences that might flow from a looser form of wording first became apparent in England in *Re Brightlife Ltd*[23]. In that case, Hoffman J held that a charge over book debts described as a 'first specific charge' was a floating charge, although the borrower was precluded from selling, factoring or discounting the debts without the lender's permission. The absence of a restriction in the *Siebe Gorman* form requiring the proceeds to be paid into a special bank account under the control of the lender was fatal to the lender's contention that it was a fixed charge. Although in *Re AH Masser Ltd*[24], Barron J did not consider the absence of the clause prohibiting withdrawals from the account to be crucial, it soon became apparent that any deviation from the formula employed in *Siebe Gorman* and *Re Keenan Brothers Ltd* could be fatal to the contention that the charge was a fixed charge.

[20.35] In *Re Wogan's (Drogheda) Ltd*[25], the next case in which the matter came before the Supreme Court, the vital clause, prohibiting as it did any withdrawal of monies from the account specified by the lender into which the monies collected were to be paid, without the consent of the lender, was sufficient to justify the categorisation of the charge as a fixed charge. The court rejected the proposition, which had found favour in the High Court, that the court was entitled to infer that the charge was intended to be a floating charge rather than a fixed charge from the fact that, subsequent to the execution of the debenture, no account had been specified by the lender into which the proceeds of the collection of the book debts was to be paid. This, it was said, was not an admissible guide to the interpretation of the debenture.

---

[21] [1977] 2 Lloyds Rep 142.
[22] [1985] IR 401.
[23] [1986] 3 All ER 673.
[24] [1986] IR 445.
[25] [1993] 1 IR 157.

[20.36] However, in *Re Holidair Ltd*[26], the relevant clause in the debenture, while it required the payment of the proceeds of the collection of the book debts into an account selected by the debenture holder, did not specifically prohibit any withdrawals by the company from the account in question. It was held by the Supreme Court, reversing the High Court, that, as a result, the charge was a floating charge and not a specific charge, since the company could continue to use the proceeds in the normal way for the carrying on of their business.

[20.37] In contrast, in England the Court of Appeal in *Re New Bullas Trading Ltd*[27] held that where a debenture created what was described as a fixed charge over its book debts, but allowed the company to deal with the monies standing in the account as it wished, in the absence of any direction by the lender as to how they were to be applied, the charge created remained a fixed charge. This decision, which has been severely criticised[28], was not seen to take into account what was emphasised by the Supreme Court in *Re Holidair Ltd*, ie that where the lender remains at liberty to use the proceeds of the collection of the book debts, the charge is in law a floating charge, however the parties may have chosen to describe it.

[20.38] On any view it would seem prudent for banks and other lending bodies relying on the device to adhere as closely as possibly to the form of charge actually employed in *Re Keenan Brothers Ltd*. In particular it should be noted that the fact that the charge is described as a 'fixed charge' will not be conclusive: this was the view taken by Hutton J in the Northern Ireland case of *Re Armagh Shoes Ltd*[29] and Keane J at first instance in *Re Keenan Brothers Ltd* and subsequently upheld by the Supreme Court in *Re Holidair Ltd*. Whether the charge is a fixed charge or a floating charge must be determined by considering the charge as a whole.

[20.39] As is frequently the case, the unsecured creditors who were defeated by the banks' claim in *Re Keenan Brothers Ltd* were the Revenue Commissioners: there would in any event have been nothing for the unsecured creditors. But since the enactment of s 115 of the Finance Act 1996, a fixed charge of this nature over book debts enjoys no priority over revenue debts.

Effect of a floating charge

[20.40] A floating charge usually takes the form of a charge by the company over:

---

[26] [1994] 1 IR 434.
[27] (1994) BCC 36.
[28] Goode, *Charges over Book Debts; A Missed Opportunity* 110 LQR 592
[29] [1982] NI 59.

'its undertaking, and all its property, present and future, including its uncalled capital for the time being.'

This will capture all the assets of the company, both in its ownership at the time of the debenture and which it subsequently acquires. It is, however, not necessary that the charge should extend so far: it may be confined to a class of assets, such as book debts[30].

[20.41] It is a usual feature of a floating charge that the company remains free to deal with its property in the ordinary course of business, despite the existence of the charge, until the charge crystallises. In particular, it may sell, let, mortgage, or otherwise deal with its assets and may pay dividends out of profits as if a floating charge had not been created.

[20.42] Thus, in the absence of any express prohibition in the debenture, the company may create legal and equitable mortgages prior to the crystallisation of the floating charge and, if created, they will have priority over the floating charge[31]. This is the case even though the mortgagees have notice of the existence of the floating charged[32]. As we shall see, however, it is standard practice to provide for such a prohibition[33].

[20.43] But although in the absence of such a prohibition, there is nothing to prevent the company from creating legal and equitable mortgages, it cannot create a second or subsequent floating charges to rank in priority to or *pari passu* with the existing floating charge. Such a charge would require to be authorised by the debenture[34].

[20.44] Debts, as we have seen, are among the assets which can be the subject of a floating charge. But the debenture holder cannot be in any better position in regard to such debts than the company. He becomes entitled to them, accordingly, subject to any right of set off which may arise because of debts incurred by the company in the course of its trading.

[20.45] Such a right to set off can only be exercised, however, where there is 'mutuality'. If the debts which it is sought to set off are acquired by assignment after the creation of the floating charge, there is no such mutuality and the debts cannot be set off. This was so decided by Budd J in *Lynch v Ardmore Studios*[35], following the decision of the Court of Appeal in *NW Robbie and Co Ltd v Witney Warehouse Ltd*[36].

---

[30] In *Re Yorkshire Woolcomber's Association* [1903] 2 Ch 284.
[31] *Re Florence Land Co* (1878) 10 Ch D 530; *Re Colonial Trusts Ltd* (1880) 15 Ch D 465.
[32] *Wheatley v Silkstone Co* (1885) 29 Ch 3 715.
[33] See para **[20.46]** below.
[34] *Re Benjamin Cope & Sons* [1914] 1 Ch 800; *Re Automatic Bottle Makers Ltd* [1926] Ch 412.
[35] [1966] IR 133.
[36] [1963] 3 All ER 613.

[20.46] The flexibility of the floating charge was a source of concern to lending bodies who saw their security in danger of losing its priority to a fixed mortgage created after the floating charge. It has accordingly become standard practice to insert a condition prohibiting the company from creating any mortgage or charge ranking in priority to or *pari passu* with the floating charge. Such a prohibition will be effective, unless the subsequent mortgagee can show that he was not aware of the prohibition in the floating charge.

[20.47] It is also clear, however, that even if a subsequent mortgagee can be fixed with notice of the existence of the floating charge - as he generally can be because of the requirement that the floating charge be registered[37] - he may still be entitled to priority, since he will usually be able to show that he was not aware of the prohibition. This is clear from a succession of authorities which were considered and approved by the Supreme Court in *Welch v Bowmaker (Ireland) Ltd* (above). In that case the argument on behalf of the debenture holder was that such prohibitions were common form in modern debentures and that the subsequent mortgagee should be fixed with constructive (as distinct from actual) notice of the prohibition. The doctrine of constructive notice means that a person may be deemed in law to be aware of matters of which he does not know but would have known had he made certain inquiries. Henchy J and Parke J both took the view, however, that the principle referred to was so well settled in law as to be incapable of alteration except by legislation. Parke J warned against the danger of extending the doctrine of constructive notice too far, saying

'the doctrine may be an unruly horse and should be ridden with a firm hand.'[38]

[20.48] As we shall see in Chapter 38, certain debts are given a degree of preference in the event of the company's being wound up. Thus the Revenue are entitled to one year's taxes in arrears in priority to the ordinary creditors. A person entitled to a floating charge may rely on his security and not prove for his debt in the event of a winding up, but the preferential creditors will still have to be paid in priority to the debt secured by the floating charge[39]. Similarly, where the charge crystallises by the appointment of a receiver before a winding up, the receiver must pay the preferential creditors out of the assets coming into his hands before paying any sums due for principal or interest to the person entitled to the charge[40].

[20.49] When a floating charge crystallises - by the appointment of a receiver, for example - there is an equitable assignment of the company's interest in the

---

[37] Under the Companies Act 1963, s 99.
[38] [1980] IR 251 at 262.
[39] Companies Act 1963, s 285(7)(h).
[40] See para **[20.24]** above.

property to the person entitled to the floating charge. This does not have the same consequences as a sale of the property, a distinction made clear by Kenny J in *Re Interview Ltd*[41]. This may be of considerable importance in determining the rights of parties to a hire purchase agreement or agreements of a similar nature, where the goods are in the possession of a company in receivership. In the case of such agreements, the goods remain the property of the hire purchase company throughout the currency of the agreement. If a receiver is appointed by the person entitled to the floating charge, the latter does not acquire the interest of the hire purchase company since there has been no sale to him. It follows that the hire purchase company (or supplier of the goods under a similar transaction) will be entitled to retain possession of the goods as against the receiver unless the sums owing in respect of the goods are paid by the receiver. It is also clear that this result will follow whether or not the hire purchase agreement was executed subsequent to the floating charge[42].

[20.50] Where an unsecured creditor recovers judgment against the company but has not executed the judgment, the floating charge will have priority[43]. Where, however, the creditor completely executes the judgment by a seizure or sale of the company's property before the charge crystallises, the floating charge loses its priority[44]. Similarly a landlord can distrain for rent before the appointment of a receiver[45].

[20.51] The debenture holder frequently finds today when he comes to realise his security that the suppliers of goods and raw materials to the company who have not been paid claim to be entitled to the ownership of them because of what are known as 'reservation of title' clauses. Such provisions, which have been familiar in continental jurisdictions for a long time but have only been making their appearance here and in England in recent years, also commonly stipulate that the supplier is to be entitled to enforce these rights against the proceeds of sale, where the goods have been resold, or against the finished product into which the raw materials have been converted. While they are usually referred to as *Romalpa* clauses after the English decision[46] which recognised their validity in that jurisdiction, they might be more properly referred to as *Interview* clauses in Ireland, since Kenny J had treated them as enforceable in that case some two years before *Romalpa*[47]. However, to avoid confusion, they will be referred to as *Romalpa* clauses in the ensuing discussion.

---

[41] [1975] IR 382.
[42] See *Palmer's Company Law* (25th edn), Vol 2, 13.140.
[43] *Re Opera* [1891] 3 Ch 260.
[44] *Evans v Rival Granite Quarries Ltd* [1910] 2 KB 979.
[45] *Re Roundwood Colliery Co* [1897] 1 Ch 373.
[46] *Aluminium Industrie Vaasem BV v Romalpa Aluminium Ltd* [1976] 2 All ER 552.

[20.52] Such clauses, if effective, make the suppliers for all practical purposes secured creditors at the expense of ordinary creditors. A *Romalpa* clause which is effective as against a receiver appointed under a floating charge will be equally effective as against a liquidator. It would seem to follow logically that

(1)   such clauses to be effective must be in the nature of chattel mortgages and should not be capable of enforcement unless the clause imposes on the company which buys the goods an obligation to hold the goods, any goods into which they are converted or the proceeds of sale of the goods in trust for the supplier;

(2)   the mortgage or charge thus created by the company to be enforceable must be registered under s 99 of the Principal Act[48].

[20.53] Unfortunately, these aspects of the clauses were not analysed in any depth in the *Interview* and *Romalpa* decisions; and confusion has been increased by the fact that the decisions on such clauses in both jurisdictions in subsequent years have naturally been addressed to the actual wording of the clauses in issue and the particular facts of the relevant cases. It is clear that intervention by the legislature is required to introduce a reasonable degree of certainty into the present law but recommendations by Cork to that effect have not been implemented by the English Insolvency Act 1986. In Ireland, the Law Reform Commission have made detailed proposals for reform and clarification of the law in the *Report on Debt Collection: (2) Retention of Title*.

[20.54] The crucial difficulty that such a clause presents is that in such transactions both parties - the supplier and the company - envisage that the goods will be either sold on to a third party or used in the manufacture of some product. In either case, Irish and English law as it now exists requires that there be some sort of fiduciary obligation on the company to account for the proceeds of sale or the end product in which the goods have been converted before it will allow the supplier to recover the price out of the proceeds of sale or the finished product. Where such a fiduciary relationship exists, and where it is possible to identify the property now representing the goods supplied, the law will recognise the rights of the supplier to follow or, in the language of the courts of equity, trace his claim into the property. This remedy, which was defined in a celebrated passage in the judgment of Jessel MR in *Re Hallett*[49], is undoubtedly available to the supplier in such a case. But this may very well mean that the company will have created a charge which to be enforceable must be registered under s 99 of

---

[47]   It should also be noted that their validity had been accepted in Ireland as long ago as 1868: see *Bateman v Green & King* (1868) IR 2 CL 166.

[48]   See para **[21.06]** below.

[49]   (1880) 13 Ch D 696 at 708-711.

the Principal Act. That is almost certainly the case where the goods have been sold or converted into other goods, but it may also be so where the goods are still in the possession of the company, depending on the language used in the clause in question.

[20.55] These difficulties inherent in, but not explored by, the judgments in the *Romalpa* case were illustrated by the subsequent English decisions in *Re Bond Worth Ltd*[50] and *Borden (UK) Ltd v Scottish Timber Products Ltd*[51]. In the first of these, the clause in question purported to reserve to the suppliers of yarn intended to be used by a company in the manufacture of carpets the 'equitable and beneficial ownership' in the yarn until payment. In a lengthy judgment, Slade J held that this clause meant that the suppliers had transferred the legal - as distinct from the equitable or beneficial - interest in the yarn to the company. The latter had thereupon created a charge on the yarn to the extent of their indebtedness to the suppliers. But it was in the nature of a floating charge, since the company were still at liberty to sell on the yarn or convert it into carpets. Whatever happened to the yarn, however, the charge crystallised when the company failed to pay in accordance with the terms of supply. It then attached to the yarn, the fibre into which the yarn had been converted or the proceeds of sale as the case might be. But since such a charge required registration under the English equivalent of s 99 of the Principal Act, and had not been registered, it was void.

[20.56] In *Borden*, the suppliers of resin intended to be used by the company to which it was delivered in the manufacture of chipboard stipulated that 'the ownership of the material' should remain with the suppliers until payment. It was held by the Court of Appeal that once the resin had been converted into chipboard any charge which might have been created over it by the company simply ceased to exist, since the material over which it had been created - the resin - had vanished. Two members of the court - Buckley LJ and Templeman LJ - were also of the view that even if such a charge was still in existence, it would have been void for non-registration. It should be noted that the court in that case did not have to decide whether the language used, differing as it did from the language in *Bond Worth*, was apt to create a charge although Templeman LJ seemed to incline to the view that it was.

[20.57] In *Clough Mill v Martin*[52], the Court of Appeal dealt with a clause where the rights of the supplier of yarn were spelled out in two distinct provisions. Under the first, the 'ownership of the material' was to remain with the supplier and the right was reserved to it to dispose of the material until payment in full

---

[50] [1980] Ch 228.
[51] [1981] Ch 25.
[52] [1984] 3 All ER 982.

was received or until the company sold the material in a *bona fide* transaction. Under the second, if any of the material was used in manufacture of the other goods, the 'property' in the whole of such goods was to remain in the supplier until payment. It was held that the first provision was not a charge of any sort: it was no more than a contractual term which prevented the property in the goods from passing until they were paid for or sold on by the company and in the meantime entitled the supplier to sell the goods itself if it wished. The capacity of a seller to reserve the property in the goods by such a clause had been expressly recognised by ss 17 and 19 of the Sale of Goods Act 1893. As such a clause, it did not create a charge which had to be registered. The court considered that the second provision, however, did involve the creation of a charge, although it was conceded that this did violence to the language used. In the event, since the defendant, who was a receiver appointed by a debenture holder, had allowed the company to use the yarn in the manufacture of fibre before payment had been made in full, it was held that he was liable in damages for the wrongful conversion of the yarn.

[20.58] In *Re Interview* an Irish company, EII, had agreed with a German company, AEG, to import their products under a contract governed by German law. Under the contract, AEG retained the property in the goods until they were paid for and EII agreed to assign to AEG any claims they might have against people to whom they sold the goods. Subsequently, it was arranged that another company, Interview Ltd, should acquire EII's stock of AEG products and that they should be supplied directly by AEG with its goods upon the same terms. EII transferred the AEG goods in their possession to Interview Ltd who then became liable to AEG for the price of some of the goods. This debt they purported to discharge by the payment of promissory notes. These promissory notes were dishonoured and a receiver was appointed by a debenture holder over the undertaking and assets of Interview. He applied to the court for directions as to the respective rights of the debenture holder and AEG to the goods still in the possession of Interview, the money representing the sale of such goods since his appointment and the money which was still to be recovered from people to whom the goods had been sold.

Kenny J held that the reservation of title clause was effective and that its enforcement depended on the *lex loci rei sitae*, in this case Irish law. But the question of the necessity for registration under s 99 is not dealt with in the judgment - and presumably was not raised in argument - except in relation to the money still to be recovered. Kenny J held that the relevant term in the AEG contract constituted an assignment by way of security of the book debts of Interview and as such was void for non-registration under s 99.

[20.59] In *Frigoscandia (Contracting) Ltd v Continental Irish Meat Ltd*[53], the question of non-registration appears to have been more fully argued. In that case, the facts and the agreement were relatively straightforward: the plaintiff company had delivered and installed an item of plant at the defendant company's factory. The contract provided that until payment the ownership of the plant was to remain with the plaintiff company. When the defendant company failed to pay, the plaintiff company claimed to be entitled to recover possession of the plant against a receiver who had been appointed. McWilliam J held that they were entitled to succeed: the provision was a straightforward contractual term which did not create any charge and accordingly did not require registration. Clearly this decision is to the same effect as the Court of Appeal decision in *Clough Mill Ltd v Martin* on the first provision in the contract.

[20.60] By contrast, both the facts and the terms of the contract considered in *Kruppstahl AG v Quitmann Products Ltd*[54] were somewhat complicated. In essence, the plaintiff company, a German concern, had supplied steel to the defendant company for use in the manufacture of certain goods such as pedal bins and bread bins. The terms of supply as translated from the German provided that:

> 'all goods supplied remain our property (reserved goods) until all claims are met, particularly also balances due to us on any legal grounds whatsoever. This also applies, if payments are effected in respect of specific claims.'

In addition, however, the contract provided for the possibility that the steel might be used in manufacturing the finished products before it was paid for. It was stated that:

> 'Handling and processing of the reserved goods are performed on our behalf ... The processed goods are deemed to be reserved goods ... In the case of processing, blending and mixing of the reserved goods with other goods by the buyer, (the plaintiff company) acquire a joint title to the new goods in accordance with the ratio of the invoice value of the reserved goods to the invoice value of the other goods used. If (the plaintiff company's) title lapses due to blending or mixing, the buyer assigns to us already at this stage his title to the new goods in accordance with the invoice value of the reserved goods and holds them in trust for (the plaintiff company) without charge. The thus arising joint title is the equivalent of reserved goods ...'

Some of the steel delivered was used by the defendant company in the manufacture of its products. When a receiver was appointed by a debenture holder, the plaintiff company claimed to be entitled to be a secured creditor in

---

[53] [1982] ILRM 396.
[54] [1982] ILRM 551.

priority to the debenture holder in respect of the total indebtedness to them of the defendant company. Gannon J, following Kenny J in *Re Interview*, held that while the contract itself was to be construed in accordance with German law, specific transactions effected in Ireland, such as the delivery of the steel in issue, were regulated by Irish law. Having considered the English authorities already referred to, he concluded that the property in the unworked steel remained in the plaintiff company, but that in the case of the steel used in manufacture, the defendant company were trustees of the finished products and had thereby created a charge which was void for non-registration under s 99. The plaintiff company were accordingly entitled to priority in respect of the unworked steel only.

[20.61] Where the goods remain in an identifiable state, such a problem should not normally arise. Thus in *Somers v James Allen (Ireland) Ltd*[55], a firm supplied certain ingredients to a company manufacturing and selling animal feeding compounds. The conditions of sale included a *Romalpa* clause which provided that the 'transfer of title' should not occur until they had been paid for in full. A receiver was appointed by the Agricultural Credit Corporation over the property of the company and the supplier who had not been paid claimed to be entitled to the ownership of the goods as against the receiver. The ingredients were in fact still identifiable: they had not been mixed with others or used in manufacturing compounds. For the receiver, it was argued that the intention of the parties must have been that the legal title only would remain in the supplier and that hence a registerable charge only had been created. Since it had not been registered, it was claimed that it was unenforceable. Carroll J rejected this submission, holding that it was perfectly within the competence of the parties to provide that both the legal and equitable ownership should remain in the supplier for so long as the goods were in their original state and payment had not been made. This conclusion was upheld by the Supreme Court on appeal.

[20.62] More complex questions arise where goods have been resold and the supplier claims to be entitled to the proceeds of sale. It seems clear that, even where the original agreement does not expressly oblige the buyer to account to the seller for the proceeds of sale in the event of their being resold, he will normally be under such an obligation. But the position is less clear where the proceeds of sale have been paid into the buyer's bank account and mixed with other funds. As we have seen, the existence of a 'tracing' remedy in such a case appears to depend on whether a fiduciary relationship exists between the buyer and the supplier. There are English decisions[56] to the effect that where the buyer is free to deal with the goods or the proceeds of sale as he wishes, no fiduciary

---

[55] [1984] ILRM 437.
[56] Eg, *Re Peachdart Ltd* [1983] 3 All ER 152.

relationship can be said to exist. Something more, it is suggested, is necessary to give rise to such a relationship. Thus, it could arise in the case of 'current account' clauses, ie if the supplier was entitled to retain title until all sums due by the buyer, and not simply the price of the particular goods, had been paid. The same inference could be drawn where there was an indication that the buyers were selling as agents for the suppliers or on the suppliers' account.

[20.63] The Irish decisions have, on the whole, adopted a broader approach and have found a fiduciary relationship to exist simply by reasons of the reservation of title itself[57]. However, in a recent decision - *Carroll Group Ltd v G & JF Bourke Ltd*[58] Murphy J took the view, in line with the English authorities, that more was required to raise the inference of such a relationship than the existence of such a clause *simpliciter*. The law, in the result, cannot be regarded as settled in this jurisdiction.

[20.64] Nor is it clear whether such a clause will in any event be treated as void in the case of a sale to a company because it has not been registered. It seems clear that such a clause will not be so treated where the seller retains ownership and the goods remain identifiable, as in *Somers v James Allen & Co*. In such a case, if the goods are sold to a third party, the seller's right to trace - assuming that it exists - would not appear to require registration. But if the seller has lost his title to the goods - as where they are not in their original state - then any claim he might have to the proceeds of sale would seem to be in the nature of a charge requiring registration.

[20.65] It has also become common practice in recent years for creditors who fear that their debtor intends to remove whatever assets are available to satisfy a judgment out of the jurisdiction to apply to the court for an injunction restraining the debtor from so doing. Such injunctions - known as *Mareva* injunctions[59] - are frequently granted by the courts; but it should be borne in mind that it has been held in England that the debenture holder is entitled in such circumstances to obtain an order discharging the injunction if the persons who obtained the *Mareva* injunction are unsecured creditors and there appears to be no hope of any surplus becoming available to such creditors[60].

---

[57] See, eg, *Re WJ Hickley Ltd* [1988] IR 126.

[58] [1990] ILRM 285.

[59] After an English decision in which such relief was granted, *Mareva Compania Naviera SA of Panama v International Bulk Carriers SA* [1980] 1 All ER 213.

[60] *Cretanor Maritime Co Ltd v Irish Marine Management Ltd* [1978] 3 All ER 164.

Crystallisation of floating charge

[20.66] A floating charge crystallises - ie the charge ceases to float and becomes attached to the assets over which it was granted - on the happening of one or two events:

(1)   the appointment of a receiver,[61] or

(2)   the winding up of the company.[62]

It has also been suggested that the charge may crystallise automatically if there is a default by the company and the debenture so provides. The more generally accepted view has been, however, as stated, ie that the crystallisation does not take place until the debenture holder has taken active steps to enforce his security by appointing a receiver or obtaining such an appointment from the court or the company has gone into liquidation[63].

[20.67] The proposition that there can be an automatic crystallisation on the default of the company if the debenture is in sufficiently explicit terms to permit of such a construction rests on some *dicta* in earlier English cases[64] and an express decision to that effect in New Zealand[65]. It is thought, however, that this line of authority is unlikely to be followed in Ireland. The courts here will probably incline to the view that such automatic crystallisation would present problems for other creditors who would have no actual notice of the terms of the debenture and that any such doctrine would need to be the subject of considered legislation and regulation[66].

[20.68] It has been held by the Supreme Court in *Re Holidair Ltd*[67] that a floating charge which has crystallised will decrystallise on the appointment of an examiner to the company, so that it ceases to be a fixed charge and reverts to being a floating charge. The validity of the concept of 'decrystallisation', which emerged for the first time in Ireland in this judgment, has been questioned, but the law appears to have been left unchanged by the 1999 (No 2) Act[68].

---

[61] *Nelson & Co v Faber & Co* [1903] 2 KB 367; *Evans v Rival Granite Quarries Ltd* [1910] 2 KB 979; *N W Robbie & Co v Witney Warehouse Co* [1963] 3 All ER 316.

[62] *Wallace v Universal Automatic Machines* [1894] 2 Ch 547.

[63] *Nelson & Co v Faber & Co* [1903] 2 KB 367; *Evans v Rival Granite Quarries Ltd* [1910] 2 KB 979.

[64] Summarised in *Palmer's Company Law*, Vol 1, 45-10.

[65] *Re Manurowi Transport Ltd* [1971] NZLR 909.

[66] It has, however, been held in England that a floating charge crystallises automatically if the company ceases to carry on business; *Re Woodroffes (Musical Instruments) Ltd* [1986] Ch 366.

[67] [1994] 1 ILRM 481.

[68] See further Ch 37 below.

Invalidity of floating charges under ss 288 and 289 of the Principal Act

[20.69] A company may sometimes under pressure from one of its creditors execute a floating charge in respect of its existing debts. Or it may do so at the instance of one of its own directors. In order to mitigate the risks to ordinary creditors arising from such transactions, ss 288 and 289 of the Principal Act render invalid floating charges entered into by companies within 12 months of a winding up subject to certain exceptions.

[20.70] Section 288 of the Principal Act as amended by s 136 of the 1990 Act provides that such charges are to be invalid unless it is proved that the company, immediately after the charge, was solvent. But the section does not invalidate the charge to the extent that it secures cash paid to the company or the price of goods sold or services supplied on an 'arms length' basis at the time of or subsequently to the creation of the charge and in consideration of the charge, together with interest on the amount at the rate of 5% per annum. In the case of a charge in favour of directors, 'connected persons' or a related company[69], the period is two years.

[20.71] It is to be observed that the burden of proof that the company was solvent immediately after the creation of the charge rests on the lender. In determining whether the company was solvent, the crucial factor is its ability to pay its debts as they fall due. Accordingly, where a company carries on its business after the creation of a charge, the value of its fixed and movable assets would have to be ignored in determining whether it was solvent at the critical time, since such assets would not be regarded as available to meet the company's day-to-day liabilities. However, the capacity of the company immediately after the creation of the particular charge, to borrow money on the security of another charge must be taken into account. The onus is then on the person claiming that the disputed floating charge is valid to prove that a creditor would in the particular circumstances have been prepared to advance sufficient money on the strength of a further charge to ensure the company's solvency[70].

[20.72] A company which is already running an overdraft frequently approaches its bank with a view to increasing its borrowing and, as it hopes, trading its way out of financial problems. The bank will probably insist on a floating charge in such circumstances; and if the company goes into liquidation within the year, problems may arise as to whether the additional finance was 'cash paid' within the meaning of the proviso to s 288. A further problem may arise if repayments

---

[69] For 'connected persons' see para **[27.57]** below, and for 'related companies' see para **[36.34]** below. Directors include 'shadow directors', see para **[29.17]** below.

[70] *Crowley v Northern Bank Finance Co* [1981] IR 353.

have been made prior to the winding up. Are these to be taken as payments in respect of the money secured by the charge or in respect of the earlier borrowing?

[20.73] These problems were considered by Kenny J in *Re Daniel Murphy Ltd*[71]. In that case the company had an overdraft of £9,759 with the bank on the security of an equitable mortgage of its premises. They required additional accommodation of up to £15,000 to finance their operations and the bank agreed to give them the facility if they executed a floating charge. The company agreed by letter to this. The preparation of the deed of charge took up some weeks; and about a fortnight after the executed deed was registered with the Registrar, the company went into liquidation. Between the date on which the company wrote its letter agreeing to give the floating charge and the resolution for a winding up, the company lodged £30,887 to its account while cheques amounting to £36,003 were debited.

[20.74] The first question that arose was whether money advanced by the bank before the charge was executed but after the company had agreed to give it was 'cash paid at the time of ... the charge'. Kenny J held that it was, provided that any delay in having their charge completed and registered was not intended to deceive creditors and was not unreasonable and culpable. In that case, he held that there was no intention to deceive nor had there been unreasonable delay.

[20.75] The next question that arose was whether the money lodged by the company after it had agreed to execute the charge should be regarded as being in repayment exclusively of the £15,000 which the charge was intended to secure or in repayment first of the earlier borrowing.

[20.76] Kenny J held that the rule in *Clayton's Case*[72] - that payments made on a running account should be appropriated first in discharge of the debtor's earliest liability - was applicable in such circumstances and that accordingly the repayments in question should be treated as having been made first in reduction of the pre-existing overdraft of £9,759. A similar view was taken in England subsequently in *Re Yeovil Glove Co.*[73]

[20.77] The final question that arose was whether the money advanced by the bank after the charge was executed was 'cash paid ... in consideration for the charge'. If the word 'consideration' was given its normal meaning in the law of contract, the cash advanced by the bank could not be regarded as having been paid in consideration for the charge, since the charge was consideration in the past, which under that law was not consideration at all. Kenny J took the view

---

[71]   [1964] IR 1.
[72]   [1816] I Mer 572.
[73]   [1965] Ch 148.

that the construction of the section should not be so confined and that accordingly money advanced after the charge could properly be regarded as having been paid in consideration for the charge. Again a similar view was taken in *Re Yeovil Glove Co.*

[20.78] Where as a condition of granting accommodation, a lender stipulates for the repayment of an earlier advance out of the new advance or for the discharge of some other liability out of the advance, it appears that the entire advance would still be treated as cash paid in consideration for the charge. It is true that in *Revere Trust Ltd v Wellington Handkerchief Co Ltd*[74], the Court of Appeal in Northern Ireland held that where the lender had stipulated for the immediate repayment of a previous advance of £90 out of an advance purportedly secured by the floating charge, £90 only could be regarded as having been 'cash paid' within the meaning of the section. They came to that conclusion in part at least, however, in reliance on a dictum of Astbury J that the payment of cash had to be 'absolute and uncontrolled'[75]. This dictum was expressly disapproved of by the Court of Appeal in England in *Re Matthews Ellis Ltd*[76] which was decided after the Northern Ireland case. It would appear from that decision that provided the company benefits from the cash advanced and grants the floating charge with that object in view it is immaterial that part of the advance is being utilised to reduce the company's indebtedness to the lender or some third party. It is only where no benefit at all accrues to the company that the cash paid should be disregarded. This would also appear to be consistent with the approach adopted by Kenny J in *Re Daniel Murphy*, although he contented himself with drawing attention to the discrepancy between the two decisions[77].

---

[74] [1931] NI 55.

[75] *Re Hayman Christie & Lilly Ltd* [1917] 1 Ch 545.

[76] [1933] Ch 458.

[77] [1964] IR 1 at 15.

Chapter 21

Registration of Charges

[21.01] It is important for those dealing with a company to be in a position to ascertain what charges the company has created over any of its assets. Section 99 of the Principal Act accordingly requires the registration with the Registrar of certain types of charge specified by the section. It is vital for the lender to ensure that charges governed by the section are in fact registered, since if they are not the Act declares them void against the liquidator and the other creditors.

[21.02] Unlike the English legislation, however, there is no requirement that the company itself keep a register of charges. It is an important omission, because the list of charges which must be registered under s 99, although wide-ranging, is not exhaustive. Thus, charges by deposit of bills of exchange, dock warrants or other negotiable instruments are not within s 99: nor in Ireland do they require entry in a register by the company[1]. The only obligation on the company, apart from registering charges which require registration under the Acts is to keep copies of every instrument of charge which requires registration at the registered office of the company[2]. The copies may be inspected during business hours by any creditor or member without fee. The company may in general meeting impose reasonable restrictions on this right of inspection, but must allow at least two hours in each day. If inspection is refused, every officer of the company who is in default is liable to a fine not exceeding £500. The court may also by order compel an immediate inspection.

[21.03] A company is also obliged to keep a register of debenture holders but the only entries that need to be made relate to the issue of a series of debentures ranking pari passu[3].

[21.04] Prior to the enactment of s 91 of the Principal Act, which requires the keeping of this register, it was usual to provide in the standard conditions that such a register should be kept by the company. The section gives statutory effect to this practice; but failure to keep the register does not invalidate the security.

---

[1] On the significance of this omission, see Fitzgerald, *A Consideration of the Companies Act 1948, the Companies' Act (Northern Ireland) 1960 and the Companies Act 1963*, Ir Jur (ns), Vol III, p 47.

[2] Companies Act 1963, ss 109 and 110 as amended by the Companies (Amendment) Act 1983, s 15.

[3] Companies Act 1963, s 91.

There is however a penalty (a fine not exceeding £250) for failure to keep the register. The Registrar must be notified of the place where the register is kept and of any changes in that place and again there is provision for a fine not exceeding £250 if the Registrar is not so notified within 14 days. The register must be kept at the registered office of the company or at the office where it is made up, eg the office of the company's auditors.

Charges which must be registered under s 99

[21.05] The company must register with the Registrar certain charges which are specified in s 99 of the Principal Act. Failure to comply with this section means that the security is void as against the liquidator and any creditor of the company. It is, accordingly, most important that the requirements of the Act be meticulously observed and its provisions, and the various cases decided in Ireland and England on its ambit, repay careful study.

[21.06] Section 99 of the Principal Act provides that, in the case of a charge created by the company to which the section applies, the prescribed particulars of the charge verified in the prescribed manner[4] must be delivered to the Registrar for registration within 21 days of its creation. The charges to which the section applies are set out in sub-s (3) as follows:

(a)   a charge for the purpose of securing any issue of debentures;

(b)   a charge on uncalled share capital of the company;

(c)   a charge created or evidenced by an instrument which, if executed by an individual, would require registration as a bill of sale;

(d)   a charge on lands wherever situate, or an interest therein, but not including a charge for any rent or other periodical sum issuing out of land;

(e)   a charge on book debts of the company;

(f)   a floating charge on the undertaking or property of the company;

(g)   a charge on calls made but not paid;

(h)   a charge on any ship or aircraft or any share in a ship or aircraft[5]

(i)   a charge on goodwill, on a patent or a licence under a patent, on a trade mark or on a copyright or a licence under a copyright.

It is made clear by sub-s (10) that a 'charge' in the section includes a mortgage.

---

4   Companies (Forms) Order 1964, SI 45/1964, para 3, Form No 47. The prescribed particulars are the date and description of the instrument, the amount secured, short particulars of the property charged and the names, addresses and occupations of the owners of the charge. In the case of a charge securing an issue of debentures, there must also be stated the amount and rate per cent of any commission, allowance or discount paid to any person in consideration of his subscribing to the issue or procuring subscriptions.

5   Inserted by the Companies Act 1990, s 122.

[21.07] Section 122 of the 1990 Act provides that the Minister may add new descriptions of charges to this list by regulation.

[21.08] Section 100 imposes on the company the duty to send the required particulars to the Registrar within the 21-day period, but also provides that registration of the charge may be effected by any person interested therein, eg the person who advanced the money which the charge is intended to secure. The company is also required (by s 101) to register with the Registrar any charge to which property acquired by them is subject, if it is one of the charges specified in s 99. The Registrar for his part is required by s 103 to keep, in relation to each company, a register of charges and, on payment of the prescribed fee, to enter the following particulars in the register:

(1) the date of creation of the charge;

(2) where the charge is not created by the company, the date of the acquisition of the relevant property;

(3) if the charge is a judgment mortgage, the date of creation of the judgment mortgage[6]

(4) the amount secured by the charge;

(5) short particulars of the property charged;

(6) the persons entitled to the charge.[7]

[21.09] While the company is required to deliver the necessary particulars of the charge, it is of course of the greatest importance to the person advancing money to the company on the security of the charge to ensure that the necessary particulars are delivered, preferably by delivering them himself as he is entitled to do. While the court has power to extend the time for delivering the particulars if they are not delivered within the 21 day period[8], the order giving such an extension invariably protects secured creditors who advanced money to the company before the charge was actually registered; and in any event it must not be thought that a person who fails to deliver particulars will automatically be given an extension of time. The surprising number of applications to the court for such extensions indicates that there is a laxity in complying with the time limit which could have disastrous consequences for a lender.

[21.10] Some of the charges to which the section applies are considered individually in the succeeding paragraphs, but a few general observations should

---

6 For judgment mortgages, see para **[21.36]** below.

7 In the case of the issue of a series of debentures, the only particulars that need be delivered are the total amount secured, the dates of the resolutions authorising the issue, a general description of the property charged and the date of the trust deed, if any.

8 See para **[21.41]** below

be made at the outset. First, the failure to register the charge does not affect the company's liability to repay the money which it secures to the lender: on the contrary, under s 99(1) where the charge is void for non-registration, the money secured thereby becomes immediately payable. Secondly, the section only applies to charges created by the company. Charges which come into existence by operation of law are not within its scope. Thus, in *Bank of Ireland Finance Ltd v DJ Daly Ltd (in liquidation)*[9], McMahon J held that the lien which an unpaid vendor has over land which he has sold to the company is not a registrable charge, since it comes into existence by operation of law.

[21.11] Since the word 'charge' includes mortgages, both legal and equitable mortgages of land are registrable. In the case of an equitable mortgage by deposit of title deeds, the mortgage must be registered whether it is accompanied by a memorandum in writing or not[10]. An agreement to deposit title deeds by way of security is also registrable[11].

[21.12] The Registrar must give a certificate under his hand of the registration of any charge registered in pursuance of Part IV of the Principal Act (including charges registered under s 99) stating the amount secured by the charge. Section 104 of the Principal Act provides that the certificate is conclusive evidence that the requirements of Part IV have been complied with. Thus, in *Lombard & Ulster Banking Ltd v Amurec Ltd*[12] a mortgage by a company to a bank was not registered until a lengthy period after its execution, the mortgage being left undated. The bank ultimately stamped and dated the mortgage and presented it for registration within 21 days of the date so appearing and the Registrar issued a certificate pursuant to s 104. Hamilton J rejected a claim by the liquidator of the company that the mortgage was void for non-registration, holding that he was bound by the clear terms of s 104 to treat the certificate as conclusive evidence that the requirements of Part IV, including registration within 21 days had been complied with. Hamilton J applied the same reasoning as that which found favour with the English Court of Appeal in *Re CL Nye Ltd*[13]. That view was later reaffirmed in *R v Registrar of Companies, ex parte Central Bank of India*[14] where, however, the question was left open as to whether the certificate could be

---

[9]   [1978] IR 79.

[10] *Re Wallis & Simmonds (Builders) Ltd* [1974] 1 All ER 561. This is so even though the debt secured by the deposit is owed not by the depositor but by a third party: ibid.

[11] *Re Jackson & Bassford Ltd* [1906] 2 Ch 467. Cf *Re Farm Fresh Frozen Foods Ltd* [1980] ILRM 131.

[12] (1978) 112 ILTR 1.

[13] [1971] Ch 442.

[14] [1986] 1 QB 1114.

successfully challenged in two special cases, ie where there was an error on its face and where it had been obtained by fraud.

[21.13] It is also clear that where the particulars of the amounts secured by a debenture as delivered are inaccurate and a certificate is issued pursuant to s 104, the actual terms of the debenture would be given effect to by the Court. That was so held by Costello J in *Re Shannonside Holdings Ltd*[15] where he was satisfied that the debenture (which had been lost) had secured a greater sum than that appearing in the particulars of registration.

Charges requiring registration under s 99 of the Principal Act

Charges for the purpose of securing any issue of debentures

[21.14] It has been held in New Zealand that this only applies to a charge securing a series of debentures and not to one securing a single debenture[16]. Where the debenture incorporates a floating charge that charge will of course be registrable under s 99(3)(f).

Charges created or evidenced by an instrument which if executed by an individual would be registrable as a bill of sale

[21.15] The relevant Irish legislation on bills of sale is to be found in the Bills of Sale (Ireland) Acts 1879 and 1883. Those Acts permit the registration of all assurances of personal chattels with certain exceptions. It has been held in England, however, that s 95 of the English 1948 Act (corresponding to our s 99) applies only to charges securing the repayment of money[17]. It would follow that not every transaction entered into by a company which if entered into by an individual would require registration as a bill of sale need be registered under s 99.

[21.16] Moreover, since charges only are within the scope of the section, sale and hiring transactions (including hire purchase agreements) are not registrable as bills of sale[18]. They must, however, be genuine sale and hiring transactions: if what was intended was an assignment by way of charge of the goods concerned rather than an absolute assignment, the transaction will require registration. In every case, the court looks to the whole substance of the transaction in order to see whether the parties intended to create an absolute assignment or an assignment by way of charge only[19].

---

[15] (Unreported, 20 May 1993).

[16] *Automobile Association (Canterbury) Inc v Australasian Secured Deposits Ltd* [1973] 1 NZLR 417.

[17] *Stoneleigh Finance Ltd v Phillips* [1965] 2 QB 537.

[18] *Manchester Rly Co v North Central Wagon Co* (1888) 13 App Cas 554.

[19] *Stoneleigh Finance Ltd v Phillips* [1965] 2 QB 537 at 574 per Russell LJ.

[21.17] In *Borden (UK) Ltd v Scottish Timber Products Ltd*[20] Buckley LJ expressed the view obiter that the reservation of title clause in that case, if effective, would have required registration as a bill of sale. In *Kruppstahl AG v Quitmann Products Ltd*[21], where the point arose directly, Gannon J held that the reservation of title machinery applicable to the worked steel was within s 99(3)(c).

Charges on land

[21.18] As we have seen, the word 'charges' includes mortgages, both legal and equitable.

In the case of charges on land, registration may also be necessary under two other systems of registration.

(a) Registered land

[21.19] In the case of land the title to which is registered under the Registration of Title Act 1964, s 80 of that Act provides as follows:

> '(1) Where a company registered under (the Principal Act) is registered as owner of land registered under this Act or as owner of a registered charge, the Registrar shall not be concerned with, and a person claiming under a registered disposition for valuable consideration shall not be affected by, any mortgage, charge, debenture, debenture stock, trust deed or other incumbrance created or issued by the company, unless such incumbrance is registered as a burden or protected by caution or inhibition under this Act.
>
> (2) No compensation shall be payable under s 120 by reason of a purchaser's acquiring any interest under a registered transfer from the company free of any such incumbrance not so registered or protected.'

[21.20] A legal charge of land, such as a mortgage, created by a company must accordingly be registered as a burden on the folio in the Land Registry if priority is to be successfully claimed. In the case of a floating charge, it is thought that registration as a burden is not possible: in this case, a caution or inhibition should be entered on the folio[22]. This effectively warns any person dealing with the lands comprised in the folio that no dealing should be completed without notice to the owner of the floating charge[23].

---

[20] [1981] Ch 35 at 46.

[21] [1982] ILRM 551.

[22] On the more generally accepted view of the nature of a floating charge, there is no vesting of the legal estate prior to crystallisation and there is consequently nothing in the nature of a 'burden' which can be registered: see para **[20.31]** above. Cf McAllister, *Registration of Title*, p 191.

[23] For cautions and inhibitions, see the Registration of Title Act 1964, ss 96, 97 and 98.

[21.21] Unless the registrar of titles is furnished with a certificate from the Registrar of Companies that the charge has been registered with him within the statutory period, there is entered on the folio in the Land Registry a note to the effect that the charge is subject to registration under s 99 of the Principal Act[24].

(b) Unregistered land

[21.22] In the case of unregistered land, any charge on the land may be registered in the Registry of Deeds under the Registry of Deeds Act 1707.

[21.23] In the case of both registered and unregistered land, it is possible to create an equitable mortgage by deposit of the land certificate or the title deeds without registration in the Land Registry or the Registry of Deeds. Such a mortgage will generally be entitled to priority over a subsequent incumbrance despite the absence of registration in the relevant registry. Where, however, the deposit is accompanied by an instrument in writing, it must be registered to secure priority.

[21.24] A deed or transfer which is capable of registration either in the Registry of Deeds or the Land Registry and is not registered will normally be postponed to a subsequent registered deed or transfer. There is an important exception, however, in the case of unregistered land, ie where the person taking under the subsequent deed has actual notice - either by himself or his agent - of the earlier deed[25]. A fortiori the priority will be lost in the case of fraud.

[21.25] There is no such exception in the case of notice where registered land is concerned. Section 31 of the Registration of Title Act 1964 provides that the Folio in the Land Registry is to be

> conclusive evidence of the title of the owner to the land as appearing on the register ...

It goes on to say that:

> such title shall not, in the absence of actual fraud, be in any way affected in consequence of such owner having notice of any deed, document or matter relating to the land ...

It is clear that this section excludes the exception for notice which applies in he case of unregistered land[26].

[21.26] It should also be remembered that registration is not the precise equivalent of notice. As we have seen, where a charge on land is registered under s 99, a person taking under a subsequent dealing will be fixed with notice of the

---

[24] Land Registration Rules 1972, SI 230/1972, r 114.
[25] Wylie, *Land Law*, paras 3.088-3.089.
[26] *Re Michael Walsh* [1916] 1 IR 40.

statutory particulars which have to be delivered but not with the contents of the charge[27]. Similarly, where such a charge is registered in the Land Registry or the Registry of Deeds, a person taking under a subsequent deed or transfer will not be fixed with notice of the contents of the instrument.

Charges on book debts

[21.27] This includes both present and future book debts of the company[28]. But where a negotiable instrument, such as a bill of exchange, has been given to secure the payment of a book debt, the deposit of the instrument for the purpose of securing an advance to the company is not a charge which requires registration, this being made clear by s 99(6). Thus if the bill of exchange is deposited by the company with a bank to secure a loan, this does not constitute a charge on book debts requiring registration.

[21.28] Where present and future debts due under a hire purchase or credit sales agreement are assigned as security for an advance, the transaction will be registrable as a charge on book debts. In every case, however, the court will look to the substance of the transaction; and if it is clear that an absolute assignment of the debts was intended rather than an assignment by way of security, the transaction will not be registrable[29].

[21.29] It has become a common practice for banks advancing bridging finance to purchasers of property to require their solicitors to give an undertaking to lodge the proceeds of sale of a property which they are proposing to sell with the bank in repayment of the bridging finance. It was held by McWilliam J in *Re Kum Tung Restaurant (Dublin) Ltd*[30] that where such an undertaking was given on behalf of a company it was not registrable as a charge under s 99. It was not a charge on land, being a charge on the proceeds of sale and not on the land itself; and it was not a charge on book debts[31].

Floating charges

[21.30] The nature of a floating charge has been fully explained already[32]. We have also seen that, in the case of registered land, neither the Registrar of Titles nor any person claiming under a registered disposition for valuable consideration is to be concerned with or affected by any mortgage, charge, debenture, debenture stock, trust deed or other incumbrance created or issued by

[27] Para **[20.47]** above.
[28] *Yorkshire Woolcombers' Association* [1903] 2 Ch 384; *Re Lakeglen Construction Ltd, Kelly v James McMahon Ltd* [1980] IR 347.
[29] *Stoneleigh Finance Ltd v Phillips* [1965] 2 QB 537.
[30] [1978] IR 446.
[31] See also *Farrell v Equity Bank Ltd* [1990] 2 IR 549.
[32] Para **[20.28]** above.

the company unless it is registered as a burden or protected by caution or inhibition under the Act[33]. While a floating charge probably cannot be registered as a burden, it undoubtedly can be protected by a caution or inhibition and this should also be done[34].

[21.31] In the case of registered land, a person who has been in adverse possession for twelve years is entitled to be registered as absolute owner on the expiration of that period. It was held in *Halpin v Cremin*[35] that twelve years' adverse possession ousted the rights of the owner of a floating charge even where it crystallised during the twelve year period.

[21.32] We have already seen that in certain circumstances a 'reservation of title' or *Romalpa* clause may require registration as a floating charge. This view was taken by Slade J in *Re Bond Worth Ltd*[36] and by Templeman LJ *obiter* in *Borden (UK) Ltd v Scottish Timber Products Ltd*[37]. In the latter case, Buckley LJ - also speaking obiter - took the view that it was more appropriately registrable as a corporate bill of sale[38] and a similar view was taken by Gannon J in *Kruppstahl AG v Quitmann Products Ltd*[39].

Charges on calls made but not paid

[21.33] These do not require elaboration.

Charges on ships

[21.34] Where such charges take the form of legal mortgages, the requirements of the Mercantile Marine Act 1955 must be observed.

It was held by McWilliam J in *Re South Coast Boatyard, Barbour v Burke*[40] and by the Supreme Court on appeal that a yacht was not a 'ship' within the meaning of the section.

Charges on goodwill, patents, trademarks, and copyrights

[21.35] Charges over patents and registered trademarks must also be notified to the Patents Office.

---

[33] Para **[21.20]** above
[34] Para **[21.20]** above.
[35] [1954] IR 19.
[36] [1980] Ch 228.
[37] [1981] Ch 35 at 44.
[38] [1981] Ch 35 at 46.
[39] [1982] ILRM 551.
[40] [1980] ILRM 186.

Judgment mortgages

[21.36] The judgment mortgage is a form of security peculiar to Ireland. A creditor who has recovered judgment for a sum of money may convert the judgment into a mortgage affecting any lands owned by the debtor. He then has the same rights, powers and remedies as if the land had been mortgaged to him by deed. He converts the judgment into a judgment mortgage by filing an affidavit containing the matters prescribed by the relevant statutes in the court in which he obtained the judgment[41]. He must register an office copy of this affidavit in the Registry of Deeds or, where it affects registered land, in the Land Registry. Prior to the Principal Act, such a form of security did not require registration under the 1908 Act, since it was not a charge created by the company. Cox recommended that the law should be altered by requiring the judgment creditor to send a copy of the affidavit to the Registrar within a specified time.

[21.37] The recommendation was partly implemented by s 102, which requires the creditor to cause two copies of the affidavit (certified to be correct copies by the appropriate registry) to be delivered to the company (not the Registrar as Cox had recommended) within 21 days after the date of registration as a judgment mortgage. The company must within three days of receipt of the copies deliver one to the Registrar for registration. The appropriate registry is also required to deliver a copy of the affidavit to the Registrar 'as soon as may be'.

[21.38] Cox did not make any recommendation as to what effect non-compliance with the requirement should have. The Principal Act did no more than impose a penalty on the judgment creditor and the company not exceeding £100 (now increased to £500 by the 1982 Act). There seems no reason why failure to register the charge should not have as its consequence the invalidity of the charge: whether a mortgage is created by deed or by the conversion of a judgment mortgage would seem to be irrelevant from the point of view of the other creditors of the company[42].

Charges by foreign companies

[21.39] The provisions of s 99 as to registration of charges extend to charges created on property in Ireland by companies incorporated outside Ireland which

---

[41] Judgment Mortgage (Ireland) Acts 1850 and 1858.

[42] This point was made by Deputy Gerard Sweetman in the debate on the committee stage, but seems to have been lost sight of. See also Fitzgerald, *A Consideration of the Companies' Act 1948* etc (above). Irish Jurist (NS) Vol III, 262.

have established places of business in Ireland and to judgment mortgages against such companies.

[21.40] A particular problem arises where a foreign company with an established base of business in Ireland fails to deliver to the Registrar the particulars required by s 352 of the Principal Act and creates a charge over any of its Irish assets. It was held in England in *NV Slavenburg's Bank v Intercontinental Natural Resources Ltd*[43] that, although there was no method of registering the charge in such circumstances, the obligation to deliver the particulars remained and failure to comply with it would invalidate the charge. The law has been changed in England and it is no longer necessary there to deliver particulars of the charge: it has not been altered in Ireland where apparently the practice is for the Registrar to issue a letter confirming that the particulars have been delivered since a certificate cannot be issued under s 104[44].

Extension of time and rectification of errors

[21.41] The court has jurisdiction under s 106 of the Principal Act to extend the time for registration of a charge under s 99 and to rectify any omission or misstatement in the particulars delivered.

[21.42] The court must be satisfied that the omission to register the charge within the required time or the omission or misstatement in the particulars was:

> 'accidental or due to inadvertence or some other sufficient cause or is not of a nature to prejudice the position of creditors or shareholder or the company or that on other grounds it is just and equitable to grant relief.'

[21.43] The court accordingly has a wide discretion under the section, but it is not empowered to delete an entry in its entirety[45]. Nor can the time for registration be extended when the charge has already been registered out of time because of a mistake as to the date on which it was created[46].

[21.44] The order extending the time is invariably made subject to a proviso that it is to be without prejudice to the rights of creditors acquired prior to the registration. Unsecured creditors are not protected by the proviso: it only applies to creditors who have acquired some form of proprietary interest in the property the subject of the charge. But once the company is wound up, the position is different: all the creditors of the company have an interest at that stage in the property, whether secured or not. The proviso would in such circumstances have

[43] [1980] 1 All ER 955.
[44] Courtney, *The Law of Private Companies*, para 15.047.
[45] *Re CL Nye Ltd* [1971] Ch 443.
[46] *Re CL Nye Ltd* [1971] Ch 443 at 474 per Russell LJ.

to extend to all the creditors and this would render the making of the order a futile exercise. It has accordingly been held in England in *Re Resinoid & Mica Products Ltd*[47] and *Victoria Housing Estates Ltd v Ashpurton Estates Ltd*[48] that an order extending the time cannot be made once the company has been wound up, save in the most exceptional circumstances[49].

[21.45] While the position is clear once a winding up has begun, differing views have been expressed as to whether the court is concerned on an application to extend the time for registration with the imminence of a winding up. Although it was the practice in England for the affidavit grounding the application to include averments to the effect that the company was carrying on business normally and was solvent, Romer LJ said in *Re MIG Trust Ltd*[50] that this was not necessary and that the court was not concerned with the imminence of a winding up. A different view was taken, however, by Clauson J in *Re LH Charles & Co Ltd*[51] where he required the holder of the charge to give an undertaking that in case the company should be wound up within a month and the liquidator should apply to the court within 21 days to discharge the order, he would submit to the jurisdiction of the court and abide by any order the court might make for the rectification of the register by the removal of any registration effected under the order.

[21.46] A similar order was made by Hamilton J in *Re Telford Motors Ltd*[52]. The debenture holder in that case had omitted to register his charge and was only alerted to his position when he received a notice that the company was convening a meeting with a view to passing a winding up resolution and that a creditors' meeting was being held. He thereupon applied to the court for an extension of time and this was granted by Hamilton J subject to the undertaking. The relevant particulars were duly delivered to the Registrar the morning after the Court's order. The company passed a winding up resolution that afternoon; and the liquidator in due course applied to the court for an order setting aside the registration of the charge. Hamilton J acceded to the application, pointing out that the unsecured creditors had acquired rights once the winding up order was made and were entitled to the benefit of the proviso.

[21.47] More recently, the Court of Appeal in England in *Re Resinoid & Mica Products Ltd* and *Victoria Housing Estates Ltd v Ashpurton Estates Ltd* have

---

[47] [1983] Ch 132.

[48] [1983] Ch 110.

[49] For a case in which the order was made although the winding up had probably already commenced see *Re R M Arnold & Co Ltd* [1984] BCLC 535.

[50] [1933] Ch 542.

[51] [1935] WN 15.

[52] (Unreported, 27 January 1978).

made it clear that the court is concerned on such an application with the imminence of a winding up and have disapproved of the observations of Romer LJ in *Re MIG Trust Ltd*. In the latter case, Brightman LJ cited with approval the following passages from the majority judgment in the Australian case of *Re Flinders Trading Co Pty Ltd*[53]:

'If at the date of the hearing of the application for enlargement of time for registration of a charge, there is insufficient evidence of the company's solvency or if it be made to appear that the company is unable to pay its debts as they fall due and that a winding up order is imminent and inescapable, the court ought not ... extend the time for registration of the charge.'

[21.48] It is accordingly, clear that where a winding up is imminent the court should refuse the application for extension of the time or, at least, require the giving of an undertaking in the form used in *Re Telford Motors Ltd*. It would also seem to follow that in any other case the order should only be made where there is evidence that the company is solvent and able to pay its debts as they fall due.

[21.49] As we have seen the order extending the time for registration invariably included a proviso that the order is to be without prejudice to the rights of parties acquired prior to the registration of the charge. It appears from decisions in England that a proviso in this form simply protected rights acquired after the expiration of the 21-day period. Rights acquired during the 21-day period were not protected. The reason for this was that the charge was treated as being validated *ab initio* when the time was extended[54]. A new form of proviso received the approval of the Companies Court judges in England as a result of the decision in *Watson v Duff Morgan and Vermont Holdings Ltd*[55] viz:

'That the time for registering the charge be extended until the day of ...; and this order is to be without prejudice to the rights of the parties acquired during the period between the creation of the said charge and the date of its actual registration.'

[21.50] This form of proviso avoids the somewhat anomalous consequence which followed from the old version, ie that whether charges were protected by the proviso depended on their having been created after the 21-day period rather than before. This form of proviso is also now in use in Ireland.

---

[53] [1978] 3 ACLR 318.
[54] *Re Ehrmann Bros* [1906] 2 Ch 697.
[55] [1974] 1 All ER 794.

Chapter 22

Receivers

[22.01] The remedy most usually availed of by debenture holders is the appointment of a receiver. As his title indicates, his main function is to receive or get in all the assets of the company on behalf of the debenture holder and dispose of them in due course in order to pay off the principal and interest due. In addition, he is also frequently appointed the manager of the company's affairs with power to carry on its business for as long as is necessary. The receiver may be appointed either by the debenture holder himself or by the court on the application of the debenture holder. In practice, the debenture invariably contains a provision entitling the debenture holder to appoint a receiver without recourse to the court in defined circumstances.

[22.02] The debenture usually provides that the debenture holder may appoint a receiver 'at any time after the principal moneys hereby secured become payable'. The usual form of the clause providing for the latter event is as follows:

'The principal moneys secured shall immediately become payable:

(a) if the company makes default for the period of six months in the payment of any interest hereby secured and the (debenture holder) before such interest is paid, by notice in writing to the company, calls in such principal moneys; or

(b) if an order is made or an effective resolution is passed for the winding up of the company; or

(c) if a distress or execution is levied or enforced upon or against any of the chattels or property of the company, and is not paid or discharged within five days; or

(d) if a receiver is appointed of the undertaking of the company or of any of its property or assets; or

(e) if the company ceases or threatens to cease to carry on its business.'[1]

[22.03] The debenture holder must ensure that one or more of the specified causes has arisen before taking the serious step of appointing a receiver. Sometimes his position is simplified because the company itself requests the appointment of a receiver and that request will usually be accompanied by an

---

[1] *Palmer's Company Law* (25th edn), Vol 2, 13.051.

express warning that, if a receiver is not appointed, the company will be forced to cease trading, thereby bringing ground (e) into operation. The company may adopt this attitude because to continue trading at a stage when the company appears to be insolvent may expose the directors to personal liability for the debts of the company[2]. The debenture holder has, of course, the option - frequently availed of in practice - to decline to appoint a receiver. In that event, he will simply await the inevitable winding up and rely on his fixed charge to defeat the unsecured creditors.

[22.04] The following consequences flow immediately from the appointment of a receiver by the debenture holder:

(1) A floating charge crystallises[3] and becomes a fixed charge on the assets and/or undertakings over which it was created.

(2) The powers of the company and the directors' authority are suspended in relation to the assets covered by the receivership and may only be exercised with the consent of the receiver[4].

(3) Where the receiver is appointed manager, he is entitled to carry on the business of the company.

(4) The receiver may, if he considers that the interests of the debenture holder so require, dispose of any asset of the company, including its entire undertaking.

Existing contracts remain binding on the company, but the receiver is under no personal liability in respect of them[5].

Persons disqualified from acting as receivers

[22.05] There are no qualifications required of a person who acts as a receiver. The following are, however, disqualified from so acting:

---

2   See Ch 36 below.

3   See para **[20.66]** above.

4   But note that the directors do not cease to be directors and are still bound by their duties to the company. See para **[27.80]** below. They also retain their powers as directors to the extent that these are not related to the assets over which the receiver is appointed: *Wymes v Crowley* (unreported, 27 February 1987) (Murphy J); *Lascombe Ltd v United Dominions Trust (Ireland) Ltd* [1994] 1 ILRM 227.

5   *Re Newdigate Colliery Co Ltd* [1912] 1 Ch 468; *Ardmore Studios (Ireland) Ltd v Lynch* [1965] IR 1. The receiver may ensure that such contracts are performed, however, if he thinks that this is in the interest of the debenture holder. This will not render him personally liable, unless there is a novation, ie an express acceptance by the receiver of personal responsibility. See para **[22.11]** below.

(1)   a body corporate,[6]

(2)   an undischarged bankrupt;

(3)   a person who is, or has been within 12 months of the commencement of the receivership, an officer or servant of the company;

(4)   a parent, spouse, brother, sister or child of an officer;

(5)   a partner or employee of an officer or servant;

(6)   anyone disqualified from acting as receiver of the company's holding or subsidiary companies or a subsidiary of its holding company.[7]

Categories (3) to (6) were added by s 170 of the 1990 Act.

[22.06] A person who becomes disqualified from acting as a result of these provisions automatically vacates office and must give notice in writing to that effect within 14 days to the company, the Registrar and the debenture holder or the court, where he was appointed by it[8]. A receiver appointed before the provision adding the new categories came into effect does not vacate office as a result of it.

[22.07] Anyone who acts as a receiver when disqualified from so doing is guilty of an offence and liable on summary conviction to a fine not exceeding £1,000 and, for continued contravention to a daily default fine not exceeding £50 and on indictment to a fine not exceeding £5,000 and a daily default fine not exceeding £250[9].

Receiver usually the agent of the company

[22.08] If there is no provision to the contrary in the debenture, the receiver on his appointment will be regarded as the agent of the debenture holder who appoints him. In practice the debenture invariably provides that the receiver is to be deemed to be solely the agent of the company and that the company is to be solely responsible for his acts or defaults and for his remuneration.

[22.09] Where the debenture provides that the receiver is to be deemed to be the agent of the company, the agency thus created will be terminated on a winding up[10]. In an effort to prevent this happening, the debenture sometimes confers a purportedly irrevocable power of attorney on the receiver. There is some doubt, however, as to whether such a power of attorney can be irrevocable. It appears that it can be irrevocable only when coupled with an interest; and the receiver, as

---

[6] Companies Act 1963, s 314 as amended by the Companies (Amendment) Act 1982, s 15.

[7] Companies Act 1963, s 315 as substituted by the Companies Act 1990, s 170.

[8] Companies Act 1963, s 315(2) as substituted by the Companies Act 1990, s 170.

[9] Companies Act 1963, s 315(5) as substituted by the Companies Act 1990, s 170.

[10] *Gosling v Gaskell* [1897] AC 575.

distinct from the debenture holder, rarely has any interest in the property charged[11].

[22.10] Prior to a winding up, however, there is no doubt as to the effectiveness of such a power of attorney. In *Industrial Development Authority v Moran*[12], the Supreme Court rejected an argument that the effect of s 40 of the Principal Act - which recognises the validity of deeds executed abroad under an Irish power of attorney but is silent as to the validity of such deeds when executed in Ireland - was to invalidate deeds executed by a receiver in Ireland under a power of attorney[13].

Liability of receiver on contracts

[22.11] We have seen that one of the consequences of the appointment of the receiver is that existing contracts (including contracts of employment) remain binding on the company. The receiver is not, however, personally liable in respect of such contracts, unless there is a novation, ie an agreement between the company, the receiver and the other contracting party that the receiver will assume the rights and obligations of the company under the contract[14].

[22.12] In the case of a contract entered into by the receiver after his appointment the position is quite different. Section 316(2) of the Principal Act provides that he is to be personally liable on any contract entered into by him in the performance of his functions, unless the contract provides that he is not to be so liable. This is so whether the contract is entered into by him in the name of the company, in his own name or otherwise. He is, however, entitled to be indemnified out of the assets of the company in respect of his personal liability.

[22.13] A supplier to the company may, of course, insist on payment of his outstanding account before he deals with the receiver. It was held by Costello J in *W & L Crowe Ltd v ESB; Ionos Ltd v ESB*[15] that the ESB are entitled to refuse to enter into a new supply contract with the receiver until the company's existing account is paid, even though the receiver is prepared to accept personal responsibility for future electricity charges. He held that there was no statutory entitlement to a new supply of electricity in such circumstances.

[22.14] The possibility that this might turn out to be the position in law was adverted to at the committee stage of the Principal Act and the Minister was pressed by one deputy to ensure that semi-state utilities such as the ESB were

---

[11] *Palmer's Company Law* (25th edn), Vol 3, 14.126.
[12] [1978] IR 159.
[13] Reversing the decision of the High Court, which is not reported.
[14] *Parsons v Sovereign Bank of Canada* [1913] AC 160.
[15] (Unreported, 9 May 1984), HC.

not made, in effect, preferential creditors[16]. There was, however, no provision made in the Principal Act for the position which emerged as a result of *Crowe's* case.

Duty of receiver to act in good faith and liability for negligence or fraud

[22.15] Although a receiver is usually deemed to be the agent of the company by virtue of the terms of his appointment, his primary duty is towards the debenture holder, who has appointed him to protect his interest and who is ultimately responsible for his remuneration. It follows that the receiver's relationship with the debenture holder is a fiduciary one, ie one of trust, and that he must show good faith towards the debenture holder in his conduct of the receivership. In one case, it was said that he is obliged to discharge his duties with 'punctilious rectitude'[17]. Plainly he will also be liable to the debenture holder in damages if his conduct of the receivership is negligent, ie if he is guilty of any lack of reasonable care as a result of which the debenture holder suffers loss.

[22.16] While a receiver's primary duty is to the debenture holder, he also owes certain duties to the company. In particular, he is liable to the company where he is negligent in the sale of any of the company's assets. This is made clear by s 316A of the Principal Act, inserted by s 172 of the 1990 Act, which provides that:

> '(1) A receiver, in selling property of a company, shall exercise all reasonable care to obtain the best price reasonably obtainable for the property at the time of the sale.'

[22.17] It is no defence that the receiver was acting as the agent of the company. As we have seen, the debenture usually provides that he is to be deemed to be so acting. Nor can he be compensated or indemnified by the company for any liability he incurs as a result of his failure to take reasonable care.

[22.18] This provision gives statutory effect to the law as it was understood to be in Ireland and England as a result of a number of decisions prior to the 1990 Act. The view expressed in the Australian case of *Expo International Property Ltd v Chant*[18] that the receiver is not liable for negligence provided he has acted in good faith is thus not the law in Ireland.

---

[16] *Official Report (Unrevised) of Parliamentary Debates: Special Committee on Companies Bill 1962*, Col 491.

[17] *Re Magadi Soda Company Ltd* (1925) 41 TLR 297 at 300.

[18] [1980] ACLC 34 at 43. It was also said in that case that the receiver was under a duty to account for his conduct of the receivership when it was over and this would also appear to be the position in Irish and English law: see para **[22.23]** below.

[22.19] A number of the pre-1990 decisions may still be of assistance in ascertaining how this new provision will be applied by the courts. The question usually arises where the receiver is alleged to have parted - or to be about to part - with the property of the company at an undervalue. In *Holohan v Friends' Provident and Century Life Office*[19], a mortgagee in possession was restrained by injunction by the Supreme Court from disposing of property at an undervalue, and *Casey v Intercontinental Bank*[20] also appears to recognise a duty on the mortgagee to secure the best price possible for the mortgaged property. In England, the Court of Appeal in *Cuckmere Brick Co Ltd v Mutual Finance Ltd*[21] held that a mortgagee exercising his power of sale owes a duty to the mortgagor to obtain 'the true market value'. In *Standard Chartered Bank v Walker*[22], it was held that this duty extended to the guarantor of the company's debt. In that case, Lord Denning said:

> 'if it should appear that the mortgagee or the receiver have not used reasonable care to realise the assets to the best advantage, then the mortgagor, the company and the guarantor are entitled in equity to an allowance. They should be given credit for the amount which the sale should have realised if reasonable care had been used.'[23]

[22.20] This passage was cited with approval by Carroll J in *McGowan v Gannon*[24]. In that case, she also posed the question as to whether a receiver who has tested the market and found it very bad is entitled to sell at a bargain price or is obliged to wait in the hope that there will be an upswing in the market. As the question was not argued, she left it unanswered. In England, however, in *Bank of Cyprus (London) Ltd v Gill*[25], it was held that while a mortgagee in possession was not obliged to wait for the market to rise, and could sell at any time, he was nevertheless obliged to take proper steps to secure the best available price at the time he sold. This would presumably apply also to a receiver. It would seem to follow that, while every case should be judged on its own facts, there is no general obligation on a receiver to wait for the market to rise. If he makes a reasonably prudent assessment of the market at the relevant time, he will not be held liable simply because it appears subsequently that by waiting he might have

---

[19] [1966] IR 1.
[20] [1979] IR 364.
[21] [1971] Ch 949.
[22] [1982] 3 All ER 938.
[23] [1982] 3 All ER 938 at 942.
[24] [1983] ILRM 516. A similar view was taken by O'Hanlon J in *Lambert v Donnelly* (unreported, 5 November 1982).
[25] [1980] 2 Lloyd's Rep 51.

got a better price. If the amounts are substantial and he is in serious doubt, he should not hesitate to apply to the court for directions[26].

[22.21] The question has been raised as to whether the receiver's liability to the company can be excluded by the terms of the debenture. It was held in *Expo International Property Ltd v Chant* that such a condition is ineffectual, partly on the ground that there is no receiver in existence at the time the debenture is executed. It has also been suggested - but the point has yet to be judicially decided - that a condition which purported to relieve him of liability for lack of good faith would be unenforceable as being contrary to public policy[27].

[22.22] The 1990 Act also imposed a new restriction on a receiver who is proposing to sell by private contract a 'non-cash' asset of the company of the 'requisite value' to anyone who was an officer of the company within three years prior to the date of his appointment. He can only do so where he has given at least 14 days' notice of his intention so to do to all the creditors of the company who are known to him or have been intimated by him. The restriction applies to any property other than cash which is at least £1,000 in value and which exceeds either £50,000 in value or 10% of the company's net assets[28]. A sale by public auction is clearly not affected by the restriction: a sale by tender would appear to be.

Receiver's duty to account to company

[22.23] There is no general duty on a receiver/manager to account to the company whose affairs he is managing. This is clear from the decision of Costello J in *Irish Oil and Cake Mills Ltd v Donnelly*[29] where he refused to grant a mandatory interlocutory injunction to the company to compel the receiver to furnish it with certain information. He also made it clear, however, that a duty to account may arise in a particular case, and instanced the English decision of *Smiths Ltd v Middleton*[30], where a receiver was ordered to account to the company after the receivership had come to an end.

Appointment of receiver by the court

[22.24] A receiver can be appointed by the court in an action brought by a debenture holder to enforce his security. The appointment may be made despite the fact that an appointment has already been made by the debenture holder[31].

---

[26] See para [22.38] below.
[27] *Palmer's Company Law* (25th edn), Vol 2, 14.127.
[28] Companies Act 1963, s 316A(3) inserted by the Companies Act 1990, s 172.
[29] (Unreported, 27 March 1983).
[30] [1979] 3 All ER 842.

On the appointment the same consequences ensue as on an out of court appointment[32] with one important addition. At common law, an appointment by the Court meant that the company's employees were automatically dismissed, although they did have a right to sue the company for damages for wrongful dismissal. This would appear to have changed since the enactment of the European Communities (Safeguarding of Employees Rights on Transfer of Undertakings) Regulations 1980[33]. Under the regulations, the contracts of employment of employees continue in existence after the transfer of an undertaking and it has been held in England that the equivalent regulations apply to receiverships[34].

[22.25] A receiver appointed by the court, unlike one appointed out of court, is an officer of the court. He is an agent of neither the company nor the debenture holder[35]. He does, however, occupy the same fiduciary relationship to the debenture holder[36] and is under the same duty to take reasonable care in the conduct of the receivership.

Set off following the appointment of the receiver

[22.26] The common law recognises the right of a person who owes money to another to set off against the debts money owed by the other contracting party. This principle applies to debts incurred by persons who deal with the receiver. There must, however, be 'mutuality'. Thus set off will not be allowed of debts arising under a pre-receivership contract which has no connection with the receiver's contract[37].

[22.27] The crystallisation of the floating charge upon the appointment of the receiver means that debts owing at that stage to the company vest in the debenture holder automatically. He takes them, however, subject to any rights of set off in existence at that date. Thus, in the case of debts incurred in favour of the company before the appointment of the receiver, the debtor will be allowed to set off claims against the company where (1) they arose before the debtor had notice of the crystallisation of the charge or (2) they arose out of the same contract or are closely connected with it[38].

---

[31] *Re 'Slogger' Automatic Feeder Co* [1915] 1 Ch 478.

[32] See para **[22.40]** above.

[33] SI 306/1980.

[34] *Jowett (Angus) & Co v Tailors' and Garment Western Union* (1985) IRLR 376.

[35] *Parsons v Sovereign Bank of Canada* [1913] AC 160.

[36] *Re Gent, Gent-Davis v Harris* (1889) 40 Ch D 190.

[37] *NW Robbie & Co v Witney Warehouse Co Ltd* [1963] 3 All ER 613, followed by Budd J in *Lynch v Ardmore Studios (Ireland) Ltd* [1966] IR 133.

[38] *Palmer's Company Law* (25th edn), Vol 3, 14.144.

Notification of receiver's appointment, statement of affairs, etc

[22.28] The debenture holder on the appointment of the receiver (whether by the court or under the debenture) must publish notice in the prescribed form[39] of the appointment within seven days in *Iris Oifigiúil* and in at least one daily newspaper circulating in the area where the registered office of the company is situated[40]. He must also deliver to the Registrar a notice in the prescribed form[41] of the appointment. A receiver on ceasing to act as such must also deliver a notice of that fact in the prescribed form[42] to the Registrar.

[22.29] The receiver on his appointment must give notice of it forthwith to the company. The company must then within 14 days from the receipt of the notice (or such longer period as the court or the receiver may allow) make out and submit to the receiver a statement of affairs in the prescribed form[43]. This statement must show as at the date of the receiver's appointment particulars of the company's assets, debts and liabilities, the names and residences of its creditors, the securities held by them respectively and the dates when the securities were respectively given. The statement must be made by the directors and secretary or by such one or more of the following as the receiver may specify:

(1) present and former officers of the company;

(2) those who took part in the formation of the company within the year prior to the receiver's appointment;

(3) employees of the company or those who were employees within the year period and who the receiver thinks may be capable of giving the required information;

(4) persons who are or were within the year period officers of a company which was itself an officer of the company in receivership, eg where a company was acting as secretary of the company.

The statement must be verified by affidavit[44].

[22.30] A person who fails to comply with these requirements is liable on summary conviction to imprisonment for a term not exceeding six months or a fine not exceeding £1,000 or both and on indictment to imprisonment for a term not exceeding three years or a fine not exceeding £5,000 or both. It is a defence

---

[39] Companies (Forms) Order 1964, SI 45/1964, para 3, Form 53.
[40] Companies Act 1963, s 107(1).
[41] Companies (Forms) Order 1964, SI 45/1964, Form 57a.
[42] Companies (Forms) Order 1964, SI 45/1964, Form 57a.
[43] Companies (Forms) Order 1964, SI 45/1964, Form 17.
[44] Companies Act 1963, s 319(1) and s 320.

for a person to prove to the satisfaction of the court that it was not possible for him to comply with the requirements.

[22.31] The court may also make whatever order it thinks fit on the application of the receiver or any creditor where there has been such non-compliance[45].

[22.32] In practice, directors frequently fail to comply with the duty to deliver a statement of affairs. This regrettable tendency has unfortunate consequences in the conduct of receiverships. The receiver has in such circumstances no guidance from those who may be in the best position to give it as to the value of the company's assets. Failure to deliver such a statement will moreover render much less informative the abstract which the receiver himself is required to deliver. (See below.) It is to be hoped that these enforcement provisions introduced by the 1990 Act will lead to a higher level of compliance.

[22.33] Within two months after receipt of the statement, the receiver must send a copy of it, and of any comments he sees fit to make on it, to the Registrar, the company, any trustees for the debenture holders, the debenture holders (so far as he is aware of their addresses) and (where he is appointed by the court) the court.

[22.34] Within one month after the expiration of the period of six months from the date of his appointment, the receiver must send an abstract in the prescribed form[46] containing the particulars set out in s 319(2) of the Principal Act to the Registrar. He must send a similar abstract at further intervals of six months and within one month after he ceases to be receiver. The following are the particulars which must be included:

(1)   the assets of the company of which he has taken possession since his appointment;

(2)   the estimated value of such assets;

(3)   the proceeds of sale of any such assets since his appointment;

(4)   his receipts and payments during the period of six months, and, where he has ceased to act, during the period from the end of the previous period up to the date of his ceasing to act, together with the aggregate amount of his receipts and payments during all preceding periods since his appointment.

[22.35] Where a receiver has been appointed, every invoice, order for goods or business letter issued by or on behalf of the company or the receiver or the liquidator of the company on which the name of the company appears must contain a statement that a receiver has been appointed. In the event of any default, the company and any officer of the company, liquidator or receiver who

---

45   Companies Act 1990, ss 173 and 174.
46   Companies (Forms) Order 1964, SI 45/1964, Form 57.

knowingly and wilfully authorises or permits the default is liable to a fine of £100[47].

Remuneration of a receiver

[22.36] The remuneration of a receiver appointed by the court is fixed by the court[48]. The remuneration of a receiver appointed under a power contained in a debenture may be fixed by agreement between the receiver and the debenture holder. However, the court has power to fix the amount of such remuneration also despite such an agreement[49]. It may do so on the application of a liquidator or any creditor or member of the company. The court's powers extend to fixing the remuneration for a period before the making of the order or the application and are exercisable although the receiver has died or ceased to act before the making of the order or the application. The receiver may also be ordered to account for any amount paid to himself or retained by him in excess of the amount fixed by the court, but this power may only be exercised by the court in special circumstances.

Receiver may be relieved of liability where charge defective

[22.37] A receiver who is appointed under a charge which is subsequently discovered to be not effective as a charge on the property or part of it may apply to the court for an order relieving him of general liability. The court, if it thinks fit, may make an order relieving him of liability, but in that event the person who made the appointment is personally liable[50].

Application by receiver for directions

[22.38] A receiver of a company was empowered by s 316 of the Principal Act to apply to the court for directions in relation to any particular matter arising in connection with the performance of his functions. This useful facility was extended by the 1990 Act to officers such as directors, shareholders, creditors (where the total indebtedness to them exceeds £10,000), contributories and liquidators. Employees may also apply if they comprise at least half in number of the full-time employees. The court on such an application may make such an order declaring the rights of persons before the court or otherwise as it thinks just[51]. This is a very useful form of procedure which receivers and others who

---

[47] Companies Act 1963, s 317 as amended by the Companies (Amendment) Act 1982, s 15.
[48] Rules of the Superior Courts, Ord 50, r 16(1).
[49] Companies Act 1963, s 318(1).
[50] Companies Act 1963, s 316(3).
[51] Companies Act 1963, s 316(1) as substituted by the Companies Act 1990, s 171.

are in serious doubt as to any matter arising under the receivership should not hesitate to employ. The application to the court should be made by special summons.

Resignation and removal of receivers

[22.39] A receiver appointed under an instrument such as a debenture may resign provided he gives one month's notice in writing to the holders of floating and fixed charges and the company or its liquidator. A receiver appointed by the court may only resign with the authority of the court and on such terms and conditions as the court lays down. Default in complying with these requirements is punishable by a fine not exceeding £1,000[52].

[22.40] A receiver may also be removed by the court on cause shown: the court may then appoint another receiver. Notice of such proceedings must be served on the receiver and the person who appointed him not less than seven days before the proceedings are heard and the receiver and the appointor may appear and be heard[53].

[22.41] Where a receiver has been appointed, it is very often, though not invariably, the prelude to a winding up. Problems have been caused for everyone concerned by the existence side by side of a receivership and a winding up and s 322B of the Principal Act, inserted by s 176 of the 1990 Act, seeks to deal with these difficulties. It enables the court on the application of the liquidator where a company is being wound up, either compulsorily or in a creditors' winding up, to terminate the receivership and prohibit any other receiver from acting. This can be done either generally or in respect of specified property. A copy of the application must be served on the receiver and the appointor at least seven days before the application and they are entitled to appear and be heard. The court may also rescind or vary the order on the application of the liquidator or the receiver.

Application of winding-up procedures to receivers

[22.42] Some provisions applicable in a winding-up are also applicable to a receivership. The powers conferred on the court in a winding up to order the return of assets which have been improperly transferred (conferred by s 139 of the 1990 Act) may also be exercised in a receivership. The power of the court to direct a liquidator to refer matters to the Director of Public Prosecutions with a view to the possible prosecution of officers and members of the company may also be exercised in a receivership[54].

---

[52] Companies Act 1963, s 322C as inserted by the Companies Act 1990, s 177.
[53] Companies Act 1963, s 322A as inserted by the Companies Act 1990, s 175.
[54] Companies Act 1990, ss 178 and 179.

Effect of appointment of examiner or receiver

[22.43] The appointment by the court of an examiner under the 1990 Act has important consequences so far as the power of a debenture holder to appoint a receiver is concerned. A receiver may not be appointed after the appointment of the examiner; where he has been appointed within the period of three days preceding the examiner's appointment he may be ordered to cease acting. These provisions are considered in more detail in Chapter 37 below.

Part VI
Membership of the Company

Chapter 23

Membership in General

[23.01] A member of a company limited by shares must be a shareholder in the company. Conversely, a shareholder in the company must be a member save in one exceptional case. The bearer of a share warrant need not be a member of the company[1]. In the case of a company limited by guarantee and having a share capital, a member need not be a shareholder, since there is nothing to prevent the memorandum and articles from providing for a class of members whose liability will be by way of guarantee only.

[23.02] All members of a company stand prima facie on the same footing. There is, however, nothing to prevent the memorandum and articles, as we have seen, from dividing the shares into different classes some of which carry preferential rights its to dividends or capital or both[2].

[23.03] While the shares are therefore of equal status, unless the company's constitution says otherwise, the power and influence of individual members will usually be determined by the number of shares they own in the company. Most importantly, the number of votes to which he is entitled will usually be the same as the number of shares he owns. There can be provision in the memorandum and articles for shares which do not carry voting rights, but this practice is not approved of by the stock exchange representing as it does a divorce between the ownership and control of a company.

Becoming a member

[23.04] With one exception, it is essential for a person to be placed on the register of members in order to become a member of the company. The exception is in the case of the subscribers to the memorandum: s 31(1) of the Principal Act provides that they are deemed to have agreed to become members of the company. As we have seen, it has been held that this means that they become in law members of the company, even if the company fails to place them on the register[3].

---

[1] See para **[17.36]** above.
[2] See para **[17.12]** above.
[3] See para **[9.03]** above.

[23.05] There is another exception which is an apparent exception only. On the death of a member, his personal representative may transfer his shares without being placed on the register[4]. However, it seems clear that if the personal representative elects not to be placed on the register, he never becomes a member and that there is then no member of the company who is entitled to the shares until a transfer has been executed[5].

[23.06] In the case of the subscribers to the memorandum, entry on the register is not necessary to constitute them as members. There is one instance, however, where it may not be possible to treat them as members, namely, where the company allots all the authorised share capital to the others. In that case, it is simply not possible to treat the subscribers as members since the allotment to the others is complete and effective[6]. It would appear, however, that in those circumstances the subscribers would be entitled to recover damages against the company.

[23.07] It will be seen that there are four normal methods of becoming a member: by being a subscriber, by applying for an allotment, by taking a transfer from an existing member and by transmission on death or bankruptcy. In addition, however, a person may become subject to the liability of a member without travelling any of these routes where he holds himself out, or allows himself to be held out, as a member. He may assent to his name appearing on the register of members although he has not in fact become the owner of any shares. Or he may knowingly have permitted his name to remain on the register when he is not the owner of shares. In either case, he may be regarded in law as being subject to the liability of a member, in the first instance because of his express agreement to that effect and in the second instance because he is estopped from denying the truth of his own representation[7]. It will follow, of course, that in both cases he will be liable to pay any amount that is unpaid on the shares. But without such assent, express or implied, the mere entry of his name on the register cannot impose liability on him.

Capacity to be a member

[23.08] A minor - one under the age of 18 years[8] - may be a member of a company. He may apply for shares and be allotted them, or take a transfer from an existing member. Similarly, he may succeed to shares on the death of a

---

4   Companies Act 1963, s 82.
5   See Gower, *Modern Company Law* (6th edn), p 353-4.
6   *Mackley's case* (1875) 1 Ch D 247.
7   *Sewell's case* (1868) 3 Ch App 131 at 138.
8   Age of Majority Act 1985.

member. But although in any of these cases, he is entitled to be placed on the register and owes a corresponding duty to the company as a member, including an obligation to pay any amount unpaid on the shares, he is also entitled, either during his minority or on reaching his majority, to repudiate his membership of the company. He will then cease to be under any liability in respect of the shares. He may also recover any money he has paid to the company in respect of the shares, provided there has been a total failure of consideration, ie where the shares were wholly worthless[9].

[23.09] The right which a minor has to repudiate his membership must be exercised with reasonable promptitude when he attains his majority. If he delays unduly or if he performs any act inconsistent with the repudiation, such as attending at a meeting or accepting a dividend, he will be treated as having affirmed his membership[10]. It would also appear that where the company is being wound up he may only repudiate his membership with the consent of the liquidator.

[23.10] A person of unsound mind can be a member of a company, but again, as in the case of a minor, his membership is voidable. There is nothing to prevent an alien from being a member of a company[11].

[23.11] A bankrupt may continue to be a member of a company, although his shares have vested in the official assignee. He may still attend meetings and vote, although the dividends are paid to the assignee[12].

[23.12] While a company cannot own shares in itself, it can be a member of another company. It was formerly the law that it could not hold shares in its holding company, but this restriction has been substantially lifted[13].

Register of members

[23.13] Every company must keep a register of its members. This must include the following particulars:

(1) the names and addresses of the members;

(2) in the case of a company having a share capital, a statement of the shares held by each member, distinguishing each share by its number (so long as it has a number), and the amount paid or agreed to be considered as paid on each share;

---

[9] *Hamilton v Vaughan-Sherrin etc Co* [1894] 3 Ch 589.

[10] *Lumsden's case* (1868) 4 Ch App 31 at 34; *Capper's case* (1868) 3 Ch App 458; *Cork & Bandon Rly v Cazenove* (1847) 10 QB 935.

[11] *Princess of Reuss v Boss* (1871) LR 5 HL 1761.

[12] *Morgan v Gray* [1953] Ch 83.

[13] See para **[15.36]** above.

(3)   the date at which each person was entered in the register as a member;

(4)   the date at which any person ceased to be a member.[14]

The register is open to inspection by any member of the public on payment of a small fee[15].

[23.14] The requirement that every company should keep a register of its members which would be open to public inspection was one of the major innovations of the first modern Companies' Act in 1844. Its utility was significantly reduced, however, by a provision that the company may not enter notice of any trust on the register and that no notice of a trust is receivable by the Registrar[16]. There was thus nothing to prevent a person or another company from effectively controlling the company by the use of nominees and concealing this fact from the public. The 1990 Act. however, contains stringent provisions as to the disclosure of interests in shares[17].

[23.15] It has been held in England that the register must indicate the class of shares held by each member[18].

[23.16] The entries referred to at (1), (2) and (3) above must be made within 28 days from the date on which the person agreed to become a member, or in the case of the subscribers, within 28 days from the date of registration. The entry referred to at (4) must be made within 28 days from the date when the person ceased to be a member, or if he ceased to be a member other than as a result of action by the company, eg by transferring his shares, within 28 days from the date on which evidence satisfactory to the company of the relevant occurrence is produced[19].

[23.17] The register at one stage had to be kept in a bound volume or volumes. Section 378 of the Principal Act, however, provides that it may be kept in loose leaf form, subject to precautions against falsification and facilities for discovery.

[23.18] In addition to the register, there must in the case of a company having more than 50 members be kept an index of members, unless the register itself is in such a form as to constitute an index. Within 14 days after the making of an alteration in the register, a corresponding alteration must be made in the index[20].

[23.19] Both the register and the index must be kept at the registered office of the company. If, however, the work of making up the register and index is done

[14] Companies Act 1963, s 116(1) as amended by the Companies (Amendment) Act 1982, s 20.
[15] Companies Act 1963, s 119.
[16] Companies Act 1963, s 123.
[17] See para **[24.04]** below.
[18] *Re Performing Rights Society Ltd* [1978] 2 All ER 712.
[19] Companies Act 1963, s 116.
[20] Companies Act 1963, s 117.

elsewhere, either by one of the company's officers or someone doing the work on behalf of the company, such as a firm of accountants, both may be kept in that place. It may not be kept outside Ireland. The Registrar must be notified of the place where it is kept and of any change in the place, except where the register has been kept at the registered office at all times since the company was formed[21].

[23.20] The register and index must be open to inspection by members without charge[22]. They are entitled to inspect during business hours, subject to such reasonable restrictions as the company in general meeting may impose, but so that not less than two hours in each day is allowed for inspection. The public have a similar right of inspection, subject in their case to the payment of a small fee. Any member or other person may require a copy of the register or any part of it on payment of a small fee. The copy must be sent by the company within 10 days[23]. The company may close the register for a period not exceeding 30 days in each year but must give notice of the closure by an advertisement in a newspaper circulating in the district in which the registered office is located[24]. This provision means that companies may prevent changes in membership occurring at certain times, eg during the period between the giving of notice of the annual general meeting and the meeting itself.

[23.21] Section 122 of the Principal Act enables the court in certain circumstances to order the rectification of the register. This arises where:

(1) the name of a person is entered on, or omitted from, the register without sufficient cause, or

(2) default is made in entering on the register within the 28 day period the fact of a person having ceased to be a member.

[23.22] The application may be made by a person who is not a member but is 'aggrieved' by the error, by any member or by the company itself. The court may either refuse the application, or order rectification and payment by the company of compensation for any loss sustained by any person aggrieved. The court may decide any question as to entitlement to registration, both as between members or alleged members and as between the company on the one hand and members or alleged members on the other hand. In addition, it may decide any question 'necessary or expedient to be decided for rectification of the register'.

[23.23] It has been held that the power thus given to the court to order rectification is a discretionary one[25]. Members have succeeded in having their

---

21 Companies Act 1963, s 116.
22 Companies Act 1963, s 119(1).
23 Companies Act 1963, s 119(2).
24 Companies Act 1963, s 121.
25 *Trevor v Whitworth* (1887) 12 App Cas 409 at 440.

names removed from the register under the equivalent English jurisdiction where the registration was effected as the result of a misrepresentation[26]. In such cases, however, the court will not come to the assistance of the member unless he acts with reasonable expedition. A registration effected as the result of a misrepresentation is voidable only and not void, and will not be set aside at the instance of the member if he delays unreasonably in seeking relief[27]. Moreover, once a winding up has commenced, a registration which is voidable only cannot be set aside[28]. If, however, the registration was void, ie a nullity from the beginning, it would seem that it may be set aside at any time, whether or not the winding up has begun.

[23.24] The application for rectification may he made in a summary manner by special summons grounded on an affidavit. If, however, there is a major issue to be determined, the relief should be sought in an action commenced by plenary summons. Any of the parties may be required to make discovery under the Rules of the Superior Courts: thus in *Cory v Cory*[29] a member claimed to have the register rectified on the ground that he had been induced to transfer his shares to a director at an undervalue by a fraudulent misrepresentation as to the company's financial position. The company was required to make discovery on oath of its financial records for a specified period. Where rectification is ordered, notice of the order must be given to the Registrar[30].

[23.25] The company may itself, without any application to the court, rectify any error or omission in the register. Such a rectification cannot, however, adversely affect any person without his consent. The company must also give notice to the Registrar of any rectification within 21 days, if the error or omission also occurs in any document forwarded by the company to the Registrar[31].

[23.26] Section 123 provides that:

> 'no notice of any trust, express, implied or constructive, shall be entered on the register or be receivable by the Registrar.'

This is one of the most important provisions of the Principal Act: it means that the effective control of the company may be in the hands of persons whose identity cannot be traced and who own the shares through nominees. It is usually supplemented by an article which extends the prohibition on recognising

---

[26] *Stewart's case* (1866) 1 Ch App 574.
[27] *Sewell's case* (1868) 3 Ch App 131; *Re Scottish Petroleum Co* (1883) 23 Ch D 413 at 434.
[28] *Oakes v Turquand* (1867) 2 HL Cas 325.
[29] [1923] 1 Ch 90.
[30] Companies Act 1963, s 122(4).
[31] Companies Act 1963, s 122(5).

beneficial interest to every conceivable type of such interest which could arise in relation to shares, eg:

> 'Except as required by law, no person shall be recognised by the company as holding any share upon any trust, and the company shall not be bound by or compelled in any way to recognise (even when having notice thereof) any equitable, contingent, future or partial interest in any share or any interest in any fractional part of a share or (except only as by these regulations or by law otherwise provided) any other rights in respect of any share except an absolute right to the entirety thereof in the registered holder ...' (Article 7)

[23.27] This aspect of the legislation is open to serious abuse: directors may have inside knowledge of the affairs of the company denied to some of the shareholders and it is clearly undesirable that, armed with such knowledge, they should be in a position to buy and sell shares in the company without the shareholders knowing that this is happening. The Cohen Committee, on whose report the English 1948 Act was largely based, recommended sweeping changes in this area, including a requirement that there should be compulsory disclosure of those beneficially entitled to 1% or more of the issued share capital. This was rejected by the framers of the 1948 Act as too drastic, but the Act did contain provisions requiring the company to maintain a register of directors' shareholdings and dealings and enabling the Board of Trade to appoint an inspector to investigate the true ownership of the company.

[23.28] When the Cox Committee considered this matter in 1958, they also rejected the Cohen recommendations as being impractical. They considered that the most serious abuses in the Irish context could be met by a requirement for a register of directors' shareholdings and dealings. In England the Jenkins Committee made less sweeping proposals than those which found favour with Cohen; but they did recommend that compulsory disclosure should be required in the case of shareholdings of 10% and more. They also recommended that certain option dealings by directors should be made a criminal offence. The framers of the Principal Act, however, confined themselves to implementing the recommendation of Cox. In England, the recommendations of Jenkins were implemented by the 1967 Act. The requirements as to disclosure of shareholdings generally were strengthened in that jurisdiction by the 1980 and 1981 Acts.

[23.29] Similar legislation was enacted in Ireland in the form of Part IV of the 1990 Act. Chapter 1, which governs share dealings by directors, secretaries and their families, is dealt with in paras **[27.136]** to **[27.152]** below. Chapters 2 and 3, which provide for disclosure as to individual and group acquisitions of interests in companies are dealt with in the next chapter.

[23.30] The fact that no notice of any trust may be entered on the register does not mean that equitable interests in shares cannot be created: it is perfectly possible for the person appearing on the register to hold the shares in trust for someone else, even though the company cannot be required to recognise anyone but the person named in the register as the owner. The court indeed will intervene by injunction at the instance of the equitable owner to prevent a transaction being completed which would adversely affect his interest in the shares.

Register prima facie evidence of contents

[23.31] The register is prima facie evidence of any matters directed or authorised to be inserted therein[32]. It is not conclusive evidence and, accordingly, it is always open to a person to adduce evidence that the register does not accurately record a particular matter. Moreover, a person is presumed to be aware that the person whose name appears on the register may not have consented to the registration, and that an allotment or transfer of shares may be voidable because of misrepresentation[33].

---

[32] Companies Act 1963, s 124.
[33] See para **[23.07]** above.

Chapter 24

Disclosure of Interests in Shares

[24.01] As we have seen[1], the register of members of a company cannot contain any entries as to trusts. There is, accordingly, nothing to prevent the member appearing on the register from owning the shares in trust for another person whose identity remains hidden from anyone inspecting the register. As a result, it was at one time possible for directors, privy to knowledge of the company's affairs denied to shareholders, to deal secretly in the company's shares through nominees. In consequence, the Principal Act obliged companies for the first time to maintain a register of directors' shareholdings[2] and these requirements were substantially strengthened by Part IV of the 1990 Act.

[24.02] The absence of any general obligation on persons other than directors to disclose their interests in shares became of particular significance when a take-over was being planned. It was possible for individuals to build up shareholdings in companies through nominees without the board of directors or anyone else becoming aware of the changes in ownership of the company. The controls first introduced in England in the 1967 Act - requiring disclosure by those beneficially entitled to 10% or more of the share capital - were evaded by the formation of so-called 'concert parties'. The individuals or companies effecting the take-over - soon to be given the zoological tag of 'predators' by the financial press - took care to effect their take-overs through a series of acquisitions by individuals remaining below the statutory limits, but in sum sufficient to allow them to reach a majority shareholding in the company under siege. Combined with 'dawn raids', ie acquisitions of shares effected with such speed that the market and commentators alike were unaware of the effects on a company's ownership, this led to calls in England for strengthened disclosure provisions. These are contained in Part VI of the English 1985 Act.

[24.03] Similar provisions appeared in Irish law for the first time in the 1990 Act. However, the requirements of the Stock Exchange had already introduced some degree of control: s 5 of the Regulations for the Admission of Securities to Listing required the notifications of acquisitions in excess of 5% to the exchange. Part IV of the 1990 Act, which is modelled on Part VI of the English 1985 Act, contains detailed statutory controls in this area.

---

[1] Para **[23.26]** above.
[2] See para **[27.136]** below.

[24.04] Chapter 1 of Part IV imposes obligations on directors, secretaries and their families as to the disclosure of shareholdings. Chapter 2 contains elaborate provisions for the compulsory notification of acquisitions by individuals or groups of beneficial interests in shares amounting to 5% or more of the issued share capital of public limited companies. It also seeks to ensure the similar notification of acquisitions of 5% or more as a result of arrangements, whether legally binding or informal, between individuals or groups, thus, as it hoped, dealing with the 'concert party' phenomenon. There are also provisions enabling the company to investigate the ownership of its own shares. Chapter 3, which applies principally to private companies, gives the court a new jurisdiction to order the disclosure by persons of their interests in a company's shares to persons having a financial interest in the company.

Disclosure of share acquisitions by individuals or groups

[24.05] We shall consider first the obligations on individuals to disclose acquisitions of shares in a public limited company. Such an obligation arises when an individual to his knowledge acquires an interest (or becomes aware that he has acquired an interest) in 5% or more of any class of its voting share capital.

[24.06] The circumstances in which the obligation arises are set out in detail in ss 67 to 71. It arises both when he acquires an interest and ceases to have an interest. In effect, if the result of the sale or purchase of the shares is to bring his holdings above or below the 5% level, he must notify the company in writing of that fact within five days. In addition, if his holdings had already reached the 5% level, he is obliged to notify the company of any subsequent acquisition or disposition.

[24.07] The obligation to disclose arises when the individual concerned acquires 5% or more in nominal value of the shares comprised in the 'relevant capital'[3]. This latter phrase means the issued share capital of a class carrying voting rights in all circumstances at general meetings: in this context, the fact that any voting rights are temporarily suspended is to be disregarded[4]. The notification which he is required to give the company must state the number of shares which he now has or, in a case where his holding has fallen below the 5% level, that fact[5].

The 5% threshold may be raised or lowered at any time by the Minister[6].

---

3   Companies Act 1990, s 67(1).
4   Companies Act 1990, s 67(2).
5   Companies Act 1990, s 71.
6   Companies Act 1990, s 70.

[24.08] The interest of a spouse or minor child of a person in shares in the relevant company must be taken into account in determining whether his holdings have reached the notifiable percentage[7]. So also must the interest of another company in shares in the relevant company if the directors are accustomed to act in accordance with his directions or instructions or if he controls the exercise of one-third or more of the voting power of the company at general meetings[8]. The obligation to disclose arises when the person concerned becomes aware of the acquisition or disposition of shares by a spouse or minor child or by a company so controlled by him.

[24.09] The nature of the 'interests' captured must next be considered. The relevant sections apply to 'interests of any kind whatsoever'[9]. Specifically, they apply to the following[10]:

(1)   a beneficiary under a trust, with certain exceptions;

(2)   a purchaser under a contract;

(3)   a person who is not a shareholder, but who is entitled to exercise (or control the exercise of) the rights of the shareholder or a debenture holder;

(4)   a person entitled to an option in respect of shares.

The following trust interests are not captured[11]:

(1)   the interest of a bare trustee;

(2)   an interest in remainder or reversion

(3)   any discretionary interest;

(4)   a life interest under an irrevocable settlement where the settler has no interest in the income or capital.

The following interests are also not captured[12]:

(1)   interests subsisting under unit trusts or their EU equivalents;

(2)   interests under schemes under the Charities Act 1961[13];

(3)   the interest of the President of the High Court in an estate before representation is raised;

---

[7]   Companies Act 1990, s 72.
[8]   Companies Act 1990, s 72.
[9]   Companies Act 1990, s 77(2).
[10] Companies Act 1990, s 77(3), (4), (5) and (6).
[11] Companies Act 1990, s 78(1).
[12] Companies Act 1990, s 78(1).
[13] Ie schemes under the Charities Act 1961, s 46 for the investment in common of different charitable funds.

(4)   any other interest prescribed by the Minister.

'Exempt security interests' are also excluded[14]. Hence, the disclosure obligations do not apply to shareholdings held by way of security, eg as collateral for overdrafts or other loans, by any of the following: banks, insurance companies, trustee savings banks, post office savings banks, and stockbrokers carrying on business on a recognised stock exchange.

[24.10] We next consider the disclosure obligations applicable to group acquisitions of shares. These are dealt with in ss 73 to 76.

As we saw[15], the obligation on a person to notify the company of an acquisition by him of an interest in shares bringing his shareholdings to the 5% level could be circumvented with relative ease: the acquisition could be effected by a number of people making smaller individual purchases on foot of a prearranged plan to take over the company. Accordingly, these sections provide that, for the purpose of determining whether a person is obliged to notify the company, he is also to be treated as being interested in shares which other parties to such an arrangement have acquired.

[24.11] These sections take effect when there is an agreement between two or more persons which includes provision for the acquisition by one or more of them of shares carrying voting rights in a public limited company, called 'the target company'. For the sections to apply, the agreement must impose obligations or restrictions on one or more of the parties as to the use, retention or disposal by them of their interests in the relevant shares[16]. There must also in fact be an acquisition pursuant to the agreement. Once such an acquisition is effected, the sections continue to apply so long as the agreement contains such provisions, irrespective of whether any further acquisitions take place or of any change in the parties or variation in the agreement[17].

[24.12] Evasion would also be easier if the sections applied only to legally enforceable agreements. The sections, accordingly, apply to any 'arrangement' and to 'undertakings, expectations or understandings' operative under such arrangements[18]. There must, however, be 'mutuality' for the sections to apply: there will thus be no obligation to disclose unless the parties are implementing some form of concerted strategy in which each is expected to play a role. Nor do the sections apply to agreements for the underwriting of shares[19].

---

[14] Companies Act 1990, s 78(1)(d) and (4).
[15] See para **[24.02]** above.
[16] Companies Act 1990, s 73(1).
[17] Companies Act 1990, s 73(3).
[18] Companies Act 1990, s 73(4).
[19] Companies Act 1990, s 73(5).

[24.13] Where there is an agreement to which the sections apply, a person is treated as being interested in all the shares in which the other parties to the agreement are interested, whether they were acquired pursuant to the agreement or not[20]. This includes shares in which any of the other parties are deemed to be interested because they are held by spouses, minor children or controlled companies.

[24.14] The object of the sections could be defeated by the parties deliberately keeping each other in the dark while the acquisitions are in progress and then pleading ignorance as the reason for failing to notify the company. Hence each party is obliged to notify the others of particulars of his interest where he knows that the arrangement is one relating to the acquisition of shares in a target company which is a public limited company and he also knows the facts which make the sections applicable[21]. He must do so when he becomes subject to this requirement and again whenever he makes a further acquisition or disposition which triggers the disclosure obligations binding on him as an individual[22].

[24.15] The 'concert party' provisions, as we have seen, are largely based on the corresponding English provisions. It should, however, be pointed out that doubts have arisen in that jurisdiction as to how effective such provisions are. Reporting on an investigation into certain share dealings, the Council of the Stock Exchange, while voicing their strong suspicions that a concert party had been at work, were unable to say that one existed within the meaning of the legislation. The report commented:

> '"Mutuality of expectations" or "mutual understanding" are almost impossible to prove in a court of law and unless there were legal agreements and unless those agreements are discoverable, it is probably beyond the competence of anyone to prove that there was or was not a concert party.'[23]

[24.16] The methods of enforcing the disclosure obligations imposed by Chapter 2 are prescribed in s 79. Any person who fails to fulfil the various obligations is guilty of an offence and liable on summary conviction to a fine not exceeding £1,000 or imprisonment for a term not exceeding 12 months or both or on indictment to a fine not exceeding £10,000 or imprisonment for term not exceeding three years or both. In addition, the section provides that where any such obligation is not fulfilled, no right or interest of any kind in respect of the relevant shares is to be legally enforceable. Any person affected by this latter provision may, however, apply to the court for relief which may be granted

---

[20] Companies Act 1990, s 74(1).
[21] Companies Act 1990, s 75.
[22] Companies Act 1990, s 75.
[23] Report of the Inquiry of the Stock Exchange Council into Westland plc.

where the court is satisfied that the default was accidental or due to inadvertence or some other sufficient cause or that, on other grounds, it is just and equitable to grant such relief.

[24.17] The disclosure requirements could be evaded if the relevant transactions were carried out by an agent of whose dealings the principal took care to remain ignorant. Hence, s 79(1) obliges a person to secure that such an agent notifies him immediately of any acquisitions or dispositions which give rise to an obligation to notify. There are the same criminal and civil consequences where this obligation is not fulfilled.

Notification to stock exchange of share acquisitions and dispositions

[24.18] Chapter 2 imposes, in addition to the disclosure obligations outlined above, an obligation to notify the Stock Exchange of any acquisition or disposal of officially listed shares carrying voting rights in a public limited company which brings a person's holding above or below certain specified percentages ie 10, 25, 50 and 70%[24]. These provisions carry into effect the requirements of an EU directive on the information to be published when a major holding in a listed company changes hands[25].

[24.19] All the provisions already outlined, including those relating to 'concert party' arrangements, apply to these notification requirements[26]. The Exchange must publish the relevant information within three days of its receipt, unless they are satisfied that it would be contrary to the public interest or seriously detrimental to the company concerned. They may only decide to withhold publication if they are satisfied that this will be unlikely to mislead the public in assessing the value of these shares[27].

[24.20] There are also provisions requiring the Exchange to notify the Director of Public Prosecutions if it appears to them that any person has contravened the notification requirements[28]. A member of the Exchange must similarly notify the management of the Exchange. Moreover, if it appears to a court in any proceedings that there has been a contravention which has not been reported to the DPP, it may direct the management of the Exchange to make a report[29]. There are consequential provisions requiring those concerned to assist the DPP in his investigations and any prosecution he may institute[30].

---

[24] Companies Act 1990, s 91.
[25] Council Directive 88/627/EEC of 12 December 1985.
[26] See para **[24.11]** above.
[27] Companies Act 1990, s 91(5) and (6).
[28] Companies Act 1990, s 92.
[29] Companies Act 1990, s 92.
[30] Companies Act 1990, s 92.

Register of interests in shares

[24.21] Every public limited company must keep a register of interests in its shares[31]. This register - which, it should be noted, is one which must be kept in addition to the registers of members' and directors' shareholdings - must record all the information received from persons in fulfilment of the disclosure obligations dealt with in this chapter. The nature and extent of a person's interest must, if he so requires, also be recorded. The company, however, is not to he affected by notice of, or put on any enquiry as to, the rights of any person in relation to any shares. The various requirements of the 1990 Act as to the register of directors' shareholdings in relation to such matters as where it is to be kept, how it is to be compiled and its availability for inspection are also applicable to this register[32]. There is also a provision requiring the company to continue to keep the register for a period of six years after it ceases to be a public limited company[33].

Investigation by a company of the ownership of its own shares

[24.22] A public limited company is also empowered by s 81 of the 1990 Act to carry out an investigation of the ownership of shares in the company. For this purpose, it can by notice in writing require any person whom it knows, or has reasonable cause to believe, to have been interested in any voting shares in the company within the preceding three years either to confirm the fact or notify the company whether it is so or not. The company can require particulars of any interests in the shares to be given to them, including information as to whether the persons interested are or were involved in any 'concert party' arrangement as to the shares. The provisions deeming spouses and minor children to be interested persons and defining the scope of the interests affected already considered apply also to this procedure[34]. The notice must require the information to be given within a specified time which must be reasonable. Details of the notice and of any information received are to be entered in the register of interests.

[24.23] An investigation of this nature must also be carried out by a public limited company if it is demanded by a sufficient proportion of the members. Section 83 provides that the company may be required to exercise its powers under s 81 on the requisition of members holding not less than one tenth of the issue shares carrying voting rights. Such a requisition must give reasonable

---

[31] Companies Act 1990, s 80.
[32] See para **[27.149]** below.
[33] Companies Act 1990, s 80(8).
[34] Para **[24.08]** above.

grounds for requiring the company to act. Where it is not complied with, the court can compel the exercise of the powers if satisfied that it is reasonable so to do. There is provision for the making of a report by the company on the results of the investigation which is to be made available at the registered office within a reasonable time after it has concluded. If it is not concluded within three months, an interim report must be made similarly available. Where these requirements as to the report are not met, the company and every officer in default is liable on summary conviction to a fine not exceeding £1,000 and on indictment to a fine not exceeding £10,000.

[24.24] A person who fails to give the information required by a valid notice served by a company under s 81 is guilty of an offence and liable on summary conviction to a fine not exceeding £1,000 or imprisonment for a term not exceeding 12 months or both and on indictment to a fine not exceeding £10,000 or imprisonment for a term not exceeding three years or both[35]. In addition, the court has power on an application by the company where there is such a failure to order the imposition of restrictions on the transfer of shares similar to those which may be imposed during the course of an investigation by inspectors appointed by the court[36]. The same provisions apply, including the power of the court to order the cesser of the restrictions on the application of the company or an aggrieved person.

[24.25] It should be noted that it is a defence to the criminal proceedings for a person to prove that the requirement to give information was 'frivolous or vexatious'. It was held in *Re FH Lloyd Holdings*[37] that an order restricting the transfer of shares should also be refused in such circumstances. But it was also held that to avail of its powers the company does not have to be in a position to prove that the person concerned was seeking to build up a substantial holding in the company.

Private companies: disclosure orders

[24.26] A procedure is provided under Chapter 3 of Para IV of the 1990 Act which enables potentially interested people to obtain information as to the ownership of shares in a private company. The major difference between this procedure and that applicable in the case of public companies is that it can only be put in motion by an order of the court. While in general it applies to all corporate bodies other than public limited companies, there are two important exclusions, ie industrial and provident societies and building societies.

---

[35] Companies Act 1990, s 85.
[36] See para **[35.50]** below.
[37] (1985) BCLC 293.

[24.27] Where the court makes an order under Chapter 3, the incidents of the order are the same in all material respects as a notice served under Chapter 2[38]. Unlike a Chapter 2 notice, however, a Chapter 3 order is not necessarily limited in its scope to the period of three years prior to its being made: it can be made in respect of persons interested in shares 'at present or at any time during a period specified in the order'. It applies, moreover, to debentures as well as shares.

[24.28] The persons who may apply for a disclosure order are those who have 'a financial interest' in the company. They are defined as including members, contributories, creditors, employees, 'co-adventurers', examiners, liquidators, receivers, lessors, lessees, licensers and licencees with an interest in the company or a related company[39]. An applicant can be required to give security for costs.

[24.29] The court may only make the order where it deems it just and equitable so to do and is of the opinion that the financial interest of the applicant is, or will be, prejudiced by non-disclosure. The applicant must give 10 days' notice to the company and to the person to whom the order is intended to be directed[40]. The application should be made by special summons. It is to be supported by such evidence as the court may require and the court may also direct service of notice of the application on other persons. Any disclosure order made may be subsequently varied or rescinded and the court may exempt specified persons or classes of shares from its requirements. The court may also impose such conditions or restrictions on the rights or obligations attached to the shares or debentures as it deems fit. It may also relieve any person from such conditions or restrictions if it considers it just and equitable so to do[41].

[24.30] The obligation is imposed on the applicant for a disclosure order of giving notice of its having been made. Notice must be given in the prescribed form by registered post within seven days to:

(1)   the company at its registered office;

(2)   the Registrar;

(3)   shareholders or debenture holders not resident in Ireland where the court considers they should be notified;

(4)   such other person as the court sees fit.

---

[38]   Companies Act 1990, s 98.

[39]   Companies Act 1990, s 98(6).

[40]   Companies Act 1990, s 99.

[41]   Companies Act 1990, s 101.

The applicant must also arrange for publication of notice of the making of the order within seven days in at least two daily newspapers circulating in the district in which the registered office of the relevant company is situated.

[24.31] Where the information is given to the court in compliance with the order, it is to be given by a prescribed officer of the court to the applicant and the company, either in whole or in part as the court directs, unless the court otherwise directs[42].

[24.32] Unlike Chapter 2, Chapter 3 does not create a criminal offence where there is a failure to comply with the disclosure requirements. This is presumably because non-compliance with a disclosure order will expose the offender to attachment for contempt of court. Section 103, however, provides for the non-enforceability of rights or interests in respect of shares or debentures in cases of non-compliance in terms virtually identical to the corresponding provisions in Chapter 2. There is also a similar requirement as to principals ensuring that agents keep them notified for the duration of the order of acquisitions and disposals of interests in shares or debentures effected by the agent which would or might give rise to an obligation on the principal's part to provide information in accordance with the order.

---

[42] Companies Act 1990, s 102.

Chapter 25

Meetings

[25.01] The principal control exercised by members of a company over its activities is through meetings of the members which the company holds from time to time. Such meetings are of three kinds:

(1)   the annual general meeting;

(2)   extraordinary general meetings; and

(3)   separate meetings of classes of shareholders.

[25.02] The annual general meeting, as its name indicates, must be held once a year. Extraordinary general meetings may be convened when the directors wish, but in addition a defined proportion of the members has the right to require the convening of such a meeting if they wish. Separate class meetings are usually required for the purpose of voting on proposals to vary or abrogate the rights attached to the class of shares in question[1].

[25.03] There was formerly provision for the holding of a statutory meeting within three months from the date on which a company was entitled to commence business. This requirement, which did not apply to private companies, was abolished in the case of all companies by the 1983 Act[2].

Annual general meeting

[25.04] Every company, public or private, limited or unlimited, and whether having a share capital or not, must hold a general meeting in each year as its annual general meeting in addition to any other meetings in that year; and it must be specified as such in the notices calling it. Not more than 15 months may elapse between the date of the holding of one annual general meeting and the next[3]. These requirements are contained in s 131(1) of the Principal Act.

[25.05] Special provision is made by s 131(2) for the first annual general meeting of a company. So long as this meeting is held within 18 months of the incorporation of the company, it need not be held in the year of its incorporation or in the following year.

---

[1]   See para **[17.20]** above.

[2]   Companies (Amendment) Act 1983, s 3, Sch 3.

[3]   Companies Act 1963, s 131(1).

[25.06] If the company fails to hold the meetings, the Minister has power, on the application of any member, to call or direct the calling of a general meeting. He may also give such ancillary or consequential directions as he thinks expedient, including directions modifying or supplementing the operation of the articles in relation to the calling, holding or conducting of the meeting. He may also direct that one member of the company present in person or by proxy shall be deemed to constitute a meeting[4]. This is necessary because of decisions to the effect that a 'meeting' must consist of at least two people[5].

[25.07] Where a meeting is held because of the exercise by the Minister of his powers and it is not held in the year in which the default occurred, the meeting is not to be treated as the annual general meeting for the year in which it is held, unless the company so resolve[6]. If they so resolve, a copy of the resolution must be forwarded to the Registrar within 15 days after it has been passed[7].

[25.08] Special provision has been made for single member companies which, as we have seen[8], can now be incorporated under regulation 8(1) of the European Community (Single-Member Private Limited Companies) Regulations 1994. Regulation 8(1) proves that the sole member of such a company may decide to dispense with the holding of annual general meetings and, if he or she does so, s 131 will not apply to the company.

Business at annual general meeting

[25.09] The annual general meeting of a company is a most important meeting, since it must be held whether the directors wish it to be held or not. The only matter which must be dealt with at the meeting is the laying before the meeting of the balance sheet, profit and loss account, auditors' report[9] and directors' report on the state of the company's affairs[10]. But this is simply the minimum statutory requirement: the articles may provide in addition that the following matters are to be dealt with at the meeting:

(1)   the declaration of a dividend;

(2)   the election of directors in the place of those retiring;

(3)   the re-appointment of the retiring auditors; and

(4)   the fixing of the remuneration of the auditors.

---

[4]   Companies Act 1963, s 131(3).
[5]   *Sharp v Dawes* [1876] 2 QBD 26; *Re London Flats Ltd* [1969] 2 All ER 744.
[6]   Companies Act 1963, s 131(4).
[7]   Companies Act 1963, s 131(5).
[8]   See para **[4.05]** above.
[9]   Certain companies may now be exempted from the requirement to have their accounts audited: see para **[30.110]** below.
[10] Companies Act 1963, s 148.

[25.10] If article 53 is applicable, items (1) to (4) above and the presentation of the accounts and reports are treated by implication as the 'ordinary business' of the meeting. Any other business transacted at the annual general meeting or at an extraordinary general meeting is treated by article 53 as 'special business'. But while this means that the items of 'ordinary business' are the matters which will invariably be dealt with at the annual general meeting, it does not preclude the members from raising other matters. A member is perfectly entitled to give notice of his intention to propose a resolution relating to some other matters at the annual general meeting: he does not have to join with other members in convening an extraordinary general meeting for the same day, as is frequently done.

[25.11] It should be noted that there is no requirement that the annual general meeting approve or adopt the accounts and reports. Section 148 of the Principal Act does no more than impose on the directors the duty of laying the relevant documents before the meeting.

[25.12] The profit and loss account must cover the period from the previous accounts to a date not earlier than nine months before the meeting. (In the case of the first meeting, the period runs from the date of incorporation.) The balance sheet must be as of the date up to which the profit and loss account is made up.

[25.13] A copy of the balance sheet, profit and loss account, auditors' report and directors' report must be sent to every member of the company (whether or not he is entitled to receive notices of general meetings), every debenture holder (whether or not he is so entitled) and every person, other than a member or debenture holder, who is so entitled at least 21 days before the meeting[11]. In the case of public companies, it is usual to include with the material which must be circulated a review by the chairman of the year's activities.

[25.14] The auditors' report must be read at the meeting and must be open to inspection by any of the members[12]. The auditors, if they are qualified, are automatically re-appointed at the meeting, unless

    (1)   a resolution is passed at the meeting appointing someone else instead of an auditor or expressly providing that he shall not be re-appointed, or

    (2)   an auditor has given the company notice in writing of his unwillingness to be re-appointed[13]

---

[11] Companies Act 1963, s 159(1).
[12] Companies Act 1963, s 163(2).
[13] Companies Act 1963, s 160(2).

Extraordinary general meetings

[25.15] General meetings other than the annual general meeting are called 'extraordinary general meetings'. They may be convened by the directors of the company, but in addition a most important power is given by s 132 of the Principal Act to the members to require the directors to convene such meetings. The section provides that the directors must convene an extraordinary general meeting on a requisition of members holding at the date of the requisition not less than one-tenth of such of the paid-up capital as carries voting rights at a general meeting. In the case of a company not having a share capital, the number of requisitionists must represent not less than one-tenth of the total voting rights of all the members entitled to vote at general meetings. These provisions cannot be excluded by the articles.

[25.16] The requisition must state the objects of the meeting, be signed by the requisitionists and be deposited at the registered office of the company. It may consist of several documents in like form each signed by one or more requisitions.

[25.17] If the directors do not convene a meeting (to be held within two months) within 21 days from the date of the deposit of the requisition, the requisitionists, or any of them who represent more than one-half of the total voting rights of all of them, may convene the meeting themselves. It may not be held, however, after the expiration of three months from the date of the deposit of the requisition. The requisitionists are entitled to be paid their reasonable expenses of convening the meeting by the company and the company in turn is entitled to retain the amount out of any fees or other remuneration due to the directors in default.

[25.18] The fact that the requisition contains resolutions which cannot be put before the meeting does not relieve the directors of their obligation to convene the meeting[14].

[25.19] The Principal Act also provides[15] that two or more members holding not less than one-tenth of the issued share capital, or, if the company has not a share capital, not less than 5% in number of all the members of the company may call a meeting, unless the articles provide otherwise. Since, however, the articles invariably provide for the convening of meetings by the directors alone, this is of no practical importance.

---

[14] *Isle of Wight Rly Co v Tahourdin* (1884) 25 Ch D 320.
[15] Companies Act 1963, s 134(b).

Power of court to convene meeting

[25.20] The court has a wide power under s 135 of the Principal Act to convene a meeting of the company. It may do so where for any reason it is impractical to call a meeting in any manner in which meetings of the company may be called or to conduct the meetings of the company in the manner prescribed by the articles or the Acts. The court may make the order either on the application of a director or a member who would be entitled to vote at the meeting, or of its own motion. It may order the meeting to be called, held and conducted in such a manner as it thinks fit and may give such ancillary or consequential directions as it thinks expedient. The directions that may be given include a direction that one member present in person or by a proxy shall be deemed to constitute a meeting[16]. Any meeting called, held and conducted in accordance with such an order is to be deemed for all purposes to be a meeting duly called, held and conducted.

Notice of meetings

[25.21] Not less than 21 days' notice must be given of the annual general meetings of all companies, public and private, and not less than seven days' notice of any other meeting, where the company is a private company or an unlimited company. Not less than 14 days' notice is required in the case of other meetings, where the company is a public limited company[17]. These are the minimum periods of notice prescribed by the Principal Act; the articles may provide for longer periods of notice and any such requirement must be observed. If a special resolution is being proposed, 21 days' notice must be given.

[25.22] The equivalent period in England for meetings other than the annual general meeting is 14 days and no distinction is made between public and private companies. Even this has been criticised as being too short, and in view of the overwhelming preponderance of private companies in Ireland, it would seem reasonable that the period of notice for all companies should be at least 14 days.

[25.23] If all the members of the company entitled to attend and vote at a meeting and the company's auditors agree, a meeting can be called by shorter notice than is specified in the Acts or the articles[18].

[25.24] The articles usually provide that the period of notice given is to be 'clear', ie exclusive both of the day of service and the day of the meeting (article 51). If the articles do not so provide, it would appear that clear notice must still be given, according to decisions in England, but a different view has been taken

---

16 See para **[25.06]** above.
17 Companies Act 1963, s 133.
18 Companies Act 1963, s 133(3).

in Scotland[19]. Obviously, it is better to err on the safe side in all circumstances and give the clear period of notice.

[25.25] The only persons who must be given notice are those entitled to attend, ie the members and the auditors, unless the articles otherwise provide. A member is not entitled to attend accompanied by a solicitor or some other advisor. He is, however, entitled to appoint another person as proxy to attend and vote instead of him; and the proxy need not be a member of the company[20].

[25.26] The articles usually provide for a method of service of the notice. article 133 enables it to be given either personally or by sending it to him by ordinary prepaid post at the address appearing in the register. Notice need not be given to members who are abroad[21], and in the case of deceased members, their personal representatives need not be notified unless they are on the register[22]. The articles usually provide that proceedings at a meeting are not to be invalidated by accidental omission to give notice or the non-receipt of notice (article 52). It is important to include such a provision, since otherwise a meeting could be rendered ineffective by an accidental failure to give notice. A deliberate failure to give notice will not be excused by article 52, where it is based on an erroneous view that a person is not entitled to notice[23].

In one case no notice need be given to anyone. This is where all the members of the company and the auditors agree to dispense with notice[24].

[25.27] The notice must specify the date, time and place of the meeting. This is usually expressly required by the articles (article 51), but is in any event necessary[25]. In addition, the notice must state the general nature of any special business to be transacted at the meeting. This means that a notice convening an annual general meeting need not specify the ordinary business of such a meeting such as the presentation of the accounts, declaration of dividend, replacement of the retiring directors, etc. It must, however, specify any other business to be transacted. In the case of an extraordinary general meeting, the notice must specify in general terms the nature of the business to be transacted, since of its nature it will not be ordinary business. The notice must also contain sufficient particulars of the business to be transacted to enable the shareholders to come to an informed decision as to how they will vote. In one Irish case, an injunction was granted to restrain the holding of a meeting where insufficient particulars

---

[19] *Re Hector Whaling Ltd* [1936] Ch 208; *Re Neil McLeod & Sons Ltd, Petitioners* 1967 SLT 46.
[20] Companies Act 1963, s 136.
[21] *Re Union Hill Silver Co* (1870) 22 LT 400.
[22] *Allen v Gold Reefs of West Africa Ltd* [1900] 1 Ch 656 at 670 per Lindley MR.
[23] *Musselwhite v Musselwhite & Co* [1962] Ch 964.
[24] *Re Express Engineering Works Ltd* [1920] 1 Ch 466.
[25] Gower, *Modern Company Law* (4th edn), p 573.

had been given[26], and in a number of English cases they have been granted to restrain the directors from implementing resolutions passed at meetings where insufficient particulars had been given[27].

Resolutions

[25.28] The decisions of a company must take the form, generally speaking, of *resolutions,* ie specific proposals formally advanced by persons entitled to do so and voted upon at duly convened meetings. They are in law of two kinds, *ordinary* and *special* resolutions. Ordinary resolutions may be proposed at the meeting and require only a simple majority of the members present and entitled to vote to be effective. Special resolutions must be passed by not less than three fourths of the votes cast by members who being entitled to vote in person do so (or where proxies are allowed, do so by proxy). In addition not less than 21 days' notice must be given of the intention to propose the resolution[28]. Some of the most important acts which a company may perform may only be done by special resolution.

[25.29] There are also resolutions of which extended notice must be given. They are:

(1)   resolutions under s 182 of the Principal Act removing a director from office, and

(2)   resolutions under s 161(1) of the Principal Act providing that a retiring auditor shall not be re-appointed or that another person shall be appointed in place of a retiring auditor.

These resolutions remain ordinary resolutions, ie they can be passed by a simple majority unless the articles otherwise provide. But at least 28 days' notice of the intention to move them must be given to the company. The company must in turn give notice to the members of the resolution at the same time and in the same manner as it gives notice of the meeting at which the resolution is to be proposed. If this is not practicable, it must give notice to the members either by an advertisement in a newspaper circulating in the district in which the registered office is situated or by any other mode allowed by the articles not less than 21 days before the meeting.

[25.30] If after notice of such a resolution has been given, a meeting is called for a date 21 days or less after the date of the notice, the notice is deemed by s 142(2) to be in time for the purposes of the section, even though not within the time specified by sub-s (1). This prevents the directors, on receiving such a

---

[26] *Jackson v Munster Bank* 13 LR (Ir) 118.

[27] *Palmer's Company Law* (25th edn), Vol 1, 79.08.

[28] Companies Act 1963, s 141(1).

proposal, from calling a meeting within a period shorter than the 28 days and then arguing that the resolution is invalid because of insufficient notice.

[25.31] There is nothing to prevent the articles from providing that particular resolutions must be passed by prescribed majorities or that a particular form or length of notice must be given in the case of certain resolutions.

[25.32] There is no equivalent in Irish law to the extraordinary resolution in English law, ie a resolution which must be passed by the same majority as is required for a special resolution but of which 21 days' notice need not be given.

No requirement that resolutions be circulated to members

[25.33] Where a meeting has been duly convened on a proper notice by the directors, they are not obliged to circulate any resolutions of which the company is given notice to the general body of members. If the members proposing such resolutions wish to ensure that adequate notice is given of their proposals, they must undertake themselves the somewhat expensive and time consuming process of circulating their fellow members. There is no equivalent to s 140 of the English 1948 Act which enables a defined proportion of the members to require the company to give notice of resolutions which they intend to move at the next annual general meeting. In addition, they can require the company to circulate the members with a statement of not more than 1,000 words with respect to the business to be transacted at any meeting. These provisions have been criticised as being somewhat inadequate but it would seem desirable that some provision of this nature should be introduced in Ireland.

Proceedings at meetings

[25.34] It has been held that generally speaking to constitute a meeting at least two people must be present. This applies to general meetings of companies, subject to certain exceptions. A meeting of a class of shareholders may take place with only one shareholder attending, if he is the only shareholder of that class. And, as we have already seen[29], in two instances, the Principal Act provides that one person present in person or by proxy may constitute a meeting, ie where a meeting is convened by the Minister or the court and a direction to that effect is given.

[25.35] For a valid meeting to take place, a quorum must be present. Where the articles make no provision for a quorum, two members personally present in the case of a private company and three in the case of a public company constitute a quorum[30]. Article 54 provides for a quorum of three members 'present in

---

[29] See paras **[25.06]** and **[25.20]** above.
[30] Companies Act 1963, s 134(c).

person'. Where this wording is used, proxies cannot be taken into account in reckoning whether a quorum is present. Article 5 in Part II (applicable to private companies) provides that 'two members present in person or by proxy' are to be a quorum.

[25.36] If there is no quorum present, no valid meeting may be held. The articles usually provide in such circumstances that if, after half an hour, there is still no quorum, the meeting is to be adjourned - or in the case of a requisitioned meeting, dissolved - and that at the adjourned meeting the members present shall be a quorum (article 55). This means that, at the adjourned meeting, two members only constitute a quorum and one of them may be present by proxy. It has even been suggested that in these circumstances, one person may constitute a quorum, but this can hardly be correct, since there is then no 'meeting'.

[25.37] The articles usually provide that the directors may elect a chairman of their meeting (article 104) and that the chairman is also to preside as chairman at every general meeting (article 56). They also usually provide that if the chairman is not present within a specified time at a general meeting or is unwilling to act, the directors present shall choose one of their number to be chairman. If there is no person entitled to act as chairman under such provisions, the first business of the meeting will be to elect one of the members present to be chairman.

[25.38] The chairman is responsible for the proper conduct of the meeting, for ensuring that order is kept and for deciding any points of order that may arise. It is his duty to ascertain the sense of the meeting with regard to any question before it. He must conduct the meeting fairly and ensure that all persons entitled to speak are given a reasonable opportunity of doing so. At meetings of public companies, he will invariably be flanked by the company's solicitor, and this is also a prudent precaution at meetings of private companies.

[25.39] Where the articles provide that the chairman 'may' adjourn the meeting, this gives him a discretion as to whether he will adjourn it or not. Where article 58 is applicable, he may only adjourn with the consent of a meeting at which a quorum is present and must adjourn if directed to do so by the meeting. In *Kinsella v Alliance and Dublin Gas Consumer's Company*[31] (which is discussed in more detail in para **[25.57]** below), where there does not appear to have been any equivalent to article 58, Barron J held that the chairman had no power to adjourn a meeting contrary to the wishes of the majority. It has been held in England that where a chairman wrongfully purports to adjourn a meeting, the members are entitled to elect another chairman and proceed with the meeting[32].

---

[31] (Unreported, 5 October 1982).
[32] *National Dwellings Society v Sykes* [1894] 3 Ch 159.

[25.40] Resolutions must be proposed by the chairman or some other member. They need not be seconded. As we have seen, 21 days' notice must be given of special resolutions, and in the case of the removal of directors or auditors extended notice of 28 days must be given. Ordinary resolutions may be proposed at the meeting.

[25.41] An amendment may be proposed to resolutions other than special resolutions. The latter can only be passed in the terms of which notice was given and accordingly no amendment is permissible, unless it is an amendment which does not affect the substance of the resolution, eg an amendment designed to correct clerical errors in the notice[33]. In the case of ordinary resolutions of which notice has been given to the members in the notice convening the meeting, an amendment may only be permitted if it is within the scope of the original resolution[34]. Thus if the notice is of a resolution to increase the remuneration of the directors by £5,000 a year, there could be no objection to an amendment proposing an increase of £3,000 a year. But if the amendment proposed an increase of £10,000 a year, it would be clearly out of order, since members might have stayed away in the belief that the lower remuneration only would be voted to the directors.

[25.42] The procedure for dealing with amendments is the same as at any other properly conducted meeting, ie the amendment should be voted on first. If it is carried, the chairman puts the resolution as amended to the meeting. If it is defeated, the unamended resolution is put.

Voting at meetings

[25.43] Unless the articles otherwise provide, all questions arising at a meeting must be decided in the first place by a show of hands[35]. Thus each member present at the meeting and entitled to vote has one vote only; and this is so irrespective of the number of shares which he holds. Not every member present may be entitled to vote, if the shares are divided into voting and non-voting shares. It is the chairman's duty to count the hands and he must in doing so disregard non-members and members without voting rights. A member who holds proxies for other members is entitled to be counted once only[36]. A non-member, however, holding a proxy may be counted.

[25.44] Clearly a vote on a show of hands is not an entirely satisfactory method of ascertaining the members' wishes since the extent of the members'

[33] *Re Moorgate Mercantile Holdings* [1980] 1 All ER 40.
[34] *Re Betts & Co Ltd v Macnaghton* [1910] 1 Ch 430.
[35] *Re Horbury etc Co* (1879) 11 Ch D 109.
[36] *Ernest v Loma Gold Mines Ltd* [1897] 1 Ch 1.

shareholdings is disregarded. For this reason, s 137 of the Principal Act protects the right (recognised at common law) of members to demand a poll. It provides that any provision contained in a company's articles which excludes the right to demand a poll on any question is to be void. The only exceptions are the election of a chairman and voting on adjournments. A provision in the articles is also void, if it requires a demand for a poll to be made by more than five members having the right to vote at the meeting or a member or members representing not less than one-tenth of all the members having the right to vote at the meeting or holding shares paid up to the extent of at least one-tenth of the total paid up on all the shares conferring the right to vote. It follows that a provision in the articles enabling an effective demand for a poll to be made by a lesser proportion of the members is valid. Thus article 59 permits a valid demand for a poll to be made by three members present in person or by proxy. That article also permits a valid demand for a poll to be made by the chairman, and he should not hesitate to exercise this power where there is any doubt as to whether a vote on a show of hands truly represents the majority view of the members on a matter of importance.

[25.45] The articles usually provide that on a poll every member shall have one vote for each share which he holds (article 63). Section 138 of the Principal Act enables a member entitled to more than one vote to use his votes in different ways. He may thus cast some of his votes for a resolution and some against it. This provision enables persons holding shares for a number of different principals to cast them in accordance with the wishes of their principals.

[25.46] When the poll is demanded, it is a matter for the chairman to fix the time and place at which it will be held. If, however, the articles provide that it is to be taken immediately, it should be taken as soon as practicable in all the circumstances[37]. It is usual and proper for the chairman to appoint scrutineers to examine and count the votes and report the result to him[38].

[25.47] If the poll is not completed on the day on which it is begun, it must be continued on another day: the chairman is not entitled to close the poll while there are still members present who wish to vote[39]. The poll may be invalidated if a person entitled to vote is excluded[40].

[25.48] The common law did not recognise any right of a member to appoint a proxy to vote on his behalf at a meeting. It was, however, the usual practice for articles to authorise voting by proxy. Section 136 of the Principal Act gives a

---

[37] *Jackson v Hamlyn* [1953] Ch 577 at 589.
[38] *Wandsworth & Co v Wright* (1870) 22 LT 404.
[39] *R v St Pancras* (1839) 11 Ad & El 15.
[40] *R v Lambeth* (1839) 8 Ad & El 356.

member of a company having a share capital who is entitled to attend and vote at meetings the right to appoint a proxy (who need not be a member) to attend and vote instead of him. The proxy so appointed has the same right as the member to speak at the meeting and to vote on a show of hands and on a poll. It should be noted that this provision is in wider terms than the corresponding provision in the English 1948 Act which gives the proxy the right to speak at a meeting only in the case of a private company. The restriction of the right to appoint a proxy to companies having a share capital is contrary to the recommendation of Jenkins on this matter and seems difficult to justify. However, sub-s (2) provides that the articles may authorise voting by proxy in a company without a share capital. Sub-section (2) also provides that a member of a company may appoint one proxy only, unless the articles otherwise provide. Again, a difference between the Principal Act and the 1948 Act should be observed: under the latter, there is no such restriction in the case of a public company. The restriction appears unnecessary in the case of any company: it seems unreasonable that a member unable to attend should have his voting power reduced. Moreover, the restriction deprives the nominee shareholder of the ability to give effect to the differing wishes of a number of beneficial owners.

[25.49] The section also requires the notice convening the meeting of a company having a share capital to include a statement (which must be given 'reasonable prominence') that a member entitled to attend and vote is entitled to appoint a proxy, or, where it is allowed, more than one proxy, to attend, speak and vote instead of him and that a proxy need not be a member. If there is default in complying with this requirement every officer of the company in default is liable to a fine not exceeding £250[41].

[25.50] The section also provides that where invitations to appoint proxies are sent to members at the company's expense, and are sent to some members only, every officer of the company who knowingly and wilfully authorises or permits their issue is liable to a fine not exceeding £500. He is not liable, however, if he simply issues a proxy form or a list of persons willing to act as proxies to a member at his request, provided proxy forms or lists are available to all members on request.

[25.51] The company's articles cannot effectively require the instrument appointing the proxy to be lodged with the company more than 48 hours in advance of the meeting or adjourned meeting[42].

[25.52] In the case of public companies, proxies are invariably 'two way' proxies, ie they enable the member to include in the proxy form an instruction to

---

[41] Companies Act 1963, s 136 as amended by the Companies (Amendment) Act 1983, s 15.
[42] Companies Act 1963, s 136(4).

vote for or against the particular proposal. In the absence of any such direction, the proxy may exercise his discretion in deciding which way to exercise the vote. Gower raises the interesting question as to whether they are legally obliged to exercise the authority conferred on them: he suggests that in general there is no such contractual or equitable obligation on a proxy, but that it may arise where, for example, the proxy is remunerated or is present in a professional capacity, eg as an accountant or solicitor[43]. Directors, however, must always exercise proxies in accordance with the members' instructions.

[25.53] The appointment of a proxy can be revoked by the member at any time before the proxy has voted, unless it is made for valuable consideration and is expressed to be irrevocable[44]. In addition, it is automatically revoked by the death of the member before its exercise. The articles usually provide, however, that a vote by proxy is to be valid notwithstanding the previous death or insanity of the member, the revocation of the proxy or the transfer of the shares to which it relates, unless notice in writing of the relevant fact is received by the company at its registered office before the meeting or adjourned meeting begins (article 73).

[25.54] There are special provisions in the Principal Act for companies which are members of other companies. Section 139 provides that a body corporate may by resolution of its directors or other governing body authorise such a person as it thinks fit to act as its representative at any meeting of the company.

[25.55] All the principles relating to the conduct of general meetings of the company - the giving of notice, the election of the chairman, voting, proxies etc - which have been explained in the preceding paragraphs apply in the same way to separate meetings of classes of shareholders.

[25.56] The only persons entitled to vote at meetings are members or their proxies, and some members may of course be precluded from voting because their shares do not carry voting rights. It is also clear that it is entirely a matter for the member as to how he votes. The company has no power to go behind his vote, as it were, and is bound to recognise it even though the member is obviously voting against the interests of the company. Nor can it decline to give effect to it, because the member in voting as he does is in breach of a contractual obligation to someone else[45] or is even defying a court order[46]. But a majority of the company cannot by their votes commit a fraud on the minority, a subject which is discussed further in the next chapter.

---

43 Gower, *Modern Company Law* (6th edn), pp 581.
44 *Spiller v Mayo (Rhodesia) etc* [1926] WN 78.
45 *Palmer's Company Law* (25th edn), Vol 1, para 7.609.
46 *Northern Counties Securities Ltd v Jackson & Steeple Ltd* [1974] 2 All ER 625.

[25.57] It is clear from a number of English decisions that the register of members is the only evidence of a member's right to attend and vote[47], but what is the position if the company fails to register as a member a person who is entitled to be registered? This question arose in *Kinsella v Dublin Gas Consumers' Company*. In that case, a number of members of the defendant company were seeking to gain control of it and remove the board of directors. The company was incorporated under a private Act and the relevant regulations were contained in the Companies Clauses Consolidation Act 1845. Under the Act each member had one vote for each share held by him up to ten, one additional vote for every five shares beyond the first ten shares up to one hundred and an additional vote for every ten shares held by him beyond the first hundred shares. The original shares which had a nominal value of £10 had long since been converted into stock and references in the Act to a vote per share or multiples of shares were accordingly references to votes per multiples of stock of £10 denomination.

The plaintiff and his supporters requisitioned an extraordinary general meeting with the object of removing the directors and replacing them with their nominees. Some of the stockholdings were comparatively large, and it was quickly apparent to the plaintiffs' camp that they might win the coming trial of strength if their holdings were sub-divided into smaller units. In addition, since the company was a public company, they availed of the time to make purchases of additional stock. In the result, a large number of transfers were received for registration in the month preceding the meeting and the company employed a firm of accountants to cope with the problem of registering them all. This process of registering all the transfers was not completed by the accountants in time for the meeting and it was found as a fact that this was simply because of the amount of paper work involved and was not due to any lack of good faith on the part of the officers of the company or the accountants. Only the registered stockholders were allowed to attend and vote at the crucial meeting and in the event the plaintiffs' resolutions were defeated. The plaintiffs then issued proceedings claiming that the proceedings at the meeting were invalid. Barron J dismissed their claim; he considered that he should follow the English decisions which made it clear that only members appearing on the register could vote. He also held that the chairman had no power to adjourn the meeting (so that the process of registration could be completed) in defiance of the wishes of the meeting.

[25.58] It does not seem satisfactory that a person who has acquired an absolute right to be entered on the register should be deprived of one of his most

---

[47] Eg *Pender v Lushington* (1877) 6 Ch D 70; *Wise v Lansdell* [1921] Ch 420 at 430.

important rights - the right to attend and vote - because of the company's failure, albeit *bona fide* to place him on the register. While it is not clear from the judgment whether the chairman actually proposed the adjournment, that would seem to have been an appropriate course for him to have taken in the circumstances. If the proposal for an adjournment was voted down by those present then that would seem to be an improper use of their powers which the court would be entitled to correct in accordance with the principles explained in the next chapter. In the circumstances of *Kinsella*'s case, the course followed might well have been categorised as a fraud on the majority, but absent majorities presumably are also entitled to protection as much as present minorities. If the chairman failed to put any proposal for an adjournment to the meeting, that again would seem to invalidate the proceedings, since a chairman should at least ascertain the sense of the meeting on so important a matter and is hardly entitled to assume that the result was a foregone conclusion. But, as we have seen, it is a fundamental principle of law that membership is not complete until registration, and this was clearly the major factor which influenced the court in applying the earlier authorities.

Defamatory statements

[25.59] Defamatory statements made by members or directors of a company at a general meeting of the company are privileged and are accordingly not actionable in the absence of malice[48]. Fair and accurate reports by the press, radio and television of the proceedings of general meetings of companies are also privileged under s 24 of the Defamation Act 1961. Again the privilege is lost if the statement is published maliciously and, to avail of the defence successfully, a reasonable explanation or contradiction of the defamatory statement must be published.

Minutes of meetings

[25.60] Section 145 of the Principal Act requires minutes to be made and kept of the proceedings at all general meetings of the company and for penalties in the event of such minutes not being made and kept. As with the register of members, they need not be kept in a bound volume: they may be kept in looseleaf form subject to precautions against falsification and facilities for discovery.

[25.61] The minutes must be signed by the chairman of the meeting at which the proceedings took place or the chairman of the next succeeding meeting. When so signed they are *prima facie* evidence of what occurred at the meeting. It follows that properly signed minutes may always be adduced as evidence of the

---

48 *Pittard v Oliver* [1891] 1 QB 474.

proceedings, but also that evidence may in turn be adduced to establish that they are not in some respects a correct record. Nor are they the only evidence: if a particular matter is not recorded in the minutes, it may be proved by some other method, such as oral evidence by a person who was present[49].

[25.62] Section 145(3) provides that when the minutes have been properly made and signed, a rebuttable presumption arises that the meeting to which they refer has been duly convened and held, that all proceedings at it have been duly conducted and that all appointments of directors or liquidators made at it are valid.

[25.63] The records containing the minutes must be kept at the registered office of the company. They are open to inspection by members of the company during business hours without charge subject to such reasonable restrictions as the company may by its articles or in general meeting impose but so that not less than two hours in each day is allowed for inspection. Creditors or members of the public are not entitled to inspect them. The member is also entitled on payment of a small fee to copies of the minutes. When an inspection or copies are refused by the company, it is liable to a fine not exceeding £125 and the court may also require the immediate production of the minutes or copies in question[50].

---

[49] *Re Fireproof Doors Ltd, Umney v Fireproof Doors Ltd* [1916] 1 Ch 142.
[50] Companies Act 1963, s 146 as amended by the Companies (Amendment) Act 1982, s 15.

Chapter 26

Majority and Minority Rights

[26.01] We have seen in the preceding chapter that many of the most important decisions of the company may be taken by a simple majority: some, such as the amendment of the articles, require a three-fourths majority. The Acts thus enshrine the democratic principle of majority rule, which itself was recognised by the common law as applicable to all corporations aggregate[1]. Clearly, a majority in a company may be guilty of behaviour which is detrimental to the interests of a minority and yet strictly within the legal powers of the majority. In this chapter, we examine the somewhat tortuous methods by which the law has sought to protect such minorities, while at the same time recognising the right of the majority to conduct the business of the company in what they see as its best interest.

The rule in *Foss v Harbottle* and its exceptions

[26.02] In the early days of the companies' legislation, a difficulty arose as to the right of an individual member to sue where he complained that the majority were acting in a manner which was damaging to the company or at least to the minority of which he was a member. In the leading case of *Foss v Harbottle*[2], it was laid down that only the company could maintain proceedings in respect of wrongs done to it. Neither the individual shareholder nor any group of shareholders had any right of action in such circumstances. The rule was based on the following practical considerations:

(1)   If individual members were allowed to bring proceedings to redress wrongs done to the company, the result would be a multiplicity of actions. Accordingly, such actions could only be brought with the authority of a meeting of the company and this effectively meant that only the company could sue.

(2)   If the action complained of was one which it was within the powers of the company in general meeting to sanction, then even though it may

---

[1]   *A-G v Davey* (1741) 2 Atk 212. For an interesting discussion of the evolution of the rule, see Hand, *The Development of the Common Law Principle of Majority Rule in Arbitration of Matters of Public Concern*, Ir Jur (ns), Vol IV 74.

[2]   (1843) 2 Hare 461. The generally accepted statement of the rule in modern case law is by Jenkins LJ in *Edwards v Halliwell* [1950] 2 All ER 1064 at 1066.

have been irregular, proceedings would be futile since the company could always ratify it at a general meeting.

[26.03] In *Foss v Harbottle*, the company in general meeting refused to take any action against directors who were alleged by the minority shareholders to have committed fraudulent acts. The court dismissed an action by the minority shareholders against the directors in which it was sought to compel them to make amends to the company. It was held that only the company could maintain such proceedings.

[26.04] The principle has been repeatedly applied in cases since then. Thus, in *MacDougall v Gardiner*[3] an individual shareholder suing on behalf of himself and all the other shareholders - except the directors - complained that the chairman had ruled that no poll could be demanded and that this was in breach of the articles. His complaint was rejected on the ground that the litigation should have been in the name of the company, since it was for the majority to decide whether they wished to complain or not. This might seem at first sight to be the explanation of the decision in *Kinsella v Alliance and Dublin Gas Consumers Co*[4] which was referred to in the last chapter. There the court declined to intervene when a meeting proceeded to vote on resolutions, although the company had failed to register a substantial body of members who were unable to vote as a result. The court held that the chairman had no power to adjourn the meeting in defiance of the wishes of the majority present in order to allow the process of registration to be completed, but that there was nothing to prevent the aggrieved members from taking steps to have another meeting convened. It does not appear, however, that the point was taken against the plaintiffs that the litigation should have been in the name of the company and neither *Foss v Harbottle* nor *MacDougall v Gardiner* is referred to in the judgment.

[26.05] A recent and more apposite example of the application of the principle is the decision in *O'Neill v Ryan*[5]. The plaintiff in that case was the chief executive of and a minority shareholder in Ryanair Ltd. Following disputes with the company, he was removed from his position and then instituted a series of proceedings against both his former employers, the principal shareholder in Ryanair, Thomas Anthony Ryan, and Aer Lingus. One of the major allegations made by the plaintiff was that Mr Ryan and Aer Lingus had entered into agreements to contravene or circumvent the competition regulations of the European Union, particularly those relating to the deregulation of air fares. As a result of what he alleged was a tortious conspiracy of this nature, the plaintiff

---

[3]   (1875) 1 Ch D 13.
[4]   (Unreported, 5 October 1982).
[5]   [1990] ILRM 140; [1993] ILRM 557.

claimed that Ryanair's interests had been adversely affected and that the value of his own shareholding in the latter company had been reduced.

[26.06] It was pleaded on behalf of Mr Ryan and Aer Lingus that these allegations were essentially of wrongs done to Ryanair and not the plaintiff personally. In the result, it was submitted, the action could not be maintained having regard to the rule in *Foss v Harbottle*. On behalf of the plaintiff, it was claimed that, even if the rule applied, it could not be invoked where it would have the effect of denying the plaintiff a remedy for a breach of the law of the European Union.

[26.07] Lynch J described the circumstances as 'a classic case to which the rule in *Foss v Harbottle* applies'. He rejected the submission that to apply the rule was to deny the plaintiff his rights under community law: the relevant articles of the Treaty of Rome were not rendered inapplicable by virtue of the rule, since it remained open to Ryanair to claim damages for any alleged wrong which it had suffered. The relevant rules of national law remained applicable in such circumstances, provided the enforcement of the articles was not wholly or substantially negatived. The learned judge, accordingly, granted an application to strike out the plaintiff's statement of claim as disclosing no cause of action.

[26.08] The plaintiff had also presented a petition under s 205 of the Principal Act claiming that the company's affairs were being conducted in a manner oppressive to him and in disregard of his interests as a member. He also appealed to the Supreme Court from the decision of Lynch J but, by the time the appeal came on for hearing, the s 205 proceedings had been settled, one of the terms of the settlement providing for the acquisition by some of the defendants of the plaintiff's shares. Accordingly, when the appeal was heard, he was no longer a shareholder.

[26.09] The Supreme Court unanimously upheld the finding of Lynch J that the case fell within the rule in *Foss v Harbottle* and that the plaintiff could not rely on the Treaty of Rome as excluding the operation of the rule, since it remained open to Ryanair to sue for damages. The court also rejected a claim by the plaintiff that, even if he could not rely on damage suffered by the company, EU law required that the domestic law should afford him a remedy in respect of the damage to him as a shareholder. It was pointed out that he in fact enjoyed such a remedy, ie a petition under s 205 of which he had availed.

[26.10] Four clear exceptions have been established to the rule in *Foss v Harbottle*:

(1)   The majority cannot commit an act which is illegal or *ultra vires* the company. An individual shareholder may always bring proceedings in respect of such an act.

(2)   There are certain decisions for which more than a simple majority is required. In such cases, if the company purports to act on the strength of a decision by a simple majority, the individual shareholder is again entitled to sue.

(3)   Certain actions of the company may purport to abridge or abolish the individual rights of a member. In such a case, the member concerned is entitled to sue.

(4)   If a majority who are in control of a company commit a fraud on the minority, the minority, or an individual member acting on their behalf, may maintain proceedings in respect of the fraud.

[26.11] The first two of these exceptions are almost self-explanatory. In recent times, however, it has been held in England that the first is subject to an important qualification. In two cases - *Taylor v NUM*[6] and *Smith v Croft (No 2)*[7] - it has been decided that, while the rule in *Foss v Harbottle* has no application where the plaintiff seeks to restrain an intended act which is *ultra vires* the company, it does apply where the act has already been committed and the plaintiff brings his suit in the name of the company to recover the damage which it has sustained as a result of the *ultra vires* act. The reason, it was said, is that in the case of acts in the past it is always within the power of the company to refrain from suing. The company might decide in good faith, the arguments runs, that no action should he brought because, for example, the defendants were no mark or the publicity might be damaging to the company.

[26.12] It is respectfully submitted that the reason given is unconvincing. Where a majority in control of a company decides to apply its funds or property in an unlawful manner and override the protests of the minority, it can hardly be an answer to the latter's claim that the majority could in any event decide that the company should take no action. If the view taken in these two cases is correct, it would seem to apply equally where the directors have wrongfully diverted profitable opportunities to which the company was entitled into their own hands. In such cases, the transactions in question have been set aside at the suit of a minority, even though they had been confirmed by a majority, the reason being that a majority in control cannot commit a fraud on the minority. It would be no answer in the latter case for the majority to claim that they were saving the company from embarrassing or expensive litigation.

[26.13] The majority decisions of the company cannot adversely affect the individual rights of a member. When a person becomes a member of a company, he enters into a contract with the company by virtue of which he becomes

---

6   (1985) BCLC 232.
7   [1988] Ch 114.

entitled to the rights of membership in return for the amount which he pays for his shares or agrees to guarantee. The contract has one unusual feature, namely that the company can unilaterally alter its terms by amending the articles of association. It cannot, however, deprive the member of the right to remain a member of the company with all the rights and privileges of such membership. In addition, the Acts confer certain additional important rights on the individual members, such as the right to receive the accounts and reports, to petition for the winding up of the company etc. None of these individual rights of the members may be taken away or abridged by the company.

[26.14] These individual membership rights, which cannot be interfered with, must be carefully distinguished from the corporate membership rights of the members, which can. A consequence of the contract of membership is that the individual member by his contract agrees with respect to some of the rights of membership to accept as binding the decisions of the majority of the members. These rights are known as corporate membership rights. Thus a decision to increase the capital of the company may affect the amount of the dividend, one of the corporate rights of all the members, but a member has no legal grievance if a majority of the members decide on such a course, provided the requirements of the Acts and the articles are observed.

[26.15] The rule has no application where the majority in control commit, or attempt to commit, a fraud on the minority. 'Fraud' in this context does not necessarily involve any element of dishonesty, let alone criminality. The word is used more in the sense in which courts of equity were traditionally prone to use it: in such courts, it was usually possible to obtain relief where a person entrusted with powers to be exercised on behalf of others used them for some other purpose. Those courts described conduct of that nature as 'a fraud on the power' and it is in that general sense that it is used here. Within certain limitations, the majority of the members in exercising their control over the company owe a fiduciary duty to the members as a whole to use that control for the benefit of the company as a whole. The major limitation that has to be remembered is that it is for the company, and not for the court, to determine what is in the best interests of the company. If the members by a majority reach a conclusion in good faith that a particular course is in the interests of the company as a whole, their decision will not be interfered with by the court, even though it may have a detrimental effect on the interests of the minority. We have already seen how this principle has been applied in the case of alterations effected by the majority to the articles of the company[8].

---

[8] Para **[6.15]** above.

[26.16] The cases in which the question arose of whether the conduct complained of constituted a fraud on the minority were in the main of a type described in the English textbooks as 'expropriation' cases. Two categories of such cases should be distinguished. In the first, some of the shareholders are compelled to sell their shares to the majority as the result of an amendment effected in the articles by the latters' use of their voting power. These cases have already been fully discussed[9]. In the second, the majority have made use of their controlling position to divert the company's property into their own hands to their profit.

[26.17] Thus in *Cooks v Deeks*[10], directors of a railway construction company made use of their privileged position to secure for themselves the benefit of a contract for the building of a railway which should have gone to the company itself. They then used their majority voting position to obtain the passing of a special resolution endorsing their action. The transaction was set aside as being a fraud on the minority.

[26.18] Cases have also arisen in which the majority have not made a profit for themselves out of the transaction in question, but have simply parted with some property without the company's deriving any material or financial benefit from the transaction. The majority may, for example, decide to make a contribution to charity. Or they may decide to award pensions or gratuities to retiring employees. It is thought that where such an action is expressly authorised by the memorandum or articles, it will not be vulnerable to a challenge by a disgruntled minority[11]. In modern conditions, moreover, tax considerations may also make such donations justifiable as being in the company's interests. It might also be argued that in some cases they are ultimately in the company's interest on the ground that they are desirable because of, for example, good management-labour relations. But where such actions are not expressly authorised by the memorandum or articles, they may undoubtedly be declared unlawful, at all events where they cannot be justified by considerations such as tax advantages or the necessity to preserve the goodwill of employees or trade unions. The often quoted observations of Bowen LJ that 'charity cannot sit at the boardroom table' and that 'there are to be no cakes and ale except for the benefit of the company'[12] still retain much of their vitality, as the cases show.

---

[9] Para **[6.16]** et seq above.

[10] [1916] 1 AC 554.

[11] *Charterbridge Corpn Ltd v Lloyds' Bank Ltd* [1970] Ch 62; cf *Northern Bank Finance Corpn Ltd v Quinn and Achates Investment Co* [1979] ILRM 221.

[12] *Hutton v West Cork Rly Co* (1883) 23 Ch D 654 at 673.

[26.19] In *Parke v Daily News*[13], for example, the owners of two English newspapers sold their interests in them and then wished to distribute the purchase price among the employees who would become redundant as a result of the sale. They were restrained from so doing at the suit of an individual shareholder on the ground that the directors were obliged to act in the interest of the shareholders alone. It is to be noted that the proposed distribution was not authorised by the memorandum or articles and that it could not be justified as being ultimately in the company's interest on the basis mentioned in the preceding paragraph since the business was about to cease.

[26.20] A similar conclusion was reached by Carroll J in *Roper v Ward*[14]. In that case, a social and recreational club which owned valuable grounds in Dublin sold them and then proceeded to wind itself up voluntarily and appoint the plaintiff as liquidator. (The club was incorporated as a company limited by guarantee not having a share capital.) It was obvious that there would be a surplus available for distribution and a meeting of the company decided that certain persons who were not members (although former employees of the business in connection with which the club was established) should be entitled to participate in the distribution. The liquidator having sought the directions of the court on these and other matters, it was held by Carroll J that even a majority of the company present and voting could not give away the company's assets in this manner.

[26.21] Section 52 of the 1990 Act requires directors to have regard to the interests of the company's employees as well as its members. The scope of the provision remains unclear, but it seems at least doubtful whether it would apply in cases such as those just mentioned where the persons benefiting were no longer employees of the company.

[26.22] The principles discussed in the preceding paragraphs were applied by the Supreme Court in *Re Greendale Developments Ltd (In Liquidation) No 2*[15]. In that case, the liquidator of a company had issued misfeasance proceedings under s 298(2) of the Principal Act seeking the repayment by one of the directors of sums alleged to be owed by him to the company. The company, it was said, had paid monies to the director or for his benefit and had received nothing in return. Costello P found in favour of the liquidator and ordered the director to repay the sums, but on appeal to the Supreme Court it was argued on behalf of the director that all the shareholders had assented to the transactions in question

---

[13]   [1961] 1 All ER 695.
[14]   [1981] ILRM 408.
[15]   [1998] 1 IR 8.

and hence, even if they were not for the company's benefit, they had been effectively validated.

[26.23] In *Buchanan Ltd v McVey*[16], Kingsmill-Moore J, sitting as a High Court judge had held that, if all the members of a company agreed to a certain course, then, however informal the agreement, it would bind the company, provided the transaction was honest and intra vires the company. That decision was upheld on appeal by the former Supreme Court. In *Greendale*, counsel on behalf of the director argued that the principle also applied where the transaction was not for the benefit of the company, since all the shareholders could take such a step if they were so minded, citing in support the decision of Gavan Duffy P in *Re SM Barker Ltd*[17].

[26.24] The argument was rejected by the Supreme Court, Keane J pointing out that, while all the shareholders in *Re SM Barker Ltd* had assented to the impugned transaction, they were being sued in misfeasance proceedings as directors of the company and not in respect of any profits made by them as shareholders. It was for that reason that Gavan Duffy P refused the liquidator the relief sought and the case was not authority for the proposition that payments or transfers of property which did not benefit the company and hence were beyond its powers could be validated by the assent of all the shareholders[18].

[26.25] The reach of the fourth exception to the rule in *Foss v Harbottle* was further considered by the Supreme Court in *Crindle Investments v Wymes*[19]. That case was part of a huge complex of litigation that resulted from the discovery of a vast lead and zinc ore body near Navan in the 1970s. The contending parties were the company (originally Canadian owned) which discovered the mine, the proprietors of the Bula Group (Irish citizens) who had purchased adjoining land under which the mine extended, the Minister who had granted the relevant licences and had also acquired a minority holding in Bula and the banks who had advanced large sums to Bula to finance their operations. The owners of Bula, other than the Minister, began proceedings in the High Court against all the other parties claiming damages under a number of headings. When the first set of proceedings came on for hearing in the High Court, settlement proposals were made which were accepted by two of the four Bula owners. The remaining two, however, who were in the majority, refused to accept the offer. The minority thereupon sought relief in separate proceedings in the High Court under s 205 of the Principal Act claiming that the conduct of the majority in rejecting the settlement offer was so unreasonable as to constitute oppression[20]. That claim

---

[16] [1954] IR 89.

[17] [1950] IR 123.

[18] For a criticism of the decision, see Forde, *Company Law in Ireland* (3rd edn), para 3.76.

[19] [1998] 4 IR 567.

succeeded in both the High Court and the Supreme Court, an order being made that the minority should be in control of any future negotiations. However, the majority were also maintaining personal claims against the other parties and the latter had insisted that those claims must also be compromised if the proceedings were to be settled. The High Court, upheld by the Supreme Court, took the view that the majority could not be required in s 205 proceedings to abandon their personal claims.

The minority then instituted plenary proceedings in which they claimed *inter alia* that damage was being done to the Bula company by the refusal of the majority to agree to a reasonable settlement of their personal claims and that, accordingly, they were entitled to an order restraining the majority from maintaining their personal claims. They said that the conduct of the majority constituted a fraud on the minority which brought the case within the fourth exception to the rule in *Foss v Harbottle*. The Supreme Court rejected this argument, however; it was pointed out that it was an essential condition that the majority were seeking to appropriate benefits to themselves to the detriment of the company as a whole. In the present case, the majority would benefit from their conduct only in the event of what was seen by the minority as their intransigence resulting in a successful outcome of the proceedings, an outcome which would be to the benefit of the company as a whole, including the minority. Hence, their conduct, however unreasonable it might appear, would not come within the fourth exception to the rule in *Foss v Harbottle*.

[26.26] There are passages in some judgments which suggest that there is a fifth exception to the rule in *Foss v Harbottle*, ie where it is necessary to permit such an exception 'in the interests of justice'. In *MacDougall v Gardiner*, Jones LJ had said that there must be something 'illegal, oppressive or fraudulent' to exclude the application of the rule[21]. In *Burland v Earle*[22], Lord Davey said that the cases in which the minority could sue were confined to those in which the actions complained of were

> 'of a fraudulent character or beyond the powers of the company'.

[26.27] But the principle was stated in somewhat wider terms by Jessel MR in *Russell v Wakefield Waterworks Co*[23] where he said that the rule is not an inflexible rule and it will be relaxed where necessary in the interest of justice.

---

[20] See para **[26.38]** et seq below
[21] (1875) 1 Ch D 13 at 21.
[22] [1902] AC 83.
[23] [1875] LR 20 Eq 474.

[26.28] Again in *Heyting v Dupont*[24], Harman LJ stated that there are cases which suggest that the rule is not a rigid one and that an exception will be made where the justice of the case requires it.

[26.29] The question was considered by Hamilton J in *Moylan v Irish Whiting Manufacturers Ltd*[25]. In that case, the plaintiff was a director and chairman of the defendant company. Following a disagreement with his fellow directors, a resolution was proposed at the annual general meeting of the company for his replacement as a director and chairman. The resolution was carried and the plaintiff then issued proceedings claiming that it was invalid on a number of grounds. Hamilton J found that there had been irregularities in the notice convening the meeting and the manner in which it had been conducted, but that the meeting had given its approval to the course adopted. Having referred to *Foss v Harbottle* and *MacDougall v Gardiner*, he concluded that there had been nothing 'illegal, oppressive or fraudulent' in the proceedings of the majority and that, accordingly, the plaintiff was not entitled to relief. More significantly, however, he expressed his general view as follows:

> 'Having regard to the provisions of Bunreacht na hEireann, I am satisfied that an exception to the rule must be made when the justice of the case demands it.'

[26.30] There is, accordingly considerable authority for the proposition that the exceptions to the rule are not confined to the four generally accepted cases. But it should be noted that in *Moylan*'s case the learned judge was clearly satisfied that the justice of the case did not require the intervention of the court and it may be that his observations might be regarded as *obiter*. It would also seem that the remark of Harman LJ quoted above is not a sufficient basis for allowing further exceptions to the rule: he was content to say that the facts of the case did not permit of any extension of the exceptions without laying down any general proposition. In *Prudential Assurance Co v Newman Industries Ltd*[26] the Court of Appeal made it clear that in their view 'the interests of justice' is not a convincing practical test.

[26.31] In *O'Neill v Ryan*[27], the Supreme Court left open the question as to whether the 'interests of justice' exception existed. It was conceded on behalf of the plaintiff that his claim did not come within any of the four exceptions to the rule, but it was argued that it did come within the exception required by the 'interests of justice'. In his judgment, Blayney J, with whom the other members of the court agreed, said that the plaintiff's claim in that case was in respect of

---

[24] [1964] 2 All ER 273.
[25] (Unreported, 14 April 1980).
[26] [1982] Ch 209.
[27] See para **[26.05]** above.

damage to his shareholding in company and not in respect of damage to the company itself. To allow the plaintiff to bring a personal action in respect of the damage to his shareholding would be to subvert the rule in *Foss v Harbottle*, as had also been held by the Court of Appeal in *Prudential Assurance Co v Newman Industries Ltd*. The question as to whether, assuming the damage was to the company as opposed to the individual shareholder, the shareholder could avail of the 'interests of justice' exception remains undecided.

[26.32] It is thought that the exceptions to the rule are so clearly defined that in practice the Irish courts would be reluctant to extend them. In support of this approach, it may be pointed out that, provided the term 'fraud' is given its wider equitable meaning, the number of cases in which the invocation of the 'justice of the case' formula is necessary must be so few as not to justify the making of additional exceptions, with the undesirable consequence of uncertainty as to what the law is.

[26.33] While the nature of the rule in *Foss v Harbottle* and its exceptions are clear enough - subject to the possibility just mentioned of a rather vague fifth exception - its application in practice has given rise to procedural problems which must now be considered.

[26.34] The first problem is well illustrated by *Nash v Lancegaye Safety Class (Ireland) Ltd*[28]. In that case, the plaintiff was a director and shareholder in the defendant company. He had persuaded the second defendant, JR, to become a director and shareholder, but in subsequent years differences developed between the two and this ultimately resulted in an allotment of shares in the company (which was a public company) being made by the directors (either relations or supporters of JR) to JR of 15,000 preference shares. The allotment was opposed by the plaintiff as not being a *bona fide* exercise by the directors of their powers. The plaintiff requisitioned an extraordinary general meeting of the company to consider and vote upon resolutions removing the other directors from office and appointing new and additional directors. It was clear that if the disputed 15,000 shares were voted, JR and his supporters would have an effective majority at the meeting. The plaintiff accordingly issued proceedings claiming that the allotment was an improper use of the directors' powers and that it should be set aside.

Dixon J found that the allotment was an improper use by the directors of their powers: it had not been made by them in good faith in the interests of the company as a whole but rather to ensure that the company would in future be controlled by JR's family. *Foss v Harbottle* was relied on by the defendants, who contended that the action was premature: the plaintiff should have awaited the

---

[28] (1958) 92 ILTR 11.

outcome of the requisitioned meeting which might well have endorsed the directors' action. This argument was rejected by Dixon J who said that it overlooked the 'fundamental point' that it was precisely the question whether the 15,000 votes could be used at the meeting that was in issue. He accordingly found in favour of the plaintiff.

[26.35] The difficulty adverted to by Dixon J in allowing the shareholders to decide whether the directors' action should be endorsed was neatly avoided by Buckley J in the subsequent English decision of *Hogg v Cramphorn Ltd*[29]. The facts were not dissimilar: the directors in an effort to ward off an attempt to secure control of the company devised a scheme of allotment which Buckley J found to have been an improper - although not *mala fide* - use of their powers. But since it would have been within the capacity of the company in general meeting to endorse their actions, he allowed the case to stand over until such a meeting was held, subject, however, to an undertaking that the disputed shares would not be voted at the meeting. In the event, the meeting endorsed the directors' actions by a comfortable majority. The distinction between this case and the *Lancegaye* case is that in the latter the battle lines had already been drawn: it was quite clear that without the disputed votes the JR camp would not have won[30].

[26.36] The second problem arises where a minority of shareholders wish to bring proceedings, relying on the exception to the rule which permits such an action to be brought where a majority in control of the company are committing a fraud on the minority. Since in such a case the allegation is of damage to the company itself rather than a violation of an individual shareholder's rights, the proceedings should logically be brought by the company itself. Since this, however, is precisely what the majority will not allow, an exception is allowed to the normal legal principle that it is not permissible to institute proceedings based on a wrong done to another party. One or more of the aggrieved minority may in such circumstances bring what has come to be known as a derivative action, ie one that derives from the injury to the company rather than the injury to individual shareholders.

[26.37] Two major difficulties can arise in such derivative actions. In the first place, there may not in fact be a majority in favour of the allegedly fraudulent conduct: thus, the claim may be that a particular transaction entered into by the directors is to their own benefit and not to that of the company (as in *Cooks v Deeks*[31]) but the company in general meeting may, for all the court knows, decline to ratify the transaction and may authorise the necessary proceedings to

---

[29] [1967] Ch 254.
[30] See also *Bamford v Bamford* [1970] Ch 212.
[31] [1916] 1 AC 554.

be taken. It is accordingly important for the aggrieved shareholder to take all the steps open to him to convene an extraordinary general meeting before he issues proceedings. If he and his supporters do not command enough shares or voting strength to do so, the court may, as we have seen, convene a meeting itself and would probably do so before embarking on a lengthy trial of the merits in a case where it had not been clearly established that the wrongdoers were in control.

[26.38] The second difficulty arises from the fact that it may not be possible to determine whether the majority are perpetrating a fraud until the entire action has been heard. If it should transpire at that stage that there has been no fraud, it should logically follow that the action should never have been allowed to proceed, since it does not come within the permitted exceptions to the rule in *Foss v Harbottle*.

[26.39] The Court of Appeal in England in *Prudential Assurance Co v Newman Industries Ltd*[32] said that the proper course in such circumstances is for the court to determine as a preliminary issue whether the case falls within the exception to the rule. This, they said, should be done by requiring the plaintiff to make out a prima facie case as to the alleged fraud. It is submitted, however, that this underestimates the difficulty involved in resolving what are often vigorously contested issues of fact at an interlocutory stage. It is unfortunate that the court's attention does not appear to have been directed to the emphasis laid by the House of Lords in *American Cyanamid Co v Ethicon Ltd*[33] on the undesirability of such an approach in the case of interlocutory injunctions. A similar approach was adopted by the Supreme Court in *Minister for Energy v Campus Oil Ltd*[34] and it is thought would render it unlikely that the approach adopted in *Prudential Insurance Co v Newman Ltd* would be adopted in Ireland. It is true that in the result a great deal of court time may be taken up and substantial costs incurred in the investigation of what turns out to have been an unjustified allegation of fraudulent conduct. But this is a necessary hazard of many other forms of litigation and there seems no good reason why in derivative actions of the nature under discussion the court should depart from its customary approach of permitting the action to proceed on the assumption that the plaintiff had not alleged such conduct in his pleadings without at least being in a position to present an arguable case. The plaintiff, after all, is the person who is likely to suffer in costs if the plea is unsustainable. The impracticability of adopting any other course was graphically demonstrated in *Smith v Croft (No 2)*[35] where the court of first instance in endeavouring loyally to apply the *Prudential Insurance*

---

[32] [1982] Ch 209.
[33] [1975] AC 396.
[34] [1983] IR 88.
[35] [1988] Ch 144.

Co Ltd technique found itself in the midst of what counsel for the plaintiff described as a 'procedural shambles'. In the event, the 'preliminary' issue took 17 days to resolve.

[26.40] While the action is a derivative action taken because of damage to the company, it may also take the form of a representative action as well: there is nothing to prevent the shareholder from taking the action on behalf of a number of shareholders and seeking a representative order under the Rules of the Superior Courts. It has also been held in England that it is open to the court in such an action to order that the company should indemnify the plaintiff against the costs of the action where it was reasonable and prudent in the company's interests to bring the action and he does so in good faith. The court also held that the plaintiff's costs should be paid by the company irrespective of the outcome of the case[36].

[26.41] It is also possible for the minority shareholder to sue in the name of the company and thus enable the issue of whether the case is truly outside the rule in *Foss v Harbottle* to be decided on an application for a stay of the proceedings. This procedure is rarely availed of nowadays.

[26.42] One further point should be noted. The principle of majority rule no doubt justifies the proposition that the majority are entitled to take whatever actions they believe in good faith to be necessary in the interests of the company and precludes a minority from challenging their decision save in the exceptional cases already discussed. But it is submitted that this principle does not absolve the majority from giving a fair hearing to the view of the minority before taking a decision and it may be that a literal adherence to the requirements of the Acts and the articles would not be a defence if in fact there was a want of fairness in the manner in which the decision was taken, apart altogether from its intrinsic merits or demerits. As Hamilton J hinted in *Moylan*'s case, the rule in *Foss v Harbottle* must be applied in Irish courts in the light of the Constitution, and artificial bodies such as companies which owe their existence and privileges to Acts enacted after the coming into force of the Constitution must expect to have their activities scrutinised in that context. It is to be presumed under our law that the Oireachtas intended that powers conferred on the majority of the company would be exercised by them in accordance with the principles of natural justice, which in an appropriate case would require giving the minority at least an opportunity to be heard[37]. The observation of Megarry J in *Gaiman v National Association for Mental Health* that:

---

36 *Wallersteiner v Moir (No 2)* [1975] QB 373.
37 Cf *Glover v BLN Ltd* [1973] IR 388 at 425.

'these duties (of directors towards the corporation) may be inconsistent with the observance of natural justice and accordingly the implication of any term that natural justice should be observed may be excluded'[38]

should be seen in this light.

Alternative remedy in case of oppression

[26.43] Unless the minority shareholder could bring himself within one of the exceptions to the rule in *Foss v Harbottle*, his only remedy until the enactment of s 205 of the Principal Act was to present a petition for the winding up of the company. There was no doubt as to the jurisdiction of the court to order the winding up of the company where it was 'just and equitable' to do so and this could clearly apply to a situation in which a minority were being treated oppressively. But it was frequently not in any one's interests to have a winding up: the assets might have to be sold at less than their real value, the business brought to an end and people thrown out of work. With a view to remedying this situation, the Principal Act, following the recommendations of Cox, provided in s 205 for what has become known as 'alternative remedy' in cases of oppression.

[26.44] The section, which is modelled (with one important variation) on s 210 of the English 1948 Act, enables any member of a company who complains that its affairs are being conducted in a manner oppressive to him or any of the members (including himself) or in disregard of his or their interests as members or that the directors' powers are being exercised in a similar fashion to apply to the court for an order designed to remedy the state of affairs complained of without actually winding up the company.

[26.45] If the court is of the opinion that the complaint is well founded, it may make a number of different orders with a view to bringing the state of affairs complained of to an end. In general terms it may prohibit or direct any act, cancel or vary any transaction, and provide for the regulation of the conduct of the company's affairs in the future. Specifically - and this is the remedy most often sought in practice - it may order the purchase of the shares of any member of the company by other members or by the company itself. Where the order provides for the purchase of the shares of any of the members by the company, the court may also order the reduction of the company's capital. The memorandum and articles may also be altered by the order, in which case the company may not make any further alteration or addition inconsistent with the order without the leave of the court.

[26.46] Although the section is under the cross-heading 'Minorities', it should be noted that it is not confined in its terms to a complaint by a member of an

---

[38] [1971] Ch 317 at 335.

allegedly oppressed minority. In addition to the Minister, the application may be made by any member of a company who complains of oppression. While the section is most frequently availed of by minority shareholders, there is nothing to prevent the majority - or those entitled to 50% of the shares or votes - from applying for relief under the section. It should also be borne in mind that while the more probable outcome of an application for relief which can only be met by an order for the purchase of members' shares is an order requiring the majority to buy out the minority, there is nothing to prevent the court from making an order enabling the minority to buy out the majority.

[26.47] Under the corresponding section of the English 1948 Act (s 210) the court had to be satisfied that it would be prepared to wind up the company on the 'just and equitable' ground before it could grant the alternative remedy. No such precondition to relief appears in s 205 of the Principal Act and it has now been dispensed with in England by s 75 of the 1980 Act. This is in accordance with the recommendation of Jenkins and the good sense of the draftsman of the Principal Act in not making it an essential precondition to relief is demonstrated by the experience in England since 1948 which led to a somewhat narrow approach to the granting of relief under s 210.

[26.48] The provision of relief of this nature would have seemed peculiarly appropriate in Ireland for two reasons. In the first place, it is a form of relief which is most likely to be invoked by shareholders in small private companies, an extremely prevalent form of business organisation in Ireland. In the second place, the volatile and quarrelsome Irish temperament makes the possibility of internecine warfare between shareholders in such companies more likely than in the neighbouring jurisdiction. It is all the more surprising, therefore, to find that so few decisions have been given by the Irish courts on the section since its enactment. Experience suggests, however, that while recourse to the section is more frequent than the number of decisions would indicate, a great many applications are settled without the court being called upon to adjudicate. The section has in fact proved to be most effective as an *in terrorem* weapon to be brandished at obdurate and unreasonable shareholders.

[26.49] It is presumably for this reason that the first recorded Irish decision on the section was not given until 1974 when Kenny J gave judgment in *Re Westwinds Holdings Ltd*[39] and that there have been so few recorded cases in which relief has been granted under the section. In the result, there is a dearth of Irish authority on the section: and English decisions must be treated with caution both because there is a significant difference in the wording of the section and

[39] (Unreported, 21 May 1974).

because the Irish courts are unlikely to adopt as restrictive an approach to operating the section as has been the case in England[40].

[26.50] The first matter to be considered is the category of persons entitled to relief under this section.

[26.51] As we have seen, to obtain relief under the section, the member has to establish that the company's affairs are being conducted in a manner oppressive to him or any of the members (including himself) or in disregard of their interests as members. It has been held in England in *Re Bellador Silk Ltd*[41] and *Re Lundie Brothers Ltd*[42] that a petition cannot succeed under the section where the oppression complained of is not oppression of the member in his capacity as member, but in some other capacity, eg as a director or a creditor. There has been no Irish decision on the point, but there can be little doubt that this narrow construction would have consequences which the legislature can hardly have intended in this jurisdiction. The typical Irish company is the small private company, in which there is frequently only a handful of shareholders. It is quite common to find that all the shareholders are actively involved in the management of the company and that they are also directors. If disputes break out, they frequently come to a head with the attempted exclusion of one of the directors or shareholders from further participation in the affairs of the company, beginning with his removal from his office as a director. At that point, the shareholder will have no means of finding out how the company's day-to-day affairs are being conducted, other than by convening an extraordinary general meeting of the company. This may be, and frequently is, part of the strategy by the other shareholders to run the company to their own advantage without regard to the excluded member's interests. It seems wrong that in these circumstances the excluded shareholder should not be able to obtain relief under s 205 and yet this would appear to be the effect of the decisions referred to. On this view it is only where the shareholder can point to some additional course of conduct which can be regarded as oppressive to him as a member that the court will come to his assistance.

[26.52] Even on a literal reading of the section, it could be argued with some degree of plausibility that this is not a correct construction. It is noteworthy that the draftsman uses the words 'as members' only in the second limb of the sub-section dealing with a disregard of the interests of the member. Those words are not used in the first limb dealing with the conduct of the affairs in a manner oppressive to the members. If the draftsman found it necessary to use those

---

[40] There have, of course, been cases in which extemporary judgments were delivered: the comment in the text is confined to cases in which a written judgment survives.
[41] [1965] 1 All ER 667.
[42] [1965] 2 All ER 692.

words in the second limb and deliberately omitted them in the first limb, it would seem to follow logically that it is only where a case is being made under the second limb that the offending conduct must relate to the applicant's position as a member. It is true, of course, that there is no obvious reason why such a distinction should have been made by the draftsman, but that is perhaps a demonstration of the unsatisfactory consequences that flow from too literal a reading of the sub-section. Since in many small private companies, his appointment as a director may have been as much an inducement to him to make his investment as the allotment of shares to him, it would seem reasonable to treat his removal as a director as being capable in certain circumstances of constituting oppressive conduct.

[26.53] Surprisingly s 459 of the English Act of 1985, which has now replaced s 210 of the English Act of 1948, fails to make it clear that oppression need not be of the member in his capacity as member. However, there are indications that a more liberal interpretation is being given to the section[43].

[26.54] What constitutes 'oppressive' conduct within the meaning of the section? There has been no attempt at a definition of it in the Irish decisions already referred to but in *Greenore Trading Company Ltd*[44], Keane J adopted the definition of Viscount Simonds in *Scottish Co-operative Wholesale Ltd v Meyer*[45] of such conduct as 'burdensome, harsh and wrongful'. It has also been said to denote some lack of probity or fair dealing towards one or more members of the company[46].

[26.55] It has been suggested that the conduct complained of must affect some legal right of the applicant, perhaps on the basis that the third of Viscount Simonds' triad of adjectives connotes conduct which is not only wanting in fairness but is also tainted with illegality. It is thought, however, that this is not correct and that the section is designed to assist victims of conduct which, although not unlawful, is unfairly detrimental to their positions as members. It is also clear of course that conduct which is unlawful is within the section, provided that it is properly described as oppressive: the fact that there may be another remedy available to the applicant does not preclude him from obtaining relief under the section.

[26.56] An interesting example is afforded by *Re Greenore Trading Company Ltd*. There the applicant originally owned one-third of the issued share capital which was £24,000. One of the other shareholders, B, who was the manager of

---

43 See *Re a Company* (1988) BCLC 374.
44 (Unreported, 28 March 1981).
45 [1959] AC 324 at 342.
46 *Re Jermyn Street Turkish Baths Ltd* [1971] 3 All ER 184.

the company, agreed to sever his connection with the company. He also owned a third of the shares, and he agreed to transfer them to the third shareholder, V, for £22,500. V, however, only paid £8,000 from his own resources: the balance of the money was provided by the company itself. It was claimed that this was because the balance represented compensation to B for his loss of employment. The transaction was, however, clearly unlawful: if it was compensation for loss of office, it should have been disclosed to the applicant and approved of by the company in general meeting[47]. If it was not, it represented the giving of financial assistance for the purchase of the company's shares contrary to s 60 of the Principal Act. Keane J held that the transaction constituted oppressive conduct and ordered the purchase of the applicant's shares by V. In that case, the applicant might have launched a derivative action under the exception to the rule in *Foss v Harbottle* on the ground that V had been guilty of conduct amounting to fraud and that he was in control of the company. But that could only have resulted in the impugned transaction being set aside. The applicant would have remained a member of a company whose affairs were being conducted in a manner oppressive to him, the very position s 205 is designed to put an end to.

[26.57] It has also been held by Plowman J in *Re Westbourne Galleries Ltd*[48] that an isolated act of oppression is not sufficient to bring the section into operation. In *Westwinds Holdings Ltd*, however, Kenny J held that a single act could constitute oppression, although it should be noted that *Re Westbourne Galleries Ltd* was not referred to. In *Greenore Trading Company Ltd*, Keane J referred to the decision in *Re Westbourne Galleries Ltd* but did not find it necessary to apply it, since there had been more than one act of oppression. The law is accordingly as stated by Kenny J and in an appropriate case a single act of oppression may be sufficient.

[26.58] In *Re Williams Group (Tullamore) Group Ltd*[49] the application of these principles enabled the applicants to obtain relief. The articles of association of the company provided, somewhat unusually, that so long as there were preference shareholders, the ordinary shareholders did not have the right to attend and vote at general meetings. Over the years, the ordinary shareholders had received substantial dividends, whereas the preference shareholders were confined to a fixed dividend. In order to distribute windfall profits and redress the imbalance, it was proposed to issue a new class of share, each of which would qualify for a single dividend of £1 over and above the usual dividend. As a result, the preference shareholders would obtain a sum of £133,340 which would otherwise be available for distribution among the ordinary shareholders.

---

[47] Companies Act 1963, s 186: see para **[30.54]** below.
[48] [1970] 3 All ER 374 at 385a.
[49] [1986] IR 217.

325

The ordinary shareholders applied for relief under s 205. Barrington J held that the resolutions proposing the issue of a new class of shares which would carry a dividend of £1 were carried in disregard of the interests of the ordinary shareholders. Applying the principles already referred to, he held that it was immaterial that a single act of oppression was involved. Accordingly, he granted the relief claimed in the petition and set aside the scheme.

[26.59] It was held by the Court of Appeal in *Re Jermyn Street Turkish Baths Ltd*[50] that the oppression complained of must be operative at the time when the application is launched, because the section uses the words 'are being conducted ...'. This again seems an unnecessarily narrow construction of the section. The result of the oppressive conduct complained of may be that the company has simply ceased to function. This was the situation in *Scottish Wholesale Society Ltd v Meyer* and yet the House of Lords found no difficulty in upholding the lower courts' finding that there was oppressive conduct within the meaning of the section. Similarly in *Re Greenore Trading Co Ltd*, Keane J was satisfied to treat the refusal of the majority to put an end to the state of affairs brought about by the acts of oppression as itself constituting oppression within the meaning of the section.

[26.60] It has been held in England that the section cannot be relied on where the company is insolvent, since in that event the applicant will have no tangible interest in the company[51]. It is thought, however, that this would not apply in Ireland: the English approach is based on the fact that the applicant must be in a position to establish that he would be entitled to an order for the winding up of the company on the 'just and equitable' ground, and that such an order cannot be made on the application of a contributory where there is no possibility of there being any surplus assets available. As we have seen, the Irish section does not contain this requirement.

[26.61] In *Re Five Minute Car Wash Service Ltd*[52], the Court of Appeal held that a complaint of unwise, inefficient or careless conduct was not sufficient to justify the granting of relief under the section. Again it must be at least doubtful whether this approach would be adopted in Ireland. If the affairs of the company are being conducted in a manner which has seriously detrimental consequences for the applicant, it would seem reasonable to describe such conduct as oppressive to the applicant even though those in control may have genuinely believed that what they were doing was right. Similarly, it would seem reasonable to treat an unwise or careless handling of the company's affairs as

---

[50] [1971] 3 All ER 184.
[51] *Re Bellador Silk Ltd* [1965] 1 All ER 667.
[52] [1966] 1 All ER 242.

constituting a disregard of the applicant's interests, no matter how good the motives of those in control might be.

[26.62] The application is made by petition grounded on an affidavit[53]. The petition should make clear the nature of the relief sought, and the affidavit without being unduly prolix, should depose to the matters on which the petitioner relies in detail. If the respondent files an affidavit in reply which puts the essential facts in issue, the next stage will be for the petitioner to bring a motion for directions, and at that stage, if it appears appropriate, the court can direct the trial of issues on oral evidence.

[26.63] The court has jurisdiction to order the hearing, or any part of it, to be in camera, if it is of the opinion that the proceedings would involve the disclosure of information the publication of which would be seriously prejudicial to the legitimate interests of the company[54].

[26.64] Orders for *in camera* hearings were made until recently almost as a matter of course. The application for a private hearing was indeed usually unopposed. But this tendency was sharply arrested by the Supreme Court decision in *Re R Ltd*[55]. In that case, the applicant for relief was a substantial shareholder who alleged that he had been unfairly dismissed from his position as chief executive of the respondent company. His petition under s 205 was supported by an affidavit setting out certain sensitive commercial information. An order for an *in camera* hearing was made in the High Court on the application of the company and one of the directors. The Supreme Court, however, held that, while the court of trial might be justified in ordering so much of the hearing as involved the disclosure of sensitive commercial information to be held in private, it did not follow that the entire trial should be so held. Having regard to the requirement of the Constitution that justice should be administered in public save in such special and limited cases as may be prescribed by law[56], the court were of the view that such an order could only be made where it was necessary in order to do justice between the parties. It followed that it would not be sufficient to establish that the precondition in s 205(7) - the probability of serious prejudice to the legitimate interests of the company - had been met in order to justify a private hearing. It would also be necessary to establish to the court's satisfaction that the case was one in which justice could be done only in a private hearing.

---

[53] Rules of the Superior Courts, Ord 75, r 4.
[54] Companies Act 1963, s 205.
[55] [1989] IR 126.
[56] Article 34.1.

[26.65] It was made clear in the later decision of the Supreme Court in *Irish Press plc v Ingersoll Irish Publications Ltd (No 1)*[57] that the effect of the decision in *Re R Ltd* was that an order for the holding *in camera* could only be made where two conditions were met, ie:

(1)   the court was of the opinion that the hearing of the proceedings or at least part of them would involve the disclosure of information the publication of which would be seriously prejudicial to the legitimate interests of company;

(2)   the court was satisfied that to hold the hearing or that particular part of it in public would prevent justice being done.

It was also made clear that the court could not make such an order merely on the consent of all the parties concerned in the petition.

In his judgment, Finlay CJ said that a court in reaching a conclusion as to whether the criteria laid down for hearing the petition in private had been met would have to bear in mind that the power of the Oireachtas to provide in legislation for the hearing of cases *in camera* was confined to 'special limited cases'. It followed that, in most cases, an applicant would probably have to establish to the satisfaction of the court:

(1)   if he were the petitioner, that a public hearing would damage his shareholding in the company to such an extent that the court would, as a result, be incapable of affording a just remedy to him under s 205(3); or

(2)   if he were the respondent, that a public hearing would damage his shareholding to such an extent that even the dismissal of the petition and an award of costs in his favour against the petitioner would not afford him a just remedy; or

(3)   in either case that, irrespective of the result, the damage to the shareholding of the petitioner or the respondent, as the case might be, as a result of the public hearing would so outweigh the advantage of succeeding in the petition that the petitioner or the respondent in the reasonable, prudent protection of his shareholding would have to refrain from tendering evidence which would probably influence the resolution of the issues and the achieving of a just result.

[26.66] The threshold requirements for an *in camera* hearing have thus been set at a significantly high level. It may be that businesses as a result may be forced into damaging compromises in order to avoid harmful publicity. But the decisions are a salutary reminder that incorporation under the Acts, with all its

---

[57]   [1994] 1 IR 176.

possible benefits, including limited liability, is a statutory privilege and the underlying philosophy of the legislation has always been to subject companies to the maximum degree of public scrutiny consistent with their efficient operation.

[26.67] It should finally be noted that the alternative remedy is only available where the court is satisfied that it will bring to an end the state of affairs of which the petitioner complains. If this cannot be achieved, it may be necessary to wind up the company on the 'just and equitable' ground[58]. This was the course taken by Gannon J in *Re Murph's Restaurants Ltd*[59] where he came to the conclusion that a restaurant business had been operated by three persons on a basis of mutual trust and confidence, that this basis had completely disappeared and that the company could not be kept in being on the basis on which it had originally been established.

---

[58] See para **[36.27]** below.
[59] [1979 IILRM 141.

Part VII
Administration of the Company

Chapter 27

The Directors

[27.01] The separation of ownership and control is a central feature of company law. The company is owned by the members, but its activities are controlled by persons who act on their behalf and who are called 'the directors'. It is important to bear this distinction in mind, even though in Ireland in a significant number of private companies the distinction is a theoretical one, the members and the directors being one and the same.

[27.02] The directors of today are the descendants of the trustees of the deed of settlement who were a feature of the companies formed before the emergence of the modern legislation in the nineteenth century[1]. It should not be thought, however that they are trustees today in the sense in which that expression is used by courts of equity or in legislation. The typical trustee is appointed because it is thought desirable to vest the ownership of property in him of which the person entitled - the beneficiary - should not be in unfettered control, because, for example, he is a minor. A trustee in this sense will never be blamed for acting in a conservative fashion: in particular, he will be expected to approach the investment of the trust property with caution. Nor will he be expected to take a particularly active role in relation to the trust in many cases.

[27.03] In contrast, company directors whether they be full time (or 'executive directors' as they are usually called) or part time are not expected to adopt this approach. The taking of occasional risks is a normal feature of a well-managed business. Moreover, the executive director is expected to devote his working life to the company and even the part-time director, as we shall see, cannot adopt as detached a role as the conventional trustee. Hence, the reluctance of courts to describe directors as 'trustees'. At the same time, the law has recognised the confidence - using the word in its old-fashioned sense which imports a flavour of trust - which shareholders place in the directors who are responsible for the day-to-day management of the company. The authorities in this context have drawn extensively on the concept of the 'constructive trust' developed by courts of equity to accommodate circumstances where no conventional trust exists but it would be inequitable for a person to retain property for himself to which another has a claim[2]. Thus, directors have been required to yield up to

---

[1]   See para [2.08] above.
[2]   See para [27.102] below.

companies benefits which they acquired as a result of their position as directors. In this area of the law, they have been classified, with other categories in whom such confidence is placed (eg partners, solicitors and bankers), as fiduciaries - a genus which at once includes and is wider than conventional trustees.

[27.04] The duty owed by a director as such a fiduciary is to act in good faith in the interest of the company as a whole[3]. It is not a duty owed to the individual shareholder as such. Nor do the directors owe any duty to the creditors of the company at common law. In both these areas, however, the legislature has introduced significant changes in the law from the enactment of the Principal Act in 1964 onwards. The individual shareholders were given the valuable right by that Act of obtaining relief from the court where they could establish that the company was using its powers oppressively, usually at the instance of the directors[4]. And the power of the court to declare the directors personally liable for the debts of the company where it has been guilty of 'fraudulent trading' were increased and strengthened by the 1990 Act[5].

[27.05] The cases have also laid stress on the need for directors to avoid conflicts of interest arising and, where they do arise, of making full disclosure to the company. These requirements of the common law were significantly strengthened by the 1990 Act. Many of these requirements of the 1990 Act extend not merely to directors but to 'shadow directors'. This is a new concept in company law: a 'shadow director' is defined by s 27 as:

> 'a person in accordance with whose directions or instructions the directors of a company are accustomed to act.'

[27.06] But a person on whose professional advice directors are accustomed to act, such as a solicitor or accountant, is not a shadow director by reason only of that fact.

[27.07] The articles of association usually provide that the day-to-day management of the company is to be carried on by one of the directors, who is called the managing director. His position should be distinguished from that of the chairman of the board of directors, who frequently also acts as chairman of the meetings of members.

[27.08] In addition, articles frequently provide for directors who are to be life or permanent directors. In the case of a public company, such directors may still be removed by an ordinary resolution of the company; but in the case of a private company, they cannot be so removed[6]. This is a major difference between Irish

---

3   *Clark v Workman* [1920] 1 IR 107.
4   See Ch 26 above.
5   See Ch 33 below.
6   Companies Act 1963, s 182.

and English law: in the latter jurisdiction the security of tenure of life directors of private companies was removed by the 1948 Act. In the case of a public company, the only effect of giving directors a special label, such as 'life' or 'permanent' is that they do not automatically retire by rotation and offer themselves for re-election, as is the case with other directors.

[27.09] The articles also sometimes provide for a 'governing' director. It is not clear what legal significance, if any, is added to the office by such an adjective.

[27.10] Every company, public and private, must have at least two directors[7]. The law is thus not the same as in England where only one director is required in the case of a private company. The retention of the requirement that there be at least two directors is somewhat anomalous, having regard to the fact that, since 1994, a company may consist of only one member. Every company must also have a secretary, who may be one of the directors. A body corporate may not be a director[8]: here again the law differs from England where there is no such prohibition. While there is a statutory minimum number of directors, there is no statutory maximum.

[27.11] The first directors of the company must be named in a statement delivered to the Registrar pursuant to s 3 of the 1982 Act. In addition, in the case of private companies, it is usual for the articles of association to name the first directors. The articles invariably provide for the method of appointment and retirement of directors.

[27.12] In the case of a company limited by guarantee - which is usually formed for the purpose of carrying on some charitable or non-profit-making activity - it is common to entrust the management of the company to a committee or council elected by the members rather than to a board of directors. All the rules set out in this chapter apply to the members of such committees and councils, since s 2 of the Principal Act defines directors as including:

'any person occupying the position of director by whatever name called.'

One director to be resident in Ireland

[27.13] The Principal Act and the 1990 Act contain prohibitions on certain persons acting as directors of companies which are dealt with in more detail below. The 1999 (No 2) Act introduced a new restriction: except in specified circumstances, one at least of the directors must now be resident in the State. In the case of companies formed after the coming into force of the relevant section, this restriction takes immediate effect. In the case of companies formed before it

---

[7] Companies Act 1963, s 174.
[8] Companies Act 1963, s 176.

came into force, it takes effect 12 months after the coming into force of the section[9].

[27.14] This enactment was promoted by concern that directors of a company who are not resident in Ireland could not be successfully prosecuted for breaches of the companies legislation. The restriction, accordingly, will not apply to a company which enters into a bond up to a value of £20,000 securing the payment of any fine imposed on the company in respect of offences under the Acts or fines and penalties under the Taxes Consolidation Act 1997.

[27.15] Where a person ceases to be a director of a company and, at the time of that cessation, he or she is resident in the State and, to his or her knowledge, no other director of the company is so resident, he or she must, within 14 days, notify the Registrar in writing of those facts.

[27.16] An exemption from these requirements is allowed when the Registrar certifies, in an application made by the company, that:

'the company has a real and continuous link with one or more economic activities that are being carried on in the State'.

Such a company, accordingly, can operate without any director resident in Ireland.

[27.17] The company must tender 'proof' to the Registrar that it has such a link. That can take the form of a written statement from the Revenue Commissioners given to the company within the period of two months preceding the application that that body has 'reasonable grounds' for believing that the company meets the requirements for the granting of a certificate.

[27.18] If the Registrar, as a result of information coming into his possession, is of the opinion that a company which has been granted a certificate under these provisions has ceased to have the 'real and continuous link' which they require, he must revoke the certificate. The information referred to can include a notice to that effect from the Revenue Commissioners.

[27.19] Whether a person is 'resident in the State' at a particular time for the purpose of these provisions is determined by a method somewhat similar to that employed in tax legislation. He will be treated as so resident where he was present in the State for a period of 183 days or more in the immediately preceding year. Alternatively, he will be treated as so resident, where he was present in the State for a period of 280 days or more in the immediately preceding two years. But if in either of those years he was present in the State for

---

[9]   Companies (Amendment) (No 2) Act 1999, s 43. This section came into force on 18 April 2000.

a period of only 30 days or less, he will not be regarded as resident in the State at the particular time.

Limitation on number of directorships

[27.20] Section 45 of the 1999 (No 2) Act imposed for the first time a limitation on the number of companies of which a person can be a director at any one time. It would seem that the principal objective is to limit the extent to which companies can be formed which have no real connection with Ireland.

[27.21] Sub-section (1) provides that a person shall not be at a particular time a director of more than 25 companies. However, in reckoning the number of companies of which a person is a director, companies in respect of which the Registrar has certified under s 44 that they have a real and continuous link with an economic activity being carried on in the State are excluded: so too are public limited companies and public companies within the meaning of the 1982 Act.

[27.22] There are also excluded companies coming within the Second Schedule to the Act, such as companies quoted on the Stock Exchange, investment companies, etc and companies which have a licence to carry on banking or are exempt from the requirement to have such a licence. Such companies are only excluded, however, where notice in the prescribed form has been given to the Registrar that they fall within one of these categories and the Registrar certifies in writing that they do. The Registrar may accept a statutory declaration by an officer of the company in the prescribed form that the company falls within one of the categories as sufficient evidence that it does so.

[27.23] When the Registrar refuses to certify that the company falls within one of the categories, the company or the person concerned may appeal to the Minister. He may either confirm the Registrar's decision or certify that the company does fall within the particular category. Alternatively, the Minister may confirm the decision of the Registrar but direct that the company is to be left out of the reckoning, where he is satisfied that to do otherwise would cause 'serious injustice or hardship' to the person concerned and that such a direction would not operate 'against the common good'.

[27.24] The exclusion of such companies, subject to these elaborate safeguards, reflects the importance attached to encouraging the development of Dublin as a financial centre which has been a feature of the policies of successive governments since the establishment of the International Financial Services Centre.

[27.25] Where a person becomes or remains a director or shadow director of one or more companies in contravention of these provisions, he is guilty of an offence which may be prosecuted summarily by the Registrar. There is also a provision that the appointment of a person as a director of a company in contravention of the sub-section is to be void.

Appointment and retirement of directors

[27.26] The subsequent directors of the company must be appointed in the manner provided by the articles: if no method of appointment is prescribed, they must be elected by the members in general meeting. Unless all the members present at the meeting agree to it, it is not permissible to propose the election of two or more directors by a single resolution[10]. This is to ensure that the members are not presented with a 'slate' of candidates, some of whom they may approve of and some not, obliging them to elect or reject them all. It may be noted that in Ireland the prohibition on such composite resolutions extends to all companies, whereas in England it is confined to public companies.

[27.27] Where the articles provide that additional directors are to be appointed by the board of directors, the company in general meeting has no power to make such appointments: it can, however, amend the articles by special resolution to give itself such power[11]. The articles sometimes provide for the appointment by the directors of alternate directors, ie directors who may act in the place of the directors when they are absent. Such alternate directors, when their appointment takes effect, have in law the same status as the directors whom they replace.

[27.28] The articles usually provide that the directors shall have power to fill casual vacancies in their number (Article 98). This enables the directors to fill any vacancy other than one that arises through a director retiring by rotation or through the expiration of the period for which he was to hold office.

[27.29] A director does not have to own any shares in the company. The articles sometimes provide that the directors are to hold a specified number of shares known as qualification shares. Where this is the case, s 180 of the Principal Act requires the director to obtain the necessary shares within two months after his appointment or within such shorter time as the articles may specify.

[27.30] The articles usually provide for the automatic vacation by a director of his office on the happening of certain events. Thus article 91 provides that he is to vacate office if inter alia he

(1)   becomes of unsound mind;

(2)   resigns his office by notice in writing to the company;

(3)   is convicted of an indictable offence; or

(4)   is absent from meetings of the directors for more than six months without their permission.

---

10 Companies Act 1963, s 181.
11 *Blair Open Hearth Furnace Co v Reigart* (1913) 108 LT 665.

Removal of directors

[27.31] The directors of the company may be removed at any time by ordinary resolution of the company in general meeting. This crucial power of ultimate control is given by s 182 of the Principal Act and cannot be removed or abridged by the articles. It is, as we have seen, subject to one major qualification in Ireland: directors of private companies holding office for life cannot be removed under the section.

[27.32] A further important qualification of the rule was recognised recently by the Supreme Court in *McGilligan v O'Grady*[12]. The plaintiff had entered into an agreement with the defendants under which arrangements were made for an investment in the third named defendant company. One of the terms of the agreement was the plaintiff was to be a director of a particular company. Following disputes between the parties, an extraordinary general meeting was convened for the purpose of considering a resolution removing the first named plaintiff from his office as a director. The plaintiffs instituted two sets of proceedings, one of them being a petition pursuant to s 205 of the Principal Act claiming that the affairs of the company were being conducted in a manner oppressive to the plaintiffs and in disregard of their interests and an order directing the company to purchase the beneficial shareholding of each of the petitioners or, in the alternative, an order winding up the company. The High Court (O'Donovan J) granted an interlocutory injunction which *inter alia* restrained the defendants from removing the first named plaintiff as a director.

It was argued on behalf of the defendants that the granting of an injunction in those terms was inconsistent with the power of ultimate control given to the shareholders by s 182 of the Principal Act. However, the Supreme Court upheld the High Court, pointing out that the essence of the s 205 procedure was to afford relief to a shareholder whose interests were being disregarded, even though the action of the majority was otherwise perfectly lawful.

[27.33] Extended notice - ie at least 28 days notice[13] - must be given of any resolution to remove a director under s 182 and notice of the resolution must be sent to the director concerned, who is then entitled to be heard on the resolution at the meeting. This is so, whether or not he is a member of the company. He is also entitled to make representations in writing to the company when he receives a notice of such a resolution, but they must be of reasonable length. Provided

---

[12] [1999] 1 IR 346. Doubts were expressed by Keane J as to the correctness of an earlier High Court decision in *Feighery v Feighery & Co* [1999] 1 IR 321 and an English decision of *Bentley-Stevens v Jones* [1974] 1 WLR 638 which appeared to suggest a different view of the law.

[13] See para **[25.29]** above.

that they are received in time, the company must state that such representations have been received in any notice of the resolution given to members and must send a copy of them to every member to whom notice of the meeting is sent. If they are not received in time, or if the company fails to send them to members, the director is entitled to require them to be read out at the meeting. There is also a provision designed to ensure that the rights conferred by the section on directors are not abused to secure 'needless publicity for defamatory matter': the court, on the application either of the company or of any person who claims to be aggrieved, may declare in such circumstances that the representations need not be sent out or read at the meeting and may require the director concerned to pay the company's costs.

Directors' service contracts

[27.34] As we have seen, one of the directors - traditionally called the managing director - will normally be responsible for the day-to-day management of the company. In larger companies, he is often described today as the 'chief executive'. In addition, in such companies, there are usually full-time directors with executive responsibilities, variously described as the 'financial executive', 'technical executive' or whatever. If such directors are removed from office, it does not follow in every case that they cease to be employees of the company. That depends in turn on whether they are employed under a contract and, if they are, what its terms are. If, moreover, as a result of the removal from office the contract of employment does terminate - because, for example, the contract itself so provides - that does not leave the dismissed director without a remedy in an appropriate case. This is made clear by s 182(7) of the Principal Act which, as we have seen, is the section enabling the company in general meeting to remove directors. It provides that:

> 'Nothing in this section shall be taken as depriving a person removed thereunder of compensation or damages payable to him in respect of the determination of his appointment as director or compensation or damages payable to him in respect of the determination of any appointment terminating with that as director ...'

[27.35] In many cases, and again this is particularly so in larger companies, there is a written contract of service with executive directors. Usually this provides that the director is to be employed as an executive for a fixed term of years. It will also generally provide for circumstances in which it can be terminated at an earlier stage by either party. The law itself will also imply in every such contract the right of either party to treat it as repudiated by the conduct of the other. Thus, a director may by behaving dishonestly or declining to carry out his duties render himself liable to peremptory dismissal even though the term of the contract has not expired.

[27.36] Where the company purports to terminate the director's employment before the end of the term without any such justification, he will be entitled to damages for wrongful dismissal in accordance with normal legal principles.

[27.37] Moreover, even in cases where grounds justifying dismissal have arisen, the company may still be liable in damages if they have failed to observe the requirements of natural justice in relation to the dismissal. Thus, it was held in *Glover v BLN Ltd*[14] that where a managing director has a service contract for a fixed term which provides for his dismissal before the expiration of the term for misconduct, the contract may be read subject to an implied requirement that any inquiry into such misconduct and any determination made as to such misconduct observes the requirements of natural justice, or 'fair procedures', to use the term more often employed in Irish cases today. Thus, in *Glover*'s case the plaintiff, who was a technical director of four companies, had a service contract which provided that he could be dismissed without compensation if guilty of any serious misconduct or serious neglect of his duties which in the unanimous opinion of the directors of the holding company injuriously affected the business or property of any of the group. In the High Court, Kenny J found that there had been in one respect serious misconduct on the plaintiff's part but that, as he had not been given notice of the charges against him his dismissal was invalid. The finding as to serious misconduct was not challenged in the Supreme Court and that court also found that his dismissal was invalid. Unlike the High Court judge, however, the majority did not base their conclusion on the fact that the plaintiff was the holder of an office: it was sufficient that the plaintiff was employed under an agreement which necessarily imported the concept of 'fair procedures' into any dismissal procedures. Walsh J invoked Article 40.3 of the Constitution, saying:

> 'Public policy and the dictates of constitutional justice require that statutes, regulations or agreements setting up machinery for the taking of any decisions which may affect rights or impose liabilities should be construed as providing for fair procedures.'[15]

It should also be noted that it has been held by the Supreme Court that a company in seeking to terminate a director's contract of employment cannot rely on a breach of contract or misconduct on his part which was unknown to them at the time of the purported dismissal[16].

[27.38] So far, we have been considering the cases in which the executive director has a written contract of service. If he has not such a contract, the courts

---

[14]   [1973] IR 388.

[15]   [1973] IR 388 at 425.

[16]   *Carvill v Irish Industrial Bank Ltd* [1968] IR 325.

will usually be in a position to infer the existence of a contract, although not necessarily one for a fixed term. The law was thus stated by O'Keeffe J, speaking for the Supreme Court in *Carvill v Irish Industrial Bank Ltd*:

> 'It appears to me that a person who is a director, and who is appointed by the board of directors to the office of managing director, must be deemed to hold that office under some contract, express or implied. The contract may be for a fixed term, in which case it cannot properly be terminated before the expiration of that term without a liability to pay damages. It may be for no fixed term and, indeed, may be for so long only as the person holds office as director, in which case, if the person concerned ceases to be a director, his office as managing director also comes to an end.'

In that case, the court declined to interfere with the finding of the High Court judge that the plaintiff was employed as managing director under an implied contract by virtue of which his employment could be terminated at any time on a year's notice. It was also held that such a contract could be inferred from the conduct of the parties even though there was no formal resolution appointing the plaintiff managing director. Clearly the reasoning of this case would apply to the other forms of 'executive directors' with which we are also concerned.

[27.39] In such a case, however, it may be that the articles of association will permit the peremptory dismissal of the director without affording him any rights of action. This was the position in *Read v Astoria Garage Streatham Ltd*[17] where the plaintiff's claim for wrongful dismissal failed because the articles provided that

> '(the managing director's) appointment shall be subject to determination *ipso facto* if he ceases from any cause to be a director or if the company in general meeting resolve that his tenure of the office of managing director or manager be determined.'

[27.40] An earlier decision of the Court of Appeal, *Southern Foundries (1926) Ltd v Shirlaw*[18] was distinguished on the ground that in that case:

(1)   there was a contract independently of the articles and

(2)   the relevant removal provisions were not contained in the articles at the date of the contract.

[27.41] In *Carvill's* case, the relevant removal provisions of the articles were qualified by the words 'subject to the provisions of any contract between him and the company' and the Supreme Court held accordingly that the plaintiff's right of action for wrongful dismissal was not affected.

---

[17]   [1952] Ch 637.
[18]   [1940] AC 701.

[27.42] The dismissal of a director who is an employee of the company may also afford him rights under the Unfair Dismissals Act 1977. This provides for the payment of compensation to an employee who is unfairly dismissed and for his re-instatement in his position if the tribunal adjudicating on his complaint considers that appropriate. It also provides for his re-engagement, where that is appropriate, in an equivalent position. Presumably in the case of a managing director, re-instatement would not be possible without the consent of a majority of the members, having regard to the provisions of s 182 of the Principal Act. 'Re-engagement' (eg as general manager but not as managing director) would presumably be available as a remedy in an appropriate case.

[27.43] It will be seen that developments in legislation and the courts have not made life easier for companies who find themselves saddled with incompetent or even dishonest executives. The problem is greatest in larger companies where the divorce between ownership and day-to-day management is more pronounced: shareholders are understandably exasperated to find that they cannot get rid of such an employee except by paying him substantial compensation and this even though he may have been retained on such generous terms solely because of a decision by his fellow directors.

[27.44] The balance was redressed to some extent by s 28 of the 1990 Act. This provides that a contract of employment entered into by a company with a director for a fixed term exceeding five years must be approved by a resolution at a general meeting of the company. The section takes effect where a contract to employ a director for a period of more than five years cannot be terminated by the company by notice or can be so terminated only in special circumstances. It also applies to a director of a holding company who has such a contract with any of the companies in the group: in his case, it must be similarly approved by the holding company. If a contract has more than six months to run and the company enters into a further contract, the unexpired period of the first contract must be taken into account in reckoning whether the five-year period has been exceeded. A written memorandum of the agreement including the term specifying its length must be available for inspection by the members at the registered office for a period of not less than 15 days prior to the meeting and at the meeting itself[19].

[27.45] Where a company enters into a contract which contravenes this section, the contract is void to that extent and must be read as though it contained a term entitling the company to terminate it at any time on the giving of reasonable notice[20].

---

[19] Companies Act 1990, s 28(4).
[20] Companies Act 1990, s 28(5).

[27.46] The 1990 Act also contains provisions intended to ensure that the shareholders can obtain information as to any service contract the company may have with directors. The company is obliged to keep at its registered office a copy of every contract of service with a director or a director of a subsidiary[21]. The copy may also be kept at the company's place of business or, where the register of members is not kept at the registered office, at the place where it is kept. It must be open to inspection by the members during business hours, subject to any reasonable restrictions that the company in general meeting imposes but so that it is open for at least two hours each day. Where there is no contract in writing, a memorandum of its terms must be kept in the same manner for inspection by members. In any case where inspection is refused, the court may compel an immediate inspection.

[27.47] Where there is a breach of these requirements, the company and any officer in default is liable on summary conviction to a fine not exceeding £1,000 and in the case of continuing breach a daily default fine not exceeding £50. There is an exemption from the requirements of the section in the case of a contract with less than three years to run or which can be terminated by the company within 12 months without payment of compensation.

[27.48] It should also be noted that there is nothing to prevent the articles from conferring on the board of directors the power to remove one or more of their number from office. Where such a power is given, the director may be removed, not only by a resolution of the company, but also by a valid resolution of the board of directors. This is made clear by s 182(7) which provides that nothing in the section is to be taken as derogating from any power to remove a director which may exist apart from the section[22].

Remuneration of directors

[27.49] A director has no right as such to remuneration for acting as director. The articles usually provide, however, for the determination by the company in general meeting of the remuneration to be given to the directors (article 76).

[27.50] The amount of the remuneration is a matter for the company and it does not have to be paid out of profits[23]. Nor does the fact that the remuneration was paid at a time when the company was insolvent render it unlawful. If, however, the remuneration is so excessive as to constitute a gift not authorised by the company's constitution or if it amounts to a disguised return of capital, it may be unlawful[24]. If a director accepts remuneration in excess of what is authorised by

---

[21] Companies Act 1990, s 50.
[22] Cf *Lee v Chou Wen Hsien* [1985] BCLC 45.
[23] *Harvey Lewis's Case* (1872) 26 LT 673.
[24] *Re Holt Garage (1964) Ltd* [1982] 3 All ER 1016.

the articles, he commits a misfeasance and can be compelled to repay the amount of the excess to the company or its liquidator[25].

[27.51] The Principal Act also contains strict requirements as to the disclosure of the amount of the remuneration - and other payments to directors - in the annual accounts[26].

[27.52] The articles usually provide that the remuneration is to be deemed to accrue from day to day. It follows from this that where the director's employment is determined during the course of a year, he is entitled to an apportioned part of his salary for the part of the year during which he was a director. Where the articles contain no such provision, there is a divergence of view as to whether the remuneration is to be apportioned, but the better view would appear to be that in such circumstances the Apportionment Act 1870 applies and the remuneration should be apportioned[27].

[27.53] The articles usually provide for the payment of expenses to directors (article 76). Such a provision is of particular importance in the modern company, because of the relief afforded to income tax payers in respect of such expenses where they are 'wholly, exclusively and necessarily' incurred in the performance of duties as directors[28]. The usual provision is that the directors may be paid all travelling, hotel and other expenses properly incurred by them in attending and returning from meetings of the directors and general meetings of the company or in connection with the business of the company. Again the amount of such expenses paid must be disclosed in the accounts[29].

Loans to directors

[27.54] The Principal Act contained no restrictions on the making of loans by the company to directors, although particulars had to be disclosed in the accounts[30]. In Ireland, the principal victims of this gap in the law were the creditors of private limited companies who frequently found, when the company got into financial difficulties, that it had made loans to its directors with no sensible commercial basis.

[27.55] Section 31 of the 1990 Act now prohibits the making of loans by companies to directors and brings within its net a wide range of similar

---

25 *Re Oxford Society* (1887) 35 Ch D 502.
26 See para [30.54] below.
27 *Palmer's Company Law* (25th edn), Vol II, 8.045-7.
28 Income Tax Act 1967.
29 See para [30.55] below.
30 See para [30.54] below.

transactions. There are, however, important exemptions which are noted in more detail below.

[27.56] The provisions, are lengthy and complex, but three main strands can be isolated. There is, first, the range of transactions intended to be captured, secondly, the various exemptions and, thirdly, the methods of enforcement.

[27.57] Section 31(1) prohibits the making of a loan by a company to a director of the company or of its holding company. In addition, companies may not enter into the following transactions with directors or directors of their holding companies:

(1)   'quasi-loans', ie transactions where one person ('the creditor') pays or agrees to pay a sum for another ('the borrower') or reimburses or agrees to reimburse expenditure incurred by the borrower;

(2)   'credit transactions', ie hire purchase agreements, leasing transactions etc;

(3)   guarantees or provision of security in connection with loans, quasi-loans or credit transactions made by other persons for the benefit of such directors.

These prohibitions extend to 'shadow directors'[31]. In addition, they apply to such transactions when they are made for 'a person connected with a director', ie:

(1)   a spouse, parent, brother, sister or child of the director;

(2)   the trustee of any trust of which the director, his spouse or any of his children or any body corporate which he controls are the principal beneficiaries;

(3)   a partner of the director[32];

(4)   the sole member of a single member company[33].

None of these are treated as 'connected', however, if they are also directors of the company in question.

[27.58] There are further wide ranging provisions designed to prevent evasion. The company cannot 'take over' a transaction which, if it had been entered into by the company, would have been in breach of s 31[34]. Nor can it take part in an arrangement whereby someone else makes the loan or whatever to the director and gets a corresponding benefit from the company[35].

---

[31]   See para **[27.05]** above.

[32]   Companies Act 1990, s 26(1).

[33]   European Community (Single-Member Private Limited Companies) Regulations 1994, SI 275/1994.

[34]   Companies Act 1990, s 31(2).

[35]   Companies Act 1990, s 31(3).

[27.59] We turn next to the exemptions. The prohibitions do not apply where the 'value of the arrangement' and the total outstanding under any other arrangements by the company with the director or a connected person is less than 10% of the company's 'relevant assets'[36]. An 'arrangement' is in effect a loan, quasi-loan or credit transaction. It would seem, accordingly, that the company's liabilities under guarantees in the director's favour are not to be taken into account in determining whether the exemption applies.

[27.60] The 'value of the arrangement' is relatively straightforward: in most cases, it is simply the principal of the loan or quasi-loan, or (in the case of credit transactions) the price the goods would have been sold for in an ordinary commercial transaction. But if the liability of the director under the arrangement cannot be expressed in money terms (because it is unascertainable or for some other reason) it is to be assumed that it exceeds £50,000[37]. The company's 'relevant assets' are its 'net assets', ie the aggregate of its assets less the aggregate of its liabilities as determined by reference to the accounts prepared and laid in accordance with the Acts for the last financial year in which such accounts were laid[38]. If no such accounts were laid, the amount of the assets is taken to be the amount of the company's called up share capital.

[27.61] There are then exemptions for transactions involving companies within the same group of companies (ie a holding company and its subsidiaries) as, for example, where one of the companies makes a loan to another in the group: in such cases, the fact that a director of one company in the group is associated with another does not render the transaction illegal under s 31[39]. Similarly, a subsidiary may enter into such transactions with its holding company without violating s 31[40].

[27.62] The advancing of money by a company to a director for reasonable expenses is specifically exempted by s 36. A company may provide its directors with funds to meet vouched expenditure properly incurred or about to be incurred for the purposes of the company or to enable him properly to perform his duties as an officer of the company. But any liability incurred as a result must be discharged by the person concerned within six months. Breach of this latter requirement is an offence punishable on summary conviction by a fine not exceeding £1,000 or, on indictment, not exceeding £10,000.

---

[36] Companies Act 1990, s 32(1).
[37] Companies Act 1990, s 25(5).
[38] Companies Act 1990, s 29(2).
[39] Companies Act 1990, s 34.
[40] Companies Act 1990, s 35.

[27.63] Finally, companies are exempted from the prohibition against loans, quasi-loans or credit transactions where the transaction involved is in the ordinary course of its business, eg banking, hire purchase, money-lending etc[41]. But the loan or other facility must not afford the director concerned any special treatment: it will only attract exemption if its value is no greater and the terms no more favourable than that which the company would offer in respect of a person of the same financial standing unconnected with the company.

[27.64] The third feature of these new provisions is the method by which they are to be enforced.

[27.65] A director or person connected with him who enters into any of the prohibited transactions is liable to account to the company for any gains he made as a result, as is any director who authorised the transaction[42]. They must also indemnify the company against any loss or damage which it suffered[43]. A director is not liable if he shows that he took all reasonable steps to secure compliance with s 31. A person connected with the director is relieved from liability if he shows that at the time of the transaction he did not know the circumstances which rendered it illegal[44].

[27.66] A prohibited transaction is voidable at the instance of the company, ie it can be set aside by the company but unless and until that happens remains valid[45]. It cannot be avoided by the company in three cases:

(1)   where restitution of any money or other assets which was the subject of the arrangement is no longer possible;

(2)   where the company has been indemnified by the director or connected person;

(3)   where rights acquired bona fide, for value and without notice of the contravention by a person other than the person for whom the transaction was made would be affected by the contravention[46].

[27.67] If the company is subsequently wound up and is unable to pay its debts, and the court considers that a transaction prohibited by s 32 'contributed materially' to its insolvency or has 'substantially impeded the orderly winding up' of the company, the court may declare that any person for whose benefit the transaction was made is to be personally responsible, with or without limitation of liability, for all or a specified part of the debts and other liabilities of the

---

41   Companies Act 1990, s 37.
42   Companies Act 1990, s 38(2)(a).
43   Companies Act 1990, s 38(2)(b).
44   Companies Act 1990, s 38(3).
45   Companies Act 1990, s 38(1).
46   Companies Act 1990, s 38(1).

company[47]. In deciding whether to make such an order, the court is to have regard to whether, and to what extent, any outstanding liabilities under the arrangement were discharged before the winding up. The court is also to have regard to the extent to which the arrangement contributed materially to the insolvency or impeded the winding up.

[27.68] An officer who authorises or permits a company to enter into a transaction which he knows, or has reasonable cause to believe, contravenes s 31 is guilty of an offence. A person who procures a company to enter into such a transaction with a similar knowledge or belief is also guilty of an offence. In each case, he is liable on summary conviction to a fine not exceeding £1,000 or imprisonment for a term not exceeding 12 months or both and on indictment to a fine not exceeding £10,000 or imprisonment for a term not exceeding three years or both[48].

Other transactions with directors

[27.69] The 1990 Act imposes restrictions on other transactions from which directors might benefit to the detriment of the shareholders or creditors. The first category to be considered is those under which the directors acquire substantial assets of the company, such as land or buildings, or the company acquires such assets from the directors. In this case, the transactions are not prohibited, but to be effective must be approved by a resolution of the company in general meeting[49]. Where the director is the director of a holding company, the resolution must be passed by that company. Transactions with a 'connected person' (defined as in the case of loans etc)[50] are similarly affected.

[27.70] The relevant section applies to 'non-cash assets' of a specified value. It will not apply unless the value is not less than £1,000 and exceeds £50,000 or 10% of the company's 'relevant assets'[51]. The 'relevant assets' are defined in the same manner as in the case of the loan provisions[52].

[27.71] There are also similar provisions intended to secure the enforcement of these requirements, ie enabling the company to avoid the transaction and requiring the director to account to the company for any gain and to indemnify the company[53]. In this case, however, contravention of the section is not a criminal offence. Moreover, while the circumstances in which the transaction

---

[47] Companies Act 1990, s 39.
[48] Companies Act 1990, s 40.
[49] Companies Act 1990, s 29(1).
[50] See para **[27.57]** above.
[51] Companies Act 1990, s 29(2).
[52] See para **[27.60]** above.
[53] See para **[27.65]** above.

may be avoided by the company are similar to those in the case of loans, the transaction is not voidable if it is affirmed within a reasonable time by the company in general meeting (or where appropriate by its holding company)[54].

[27.72] All of these requirements apply to 'shadow directors'[55] of companies in the same manner as they do to directors.

[27.73] It should be noted that the section applies irrespective of whether the transaction in question is an 'arms length' transaction, ie one in which the full market value of the property is paid and where the director secures no advantage from his connection with the company.

[27.74] The second category of transactions affected are those where a director buys options in the shares of the company. Such options, which give the director the right to buy or sell his own company's shares at a specified time in the future at a fixed price, are clearly capable of abuse, since they enable unscrupulous directors to make use of their special knowledge of the company's affairs to their benefit and the shareholders' detriment. In contrast to the transactions mentioned in the preceding paragraph, such contracts are now absolutely prohibited. Any director who buys an option to buy or sell 'relevant shares' is guilty of an offence, 'relevant shares' being defined as shares in the company of which he is a director and shares in any subsidiary of the company or in its holding company, or in any of the other subsidiaries of the holding company, which are traded in any stock exchange here or abroad. There is a similar prohibition against buying options in debentures of the company or its associated companies[56].

[27.75] Any director buying such options is guilty of an offence and liable on summary conviction to a fine not exceeding £1,000 or a term of imprisonment not exceeding 12 months or both and on indictment to a fine not exceeding £10,000 or imprisonment for a term not exceeding three years or both.

[27.76] Again, these requirements apply to 'shadow directors'[57] in the same manner as they do to directors.

Powers and duties of directors

[27.77] The powers of the directors are those which the company has delegated to them. If, as is usually the case, the articles provide that the directors may exercise all the powers of the company which are not by the Acts or the articles required to be exercised by the company in general meeting (Article 80), the

---

54 Companies Act 1990, s 29(3)(c).
55 See para **[27.05]** above.
56 Companies Act 1990, s 30.
57 See para **[27.05]** above.

delegation is unrestricted, and the board of directors can do whatever the company could do. They cannot, of course, do anything which is illegal or ultra vires, any more than the company in general meeting can.

[27.78] It follows that the company cannot, in general meeting, validly set aside an action taken by the directors within the powers conferred on them by the articles. Equally the company cannot itself in general meeting take any step which by virtue of its articles it has delegated to the directors.

[27.79] But although the directors, once the powers have been delegated to them, can do anything which the company can do, this does not mean that the company cannot ultimately control the directors, if it wishes. In the first place, the company may always amend the articles of association by special resolution so as to circumscribe the powers of the directors in any way it thinks fit. In the second place, the company may always by ordinary resolution remove all or any of the directors except a life director. And even in the case of a life director, he can always be removed if there is a majority sufficient to effect the necessary amendment of the articles.

[27.80] We have seen that directors occupy a fiduciary position towards the company. This means that they must always act in good faith in the interests of the company as a whole. The test in other words is subjective: if the directors genuinely believe that what they are doing is in the interests of the company as a whole, the court will not interfere with their decisions even though they might appear objectively to be detrimental to the company[58].

[27.81] The duty is owed by the directors to the company as a whole and not to the individual shareholders. This was first established by the leading case of *Percival v Wright*[59]. A director purchased shares from a member and did not disclose to him that the directors were aware that negotiations were in progress for the purchase of all the shares at a higher figure. When the member sought to make the director account for the profit on the shares, it was held by Swinfen Eady J that he could not succeed: there had been no breach of duty on the part of the director to the company. If, however, the directors can be regarded in a particular transaction as acting on behalf of individual shareholders, ie if they are in effect acting as the agent of individual shareholders, they will owe them a duty to act in their interests[60].

[27.82] It was also made clear in the Scottish case of *Dawson International plc v Coets Paton plc*[61] that this legal principle may entitle the directors of a public

---

[58] *Re Greshem Life Assurance Soc* [1872] LR 8 Ch 446 at 449.
[59] (1902) 2 Ch 421. But note that the plaintiff in that case would succeed today under the 'insider dealing' provisions of the Companies Act 1990: see para **[34.05]** below.
[60] *Allen v Hyatt* (1914) 30 TLR 444.

company which is involved in a take-over battle to act in a way which may be disadvantageous to shareholders wishing to dispose of their shares, if they believe that so to act is in the interest of the company. Lord Cullen observed:

> 'What is in the interests of current shareholders who are sellers of their shares may not necessarily coincide with what is in the interests of the company. The creation of parallel duties could lead to conflict. Directors have but one master, the company'.

[27.83] Since the duty is owed to the company as a whole, it is not fulfilled where the directors act in the interests of a section only of the members[62]. Nor is it sufficient to act in the short term interests of the company alone without regard to its long term interests on the basis that the duty is confined to the existing body of members: the directors must take into account the long term and short term interests of the company[63].

[27.84] Some modern authorities indicate that, in any event, the rule in *Percival v Wright* is not as inflexible as was previously thought. In the New Zealand case of *Coleman v Myers*[64], it was said by the Court of Appeal that directors of a private company, who withheld information as to the value of their shares from members of their family, who were also shareholders, when they were seeking to acquire those shares, had acted in breach of a fiduciary duty. Woodhouse J said that it was not the law that anyone holding the office of a company director was for that reason alone to be relieved from what would otherwise be regarded as a fiduciary responsibility owed to shareholders in the same company. He indicated the factors which would be relevant in determining whether a fiduciary duty existed as follows:

> '... dependence upon information and advice, the existence of a relationship of confidence, the significance of some particular transaction for the parties and, of course, the extent of any positive action taken by or on behalf of the director or directors to promote it.'

That approach was expressly approved in Ireland by the High Court and the Supreme Court in *Crindle Investments v Wymes*[65], although on the facts of the case, it was found that a fiduciary duty did not exist.

---

[61] [1989] BCLC 233.
[62] *Report of the Second Savoy Hotel Investigation*, HMSO, June 1954; *Gaiman v National Association for Mental Health* [1971] Ch 317 at 330.
[63] *Report of the Second Savoy Hotel Investigation*, HMSO, June 1954; *Gaiman v National Association for Mental Health* [1971] Ch 317 at 330.
[64] [1977] 2 NZLR 225.
[65] [1998] 4 IR 567.

[27.85] It has also been made clear by the Supreme Court in recent times that, in the case of an insolvent company, the duty owed by the directors to the company is effectively transposed into a duty to act in the interests of the company's creditors. That approach had been adopted in the Australian case of *Kinsela v Russell Kinsela Property Ltd*[66] and was applied by both the High Court and the Supreme Court in *Re Frederick Inns Ltd*[67].

In the latter case, the directors of a group of companies, which were insolvent, sold assets of some of the companies and paid the Revenue Commissioners, not only the sums owed by the company in question but also those owed by other companies in the group. Lardner J held that the payments to the Revenue were in breach of the duty which the company and directors owed to the general creditors of the insolvent companies and his decision was upheld by the Supreme Court.

[27.86] Section 52 of the 1990 Act imposed for the first time on the directors a duty to have regard to the interests of the company's employees in general, as well as the interests of the members. This provision is in similar terms to s 309 of the English 1985 Act and, while the motives which prompted it are understandable, it suffers from the same probably inescapable defect as its English counterpart. There is no guidance as to how the board are to resolve the conflict which may arise between those interests and the interests of the shareholders which they must also protect. In practice, a management which regularly disregards the interests of its employees will find itself in difficulties anyway and the occasions on which it is in the shareholders' interests to antagonise the workforce must be rare.

[27.87] A director cannot validly enter into a contract which fetters his discretion in some way and thereby inhibits him from exercising his functions in the interests of the company as a whole. Thus, in *Clark v Workman*[68] directors who gave an undertaking to look after the interests of a third party were held to have acted improperly.

---

[66] [1986] 4 NSWLR 722

[67] [1991] ILRM 582; [1994] ILRM 387. It has been suggested that the duty should still be regarded as one owed by the directors to the company and that this is consistent with their also being required to take into account the creditors' interests: see Fealy, *The Role of Equity in the Winding Up of a Company* (1995) 17 DULJ 18. At least where the company is insolvent (the situation which had arisen in *Re Frederick Inns Ltd*) it is not easy to see why so refined a distinction should be observed by the courts. As to the finding by the Supreme Court that the company had ceased to be the beneficial owner of its assets because of its insolvency, which is also criticised in that article and in Forde, *Company Law in Ireland* (3rd edn), para 16.08, see para **[36.93]** below.

[68] [1920] 1 IR 107.

[27.88] The position of nominee directors - ie those who have been appointed to represent some special interest - should be noted. It has been held in England that the terms on which they are appointed do not absolve such directors from their duty to act in the interests of the company as a whole[69]. But Australian decisions have also indicated that the courts will have regard to the fact that the appointment of the director on those terms may well have been a decision taken in good faith in the interests of the company. So where a director is appointed to represent the interests of a secured creditor, he will not necessarily be acting in breach of his duties to the company by taking steps to enforce the security[70]. And where directors are appointed to represent the interests of different groups in joint ventures, nominees who act in the interests of their principals would seem not to be in breach of duty, unless it can be inferred that they would have acted in the same way even if they thought that their action was not in the interests of the company: per Jacobs J in *Re Broadcasting Station 2GB Ltd*[71].

[27.89] The powers conferred on the directors by the articles, however unrestricted the language used, may only be used for the purposes for which they are conferred. Thus, the power to issue shares in the company may not be used by the directors for the purpose of maintaining their control, or their friends' control, of the company or in order to defeat the wishes of the majority of the shareholders[72]. The directors may genuinely believe that by ensuring their future dominance over the company, they are also securing its well-being, but that does not entitle them to use the power to issue shares for a purpose for which it was not intended, ie the maintenance of their control, as distinct from one of the purposes for which it is conferred, eg the raising of new capital.

[27.90] An example is afforded by *Nash v Lancegaye (Ireland) Ltd*[73], the facts of which have already been stated[74]. In that case Dixon J set aside an issue of shares which he found had been made by a majority of the directors with a view to ensuring the continued control of the company by a particular family.

[27.91] The principle is also seen in operation in *G & S Doherty Ltd v Doherty*[75]. GD, who had considerable experience of the advertising business, came to an arrangement with three people he knew as a result of which each invested money in a company of which GD was the principal shareholder and the managing director. Henchy J found as a fact that all were agreed that GD would in effect

---

[69] *Scottish Co-operative Wholesale Society Ltd v Meyer* [1959] AC 324.

[70] *Levin v Clark* [1962] NSWR 68.

[71] [1964/5] NSWR 1648.

[72] *Punt v Symons & Co* [1903] 2 Ch 506; *Piercy v S Mills & Co* [1920] 1 Ch 77.

[73] (1958) 92 ILTR 11.

[74] Para **[26.34]** above.

[75] (Unreported, 4 April 1968 and 19 June 1968); Supreme Court (unreported, December 1969).

run the business: the others, although directors, were not concerned with the day-to-day management. The company made major losses in its early years and the other directors were anxious to sell their shares to GD. He attempted to pay part of the agreed purchase price with funds of the company. The other directors convened a meeting which was not attended by GD and at which they removed him from office. Henchy J held that in view of GD's misconduct and mismanagement his fellow directors were entitled to take this course. But they also made a new allotment of shares in which GD was unable to participate and which reduced him to the status of a minority shareholder. Henchy J held that this allotment was an improper use of their fiduciary powers, since its sole object was to remove GD from any significant role in the company and hence was not made in good faith for the benefit of the company as a whole.

[27.92] It has also been held in England that the directors cannot use the power to issue new shares as a means of blocking a takeover hid of which they disapprove but which a majority of the shareholders wish to accept. In *Howard Smith Ltd v Ampol Petroleum Ltd*[76], the directors of a company called RW Miller (Holdings) Ltd were held to have acted unlawfully when they used their powers with this in view. More than 50% of the shares in Millers were owned jointly by Ampol and another company, Bulkheads Ltd. Ampol made a takeover bid, which was rejected, and this was followed by a takeover bid at a higher figure by Howard Smith Ltd. Ampol and Bulkheads then issued a joint statement that they would not co-operate in any takeover by Howard Smith or any other firm. The directors riposted by allotting a sufficient number of new shares in the company to Howard Smith to make them majority shareholders.

Lord Wilberforce, giving the advice of the Judicial Committee of the Privy Council, said that the mere fact that the issue was not needed for the raising of new capital did not of itself make it an unlawful use of the directors' powers. But the powers were nonetheless being used for an improper purpose, ie the transfer of power to a new majority of shareholders. The case could no doubt have been decided on the basis that the powers were being used for a purpose for which they were not conferred, as in the *Lancegaye* case and the earlier English decision of *Hogg v Cramphorn*[77], Lord Wilberforce, however, took the view that the use of the power in this instance was improper not merely because it was being used for a purpose for which it was not intended but because its use in the manner impugned violated a fundamental principal of company law, ie the constitutional separation of powers between the shareholders on the one hand and the directors on the other. The directors could not by the issue of new shares abolish the position of the majority.

---

[76] [1974] AC 821.
[77] [1967] Ch 254.

[27.93] The fact that some shareholders because of some distinguishing factor common to them are excluded from an allotment will not of itself render the allotment an unlawful exercise of the directors' powers, if the allotment is in general a bona fide use of their powers for the good of the company as a whole. In *Mutual Life Insurance Co of New York v The Rank Organisation Ltd*[78], the directors excluded foreign shareholders from participation in a new allotment, not because they wished to discriminate against them but because they considered that there would be technical problems in extending the new issue to them. It was held that this was not an improper use of their powers and the decision was applied to somewhat similar circumstances by Carroll J in *Afric Sive Ltd v Gas and Exploration Ltd*[79].

[27.94] It is always open to the directors of a private company to ward off an attempt by outsiders to take over the company by using their powers to refuse to register transfers. Provided the directors exercise the discretion given to them in this area by the articles in good faith in what they believe to be the interests of the company, their decisions will not be set aside by the court[80]. In the case of many private companies of a relatively small and intimate nature - what are sometimes called quasi-partnership companies - the very basis of the company may be the confinement of the business to a relatively small number of people, such as, for example, the members of a family. In such a case, a refusal of the directors to register transfers to outsiders will be peculiarly difficult to challenge.

[27.95] It should be remembered that there are now important statutory restrictions on the powers of the directors to issue shares. These have already been explained in Chapter 8; it is sufficient at this point to recall that the directors cannot now exercise the power of the company to issue shares unless they are authorised so to do by:

(1)   the company in general meeting, or

(2)   the articles.

Moreover, where the company is so authorised, the authority will expire at the end of five years from the date on which it is conferred, unless it is renewed by a resolution of the company in general meeting.

In addition, the shareholders of the company have now a right of pre-emption when new shares are being issued.

---

[78]   (1985) BCLC 11.
[79]   (Unreported, 30 January 1989), HC.
[80]   See para **[27.89]** above.

[27.96] The directors owe a duty to the company to exercise skill and diligence in the discharge of their functions. This is a general principle, but the courts in a succession of cases of which the most important is still the decision of Romer J in *City Equitable Fire Insurance Company Ltd*[81], have broken it down into a number of sub-propositions, most of them tending to limit or modify the extent of the duty owed by directors.

A director need not exhibit in the performance of his duties a greater degree of skill than may reasonably be expected from a person of his knowledge and experience

[27.97] Thus a person who is appointed a director without possessing any particular knowledge or expertise which might be useful in the conduct of the company's business cannot be held responsible for any loss the company may sustain as a result of his lack of knowledge or expertise. A director of a life insurance company, for example, who is not an actuary or a physician cannot be expected to have the knowledge or skill expected of those professions[82].

A director cannot be held responsible for errors of judgment as such

[27.98] The day-to-day conduct of business demands that risks be taken on occasions. The law does not expect infallibility from directors or from anyone else and if a director makes a decision in what he genuinely believes to be the best interests of the company, the fact that it subsequently proves to be mistaken (frequently with the benefit of hindsight) will not of itself be a ground for setting it aside[83].

A director is not bound to give continuous attention to the affairs of his company

[27.99] In particular while the failure of a director to attend board meetings with reasonable regularity is a breach of his duty to take care, he is not under a duty to attend every board meeting[84]. Moreover, what constitutes 'reasonable regularity' will depend very much on the circumstances of the particular case. The position of the managing director is, of course, obviously different. In the case of other directors, intermittent attention only to the affairs of the company is required, and the mere failure of a director to attend a number of board meetings will not of itself render him liable for some irregular action taken by the board in his absence[85]. In England, many persons are appointed to boards simply because they possess a title, and the practice is not unknown in Ireland, where it is also

---

[81] [1925] Ch 407.
[82] Per Romer J in *City Equitable Fire Insurance Ltd* [1925] Ch 407.
[83] *Re Brazilian Rubber Plantations and Estates Ltd* [1911] 1 Ch 425 at 437.
[84] *Perry's Case* (1876) 34 LT 716.
[85] *Marquis of Bute's Case* [1892] 2 Ch 100.

quite common to find persons appointed to boards because they are well known public figures. Clearly, the specialised attention which such directors are expected to give to the affairs of the company will be less than the attention expected of directors with a distinctive knowledge or expertise. But in *Jackson v Munster Bank*, a director who was not expected to give full time attention was held responsible for breaches of trust by his fellow directors where there were circumstances which should have aroused his suspicions[86].

A director is in general justified in leaving duties to be performed by another official of the company where such duties may properly be left to such an official having regard to the provisions of the articles and the exigencies of the business

[27.100] In the words of Lord Halsbury LC in *Dovey v Cory*[87]

'The business of life could not go on if people could not trust those who are put into a position of trust for the express purpose of attending to details of management.'

There is one qualification to this principle. A director will not be able to escape responsibility where there were grounds for suspicion as to the official concerned[88].

Negligence need not be 'gross negligence'

[27.101] A director will be liable for negligence in its ordinary sense. It was at one time said that a director was only liable for what was called 'gross negligence', but it is clear from later decisions[89] that this is not so and that the standard to be applied is the one generally applicable to all types of negligence, ie a failure to take reasonable care in circumstances where the director was under a duty to take care.

Liability of directors to account for benefits

[27.102] We have seen that directors, although not trustees in the conventional sense, can be required to account to the company for benefits which they have received as a result of their position as directors. Because of the fiduciary relationship which exists between them and the company, the law will in such circumstances impose a constructive trust on such benefits and enforce the trust at the instance of the members. We now consider this principle in more detail.

---

[86] (1884-5) 13 LR (Ir) 118.
[87] [1901] AC 477 at 456.
[88] *City Equitable Fire Insurance Company Ltd* [1925] Ch 407 at 429 per Romer J.
[89] *Re Brazilian Rubber Plantations and Estates Ltd* [1911] 1 Ch 425; *City Equitable Fire Insurance Company Ltd* [1925] Ch 407.

[27.103] The classical example of the constructive trust in equity was the renewal of a lease. If a lessee was entitled to have his lease renewed and happened to be a trustee, he could not enjoy the renewed lease in his own right: he had only obtained the right of renewal because he was a trustee and equity insisted that he held the renewed lease also in trust for the beneficiary. In the leading case of *Keech v Sandford*[90] (also known as the *Romford Market* case) the trustee held a leasehold interest in the profits of a market on behalf of an infant. When the lease of the market expired, the owner of the market refused to renew the lease in favour of the infant, but was willing to grant one to the trustee personally. The trustee accepted the lease, but it was held that he was obliged to pay to the infant the profits he received.

[27.104] It was immaterial in such a case that the donor would probably have been perfectly happy for the trustee to have the benefit of the lease if the object of his benevolence could not. It was equally immaterial that the conduct of the trustee was not in any way dishonest or fraudulent. These austere principles were applied with equal rigour by the Irish courts in cases such as *Gabbet v Lowder*[91]. In time, they came to be applied to other categories of person who could be regarded as having been in a fiduciary capacity when they acquired the benefits, whatever they might be. Among these categories is the company director.

[27.105] The leading modern case on the topic is the decision of the House of Lords in *Regal (Hastings) Ltd v Gulliver*[92], which graphically illustrates the unbending attitude of the law towards benefits acquired by directors from their position. The company owned one cinema and the directors decided to acquire three others with a view to selling all three as a going concern. A subsidiary was formed with a view to taking a lease of the other two. In order to provide the subsidiary with sufficient paid up capital to satisfy the lessors, the directors took up a number of shares in the subsidiary themselves. They then sold the shares in both the company and its subsidiary. The sale of their shares in the subsidiary realised a profit for them and when the new owners of the company became aware of this, proceedings were instituted against the directors by the company claiming that the profit belonged to the company. There was no suggestion that the directors had acted otherwise than in good faith or that what they had done was other than for the benefit of the company: had they not agreed to take up shares in the subsidiary, the lease would not have been granted to the subsidiary on the strength of the capital which the company itself was in a position to subscribe. The company's action failed for these reasons in the Court of Appeal but succeeded in the House of Lords. It was held that where directors during the

---

[90] (1726) S & L Cas Ch 61.
[91] (1883) 11 Lr (Ir) 295.
[92] [1942] 1 All ER 378.

course of their management of the company avail of their opportunities and special knowledge and as a result obtain a profit, they must account to the company for that profit, even though there was nothing improper in what they did and the company did not suffer as a result.

[27.106] The same principle was applied in *Industrial Development Consultants Ltd v Cooley*[93]. The defendant was the managing director of the plaintiff firm which offered to its customers a wide range of construction services, including those of architects, engineers and project managers. The plaintiffs had discussions with a potential customer about the possibility of their designing buildings for it. Their proposals were rejected, but at the suggestion of the customer, the defendant, who was himself an architect, obtained his release from his contract of employment with the plaintiffs on the pretext of being ill and then entered into a lucrative contract for precisely the same work. He was held to be a constructive trustee of the profits for the firm.

[27.107] To the same effect is the Canadian decision of *Canadian Aero Services Ltd v O'Malley*[94] where the president and vice-president of the plaintiff company had been engaged on their behalf in negotiating for a large aerial survey and mapping contract with the government of Guyana. Instead of securing the contact for their company, they resigned and obtained it for a new company which they formed for the purpose. The Supreme Court of Canada held that both the new company and the executives were liable in damages to the plaintiff company.

[27.108] There is no reported Irish decision expressly applying the principle in *Keech v Sandford* to company directors, but it is a reasonably safe assumption that the same approach would be adopted as in the English and Canadian decisions just discussed. The position is much less clear if the directors seeking to appropriate business opportunities of this nature for themselves take the precaution of obtaining beforehand the approval of a general meeting of the company. It might be thought that the directors in such a case had rendered themselves immune to a subsequent challenge. That view gains some support from a dictum of Lord Russell of Killowen in the *Regal (Hastings)* case, but it is also in potential conflict with another principle of company law.

[27.109] It is clear that where the majority of the shareholders in a company use their controlling position in a company to make a profit for themselves which might otherwise have been available to the company, the resulting transaction may be set aside as a fraud on the minority. In cases such as *Regal (Hastings)*, the board of directors may well control a majority of the shares and it seems

---

[93] [1972] 2 All ER 162.
[94] [1974] SCR 592.

clear that where that is so they cannot protect themselves by obtaining a resolution sanctioning their behaviour. But if they do not have a majority and secure the approval of the company after a full disclosure of the relevant circumstances, there would seem no ground for setting aside the transaction at the behest of disgruntled shareholders to whom the control of the company subsequently passes.

Contracts by directors with the company

[27.110] Because a director is in a similar position to a trustee, he cannot enter into a contract with the company and, if he does so, the contract is voidable at the instance of the company, ie it is valid unless and until it is set aside by the company. The same applies to a contract by the company with a company or firm in which he has an interest. This principle was laid down by the House of Lords at an early stage in *Aberdeen Rly Co v Blaikie Bros*[95]. But it was clear that it did not apply where the contract was authorised or ratified by a general meeting of the company. Nor did it apply where the articles themselves authorised such transactions, as they usually do, subject to the director's disclosing his interest to his fellow directors, not voting in respect of the transaction and not being counted in the quorum at the relevant board meeting[96].

[27.111] These common law rules are supplemented by the requirements of s 194 of the Principal Act. These oblige the director to disclose the nature of his interest in such a contract or proposed contract at a meeting of the directors. In the case of a proposed contract, the disclosure must be made at the meeting at which the question of entering into the contract is first considered. If he is not interested at that date, the disclosure must be made at the next meeting held after he becomes so interested. Where he becomes interested in the contract after it has been made, the disclosure must be made at the next meeting held after he becomes so interested. As amended by s 47 of the 1990 Act, these requirements apply to loans, quasi-loans, credit transactions and the provision of guarantees or securities for directors, shadow directors[97] or persons connected with them[98].

[27.112] The section provides for the adequacy for its purposes of a general notice by a director to the effect that:

    (1)   he is a member of a specified company or firm and is to be regarded as interested in any contract which may thereafter be made with that company or firm; or

---

[95] (1854) 1 Macq 461.
[96] Articles 84 and 85.
[97] See para **[27.05]** above.
[98] See para **[27.57]** above.

(2)   he is connected with a specified person within the meaning of s 25 of the 1990 Act and is to be regarded as interested in any contract which may thereafter be made with that person.

[27.113] The section also requires that copies be entered in a book kept for that purpose of such declarations and notices within three days. It must be open for inspection without charge to the directors, members, auditors and secretary at the registered office. It must also be produced at every general meeting of the company and at any meeting of the directors where a request for its production is made in sufficient time by one of the directors.

[27.114] A director who fails to comply with this section is liable to a fine of £500, as is any officer of the company who is in default as to the recording requirements. The court can compel an inspection or production of the book where it is refused.

[27.115] These requirements also apply to 'shadow directors' by virtue of the 1990 Act. In their case, however, the interest is to be disclosed, not by a declaration at a meeting of directors, but by a specific notice given before the meeting at which he would have been required to make a declaration if he were a director or by a general notice similar to that which directors are entitled to give.

[27.116] It has been held in England that disclosure to an executive committee of the board of directors is not a sufficient compliance with the section. Nor is it enough to show that all the directors were aware of the transaction: there must be disclosure at a duly convened full board meeting[99].

Remedies against directors

[27.117] Where a director has been guilty of negligence in the conduct of his office, he is liable to the company for the damage that results. This liability may be enforced against him in the ordinary way by an action brought by the company. It will be remembered, however, that under the rule in *Foss v Harbottle*, such an action must be brought by the company itself and cannot in general be maintained by a group of shareholders[100].

[27.118] Where the director has been guilty of some breach of trust or where he has derived some benefit from the company for which he is liable to account, the company may enforce their rights against him either by a common law action or in proceedings claiming equitable relief such as a declaration, injunction or an account, as may be appropriate.

---

[99] *Guinness plc v Saunders* [1988] 2 All ER 940.
[100] See para **[26.02]** above.

[27.119] Apart from these remedies, a special remedy is available against a director when the company is wound up. Under s 298 of the Principal Act, the court may compel any director who has misapplied or retained or become accountable for any money or property of the company or who has been guilty of any misfeasance or breach of trust to repay or restore the money or property. This remedy - known as 'misfeasance proceedings' - is considered in more detail in Chapter 38 below.

Relief from liability as director

[27.120] Directors are entitled as agents of the company to be indemnified by the company in respect of any liabilities incurred by them in the management of the company's business. In addition, it was usual for the articles to exempt the directors from liability for any losses sustained by the company other than those incurred as a result of their 'wilful default' or actual dishonesty. Section 200 of the Principal Act, however, provides that any such provision is to be void except in relation to liability incurred by the director in defending criminal or civil proceedings in which he succeeds or is acquitted or in connection with an application under s 391 of the Principal Act in which he obtains relief from the court. That latter section enables the court to relieve any officer or auditor of the company from liability for any negligence, default, breach of duty or breach of trust, where:

(1) the officer or auditor has acted honestly and reasonably, and

(2) it appears to the court that, having regard to all the circumstances, he ought fairly to be excused.

Meetings of directors

[27.121] The management of the company is vested in the board of directors and decisions affecting its management must accordingly be taken, generally speaking, at properly convened and regularly conducted meetings of the board. The articles usually provide, however, for the appointment by the directors of one of their number to be managing director (article 110) and for the entrusting to him of such powers exercisable by them as they think fit (article 112). Moreover, the articles usually provide that a resolution signed by all the directors entitled to receive notice of a meeting of directors is to be as valid as if it has been passed at a meeting duly convened and held (article 109).

[27.122] The requirements as to the convening of meetings, the quorum for such meetings, voting, the election of a chairman and the general conduct of the meeting are all usually dealt with in the articles. They normally provide that the directors, 'may meet together for the despatch of business, adjourn and otherwise regulate their meetings as they think fit.' (Article 101.)

They also usually provide that a director may, and the secretary shall on the requisition of a director, convene a meeting at any time (Article 101). The normal provision as to a quorum is that it is to be fixed by the directors and, if not so fixed, is to be two (Article 102). If the articles so provide - and they generally do - the continuing directors may act notwithstanding any vacancy in their number. They may also stipulate, however, that where the directors are insufficient in number to constitute a quorum, they may only meet for the purpose of increasing their number to the number necessary for a quorum or for the purpose of convening a general meeting of the company but for no other purpose (Article 103).

[27.123] Every director is entitled to be given notice of a meeting and the notice must be given within a reasonable time. The only exception is where the director is abroad: it is usual to provide in the articles (Article 101) that the directors may resolve not to give notice of meetings to directors absent from the state who are normally resident in the state, but even without such a provision, it is probably not necessary to give notice to directors so absent[101].

[27.124] A meeting of which due notice is not given or at which a quorum is not present is irregular and its decisions will not be valid. It must be remembered, however, that under the rule in *British Royal Bank v Turquand*, an outsider dealing with the company will not be affected by such an irregularity of which he has no notice since it is part of the 'indoor management' of the company of which he is not presumed to be aware[102].

[27.125] Where the directors of a company wrongfully exclude one of their number from their proceedings, he has a right of action against them, at all events where he has a proprietary interest in the company in the form of shares. This was so decided by Budd J in *Coubrough v James Panton & Co*[103], distinguishing an earlier English decision of *Harben v Phillips*[104]. In that case the director could only be removed by an extraordinary resolution of the company and the other directors did not have a majority sufficient to remove him.

[27.126] Extraordinary resolutions were abolished by the Principal Act but the articles may still provide for the appointment of life directors. In such a case, a special resolution amending the articles could be necessary before the directors

---

[101] *Halifax Sugar etc Co v Francklyn* (1890) 59 LJ Ch 591.
[102] See para **[12.34]** above.
[103] [1965] IR 272.
[104] (1883) 23 Ch D 14.

could be removed, and if the other directors did not command the necessary majority, the decision in *Coubrough v James Panton & Co* could still be applicable.

[27.127] Minutes must be kept of the proceedings and meetings of directors[105]. The provisions applicable to the keeping of minutes of meetings of the company are also in general applicable to minutes of meetings of directors[106].

Register of directors

[27.128] Section 195 of the Principal Act required companies to maintain a register of directors and secretaries. These provisions have now been replaced by the more detailed requirements of the 1990 Act and the 1999 (No 2) Act.

[27.129] The register must contain the following information relating to each director:

(1)   his present forename and surname and any former forenames and surnames;

(2)   his date of birth;

(3)   his usual residential address;

(4)   his nationality;

(5)   his business occupation, if any; and

(6)   any other directorships held by him here or abroad or formerly held by him[107].

The obligation to give details of directorships of companies abroad and directorships formerly held was imposed for the first time by 1990 Act. The latter requirement is limited to directorships held within the preceding ten years. Nor is it necessary to include directorships in the company's holding company, its fellow subsidiaries or its own subsidiaries.

[27.130] The 1990 Act imposed a further new obligation on companies. They must notify the registrar within 14 days of any change among their directors or secretary or of any change in the particulars in the register[108].

[27.131] The 1999 (No 2) Act provides for any default by the company in giving the required notification to the Registrar, where the change takes the form of the resignation or removal of a director or secretary. Where that happens, the person concerned may serve on the company a notice requesting it to send to the

---

[105] Companies Act 1963, s 145.

[106] See para **[25.60]** above.

[107] Companies Act 1963, s 195 as substituted by the Companies Act 1990, s 51.

[108] Companies Act 1963, s 195(6).

registrar forthwith the notification of his having ceased to be a director or secretary and stating that, if the company fails to comply with that request within 21 days of the service of the notice, he will forward to the registrar and every officer of the company a copy of his notice of resignation or any other documentary proof of his having ceased to be such a director or secretary, together with (in the case of the notice to the Registrar) any additional information that may be prescribed and (in the case of the officers) a written request that they take such steps as will ensure that the failure of the company to comply with the notice continues no further. The prescribed information may include a statutory declaration made by the person concerned stating the names of the person who are officers of the company[109].

[27.132] If the company fails to comply with the request, the person concerned may forward to the Registrar and the officers of the company a copy of the notice of resignation or other documentary proof of his having ceased to be a director or secretary, provided that he also forwards to the Registrar the required additional information and to the officers a written request to ensure compliance with the notice. Where these steps are taken by a director or secretary who has resigned or been removed, the Registrar is precluded from considering any other notice of resignation or documentary proof of his having ceased to be a director or secretary[110].

[27.133] The 1999 (No 2) Act also provides that, where as a result of the operation of these provisions there are no persons recorded in the office of the Registrar as being directors of the particular company, this is to afford the Registrar good grounds for believing that the company is not carrying on business and, accordingly, for exercising his power under s 311 of the Principal Act to strike the company of the register as being defunct[111].

[27.134] The register must be open to inspection by any member of the company without charge during business hours, subject to such reasonable restrictions as the company in general meeting or by the articles may impose but so that it is open for at least two hours each day. It must be similarly open to inspection by any person other than a member on payment of a fee not exceeding one pound. Where an inspection is refused, the court may order an immediate inspection[112].

[27.135] Each director and secretary is required to give information to the company as soon as may be of such matters as may be necessary to enable the

---

[109] Companies Act 1963, s 195 as amended by the Companies (Amendment) (No 2) Act 1999, s 47
[110] Companies Act 1963, s 195 as amended by the Companies (Amendment) (No 2) Act 1999, s 47.
[111] Companies (Amendment) (No 2) Act 1999, s 48.
[112] Companies Act 1963, s 195(10) and (13).

company to comply with these requirements. If they fail to do so, they are liable on summary conviction to a fine not exceeding £1,000 and on indictment to a fine not exceeding £10,000. In the case of any other contravention of the section, the company and every officer in default is liable to a fine not exceeding £1,000 and, for continued contravention, to a daily default fine not exceeding £50[113].

Disclosure of share dealings by directors and their families

[27.136] The Principal Act required companies to maintain a register of directors' shareholdings. This relatively simple provision was replaced by the far more elaborate machinery contained in Part IV of the 1990 Act. This obliges directors and secretaries to notify the company in writing of their interests in the company's shares and of any dealings by them in those shares. 'Interest' for this purpose is widely defined so as to bring within the ambit of the provisions interests held in trust, contractual and option arrangements and other indirect methods of controlling share interests. They also apply to interests held by the spouses and minor children of directors. There are also requirements as to the register to be kept and provisions for an investigation by the Minister where he thinks there have been contraventions of the relevant sections.

[27.137] Section 53 imposes the essential obligation: the remainder of Chapter I of Part IV is devoted to elaborating the nature of the interests affected, detailing the persons to whom Chapter 1 applies and providing for recording, publication and enforcement.

[27.138] A director or secretary of a company is required by s 53 to notify the company in writing of the fact that he is interested in shares or debentures of the company and the number of shares of each class and the amount of debentures of each class in which he is so interested. The obligation extends to shares and debentures in the company's holding company, its fellow subsidiaries and its own subsidiaries. He must further notify the company of the occurrence of any event as a result of which he ceases to be interested or becomes interested in any such shares or debentures, specifying the number or amount and class of shares and debentures involved in each case.

[27.139] He is also obliged to notify the company of the following:

(1) the entering into by him of any contract to sell any such shares or debentures;

(2) the assignment by him of a right granted to him to subscribe for shares or debentures in the company;

---

[113] Companies Act 1963, s 195(12) and (14).

(3)   the grant to him by the company's holding company, subsidiary or fellow subsidiary of a right to subscribe for shares or debentures and the exercise and assignment of such a right.

All these requirements also apply to shadow directors[114].

[27.140] The requirements of s 53 do not apply to dealings which occurred before the section came into force[115]. But persons affected by the section were obliged to notify the company in writing of their interests within five days of its coming into force. Where the persons concerned are unaware of their interests, the obligation to notify becomes operative within five days of their becoming so aware. The obligation to notify the company of the various 'events' specified in s 51, ie dealings of different types, arises five days after their occurrence or five days after the day on which the person concerned becomes aware of their occurrence[116].

[27.141] Where the event to be notified is a contract for the sale or purchase of shares or debentures, the notification to be effective must state the price[117]. Where it is the assignment of a right to subscribe for shares or debentures in the company or one of its associated companies, the consideration (if any) must be stated or the fact that there is no consideration. Where it is the grant of a right to subscribe for shares or debentures, it must state

(1)   the date,

(2)   the period within which it is exercisable,

(3)   the consideration (if any) or the fact that there is none and

(4)   the price of the shares or debentures.

Where it is the exercise of such a right, it must state the number or amount of shares or debentures taken up and the persons in whose name they are registered.

[27.142] The nature of the 'interests' captured must next be considered. Chapter I applies to interests 'of any kind whatsoever', irrespective of any restraints or restrictions to which they are subject. Specifically, it applies to the interests of the following[118]:

(1)   a beneficiary under a trust, with certain exceptions;

(2)   a purchaser under a contract;

---

[114] See para **[27.05]** above.
[115] On 1 August 1993.
[116] Companies Act 1990, s 56.
[117] Companies Act 1990, s 57.
[118] Companies Act 1990, s 54.

(3)   a person who is not the shareholder or debenture holder but is entitled to exercise (or control the exercise of) the rights of the shareholder or debenture holder;

(4)   a person entitled to an option in respect of shares.

[27.143] The following interests are not captured[119]:

(1)   the interest of a bare trustee;

(2)   an interest in remainder or reversion;

(3)   any discretionary interest;

(4)   a life interest under an irrevocable settlement where the settler has no interest in the income or property.

[27.144] The following interests are also not captured[120]:

(1)   interests subsisting under unit trusts or their EU equivalent;

(2)   interests under schemes under the Charities Act 1961[121]

(3)   interests held by stockbrokers acting as such;

(4)   any other interests prescribed by the Minister.

[27.145] The interest of a spouse or minor child of a director or secretary is treated as the interest of the director or secretary for the purposes of s 53.

[27.146] A person is also treated as 'interested' for the purpose of s 53 where the shares are held by a company which is (or whose directors are) accustomed to act in accordance with his directions or instructions or where he is entitled to exercise, or control the exercise of, one-third or more of the company's voting power at general meetings[122].

[27.147] Where a person to whom s 53 applies fails to notify the company within the prescribed time, his rights and interests in relation to the relevant shares are unenforceable. He may, however, apply to the court for relief[123]. This may be granted where the court is satisfied that the default was accidental or due to inadvertence or some other sufficient cause or where it is satisfied that it would be just and equitable to grant relief. But relief may not be granted where the default is due to any deliberate act or omission on the part of the applicant. These 'unenforceability' provisions do not apply where the notifiable event is the person's ceasing to be interested in the shares or debentures.

---

[119] Companies Act 1990, s 55(1)(a) and (c).

[120] Companies Act 1990, s 55(1)(h).

[121] Ie schemes under the Charities Act 1961, s 46 for the investment in common of different charitable funds.

[122] Companies Act 1990, ss 64; 54(5) and (6).

[123] Companies Act 1990, s 58(3), (4) and (5).

[27.148] Every company must keep a register for the purposes of s 53[124]. This register now replaces the register of directors' shareholdings which companies were formerly required to maintain under s 190 of the Principal Act. The company must enter in the register all information received from directors or secretaries or shadow directors pursuant to s 53. Where it grants a director, shadow director or secretary the right to subscribe for shares or debentures it must enter:

(1)   the date of the grant,

(2)   the period during which the right is exercisable,

(3)   the consideration (if any) for the grant or the fact of there being none and

(4)   the description of the shares or debentures involved, the number or amount and the price.

Particulars must also be entered when the right is exercised. The entries must be made within three days[125].

[27.149] The register must be kept at the registered office, or, if the register of members is not kept there, at the place where it is kept. It must be open for inspection during business hours (subject to such reasonable limitations as the company in general meeting may impose but so that not less than two hours in each day is allowed for inspection) by members without charge and by others on payment of a fee not exceeding 30p. A copy of the register or any part of it must be sent to any member who requires it within ten days on payment of a small fee. The register must be produced 15 minutes before the annual general meeting and remain open and accessible to any person attending the meeting. Where an inspection or the sending of copies is refused to a person entitled, the court can order an immediate inspection or the sending of copies[126].

[27.150] The register must be made up so that the entries against individual names appear in chronological order. Unless it is kept in such a way as to constitute in itself an index, the company must keep a proper index[127].

[27.151] There are also provisions requiring a company whose shares are dealt in on a recognised stock exchange to notify the exchange of information supplied to them in pursuance of s 53 relating to the shares or debentures and enabling the stock exchange to publish the information[128]. The notes to the

---

[124] Companies Act 1990, s 59.
[125] Companies Act 1990, s 60(2).
[126] Companies Act 1990, s 60(5), (6), (8) and (11).
[127] Companies Act 1990, s 60(7).
[128] Companies Act 1990, s 65(1).

annual accounts or the directors' report annexed thereto must also contain details of directors' shareholdings[129].

[27.152] Various penalties are provided for contravention of the disclosure requirements in Chapter I of Part IV, ranging from a fine on summary conviction not exceeding £1,000 to imprisonment for a term not exceeding three years. In addition, the Minister is given power to appoint one or more inspectors to carry out an investigation and report to him if it appears to him that contraventions may have occurred[130].

[27.153] Section 196 of the Principal Act requires certain particulars of directors to be given in all business letters in which the company's name appears. The particulars, which must be legible, are:

(1)   the present Christian name, or the initials thereof, and present surname;

(2)   any former Christian names and surnames; and

(3)   his nationality, if not Irish.

The Act does not apply to companies registered under the 1908 Act which were registered before 23 November 1916 (the date of the coming into force of the Registration of Business Names Act 1916). The Minister may also exempt companies from the obligations of the section if he thinks it expedient so to do. If a company makes default in complying with the section, every officer who is in default is liable on summary conviction to a fine not exceeding £125[131]. No proceedings may be instituted, however, without the consent of the Minister.

Disqualifications and restrictions

[27.154] Under the Principal Act, apart from bodies corporate, undischarged bankrupts and auditors to the company, the only people who could not act as directors were those who were expressly prohibited from so doing by a court order made after they were found guilty of fraud or dishonesty. The requirements of the law in this area were significantly strengthened by Part VII of the 1990 Act. Directors of insolvent companies which are wound up may only act as directors of other companies under severe restrictions. The circumstances under which a person may be prohibited from acting as a director are greatly extended, as are the criminal penalties and consequences in civil proceedings for those who are in breach of the requirements of the Acts in this area.

---

[129] Companies Act 1990, s 63.
[130] Companies Act 1990, s 66.
[131] Companies Act 1963, s 196(4) as amended by the Companies (Amendment) Act 1982, s 15.

[27.155] The restrictions on directors of insolvent companies are set out in Chapter 1 of Part VII. In effect, unless they can satisfy the court that their actions were honest and reasonable, they must be prohibited from acting as directors for five years save where the new company meets certain requirements as to its paid up capital.

[27.156] These provisions come into effect where a company is being wound up and it is

(1)   proved to the court at the commencement of the winding up that it is unable to satisfy its debts or

(2)   the liquidator certifies, or it is otherwise proved, to the court during the course of the winding up that it is unable to pay its debts[132].

[27.157] The court must declare that any director or 'shadow director'[133] of such a company (or anyone who was such within 12 months prior to the commencement of the winding up) is not to act as a director or secretary or be concerned in the promotion or management of any company for a period of five years unless the company meets the specified requirements as to its paid up capital. But the order is not to be made where the court is satisfied that:

(1)   the person concerned has acted honestly and reasonably in relation to the conduct of the affairs of the company and there is no other reason why it would be just and equitable to subject him to these restrictions; or

(2)   the person concerned was a director solely because he was nominated as such by a financial institution in connection with the giving of credit to, or the purchase of shares in, the company by that institution[134].

[27.158] The limited nature of the exemptions in (2) should be noted. Save in the case of nominees of banks and other financial institutions, there is no general exemption for part-time directors. Thus, solicitors or accountants who are frequently nominated to the boards of companies without having any significant financial involvement in them are potentially liable to the new disqualification provisions.

[27.159] The exemption from disqualification in the case of (2) does not apply, however, if the company or any of the directors has given a personal or individual guarantee of repayment[135].

---

[132] Companies Act 1990, s 149(1).
[133] See para **[27.05]** above.
[134] Companies Act 1990, s 150(2)-(6). There is also an exemption for investment companies prescribed by the Minister.
[135] Companies Act 1990, s 150(2).

[27.160] Directors who are affected by these provisions cannot act as directors of other companies during the five year period unless, in the case of a public limited company, the nominal value of the allotted share capital is at least £100,000 or, in the case of a private company, £20,000 and in either case each allotted share and any premium is fully paid up in cash[136].

[27.161] There are ancillary provisions precluding the company of which such a person becomes a director from making use of the machinery provided under s 60 of the Principal Act (whereby a company may provide financial assistance for the purchase of its own shares) and subjecting it to the same restrictions as are imposed by the 1983 Act on public limited companies in making allotments of shares other than for cash. Where such a company allots a share which is not fully paid up, it is to be treated as if the whole of its nominal value and any premium had been received, but the allottee is liable to pay the company in cash the full amount which should have been received less the amount of any consideration paid[137].

[27.162] It was pointed out by Murphy J in *Business Communications Ltd v Baxter & Parsons*[138] that there is a strange lacuna in these provisions. Neither the legislation nor the rules impose any duty on any person to apply to the court for an order, in the case of an insolvent company, prohibiting the persons concerned from acting as directors for five years, save where the requirements as to its paid up capital are met or where the court is satisfied that they come within the exempting provisions. This difficulty has been met in the case of compulsory liquidations by the court directing official liquidators to bring the appropriate application against the directors of insolvent companies. It was pointed out that there was no comparable machinery available in the case of voluntary liquidations.

[27.163] In the same case, Murphy J drew a distinction between the burden of proof required of directors under these provisions and the burden of proof resting on the director under Chapter 2 of Part VII to satisfy the court that he should not be disqualified from acting as a director. He considered that a much stronger burden of proof rested on the directors in the latter case. In the case in question, he was satisfied that their continuing to trade for a period of more than six months was 'imprudent in the extreme' and he rejected their plea to be treated as exempt from disqualification under s 150.

---

136 Companies Act 1990, s 150(3).
137 Companies Act 1990, s 156.
138 (Unreported, 21 July 1995), HC, noted in Commercial Law Practitioner, October 1995 at p 238.

[27.164] In a case decided on the same day, *Re Costello Doors Ltd*[139], the same learned Judge held that the maintenance of proper books and accounts and the employment of appropriate experts would 'go a long way to discharge the onus of showing that the directors behaved responsibly'[140].

[27.165] In *Re Verit Hotel and Leisure (Ireland) Ltd, Carway v Attorney General*[141], an application was made by a liquidator under these provisions. The liquidator, in bringing the application, relied on the certificate provided for under s 149(1). The plaintiff challenged the constitutionality of the irrebuttable presumption of insolvency under s 149(1)(b) on the ground that it was contrary to the principles laid down in *Maher v the Attorney General*[142] and the *State (McEldowney) v Kelleher*[143]. It was held by Carroll J that there was no provision that the liquidator's certificate was to be conclusive and hence that there was no irrebuttable presumption as to insolvency. The certificate was simply a preliminary step in the proceedings in which the court had to be satisfied that the directors had acted honestly and responsibly and there was nothing to prevent the directors in those proceedings from raising questions as to the company's alleged insolvency.

[27.166] There is no obligation on the liquidator to notify the persons affected by these provisions of the fact that they are so affected. If, however it appears to him that the interests of another company or its creditors may be placed in jeopardy because a director liable to be disqualified under this Part is acting as a director of it or is concerned in its promotion or formation, he must notify the court of his opinion and the court may make: 'whatever order it sees fit'[144]. A liquidator in breach of these requirements is liable on summary conviction to a fine not exceeding £1,000 and for continued contravention to a daily default fine not exceeding £50 and on conviction on indictment to a fine not exceeding £10,000 and for continued contravention to a daily default fine not exceeding £250[145].

[27.167] A person affected by these provisions may apply to the court for relief within not more than one year after the service of a notice on him by the liquidator. The court may give him relief in whole or in part against the

---

[139] (Unreported, 21 July 1995), HC, noted in Commercial Law Practitioner, October 1995 at p 238.
[140] See also *Re Cavan Crystal Group Ltd (In Receivership)* (unreported, 26 April 1996) (Murphy J), noted in Commercial Law Practitioner, November 1996 at p 266.
[141] (Unreported, 3 July 1996), HC, noted in Commercial Law Practitioner, September 1996.
[142] [1973] IR 14.
[143] [1983] IR 289.
[144] Companies Act 1990, s 151(1) and (2).
[145] Companies Act 1990, s 151(3).

restrictions on such terms and conditions as it sees fit if it deems it just and equitable to do so[146].

[27.168] Section 154 provides that the provisions of Chapter 1 are to apply 'with necessary modifications' to a receiver of the property of the company.

[27.169] Chapter 2 of Part VII provides for an extensive range of circumstances in which persons are disqualified either automatically or by court order from acting as directors.

[27.170] Where a person is convicted on indictment of any indictable offence in relation to a company or one involving fraud or dishonesty, he is automatically disqualified for five years from the date of the conviction from acting as director, auditor, or other officer, receiver, liquidator or examiner[147] of any company or from being concerned in any way in the promotion, management or formation of any company. The court has a discretion, on the application of the prosecutor, to substitute another period of disqualification, either shorter or longer[148].

[27.171] This provision applies in criminal proceedings only. But the court has a wide discretion in other proceedings to disqualify people from so acting, either of its own motion or on an application for such period as it thinks fit[149]. It can do so where:

(1) a person has been guilty of any fraud in relation to a company, its members or creditors, while acting as promoter, auditor, officer, receiver, liquidator or examiner of the company;

(2) a person has been guilty, while acting in any of the roles mentioned in (1), of a breach of his duty as such;

(3) a person has been declared personally liable for a company's debts because of fraudulent or reckless trading[150];

(4) a person's conduct in any of the roles mentioned in (1) makes him unfit to be concerned in the management of a company;

(5) in consequence of an inspector's report under the Acts[151] a person is similarly unfit;

(6) a person has been persistently in default in making returns, giving notices or filing documents with the Registrar.

---

[146] Companies Act 1990, s 152.
[147] For examiners generally, see Ch 37 below.
[148] Companies Act 1990, s 160(1).
[149] Companies Act 1990, s 160(2).
[150] See Ch 33 below.
[151] See Ch 35 below.

A person is conclusively presumed to have been persistently in default for the purpose of (6) if he has been found guilty of three or more such defaults.

[27.172] An application for such an order may be made in any proceedings, civil or criminal, or independently under s 160. Such an application may be made by the Director of Public Prosecutions or any member, contributory, officer, employee, receiver, liquidator, examiner or creditor of the relevant company, but only the DPP may apply on ground (5) and only the DPP and the Registrar under ground (6)[152].

[27.173] The following are also prohibited from acting as directors:

(1)   undischarged bankrupts;

(2)   a body corporate;

(3)   the auditor of the company (or of its holding company or any of its subsidiaries)[153].

[27.174] Any person convicted of the offence of acting as director while an undischarged bankrupt is deemed to be subject to a disqualification order from the date of the conviction[154].

[27.175] A person who acts as a director when prohibited from doing so by any of these provisions is guilty of an offence and liable on summary conviction to a fine not exceeding £1,000 or imprisonment for a term not exceeding 12 months or both and on conviction on indictment to a fine not exceeding £10,000 or imprisonment for a term not exceeding three years or both. In addition, if not already subject to a disqualification order, he is deemed to be subject to one. The term of an existing disqualification order is to be extended for ten years or such other period as the court, on the application of the prosecutor, orders[155].

[27.176] There are also extensive consequences in civil law following contraventions of the restriction and disqualification provisions. A company is entitled to recover any remuneration or other consideration which they have paid to a person who acted as a director in breach of the provisions. Where a person is convicted of an offence under s 161 and the company is being wound up at the time or goes into liquidation within 12 months, the court may declare the convicted person personally liable without limitation of liability for all or any

---

[152] As to the principles to which a court should have regard in exercising its discretion, see *Re Lo-Line Electric Motors Ltd* (1988) BCLC 698.

[153] Companies Act 1963, s 183 as substituted by the Companies Act 1990, s 169; Companies Act 1963, s 176; Companies Act 1963, s 162(5)(a) as substituted by the Companies (Amendment) Act 1982, s 15.

[154] Companies Act 1963, s 183(2).

[155] Companies Act 1990, s 161.

part of the debts or other liabilities of the company. The application may be made by the liquidator or any creditor. The Court may grant relief[156].

[27.177] There are also stringent requirements in the 1990 Act as to the giving of information by directors where they are charged with an offence relating to the company. These requirements also apply to any charge or proceedings against a director involving fraud or dishonesty. In all such cases he must give notice in writing to the court before the hearing of:

(1)   the names of all companies of which he is a director;

(2)   the names of all companies of which he was a director within the preceding 12 months;

(3)   the dates and duration of any period during which he has been subject to a disqualification order.

[27.178] These obligations also apply to shadow directors[157]. Any person in breach is liable on summary conviction to a fine not exceeding £1,000 or imprisonment for a term not exceeding 12 months or both or on indictment to a fine not exceeding £10,000 or imprisonment for a term not exceeding three years or both.

---

[156] Companies Act 1990, s 163.

[157] Companies Act 1990, s 166. For 'shadow directors', see para **[27.05]** above.

Chapter 28

The Secretary

[28.01] Every company formed under the Acts is required to have a secretary. He may be one of the directors; but it should be noted that where something is required or authorised to be done by a director and the secretary, such as the execution or witnessing of a document, it cannot be done by the same person acting both as director and as, or in the place of, the secretary[1].

Functions of secretary

[28.02] The functions of the secretary are not defined by the Acts. They are, however, clearly administrative rather than managerial. The secretary is normally the person responsible for ensuring that the company complies with the requirements of the Acts, and it is accordingly a reasonably onerous position. He will be expected to attend to the following matters in particular:

(1)   keeping charge of the register of members, register of directors and secretaries, register of debentures and register of directors' shareholdings;

(2)   making the annual return to the Registrar;

(3)   keeping the minutes of general meetings and of meetings of the board of directors;

(4)   notifying the Registrar of any alterations in the memorandum and articles:

(5)   giving notice to members of meetings;

(6)   furnishing the Registrar with particulars of charges entered into by the company.

Appointment of secretary

[28.03] The secretary may be named in the memorandum or articles of association. It is more usual, however, for him to be appointed by the members of the company or the directors. He must in any event be named in the statement required to be delivered to the Registrar with the memorandum by s 3 of the 1982 Act.

---

[1] Companies Act 1963, s 177.

[28.04] Prior to the enactment of the 1990 Act, the secretary did not have to be qualified in any way. This is still the position in the case of private companies. In the case of public limited companies, s 236 obliges the directors to take all reasonable steps to ensure that the secretary has 'the requisite knowledge and experience of the functions' of secretary. In addition, a secretary appointed after the section came into effect must be a member of a body recognised by the Minister, unless he appears to the directors capable of discharging his functions by reason of his holding a particular office or being a member of any body. These additional requirements do not apply to persons appointed before the section came into effect or to persons who have been secretaries of other companies for at least three of the five years preceding their appointment.

[28.05] The position may be occupied by a body corporate, and it is quite common for companies to avail of this power to appoint a firm of accountants or consultants to act as secretary. The Principal Act also provides that anything required or authorised to be done by or to the secretary may be done by or to any assistant or deputy secretary capable of acting, if the office of secretary is vacant or there is no secretary capable of acting[2].

Implied authority of secretary to act on behalf of the company

[28.06] A secretary may be expressly authorised to enter into a particular transaction on behalf of the company, in which case it will be binding on the company. He may also bind the company by entering into a contract which is within his apparent authority as secretary, whether it has been expressly authorised or not[3]. Thus, it would normally be regarded as within his authority to enter into contracts relating to the administrative aspect of the company's affairs, such as the management of its office. He would not normally be regarded as having authority to enter into ordinary commercial contracts for the purchase of materials, the placing of orders, etc. His position in this context should be contrasted with that of a managing director who has implied authority to enter into a wide range of commercial contracts[4].

---

[2] Companies Act 1963, s 175(2).
[3] See para **[12.25]** above.
[4] See para **[12.27]** above.

Chapter 29

The Annual Return

[29.01] Every company formed under the Acts, public or private, limited or unlimited, is obliged to make an annual return to the Registrar setting out certain matters specified in the Principal Act[1]. This, in theory, was one of the most important requirements of the law applicable to companies, because the basis of that law, as we have seen, is that the public should have access to the details of the ownership, finances and officers of companies granted the privilege of incorporation. However, in practice its importance was greatly reduced by the fact that private companies were entirely exempted from supplying the information which would probably have been of most value, ie the annual accounts. This exemption was removed in the case of larger companies by the 1986 Act.

Matters to be included in the return

[29.02] The information required to be set out in the return differs depending on whether the company has a share capital or not. In the case of all companies, it must include:

(1)   the address of the registered office;

(2)   where the register of members is kept and if not kept at the registered office, the address where it is kept;

(3)   where the register of debenture holders is kept and if not kept at the registered office, the address where it is kept;

(4)   a statement of the total indebtedness of the company in respect of all mortgages and charges required to be registered under s 99 of the Principal Act;

(5)   the same particulars relating to directors and secretaries as are required to be contained in the register of directors and secretaries[2].

[29.03] In the case of companies having a share capital, the following information must also be given:

---

[1]   Companies Act 1963, ss 125-129.
[2]   See para **[27.129]** above.

(1) a summary of the share capital, distinguishing between shares issued for cash and issued as fully or partly paid up otherwise than in cash;

(2) a list of the members of the company and those who have ceased to be members since the last return;

(3) the number of shares held by each member and (in the case of a private company) details of shares transferred since the last return[3].

[29.04] The detailed provisions as to such information are set out in Part I of the Fifth Schedule to the Principal Act. Part II contains the form in which the return must be made. In the case of the share capital, it is necessary to show:

(1) the amount of the capital and the number of shares into which it is divided;

(2) the number of shares taken up to the date of the return;

(3) the amount called up on each share and the total of calls received and calls unpaid;

(4) the total commission paid in respect of any shares or debentures;

(5) the discount allowed on the issue of any shares or so much of it as has not been written off; and

(6) the total of shares forfeited.

[29.05] The list of members must give their addresses and occupations. It is to be made up as of the 14th day after the annual general meeting for that year. Where the company has given all the required particulars as to members and transfers of shares in its returns for the previous five years, it is only required to give details of new members, persons ceasing to be members and shares transferred since the last return. If the names of the members are not set out in alphabetical order, there must be an index for easy reference.

Documents to be annexed to the return

[29.06] In the case of all limited companies, public and private, with some qualifications in the case of certain exempted private companies, the following documents must be annexed to the return:

(1) A written copy certified by a director and secretary to be a true copy of the balance sheet and profit and loss account laid before the annual general meeting of the company held during the period to which the return relates.

---

[3] Companies Act 1963, s 125.

(2) Copies similarly certified of the reports of the auditors on, and the directors accompanying, the balance sheet and profit and loss accounts.

(3) Whenever these documents are in a language other than Irish or English a translation in Irish or English certified in the prescribed manner to be a correct translation.

[29.07] The requirement that there be annexed to the return a certified copy of the report of the auditors on the balance sheet and profit and loss account does not apply to a private company which is exempted from the requirement to have its accounts audited by virtue of s 32 of the 1999 (No 2) Act[4].

[29.08] Until the enactment of the 1986 Act, private companies were entirely exempt from the requirement to annex the balance sheet and profit and loss accounts, together with the accompanying reports, to the annual return of the company. The relevant sections of the 1986 Act are intended to give effect to the requirements of the Fourth EU Directive by ending the privileged position of private companies in this area, but there are important exemptions in the case of what are described as 'small' and 'medium-sized companies'.

Small companies

[29.09] A company is a 'small company' for this purpose where in the relevant financial year it satisfies any two of the following three conditions:

(1) its 'balance sheet total' (ie the value of its fixed and current assets as appearing in the balance sheet) does not exceed £1,500,000;

(2) the amount of its turnover does not exceed £3,000,000;

(3) the average number of the persons employed by the company does not exceed 50[5].

[29.10] Such a company is exempted from the requirement to annex a copy of the profit and loss account and the directors' report to the return[6]. It may also annex an 'abridged' balance sheet[7], ie one which merely gives the value as it

---

4   Some private companies may now be exempted from the requirement to have their accounts audited: see para [30.110] below.
5   Companies Act 1986, s 8 as amended by the European Community (Accounts) Regulation 1993, SI 396/1993, reg 4. The 'average number' of employees is calculated by taking the number of persons under contracts of service with the company f or each week of the relevant financial year, adding them together and dividing the result by the number of weeks. This is the method prescribed by para 42(4) of Part IV of the Schedule to the Companies Act 1986 which sets out the information which must he given by way of notes to the annual accounts.
6   Companies Act 1986, s 10(1).
7   Companies Act 1986, s 10(2).

appears in the balance sheets of the following items, without any further breakdown:

(1) Fixed assets:
   (a) intangible assets;
   (b) tangible assets;
   (c) financial assets.

(2) Current assets:
   (a) Stocks;
   (b) Debtors;
   (c) Investments;
   (d) Cash at bank and in hand.

(3) Creditors;

(4) Capital and reserves:
   (a) Called up share capital;
   (b) Share premium account;
   (c) Revaluation reserve;
   (d) Other reserves;
   (e) Profit and loss account;

(5) Provisions for liabilities and charges.

Medium-sized companies

[29.11] A company is a 'medium-sized company' for this purpose where in the relevant financial year it satisfies any two of the following three conditions:

(1) its balance sheet total (as defined above) does not exceed £6,000,000;

(2) its turnover does not exceed £12,000,000;

(3) the average number of persons employed by the company does not exceed 250[8].

[29.12] Such a company may also annex an 'abridged' balance sheet to its return, but in its case the number of items the separate value of which may be omitted is significantly less[9]. It must also annex both the auditors' and the directors' reports to the return. The profit and loss account must also be annexed, but in this case the company is not required to give separate details of

---

[8] Companies Act 1986, s 11 as amended by the European Community (Accounts) Regulation 1993, SI 396/1993. For the method of calculating the number of employees see n 5, p 385.

[9] See para **[30.27]** below.

their turnover and costs of production but may simply combine them under the heading 'gross profit or loss'.

[29.13] Because the assets, turnover and payroll of companies may change from year to year, s 9 of the 1986 Act provides rules for determining whether in any particular year a small or medium sized company should be reclassified as another form of company.

[29.14] Although small and medium sized companies are enabled to annex abridged balance sheets to the annual return, it should be borne in mind that there is an over-riding requirement under the Acts applicable to all companies that the balance sheet should give a true and fair view of the state of affairs of the company. This requirement is considered in more detail in the next chapter: for the moment, it is sufficient to note that it applies also to the balance sheet annexed to the return and hence may necessitate more disclosures in the case of small and medium sized companies than would be involved if they confined themselves to the relevant abridged format. It should also be noted that the obligations imposed on companies in regard to annexing the accounts to their returns and presenting them to the annual general meeting are quite distinct. Hence, as we shall see in the next chapter, medium-sized companies cannot present the abridged accounts to their members.

[29.15] The 1986 Act retains the exemption from the requirement to annex these documents to the annual return provided by the Principal Act in the case of certain companies with charitable objects. A specified company not having a share capital and formed for charitable purposes is so exempt either altogether or for a limited period where the Commissioners for Charitable Donations and Bequests so order[10]. So too, it would seem, is a company not having a share capital which is formed for an object which is charitable and which is:

> 'under the control of a religion recognised by the State under Article 44 of the Constitution, and which exercises its functions in accordance with the laws, canons and ordinances of the religion concerned.'

This provision appeared in s 128(4)(c) of the Principal Act and s 2(2) of the 1986 Act says baldly that the latter Act is not to apply to a company to which s 128(4)(c) of the Principal Act applies. The provisions of Article 44 of the Constitution referred to were, however, deleted by referendum in 1972 and, accordingly, the scope of this exemption is not clear. If it is intended to apply only to those religions specified in Article 44, it is of dubious constitutionality, since Article 44 also guarantees that the State will not enact laws which discriminate between religions[11]. If the reference to s 128(4)(c) is to be read as a

---

10   Companies Act 1963, s 128(5).
11   Cf Hogan & Whyte, *Kelly: The Irish Constitution* (3rd edn, 1994), p 1095.

reference to the section shorn of the words 'recognised by the State under Article 44 of the Constitution' it would presumably encompass sects and cults which have attracted unfavourable scrutiny in other contexts, such as the Moonies. It is far from clear why the exemption has been retained in any form, since a religious community in good standing should have no difficulty in obtaining the necessary order from the Charitable Commissioners under s 128(5) of the Principal Act. It would also in many cases qualify for exemption as 'a company not trading for the acquisition of gain by the members' to which the 1986 Act does not apply.

[29.16] It should be noted that the exemption of such companies from the requirements of the 1986 Act means that they are also relieved of the more onerous requirements of that Act as to the form and contents of the balance sheet and profit and loss account[12].

[29.17] Certain categories of company, which were exempted from the requirements of the Principal Act as to the annexing of their accounts to the annual return, retain their exemption under the 1986 Act. Insurance companies, which are the holders of authorisations under the relevant EU regulations, do not have to annex the documents in question[13]. Since they are subject to the strict public supervision of their affairs required by the Insurance Acts 1909 to 1983, this is understandable. More contentious is the continued exemption of foreign companies. Under s 354 of the Principal Act, such a company where it establishes a place of business in Ireland is obliged to deliver copies of its accounts to the Registrar, unless there are provisions in its constitution that would entitle it to rank as a private company if it was registered in the State. Despite severe criticism, this was left untouched by the 1986 Act.

[29.18] There are also special provisions in the 1986 Act dealing with subsidiaries of companies in other member states of the European Union, which are intended to implement other requirements of the Fourth Directive. Such companies are exempted from the requirement to annex their accounts to the return provided certain conditions are met, ie:

(1)   all the shareholders in the subsidiary declare their consent;

(2)   there is in force an irrevocable guarantee by the holding company of the subsidiary's liabilities in respect of the relevant financial year;

(3)   the annual accounts for the subsidiary are consolidated with the holding company's for the relevant year;

---

[12] As to which, see Ch 30 below.

[13] Companies Act 1986, s 2(3). The regulations in question are the European Communities (Non-Life Insurance) Regulations 1976, SI 115/1976 and the European Communities (Life Assurance) Regulations 1984, SI 57/1984.

(4) a notice stating that the company has availed of the exemption and a copy of the guarantee and notification, together with a declaration by the company that all the shareholders have declared their consent, is annexed to the return;

(5) the group accounts of the holding company are drawn up and audited in accordance with the Fourth Directive and annexed to the subsidiary's return[14].

Certificates to be sent by private company with return

[29.19] A private company must send with its return the following certificates signed by a director and the secretary:

(1) a certificate that the company has not, since the date of its last return, or in the case of a first return since the date of incorporation, issued any invitation to the public to subscribe for shares or debentures of the company;

(2) where the number of members exceeds 50, a certificate that the excess consists wholly of persons who under the Acts are not to be included in reckoning the number of 50, ie employees or former employees of the company[15].

Default in making return

[29.20] The return must be completed within 60 days after the annual general meeting for the year and the company must forthwith forward to the Registrar a copy signed by a director and the secretary. If the company fails to comply with these requirements, both the company and every officer in default is liable to a fine not exceeding £500. Proceedings in relation to such offences may be brought and prosecuted by the Registrar[16].

[29.21] An additional power was conferred on the Registrar in the event of a default by a company in relation to the return by s 12 of the 1982 Act. That has now been replaced by the more stringent provisions of s 46 of the 1999 (No 2) Act.

---

14 Companies Act 1986, s 17. Two features of this exemption should be noted. First, it leaves unaffected the general exemption of foreign companies mentioned in the preceding paragraph. Secondly it would appear not to be availed of very much in practice. Understandably, such companies are reluctant to enter into such guarantees and in any event are used to the publication of accounts.

15 Companies Act 1963, s 129.

16 Companies Act 1963, s 127 as amended by the Companies (Amendment) Act 1982, s 15.

[29.22] If a company has failed for one or more years to make a return, he may write to it by registered post stating that, unless all the outstanding returns are delivered to him within one month of the date of the letter, a notice will be published in *Iris Oifigiúil* with a view to striking the name of the company off the register. Unless he receives all the outstanding returns within one month or an answer to the effect that the company is not carrying on business, he may publish in *Iris Oifigiúil* a notice stating that, at the expiration of one month from the date of that notice, the name of the company will be struck off the register and the company dissolved. At the expiration of the time mentioned in the notice, the Registrar may, unless cause to the contrary is previously shown by the company, strike its name off the register and he must then publish a notice to that effect in *Iris Oifigiúil*. Upon the publication of the notice, the company is dissolved.

[29.23] Section 46 provides for a similar procedure where the Revenue Commissioners notify the Registrar in writing that a company has failed to deliver a statement which it was required to deliver under s 882(3) of the Taxes Consolidation Act 1997 inserted by s 83 of the Finance Act 1999.

That section provides that every company incorporated in the State or which begins to carry on a trade, profession or business in the State shall within 30 days from the date on which it begins to carry on such a trade, profession or business, give specified particulars to the Revenue Commissioners in writing. The particulars are:

(1)   The name of the company.

(2)   The address of the company's registered office.

(3)   The address of its principal place of business.

(4)   The name and address of the secretary of the company.

(5)   The date of commencement of the trade, profession or business.

(6)   The nature of the trade, profession or business.

(7)   The date up to which accounts relating to such trade, profession or business will be made up.

(8)   Such other information as the Revenue Commissioners consider necessary for the purposes of the Tax Acts.

[29.24] In the case of companies which are incorporated, but not resident, in the State, there are provisions requiring such a company to furnish the name of the territory in which the company is, by virtue of its law, resident for tax purposes and the names of the ultimate beneficial owners of the company. In the case of a company that is neither incorporated nor resident in the State but which carries on a trade, profession or business in the State, the following particulars must be furnished:

(1)   the address of the company's principal place of business in the State;

(2)   the name and address of the agent, manager, factor or other representatives of the company; and

(3)   the date of commencement of the company's trade, profession or business in the State.

[29.25] Where a company fails to deliver a statement which it is required to deliver under s 882(3) of the 1997 Act, the Revenue Commissioners may give notice in writing to that effect to the Registrar. They are expressly relieved of any obligations as to secrecy or other restrictions upon disclosure of information in the event of such a default by the company.

[29.26] Where the Registrar receives such a notice from the Commissioners, he may write to the company by registered post stating that, unless the company delivers the requisite statement to the Revenue Commissioners within one month, a notice will be published in *Iris Oifigiúil* with a view to striking the name of the company off the register. In the event of a failure by the company to deliver the statement within one month from the sending of the letter, the same consequences follow as to striking the name of the company off the register and its dissolution.

[29.27] Where the name of a company is struck off the register and it is dissolved under any of these provisions, the liability of the directors, officers and members continues and the jurisdiction of the court to wind up the company is unaffected.

[29.28] Both the Principal Act and the 1982 Act contained provisions for an application to the court by the company or any creditor or member of the company, who feels aggrieved by its having been struck off, with a view to having the name of the company restored to the register. This procedure is still available under s 46 of the 1999 (No 2) Act, but subject to important changes.

[29.29] If any member, officer or creditor of the company is so aggrieved, such an application may be made to the court. It must, however, be made on notice, not merely to the Registrar, but also to the Revenue Commissioners and the Minister for Finance. As before, this must be made within 20 years of the publication of the notice in *Iris Oifigiúil*. The court, if satisfied that it is just to make the order, may order that the name of the company be restored to the register. Upon an office copy of the order being delivered to the Registrar, the company is deemed to have continued in existence as if its name had not been struck off. The court may also give such directions as seem just with a view to placing the company and all other persons in the same position as if the company had not been struck off[17].

[29.30] Where the court makes such an order, it now has power to make what is described as an 'alternative order'. This may include a provision that the officers of the company, or any one or more of them specified in the order, are to be liable for the whole or part of any debt or liability incurred by or on behalf of the company during the period when it stood struck off the register.

[29.31] Where the application for a restoration order is made by a member or officer of the company, the order must provide that it is not to take effect unless, within one month from the date of the order, all outstanding annual returns or outstanding statements required by s 882 of the 1997 Act, are delivered to the Registrar or the Revenue Commissioners, as the case may be. Where the order is made on the application of a creditor, the court must direct that one or more specified members or officers of the company deliver all outstanding returns or outstanding statements to the Registrar or the Revenue Commissioners within a specified period.

[29.32] An application to the court for an order restoring a company to the register may also be made by the Registrar on notice to every person who to his knowledge is an officer of the company before the expiration of the 20-year period from the publication in *Iris Oifigiúil* of the relevant notice. The court, when the application is by the Registrar, may give similar directions as in the case of an application by an officer, member or creditor including an 'alternative order'. There is no provision, however, for making the order conditional upon the furnishing of outstanding returns or statements under s 882 of the 1997 Act. Presumably, it was envisaged that such an application would only be made by the Registrar where all outstanding returns had been delivered or outstanding statements furnished to the Revenue Commissioners.

[29.33] Under s 311 of the Principal Act, which was inserted by s 246 of the 1990 Act, the Registrar himself may make the order restoring the company to the Registrar if an application is made by the company within 12 months of the publication of the notice in *Iris Oifigiúil*. There is a similar provision in s 46 of the 1999 (No 2) Act where the company has been struck off because of its failure to deliver a statement to the Revenue Commissioners under s 882 of the 1997 Act. Such an order, however, may only be made in that case where the

---

[17] Note that the provisions of the section are without prejudice to the general power of the Registrar to strike a defunct company off the register under the Companies Act 1963, s 311. That section contains similar machinery entitling the Registrar to strike off a company where he has reasonable cause to believe that it is not carrying on business.

Registrar has received confirmation from the commissioners that all the outstanding statements have been delivered to them.

[29.34] In an interesting innovation, the Circuit Court is now given a jurisdiction to hear applications for the restoration of companies to the register. Its jurisdiction is, however, confined to cases where the application is made either by a creditor or by the Registrar. In the case of an application by a creditor, it is to be made to the Judge of the Circuit Court for the circuit in which the registered office of the company was situated immediately before it was struck off. If no office was registered at that time, it is to be made in the circuit in which the creditor resides. In the case of a creditor residing outside the State it is to be made to the Dublin Circuit Court, as is an application by the Registrar.

Chapter 30

Accounts and Audit

[30.01] Until the Principal Act came into force in 1964, there was no legal obligation on Irish companies to keep proper books of accounts. This is not to say, of course, that such books were not kept in practice: any careful businessman would recognise the importance of keeping a proper record of all the firm's finances on a day-to-day business. But the absence of any express requirement of the law in this area gave rise to understandable concern. The Principal Act introduced major changes in the law: for the first time, all companies formed under the Acts were expressly required to keep proper books of accounts and there were important new provisions as to the information to be included in the accounts which are laid before the members.

[30.02] More recently, the 1986 and 1990 Acts introduced significant changes. Those contained in the 1986 Act for the most part give effect to the requirements of the Fourth EU Directive. We have seen in the last Chapter that this Act ended the total exemption of private companies from the requirement that the annual accounts be annexed to its annual return. In addition, it imposes more stringent requirements as to what must be disclosed in accounts, including details of accounting policies, methods of valuations and operation costs.

[30.03] One of the most important requirements of the Principal Act was that the accounts of all companies, public and private, must be audited by properly qualified auditors. These provisions were supplemented by the 1990 Act, which contains new requirements as to the qualification, powers and duties of auditors.

[30.04] In 1994, a Task Force on Small Business recommended that auditing of accounts should no longer be required in the case of a business with a small turnover on the ground *inter alia* that the costs of auditing were out of proportion to the benefit to such companies, their customers, banks, and interested third parties. The recommendation was supported by the Company Law Review Group. The 1999 (No 2) Act has now introduced a degree of exemption for small companies from the auditing requirement, which is considered in more detail at para [30.110] below.

[30.05] In considering the requirements of the Acts in this area, it is necessary to distinguish between the basic records which companies are obliged to maintain and information which companies are required to prepare and, in some instances, publish.

[30.06] Companies are required to maintain books of account in which are recorded, on a day to day basis, the finances of the company. The directors are charged with the responsibility of preparing a balance sheet and a profit and loss account to be laid before the members annually in general meeting[1]. This balance sheet will be prepared from the books of account of the company and can be viewed as the means by which the directors render an account to the shareholders of their financial stewardship.

[30.07] In practice, many companies will prepare balance sheets and profit and loss accounts at more frequent intervals than a year for internal use in managing and controlling the enterprise. In addition, it is now normal practice to produce at regular intervals budgets, cash flows and other such information as part of the internal management control system.

[30.08] The auditors are required to report to the members on every balance sheet and profit and loss account laid before the members annually and to frame their report in accordance with the requirements of the Seventh Schedule to the Principal Act. To that end, they will carry out an examination of the books of account and other financial records of the company.

[30.09] There are special provisions as to the preparation of 'group accounts' in the case of companies having subsidiary companies, ie companies either owned or effectively controlled by them.

Books of account

[30.10] The statutory obligation to keep proper books of account imposed on companies by s 147 of the Principal Act was replaced by the more elaborate provisions of s 202 of the 1990 Act. Companies must keep proper books of account 'on a continuous and consistent basis'. The use of this phrase for the first time reflects the increasing recognition in legislation of the desirability of companies complying with the relevant standards and requirements of the accountancy professions and not departing from them to any significant degree without good reason. Advances in technology are reflected in the sanctioning of such books of account being kept 'in the form of documents or otherwise'. In many companies today, the bound ledger has been replaced by a computerised system with the information maintained on magnetic tape or disc and printouts provided on computerised stationery. The sensible course to follow is to ensure that, whatever records are kept, they record the transactions in such a way that they can be understood and traced through the system at a later stage. Specifically, they must be kept in such a manner that they comply with the 1990 Act requirements, ie they must

---

1   Companies Act 1963, ss 148 and 159.

(1)   correctly record and explain the transactions of the company;

(2)   enable the financial position of the company to be determined at any time with reasonable accuracy;

(3)   enable the directors to ensure that the balance sheets and profit and loss accounts or income and expenditure accounts of the company comply with the requirements of the Acts;

(4)   enable the accounts of the company to be readily and properly audited.

[30.11] The somewhat bald requirements of s 147 of the Principal Act as to what the books of account are to contain were replaced in the 1990 Act by provisions which spell out these obligations in more detail. Without prejudice to the generality of the requirements mentioned in the preceding paragraph, they must record

(1)   all sums of money received and expended from day to day by the company and the matters in respect of which the receipt and expenditure takes place;

(2)   the assets and liabilities of the company;

(3)   if the company's business involves dealing in goods:
    (a) all goods purchased and sold (except those sold for cash by way of ordinary retail trade), showing the goods, the sellers and the buyers in sufficient detail to enable each to be identified and all the relevant invoices;
    (b) stock held by the company at the end of each financial year and stocktakings from which such statements of stock are prepared;

(4)   if the company's business involves the provision of services, the services provided and the relevant invoices.

[30.12] Proper books of account are deemed to be kept if they comply with all these requirements and, in addition, give 'a true and fair view of the state of affairs' of the company and explain its transactions. The expression 'a true and fair view', which was also used in the Principal Act, has never been further defined. We shall consider it in more detail when we deal with another important context in which it occurs, ie the annual accounts of the company[2].

[30.13] The books of account must be kept at the registered office of the company or such other place as the directors think fit. They must be available for inspection by the directors at reasonable times[3]. Where they are kept at a place outside Ireland - as they may be - accounts and returns must be sent at intervals

---

2   See para **[30.20]** below.

3   The inspection may be carried out on behalf of a director by an accountant: per Kenny J in *Healy v Healy* [1973] IR 309.

not exceeding six months to a place in Ireland where they must be open to inspection by the directors at all reasonable times. Such accounts and returns must disclose with reasonable accuracy the financial position of the company and enable the balance sheet and profit and loss account of the company to be prepared in accordance with the Principal Act.

[30.14] There are penalties provided for directors who fail to take reasonable steps to secure compliance by the company with the requirements as to keeping books of accounts or who, by their own wilful acts, are the cause of the company being in default. They are liable on summary conviction to imprisonment for a term not exceeding six months or to a fine not exceeding £500 or both[4]. But where a person is charged with failing to take reasonable steps to secure compliance, it is a defence to prove that he had reasonable ground for believing, and did believe, that a competent and reliable person was charged with the duty of seeing that the requirements were complied with and was in a position to discharge that duty. Moreover, a person may not be sentenced to imprisonment unless the court is of the opinion that the offence was committed wilfully.

[30.15] These provisions, which replaced corresponding provisions in the Principal Act, were strengthened by ss 203 and 204 of the 1990 Act. Section 203 enables a court to impose severe penalties on the officers of a company which is being wound up and is unable to pay its debts if proper books of account have not been kept by the company. If the court considers that this failure has:

(1)   contributed to the company's inability to pay all its debts;

(2)   resulted in 'substantial uncertainty' as to the assets and liabilities of the company; or

(3)   'substantially impeded' the orderly winding up of the company;

every officer of the company in default is guilty of an offence and liable on summary conviction to a fine not exceeding £1,000 or imprisonment for a term not exceeding six months or both and on conviction on indictment to a fine not exceeding £10,000 or imprisonment for a term not exceeding five years or both. This section clearly imposes a serious responsibility on directors among others to ensure that proper books of account are kept and it is important to note that the obligation extends to 'part time' or non-executive directors. There is, however, a defence provided for officers who show that they took 'all reasonable steps' to ensure that the company complied with its duty or had 'reasonable grounds' for believing that:

'a competent and reliable person acting under the supervision and control of a director of the company who has been formally allocated such responsibility was

---
[4]   Companies Act 1963, s 147(6) as amended by the Companies (Amendment) Act 1986, s 15.

charged with the duty of ensuring that the section was complied with and was in a position to discharge that duty.'

[30.16] Section 204 provides that where the circumstances giving rise to criminal liability under s 203 arise, the court may, if it thinks proper to do so, declare that any officer or former officer of the company in default is to be personally liable, either without limitation or to a specified extent, for the debts and other liabilities of the company. The application may be made by the liquidator or any creditor or contributory. There is again a defence available for officers or former officers in similar terms to that available to the criminal charge. The court also has wide powers to make a person's liability under the section a charge on any debt or obligation of the company to him or on any mortgage or charge he, or someone of his behalf, may have over the assets of the company. A charge imposed by the section may also be extended to assignees of the person, except those who gave valuable consideration and acted in good faith and without notice of the matters giving rise to the imposition of the charge.

[30.17] In *Mehigan v Duignan*[5], an application was made under s 204 by an official liquidator of a company for an order declaring the respondent, a director and shareholder, to be personally liable for the debts of the company. The company was insolvent and Shanley J found that proper books of account had not been kept. He pointed out that, on its face, s 204 appeared to allow the court in the exercise of its discretion to impose unlimited liability on an officer of a company where the contravention under s 202 had not in itself resulted in any loss to the company, but had substantially impeded the orderly winding up of the company or resulted in substantial uncertainly as to it assets and liabilities. He added, however, that:

'There may be circumstances where, if the court's discretion is exercised in this way, the result achieved would be so harsh, unfair and disproportionate, having regard to the wrong committed, as to constitute an unjust attack on the personal rights of the affected officers.'

Shanley J went on to say that, in his view, the court in the exercise of its discretion must have regard (but not necessarily exclusively) to the extent to which the contravention of s 202 resulted in financial loss and, if it did, whether or not such losses were reasonably foreseeable by the officer as a consequence of the contravention.

Shanley J also held, following the decision of the Supreme Court in *Banco Ambrosiano SP v Ansbacher & Co Ltd*[6] that, in deciding whether to impose liability under s 204, no higher degree of probability of a contravention of s 202

5   [1997] 1 IR 340.
6   [1987] ILRM 669.

was required than in any other civil matter. In that case, he found that losses sustained by the company resulting from the contraventions of s 202 were reasonably foreseeable by the respondent and, accordingly, he made the order sought.

[30.18] Records required to be kept under s 147 must be preserved by the company for a period of six years after the dates to which they relate.

The annual accounts

[30.19] The directors are required by the Principal Act to prepare, or have prepared, a balance sheet and profit and loss account which they must lay before the annual general meeting of the company[7]. To these documents must be attached the directors' report[8] and auditors' report[9]. The information contained in the annual accounts must include the information specifically set out in the Schedule to the 1986 Act, which for this purpose replaced the Sixth Schedule to the Principal Act.

[30.20] The 'over-riding requirement', however, of the legislation (to use the phrase actually employed by s 3 of the 1986 Act) is that the annual accounts should give a 'true and fair' view of the 'state of affairs' of the company at the end of its financial year (in the case of the balance sheet) and of the profit or loss of the company for the financial year (in the case of the profit and loss account). The expression 'true and fair' view has never been further defined and, in particular, the distinction between 'true' and 'fair' in this context further explained. (Can an untrue view ever be 'fair'?) Moreover, there may be more than one 'true and fair' view of any given situation. It is probably safe to say that, as a general rule, annual accounts which do not contain any material error, are not misleading in any material manner and comply with generally accepted accountancy standards will meet the 'true and fair' requirement. As we shall see, in a number of respects the 1986 Act gave statutory effect to such standards.

[30.21] It was pointed out in the first edition that it might sometimes be necessary to supply information in the accounts additional to that required by the relevant schedule in order to meet the 'true and fair' requirement. It might even, in exceptional circumstances, be necessary to depart from those requirements. This approach (which obviously reflected prudent accountancy practice) was given statutory form in s 3 of the 1986 Act. Section 3(1)(b) provides that where a balance sheet or profit and loss account drawn up in accordance with ss 4 and 5 and the Schedule would not provide sufficient

---

[7] Companies Act 1963, s 148.
[8] Companies Act 1963, s 158.
[9] Companies Act 1963, ss 157 and 163.

information to give a true and fair view, any necessary additional information is to be provided in the balance sheet or profit and loss account or in a note to the accounts. Section 3(1)(d) provides that where, owing to 'special circumstances', the preparation of accounts of a company in accordance with ss 4 and 5 and the Schedule would prevent a true and fair view being given, (even with the additional information just mentioned), the directors must depart from the requirements of the Schedule to the extent necessary to give a true and fair view. Where they do so, however, they must attach a note to the accounts giving details of the particular departures, the reasons and the effect on the accounts. It should be pointed out, however, that the cases in which it is necessary for the directors to depart from the requirements of the Schedule are in practice very few.

[30.22] The importance has been mentioned more than once in this Chapter of complying with accepted accountancy standards when preparing accounts. Statements of Standard Accounting Practice (abbreviated to SSAP) are issued from time to time by the Consultative Committee of Accounting Bodies which represents the major accountancy institutions[10]. These statements set out approved methods of accounting for application to all financial accounts which are intended to give a true and fair view of the financial position and profit or loss. Members of the professions represented are required to use their best endeavours to ensure that accounting standards are observed and that significant departures found to be necessary are adequately disclosed and explained.

[30.23] It should also be remembered that methods of financial accounting change from time to time. New accounting standards are issued and established and standards reviewed and updated with the object of improving them in the light of new needs and developments.

[30.24] Certain specified accounting principles must be used in preparing the accounts which are set out in s 5 of the 1986 Act.

(1) The company is to be presumed to be carrying on business as a going concern.

(2) Accounting policies must be applied consistently from one financial year to the next.

(3) The amount of each item must be determined on a prudent basis. In particular,
    (a) only profits realised at the balance sheet date may be included in the profit and loss account
    (b) all liabilities and losses which have arisen or are likely to arise in respect of the relevant financial year or any previous year must be

---

[10] These are now supplemented by the standards prescribed by the Financial Reporting Council ('FRS').

taken into account, including those only becoming apparent between the balance sheet date and the signing of the balance sheet in accordance with s 156 of the Principal Act.

(4)   All income and charges for the relevant year must be taken into account without regard to the date of receipt or payment.

(5)   In determining the aggregate amount of any item, the amount of each asset or liability must be determined separately.

The balance sheet

[30.25] A company's balance sheet, as we have seen[11], sets out the capital and reserves of the company and the manner in which they are represented by the assets of the company. It has been repeatedly emphasised that it is not designed to provide a reliable guide to the worth of the company. Essentially it is a historic document intended to indicate the extent of the investment of the shareholders in the company and how that investment has been employed. Moreover, its utility as a guide to the company's worth is further affected by the fact that, in the case of fixed assets, their value in the balance sheet may be stated at the cost of acquisition, although their current value may be higher as a result of inflation. While the Schedule to the 1986 Act gives companies the option of adopting what is called current cost valuation, ie the current market value of the asset, the historic cost method is still permissible. It should, however, be noted that, whichever method is adopted, there must also be provision for depreciation or diminution in value.

[30.26] The 1986 Act contains elaborate requirements as to the contents of balance sheets which are far more detailed than those formerly applicable. Companies must elect to prepare their balance sheets in one of two formats. Format I is the 'vertical' form which we have used as our illustration in Chapter 14 above. Format 11 is the 'horizontal' form. While the layout is different, however, the statutory requirements as to the items to be included are virtually identical. The 'vertical format' is that more favoured by the accountancy professions in these islands. But whichever format is used, the directors must adopt the same format in following years, unless, in their opinion, there are 'special reasons' for a change, in which case the reasons for the change, together with full particulars of the change, must be given in a note to the accounts in which the new format is first adopted[12].

[30.27] The directors of a 'small company' may draw up an abridged balance sheet. We have seen in the last chapter how such a company is defined and the

---

[11]   See para **[14.09]** above.

[12]   Companies Act 1986, s 4.

extent of the permitted abridgement[13]. The directors of a 'medium-sized company' as there defined may also draw up an abridged balance sheet, but in their case the permitted omissions are far fewer. Thus, they must disclose the value of the individual items making up the tangible fixed assets of the company under the following headings:

(1)   land and buildings;

(2)   plant and machinery;

(3)   fixtures, fittings, tools and equipment;

(4)   payments on account and assets in course of construction[14].

[30.28] In contrast, small companies need only show the aggregate value of all the tangible fixed assets. Again, a medium-sized company must show the breakdown of its creditors, giving separately the amounts owed under debentures, by way of bank loan and overdrafts, to trade creditors and to other creditors, including tax and social welfare. A small company need show only the total owed to all creditors. There is a further major difference. Medium-sized companies must present a full and unabridged balance sheet to the annual general meeting: the exemption is confined to the balance sheet annexed to the return.

[30.29] The basic obligation on small companies is to do no more than present an abridged balance sheet to its members and annex the balance sheet similarly abridged to its return. But it should always be remembered that the overriding requirement remains that the balance sheet gives a true and fair view of the state of affairs of the company and this may necessitate additional disclosures and explanations in particular cases.

[30.30] The 1986 Act contains detailed provisions (in Part V of the Schedule) as to the information that must be supplied by way of notes to the accounts. In the case of the balance sheet, this information relates to the following topics:

(1)   Share capital and debentures;

(2)   Fixed assets;

(3)   Financial assets and investments held as current assets;

(4)   Reserves and provisions;

(5)   Details of indebtedness;

(6)   Guarantees and other financial commitments.

[30.31] These requirements are far more detailed than those contained in the Principal Act. It is not intended to set them out in full: the Schedule should be

---

[13] See para **[29.09]** above.

[14] Companies Act 1986, s 11(2).

consulted where necessary. Some of its more important features, however, deserve mention.

(a) Share capital and debentures

[30.32] Particulars must be given, not merely of the authorised share capital, but of any allotments that have been made during the relevant financial year, including the reasons for the allotment. There is a similar requirement in the case of debentures.

(b) Fixed assets

[30.33] While it was necessary prior to the 1986 Act to distinguish between fixed and current assets, there could be difficulty in ascertaining whether particular assets should be regarded as fixed or current. Thus, investments in property were treated as fixed assets by some companies, while others preferred to treat them as current, particularly if it was intended to realise them at an early date. The Schedule to the 1986 Act provides that assets are to be treated as fixed assets if they are intended for use on a continuing basis in the company's activities and that any assets not intended for such use are to be treated as current assets. The difficulty referred to is recognised by the creation of a new category of assets called 'financial assets and investments held as current assets'.

[30.34] There are detailed requirements as to stating (in the case of fixed assets) their value (whether on the historic cost or current cost basis) and as to provision for diminution in value or depreciation. Where the historic cost method is employed, the amount stated is to be the purchase price or production cost. If it has what is called 'a limited useful economic life', the amount must be reduced systematically over the life span. (If it is thought that it will have a residual value at the end of the period, the amount to be written off over the period is the purchase price or production cost less that value.) But if the reduction in value in any year of a fixed asset is estimated to be permanent, the amount must be correspondingly reduced in the balance sheet, irrespective of whether it has a limited economic life.

[30.35] Where the current cost method is employed, the amount stated is to be the market value at its last valuation or the current cost. 'Current cost' is not defined but is presumably the cost of replacing the asset at current market prices. The same depreciation rules then apply as in the case of the historic cost method, but the starting point for calculating the depreciation each year is the last valuation. Where the revaluation of the asset has resulted in a profit or loss the amount involved must be credited or debited as appropriate to a special reserve called the 'revaluation reserve'.

[30.36] It should be observed that a company does not have to adopt one set of rules exclusively. A company may decide to value particular assets in accordance with either method[15].

[30.37] In the case of 'financial assets and investments held as current assets', the market value of investments must be stated if it is different from the amount at which they are valued in the balance sheet. Where the market value is in the accounts taken to be higher than the stock exchange value, both must be stated.

(c) Reserves and provisions

[30.38] Reserves are one of the items in the balance sheet which have tended to arouse controversy, since the manner in which they are treated can distort the company's true financial position. It is not surprising to find that the Schedule contains detailed requirements in this area.

[30.39] As we have seen[16] every balance sheet contains an item headed 'capital and reserves'. Except in the case of small private companies, this must be further sub-divided. Among the specified items are the 'revaluation reserve' already referred to and 'other reserves'. This latter item is further sub-divided into headings, two of which relate to the company's liability to redeem or repay shares, one to reserves which must be maintained because of a provision to that effect in the articles and a final item headed again 'other reserves'.

[30.40] It is the last heading which concerns us at this point. Where the company's profit and loss account shows a profit in any year, that profit may be dealt with, broadly speaking, in two ways. It may be distributed by way of dividend or it may be transferred to the reserves section of the balance sheet. Where it is transferred to reserves, it will form part of the 'other reserves' just mentioned.

[30.41] Provisions must be charged in the profit and loss account in arriving at the profit and loss for the year. 'Provisions' are again sub-divided, this time into pensions and other obligations, taxation (including deferred taxation) and 'other provisions'. The last phrase includes sums retained by way of providing for any known liability the amount of which cannot be determined with substantial accuracy. In this context, liability includes expenditure which has been contracted for and disputed and contingent liabilities. But a sum which has been set aside for the purchase of new property or to meet unknown contingencies is considered as a reserve.

---

[15] It should be noted, however, that it has been held by Carroll J that for tax purposes the accounts must be prepared on the historic cost basis: see *Carroll Industries plc v O'Cualachain* [1988] IR 705.

[16] See para **[14.09]** above.

[30.42] Unless it is restricted from so doing by the articles and provided the requirements of s 45 of the 1983 Act (which are discussed in detail in the next Chapter) are observed, a company is free to distribute by way of dividend part or all of its reserves provided they are realised. However, in practice most companies retain some or all of the reserves for future working capital requirements and to provide a safety net should the company get into trouble.

(d) Details of indebtedness

[30.43] We have already seen that small private companies need only state the total of debts due by them without any further breakdown. However, even in their case the balance sheet must distinguish between debts which must be paid within a year and longer term indebtedness. In the case of these companies, the debts must not only be broken down in the manner already indicated, but particulars must be given of longer term borrowing by the company, which for this purpose means debts which are not repayable by instalments and do not fall due until the expiration of five years after the end of the relevant financial year.

Profit and loss account

[30.44] Every company, as we have seen, is required to draw up a profit and loss account in each year, although in the case of small companies it does not have to be annexed to the annual return. The title of the document is almost self-explanatory: it is a statement of the profits and losses of the company since the last such statement, made up to a date which must not be more than nine months before the meeting at which it is presented. As we have seen, such a statement must in every case be annexed to the balance sheet and presented to the annual general meeting of the company in each year. The Schedule to the 1986 Act imposed significant new requirements as to what is to be contained in the profit and loss account, but there are important exemptions in the case of small and medium sized private companies.

[30.45] The profit and loss account is to be drawn up in one of four formats set out in the Schedule. They should be consulted for matters of detail, but it can be said at the outset that Formats 1 and 2 most closely reflect accountancy practice in these islands. All four formats represent a new departure in our company law in requiring details of turnover and operating costs to be given. As to the differences between Formats 1 and 2, Format 1 can he said to adopt a 'functional' approach in requiring 'distribution costs' and 'administrative expenses' to be specified, whereas Format 2 simply requires the character of the relevant expenditure to be stated, for example, 'wages and salaries'. Similarly, Format 1 uncompromisingly stipulates that 'costs of sales' be set out: Format 2 takes refuge in the vaguer 'other operating charges' which can include expenses not normally referable to cost of sales.

[30.46] Small and medium-sized companies are exempted from the more stringent of these requirements. They may combine the turnover and operating costs in one item, the 'gross profit or loss'. Medium-sized companies, unlike small companies, must annex the profit and loss account to their return, but can make use of this abridged version for that purpose. Again, in every case, it is to be noted that the 'true and fair' view requirement may necessitate additional disclosures or explanations.

Exceptions for certain companies

[30.47] Certain types of companies are exempted from the general requirements of ss 3, 4 and 5 of, and the Schedule to, the 1986 Act. They are:

(1)　banks holding a licence under the Central Bank Acts 1971 to 1989;

(2)　trustee savings bank certified under the Trustee Savings Banks Acts 1863 to 1965;

(3)　hire purchase companies;

(4)　companies engaged in accepting deposits or granting credit for their own account,

(5)　the ACC bank plc;

(6)　the ICC bank plc;

(7)　insurance companies authorised under the relevant EU Regulations[17].

Other requirements as to accounts

[30.48] The Principal Act requires certain documents to be annexed to the balance sheet[18]. They are:

(1)　the profit and loss account;

(2)　a report by the directors; and

(3)　the auditor's report.

[30.49] The directors' report is 'on the state of the company's affairs', and it must state the amount (if any) which they recommend should be paid by way of dividend and the amount (if any) which they propose to carry to reserves. It must also deal, so far as is material to the appreciation of the state of the company's affairs, with any change during the year in the nature of the company's business or the business of any of its subsidiaries or in the classes of business in which the company has an interest. It must also contain a list of the company's subsidiaries and of companies in which the company has a shareholding in excess of 20%

---

[17]　Companies Act 1986, s 2(2).

[18]　Companies Act 1963, s 157.

carrying voting rights. The report must be signed on behalf of the directors by two of their number.

[30.50] If a director fails to take all reasonable steps to comply with the requirements of the Principal Act as to the report, he is liable on summary conviction to imprisonment for a term not exceeding six months or to a fine not exceeding £500[19]. It is a defence for the director to prove that he had reasonable ground to believe and did believe that a competent and reliable person was charged with the duty of seeing that the provisions of the Act were complied with and was in a position to discharge that duty. Moreover, a person may not be sentenced to imprisonment unless the court is of the opinion that the offence was committed wilfully.

[30.51] The directors' duties as to the report were further elaborated in the 1986 Act[20]. As a result, the report must contain in addition:

(1)   a 'fair review' of the development of the business of the company in the relevant year;

(2)   particulars of any 'important events' affecting the company which have occurred since the end of that year;

(3)   an indication of likely future developments in the business of the company;

(4)   an indication of the research and development activities of the company (if any).

These obligations also apply where the events or activities in question are those of subsidiary companies.

[30.52] Another requirement of the 1986 Act is that the report must contain particulars of any acquisition by the company of its own shares in the relevant year whether as a result of the company's using the machinery for that purpose provided by the 1983 Act or by other methods such as forfeiture, surrender in lieu of forfeiture or lien[21].

[30.53] It should be noted that the Safety Health and Welfare at Work Act 1989 imposes on directors a duty to include in their report 'an evaluation of the extent to which the policy set out in a safety statement was fulfilled during the period in time covered by the report'.

[30.54] The Principal Act also requires particulars of the directors' salaries and other payments to them to be given in the accounts or in a statement annexed thereto[22]. The particulars required are:

[19] Companies Act 1963, s 158(7) as amended by the Companies (Amendment) Act 1982, s 15.
[20] Companies Act 1986, s 13.
[21] Companies Act 1986, s 14.
[22] Companies Act 1963, s 191.

(1)   the aggregate amount of the directors' emoluments;

(2)   the aggregate amount of directors' or past directors' pensions;

(3)   the aggregate amount of any compensation to directors or past directors for loss of office.

[30.55] 'Emoluments' includes sums paid by way of expenses allowances insofar as those sums are charged to income tax. They also include benefits received by directors otherwise than in cash (which must be valued in money terms) and contributions paid in respect of them to pension schemes. The sums paid by way of compensation for loss of office which must be shown in the accounts include sums paid in respect of the loss of any office in the company and in any subsidiary.

[30.56] Particulars of the relevant salaries and other payments must be given whether the sums are paid by the company, its subsidiaries or any other person. If the requirements of the Acts are not met, the auditors must include in their report, so far as they reasonably can, a statement giving the necessary particulars.

[30.57] As we have seen[23], the 1990 Act introduced for the first time into Irish company law stringent restrictions on the making of loans by companies to their directors. Such restrictions extend, not merely to loans as such, but also to 'quasi-loans' where the 'lender' pays money owed by the director to a third party and 'credit transactions' where the 'creditor' supplies goods or services under a hire purchase agreement or similar transaction or leases land to the director. As a logical corollary, the requirements of the Principal Act as to the disclosure of loans to directors have now been elaborated so as to take account of the new provisions as to loans, quasi-loans and credit transactions.

[30.58] All such 'transactions and arrangements', as they are called, must now be disclosed in the annual accounts[24]. Thus, in the specified circumstances where such transactions are permitted (as where the total indebtedness of the director to the company is less than 10% of its assets) they must be disclosed in the accounts. They must, moreover, be disclosed by way of notes to the accounts, thus ensuring, it may be hoped, that they do not escape casual or uninformed scrutiny of the accounts. There are exemptions, considered in more detail below, where the total amounts involved do not exceed £2,500. There are also special provisions in the case of licensed banks.

[30.59] The 'transactions and arrangements' affected extend not merely to the loans, quasi-loans and similar transactions referred to in Part III of the 1990 Act.

---

[23] See para **[27.57]** above
[24] Companies Act 1990, ss 41 and 42.

They also include other transactions in which a director or a person connected with him has 'a material interest'. The range of affected transactions which must, accordingly, be disclosed is as follows:

(1)   loans;

(2)   quasi-loans;

(3)   credit transactions;

(4)   guarantees or securities entered into or provided in connection with any of the above;

(5)   agreements to enter into any of the transactions specified above;

(6)   any other transaction or arrangement with the company in which a director has a 'material interest'.

[30.60] An 'interest' for the purpose of these provisions is not 'material' if a majority of the other directors, having considered the matter, are of the opinion that it is not. Whether such an 'opinion' could be reviewed by the court where there was arguably no basis on which it could reasonably have been formed is uncertain. There are recent decisions by the High Court to the effect that the judicial review procedure established by the Rules of the Superior Courts in 1986 is not confined to public law matters, but the Supreme Court, while expressly reserving the question, have expressed doubts *obiter* as to whether they were correctly decided[25].

[30.61] 'Directors' in these provisions includes the 'shadow directors' extensively defined in Part III[26]. Transactions with a 'person connected with a director' are also affected.

[30.62] The particulars to be disclosed in the accounts are set out in detail in ss 41 and 42. They include matters such as the name of the borrower and (in the case of a 'connected person') the relevant director, the amount of the loan and any unpaid interest and the amount of any provision made in the accounts for a default in repayment. In the case of any officers of the company, the accounts must also disclose the total sums outstanding during the relevant year.

[30.63] The exemptions must next be considered. Particulars do not have to be disclosed in the accounts where the total amount involved does not exceed £2,500.

[30.64] In the case of transactions or arrangements in which the person concerned has a material interest, disclosure is not required where:

---

[25]   *O'Neill v Iarnród Éireann* (unreported, 3 July 1990).
[26]   See para **[27.05]** above.

(1)   the amount involved does not exceed £1,000, or

(2)   if more, does not exceed either £5,000 or 1% of the value of the net assets of the company for the relevant period.

The Minister has power to alter by order any of these financial limits.

[30.65] In the case of licensed banks, particulars need not be disclosed in the annual accounts. But the bank must have a statement of the same particulars available for the shareholders at its registered office for a period of at least 15 days ending with the date of the annual general meeting. The statement must also be available for inspection by the shareholders at the annual general meeting. These requirements do not apply, however, where the transaction in question:

(1)   is entered into by the bank in the ordinary course of its business; and

(2)   the value is no greater and the terms no more favourable than those which the bank ordinarily offers (or might reasonably be expected to offer) to a person of the same financial standing but unconnected with the bank.

[30.66] In addition (except in the circumstances just mentioned), the bank must maintain a register containing a copy of every transaction which it would be obliged to disclose under these provisions if it were not a bank, or, if it is not reduced to writing, a written memorandum of its terms.

[30.67] The directors are also obliged to give notice in writing to the company of such matters as may be necessary for the purpose of enabling the company to give particulars in the accounts of salaries and other payments to directors and of loans to directors[27].

[30.68] Every balance sheet and profit and loss account of a company must be signed on behalf of the directors by two of the directors. Where it is either issued, circulated or published unsigned, the company and every officer in default is liable to a fine not exceeding £500. This does not preclude the company, however, from issuing, publishing or circulating a fair and accurate summary of the balance sheet and profit and loss account where the full document has been signed[28].

Group accounts

[30.69] The requirement that a public company should send copies of its accounts to the Registrar with the annual return imposed by the 1908 Act was rendered significantly less effective by the fact that no such obligation rested on

---

[27] Companies Act 1963, s 193.

[28] Companies Act 1963, s 156 as amended by the Companies (Amendment) Act 1982, s 15.

a private company which was a subsidiary of the public company. This anomaly was first tackled in England in 1929 but it was not until the enactment of the Principal Act that there was any attempt to deal with the problem in Ireland. That Act required 'holding companies', as they are called, to incorporate in their own published accounts the financial position and results of their 'subsidiaries', ie companies which are effectively owned or controlled by the holding company. These 'group accounts', as they are called, must normally take the form of consolidated accounts showing the state of affairs of the entire group comprising the holding company and all its subsidiaries.

[30.70] The significance in Ireland of these requirements was somewhat reduced by the fact that private companies which were holding companies were not required to prepare group accounts. This was not illogical, having regard to the exemption of private companies from the requirement to send accounts with the annual return to the Registrar.

[30.71] Following the ending of that total exemption, which was the result of the 1986 Act, private companies which were holding companies were obliged to give certain information in their annual accounts relating to their subsidiaries. They were not obliged, however, to prepare group accounts although, if they did, they had to furnish any member of the company who requested it with a copy of the latest balance sheet of each of the subsidiaries which had been sent to the members of that subsidiary.

[30.72] While the Principal Act set out requirements which were, in general, to be observed in the preparation and presentation of group accounts, there were also provisions in the Act enabling the directors of any company, public or private, to adopt a different form for the accounts where they were of the opinion that it would better serve the purpose of presenting the accounts, or equivalent information, or its better appreciation.

[30.73] The legal requirements as to the preparation and presentation of group accounts were radically altered as a result of the enactment of the European Communities (Companies) (Group Accounts) Regulations 1992[29], which implemented in Ireland the provisions of the Seventh EU Company Law Directive. They should be read in conjunction with the European Communities (Accounts) Regulations 1993[30].

[30.74] Three major changes were effected by the Regulations. First, the total exemption hitherto enjoyed by private companies from the obligation to prepare group accounts was ended. Secondly, significantly broader criteria were

---

[29] SI 201/1992.
[30] SI 396/1993.

introduced for determining whether one company was a subsidiary of another. Thirdly, the requirements laid down in the Regulations and the Principal Act as to the form group accounts were to take could no longer be departed from by the directors.

[30.75] Before we proceed to consider the provisions of the Principal Act and the Regulations in more detail, it should be noted that the Regulations are not confined in their application to bodies corporate as such and companies incorporated under the Companies Acts. As is frequently the case with EU directives and regulations, they apply to 'undertakings', which include partnerships and other unincorporated bodies.

[30.76] Under the 1992 Regulations, the following parent undertakings are obliged to present group accounts in accordance with the regulations.

    (1)   companies limited by shares;

    (2)   companies limited by guarantee;

    (3)   unlimited companies or partnerships, where all the members which do not have a limit on their liability are either:

        (a) companies limited by shares or guarantees;

        (b) equivalent bodies not governed by the law of the State;

        (c) any combination of (a) or (b);

        (d) themselves unlimited companies or partnerships of this kind governed by the law of the State; or

        (e) themselves equivalent bodies of this kind, governed by the laws of an EU member state.

[30.77] The exemptions from the requirement to prepare and present group accounts must next be considered. First, private companies may be exempted depending on their size. Regulation 7 of the 1992 Regulations provides that a parent undertaking which is a private company need not comply with the requirement to prepare and present group accounts where it meets two of the following three conditions;

    (1)   the balance sheet total of the parent undertaking and its subsidiary undertakings together does not exceed £6 million;

    (2)   the amount of the turnover of the parent undertaking and its subsidiary undertakings together does not exceed £12 million.

    (3)   the average number of persons employed by the parent undertaking and its subsidiary undertakings together does not exceed 250.

[30.78] The exemptions will not apply where:

(1) any shares, debentures or other debt securities of the parent undertaking or of one of its subsidiary undertakings have been admitted to official listing on a stock exchange established in a member state;

(2) The parent undertaking or any of its subsidiary undertakings is one of the financial institutions listed in reg 6(2) such as a bank, a trustee savings bank, a hire purchase company, etc.

[30.79] Parent undertakings are also exempted from the obligation to prepare group accounts where the parent undertaking is itself a subsidiary of another undertaking established under the laws of the member state of the EU and all its shares or 90% of them are held by that parent undertaking. The remaining shareholders in the exempted parent must also have approved of the exemption. Again, this exemption does not apply to a parent undertaking whose shares, debentures, or other debt securities have been admitted to official listing on a Stock Exchange established in the EU.

[30.80] The following conditions must be met before an undertaking can avail of the exemption referred to in the last paragraph:

(1) The exempted parent and all its subsidiary undertakings must be dealt with in the group accounts prepared by the parent undertaking.

(2) These group accounts and the report of the directors of the parent undertaking must be prepared and audited according to the law of the member state in which it is established and in accordance with the Seventh Directive.

(3) There must be annexed to the next annual return of the exempted parent the group accounts referred to in (1) above, the directors' report and the auditor's report.

(4) The notes on the annual accounts of the exempted parent must disclose the name and registered office of the parent undertaking and the exemption from the obligation to draw up group accounts and a directors' report.

(5) There must be annexed to the group accounts, the directors' report and auditor's report a translation in the English or Irish languages of any of these documents that are not in either of those languages.

[30.81] An exemption is also available to a parent undertaking where that parent undertaking is a subsidiary undertaking of another undertaking established under the law of a member state, but less than 90% of its shares are held by that parent undertaking so that the exemption set out in the earlier paragraph does not apply. Such an undertaking will be exempted unless shareholders or members holding an aggregate of 10% or more in nominal value of the total share capital request the preparation of group accounts not less than six months before the end of its financial year. Again, this exemption will only be available if the conditions set out in the last paragraph are met and it will not apply to a parent undertaking any of whose shares, debentures or other debt securities have been admitted to official listing on a stock exchange established in a member state.

[30.82] Under the Principal Act, the directors of the holding company are required to ensure that, except where there are good reasons against it, the financial years of each of its subsidiaries are to coincide with the company's own financial year. The Minister has power on the application or with the consent of the directors to direct that the holding of an annual general meeting, the making of the return and the submission of the accounts to the meeting be postponed from one calendar year to the next with a view to enabling the subsidiary's financial year to end with that of its holding company. A director who fails to take all reasonable steps to secure compliance by the company with the requirements as to the financial year is liable on summary conviction to a fine not exceeding £250.

[30.83] The 1992 Regulations contain further provisions in this area. They provide that group accounts must be drawn up as of the same date as the annual accounts of the parent undertaking. If the financial year of a subsidiary undertaking dealt with in the group accounts differs from that of the parent undertaking, the group accounts are to be drawn up from the accounts of the subsidiary undertaking for its financial year last ending before the end of the parent undertaking's financial year, provided that year ended no more than three months before that of the parent undertaking. Alternatively, the group accounts are to be drawn up from interim accounts prepared by the subsidiary undertaking as at the end of the parent undertaking's financial year. Under reg 5(1) at the end of its financial year, a parent undertaking must prepare group accounts in accordance with the Regulations and the accounts are to be laid before the annual general meeting at the same time as the undertaking's annual accounts are so laid.

[30.84] Under reg 13 of the 1992 Regulations, group accounts must consist of:

(1)   a consolidated balance sheet dealing with the state of affairs of the parent undertaking and its subsidiary undertakings as a whole;

(2)   a consolidated profit and loss account dealing, as provided for in the Regulations, with the profit or loss of the parent undertaking and its subsidiary undertakings as a whole, and

(3)   notes on the accounts giving additional information required by the Regulations.

[30.85] By consolidated accounts are meant accounts in which the assets and liabilities, profits and losses of the subsidiary undertakings and the parent undertaking are grouped together under the appropriate headings. As we have already noted, these requirements can no longer be departed from by the directors, as was the case under the provisions of the Principal Act.

[30.86] As in the case of individual accounts, the group accounts must give a 'true and fair view' of the state of affairs as at the end of the financial year and the profit or loss for the financial year of the parent undertaking and subsidiary undertakings as a whole. If the accounts as drawn up in accordance with the regulations would not give such a 'true and fair view', the necessary additional information must be provided in the accounts.

[30.87] The 1992 Regulations provide that, in certain circumstances, a subsidiary undertaking need not be included in group accounts. Thus, it need not be included where that is not necessary for giving a true and fair view of the state of affairs of the group as a whole. Nor need it be included where:

(1)   severe long term restrictions substantially hinder the parent undertaking in the exercise of its rights over the assets or management of the subsidiary;

(2)   the information necessary cannot be obtained without disproportionate expense or undue delay; or

(3)   the shares of the subsidiary are held by the parent undertaking exclusively with a view to their subsequent resale.

[30.88] Other subsidiary undertakings *must* be excluded from the group accounts, ie where their activities are so different from those of the other undertakings that their inclusion would be incompatible with the obligation to give a true and fair view. The reasons must, however, be disclosed in the notes to the group accounts.

[30.89] Regulation 15 provides that the Schedule to the 1986 Act, the requirements of which are considered in detail above, are to apply to group accounts prepared in compliance with the 1992 Regulations as they apply to annual accounts prepared under that Act, subject to any necessary modifications to take account of differences between group accounts and annual accounts or the provisions of the Regulations.

[30.90] Thus, as we have seen, certain subsidiary undertakings need not be included in group accounts or must be excluded from such. However, the Regulations also provide that all such subsidiary undertakings are to be treated as a subsidiary undertaking of the group. As a result, they are captured by the provisions of para 45 of the Schedule, which requires amounts attributable to dealings with or interests in a parent undertaking or subsidiary undertaking to be shown as separate items in the balance sheet or in a note to the company's accounts. Similarly, a parent undertaking which is itself a subsidiary undertaking is to be treated as a subsidiary undertaking of the grandparent undertaking (if it can be so described) and the references in para 45 to 'fellow subsidiary undertakings' are to be construed accordingly. (Paragraph 45 requires amounts attributable to dealings with or interests in fellow subsidiary undertakings to be similarly shown as separate items.)

[30.91] Another departure is permitted in the case of the treatment of 'stocks' in the balance sheet. These need not be divided into separate categories such as raw materials, work in progress, etc if the directors think that undue expense would be thereby incurred: they may simply be shown as a single item under the heading 'stocks'.

[30.92] A parent undertaking is not required to prepare an individual profit and loss account where it is required to prepare and does prepare group accounts in accordance with the regulations. However, the notes to the undertaking's individual balance sheet must show the profit or loss for the financial year determined in accordance with the 1986 Act and the fact that the undertaking has availed of this exemption must be disclosed in its individual accounts and in the group accounts.

[30.93] Where the composition of the undertakings dealt with in the group accounts has changed significantly in the course of a financial year, the group accounts must include information which makes the comparison of successive sets of group accounts 'meaningful'.

[30.94] There are also provisions in the regulations dealing with 'joint ventures'. Where a parent undertaking or one of its subsidiaries dealt with in the group accounts manages another undertaking jointly with one or more undertakings which are not so dealt with, the other undertaking - described as a 'joint venture' - may be 'proportionally' consolidated in the group accounts. This means that it is to be dealt with in proportion to the rights held in its capital by the parent undertaking or subsidiary being dealt with in the group accounts.

[30.95] There are further provisions in the regulations concerning 'associated undertakings'. These are undertakings in which a parent or subsidiary undertaking dealt with in the group accounts has a 'participating interest' and over whose operating and financial policy it exercises a 'significant influence'. Where an undertaking holds 20% or more of the voting rights in another undertaking, it is to be presumed to exercise such an influence unless the contrary is shown. A subsidiary undertaking or a joint venture which has been proportionately consolidated in accordance with the regulations cannot be an associated undertaking.

[30.96] The interest of an associated undertaking and the amount of the profit and loss attributed to that interest is to be shown in the group accounts by way of the 'equity method' of accounting. In particular, the goodwill is to be dealt with in accordance with the Schedule to the 1986 Act, ie its value is to be reduced for depreciation over a specified period chosen by the directors, which is not to exceed the useful economic life of the goodwill in question.

[30.97] The 1992 Regulations also require that transactions between the different undertakings within the group are not taken into account in the group accounts, as this would not give a true and fair view of the state of affairs of the group as a whole. Regulation 25 requires the group accounts to show the assets, liabilities, state of affairs and profit or loss of the group as if it consisted of a single undertaking. Hence, debts and claims between the undertakings must be eliminated from the accounts: similarly, income and expenditure relating to transactions between the undertakings must also be eliminated from the accounts. Where profits and losses resulting from transactions between the undertakings are included in the book value of assets, they must also be eliminated from the accounts.

[30.98] The valuation methods contained in the Schedule to the 1986 Act apply to the amounts included in the group accounts and must be applied consistently within the accounts. The parent undertaking must also apply the same methods of valuation in drawing up group accounts as it applies in drawing up its annual accounts. The directors, however, may depart from this requirement where they think that is necessary to give a true and fair view. The reasons for such a departure must be disclosed in the notes to the group accounts.

[30.99] When the assets and liabilities of an undertaking dealt with in the group accounts have been valued by a different method from that being used in the group accounts, they must be revalued in accordance with the method used in the group accounts. Such a revaluation need not be made, however, where it is not material to the purpose of giving a true and fair view or where, in the opinion of the directors, there are special reasons for departing from this requirement. Any such departure and the reasons therefor must be stated in the notes to the group accounts.

[30.100] In addition to the information which must be supplied by way of notes to the accounts under the Principal Act and the 1986 Act, the Regulations require further information to be supplied in the case of group accounts. They relate to the following topics:

(1)   acquisitions of undertakings;

(2)   the basis on which currencies have been translated into other currencies in the group accounts;

(3) details of debts owed by the group, eg whether they are repayable by instalments;

(4) the number of persons employed in the financial year by each of the undertakings;

(5) the aggregate amount of staff costs, save insofar as the amount is stated in the group profit and loss account;

(6) the information as to pension commitments, emoluments and compensation required in the case of individual accounts which extend, in the case of group accounts, to commitments, emoluments and compensation relating to directors or past directors of the parent undertaking in respect of duties relating to the parent undertaking, to any of its subsidiary undertakings or to undertakings proportionally consolidated in accordance with the Regulations or to associated undertakings;

(7) transactions, arrangements and agreements entered into by a director of the parent undertaking with an undertaking proportionally consolidated or an associated undertaking.

[30.101] Information must also be given in relation to each undertaking dealt with in the group accounts, including its name and registered office, the aggregate of the qualifying capital interests held in the undertaking by each of the undertakings and which of the provisions set out above gave rise to the undertaking being dealt with in the group accounts. This information must also be given in respect of every undertaking which has been excluded from the group accounts by virtue of the exemptions already dealt with, every associated undertaking, every undertaking that has been proportionally consolidated and every undertaking of 'substantial interest'.

[30.102] The 1992 Regulations also contain requirements as to the accounting method which is to be adopted where an undertaking becomes a subsidiary undertaking of a parent undertaking. This is described as an 'acquisition' and is to be accounted for by what is called 'the acquisition method' of accounting, unless the conditions of accounting for it as a 'merger' are met and the 'merger method' of accounting is adopted.

[30.103] The acquisition method of accounting is as follows. The 'identifiable assets and liabilities' of the acquired undertaking are to be included in the consolidated balance sheet at their fair values as of the date of acquisition. By 'identifiable assets or liabilities' is meant the assets or liabilities which are capable of being disposed of or discharged separately, without disposing of a business of the undertaking. Under this method, the income and expenditure of the acquired undertaking are to be brought into the group accounts only as from the date of acquisition. There is to be set off, against the cost of acquiring the interest in the shares of the undertaking, the interest of the acquiring undertakings in the adjusted capital and reserves of the acquired undertaking. If the resulting amount is positive, it is to be treated as goodwill and the provisions in the Schedule to the 1986 Act in relation to goodwill (which as already mentioned, require the consideration for any goodwill to be depreciated over a period chosen by the directors) are to apply. If the resulting amount is negative, it is to be treated as 'a negative consolidation difference'.

[30.104] The cost of acquisition is the amount of any cash consideration and the fair value of any other consideration, together with such amounts (if any) in respect of fees and other expenses of the acquisition as the parent undertaking may determine. The adjusted capital and reserves of the acquired undertaking are its capital and reserves at the date of the acquisition after adjusting the identifiable assets and liabilities to fair values as of that date.

[30.105] The merger method of accounting may only be adopted where:

(1)   at least 90% of the nominal value of the relevant shares in the acquired undertaking are held by or on behalf of the acquiring undertaking;

(2)   this proportion was attained pursuant to an arrangement under which the acquiring undertaking issued equity shares;

(3)   the fair value of any consideration other than the issue of equity shares did not exceed 10% of the nominal value of the equity shares issued.

'Relevant shares' are those carrying an unrestricted right to participate both in distributions and in the assets of the undertaking upon liquidation.

[30.106] The merger method of accounting is as follows. The assets and liabilities of the acquired undertaking are to be brought into the group accounts at the figures at which they stand in that undertaking's accounts, subject to any adjustment authorised or acquired by the Regulations. The income and expenditure of the acquired undertaking are to be included in the group accounts for the entire financial year, including the period before the acquisition. Corresponding amounts are to be shown in respect of the previous financial year as if the undertaking had been included in the consolidation throughout that year. The nominal value of the issued share capital of the acquired undertaking held by the acquiring undertaking is then set off against the appropriate amount in respect of the shares issued by the undertakings as part of the arrangement already referred to and the fair value of any other consideration involved. The balance is to be shown as an adjustment to the consolidated reserves.

[30.107] It will be seen that, where the merger method can be and is employed, no problem arises if there is a difference between the nominal value of the shares issued by the acquiring undertaking and the nominal value of the shares being acquired. Any such difference is simply reflected in an adjustment in the reserves. However, since there is no provision for 'merger relief' as there is in the United Kingdom, it would seem to follow that pre-acquisition profits must be transferred to the share premium account and will not be available for distribution by way of dividend[31].

The merger method has been used infrequently in practice in Ireland and the United Kingdom[32].

Auditors

General

[30.108] Since the enactment of the Principal Act in 1964, all companies have been obliged by law to submit their accounts at least once a year to scrutiny by an independent, professionally qualified auditor. Until then, only public companies were under such a duty. The importance of the audit has grown significantly since then because of a number of factors: the increasing tendency of wrongdoers to avail of the corporate structure and limited liability for illegal purposes, the greater complexity of the laws governing the preparation of accounts and the extent to which accountancy has become a sophisticated and highly specialised profession. In the result, the legal requirements as to the audit have, not surprisingly, been the subject of much attention both by the legislature and the courts in recent years.

[30.109] The principal object of the audit is to ensure that the company's accounts give a true and fair view of the state of the company's affairs for the relevant period, that they comply with the requirements of the Acts and that they give shareholders, creditors and others dealing with the company the information they should have for their own protection. Apart altogether from the special interests of shareholders and creditors, there is a general public interest in the maintenance by companies of proper accounts. This is particularly the case in Ireland, where so many companies, including relatively large organisations, are private companies whose accounts in the result do not attract the same scrutiny as public companies.

[30.110] As we have noted, however, concern was expressed by the Task Force on Small Business that the requirement that the accounts of all companies should be audited, irrespective of their size, was unduly onerous in the case of small businesses and their recommendations for a change in the law were endorsed by the Company Law Review Group. The 1999 (No 2) Act now

---

[31] See para **[9.55]** above.

[32] Doubts, it would seem, persist as to its legality despite the Regulations: see Brennan and Pierce, *Irish Company Accounts, Regulation and Reporting.*

provides for some degree of exemption, although not to the same extent as that recommended by the Task Force.

[30.111] A company will be eligible for exemption where the amount of its turnover does not exceed £250,000, its balance sheet total does not exceed £1,500,000 and the average number of persons employed by the company does not exceed 50. The exemption is only available to a company which has submitted its annual return on time in the current and preceding financial year. The exemption is not available in the case of a 'parent undertaking' or a 'subsidiary undertaking' or the holder of a licence to carry on business as a bank or an insurance undertaking or publicly quoted companies on the stock exchange and similar businesses. The exemption is only available where the directors of the company are of the opinion that it will satisfy these conditions in respect of a particular financial year and that the company should avail itself of the exemption; the decision to that effect must also be recorded in the minutes of the meeting concerned. Except where the financial year is the first year of the company, the company must also have met the same conditions in respect of the preceding financial year. Where the company avails itself of the exemption in a financial year, the balance sheet must contain a statement by the directors of the company to that effect. The company may not avail itself of the exemption where members of the company holding shares that confer, in aggregate, not less than 1/10th of the total voting rights in the company, so request.

[30.112] Where the company decides to terminate the appointment of an auditor because they are availing of the exemption, the auditor must, within 21 days of being notified by the company of that decision, serve a notice on the company. That notice must either state that there are no circumstances connected with the company's decision which the auditor considers should be brought to the notice of the members or creditors of the company or, if there are such circumstances, a statement of them. The auditor must also send a copy of that notice to the Registrar and the company in turn must send the notice to everyone entitled to be given copies of documents under s 9(5) of the Principal Act. The copies need not be sent to such persons where the Court, on an application being made, is satisfied that it contains material which has been included to secure needless publicity for defamatory matter.

[30.113] Where an exemption ceases to have effect in relation to a company, the directors of the company must appoint an auditor to the company as soon as may be after the circumstances have arisen which have lead to the exemption ceasing to have effect.

[30.114] We examine first the qualifications of auditors in respect of which the 1990 Act contained new provisions implementing the requirements of the Eighth EU Directive. Then we deal with the manner in which they may be appointed and removed in respect of which the 1990 Act also contained new and elaborate provisions. Finally we consider the duties and powers of auditors and the circumstances in which and the persons to whom they are liable for negligence in the performance of their duties.

Qualifications of auditors

[30.115] The qualifications required before a person can act as the auditor of a company are set out in s 187 of the 1990 Act. It provides that only the following can so act:

(1)   members of bodies of accountants recognised by the Minister for the purposes of the section who hold valid practising certificates from such bodies;

(2)   persons holding accountancy qualifications granted by bodies of accountants which are, in the opinion of the Minister, of a standard not less than that required for membership of the recognised bodies and which would entitle them to be granted practising certificates by the bodies in question and who are authorised by the Minister to be so appointed;

(3)   persons who were members on 31 December 1990 of bodies of accountants recognised under s 162(1) of the Principal Act;

(4)   persons authorised by the Minister so to act before 3 February 1983 and still so authorised;

(5)   during a transitional period, persons undergoing professional or practical training[33];

(6)   persons declared by the Minister to be so qualified who hold either a qualification entitling them to audit accounts under the law of a specified foreign country or a specified accountancy qualification recognised under the law of another country[34].

[30.116] The bodies recognised by the Minister under the Principal Act are:

(1)   The Institute of Chartered Accountants in Ireland;

(2)   The Institute of Chartered Accountants in England and Wales;

(3)   The Institute of Chartered Accountants of Scotland;

(4)   The Institute of Certified Public Accountants in Ireland;

(5)   The Chartered Association of Certified Accountants.

---

[33] Companies Act 1990, s 188.
[34] Companies Act 1990, s 190.

Those who were members of any of these bodies on 31 December 1990 are, accordingly, qualified to act as auditors. Under s 191(1) of the 1990 Act, such bodies were given a period of three months from the commencement of the section within which to satisfy the Minister that they met certain requirements: in the event of their being met, they are entitled to have their recognition renewed. Similarly, any other body that satisfies the Minister as to these matters may be granted recognition. In the event of any of the existing bodies failing to satisfy the requirements, their recognition must be withdrawn.

[30.117] The requirements of s 191(1) are as follows:

(1)   The standards relating to training, qualifications and repute required by the body for the awarding of a practising certificate must be not less than those prescribed by specified articles of the Eighth EU Directive.

(2)   The Minister must be satisfied as to the standards the body applies in the areas of ethics, codes of conduct and practice, independence, professional integrity, technical standards and disciplinary procedures.

[30.118] The relevant articles of the Directive - Articles 3 to 6, 18 and 19 - may be briefly summarised. They stipulate that only persons 'of good repute' who are not carrying on activities incompatible with statutory auditing are to be 'approved persons' for carrying out such audits. To qualify as such, they must have attained university entrance level and completed a course of theoretical instruction, undergone practical training and passed an examination of professional competence of university final examination level recognised by the State. The subjects to be included are specified in Article 6 and it is also stipulated that a trainee must complete a minimum of three years' practical training in *inter alia* the auditing of annual accounts, consolidated accounts or similar financial statements.

[30.119] There are also provisions in the 1990 Act empowering the Minister to consult with any person or body as to the conditions imposed or standards required by the respective professional bodies. The Minister may also require a recognised body of accountants to prepare and submit to him for his approval codes of professional conduct for its members.

[30.120] The following categories are disqualified from being appointed as auditors

(1)   officers and servants of the company (which would include the directors and secretary);

(2)   a person who has been an officer or servant during a period in respect of which accounts would have to be audited by him if he were an auditor;

(3) a parent, spouse, brother, sister or child of an officer of the company;

(4) a person who is a partner of or in the employment of an officer of the company;

(5) a person who is disqualified from acting as an auditor of the company's holding company or one or more of its subsidiaries;

(6) a body corporate.[35]

[30.121] These categories are set out in s 187(2) of the 1990 Act which replaced s 162 of the Principal Act. The range of disqualified persons is significantly greater as a result. In particular, it should be noted that members of the immediate families of officers and servants of the company may not act as its auditors. In addition, it is no longer possible for the partner or employee of an officer of a private company to act as its auditor. The penalties for acting when disqualified have also been greatly strengthened: the offender is liable on summary conviction to a fine not exceeding £1,000 and, for continued contravention, to a daily default fine not exceeding £50 and on indictment to a fine not exceeding £5,000 and, for continued contravention, to a daily default fine not exceeding £100.

Appointment, removal, resignation and remuneration of auditors

[30.122] Every company must appoint an auditor or auditors at each annual general meeting to hold office until the next annual general meeting. The first auditors may be appointed by the directors at any time before the first annual general meeting and hold office until the conclusion of that meeting. The company may, however, remove such auditors at a general meeting and substitute for them persons who have been nominated for appointment by any member of the company and of whose nomination notice has been given to the members not less than 14 days before the date of the meeting[36].

[30.123] Until recently this was the only power which the shareholders had to remove auditors. (They could, however, decline to reappoint a retiring auditor.) Under the 1990 Act, however, any auditors, and not merely those first appointed, can be removed at any time by the company. This can be done by an ordinary resolution at a general meeting and the auditor thus removed may be replaced by any other qualified person nominated by any member of whose nomination notice has been given to the members. 'Extended notice' must be given of a resolution to remove an auditor and the auditor has certain rights to be heard by the members in relation to his removal. Both these topics are dealt with in more detail below.

---

[35] Companies Act 1990, s 187(2).
[36] Companies Act 1963, s 160.

[30.124] At every annual general meeting a retiring auditor, however appointed, must be re-appointed without any resolution being passed unless:

(1)   he is not qualified for re-appointment;

(2)   a resolution has been passed at that meeting appointing someone instead of him or providing expressly that he is not to be re-appointed; or

(3)   he has given the company notice in writing of his unwillingness to be re-appointed[37].

[30.125] The directors or the company in general meeting may fill casual vacancies in the office of auditor, ie vacancies occurring as a result of death or disqualification during the course of the year, but while any vacancy continues, the surviving auditor or auditors may continue to act[38].

[30.126] 'Extended notice' - ie at least 28 days' notice[39] must be given of:

(1)   a resolution at the annual general meeting proposing the appointment of someone other than the retiring auditors as auditor or providing expressly that a retiring auditor is not to be re-appointed;

(2)   a resolution at a general meeting removing an auditor before the expiration of his term of office;

(3)   a resolution at a general meeting of a company filling a casual vacancy in the office of auditor.

[30.127] In the case of all such resolutions, the auditor whose replacement is envisaged must be sent a copy of the intended resolution. Where the resolution proposes the removal of an auditor or that a retiring auditor be not re-appointed or that he be replaced, the auditor affected has certain rights to be heard in his own defence by the meeting. He may make representations in writing (which cannot be unreasonably lengthy) to the company and request that the members of the company be notified of them. Where he avails of this right, the company must state that the representations have been received in the notice given to the members of the resolution. The company must also send a copy of the representations to every member of the company to whom notice of the meeting is sent. If a copy of the representations is not sent out because it is received too late or because of the company's default, the auditor may require them to be read out at the meeting. There is also provision for an application to the court to prevent the auditor's right to make representations being abused. Where the court is satisfied that the rights are being used to secure 'needless publicity for

---

[37] Companies Act 1963, s 160(2).

[38] Companies Act 1963, s 160(4).

[39] See para **[25.29]** above.

defamatory matter' the representations need not be sent out or read at the meeting and the auditor may be ordered to pay the company's costs of the application[40].

[30.128] An auditor who has been removed is given the additional right by the 1990 Act to attend a meeting of the company in person. He can attend both the annual general meeting at which, but for his removal, his term would have expired and the general meeting at which it is proposed to fill the vacancy caused by his removal. He is also entitled to receive any notices or communications relating to such a meeting which a member is entitled to receive. He is also entitled to be heard at any such meetings on any part of the business which concerns him as a former auditor[41].

[30.129] The underlying philosophy of all these provisions is to guard against the removal of auditors whose zeal in discharging their statutory duties may prove awkward for the directors. At the same time, they are intended to give some form of control to the shareholders, enabling them to remove auditors who go to the other extreme of undue compliance with the directors' wishes. Obviously the directors and shareholders may frustrate these objectives, at least for a time, by simply not appointing any auditors. The Principal Act sought to meet this by empowering the Minister to appoint auditors where this happened, but made no provision for a situation in which no one was aware of the non-appointment. Section 183 of the 1990 Act is intended to bridge this gap by requiring the company to give notice to the Minister that his powers have become exercisable within a week of this happening. Similarly, the company must give notice to the Registrar of any resolution removing an auditor within 14 days of the meeting at which the resolution was passed. If the company fails to give these notices, they and every officer in default are guilty of an offence and liable on summary conviction to a fine not exceeding £1,000.

[30.130] Until recently, an auditor could not retire during the year. He was obliged to wait until the annual general meeting at which stage he can, as we have seen, signify his unwillingness to be re-appointed. Even then, he could not draw the attention of the members, or the wider public, to any circumstances which prompted his resignation and which he might consider should be known to those concerned. The 1990 Act provided machinery for the first time which enables auditors concerned with the manner in which a company's affairs are being conducted to resign without waiting for the annual general meeting and to indicate the reasons for their resignation.

---

[40] Companies Act 1963, s 161 as amended by the Companies Act 1990, s 184.
[41] Companies Act 1963, s 161 as amended by the Companies Act 1990, s 184.

[30.131] Section 185 enables an auditor to resign by serving a notice to that effect on the company. The notice takes effect on the day specified in the notice. It must contain either a statement to the effect that there are no circumstances connected with the resignation which he considers should be brought to the notice of the members or creditors or a statement of any such circumstances. The auditor must send a copy of the notice within 14 days after its service to the Registrar. Where it states that there are circumstances which should be brought to the attention of the members or creditors, the company must sent a copy within 14 days from service to every person who is entitled to be sent copies of the accounts. Failure to circulate a notice is a criminal offence rendering the company and every officer in default liable, on summary conviction, to a fine not exceeding £1,000 or imprisonment for a term not exceeding 12 months or to both or, on indictment, to a fine not exceeding £10,000 or imprisonment for a term not exceeding three years or to both. The notice need not be circulated, however, where the court, on the application of the company or any person claiming to be aggrieved, is satisfied that it contains material which has been included to secure 'needless publicity for defamatory matter'. The court may order the company's costs of such an application to be paid by the auditor.

[30.132] An auditor resigning under these provisions may also requisition the holding of a general meeting of the company for the purpose of considering any account and explanation he may wish to give the meeting of the circumstances connected with his resignation[42]. He may also request the company to circulate to its members a further statement in writing prepared by him as to those circumstances. The company must then in its notice of the meeting state that such a statement has been made by the auditor and send a copy to the Registrar and the persons entitled to receive the balance sheet. There are similar provisions rendering non-compliance by the company and its officers a criminal offence and enabling the court to order that a notice intended to give needless publicity to defamatory matter need not be circulated.

[30.133] An auditor who has resigned under these provisions has the same right to attend and be heard at the relevant meetings of the company as an auditor who has been removed.

[30.134] Where an auditor is appointed by the directors or the Minister, his remuneration is fixed by the directors or the Minister as the case may be. In all other cases, his remuneration must be fixed by the company in general meeting or in such manner as the company at the annual general meeting may determine. It is common practice for the annual general meeting to resolve that the auditors' remuneration be fixed by the directors.

---

[42] Companies Act 1990, s 186.

Status and duties of auditors

[30.135] It has been held in England that an auditor appointed under the section corresponding to s 160 of the Principal Act is an 'officer' of the company[43]. It would seem, however, that while he may be regarded as an agent of the company when carrying out his duties under the Acts, such as the audit, he is not an agent for other purposes[44].

[30.136] The statutory duty of the auditors is to make a report to the members on the accounts examined by them, and on every balance sheet, profit and loss account and all group accounts laid before the company in general meeting during their term of office[45]. The matters which must be dealt with are set out in the Seventh Schedule to the Principal Act. The auditors must state:

(1)   whether they have obtained all the information and explanations which to the best of their knowledge and belief were necessary for the purposes of the audit;

(2)   whether, in their opinion, proper books of account have been kept by the company, so far as appears from their examination of those books, and proper returns adequate for the purposes of their audit have been received from branches not visited by them;

(3)   whether the company's balance sheet and (unless it is framed as a consolidated profit and loss account) profit and loss account dealt with by the report are in agreement with the books of account and returns;

(4)   whether, in their opinion and to the best of their information and according to the explanations given to them, the accounts give the information required by the Acts in the manner so required and give a true and fair view

(a) in the case of the balance sheet of the state of the company's affairs as at the end of its financial year; and

(b) in the case of the profit and loss account, of the profit or loss for its financial year

or, as the case may be, give a true and fair view thereof subject to the non-disclosure (which must be indicated in the report) of any matters which are not required to be disclosed in the case of banking and discount companies, assurance companies and other companies prescribed by the Minister[46];

---

[43]   *R v Shacter* [1960] 2 QB 252.
[44]   *Re Transplanters (Holding Companies) Ltd* [1958] 2 All ER 711.
[45]   Companies Act 1963, s 163.
[46]   See para **[30.19]** above.

(5) in the case of a company which is a holding company and which submits group accounts whether, in their opinion the group accounts have been properly prepared in accordance with the Acts so as to give a true and fair view of the state of affairs and profit or loss of the company and its subsidiaries dealt with thereby, so far as concerns members of the company, or as the case may be, so as to give a true and fair view thereof subject to the non-disclosure (which must be indicated in the report) of any matters which are not required to be disclosed in the case of banking and discount companies etc.

[30.137] If the auditors are not satisfied as to any of these matters, it is their duty to make their reservations clear by making the relevant statement subject to an appropriate qualification. In deciding whether any statement should be qualified, the auditors must use their own judgment and express their own opinion: if they do so and for that purpose use the skill and care which might reasonably be expected of them as competent and careful auditors, they will have performed their statutory duty[47].

[30.138] The auditors are also required under s 15 of the 1986 Act to consider whether the information given by the directors in their report is consistent with the accounts for the relevant year and to state in their report whether, in their opinion, such information is consistent with the accounts.

[30.139] In modern circumstances more will frequently be expected of auditors than the statutory minimum: it is now standard practice, for example, for them to furnish a commentary on the company's finances to the directors.

[30.140] The auditor's responsibility is an onerous one. But, in the celebrated phrase of Lopes LJ, the law treats the auditor as 'a watchdog, not a bloodhound'[48]. He must ensure that there are not errors in the accounts and that they are not in any way misleading. But he is not a detective and is not expected to approach the audit on the assumption that the company has been dishonestly managed. Perhaps the most acceptable modern statement of his responsibility is by Lord Denning:

'His vital task is to take care to see that errors be not made, be they errors of computation, or errors of omission or commission, or downright untruths. To perform this task properly he must come to it with an inquiring mind - not suspicious of dishonesty, I agree - but suspecting that someone may have made a mistake somewhere and that a check must be made to ensure that there has been none.'[49]

---

47 *Palmer's Company Law* (25th edn), Vol 2, 9.522.
48 *Re Kingston Cotton Mill Co (No 2)* [1896] 2 Ch 279 at 288.
49 *Fomento (Sterling Area) Ltd v Selsdon Fountain Co* [1958] 1 All ER 11.

[30.141] Thus in *Thomas Gerrard & Sons Ltd*[50], auditors were held liable where a managing director had falsified the accounts by altering invoices and the auditors, having come across the altered invoices, failed to make sufficiently exhaustive inquiries.

[30.142] The auditor is required to perform his duty with reasonable skill and care. The standard expected of him is that which would be expected of any careful and competent auditor. In modern circumstances, where both accountancy and auditing practices have become stricter, this may involve a different standard in specific areas than is suggested by the older English authorities. Thus, while Lopes LJ in the case already referred to, said that it was not the duty of the auditor to take stock – 'he its not a stock expert[51]' - this would have to be treated with some caution today where a more vigilant role is expected of auditors in relation to stock-taking[52]. They are required to ensure that such assets are appropriately valued and must have regard, for example, to retention of title clauses, particularly where unmixed goods are involved[53].

[30.143] The 1990 Act imposed on auditors for the first time an express duty to take certain positive steps in the event of their taking the view that all is not well with the way in which the company is keeping - or not keeping - its accounts. If they form the opinion that the company is contravening their obligations in relation to the keeping of proper accounts (as laid down in s 202 of the 1990 Act), they must serve a notice to that effect on the company 'as soon as may be' and must also notify the Registrar not more than seven days later of the notice. Failure to take such steps is a criminal offence punishable on summary conviction by a fine not exceeding £1,000 or imprisonment for a term not exceeding 12 months and, on indictment, to a fine not exceeding £1,000 or a term of imprisonment not exceeding three years or both[54].

Rights of auditors

[30.144] For the purpose of carrying out his duties, the auditor has a right of access at all reasonable times to the books, accounts and vouchers of the company. He is also entitled to require from the officers of the company such information and explanations as he thinks necessary for the performance of those duties. He is also entitled to attend any general meeting of the company and has the same right to receive notices and other communications relating to general meetings as the members. He is entitled to be heard at any general

---

[50] [1968] Ch 455.

[51] *Re Kingston Cotton Mill Co (No 2)* [1896] 2 Ch 279 at 289.

[52] *Palmer's Company Law* (25th edn), Vol 2, 9.546.

[53] See para **[20.51]** above.

[54] Companies Act 1990, s 194.

meeting which he attends on any part of the business which concerns him as auditor[55].

[30.145] In the case of a holding company, the 1990 Act imposes an express duty on its subsidiaries (where they are incorporated in the State) to give to the auditors of the holding company such information and explanations as they may reasonably require for the purposes of their duties as such auditors. Where the subsidiary is outside the State it is the holding company's duty, if required by its auditors to do so, to take all such steps as are reasonably open to it to obtain such information and explanations. If a company or auditor fails to comply with these requirements within five days, they and every officer in default are guilty of a criminal offence and liable, on summary conviction, to a fine not exceeding £1,000 and, on indictment, to a fine not exceeding £10,000. It is a defence, however, for a person to show that it was not reasonably possible for him to comply within the five day period and that he complied as soon as was reasonably possible after that period[56].

[30.146] The rights conferred in these areas by the Acts on auditors cannot under any circumstances be modified or abridged by the memorandum or articles of association.

Penalties for false statements to auditors

[30.147] The 1990 Act creates in s 197 a new criminal offence in wide ranging terms where false statements are made to the auditors of a company. An officer (and in this context the expression covers any employee) who knowingly or recklessly makes a statement to which the section applies that is 'misleading, false or deceptive' is guilty of the offence which is punishable, on summary conviction, with a fine not exceeding £1,000 or imprisonment for a term not exceeding twelve months or, on indictment, to a fine not exceeding £10,000 or imprisonment for a term not exceeding three years or both.

[30.148] The section applies to any statement, oral or written, which conveys, or purports to convey, any information or explanation which the auditors require or are entitled to require under the Acts as auditors. It is also an offence punishable in the same manner for an officer to fail to provide any information or explanations that the auditors require as auditors of the company or of its holding company within two days of its being required where it is within his knowledge or procurement. In this case, there is, however, a defence available that it was not reasonably possible for him to comply with the requirement within the two day period but that he complied as soon as it was reasonably possible to do so after the expiration.

---

[55] Companies Act 1963, s 163.
[56] Companies Act 1990, s 196.

Liability of auditors

[30.149] Where the auditor fails to perform his duties with reasonable skill and care he will be liable to the company for any damages which it may sustain as a result of his negligence.

[30.150] It is also clear, in the light of modern decisions, that the auditor will be liable to any other persons to whom he owes a duty of care when performing his statutory duties. Prior to the decision of the House of Lords in *Hedley Byrne & Co v Heller and Partners*[57], it had been thought that an action for damages for a negligent misstatement could only be maintained by persons to whom the person making the statement owed a duty in contract or a fiduciary duty. That decision established that the liability was not so confined: the court expressly approved the dissenting judgment of Denning LJ in *Candler v Crane Christmas & Co*[58] in which he held that accountants could be held liable to persons other than their clients for negligence in the preparation of auditing of accounts. Specifically, he was of the view that they were liable where they knew at all relevant times that their employer required the accounts to show them to a third party so as to induce him to act on them, and the accounts were then presented to the third party who proceeded to act upon them to his detriment. The same principle has been applied in at least three cases in Ireland[59].

[30.151] It was suggested in the first edition that the principle referred to in the last paragraph was capable of radical extension. It was pointed out that a number of English decisions appeared to recognise a potential liability on the part of those who issue documents of a particular character on which a relatively undefined category of persons may rely, such as certificates by local authorities as to the safety of foundations. These decisions - *Dutton v Bognor Regis Building Co*[60] and *Anns v Merton London Borough Council*[61] - were applied by the Supreme Court in *Siney v Dublin Corpn*[62]. It was said in the first edition that:

> 'It may be argued in the future that if a purchaser of whose existence the local authority was unaware when it issued a certificate to a builder can sue the authority when the relevant inspection was carried out negligently, there is no reason in principle why an auditor who issues a misleading report following a negligent audit may not be similarly liable to a prospective investor who relies on

---

[57] [1964] AC 465.
[58] [1951] 2 KB 164.
[59] *John Sisk & Son Ltd v Flinn* (unreported, 18 July 1984) (Finlay P); *Kelly v Haughey Boland & Co* [1989] ILRM 373; *Golden Vale Co-op Ltd v Barrett* (unreported, 16 March 1987) (O'Hanlon J).
[60] [1972] 1 QB 373.
[61] [1978] AC 728.
[62] [1980] IR 400.

that report, even though he had no reason to anticipate that the accounts were being audited for anything other than the usual statutory reasons.'

[30.152] However, in *Caparo Industries plc v Dickman*[63] the House of Lords firmly and unanimously rejected an attempt in that jurisdiction so to extend the liability of auditors. The plaintiffs, who already owned shares in a public company, launched a successful take-over bid shortly after the publication of the company's audited accounts. The plaintiffs said that they had made their take-over bid in reliance on the accounts which, they claimed, were seriously misleading. On the trial of a preliminary issue as to whether the auditors would be liable in the event of the plaintiffs establishing their allegation, Lawson J held that they would not be so liable. His decision was reversed by a majority of the Court of Appeal, but restored by the House of Lords.

The law lords declined to accept that auditors owed a duty of care to all prospective investors. Nor did they owe a duty to individual shareholders. (The plaintiff company came within both categories.) They pointed out that the carrying out of the audit was part of a general legislative scheme designed to protect the company itself and make available to those having an interest in its financial progress and stability the necessary information as to its affairs. It was not intended for the benefit of the public at large or potential investors. The fact that the statement of its affairs was put into general circulation did not render the auditors liable as the makers of the statement to the world at large: it might well be relied on by strangers for any one of a variety of purposes which the makers had no specific reason to anticipate. Subjecting them to liability so unrestricted in its scope would, it was said, expose them, in Cardozo J's celebrated formulation, to

'liability in an indeterminate amount for an indeterminate time to an indeterminate class.'[64]

It was also held that, while the auditors owed a duty of care to the shareholders as a body, they did not owe such a duty to them as individuals: the appropriate remedy for a breach of the auditors' duty was an action by the company itself.

[30.153] In its general approach to this problem, the House of Lords was clearly influenced by a developing tendency to move away from the broad statement of liability in negligence adopted by Lord Wilberforce in *Ann's* case, a development which culminated in the reversal of both *Dutton's* case and *Ann's* case by the same tribunal[65]. That statement of the law had treated liability as arising in every case where the relationship of proximity was such as to render it likely that

---

[63] (1990) BCLC 273.

[64] *Ultramares Corp v Touche* (1931) 255 NY 170 at 179.

[65] *Murphy v Brentwood District Council* [1990] 2 All ER 908.

damage would result from the defendant's carelessness, unless there were any countervailing considerations. Even before the two cases in question were reversed, doubts had been expressed as to whether the statement was too broad and in *Caparo Industries plc v Dickman*, Lord Bridge expressed his preference for a more traditional approach, stated in an Australian case[66] by Brennan J as follows:

'It is preferable in my view that the law should develop novel categories of negligence incrementally and by analogy with established categories rather than by a massive extension of a prima facie duty of care restrained only by indefinable "considerations which ought to negative, or to reduce or limit the scope of the duty or the class of persons to whom it is owed".'

[30.154] It remains to be seen whether a similar approach would be adopted in this country. The Supreme Court in *Ward v McMaster*[67] held that a local authority were liable for the negligence of a surveyor employed by a local authority where the house purchaser to the knowledge of the authority was relying on his report. It is interesting to note that, although a similar view was taken by the House of Lords, the decisions were distinguished in *Caparo's* case on the ground that in such a case advice is given for the purpose of a particular transaction and the adviser knows or ought to know that it will be relied on by a particular person or class of persons in connection with that transaction. This was contrasted with the duty of care owed to an unrestricted class which was claimed to exist in *Caparo's* case. However, in the absence of any detailed analysis in any of the decisions in Ireland of the underlying policy considerations, it cannot be predicted with any great confidence in which direction the law may evolve.

---

66 *Sutherland Shire Council v Heyman* (1985) 60 ALR 1.
67 [1988] IR 337.

Chapter 31

Dividends and Distribution of Profits

[31.01] We have seen that one of the rights of a shareholder is to be given a share of the company's profits at periodical intervals in the form of a money payment called a dividend. The payment of dividends is generally regulated by the memorandum and articles; but there are also certain legal principles applicable which are explained in this chapter. In particular, it is a fundamental principle that dividends cannot be paid out of the capital of the company, since this would have as its consequence an unauthorised reduction of the company's capital.

[31.02] It follows that dividends can only be paid out of the profits of the company. But it does not follow that whenever the company makes a profit, the shareholder is automatically entitled to a dividend: the company may decide not to distribute some or all of its profits in a particular year but instead to carry them to its reserves. A distinction has to be drawn, accordingly, between profits which are available for dividend and those which are not.

[31.03] These rules governing the payment of dividends might seem reasonably straightforward. Their application in practice, however, was not so simple; in particular there was room for a wide difference of opinion as to what were profits available for distribution. If a company sold some of its circulating or current assets, eg its stock in trade, for more than they cost, the surplus was usually a profit available for distribution. But what of the sale of a fixed asset, eg a factory building? Was the surplus on such a sale a profit available for distribution? If it was, did the same result follow when there was no sale and the asset was simply re-valued in the balance sheet: could such an unrealised capital profit, as it was called, be treated as a profit available for distribution? There were also difficulties in determining what were fixed assets and what were current assets: shares held by an investment company, for example, might reasonably be regarded as coming within either category.

[31.04] There was also the question of losses from previous years and how they were to be dealt with. Could a company take its accounting year in isolation and simply set off profits against losses in that year without taking into account losses made in previous years before calculating the amount available for distribution?

[31.05] The answers to many of the questions posed in the last paragraphs will be found in the 1983 Act. Part IV of that Act under the heading 'Restrictions on distributions of profits and assets' contained important new provisions in this area. In general, they are intended to implement the relevant requirements of the Second EU Directive which was concerned, as we have seen, with the maintenance by companies of their capital[1].

General power of company to pay dividends

[31.06] Every company has an implied power to apply its profits to the distribution of dividends among its members. Such a power exists, in other words, whether or not it is conferred on the company by its memorandum or articles[2]. It does not follow, however, that a company must apply its profits for that purpose; as we have seen, it is perfectly entitled to carry some or all of its profits to reserves or to provide for contingencies.

[31.07] The articles usually provide in what proportion dividends are to be paid as between members. As we have seen, the company is normally given power to issue preference shares which entitle the holders to the payment of a dividend - usually of a fixed percentage of the profits available for distribution - in priority to the other shareholders. Subject to any special provisions of this nature, the shareholders are entitled to participate in the profits of the company in proportion to their respective interests therein. The better view appears to be that this means in proportion to the amount actually paid up on their shares and not in proportion to the nominal value of the shares.

Declaration of dividend

[31.08] A dividend does not become payable to the shareholder unless it is declared by one of the organs of the company[3]. There is no requirement in the Acts as to which organ is to declare the dividend, but the usual practice is to provide in the articles that it is to be declared by the company in general meeting and is not to exceed such amount as is recommended by the directors (Article 116). In addition, the directors are usually empowered to pay such interim dividends as appear to them to be justified from the profits of the company. Such an interim dividend is to be distinguished from the final dividend declared by the company at its annual general meeting.

[31.09] As we have seen, a dividend is only payable out of profits available for distribution, and any provision in the articles to the contrary is of no effect. In practice, the articles usually provide expressly that dividends are payable only out of profits (Article 118).

---

[1] See para **[3.12]** above.
[2] See para **[17.40]** above.
[3] See para **[17.40]** above.

Enforcing the payment of dividends

[31.10] When the dividend is declared, it becomes a liability of the company and the shareholder may recover the amount by action if it remains unpaid[4]. The limitation period under the Statute of Limitations 1957 is six years from the date on which the dividend is declared and not twelve years, since it is a simple contract debt as distinct from a speciality debt[5]. If the company is wound up, a dividend in arrears has no priority over other simple contract debts[6].

Apportionment of dividends

[31.11] The provisions of the Apportionment Act 1870 apply to dividends. It follows that when there is a transmission - eg on the death of the shareholder - during a period in respect of which dividends are subsequently paid, the dividends will be apportioned. If, for example, a shareholder leaves his shares to AB and the residue of his estate to CD, AB will be entitled to the dividends as from the date of death - from which date the will speaks - but the portion prior to the death will belong to CD as part of the residue. It is always possible, of course, for a testator or settler to exclude apportionment by the express terms of the will or settlement.

Dividend warrants

[31.12] Payment of dividends in the case of a public company is usually made by a dividend warrant in the form of a printed cheque drawn on the company's bank. Tax is deducted by the company before paying the dividend, but the warrant usually has attached to it an advice note which can be presented to the Revenue Commissioners to support a claim for the refund of any tax to which the shareholder may be entitled.

Dividend mandates

[31.13] It is a common practice for public companies today to encourage the payment of dividends directly to the shareholder's bank. This is done by a dividend mandate in a standard form which is signed by the shareholder and authorises the payment of the dividend into the shareholder's bank account.

---

[4] *Re Severn and Wye and Severn Bridge Co Rly* [1896] 1 Ch 559.
[5] *Re Compania de Electricidad de la Provincia de Buenos Aires Ltd* [1978] 3 All ER 668.
[6] As to preference shares, see para **[17.38]** above.

Scrip dividend

[31.14] A company may offer its shareholders a choice between a cash dividend and a scrip dividend. If the shareholder opts for the latter, he is allotted an appropriate number of ordinary shares in the company in lieu of the dividend and the shares are treated as fully paid up. In times of inflation, it is an attractive option for a shareholder and it has also advantages for the company since it eases its liquid cash position and increases its capital.

Dividends must not be paid out of capital

[31.15] This, as we have seen, is a fundamental rule. It does not, however, mean that the company may only pay dividends out of profits earned in the current year. If profits have been accumulated as such - ie carried to reserve and not capitalised - the rule does not prevent the company from distributing them as dividend. What it does mean is that the company is precluded from paying a dividend which would be in excess of the available reserves and hence cause a loss of capital. It does not mean that losses of capital sustained in the ordinary course of business must be replaced before a dividend is declared.

Restrictions on the distributions of profits and assets

[31.16] Not all 'profits' are profits available for distribution. There was formerly some uncertainty as to what were profits so available. The 1983 Act, implementing the Second EU Directive and closely modelled on the English Act sets out detailed requirements in this area. The Act prohibits the making of a distribution except out of profits available for that purpose and goes on to set out criteria for determining what are such profits.

[31.17] It must be borne in mind that a 'distribution' of profits may take forms other than the payment of dividends and 'distribution' is accordingly specially defined. Section 51 provides that it means every distribution of a company's assets, whether in cash or otherwise, except:

(1)   an issue of fully or partly paid up bonus shares;

(2)   the redemption or purchase of shares;

(3)   a reduction of the share capital authorised under s 72 of the Principal Act; and

(4)   a distribution of assets on a winding up.

[31.18] A company's profits available for distribution within this special meaning are 'its accumulated, realised profits ... less its accumulated realised losses ...'[7]. The profits, however, may not include profits previously utilised either by distribution or capitalisation. The realised losses do not include amounts previously written off in a reduction or reorganisation of the capital.

[31.19] It will be noted that it is only realised profits which are available. The Principal Act provides that a capital surplus arising on a revaluation of unrealised fixed assets is not available for distribution[8]. A realised profit arising from the actual sale of capital assets is, however, available for distribution, provided the profit has not been previously utilised either by a distribution or a capitalisation.

[31.20] Some modifications of the principles laid down by these new provisions must next be noted.

(1) Where fixed assets are revalued and a surplus arises, the difference between the depreciation charge based on the revalued amount and the depreciation charge based on the cost may be treated as available for distribution. For example, machinery belonging to the company originally costs £100,000 and is being depreciated at the rate of £20,000 annually. At the beginning of the third year, the machinery is revalued to £75,000 and the annual depreciation charge is revised to £25,000 for the remaining three years. The company is entitled to treat £5,000 (being the additional depreciation each year) as available for distribution[9].

(2) In determining whether a company has made a profit or loss in respect of a particular asset, the company may be in the difficulty that it has no record of its original cost: where this is the case, or where such a record cannot be obtained without unreasonable expense and delay, the cost of the asset is taken to be the earliest record valuation available after its acquisition by the company[10].

[31.21] 'Realised losses' must next be considered. Obviously a debit balance on the profit and loss account is a 'realised loss'. In addition, s 45(4) states that, subject to one important proviso, any amount written off or retained for depreciation, diminution or renewal of assets or retained as a provision for known but unquantifiable liabilities is to be treated as a realised loss. Such amounts accordingly must be treated as losses in determining the amount available for distribution and they include not only the current losses but also the accumulated losses from previous years.

---

[7]   Companies (Amendment) Act 1983, s 45(2).
[8]   Companies Act 1963, s 149(6).
[9]   Companies (Amendment) Act 1983, s 45(6).
[10]   Companies (Amendment) Act 1983, s 45(7).

[31.22] The exception arises where there is a revaluation of all the fixed assets - or all the fixed assets other than goodwill - and provision is made for the diminution in value of any of the assets. Such a diminution in value need not be treated as a realised loss. Moreover, even when there is not a revaluation as such of all the assets, but the directors have at least considered the value of each asset, the exception applies, with an important proviso: the directors must be satisfied that the aggregate value of the assets at least equals their value as stated in the accounts. Subject to that proviso, a fixed asset may be written down in the books and not give rise to a realised loss, without the necessity for a full revaluation of all the fixed assets of the company.

Restrictions on public limited companies

[31.23] When a company's assets exceed its liabilities, the balancing figure on the liabilities side, as we have seen[11], consists of the called up share capital and reserves of the company (if reserves have been accumulated). If the surplus of the assets over liabilities is less than the called up share capital, it might seem contrary to principle for the company to declare a dividend. It was, however, the law prior to the 1983 Act that a company could legitimately pay a dividend in such circumstances since the share capital, although appearing on the liabilities side of the balance sheet, was not a liability of the company. Now, however, a public limited company is prohibited by Part IV of the 1983 Act from making a distribution unless the amount of its net assets (ie its aggregate assets less its aggregate liabilities) equals or exceeds the aggregate of its called up share capital and undistributable reserves and the distribution does not reduce the amount of those assets to less than the aggregate. This again is in pursuance of the objective of the EU Directive which, as we have seen, is concerned with the maintenance by companies of their capital.

[31.24] 'Undistributable reserves' in this context means:

(1)   the share premium account[12];

(2)   the capital redemption reserve fund[13];

(3)   the amount by which the company's accumulated, unrealised profits - so far as not capitalised - exceed its accumulated, unrealised losses so far as not previously written off in a reduction or reorganisation of capital;

(4)   any other reserve which the company is prohibited either by statute or its memorandum or articles from distributing.

---

[11] Para **[14.07]** above.

[12] See para **[14.17]** above.

[13] See para **[14.18]** above.

[31.25] An investment company, ie one which does not carry on business in the ordinary sense, but simply holds and manages shares or other interests in property for the benefit of its members, may be prohibited by its memorandum or articles from distributing any capital profit, such as a profit on the sale of shares held by it. Where such an investment company is a public limited company, it would be subject to the same limitations on distributing its profits as any other public limited company, although it is subject to a special limitation not applicable to other trading companies, ie that it cannot distribute the profits of its trade such as profits on the sale of shares. Special treatment is accordingly provided in s 47 for such a company: it may make a distribution out of the accumulated realised 'revenue' profits less the accumulated 'revenue' losses, realised or unrealised, provided its assets are at least 50% greater than its liabilities and that the distribution does not reduce its assets below that figure.

[31.26] In order to qualify as an 'investment company' for this purpose, the company must, meet certain conditions:

(1)   it must have given notice in writing which has not been revoked to the Registrar of its intention to carry on business as an investment company;

(2)   the company's business since the date of the notice must have consisted of investing its funds mainly in securities with the aim of spreading the investment risk and giving the members the benefit of the results of the management of its funds;

(3)   the company's investments after the date of the notice in any company (other than another investment company) must not have been more than 15% in value of its entire investment;

(4)   the company must not have retained since the date of the notice more than 15% of its income from securities in respect of any financial year except in accordance with Part IV of the 1983 Act;

(5)   the company must since the date of the notice have been prohibited by its memorandum or articles from distributing its capital profits.

[31.27] An investment company may not make a distribution under s 47 unless:

(1)   the company's shares are listed on a recognised stock exchange;

(2)   the company has not made a distribution of capital profits or applied any unrealised profits or capital profits, whether realised or unrealised, in paying up debentures or amounts unpaid on its issued share capital during the year immediately preceding the financial year in which the distribution is proposed to be made.

The 'relevant accounts' under the 1983 Act

[31.28] In order to determine whether a distribution may be made in accordance with Part IV of the 1983 Act, and if so the amount, regard must be had to 'relevant items' in the 'relevant accounts'. The relevant accounts, as defined by s 49, are primarily the last annual accounts, ie the accounts prepared in accordance with the Principal Act in respect of the last financial year in which accounts so prepared were laid. Where, however, the distribution is contrary to Part IV by reference only to the last annual accounts, the relevant accounts are such accounts (called 'interim accounts') which are necessary to enable a reasonable judgment to be made as to the amount of any of the relevant items. Finally, if the relevant distribution is to be made during the company's first financial year or before any accounts are laid in respect of that financial year, the relevant accounts are such accounts as are similarly necessary (in this instance called 'initial accounts').

[31.29] There are provisions requiring that, in the case of the last annual accounts and of the initial accounts, they should have been properly prepared, that the auditors should have made their statutory report and that it should have been either unqualified or qualified only in respect of non-material items. In the case of the initial accounts, a copy of them must be delivered to the Registrar. In the case of interim accounts, they must also have been properly prepared and a copy of them delivered to the Registrar.

[31.30] The 'relevant items' to be taken into account in determining whether a distribution may properly be made are profits, losses, assets, liabilities, provisions, share capital and reserves.

Consequences of unlawful distribution

[31.31] Where a distribution is made by a company to one of its members in contravention of Part IV of the 1983 Act and he knows, or has reasonable grounds for believing, that it is so made, he must repay it to the company.

Chapter 32

Mergers, Arrangements, Reconstructions and Takeovers

[32.01] Circumstances frequently arise in which a company wishes to sell its business to, or merge with, another company. Thus, company A may sell its assets and undertakings to company B, with the shareholders in company A being given shares in company B. It may also be decided to dissolve company A, leaving the business of the two companies effectively merged. Alternatively, it may be decided to form a new company, C, to whom the assets of both A and B are sold. The shareholders in A and B will be given shares in C, and A and B will then be dissolved. In this case, the two companies have simply amalgamated to form a third company.

[32.02] A company may also wish to obtain control of another company by acquiring the shares - or a sufficient number of them to ensure control - from the existing shareholders, the procedure usually known as a 'takeover' bid.

[32.03] There are also occasions on which a company, for various reasons, may wish to construct or rearrange its share capital, although there is no question of a merger or amalgamation with another company.

[32.04] Finally, there are occasions when a company may wish to come to an arrangement with its creditors for the payment of the company's debts, usually as an alternative to the company being wound up.

[32.05] Mergers, arrangements, reconstructions and takeovers are an essential feature of commercial activity in free market economies and the Principal Act contains various provisions intended to facilitate them. In the case of reconstructions, we have already noted the company's power to reduce its capital with the sanction of the court[1], to increase such capital without any sanction[2], to vary the rights attached to shares[3] and to issue redeemable shares[4]. Sections 201 and 203 contain specific provisions enabling amalgamations and arrangements to be carried out with the sanction of the court. Section 260 empowers the liquidator of a company being voluntarily wound up to transfer the assets of the

---

[1] Para **[16.11]** above.
[2] Para **[16.04]** above.
[3] Para **[17.19]** above.
[4] Para **[15.05]** above.

company to another company in exchange for shares in the other company. In this instance, the sanction of the court is not required. In the case of takeovers, s 204 provides a machinery under which a dissentient minority of the company being taken over may be compelled to sell their shares to the acquiring company, where the latter has acquired 80% of the shares[5].

[32.06] Finally the 1990 (No 1) Act introduced a procedure under which an examiner appointed by the court can bring about an arrangement. This procedure is considered in detail in Ch 37.

[32.07] The Oireachtas has also recognised, however, that the public interest may not always be served by a merger, amalgamation, or take-over. Accordingly, the Mergers, Take-overs and Monopolies (Control) Act 1978, as amended by the Competition Act 1991, provides for the investigation by the Competition Authority of mergers and take-overs in the case of companies of a certain size and their prohibition, if it appears justified from its report, by the Minister. In addition, where a merger or take-over could be regarded as restricting competition in this State contrary to the provisions of the Competition Acts 1991-1996, notice of it must be given to the Competition Authority which then decides whether it should be allowed to proceed.

[32.08] Mergers may also be affected by EU law. The 1978 Act and the Competition Acts do not apply to mergers or take-overs which are above a certain size and involve trading activities outside the State. Moreover, where the merger or take-over affects trade within a substantial part of the European Union, Articles 81 and 82 of the Treaty of Rome, prohibiting anti-competitive practices and the abuse of a dominant position within the Union, may be applicable.

[32.09] It should also be noted that, in the case of a take-over of a company whose securities are listed on the Irish Stock Exchange, the controls applicable under the Irish Take-over Panel Act 1997 and the Panel's Take-over Rules may be applicable.

Arrangements with sanction of court

[32.10] When a company proposes to enter into a 'compromise or arrangement' with its creditors or its members and obtains the sanction of the court to it under s 201, the compromise or arrangement is binding on all the creditors or members. The section is rarely availed of, however, in practice[6]. If the company

---

[5] Mergers between public limited companies - extremely rare in Ireland - are now affected by the requirements of EU law applicable in Ireland: see para **[3.13]** above.

[6] No order under the section was delivered for registration in the year 1987, the last for which figures are available: *Report of the Department of Industry and Commerce* 1987 Pl 6258.

wishes to reconstruct for the purpose of a merger or amalgamation, this can usually be done by means of a voluntary winding up, using the powers conferred on the liquidator by s 260. This avoids the necessity for an application to the court: the major disadvantage is that, in contrast to an arrangement sanctioned under s 201, it is not necessarily binding on all the members. So far as compromises or arrangements with creditors are concerned, it would seem that companies who have reached the stage where such a course becomes a possible option will normally elect for a creditors' winding up instead.

[32.11] Before the court sanctions an arrangement or compromise under s 201, a meeting must be held of the members (or class of members) or creditors (or class of creditors) whom it is sought to bind by the proposal. It is only if three-fourths of the members or creditors present at the meeting vote in favour of the compromise or arrangement that it may be sanctioned by the court. For this purpose, the court may order the convening of a meeting of the members or class of members or creditors or class of creditors whom it is sought to bind.

[32.12] Accordingly, the company will initially have to decide which class of members or creditors will be affected by the proposal, before it applies to the court for an order convening a meeting. Normally the classes that will have to be considered in the case of a proposal affecting members are the ordinary and preference shareholders; and in the case of a proposal affecting creditors, the preferential, secured and unsecured creditors. But there may be further categories to be considered and the criterion to be applied in considering whether a particular category of members or creditors constitutes a 'class' within the meaning of the section was defined as follows by Bowen LJ in *Sovereign Life Assurance Co v Dodd*[7]:

> 'It seems plain that we must give such a meaning to the term "class" as will prevent the section being so worked as to result in confiscation and injustice, and that it must be confined to those persons whose rights are not so dissimilar as to make it impossible for them to consult together with a view to their common interest'.

[32.13] In *Re Pye Ireland Ltd*[8], Costello J declined to order the convening of a meeting of the company's six classes of creditors where the proposal to be considered was being opposed by one of the creditors, ie the Revenue. The company intended, if sanction was given, to discontinue its business as a manufacturer and distributor of television and related equipment and to sell off land which it owned over a three year period in order to pay its various creditors. The Revenue were owed a substantial sum and objected to the scheme.

---

[7] [1892] 2 QB 573 at 583.

[8] (Unreported, 12 November 1984).

Costello J took the view that the Collector-General was in a special position since the debts he was seeking to collect were owed to the state and that the court should be very slow to order the holding of a meeting to consider a scheme to which he objected.

It appears that this special position for the Revenue was disclaimed by counsel when the matter was appealed to the Supreme Court and accordingly that the court did not have to express any opinion as to the correctness of Costello J's view. It was accepted that portion of the Revenue debt, amounting to one year's taxes, was entitled to priority, but since the company was willing to pay this sum the court allowed the meetings to proceed[9]. It is thought that the decision of Costello J is open to question: there seems no basis of law for according to the Revenue any special standing as a creditor other than that afforded to them under the Principal Act as a preferential creditor in respect of certain taxes.

[32.14] If the compromise or arrangement is for the purpose of, or in connection with, a scheme for the reconstruction of the company or the amalgamation of two or more companies, the court may also make provision under s 203 for:

(1) the transfer of the undertaking and of the property or liabilities of one company (called 'the transferor') to another company (called 'the transferee');

(2) the allotting or appropriating by the transferee of shares, debentures, policies, etc which, under the compromise or arrangement, are to be allotted or appropriated by it to or for any person;

(3) the continuance of legal proceedings by or against the transferee;

(4) the dissolution, without winding up, of the transferor;

(5) the provision to be made for persons who dissent from the scheme;

(6) such incidental or consequential matters as are necessary to secure that the reconstruction or amalgamation is carried out fully and effectually.

The application should be made by special summons[10].

[32.15] Before the meetings of members or creditors or class of members or creditors is held, the members or creditors concerned are entitled to be given certain information as to the proposed compromise or arrangement. Section 202 requires a statement to be sent with every notice summoning such a meeting explaining the effect of the compromise or arrangement. It must also state any material interests of the directors, whether as directors, members, creditors or otherwise, and the effect thereon of the compromise or arrangement. If notice is

---

[9] (Unreported). The judgments appear to have been ex-temporary: cf *The Irish Times*, 23 November 1984.

[10] Rules of the Superior Courts Ord 75, r 4.

given by advertisement, it must either include such a statement or a notification of the place at which, and the manner in which, creditors or members entitled to attend may obtain copies of such a statement. Any creditor or member applying for a copy of the statement in response to the advertisement must be furnished with it free of charge.

[32.16] A compromise or arrangement proposed under s 201 must not be illegal and must be within the powers of the company. Subject to this, there is no limitation on the nature of the compromise or arrangement that may be sanctioned under the section. The court must, of course, be satisfied that all the requirements of s 201 have been met. It would appear that the court must be satisfied that the scheme proposed is a reasonable one, but will not decide these issues in terms of its commercial merits, these being matters for the members or creditors[11].

Reconstruction by voluntary liquidation

[32.17] This is a method more favoured in Ireland of effecting a merger or amalgamation of two or more companies, since it does not require any application to the court. Section 260 of the Principal Act empowers the liquidator of a company being wound up voluntarily to sell or transfer either the whole or part of its business and property to another company in exchange for shares, policies and other interests in the other company. The shares, etc are then distributed among the members of the company in liquidation. The liquidator may also enter into an alternative arrangement under which the members, instead of receiving shares etc, are permitted to participate in the profits of the company to whom the business is transferred or receive some other benefit from it.

[32.18] As we have seen, a company may simply merge with another company by transferring all its assets and business to it, and may avail of s 260 for that purpose. Alternatively, two companies may decide to amalgamate and form a new company, in which case again s 260 may be employed.

[32.19] Unlike s 201, no application to the court is necessary. The procedure under s 260, however, suffers from one major disadvantage which does not affect a scheme sanctioned under s 201; dissentient shareholders are not bound by the reconstruction. Moreover, the position of creditors is entirely different: as we have seen, in the case of an arrangement sanctioned under s 201, all the creditors or class of creditors will be bound. In the case of a reconstruction under s 260, the creditors are not obliged to look to a company to whom the business is transferred for payment. It is true that the company may have denuded itself of

---

11   *Re London Chartered Bank of Australasia* [1893] 3 Ch 540.

some of its assets, but the liquidator must retain sufficient to meet any creditor's claim or obtain an adequate indemnity from the transferee company[12]. The creditors are further protected by a provision that, in the event of the company being wound up by the court within 12 months of the resolution authorising a reconstruction under s 260, the latter resolution is to be of no effect unless sanctioned by the court[13].

[32.20] It is important to bear in mind that a reconstruction under s 260 can only be effected during the course of a members' winding up. A members' winding up differs from a creditors' winding up in that the former may only take place where those responsible for the management of the company's affairs - usually the directors - file a declaration of solvency. Where such a declaration is filed, the members effectively retain control of the winding up. Where no such declaration is filed, control of the winding up is effectively vested in the creditors and exercised by them in most cases through the agency of a committee of inspection. Accordingly, if the liquidator wishes to carry out a reconstruction during the course of a creditors' winding up, he will generally be unable to do so without the consent of the creditors or their committee of inspection.

[32.21] A reconstruction under s 260 may only be carried out with the sanction of a special resolution of the company. As we have seen, if the company is ordered to be wound up within a year of the passing of the resolution, it is of no effect unless sanctioned by the court.

[32.22] Where a shareholder does not vote in favour of the special resolution, and serves notice expressing his dissent from the resolution within seven days, he may require the liquidator either to abstain from carrying it into effect or to purchase his shares. It may well be impossible for the liquidator, as a matter of law, to abstain from proceeding with the scheme, and in most cases the result will be that he is obliged to purchase the shares of the dissentient member. If a price cannot be agreed, it must be determined by arbitration under the procedure laid down in the Companies Clauses Consolidation Act 1845. This provides for the appointment by each party of an arbitrator who, if they cannot agree, appoint an umpire to resolve the dispute. If the arbitrators fail to appoint an umpire, the court may do so under the Arbitration Act 1954. It would appear that the valuation should be made on the assumption that the scheme was not carried out and that the company's assets were distributed in the ordinary way to the shareholders at the end of the winding up. It may be difficult in practice for the dissentient members to establish this value, particularly as it has been held that he is not entitled to examine the company's officers and that, in the absence of

---

[12] *Pulsford v Devenish* [1903] 2 Ch 625.
[13] Companies Act 1963, s 260(5).

fraud or proven inaccuracy, he is not entitled to discovery of the books of the company[14].

[32.23] The notice of dissent must be served at the registered office of the company. If a person does not dissent, he loses the right to be paid a fair price for his shares, but he is not obliged to accept shares in the new company. Thus, if the shares in the new company are of little value and impose certain liabilities, eg in relation to unpaid capital, on the members, the fact that a person has not dissented does not prevent him from refusing to accept the new shares[15].

[32.24] It is clear that any provision in a memorandum or articles which purports to deprive a member of his statutory right to dissent from a reconstruction under s 260 is void. It is also clear that the court will not allow the rights of dissentients to be circumvented by making an order under s 201 giving sanction to a scheme which could have been carried out under s 260[16].

[32.25] A takeover may be said to occur when one company acquires a majority of the shares in another company. This may, of course, happen as a result of an agreement between the board of directors of the two companies concerned: if the directors of the company being taken over own a sufficient number of the shares, the takeover will present few complications. The takeover which presents the most problems is the attempt by one public company to acquire the necessary majority of shares in another public company by making an offer to the shareholders in that company for the purchase of their shares at a stated figure. The offer is usually conditional upon its being accepted by a stated percentage of the shareholders: when that percentage has accepted, the offer becomes unconditional and binding upon the acquiring company. Such takeover 'bids' have, of course, been extremely common in England for many years, but are relatively infrequent in Ireland, because of the small number of public companies. It should be remembered, however, that there can be a takeover of a private company just as of a public company and students and practitioners should be familiar with the general legal principles affecting such takeovers, whether of public or private companies.

[32.26] The philosophy underlying the Acts is intended to facilitate mergers, amalgamations and takeovers subject to safeguards being provided for shareholders and creditors. (The public interest is intended to be protected by independent legislation, which is considered below.) In the case of a takeover, the company acquiring the shares (called in the Principal Act and this chapter

---

14 *Re British Building Stone Co Ltd* [1908] 2 Ch 450; *Re Glamorganshire Banking Co, Morgan's Case* (1885) 28 Ch D 620.
15 *Higg's Case* [1865] 2 H & M 657 at 665.
16 *Re Anglo-Continental Supply Co* [1922] 2 Ch 723.

'the transferee') will usually want to acquire at least 75% of the shares in the other company (called 'the transferor'). As we have seen, a special resolution of a company to be valid must be supported by at least 75% of those voting at a meeting, and some important matters may only be dealt with by means of such a resolution. Even a minority of less than 25% can, however, prove an embarrassment to the transferee company, and, accordingly, with a view to facilitating a takeover which has overwhelming support from the shareholders in the transferor, s 204 enables the transferee to acquire compulsorily the shares of a dissentient minority, where not less than 80%[17] in value of the shareholders in the transferor have agreed to the takeover.

[32.27] A company making a takeover can put in motion the machinery under s 204 where the scheme, contract or offer has become binding or approved or accepted in respect of not less than four-fifths in value of the shares affected. The offer must have been accepted by, and become binding on, the necessary majority not later than four months after the publication of the terms of the offer to the shareholders. The transferee then has a further two months (ie six months from the date of publication) within which to exercise its rights to acquire the shares of any of the dissentients. This is done by serving a notice in the prescribed form[18] on any of the dissentients who in turn may apply to the court within one month for an order setting aside the notice.

[32.28] The court may set aside the notice 'if it thinks fit'. There is no guidance in the section as to what matters may properly be taken into account by the court in exercising its discretion. It is clear, however, that the onus is on the dissentient shareholder who applies for such an order to establish that the terms of the acquisition are not fair[19]. It has also been held that it is not sufficient to establish that the offer could be improved[20]. The court would not, it is thought, be concerned with the commercial merits of the takeover or its effect on the public interest and, in exercising its discretion, must naturally give great weight to the fact that at least four-fifths of the shareholders have approved the takeover[21].

[32.29] It has also been held in England that it is not sufficient to allege that inadequate information was given to the shareholders[22], but that there is a duty on the transferee to act honestly and not to mislead the shareholders in the transferor.

---

[17] Note that only an 80% majority is required: in England, the figure is 90%.
[18] Companies (Forms) Order 1964, SI 45/1964, Form No 18.
[19] *Re Hoare & Co* (1934) 150 LT 374.
[20] *Re Grierson, Oldham and Adams Ltd* [1968] Ch 17.
[21] *Re Hoare & Co* (1934) 150 LT 374.
[22] *Re Evertite Locknuts* [1945] Ch 220 at 223.

[32.30] A different view was taken by McWilliam J in *Securities Trust Ltd v Associated Properties Ltd*[23], where he held that the shareholders in the transferor are entitled to be given 'full particulars of the transaction, its purposes, the method of carrying it out and its consequences'. It does not appear, however, that any of the earlier authorities were cited and it may be that the decision should be regarded as confined to the facts of the particular case.

[32.31] More recently, it has been emphasised by the Supreme Court that, while the court has a discretion as to the order it should make, the onus is on the dissenting shareholder to satisfy the court that the transaction should be set aside and must pay 'great attention' to the views of the majority who accepted the bid[24].

[32.32] What is the position if the transferee, at the time of the publication of the offer, owns shares already in the transferor? If the holding of the transferee at that time exceeds one-fifth, sub-section (2) provides that the transferee cannot exercise the compulsory purchase power unless it acquires four-fifths of the remaining shares and the accepting shareholders represent three-fourths in number of the holders of the remaining shares.

[32.33] It should also be noted that the time limit for giving notice to the dissenting shareholders will remain the same, even though the time within which the shareholders in the transferor company have to accept has been extended by the transferee[25].

[32.34] Even if the transferee does not wish to exercise the power of compulsory purchase under s 204, it must still give the dissentients an opportunity of selling their shares. This is provided for by sub-section (4), under which the transferee, where it has acquired four-fifths in value must, within one month, give notice of that fact in the prescribed manner[26] to any shareholders whose shares have not been acquired. They in turn may then give notice to the transferee requiring it to acquire their shares. The shares must then be acquired by the transferee on the same terms as the remaining four-fifths were acquired.

Compensation for loss of office on mergers etc

[32.35] The Principal Act contains provisions designed to ensure that any arrangement for the payment of compensation to the directors for loss of office on a merger, amalgamation or takeover is notified to the members and approved by them before it becomes effective. Section 187 renders unlawful the payment

---

[23] (Unreported, 19 November 1980).

[24] *Duggan v Stoneworth Investment Ltd* (unreported, 21 December 1999).

[25] *Musson v Howard Glasgow Associates Ltd* (1961) SLT 87.

[26] Companies (Forms) Order 1964, SI 45/1964, Form No 19.

of any compensation to a director for loss of office in connection with the transfer of the whole or part of the company's undertaking or property, unless particulars of the proposed payment (including the amount) have been disclosed to the members and the proposal approved by the members in general meeting. The disclosure must be made to all members, whether or not they are entitled to notice of meetings and must be made before the payment is made.

[32.36] Section 188 requires a director to disclose particulars of any payment made to him as compensation for loss of office in connection with a transfer of shares in the company, where the transfer results *inter alia* from an offer made to the general body of shareholders. He must take all reasonable steps to secure that the particulars are included in or sent with any notice of the offer. There is provision for a fine not exceeding £125 in the event of his not doing so and for treating any sums received by him as being held on trust for those who have sold their shares as a result of the offer.

Control of mergers and takeovers

[32.37] In the case of public companies, the requirements of the Irish Take-over Panel Act 1997 and in the rules made by the Irish Take-over Panel established under the Act will be applicable. This legislation was enacted following the separation of the Irish Stock Exchange and the London Stock Exchange in 1995. Prior to 1995, the requirements of the City Code on Take-overs and Mergers were applicable, although they had no force in law.

[32.38] The 1997 Act sets out general principles which are applicable to the conduct of take-overs. All shareholders are to be treated equally and they are entitled to receive such information and advice as will enable them to make an informed decision on the offer. The offeror (the company initiating the take-over) is required to give careful and responsible consideration to it before it is made; conversely it is the duty of the directors of the offeree (the company which is the target of the take-over) to refrain from doing anything which might frustrate the offer or deprive shareholders of the opportunity of considering the merits of the offer, unless the shareholders in general meeting so authorise. Directors of the offeree and the offeror are also under a duty to act in disregard of their personal interests and there are also requirements intended to ensure that the transaction is completed with reasonable speed. All parties are under a duty to prevent the creation of a false market in any of the securities of the offeror or offeree. The take-over rules give effect in more detail to the general principles[27].

---

[27] As to the take-over rules and other aspects of this statutory scheme, see Cahill, *Corporate Finance Law*, pp 971-977.

[32.39] There are, in addition, statutory controls on all mergers and take-overs, whether of public or private companies, where the gross assets of each of the companies involved is not less than £10 million in the most recent financial year, or, the turnover of each is not less than £20 million. These are contained in the Mergers, Takeovers and Monopolies (Control) Act 1978.

[32.40] The Act applies to 'enterprises' and these are defined by s 1(1) as meaning:

> 'a person or partnership engaged for profit in the supply or distribution of goods or the provision of services ...'

The word 'person' would include a company formed under the Acts, and subsection (1) also makes it clear that it includes a holding company.

[32.41] A merger or takeover within the meaning of the Act takes place when two or more enterprises in Ireland, at least one of which carries on business in Ireland, come under 'common control'. 'Common control' in turn is defined as existing where the decision as to how or by whom each of the enterprises is managed can be made by the same person or by the same group of persons 'acting in concert'. This general definition is supplemented by a special definition in the case of companies. Without prejudice to the general definition, companies are deemed to come under common control when one company acquires:

(1) the right to appoint or remove a majority of the board of committee of management of the other, or

(2) more than 30% of the shares carrying voting rights in the other.

(2), however, does not apply, where the acquiring company already owns more than half the shares carrying voting rights in the other company.

[32.42] It should be particularly noted that for a merger or takeover to exist, it is not necessary for one company to acquire a majority or controlling interest in another. It is sufficient if more than 30% of the shares are acquired.

[32.43] A merger or takeover is also deemed to take place where one company acquires assets of another company and as a result the acquiring company substantially replaces the other company in the business concerned.

[32.44] In certain circumstances where companies come under common control or assets are acquired, no merger or takeover will be deemed to exist for the purposes of the Act. They are:

(1) where the person making the decisions giving rise to the 'common control' assumption is a receiver or liquidator;

(2) where the person acquiring the assets is an underwriting or jobber acting as such or a liquidator or receiver acting as such;

(3)   where the companies concerned are wholly owned subsidiaries of the same holding company.

[32.45] We have already seen that the Act applies only to mergers and takeovers affecting enterprises with assets or turnover exceeding the statutory figures. Where, however, the Minister is of the opinion that the exigencies of the common good so warrant, he may declare that the Act is to apply to a particular merger or takeover even though the statutory figures are not exceeded.

[32.46] In order to prevent the Minister being presented with a *fait accompli* which might be difficult and complex to undo, the Act provides in s 3 for the automatic deferral of the implementation of a merger or takeover until the Minister has had an opportunity of considering whether he should make a prohibition order under s 9. Accordingly, the section provides that the title to the assets or shares concerned in the merger or takeover is not to pass until

(1)   the Minister has stated that he has decided not to make a prohibition order; or

(2)   the Minister has made a conditional order; or

(3)   a period of three months has elapsed from the date of the notification to the Minister of the proposal or the date on which the Minister receives further information in response to a request;

whichever of these three events happens first.

[32.47] Moreover, s 14 provides that an order under s 201 or 203 of the Principal Act is not to be made in respect of a merger or takeover to which the 1978 Act applies until either:

(1)   the Minister has stated in writing that he has decided not to make a prohibition order; or

(2)   the Minister has made a conditional order; or

(3)   a period of three months has elapsed from the date of the notification to the Minister of the proposal or the date on which the Minister receives further information in response to a request;

whichever of these events happens first.

[32.48] Each of the enterprises involved and having knowledge of the proposal must notify the Minister in writing of it within one month or such other period as the Minister may specify. The Minister may then, within one month of the notification, or the last of the notifications, request further information in writing from any one or more of the enterprises which must be provided within the period specified by the Minister. A notification is not valid where any information provided or statement made is false or misleading.

[32.49] Where there is a breach of these provisions, any officer of the company who authorised the breach is guilty of an offence and liable on summary conviction to a fine not exceeding £1,000 and, for continued contravention, to a daily default fine not exceeding £100. He is liable on indictment to a fine not exceeding £200,000 and a daily fine not exceeding £20,000.

[32.50] The next step is for the Minister to decide whether he should refer the proposal to the Competition Authority for investigation. Such a reference must be made, if at all, within 30 days of the notification of the proposal or the receipt by him of further information requested by him. The Authority in making their report are required to assess whether the proposal:

> 'would be likely to prevent or restrict competition or restrain trade in any goods or services and would be likely to operate against the common good'.

[32.51] The Minister, in deciding whether to make a prohibition order is confined to considering whether the 'exigencies of the common good' warrant such action. This is a somewhat elastic concept, but both the Authority in making their report and the Minister in making his decision, are required to take into account certain specific criteria set out in the Act as follows:

(1)   Continuity of supplies or services.

(2)   Level of employment.

(3)   Regional development.

(4)   Rationalisation of operations in the interests of greater efficiency.

(5)   Research and development.

(6)   Increased production.

(7)   Access to markets.

(8)   Shareholders and partners.

(9)   Employees.

(10)   Consumers.

[32.52] When the Minister has received and considered the Authority's report, he then decides whether the 'exigencies of the common good' warrant the prohibition of the proposal either absolutely or except on specified conditions. Before doing so, he must consult with any other Minister appearing to him to be concerned, and he must also have regard to any relevant international obligations of Ireland. The order must state the reasons for its being made.

[32.53] One of the conditions to which an order permitting a proposal may be made subject is one that the proposal is to take effect within 12 months of the making of the order. A conditional order may also be retrospective in its effect.

[32.54] Every such order must be laid before each House of the Oireachtas and if a resolution annulling the order is passed by either such house within the next 21 days on which the house has sat after the order is laid before it, the order is to be annulled, but without prejudice to the validity of anything done thereunder previously.

[32.55] Where a sale of shares is rendered invalid as a result of such deferral, the vendor is entitled to recover damages from the purchaser unless the purchaser satisfies the court that before the purported sale he notified the vendor of circumstances relating to the proposed sale which gave rise to the possibility of such an invalidity.

[32.56] Even where the Minister has not referred a proposed merger or take-over to the Competition Authority, that body has taken the view that a merger may violate s 4(1) of the Competition Act 1991 as being an 'agreement' restricting competition in the State. Under the mechanism established by that Act, such agreements are unlawful unless they are given the appropriate licence by the Competition Authority. Accordingly, a merger which has not been the subject of a reference by the Minister under his powers, may still require a licence from the Authority before it can be lawfully brought to completion.

[32.57] It is also been held that Article 82 of the Treaty of Rome, which prohibits what was called the 'abuse of a dominant position within the Common Market' by one or more undertakings, entitles the Commission to control or prohibit mergers. The statement in the second edition that its practical significance in the Irish context was limited since the dominant position must be within the Common Market or a substantial part of it, eg one of the larger member states such as the UK or France, is incorrect. Thus, the Article prohibits the abuse of a dominant position held by a particular undertaking, not merely in Ireland, but even in a reasonably significant part of Ireland, eg County Kerry.

[32.58] As already pointed out, large mergers in the European Union are now removed from the ambit of domestic legislation under the EC Mergers Regulations. However, that Regulation and indeed the entire field of both EU and domestic competition law, which applies to undertakings other than companies, is outside the ambit of this book. There are a growing number of excellent specialised works on these topics to which students and practitioners should refer[28].

---

[28] Cahill, *Corporate Finance Law*; Whish and Sufrin, *Competition Law*; Maher, *Competition Law, Alignment and Reform*; Clarke, *Takeovers and Mergers Law*.

Chapter 33

Fraudulent and Reckless Trading

[33.01] The provision in the Principal Act[1] that directors and others could be made personally liable in a winding up for the debts of a company where they could be shown to have been guilty of 'fraudulent trading' was in theory a major inroad into the principle of limited liability. The same conduct also constituted a crime. This provision had, however, been introduced on the recommendation of Cox to deal with one particularly blatant form of fraud which had prompted similar legislation in England. Directors of an insolvent company who had floating charges had been known to order goods in the knowledge that they could not be paid for but would represent at least some security in the event of the company being liquidated. This was the sort of practice aimed at by s 297, but it was seldom availed of by liquidators until recent years. A series of decisions did, however, indicate that its scope might be somewhat wider than had been thought[2].

[33.02] The 1990 Act enlarged significantly the operation of the fraudulent trading machinery. Three major changes were introduced. It is no longer necessary in every case to establish 'fraud' (a notoriously difficult burden to undertake) in order to render the persons concerned liable for the debts: 'recklessness' may suffice. The application can be made whether or not there is a winding up in being. And the penalties for the crime of fraudulent trading were increased.

[33.03] The object of these provisions is relatively clear. They are intended to ensure that the protection of limited liability will not be available to traders who carry on business with the intention of defrauding their creditors or who do so in circumstances where any reasonable person would know that there is no real prospect that the creditors will be paid. Clearly, the philosophy that underlies the provisions is that honest and responsible people should not be penalised simply because their businesses have failed, but that the dishonest and the irresponsible should not escape liability for the debts they have run up.

---

[1]   Companies Act 1963, s 297.
[2]   See para **[33.18]** below.

Civil liability for fraudulent or reckless trading

[33.04] Section 297 of the Principal Act has, as a result of the 1990 Act, been replaced by two separate sections, s 297 and s 297A[3]. Section 297A provides that specified persons are to be personally responsible without limitation of liability for all or part of a company's debts or liabilities in defined circumstances. Section 297 imposes criminal liability on persons found guilty of fraudulent trading.

[33.05] The civil liability imposed by s 297A can take two forms. First, an officer of the company, such as a director, can be declared to be personally responsible, without any limitation of liability, for all or part of the debts of the company, where it appears that, while he was an officer, he was knowingly a party to the carrying on of the business of the company in a reckless manner. Secondly, any person, whether an officer or not, can be made similarly liable if he was knowingly a party to the carrying on of any business of the company with intent to defraud its creditors or for any fraudulent purpose.

[33.06] The application can be made in the course of the winding-up of the company by the receiver, liquidator, or any creditor or contributory[4]. It can also be made, however, by any of these parties where there is no winding-up, but either:

(1)   an execution of a judgment in favour of a creditor has been returned unsatisfied; or

(2)   it is proved to the satisfaction of the court that the company is unable to pay its debts, taking into account its prospective and contingent liabilities;

and in either case the reason or the principal reason for its not being wound up is the insufficiency of its assets[5]. This provision is intended to provide for the many cases which can arise in which there are grounds for believing that the company has been trading recklessly or fraudulently but its assets are either non-existent or are not enough to pay the costs of a winding-up. The application can also be made by an examiner who has been appointed under the provisions of the 1990 (No 1) Act.

[33.07] Where, however, the application is made in respect of alleged reckless trading, the order can only be made where the company is deemed to be unable to pay its debts because one or more of the circumstances mentioned in s 214 of the Principal Act has arisen, of which the most common is that a creditor to

---

[3]   Inserted by the Companies Act 1990, ss 137 and 138.

[4]   Companies Act 1963, s 33.

[5]   Companies Act 1990, s 251.

whom the company is indebted in the sum of £1,000 or more has not been paid his debt for a period of three weeks after a written demand[6].

[33.08] In the case of reckless trading, it must also be shown that the applicant, 'being a creditor or contributory of the company, or any person on whose behalf such application is made,' suffered loss or damage as a result of the behaviour in question[7].

[33.09] We shall deal first with 'reckless' trading, bearing in mind that, in this respect, liability is confined to the officers of the company. 'Officer' in this context includes, in addition to directors and secretaries, 'shadow directors'[8], auditors, liquidators and receivers.

[33.10] 'Reckless' trading is not defined, but sub-s (2) gives some additional guidance by providing (without prejudice to the generality of the expression) that an officer may be deemed to be knowingly a party to reckless trading in either of the following circumstances:

(1) where he was a party to the carrying on of the business and, having regard to the general knowledge, skill and experience that might reasonably be expected of a person in his position, he ought to have known that his actions or those of the company would cause loss to the creditors;

(2) where he was a party to the contracting of a debt by the company and did not honestly believe on reasonable grounds that the company would be able to pay the debt when it fell due for payment as well as its other debts (taking into account contingent and prospective liabilities)[9].

[33.11] In deciding to make an order where the officer concerned is alleged to have been party to the contracting of a debt by the company where he did not honestly believe that it could be paid, the court is to have regard to whether the creditor was aware at the time of the company's financial state of affairs.

[33.12] The court has also power to relieve any person of liability in whole or part where it appears that the person concerned has acted 'honestly and reasonably' in relation to the affairs of the company or any matter on the ground of which a declaration is sought. The adverb 'reasonably' should be noted: a person who has acted honestly throughout may still be found liable if his conduct has been unreasonable.

---

6   Companies Act 1963, s 297A(3).
7   Companies Act 1963, s 297A(3).
8   See para **[27.05]** above.
9   Companies Act 1963, s 297A(2).

[33.13] There has been much controversy in the area of the criminal law in recent years as to whether the term 'reckless' should be interpreted in an objective or subjective manner. Construing it objectively would mean in effect the court deciding whether the hypothetical 'reasonable man' would have acted in the particular way, whereas construing it subjectively would mean deciding whether the person concerned genuinely believed he was not acting recklessly, however unreasonable his behaviour might seem viewed objectively[10].

[33.14] The decision of the High Court in *Re Hefferon Kearns Ltd (No 2)*[11] made it clear that, in the circumstances envisaged in sub-ss (a) and (b), recklessness is to be determined objectively. Lynch J pointed out that the inclusion of the word 'knowingly' in sub-s (1) indicated that an officer of the company could not be regarded as guilty of reckless trading unless he was carrying on the business in a manner which he knew very well involved an obvious and serious risk of loss or damage to others. However, sub-ss (a) and (b) extended the application of sub-s (1) to circumstances where he ought to have known that his actions would cause loss to the creditors or where he did not honestly believe on reasonable grounds that a company could be able to pay a particular debt when it fell due. The objective nature of the test of recklessness was emphasised by sub-s (6) empowering the court to relieve any person of liability where it appeared that he had acted 'honestly and reasonably'. As the learned judge put it:

> 'The objective nature of the test of recklessness is emphasised by sub-section 6 which presupposes that a director may be reckless, although he acted honestly and responsibly. The plaintiff must show that the defendants took an unjustified risk, but that is to be assessed on the basis of what they ought to have known and not merely on what they in fact knew. Merely continuing with the business when that fact involved an unjustifiable risk and caused loss to creditors is enough'.

[33.15] In practical terms, accordingly, it would appear that a person who continues to trade or incurs specific liabilities in a foolishly optimistic belief that he will get out of his difficulties may be held to have traded 'recklessly'. If, however, he has acted in a manner in which the average reasonable person would have done in his particular circumstances, it would seem that he would not be held liable, however ill advised his actions may appear to be in retrospect.

[33.16] Personal liability for the company's debts can also be incurred by any person who was knowingly party to the carrying on of any business of the company with intent to defraud the creditors of the company or any other person or for any other fraudulent purpose. This provision is in precisely the same terms

---

[10] See *DPP v Murray* [1977] IR 360; *R v Caldwell* (1982) AC 341; Law Reform Commission Report on Malicious Damage, pp 79/80.
[11] [1993] 3 IR 191.

as the (now replaced) s 297(1) of the Principal Act. Accordingly, the authorities on that sub-section can safely be referred to when it is being considered.

[33.17] Unlike the 'reckless trading' provision, this extends to any person who was knowingly party to the fraudulent trading and is not confined to the officers. It was held in England in *Re Wm C Leitch Bros Ltd*[12] that where the company carried on business and incurred debts and there was to the knowledge of the directors no reasonable prospect of the creditors being paid, it was, in general, a proper inference that the company was carrying on business with intent to defraud. But the High Court in Australia took a stricter view of the onus of proof and said that an express intention to defraud was required[13]. As we have seen, if it could be shown that there was no reasonable prospects of the creditors being paid, a case would probably now lie against the directors for reckless trading.

[33.18] Normally, one would expect to find a pattern of continuous fraudulent trading where an order is made under this provision. Thus, in *Re Aluminium Fabricators Ltd*[14], O'Hanlon J found that the directors of a company had deliberately maintained a dual system of bookkeeping in order to conceal from their auditors, the Revenue and their creditors generally the fact that they were siphoning off the assets of the company for their own benefit. In *Re Kelly's Carpetdrome Ltd*[15], Costello J found that the controller of the company had arranged for the destruction of records and the transfer of assets into other hands with a view to defrauding the Revenue. In both cases, the persons responsible were held to be personally liable for all the company's debts.

[33.19] But it is also clear that a single transaction may be enough to justify the making of an order under this provision. In *Re Hunting Lodge Ltd*[16], an application was made for such an order when two directors, RP and his wife, JP, had arranged for the sale of the only remaining asset of the company to O'C, P Co being used by O'C as a vehicle for completing the transaction. The sale price was £480,000, but there was a secret arrangement for the payment of £200,000 by O'C directly and not into the company's account. This money was lodged by RP in a building society in fictitious names. At the time of this transaction, the company was insolvent. Carroll J held that the words 'any business of the company' were not synonymous with trading: a single transaction which was entered into with the intention of defrauding the company's creditors could bring the provision into operation. Since it was clear that the object of the transaction

---

[12] [1932] Ch 71.
[13] *Hardie v Hanson* (1960) CLR 451.
[14] (Unreported, 13 May 1983).
[15] (Unreported, 1 July 1983).
[16] [1985] ILRM 75.

was to ensure that the sum of £200,000 was paid to RP rather than to the creditors, an order could be made under the provision.

[33.20] Although, as we have seen, the provisions as to fraudulent trading extend to persons other than directors, in their case mere inaction is not enough. The failure of the company's secretary or financial adviser to warn the directors of the company's insolvency and its possible consequences was held to be an insufficient ground for an order in *Re Maidstone Building Provisions Ltd*[17]. Under the new provisions, however, he could perhaps have been found liable for reckless trading as an officer of the company. In *Re Hunting Lodge Ltd*, Carroll J found that not merely RP and JP were liable but also O'C and P Co on the ground that they had actively participated in the fraudulent transaction.

[33.21] The judgment against the persons concerned, whether for reckless or fraudulent trading, is for a fixed sum which then becomes part of the assets[18]. The court may, however, order that sums recovered under the section are to be paid to specified persons or classes of persons (such as for example creditors of a particular class) in defined proportions and in such priority as the order specifies. It may also charge the liability of the persons concerned against any security which they may hold from the company[19]. A director may also be disqualified from acting as a director of any company for such period as the court specifies in the order[20].

[33.22] Doubts that had been expressed as to whether provisions of this nature are repugnant to the Constitution, because they in effect subject persons to a trial on criminal charges without the protection normally afforded by the criminal law, were resolved in the case of *O'Keeffe v Ferris*[21]. In the High Court, Murphy J concluded that, while the provisions were perhaps anomalous, it did not seem to him that the sanction was necessarily criminal. The Oireachtas had clearly intended to create a civil offence which could be invoked so as to recover compensation from a group of wrongdoers for the benefit of those who were wronged. It was the clear intention of the Oireachtas that this should be a civil remedy and not a criminal one. However, he also said:

'The sub-section confers a wide discretion on the court and it must be assumed that the court will exercise those powers, not merely in a responsible but also in a constitutional fashion. If the Constitution does require that in civil proceedings the burden imposed on the defendants should in general be commensurate with the loss suffered by the plaintiff (or the class whom the plaintiff represents) then

---

17 [1971] 3 All ER 363.
18 *Re Williams C Leitch Bros (No 2)* [1933] Ch 261.
19 Companies Act 1963, s 297A(7).
20 See para [27.171] above.
21 [1993] 3 IR 165.

it must be assumed that the sub-section will be so construed and applied. It had already been decided in the *Leitch* case that the courts should declare the particular amount payable by any given defendant and it seems to me that this is a desirable and proper interpretation of this section and its predecessor. It is important that the defendant should know the extent of his liability'.

The learned judge also rejected a submission that the determination in civil proceedings of the responsibility of a defendant who could also be prosecuted for a criminal offence arising out of the same facts was constitutionally frail.

[33.23] These conclusions were upheld on appeal by the Supreme Court. O'Flaherty J, giving the judgement of the court, said that:

'While much stress has been laid by counsel for the plaintiff on the need to protect the citizen from injustice in the course of proceedings, the entitlement of victims of wrongdoings to be safeguarded is something to which the court must also have regard and the court, therefore, upholds the paramount objective of this legislative provision, which is to protect those who may have been wronged'[22].

Criminal liability for fraudulent trading

[33.24] Section 297 of the Principal Act, as inserted by s 137 of the 1990 Act, provides that, where in the course of the winding up of a company, it appears that any business of the company has been carried on with intent to defraud creditors of the company or creditors of any other person or for any fraudulent purpose, any person who was knowingly party to the carrying on of the business in that manner is guilty of an offence. He is liable on summary conviction to imprisonment for a term not exceeding 12 months or to a fine not exceeding £1,000 or both and on indictment to imprisonment for a term not exceeding seven years or to a fine not exceeding £50,000 or both.

[33.25] A prosecution can also be brought under this section where no winding up has taken place if the conditions mentioned in para **[33.06]** above as to the insolvency of the company in general terms are met.

---

[22] [1997] 3 IR 463.

Chapter 34

Insider Dealing in Shares

[34.01] 'Insider dealing' is not a new phenomenon. Since the earliest days of markets in shares, profits have been made by those in possession of information not generally available. Sometimes the killing has been the result of a tip from someone in the company; sometimes it has been the insider himself who has been the beneficiary. As we have seen[1], the courts developed doctrines which helped to make directors accountable when they benefited themselves at the expense of the general body of shareholders. The legislature, moreover, has intervened to an increasing extent to ensure that directors' dealings in shares in their own or related companies are fully disclosed and has extended these obligations to a wide range of people connected with directors[2]. In addition, dealings by directors in share options in their own and related companies were rendered criminal[3].

[34.02] Part V of the 1990 Act was intended to close another gap in this area of company law. Although directors and others could be forced to yield up such profits for the benefit of the company itself, the individual shareholder had, in general, no remedy, even where he was clearly at a loss and even though 'insider dealing' as it came to be called, could expose directors to civil proceedings in certain circumstances. Moreover, it did not generally result in criminal liability.

[34.03] In recent decades, the stock exchanges in the United Kingdom and Ireland sought to control insider dealing by means of regulations[4]. Statutory controls were first introduced in England by the 1980 Act. The relevant legislation in that jurisdiction is now Part V of the Criminal Justice Act 1993. Those provisions, however, impose criminal liability only, unlike Part V of our 1990 Act which affords a civil remedy to those who can prove loss as a result of insider dealing.

[34.04] Although the English legislation has been in place since 1980, there had only been 33 prosecutions in that jurisdiction up to the end of the first quarter of 1994. Fourteen pleaded guilty and only nine were convicted after pleading not

---

[1]   See para **[27.102]** above.
[2]   See para **[27.136]** above.
[3]   See para **[27.74]** above.
[4]   See the 'core rules' made under the Financial Services Act as amended by the Companies Act 1989.

guilty[5]. In the far smaller Irish exchange it must be doubtful whether there is a problem of sufficient dimensions to justify the relatively complex provisions of Part V. However, the co-ordination of regulatory measures in this area in the EU generally probably made such legislation here inevitable[6]. It might also have been thought that the criminal provisions in particular might discourage the carrying on of insider dealing from a base inside this jurisdiction[7].

Unlawful dealings by 'insiders'

[34.05] Section 108 of the 1990 Act is the basic provision which prohibits share dealings by 'insiders'. (The expression insiders is not used in the Act itself, although it appears both in the heading to Part V and the marginal note to s 108.) It renders unlawful dealings in securities of a company by a person who has been 'connected with' that company within the past six months where the person concerned is in possession of information which is not generally available but, if it were, would be likely materially to affect the price of the securities. (We shall call it in this chapter 'relevant information'.) These offenders can be described as 'primary insiders'. However, the prohibitions also extend to 'secondary insiders', ie those who receive the relevant information from the primary insiders.

[34.06] It should be noted that the section renders unlawful the use of information of which the dealer is 'in possession'. This is in contrast to the English legislation which uses the expression 'obtained'. In that jurisdiction, an argument was advanced which proved ultimately unsuccessful that a person committed no offence who simply received information but took no active steps to obtain it[8]. In view of the difference in wording, the argument would be even less likely to succeed in Ireland.

[34.07] The key expressions in the section are defined in sweeping terms. 'Dealing' covers not merely acquiring, disposing of, subscribing for or underwriting securities: it extends to making or offering to make an agreement relating to any of these activities and inducing or attempting to induce any other person to do the same. It covers in the same way an agreement the purpose of which is to secure a profit or gain to a person who acquires, disposes of, subscribes for or underwrites the securities or to any of the parties to the agreement. 'Securities' are defined as shares, debentures or other debt securities issued or proposed to be issued in Ireland or elsewhere and for which dealing

---

5   See Hannigan, *Insider Dealing* (2nd edn, 1994), p118 et seq.
6   European Community Directive 89/592, co-ordinating regulations on insider dealing.
7   At the time of writing, there would appear to have been no criminal or civil proceedings brought in this jurisdiction in respect of insider dealing.
8   *R v Fisher* [1989] 2 All ER 1.

facilities are provided on a recognised stock exchange. Hence, shares in a private company are not affected, but with that limitation the definition extends to rights, options and obligations in all such securities and to such other interests as the Minister may prescribe.

[34.08] The expression 'a person ... connected with a company' is also widely defined. It means:

(1)   officers of the company and its related companies;

(2)   shareholders in the company and its related companies;

(3)   persons occupying positions that may reasonably be expected to give them access to the relevant information because:

    (a) there is a professional business or other relationship between them and the company or its related companies;

    (b) they are officers of 'substantial shareholders' in the company or its related companies.

In turn, these expressions are elaborated. 'Officers' include directors, secretaries, employees, liquidators, examiners, auditors and receivers. Moreover, 'shadow directors', ie those on whose instructions the directors are accustomed to act, are also included. A 'related company' is a subsidiary or holding company of the company or a subsidiary of its holding company.

[34.9] It will be observed that those who acquire the relevant information because of some professional or business relationship, such as solicitors, accountants, bankers etc are brought within the ambit of the section. Such persons are affected whether they have access to the relevant information because of a private occupation or because they hold a public office.

[34.10] As we have seen, the prohibitions in s 108 extend not merely to the primary insiders discussed in the preceding paragraph, but to secondary insiders as well. Those who are not 'connected with' the company but are in possession of relevant information received, directly or indirectly, from someone who is, are also prohibited from dealing in the securities, if they are aware, or ought reasonably to be aware, that the person concerned is himself prohibited from dealing. An insider, whether he is of the primary or secondary category, is also precluded from passing on the relevant information to any other person, if he knows or ought reasonably to know, that the other person will make use of the information for the purpose of dealing in the securities or causing or procuring another person to deal in the securities.

[34.11] A primary insider is also precluded from dealing in securities of a company other than the one with which he is connected where, because of the connection, he is in possession of relevant information relating to the other company and the information relates to a transaction involving both companies or the fact that such a transaction had been, but is no longer, contemplated.

[34.12] It is also unlawful for primary or secondary insiders to cause or procure any other person to deal in the relevant securities.

[34.13] A company is prohibited from dealing in securities when one of its officers is so precluded, whether as a primary or secondary insider. But this does not apply where the decision to enter into the transaction was taken by a person on its behalf other than the officer concerned, there were written arrangements in operation to ensure that the information was not communicated to that person and that no advice was given to him by a person in possession of such information, and no such information or advice was in fact given.

[34.14] The prohibition does not extend to an agent acting pursuant to specific instructions to effect the dealing, provided he does not give any advice to his principal in relation to dealings in securities of the same class.

Civil liability for insider dealing

[34.15] It is sometimes said that insider dealing is a 'victimless offence': the insider doubtless reaps a profit not available to others, but that is hardly a reason for regarding the others as all victims. This is not the whole truth: the person who sells his shares is getting less than he would if he knew the facts of which the insider is aware and, to that extent, can properly be regarded as being at a loss. Part V, accordingly, seeks to ensure a remedy for those who can show that they have been injured by the relevant insider dealing.

[34.16] Where a person deals in securities in breach of s 108, or causes or procures another to do the same, he is under a twofold potential liability. He is liable to compensate any other party to the transaction who was not in possession of the relevant information for any loss he sustains because of the difference between the price at which the securities were actually dealt in and the price at which they would have been dealt in if he had been in possession of the relevant information[9]. He is also liable to account to the company for any profit which accrues to him from dealing in the securities[10]. This latter provision can be seen as an extension of the liability already imposed at common law on directors in this area to the wide range of other persons connected with the company who are captured by Part V[11].

[34.17] Where the insider has been found liable already to pay compensation or account for profits because of the same act or transaction, the amount in

---

[9] Companies Act 1990, s 109(1).
[10] Companies Act 1990, s 109(1).
[11] See para **[27.102]** above.

question is to be deducted. The onus of proving that the liability arose from the same transaction is, however, on the insider.

[34.18] An action for the recovery of the loss or profits under this provision must be brought within two years of the completion of the transaction.

Criminal liability for insider dealing

[34.19] Anyone who deals in securities in breach of s 108 is guilty of an offence[12]. He is liable on summary conviction to imprisonment for a term not exceeding 12 months or a fine not exceeding £10,000 or both and on indictment to imprisonment for a term not exceeding ten years or a fine not exceeding £200,000 or both. It may be noted that the penalties are substantially higher than for any other offences created by the Acts.

[34.20] A person who is convicted of an offence under this provision and deals in any securities within the next 12 months is guilty of a further offence and liable to the same penalties. But no offence is committed where the relevant transaction was initiated, but not completed, before the date of the conviction, the rights of an innocent third party would be prejudiced by its non-completion and it is not in any other way unlawful[13].

[34.21] There are provisions intended to ensure that the stock exchange report cases in which they suspect insider dealing may have occurred to the Director of Public Prosecutions[14]. The obligation to report such cases is imposed on both the 'relevant authority' of the exchange and its members. A relevant authority is the board of directors, management committee or other management authority or its manager.

[34.22] If it appears to the relevant authority of the exchange that an offence under Part V has been committed, it must report the matter forthwith to the DPP. It must also give him such information and documents in its possession or under its control as he may require. If no report is made but it appears to a court hearing any proceedings that an offence has been committed, the court may on the application of any person interested in the proceedings or of its own motion, direct a report to be made.

[34.23] A member of the exchange is required to make a report to the relevant authority forthwith where he suspects that an offence has been committed. The exchange thereupon comes under the same duty to report the matter to the DPP.

---

12 Companies Act 1990, s 111.
13 Companies Act 1990, s 112.
14 Companies Act 1990, s 115.

[34.24] The stock exchange is given certain investigative powers in order to enable it to report to the DPP as to the possible commission of offences[15]. An 'authorised person' - either the manager of the exchange or a person nominated by the relevant authority - may require any person whom he or the authority have reasonable cause to believe to have dealt in securities or to have information about such dealings to give the authorised person information reasonably required in regard to

   (1)   the securities concerned;

   (2)   the company which issued them;

   (3)   his dealings in the securities;

   (4)   any other information reasonably required by the authorised person in relation to such securities or such dealings.

[34.25] Either the authorised person or the person from whom the information is sought may apply to the court for a declaration as to whether the exercise of the powers is warranted by 'the exigencies of the common good'. If the court declares that it was and the person refuses to comply with the requirement within a reasonable time, the authorised person may certify the refusal under his hand to the court and the court may, after hearing any statement which may be offered in defence, punish the offender 'in like manner as if he had been guilty of contempt of court'. It would seem that this method of enforcement is of doubtful constitutionality[16].

[34.26] The Minister can request the exchange to make use of its powers of investigation and reporting under Part V if a complaint is made to the relevant authority concerning an alleged offence and it appears to him that there are circumstances suggesting that they ought to do so. Where he makes such a request, the relevant authority must communicate to him the results of its investigations or a copy of its report as the case may be[17].

[34.27] The stock exchange must present an annual report to the Minister, detailing the number of written complaints received, the number of reports made to the DPP, the number of instances in which, following an investigation, reports were not made and such other information as may be prescribed by the Minister[18].

---

[15] Companies Act 1990, s 117.
[16] See para **[35.36]** below.
[17] Companies Act 1990, s 115(5) and (6).
[18] Companies Act 1990, s 120.

Exempt transactions

[34.28] The following transactions are exempt from the provisions of Part V prohibiting dealings in securities:

(1)   the acquisition of securities under a will or intestacy;

(2)   the acquisition of securities in a company pursuant to an employee sharing scheme;

(3)   the obtaining by a director of his share qualification;

(4)   a transaction entered into by a person in accordance with his obligations under an underwriting agreement;

(5)   transactions entered into by personal representatives, trustees, liquidators, receivers or examiners in the performance of their functions; or

(6)   transactions by way of, or arising out of, mortgages or charges on securities or mortgages, charges, pledges or liens on documents of title to securities.

The transactions other than (1) and (2) are only exempt, however, where they are entered into in good faith.

[34.29] Transactions entered into by a government minister or the Central Bank in pursuit of monetary, exchange rate, national debt management or foreign exchange reserve policies are also exempt[19].

[34.30] A person is to be regarded as having entered in good faith into the transactions to which (4) above relates, where he enters in good faith into:

(1)   an agreement to underwrite securities or

(2)   an agreement, in advance of dealing facilities being provided by a recognised stock exchange for securities, to acquire or subscribe for a specified number of those securities;

(3)   negotiations with a view to entering an agreement to which (1) or (2) above relate or

(4)   a transaction in accordance with such a person's obligations under an agreement to which (1) or (2) relates[20].

[34.31] The manipulation of the stock market with a view to stabilising the price of a new issue could be in breach of provisions of Part V of the 1990 Act prohibiting insider dealing which have been considered in this chapter. Steps taken to ensure such stabilisation might also be in breach of the obligation to disclose interests in share capital in certain circumstances imposed by ss 67 to 79 of that Act. Since, however, the stabilisation of the price of a new share issue

---

[19]   Companies Act 1990, s 110 as amended by the Companies (Amendment) (No 1) Act 1999, s 4.
[20]   Companies Act 1990, s 110 as amended by the Companies (Amendment) (No 1) Act 1999, s 4.

could be a legitimate strategy, the 1999 (No 1) Act provides for the removal of such transactions from the ambit of those provisions in the 1990 Act.

[34.32] Such transactions are exempted provided they take place in accordance with the Stabilisation Rules set out in the Schedule to the Act. These rules broadly correspond to the rules adopted in the United Kingdom by the Securities and Investment Board and apply where:

(1)   the securities are listed on a recognised stock exchange and the total cost of the securities is at least £15 million; or

(2)   the securities may be dealt with on a recognised stock exchange without a formal application; or

(3)   an application has been made to a recognised stock exchange for the securities to be dealt with on that exchange.

[34.33] The transactions entered into with a view to stabilising or maintaining the market price of such securities are only exempted where the offer or issue is at a specified price. A take over offer is not within the exemption. The rules provide that the stabilising actions can only be taken within a specified period[21].

Co-operation with other EU stock exchanges

[34.34] Part V also contains provisions intended to facilitate co-operation between stock exchanges in the member states of the EU in combating insider dealing. Where the relevant authority of the stock exchange receives a request for information from a similar authority in another member state relating to the performance of its functions under any enactment in the EU relating to unlawful dealing, the authority, so far as it is reasonably able to do so, must obtain and provide the information requested, making use of the powers already detailed where appropriate[22].

[34.35] Before complying with such a request, however, the authority must advise the Minister who may direct it not to comply on any of the following grounds:

(1)   compliance might adversely affect the sovereignty, security or public policy of the State;

(2)   civil or criminal proceedings have already been commenced in Ireland in respect of any of the acts concerned;

(3)   any person has been convicted in Ireland in respect of any such acts.

---

[21] It would appear that the Companies (Amendment) (No 2) Act 1999 was enacted in order to provide, if necessary, for the stabilisation of the market price of the shares in Telecom Éireann (now Eircom) offered to the public in July 1999. See Cahill, *Corporate Finance Law*, p 260, n 226.

[22] Companies Act 1990, s 116.

Chapter 35

Investigation of a Company's Affairs

Introduction

[35.01] The Minister has, as we have seen, a general supervisory jurisdiction over companies formed under the Acts. Both the 1908 Act and the Principal Act gave him and his predecessor power to appoint inspectors to investigate the affairs of companies. These powers were rarely availed of in practice. In many cases, those who wished to see the company's affairs investigated were frustrated creditors and they might have preferred to petition for the winding up of the company. But another factor was undoubtedly the reluctance of successive Ministers to make use of their powers. There were also serious limitations on the circumstances in which the Minister could order an investigation.

[35.02] The 1990 Act introduced sweeping changes in this area. The power to order an investigation was vested in the High Court and the limitations on the circumstances in which the investigation may be initiated were largely removed. The Minister was given new powers to investigate the ownership of companies and to require the production of documents. He may also obtain a search warrant from the District Court in order to seize documents which have been withheld from him.

[35.03] The provisions in relation to investigations are contained in Part II of the 1990 Act: this in effect replaced ss 165 to 173 of the Principal Act which were repealed.

[35.04] The new powers conferred by the 1990 Act have been availed of in a number of cases. Of these, the most notable have been the investigations ordered into the acquisition by Telecom Éireann (as it then was) of a site in Ballsbridge, events arising out of the privatisation of the Irish Sugar Company, (the Greencore investigations), and certain practices of National Irish Bank Limited which, it was suggested, were designed to facilitate tax evasion and the unfair exploitation of customers by the imposition of concealed charges.

[35.05] Following the revelation to the McCracken Tribunal of Inquiry that payments had been made by Mr Ben Dunne, when Chairman and Chief Executive of the Dunnes Stores Group, to Mr Michael Lowry and Mr Charles Haughey, the Minister also made use of her powers under the 1990 Act. The number of such investigations launched within the comparatively short period during which the new statutory regime has been in existence is striking. The inquiries have also given rise to some important Court decisions as to the interpretation of the relevant statutory provisions which are considered in more detail below.

Court order for investigation

[35.06] Section 7 of the 1990 Act confers the basic power on the court to appoint 'one or more competent inspectors' to investigate the affairs of a company. The circumstances in which such an order can be made are not specified and the only express limitations on the court's jurisdiction are as to the persons on whose application such an order can be made. They are:

    (1)   in the case of a company having a share capital, not less than 100 members or a member or members holding not less than one-tenth of the paid up share capital;

    (2)   in the case of a company not having a share capital, not less than one-fifth in number of the persons on the company's register of members;

    (3)   in any case, the company or a creditor of the company.

[35.07] Since the order can only be made on the application of one of these parties, it would seem that the court has no power to order an investigation of its own motion. It would seem, moreover, that the court cannot make such an order on the application of the liquidator during the course of a compulsory or voluntary winding up, since he is not one of the specified persons on whose application such an order can be made. It is clear, however, that the existence of a winding up is no bar to the making of the order and hence it can be made on the application of a creditor where the company is being wound up whether compulsory or voluntarily[1].

[35.08] The application must be supported by such evidence as the court may require. The inspectors appointed are to report in such manner as the court may direct. The expenses of the investigation are to be defrayed in the first instance by the Minister for Justice[2]. The court, however, can order the applicant or any company dealt with in the report to repay the Minister to such extent as it directs, but so that the amount does not exceed £100,000[3].

[35.9] In *Minister for Justice v Suicre Éireann*[4], Lynch J declined to make an order in favour of the Minister because the conduct which led to the investigation had taken place when the company, the subject of the investigation, was owned by the State.

1 Companies Act 1990, s 8(2)(a).
2 Companies Act 1990, s 13(1).
3 Companies Act 1990, s 13(1).
4 [1992] 2 IR 215.

[35.10] Frivolous or vexatious applications will presumably be discouraged by a provision enabling the court to order an applicant to provide security for these costs in a sum not less than £500 and not exceeding £100,000[5].

[35.11] The jurisdiction to order an investigation on the application of the Minister must next be considered. This power - which is expressed to be without prejudice to the more general power conferred by s 7 - can be exercised where the court is satisfied that there are circumstances suggesting:

(1)   that the company's affairs are being or *have been* conducted with intent to defraud its creditors or the creditors of any other person or otherwise for a fraudulent or unlawful purpose or in a manner which is unfairly prejudicial to some part of its members or that any actual or proposed act or omission of the company is or would be so prejudicial, or that it was formed for any fraudulent or unlawful purpose;

(2)   that persons connected with its formation or the management of its affairs have in connection therewith been guilty of fraud, misfeasance or other misconduct towards it or towards its members;

(3)   that its members have not been given all the information relating to its affairs that they might reasonably expect[6].

The words emphasised in (1) did not appear in the replaced provisions: it is a welcome change which makes it clear that the power to order an investigation is not confined to cases where the suspected misconduct is still going on. It should be noted, however, that the powers are not exercisable simply because of an apprehension on the part of creditors or members that the company is about to take some step which they see as damaging to their interests.

[35.12] The provisions as to the defraying of the expenses of the investigation by the Minister for Justice and the giving of security for costs summarised in the earlier paragraph apply in the same manner to an investigation under s 8.

[35.13] The power to make an order under s 8 extends to companies incorporated outside Ireland which carry on, or have at any time carried on, business in Ireland. Section 7 is, however, confined to companies incorporated in Ireland.

Nature of an investigation

[35.14] The investigation is into 'the affairs of a company'. The draftsman does not elaborate further: the phrase has, however, been interpreted in a decision on the corresponding English legislation as including the company's

---

5   Companies Act 1990, s 7(3).
6   Companies Act 1990, s 8(1).

'goodwill, its profits or losses, its contracts and assets including its shareholding in and ability to control the affairs of a subsidiary and perhaps in the latter regard a sub-subsidiary ...'[7]

[35.15] As in the case of an investigation under the provisions of the replaced sections in the Principal Act, the functions of the inspectors are to investigate and report. It is thus in essence a fact-finding exercise which does not of itself affect the legal rights and obligations of any individual concerned, although the publication of the report - and even the fact of an investigation having been ordered - may affect their reputations. The court, moreover, may make any order it deems fit in relation to matters arising from the report, including an order made of its own motion for the winding up of a company[8].

[35.16] Since the inspectors' reports do not determine any issues of fact or law, they are not, it is thought, exercising the judicial power of the state, when investigating or reporting, even though they are doing so in pursuance of a court order. Their functions, indeed, are more administrative than judicial or quasi-judicial in character. But it seems clear that they are obliged to observe the constitutional requirements of 'fair procedures', having regard to the consequences that may follow for individuals as a result of their report. The latter will have no redress in the form of a defamation action in respect of the contents of the report if it is published, since the publication is privileged[9]. In addition, the court may make an order in consequence of the inspectors' report which could undoubtedly affect their legal rights. Having regard to the principles laid down in *Re Haughey*[10], it would seem to follow that the inspectors must follow whatever fair procedures are appropriate, depending on the nature of the investigation.

[35.17] Thus, it may not be appropriate in every case for the inspectors to hold an oral hearing: the investigation ordered by the court may be more appropriately carried out by interviewing individuals separately and examining documents, much in the manner of a police inquiry. Even in such a case, however, it would seem essential for the inspectors to give a person or company in respect of whom they intend to make a critical finding an opportunity of answering the 'charge' before they present their report to the court. No doubt, the judge would consider himself equally bound before making any order on foot of the report, but that hardly absolves the inspectors from their duty to be fair. This was the view taken by the Court of Appeal in England in *Re Pergamon*

---

7   *R v Board of Trade, ex p St Martin's Preserving Co Ltd* [1965] I QB 603 at 613.
8   Companies Act 1990, s 12(1).
9   Companies Act 1990, s 23(3).
10 [1971] IR 217.

Press Ltd[11] where it was said that at least an outline of the charge should be given to the person concerned. It would seem to be reinforced by the views expressed by the Supreme Court as to the conduct of an inquiry under the Tribunals of Inquiry Act 1921 as amended in *Haughey v Moriarty*[12].

[35.18] That, however, would seem to be the limit of the obligation placed on the inspectors, unless they decide to hold an oral hearing. In that event, all the precautions to which the 'accused' is entitled under *Re Haughey* become applicable. He or they are not only entitled to be heard in their own defence under the *audi alteram partem* rule: they are also entitled to:

(1)   an opportunity to cross-examine witnesses[13];

(2)   an adjournment to enable them to prepare their case[14];

(3)   legal representation when the seriousness of the matter in issue or the consequences for the person concerned seem to warrant it[15].

In some circumstances, it may be a breach of the fair procedures rule to deny them access to documents which the inspectors have obtained from other parties for the purpose of the investigations[16].

[35.19] Obviously, observance of all these requirements may render an investigation unduly cumbersome. Although, as we shall see, the inspectors have power to compel the attendance of witnesses before them, the investigation may be facilitated if witnesses know that their identity will not be revealed by their having to attend an oral hearing. It would seem to defeat the object of the sections if an oral hearing were to be considered mandatory in every case. Presumably, however, if the new powers are availed of with any regularity, it will become apparent in what circumstances, arguably somewhat exceptional, the inspectors will be obliged to hold an oral hearing. Such an oral hearing need not be public, since it is not part of the administration of justice, although there is nothing to prevent it from being held in public if the inspectors consider this desirable[17].

---

[11] *Re Pergamon Press Ltd* [1971] Ch 388.

[12] (Unreported, 28 July 1998).

[13] *Kiely v Minister for Social Welfare* [1977] IR 267.

[14] *Kiely v Minister for Social Welfare* [1971] IR 21.

[15] *Re Haughey* [1971] IR 217.

[16] *Nolan v Irish Land Commission* [1981] IR 23.

[17] *Re Redbreast Preserving Co (Ireland) Ltd* 91 ILTR 12. Walsh J expressed doubts as to the correctness of this decision in *Re R Ltd* [1989] IR 126, but it would seem that his reservations were confined to the constitutional propriety of a judicial decision based on evidence heard other than in public. The inspectors' report under consideration does not necessarily result in such a decision: if it did, there might be doubts as to the constitutionality of the decision unless the inspectors conducted the hearing in public.

Powers of the inspectors

[35.20] The inspectors have wide ranging powers for the purpose of an investigation ordered by the court.

Investigation of other companies

[35.21] With the court's approval, they may extend their investigation into other related companies. (Related companies are defined in s 140 of the 1990 Act: see para **[36.34]** below.) This applies when the company in question answered that description at any relevant time[18].

Production of documents

[35.22] The officers and agents of the subject company and any other related company under investigation are under a duty to produce to the inspector all books and documents relating to the company in question in their custody or power[19]. If they consider that any other person is or may be in possession of any information concerning the relevant company, they may require that person to produce to them any books or documents relating to the company in question in his custody or power and he must then comply with that requirement[20].

Attendance and examination on oath

[35.23] The inspectors may require the officers and agents of the relevant companies and any other person whom they consider may be in possession of the information just mentioned to attend before them. They may then be examined on oath by the inspectors in relation to the company's affairs[21].

Assistance in general

[35.24] The officers and agents of any relevant company are also under a duty to give to the inspectors all the assistance in connection with the investigation which they are reasonably able to give[22]. Any person whom the inspectors consider may be in possession of the information mentioned above may also be required to give such assistance and must do so[23].

Bank accounts

[35.25] A director of a company under investigation can be required by the inspectors to produce documents, such as bank statements, relating to a bank

---

[18] Companies Act 1990, s 9.
[19] Companies Act 1990, s 10(1).
[20] Companies Act 1990, s 10(2).
[21] Companies Act 1990, s 10(4).
[22] Companies Act 1990, s 10(1).
[23] Companies Act 1990, s 10(2).

account maintained by him. This power becomes operative when the inspectors have reasonable grounds for believing that money has been paid into or out of the bank account which was the result of, or was used in, certain categories of transactions, particulars of which were not fully disclosed in the accounts or recorded in a register as required by the Acts. The transactions are:

(1)   contracts with the company or its subsidiary in which the director had a material interest;

(2)   loans, quasi-loans, credit transactions etc in favour of the director and others;

(3)   exempted lending transactions by licensed banks, particulars of which must be entered in a register by the bank[24].

[35.26] These requirements also apply where the inspectors have reasonable grounds for believing that money in an account has been in any way connected with acts or omissions constituting 'misconduct', whether fraudulent or not, on the part of the director towards the company or its members[25].

[35.27] It has been held in a number of cases that the inspectors are entitled, by virtue of these provisions, to inquire into companies, foreign or domestic, which are not even related to the company named in the order. The sole proviso is that such inquiries are relevant to the investigation of the affairs of the company named in the order of the Court or the Minister.

[35.28] Virtually all the decisions in question arose out of the investigation ordered by the Minister into the acquisition by Telecom Éireann of the premises formerly owned by Johnson, Mooney and O'Brien in Ballsbridge in 1990. The building had been bought by Telecom Éireann, then a semi-state body, for IR£9.4m having changed hands for only IR£4m two years earlier. Those engaged in the transactions, notably Dermot Desmond, a well-known Dublin financier, had used a number of interlocking companies, some of them incorporated outside Ireland, to carry into effect the sale and re-sale of the property. Because of public unease that people concerned in Telecom Éireann, might have benefited in the result from the purchase of the property by that body, the Minister originally established a committee of inquiry. That having failed to uncover all the details of the transactions, he then made use of his power under s 14 of the 1990 Act to appoint an inspector to investigate and report to him on the ownership of the company. That appointment, and the conduct of the investigation by the inspector, were the subject of a number of court challenges. While the investigation, accordingly, was not carried out under

---

24   As to these transactions, see paras **[27.57]** to **[27.60]** above.
25   Companies Act 1990, s 10(3).

an order of the court, it is clear that the principles laid down in the decisions in question are equally applicable to investigations ordered by the court.

[35.29] In *Chestvale Properties Ltd v Glackin*[26] and *Lyons v Curran*[27], it was held in the High Court by Murphy J and Blayney J respectively that the inspectors were not confined to inquiring into the affairs of the company named in the order and 'related companies'. That conclusion was upheld in *Probets v Glackin*[28] by the Supreme Court, McCarthy J observing that:

> 'If every time an inspector ran into a corporate shareholder, which happened to be a company registered outside the state, he had to cry "halt" it would make the section inoperable.'

[35.30] It was held by Costello J in *Glackin v Trustee Savings Bank*[29] that banks could not refuse to give the information sought by the inspector because to do so would be in breach of their confidential relationship with their customer. It is, however, clear that a person cannot be required to produce information in respect of which he would be entitled to claim legal professional privilege.

[35.31] It was also held by Murphy J in *Chestvale Properties Ltd v Glackin* that the relevant provisions of the 1990 Act empowered the inspectors to include in their investigations events which had occurred before the Act came into force. While acknowledging that there was a presumption that legislation was not intended to be retrospective unless that was expressly so provided, he held that it was the clear intention of the 1990 Act that it was to be retrospective.

[35.32] In the same case, Murphy J rejected a challenge to the constitutionality of the provision entitling the inspectors to inquire into the ownership of a company, holding that, while they undoubtedly abridged the private property rights of the citizen, they only did so to the extent necessitated by the exigencies of the common good.

[35.33] Section 10(5) of the 1990 Act as enacted provided that where an officer or an agent of the company or other person affected by the section refused to produce books or documents, or to attend before the inspectors or answer questions put to them in pursuance of an investigation ordered by the court, the inspectors might certify the refusal under their hand to the High Court. That court could then, after inquiring into the case, and hearing any witnesses who might be produced against or on behalf of the alleged offender and any statement

---

[26] [1993] 3 IR 35.
[27] [1993] ILRM 375.
[28] [1993] 3 IR 145.
[29] [1993] 3 IR 55.

offered in defence, punish the offender 'in like manner as if he had been guilty of contempt of court'.

[35.34] Section 10(6) provides that, without prejudice to that power, the court may, after a hearing under that sub-section, make any order or direction it thinks fit, including a direction to the person concerned to attend or re-attend before the inspector or produce particular books or documents or answer particular questions put to him by the inspector, or a direction that the person concerned need not produce a particular book or document or answer a particular question put to him by the inspector.

[35.35] It was pointed out in the second edition that sub-s (5) restored verbatim the corresponding provision in the Principal Act. The latter had been replaced by s 7 of the 1982 Act which created a criminal offence and provided for a trial either in the District Court or before a jury. It was suggested that s 2 of the 1982 Act had been enacted because of concern that the provisions in the Principal Act were repugnant to the Constitution, having regard to the decision of the Supreme Court in *Re Haughey*[30] that a similar power conferred on a Dail committee was unconstitutional because it deprived a person of his right to a trial by jury on a major charge. The reversion in the 1990 Act to the dubious procedure in the Principal Act was described as 'surprising'.

[35.36] These doubts as to the constitutionality of s 10(5) were confirmed by O'Hanlon J in *Desmond v Glackin (No 2)*[31], in which he held that so much of sub-s (5) as empowered the inspector to certify the refusal and the High Court to punish the offender was invalid having regard to the provisions of the Constitution. However, he also concluded that so much of sub-s (5) and sub-s (6) as entitled the court to direct the person concerned to produce particular books or documents or answer particular questions after the inquiry envisaged under sub-s (5) was severable and not repugnant to the Constitution. Failure to comply with such an order or direction of the court would, of course, be punishable as contempt of court in the ordinary way.

On appeal, the findings of O'Hanlon J on both issues were upheld by the Supreme Court which declined an invitation to overrule its earlier decision in *Re Haughey*.

The inspectors' report

[35.37] The inspectors must make a report to the court when they have completed their investigation. They may also present interim reports during the course of the investigation and must do so, if so directed by the court. If they

---

[30] [1971] IR 217.
[31] [1993] 3 IR 67.

become aware of matters during the course of the investigation suggesting that an offence has been committed, they may so inform the court without having to present a formal report[32].

[35.38] The court, as we have seen, may make such order as it deems fit in relation to matters arising from the report. Subject to the obvious limitation that the court could not impose a penalty on any individual without affording him the protection of a criminal trial in due course of law, there is no other qualification on the court's powers. One possible consequence which is envisaged by other provisions of the 1990 Act is the disqualification of a person from acting as an officer of any company[33]. Another would be the sending by the court to the Director of Public Prosecutions of all the papers relating to the investigation. The court is expressly empowered to order the winding up of any relevant company as a result of the report of its own motion.

[35.39] The court must furnish the Minister with a copy of the report. It may also cause the report to be printed and published and may forward a copy on request and payment of a prescribed fee to:

(1)   any member of a company which is the subject of the report;

(2)   any person whose conduct is referred to in the report;

(3)   the auditors of the company;

(4)   the applicants for the investigation;

(5)   any other person, including an employee and creditors, whose financial interests appear to be affected

(6)   the Central Bank, if the report relates wholly or partly to the affairs of a licensed bank[34].

The court may also forward a copy to the company's registered office[35].

[35.40] The court may, if it thinks proper, direct the omission from the report as published or transmitted to anyone of any particular part[36]. This will enable the court to publish the report without needlessly damaging the financial or other interests of a company or individual.

[35.41] The Act also provides that the publication of the report is to be privileged[37]. This provision was presumably prompted by doubts as to whether its publication could be regarded as part of the administration of justice, in

---

[32] Companies Act 1990, s 11.
[33] See para **[27.171]** above.
[34] Companies Act 1990, s 11(3).
[35] Companies Act 1990, s 11(3).
[36] Companies Act 1990, s 11(4).
[37] Companies Act 1990, s 23(3).

which case it would at common law be privileged. It may well be that, in ordering the publication of the report, the court may not be exercising the judicial power of the state. The judge, in ordering the investigation and publication of the report, may not be determining any issue of fact or law. The court indeed may very well take no action of any sort as a result of the report. Since it has been held on a number of occasions that the resolution of disputed issues of fact or law is one of the distinguishing characteristics of the administration of justice[38] it could be plausibly argued that no judicial function is being exercised. It was indeed held by the Court of Appeal in England that the power of the Secretary of State to order an investigation under the corresponding legislation was a purely administrative function which did not have to be exercised in accordance with natural justice[39]. It could, however, be argued that where the court orders an investigation under the new legislation, it is exercising a recognisably judicial function, since its order affects the rights of persons and companies, subjecting them to legal obligations as to the giving of evidence and, if the order is made in public, arguably affecting their commercial reputation. A *fortiorari*, the same could be said of the order that the report be published. The balance would seem to be in favour of regarding the orders made by the court - as contrasted with the investigation itself - as judicial in character, but it was clearly a safer course to provide expressly that the publication was privileged.

[35.42] The fact that, in the result, the persons affected by the contents of the report will have no recourse by way of an action for defamation against those responsible for its publication makes it all the more essential that the inspectors, in conducting their investigation, observe fair procedures. Any other approach could be challenged as failing adequately to protect the right of a person affected to his 'good name', contrary to Article 40.3 of the Constitution[40].

Investigation of ownership of company

[35.43] The 1990 Act conferred extensive new powers on the Minister to investigate the ownership of companies. The basic power is given to him by s 14 under which he can order one or more competent inspectors to investigate and report to him on its membership and otherwise with a view to determining:

> 'the true persons who are or have been financially interested in the success or failure (real or apparent) of the company or able to control or materially to influence the policy of the company.'

---

[38] *McDonald v Bord Na gCon* [1965] IR 217 at 263 *per* Kenny J.
[39] *Re Pergamon Press Ltd* [1971] Ch 388.
[40] *Re Haughey* [1971] IR 217.

[35.44] The Minister must be satisfied that there are circumstances - stated in extremely broad terms - justifying an investigation. They are:

(1)   the effective administration of company law;

(2)   the effective discharge by him of his functions under any enactment;

(3)   the public interest.

[35.45] The appointment may define the scope of the investigation and, in particular, may limit it to certain classes of shares or debentures.

[35.46] It would appear that the exercise by the Minister of this power may be judicially reviewed by the High Court and that he or she may be required to state the reasons for the investigation. In *Dunnes Stores Ireland Co v Maloney*[41], Laffoy J held that this was the case when the Minister was seeking the production of books or documents by the company under s 19 of the 1990 Act and the same considerations would seem to be applicable to the exercise of the power under s 14.

[35.47] For the purposes of the investigation, the inspectors have all the powers of inspectors under a court investigation, including the powers as to contempt of court, save the power of requiring information as to bank accounts[42]. There are the same provisions with relation to the presentation of interim and final reports, with the Minister being given the court's powers as to publication. Like the court, he may order any part of the report not to be published[43]. The publication of the report is also privileged[44].

[35.48] As already noted[45], the courts have taken an expansive view of the reach of this power: it is not confined in its operation to the named company and 'related' companies, but extends to all companies, domestic or foreign, and whether related to the named company or not, provided the investigation of the companies concerned is relevant to the investigation of the named company.

[35.49] Where it appears to the Minister that an investigation of the ownership of shares or debentures in a company is necessary on any of the grounds already mentioned, he may dispense with the appointment of inspectors and simply require the persons in a position to do so to give him the names and addresses of those interested, now or in the past, in the relevant shares or debentures. Any person who fails to give the required information, or knowingly or recklessly gives materially false information, is guilty of an offence and liable on summary

---

41 [1999] 1 ILRM 119.
42 See para **[35.20]** above.
43 See para **[35.39]** above.
44 See para **[35.41]** above.
45 See para **[35.27]** above.

conviction to a fine not exceeding £1,000 or imprisonment for a term not exceeding 12 months or both or on indictment to a fine not exceeding £10,000 or imprisonment for a term not exceeding three years or both[46].

[35.50] The powers of the Minister in carrying out such investigations could be effectively frustrated by a sale or transfer of the relevant shares. He is, accordingly, empowered by s 16 to impose restrictions on the transfer of such shares. Where he gives the appropriate directions by notice in writing in relation to the shares, the following consequences ensue:

(1)   any transfer of the shares is void;

(2)   no voting rights are exercisable;

(3)   no rights issue can be made to the holders;

(4)   except in a liquidation, no payment can be made to the shareholder of any sum due on the shares.

[35.51] Any person aggrieved by the exercise by the Minister of these powers may apply to the court for relief. Both the Minister and the court are empowered to lift the restrictions if, but only if:

(1)   either is satisfied that the relevant facts about the shares have been disclosed to the company and that no unfair advantage has accrued to any person as a result of the earlier non-disclosure; or

(2)   the shares are being sold and either approves the sale.

[35.52] The court may also order the sale of shares subject to restriction on the application of the Minister or the company and there are consequential provisions dealing with the lodgment in court and payment to those entitled of the proceeds of sale.

[35.53] An offence is also committed by any person who:

(1)   disposes or purports to dispose of any shares when he knows that their transfer is restricted;

(2)   votes, either as holder or proxy, in respect of such shares or appoints a proxy;

(3)   is a shareholder and fails to notify anyone who becomes a shareholder in respect of the shares of the restrictions, where he knows that the person concerned is unaware of them;

(4)   enters as shareholder or a person entitled to rights over the shares into an agreement avoided by the section.

---

46   Companies Act 1990, s 15.

The same penalties are applicable as are specified in para **[35.38]** above. There is, however, a provision peculiar to this section that summary proceedings may only be issued with the consent of the Minister. The Minister must publish notice of the restrictions in *Iris Ofigiúil* and at least two daily newspapers and send the notice to the company at its registered office.

Preliminary investigations and searches

[35.54] The Minister is given powers by the 1990 Act to require the production of documents relating to companies with a view to deciding whether a formal investigation under an order of the court or in exercise of his own powers is necessary. He may also require the production of such documents in an extensive range of other circumstances. These powers are reinforced by a provision enabling him to obtain a search warrant from the District Court if he suspects that documents are being withheld.

[35.55] Section 19 empowers the Minister to require the production by a company of books or documents. This may be done by the Minister or one of his authorised officers on production (if required) of evidence of his authority. The Minister may, as already noted, make such a requisition with a view to determining whether there should be a formal investigation. He may also use the power if there are circumstances suggesting that:

(1)   the affairs of the company are being or have been conducted with intent to defraud its creditors, the creditors of any other person or its members or for some other fraudulent purpose;

(2)   its affairs are being conducted in a manner which is unfairly prejudicial to some part of its members;

(3)   any actual or proposed acts or omissions on its part would be unfairly prejudicial to some part of its members or unlawful;

(4)   the body was formed for any fraudulent or unlawful purpose.

[35.56] The Minister or his authorised officers may also make similar requisitions in relation to persons who appear to be in possession of such books or documents, without prejudice to any lien. Copies of the relevant documents may be taken and the person concerned can be asked to give an explanation of any of them. He may also be required to state where the books or documents are, if they are not produced.

[35.57] Failure to comply with any of these requirements is an offence punishable in the same manner as failure to comply with the requirements of the Minister under the formal investigation. It is, however, a defence for a person to prove that the relevant books or documents were not in his possession or under his control and that it was not reasonably practicable for him to comply with the requirement.

[35.58] It was held by Laffoy J in *Dunnes Stores Ireland Co v Maloney*[47] that the exercise of this power may be judicially reviewed by the High Court. While the normal presumption applies that the power will be exercised by the Minister in a constitutional manner, the court is entitled to inquire into the manner in which it has been exercised where it is at least arguable that there were no grounds on which it could have been reasonably invoked or where fair procedures had not been observed. She further held that the Minister could be required to furnish his or her reasons for appointing an inspector: otherwise the court's power to review the reasonableness of the decision could be, as she put it, 'effectively stymied'. The Minister had sought the production of the documents following the revelation that, while the company was under the stewardship of Mr Ben Dunne, payments had been made from the company's funds to two politicians, Mr Michael Lowry and Mr Charles Haughey (in the latter case, the payments being in excess of £1,000,000). Laffoy J also held that the range of documents sought by the Minister was excessive.

[35.59] Section 20 empowers the District Justice to grant a search warrant. He may do so where he is satisfied on information on oath laid by an authorised officer that there are reasonable grounds for suspecting that there are on any premises any books or documents of which production has been required under s 19 but has not been forthcoming. The warrant is issued to a member of the Garda Síochána and any other person named in it and entitles them to enter any premises named in the information, using such force as is reasonably necessary. They may then search the premises and take possession of any books or documents which appear to have been the subject of a requisition. They may be retained for a period of three months or, if specified criminal proceedings to which they are relevant are commenced within that period, until the conclusion of the proceedings.

[35.60] There are strict limitations on the use which may be made of the seized documents. They may not be published without the company's consent to anyone except a 'competent authority' unless publication or disclosure is required:

(1)   with a view to the institution of criminal proceedings under the Acts or for any offence entailing misconduct in relation to the company's affairs or misapplication or wrongful retainer of its property;

(2)   with a view to the institution of any criminal proceedings in relation to exchange control or insurance legislation;

---

[47]   [1999] 1 ILRM 119.

(3)   for the purpose of complying with any of the requirements or exercising any of the powers in respect of inspectors' reports;

(4)   with a view to the institution by the Minister of proceedings for the winding up of the company under the Principal Act;

(5)   for the purpose of a search warrant application[48].

[35.61] The competent authorities are the Ministers for Industry and Commerce and Finance and their authorised officers, any court of competent jurisdiction, the inspectors, the Central Bank and a supervisory insurance authority[49].

[35.62] Offences are committed by any person who obstructs the exercise of an authorised right of search and seizure or who publishes books or documents except as permitted by the legislation. The penalties are the same as those outlined in para **[35.38]**[50].

Admissibility of answers and of reports in other proceedings

[35.63] Section 18 of the 1990 Act provides that an answer given by a person to a question put to him in exercise of the powers conferred by the Act may be used in evidence against him. The same applies to answers given during examinations conducted in the course of the winding up of companies, whether by the court or voluntarily. It was held in England that a person could not refuse to answer a question put to him in exercise of the powers conferred by the corresponding provisions on inspectors on the ground that he might incriminate himself[51]. It was suggested in the second edition that the position in Ireland, as in England, would be determined by common law, in the absence of any express constitutional provision protecting persons against self incrimination. It appeared to follow, that, subject to the overriding necessity to observe fair procedures[52], a person could not refuse to answer a question on the ground that the answer might incriminate him.

[35.64] Recent decisions of the Supreme Court have made it clear that the 'right of silence', as it is sometimes called in criminal proceedings, is protected by implication by Article 38.1 of the Constitution, guaranteeing the trial of all criminal offences 'in due course of law'[53]. It was held in those cases, however, that the right was not absolute and could be abridged, provided the curtailment was proportionate, ie no more than was required in order to uphold other

---

[48] Companies Act 1990, s 21(1).
[49] Companies Act 1990, s 21(3).
[50] Companies Act 1990, s 20(4).
[51] *R v Harris* [1970] 2 All ER 746.
[52] See para **[37.04]** above
[53] *Heaney v Ireland* [1994] 3 IR 593 (HC), [1996] 1 IR 580 (SC); *Rock v Ireland* [1997] 3 IR 485.

constitutional values. It was held by the Supreme Court in *Re National Irish Bank*[54] that a person could, accordingly, be required to answer a question put to him by the inspectors, even though the answer might incriminate him and might be used in evidence against him. Whether the statement could, in such circumstances, be regarded as voluntary and admissible in subsequent criminal proceedings would be a matter for the court which tried the criminal charge.

[35.65] Section 22 of the 1990 Act provides that a copy of the inspector's report is to be admissible in any legal proceedings as evidence:

(1)   of the facts set out therein without further proof unless the contrary is shown and

(2)   of the opinion of the inspector in relation to any matter contained in the report.

[35.66] In *Countyglen Ltd v Carway*[55], the plaintiff company sought to make use of an inspector's report in proceedings against members of a family who had formerly controlled the company and in which it (the company) made allegations of fraud, deceit and conspiracy. The use of the report in the proceedings was challenged on a number of grounds, including a submission that to construe the section as permitting the admission of the report in such circumstances would be unconstitutional because it would change the essentially adversarial nature of the proceedings into inquisitorial proceedings, contrary to principles of fair procedures.

[35.67] The constitutionality of the section was not challenged in those proceedings and Laffoy J held that, construed in accordance with the Constitution, the section permitted the adduction of the inspector's report as *prima facie* proof of the facts found therein and did no more than impose the burden of proof of establishing the contrary on the defendants.

Application of powers to foreign and other companies

[35.68] It should be noted that the powers of the inspectors where they are appointed by the court on the application of the Minister extend to foreign companies which carry on, or have at any time carried on, business in Ireland[56]. In addition, the power of the Minister under s 19 to require the production of documents extends to such companies and also to companies formed under previous legislation which was replaced by the Acts[57].

---

[54] [1999] 1 ILRM 321. See also *Saunders v United Kingdom* (1996) 23 EHRR 313.

[55] (Unreported, 20 February 1996), HC.

[56] Companies Act 1990, s 17.

[57] Companies Act 1990, s 19(1).

Part VIII

Winding up of Companies and Protection Orders

Chapter 36

Winding up by the Court

Introduction

[36.01] A company may in theory live forever. It may also, however, have its legal existence cut short in two ways: by being wound up or by being removed from the register.

[36.02] Strictly speaking, it is not the winding up of the company which terminates its legal existence. That only happens when the company is dissolved. But winding up, as the expression itself implies, is a necessary stage in the process which leads to dissolution.

[36.03] A winding up may take place for a variety of reasons: because the company has simply ceased to fulfil any useful purpose, because of strife among the members as to how it should be conducted, because it is insolvent, to name some. In each case, whatever the reason, the winding up is carried out by a liquidator.

[36.04] In the case of insolvent companies, the winding-up process is in many ways similar to the bankruptcy procedure in the case of an individual. The assets of the insolvent in each case are collected by an officer and distributed among the creditors in accordance with well-established rules. Some creditors, such as the Revenue, are entitled to priority for portion of their debts over the other creditors. Secured creditors may choose to rely on their securities and not avail of any distribution in the winding up or bankruptcy.

[36.05] There are also, however, important differences between the two codes. A bankruptcy is invariably carried out by a permanent officer of the court known as the Official Assignee. A liquidation is carried out by a person appointed either by the company or the court for the purpose of a specific liquidation.

[36.06] A winding up of a company which is solvent usually presents less problems than of one which is insolvent. In the latter case, there may be difficulties as to the rights of different types of creditors - ordinary, preferential and secured - and the liquidator may have to apply to the court for directions. The court may also be called upon to investigate the conduct of the company by the directors and other officers and to decide whether any such officer should be fixed with personal liability in respect of any of the company's debts.

[36.07] There are two main forms of winding up: by the court and voluntary. As the names suggest, the essential difference between the two procedures is that in the first the winding up is ordered by the court whereas in the second the members themselves decide to wind up the company. A voluntary winding up can be either a members' winding up or a creditors' winding up.

[36.08] The provisions relating to a winding up by the court (which is also sometimes called a compulsory winding up or compulsory liquidation) are contained in ss 212 to 250 of the Principal Act; those relating to a voluntary winding up (or voluntary liquidation) generally in ss 251 to 256; those relating to a members' winding up in ss 257 to 264; those relating to a creditors' winding up in ss 265 to 273; and those common to all forms of winding up in ss 206 to 211 and ss 283 to 313. Important amendments to all these provisions were effected by Part VI of the 1990 Act. The Rules of Court which prescribe the practice and procedure to be followed in winding up are contained in Order 74 of the Rules of the Superior Courts[1]. The forms to be used are contained in Appendix M to the Rules.

The High Court alone has jurisdiction in the winding up of companies[2].

Winding up by the court

[36.09] The Principal Act provides that in certain circumstances the court may order the winding up of a company on the petition of a person or body entitled under the Act to present such a petition. Such petitions are most commonly presented by or on behalf of creditors of the company.

[36.10] The essence of a typical winding up by the court is that, instead of each creditor of an insolvent company proceeding to enforce his claim for payment against the company individually, a liquidator is appointed to collect the assets of the company and enforce payment of the contributions due from the members. He then proceeds to distribute the assets among the creditors of the company in the priority prescribed by the Principal Act. The Principal Act contains provisions which prevent the taking of individual actions against the company during the winding up and which render void certain dispositions of property by which a company, aware of the imminence of the winding up, might seek to defraud its creditors.

---

[1]   SI 1986/15.

[2]   Companies Act 1963, s 212: cf *Stokes v Milford Cooperative Creamery Ltd* (1956) 90 ILTR 67.

Companies that may be wound up by the court

[36.11] All companies formed and registered under Part II of the Principal Act or registered under Part IX of the Act may be wound up by the court. In addition, the following companies are subject to this jurisdiction:

(1)   companies formed and registered under former Companies Acts[3]

(2)   companies registered but not formed under former Companies Acts[4]

(3)   unlimited companies re-registered as limited companies under former Companies Acts[5]

(4)   unregistered companies.

[36.12] Part X of the Principal Act deals with the winding up of unregistered companies. An unregistered company, in this context, does not include companies formed and registered under the Acts or under previous Companies Acts, or partnerships, associations or companies which consist of less than eight members and are formed in Ireland. Subject to this, it includes:

(1)   any partnership, whether limited or not;

(2)   any association; and

(3)   any company.

[36.13] Among unregistered companies which may be wound up by the courts are:

(1)   companies incorporated by special Act[6];

(2)   companies incorporated by royal charter (but not societies so incorporated[7];

(3)   foreign companies which have established a place of business in Ireland but have ceased to carry on business in Ireland[8];

(4)   building societies formed prior to the Building Societies Act 1874[9];

(5)   trustee savings banks[10];

(6)   friendly societies[11];

(7)   industrial and provident societies[12]

---

[3]   Companies Act 1963, s 324.

[4]   Companies Act 1963, s 325.

[5]   Companies Act 1963, s 326.

[6]   *Re Barton-upon-Humber Water Co* (1889) 42 Ch D 585.

[7]   *Re Commercial Buildings* [1938] IR 477.

[8]   Companies Act 1963, s 345(7).

[9]   *Re Ilfracombe Building Society* [1901] 1 Ch 102.

[10]   Companies Act 1963, s 344.

[11]   Friendly societies can only be wound up compulsorily: *Re Independent Protestant Loan Society* [1895] 1 IR 1; *Re Irish Mercantile Loan Society* [1907] 1 IR 98.

[12]   Industrial and provident societies, like friendly societies, can only be wound up compulsorily. See Industrial and Provident Societies (Amendment) Act 1978.

[36.14] A procedure is provided by Part IV of the Insurance Act 1936 for the winding up of insolvent insurance companies on the petition of the Minister. The Minister also has power under the Insurance (No 2) Act 1983 to apply to the court for the appointment of an 'administrator' of an insurance company which is in difficulties. Under this procedure - which has been availed of in recent times in the case of the Private Motorists' Protection Association and the Insurance Corporation of Ireland - the company is not wound up (in order to avoid its insured being left without cover) but is managed by the administrator with a view to its being restored ultimately to viability.

When a company may be wound up by the court

[36.15] The grounds on which a company may be wound up by the court are set out in s 213 of the Principal Act. Of these, the most important in practice are:

(1) that the company is unable to pay its debts;

(2) that it is 'just and equitable' to wind up the company; or

(3) that a member is being treated in an oppressive manner or his interests are being disregarded.

[36.16] In addition, the company may be wound up by the court on the following grounds:

(1) that the company has resolved by special resolution that the company may be wound up by the court;

(2) that the company did not commence its business within a year from its incorporation or suspended its business for a whole year;

(3) that the number of members is reduced, in the case of a public company, below seven.

[36.17] The most important grounds will now be considered in turn.

Inability to pay debts

[36.18] This is the most frequent ground for winding up. Section 214 of the Principal Act as amended by s 123 of the 1990 Act provides that a company shall be deemed to be unable to pay its debts in certain circumstances, ie:

(1) where a creditor has not been paid a debt of £1,000 or more within three weeks after demanding it in writing;

(2) where a judgment is unsatisfied; or

(3) where it is proved to the satisfaction of the court that the company is unable to pay its debts.

[36.19] In deciding whether it has been proved that the company is unable to pay its debts, the court will generally act on evidence that a creditor has repeatedly applied for a payment without success.

[36.20] Where the company in good faith and on substantial grounds disputes any liability in respect of the alleged debt, the petition will be dismissed. Moreover, if the matter is brought before the court before the petition is issued, its presentation will, in normal circumstances, be restrained. This is on the ground that a winding up petition is not a legitimate means of seeking to enforce payment of a debt which is bona fide disputed[13].

[36.21] It should, however, be noted that in order to have the petition dismissed or its presentation restrained, the company must establish that there is no liability in respect of the debt. Where a company admits its indebtedness in a sum exceeding £1,000 but disputes the balance - even on substantial grounds - the creditor will not normally be restrained from presenting a petition. This was so held by the High Court in *Truck and Machinery Sales Ltd v Marubeni Komatsu Ltd*[14] applying the decisions of Plowman J in *Re Tweeds Garage Ltd*[15] and the Court of Appeal in *Taylor's Industrial v M & H Plant Hire*[16].

[36.22] Keane J pointed out, however, in *Truck and Machinery Sales Ltd* that, even where the company appears to be insolvent, the court may nonetheless, in the exercise of its equitable discretion, restrain the presentation of the petition where it is satisfied that the petition is being presented for an ulterior or collateral purpose and not in good faith by a creditor forming part of a class of creditors which seeks distribution of the assets of the company for the benefit of that class in an orderly manner under the supervision of the court.

[36.23] The jurisdiction to restrain the presentation of the petition is one to be exercised only with great caution. This was the view taken by the Court of Appeal in *Bryanston Finance Ltd v Devries (No 2)*[17], which was followed by Keane J in *Truck and Machinery Sales Ltd*.

[36.24] It was also held by Keane J in *Truck and Machinery Sales Ltd* that, where a company seeks to restrain the presentation of a petition for its winding up, the tests normally applicable in an application for an interlocutory injunction

---

13 *Mann v Goldstein* [1968] 1 WLR 1091, approved of by the Court of Appeal in *Stonegate Securities v Gregory* [1980] Ch 576, adopted by O'Hanlon J in *Re Pageboy Couriers Ltd* [1993] ILRM 510.

14 [1996] 1 IRL 12.

15 [1962] Ch 406.

16 [1990] BCLC 216. The decision of the High Court in *Clandown Ltd v Davis* [1994] 2 ILRM 536 was not followed in *Truck and Machinery Sales Ltd*.

17 [1976] Ch 63.

will not necessarily be appropriate. Thus the company will have to establish at least a *prima facie* case that its presentation would constitute an abuse of process: any other approach would unduly inhibit the constitutional right of recourse to the courts[18].

'Just and equitable'

[36.25] The Court has a wide jurisdiction to wind up a company when it is of opinion that it would be 'just and equitable' to do so. The words 'just and equitable' are not *ejusdem generis* with the other grounds enumerated in s 213, so that the court is not restricted to grounds of a similar character to those specified in the other paragraphs of the section in exercising its discretion under this paragraph[19]. Moreover, while it was at one time usual for commentators on the section to specify categories of cases in which the court would exercise its discretion, it was emphasised by Lord Wilberforce in the leading modern English case, *Re Westbourne Galleries Ltd*[20] that the section conferred a general power: 'Illustrations may be used,' he said, 'but general words should remain general and not be reduced to the sum of particular instances'.

[36.26] It is also clear from that case that a winding-up order on the 'just and equitable' ground may be peculiarly appropriate to small private companies founded on a personal relationship involving mutual trust and confidence between the parties where that trust and confidence has broken down: cases involving the sort of business association which, as we have seen throughout this book, is by far the most common type of company in Ireland. Such a company is more akin to a partnership and indeed is sometimes described as a quasi-partnership company. Because the element of mutual trust is so important in such a company, the court, as Lord Wilberforce made clear, will not refuse relief simply because there may have been no breach of a legal obligation by the members whose conduct is impugned. It will be sufficient to ground a case for an order under the section if the petitioner can show that the other members have not acted in good faith towards him and have in the broadest sense acted inequitably.

[36.27] A number of passages from the speech by Lord Wilberforce in *Re Westbourne Galleries* were cited by Gannon J in *Re Murph's Restaurant Ltd*[21] and applied by him to the facts in that case. There were only three shareholders, each of them directors, and all three were actively concerned in the management

---

[18] The decision in *Truck and Machinery Sales Ltd* was upheld on appeal by the Supreme Court, *ex temp*, 13 March 1996.

[19] *Re Newbridge Sanitary Steam Laundry Co* [1917] 1 IR 67.

[20] [1973] AC 360.

[21] [1979] ILRM 141.

of the company. One of the three was removed from his office as director by the other two and effectively excluded from all further participation in the company. The company had been conducted on an extremely informal basis and the dismissed director had never been paid any dividend on his shares. He had given up regular salaried employment in order to devote himself full time to the company and Gannon J found that the reasons for his removal put forward by his co-directors were unconvincing. He made it clear that, whether or not the legal requirements had been observed in the removal of the petitioner from office, the action of his co-directors in dismissing him amounted to a repudiation of their relationship with him. He accordingly granted an order for the winding up of the company on the 'just and equitable' ground.

[36.28] A company may also be wound up on the 'just and equitable' ground where there is a complete deadlock between the shareholders and the company's activities are effectively paralysed to the detriment both of the member and the creditors. The leading case is *Re Yenidje Tobacco Co*[22], the principle of which was applied by Kenny J in *Re Irish Tourist Promotions*[23] and Murphy J in *Re Vehicle Buildings and Insulations Ltd*[24].

[36.29] Other instances in which companies have been wound up on the 'just and equitable' ground are where there has been a failure of substratum[25], ie the purpose for which the company was formed can not, or is not being, carried out, where its objects are illegal[26], and where the company is being used as an instrument of fraud[27].

Oppression of a member

[36.30] Little need be said about this ground since the circumstances in which the court will grant relief - whether in the form of a winding-up order or the alternative remedy under s 205 - have already been fully discussed in Chapter 28 above.

---

[22] [1916] 2 Ch 426.
[23] (Unreported, 22 April 1974).
[24] [1986] ILRM 239.
[25] *Re German Date Coffee Company* (1882) 20 Ch D 169.
[26] *R v Registrar of Joint Companies* (1931) 2 BK 197.
[27] In *Re Shrinkpak Ltd* (unreported, 20 December 1989), Barron J wound up company A on the application of the liquidator of company B on the ground that the assets of company B had been fraudulently diverted to company A. The judgment was extempory but is noted by Courtney, *The Law of Private Companies*, para 18.090. It might now be possible to achieve a similar result under the Companies Act 1990, s 141: see para **[36.61]** below.

Winding up of related companies

[36.31] Section 141 of the 1990 Act provides that where two or more 'related companies' are being wound up, the court may order them to be wound up together as if they were one company. As a result, the assets of all the companies in a group will be available to all the creditors, thus, as it is hoped, avoiding situations in which the extent to which creditors are paid depend on which company they were formally dealing with when in reality they considered themselves as dealing with the group. The order can be made, on the application of the liquidator of any of the companies, where the court is satisfied that it is just and equitable so to do. It can be made on such terms as the court thinks fit, but the court is required to have particular regard to the interests of those who are members of some, but not all, of the companies.

[36.32] The court must also have regard to the following matters:

(1)   the extent to which any of the companies took part in the management of the other companies;

(2)   the conduct of any of the companies towards the creditors of any of the other companies;

(3)   the extent to which the circumstances that gave rise to the winding up of any of the companies are attributable to the actions or omissions of any of the other companies;

(4)   the extent to which the businesses of the companies have been intermingled.

[36.33] The order cannot be made solely on the ground that a company is related to another company or that creditors have relied on the fact of their being related. This seems a surprisingly restrictive provision: one would have thought that it was in precisely those circumstances, ie where creditors had acted reasonably in treating the companies as a group, that it would be just and equitable to make the order.

[36.34] 'Related companies' are defined in wide-ranging terms in s 140. A company is related to another company if

(1)   the other company is its subsidiary or holding company; or

(2)   more than half in nominal value of the equity share capital is held by the other company and companies related to the other company, directly or indirectly; or

(3)   more than half in nominal value of the equity share capital is held by members of the other, directly or indirectly; or

(4)   the other company or companies related to it or the other company together with companies related to it are entitled to exercise, or control

the exercise of, more than one half of the voting power at any general meeting of the company; or

(5)   the businesses of the companies have been so carried on that the separate business of each company, or a substantial part thereof, is not readily identifiable; or

(6)   there is another company to which both companies are related.

[36.35] 'Equity share capital' is defined as the issued share capital but excluding shares which do not carry rights beyond a specified amount to dividends or the return of capital, ie in effect preference shares. For the purposes of (2) and (3), shares held in a fiduciary capacity are to be disregarded.

[36.36] A 'company' includes any body which is liable to be wound up under the Acts. Hence it includes among others building societies, friendly societies and industrial and provident societies.

The petition

General

[36.37] The machinery of a winding up by the court is set in motion by a petition which may be presented by any of the following:

(1)   the company;

(2)   any creditor;

(3)   any contributory, ie any person liable to contribute to the assets of the company in the event of its being wound up;

(4)   the Minister;

(5)   in the case of oppression, any person entitled to apply for an order under s 205.

[36.38] The right to present a petition is a statutory right which cannot be excluded by the articles of association[28].

[36.39] A company will seldom present a petition itself, since if it wishes to wind up it can pass the necessary resolution. If the directors believe that the company's affairs require investigation by the court, however, the company should present a petition; but the company in general meeting must sanction such a petition[29].

---

[28]   *Re Peveril Gold Mines Co Ltd* [1898] 1 Ch 122.
[29]   *Re Galway and Salthill Tramways Co* [1918] 1 IR 62.

Petitions by creditors

[36.40] The great majority of winding up petitions are presented by creditors of the company. A creditor, for this purpose, means any person owed a sum of money by the company, whether by virtue of the assignment to him of another's debt or otherwise. The term includes a 'contingent' or 'prospective' creditor; but such a creditor must provide security for the costs of the petition and must also satisfy the court that there is a *prima facie* case for winding up[30].

[36.41] A petitioning creditor who cannot get his debt paid has a right to a winding-up order *ex debito justiciae,* ie as a matter of right[31]. But this is subject to the inherent jurisdiction of every court to refuse relief where it considers that an application is an abuse of the court's process, an example of which was *Re Bula Ltd*[32].

A company which owned large zinc and lead deposits had never traded and owed substantial sums to a number of banks. The latter had appointed a receiver pursuant to their powers as debenture holders. When another creditor of the company was about to convert itself into a secured creditor under the judgment mortgage procedure, the banks applied for a compulsory winding-up order. This was granted by the High Court, but the order was discharged by the Supreme Court. McCarthy J, speaking for the court, said that since it was the admitted object of the petitioning banks to negative the effect of the judgment mortgage and there was no other justification for presenting the petition, it should be dismissed in the exercise of the court's discretion as an abuse of process.

[36.42] The court also has regard to the wishes of the majority in value of the creditors and if the majority objects to a winding-up order being made, the court may in its discretion refuse the order. The opposing creditors must, however, show some good reasons for their attitude[33].

[36.43] While the wishes of the creditors are normally of great importance, the court is not necessarily bound by them. If, for example, there are circumstances which suggest that the company's affairs ought to be investigated by the court, a winding-up order will be made notwithstanding the opposition of the creditors[34].

[36.44] Section 282 of the Principal Act provides that a voluntary winding up is not to be a bar to the right of any creditor to have the company wound up by the court. If, however, the majority in value of the creditors oppose such an application, it may be refused[35]. Where the court makes the order, it has power to

---

[30] Companies Act 1963, s 215.
[31] *Bowes v Hope Life Insurance and Guarantee Co* (1865) 11 HLC 389 at 402.
[32] (Unreported, 13 May 1988), SC.
[33] *Re P & J Macrae Ltd* [1961] 1 All ER 302.
[34] *Re George Downes & Co* [1943] IR 420 at 424 per Overend J.

adopt the proceedings already had in the voluntary liquidation. Otherwise, such proceedings are void.

Petitions by contributories

[36.45] A contributory, being a member of the company, has to show special circumstances in order to obtain a winding-up order. Moreover, in order to prevent people buying shares in a company with the object of wrecking it, a contributory is precluded from presenting a petition unless:

(1)   the number of members is reduced, in the case of a public company below seven members, or

(2)   his shares or some of them were either allotted to him, or have been held by him and registered in his name, for at least six months during the eighteen months before the commencement of the winding up or have devolved on him through the death of a former holder[36].

[36.46] If a voluntary winding up is in progress, this is *prima facie* a bar to the contributory's petition, because as a member of the company, he is bound by the wishes of the majority. But it is not an absolute bar and the court under s 282 will make the order, if it is satisfied that the rights of the contributory will be prejudiced by the continuation of the voluntary winding up.

Form and presentation of the petition

[36.47] The petition must state:

(1)   the incorporation of the company;

(2)   the address of its registered office;

(3)   the amount of its paid up capital;

(4)   the grounds on which the winding-up order is sought[37].

[36.48] It is presented at the central office of the High Court and retained there[38]. A sealed copy is taken out by the petitioner and it and the original petition are brought to the office of one of the registrars who appoints the time and place at which the petition is to be heard. The registrar lists the petition for hearing before one of the judges assigned by the President of the High Court for the hearing of chancery matters; and he can alter the time appointed for its hearing at any time before it is advertised[39].

---

[35]   *Re Wicklow Textiles Ltd* (1953) 87 ILTR 72.
[36]   Companies Act 1963, s 215.
[37]   Rules of the Superior Courts 1986, SI 1986/15, App M Form 2.
[38]   Rules of the Superior Courts 1986, SI 1986/15, Ord 74, r 8.
[39]   Rules of the Superior Courts 1986, SI 1986/15, Ord 74, r 9.

Service and advertisement of the petition

[36.49] Unless it is presented by the company, the petition must be served on the company at its registered office. If there is no registered office, it should be served at the principal, or last known principal, place of business of the company (if any such can be found) by leaving a copy there with any member, officer or servant of the company or, if no such person can be found there, by leaving a copy there or serving such member or members of the company as the court may direct[40]. The Rules provide for the obtaining of copies of the petition by the contributories and creditors[41].

[36.50] The petition must be advertised in the prescribed form[42] seven clear days before the hearing, once in *Iris Oifigiúil* and once at least in two Dublin daily morning newspapers or in such other newspapers as the registrar may direct[43]. Any error in the title, the name of the company (such as the omission of the word 'limited'[44]) or the date and place fixed for the hearing may render the advertisement invalid. But a trifling error in spelling, by which no one is misled, will not invalidate it[45].

[36.51] We have already seen that the court will restrain the presentation of a petition, when the petition is an abuse of the process of the court, eg where the existence - as distinct from the amount - of a debt is disputed on substantial grounds[46]. Similarly, where it is such an abuse of process, the court will restrain the publication of the advertisement by injunction.

The statutory affidavit

[36.52] Every petition must be verified by an affidavit referring thereto, known as 'the statutory affidavit'[47]. It must be made by the petitioner and sworn and filed within four days after the petition is presented. The Rules make the affidavit *prima facie* evidence of the statements in the petition[48]. The object of the affidavit is to prevent the abuse of filing unnecessarily long affidavits in support of the petition[49]. Allegations of fraud or misconduct in the petition, however, not only can but must be supported by a more detailed affidavit[50].

---

[40] Rules of the Superior Courts 1986, SI 1986/15, Ord 74, r 11.
[41] Rules of the Superior Courts 1986, SI 1986/15, Ord 74, r 13.
[42] Rules of the Superior Courts 1986, SI 1986/15, App M Form 5.
[43] Rules of the Superior Courts 1986, SI 1986/15, Ord 74, r 10(1).
[44] *Re London and Provincial Pure Ice Manufacturing Co* [1904] WN 136.
[45] *Re J & P Sussman Ltd* [1958] 1 All ER 857.
[46] See para **[36.20]** above.
[47] Rules of the Superior Courts 1986, SI 1986/15, Ord 74, r 12; App M Forms 6 and 7.
[48] Rules of the Superior Courts 1986, SI 1986/15, Ord 74, r 12.
[49] *Re Gold Hill Mines* (1883) 23 Ch D 210 at 214.

Notice of intention to appear

[36.53] Every person who intends to appear on the hearing of the petition must serve on, or send by post to, the petitioner or his solicitor or Dublin agent at the address stated in the petition notice of his intention to do so[51]. The notice must be in the prescribed form and must be served in the manner prescribed by the Rules[52]. On the day of the hearing, a list of the names and addresses of those who have given such notice (or a statement that no notice has been received) must be handed by the petitioner or his solicitor to the registrar prior to the hearing[53].

Affidavits in opposition

[36.54] Affidavits in opposition to the petition must be filed within seven days after the publication of the last of the required advertisements; and notice of the filing of every such affidavit must be given to the petitioner or his solicitor or Dublin agent on the day on which it is filed[54]. The petitioner and the opposing deponents may be cross-examined on their affidavits, but the court has a discretion as to allowing such cross-examination.

Withdrawal of petition

[36.55] The failure of the petitioner to proceed with the petition does not mean that any other person with the appropriate standing who wishes to obtain a winding-up order must start the proceedings afresh. A petitioner may consent to the withdrawal of his petition or allow it to be dismissed or the hearing adjourned. He may fail to appear at the hearing or to make any application for an order in the terms of the prayer in the petition. In any of these circumstances, the court may substitute as petitioner any creditor or contributory, who has a right to present such a petition and wishes to prosecute the petition, upon such terms as the court deems just[55].

Hearing of the petition

[36.56] Upon the hearing of the petition, the court may dismiss it with or without costs, adjourn the matter conditionally or unconditionally or make an

---

[50] *Re S A Hawken Ltd* (1950) 66 TLR (Pt 2) 138; *Re ABC Coupler and Engineering Co Ltd (No 2)* [1962] 3 All ER 68.
[51] Rules of the Superior Courts 1986, SI 1986/15, Ord 74, r 15.
[52] Rules of the Superior Courts 1986, SI 1986/15, Ord 74, r 15, App M Form 8.
[53] Rules of the Superior Courts 1986, SI 1986/15, Ord 74, r 17.
[54] Rules of the Superior Courts 1986, SI 1986/15, Ord 74, r 17.
[55] Rules of the Superior Courts 1986, SI 1986/15, Ord 74, r 18.

interim order or any order it deems just, including, of course, an order for winding up[56]. In all matters relating to the petition, the court may have regard to the wishes of the creditors and contributories and may, if it considers it expedient to do so, direct meetings to be summoned to ascertain such wishes. The procedure at such meetings is prescribed by Rules 51 to 55.

[36.57] If the company is solvent, the wishes of the contributories, being the persons chiefly interested in the assets, carry most weight; if it is insolvent, the creditors.

[36.58] Section 216 of the Principal Act provides that an order for winding up is not to be refused on the ground only that the assets of the company have been mortgaged to an amount equal to or in excess of those assets or that the company has no assets. It might seem at first sight that no useful purpose would be served by making the order in such circumstances, but in an appropriate case the court will do so, eg where the company intends to carry on business to the detriment of innocent creditors[57].

The winding-up order and its effect

[36.59] The order is to the effect that the company be wound up by the court under the provisions of the Acts[58]. The winding up dates, however, not from the date of the order but from the presentation of the petition[59]. A voluntary winding up dates from the passing of the appropriate resolution, and when a compulsory winding up is ordered after the commencement of a voluntary winding up, the winding up dates from the passing of the resolution[60].

[36.60] It is important to bear in mind that the winding-up order does not terminate the company's existence. It remains in being until the court makes an order under s 239 of the Principal Act dissolving the company.

[36.61] An immediate effect of the order is to render void and ineffective all dispositions of property (including choses in action) of the company between the commencement of the winding up (ie the presentation of the petition) and the date of the order, unless the court otherwise directs[61]. In practice, the court usually allows such dispositions to remain effective, if they are made *bona fide*

---

[56] Companies Act 1963, s 216. If a number of petitions are presented, the order is made on the first presented: *Re Bamford* [1901] 1 IR 390.

[57] *Re Clandown Colliery Co* [1915] 1 Ch 369.

[58] The prescribed form for the order is the Rules of the Superior Courts 1986, SI 1986/15, App M Form 10.

[59] Companies Act 1963, s 220(2).

[60] Companies Act 1963, s 220(1).

[61] Companies Act 1963, s 218.

and in the usual course of business[62]. Lodgments to a bank account and the payment (but not the drawing alone) of cheques on it are 'dispositions' within the meaning of the relevant section[63].

[36.62] The order also renders invalid any attachment, sequestration, distress or execution put in force against the property and effects of the company after the commencement of the winding up[64].

[36.63] Any floating charge on the undertaking of the company created within 12 months of the commencement of the winding up is rendered invalid, unless it is proved that the company was solvent immediately after creating the charge, except to the amount of cash paid to the company in consideration of the charge, with interest thereon at the rate of 5%[65]. This is an important provision, since banks and other institutions which lend moneys normally require such a floating charge to be created by the company to secure the advance. If a petition is presented within 12 months from the creation of the charge and a winding-up order made, the charge is invalid except to the extent of moneys actually advanced in consideration of the charge. In the case of 'connected persons', the period is two years. The provision has been fully dealt with in Chapter 20 above.

Staying of proceedings

[36.64] It is essential to the nature of the winding-up procedure that individual creditors should not be allowed to proceed with a multiplicity of separate actions against the company. Accordingly, the Principal Act provides that no action or proceeding can be taken against the company after the order or after the appointment of a provisional liquidator except by leave of the court and subject to such terms as the court may impose[66].

[36.65] There are many instances in which the court will exercise its power to allow proceedings to be maintained notwithstanding the winding-up order. Secured creditors are allowed to proceed with any action to enforce their security as a matter of course[67]. Other examples are proceedings in respect of fatal accidents under s 48 of the Civil Liability Act 1961[68]; for specific

---

[62] *Re Burton & Deakin Ltd* [1977] 1 All ER 631.
[63] *Re Gray's Inns Consolidated Co Ltd* [1980] 1 WLR 711; *Re Pat Ruth Ltd* [1981] ILRM 51; *Re Ashmark (No 2) Ltd* [1990] ILRM 455.
[64] Companies Act 1963, s 219.
[65] Companies Act 1963, s 288 as inserted by the Companies Act 1990, s 136.
[66] Companies Act 1963, s 222.
[67] *Lloyd v Lloyd & Co* (1877) 6 Ch 3 339.
[68] *Re Thurso New Gas Go* (1899) 42 Ch D 486 at 491.

performance[69]; and for securing the fruits of an earlier action[70]. The application for leave is made by motion on notice.

[36.66] After the presentation of the petition and before the making of the order, any creditor or contributory, in the case of an action or proceedings in the High Court or an appeal to the Supreme Court, may apply to the court in which the action, proceeding or appeal is pending for a stay of the proceedings; and, in the case of an action or proceeding in any other court, may apply to the High Court for an order restraining further proceedings. The court to which the application is made can restrain the proceedings on such terms and for such period as it thinks just[71].

Costs

[36.67] The costs of the petition are in the discretion of the court; but in the event of the winding-up order being made, the usual practice is to give the petitioner and the company their costs. It is also usual to allow one set of costs each to the creditors and contributories supporting the petition[72]. The costs are paid in the first place out of the assets of the company[73]. If the order is refused, the petitioner may have to pay the costs of any creditors and contributories who opposed the petition. But if a petitioning creditor has actually obtained judgment for his debt and fails to get a winding-up order because of opposition by the majority of creditors, costs will not usually be given against him[74].

Appeal

[36.68] Any party affected by the winding-up order, or by the court's refusal to grant one, may appeal to the Supreme Court by serving notice of appeal within 21 days from the date of the order[75]. When a company appeals from the making of a winding-up order, it can be required to give security for the costs of the appeal[76].

---

[69] *Thames Plate Glass Co v Land etc Co* [1870] LR 11 Eq 248.

[70] *Re National Provincial Insurance Corpn, Cooper v National Provincial Insurance Corpn* (1912) 56 Sol Jo 290.

[71] Companies Act 1963, s 217.

[72] *Re Humber Ironworks Company* [1866] LR 2 Eq 15.

[73] Rules of the Superior Courts 1986, SI 1986/15, Ord 74, r 128(1).

[74] *Re R W Sharman Ltd* [1957] 1 All ER 737.

[75] Rules of the Superior Courts 1986, SI 1986/15, Ord 58, r 3.

[76] Companies Act 1963, s 390.

Statement of affairs

[36.69] When the court has made the winding-up order or appointed a provisional liquidator[77], a statement must be filed in court of the company's affairs. The statement, which must be in the prescribed form[78] and verified by affidavit[79], must show:

(1)   the company's assets and liabilities;

(2)   the names, residences and occupations of the company's creditors;

(3)   the securities held by such creditors and the dates when such securities were given;

(4)   such further information as may be or as the court may require[80].

[36.70] The statement is to be filed and verified by one or more of the directors at the date of the winding-up order and by the secretary at that time. Alternatively, it can be filed and verified by such of the persons named in s 224(2) as the court may direct. It must be filed within 21 days from the date of the winding-up order or within such extended time as the court may for special reasons appoint. There are ancillary provisions in regard to penalties for not complying with the requirements of the section and the rights of contributories and creditors to copies or extracts from the statement.

[36.71] If a person who is required to make, or concur in making, such a statement, anticipates that he will incur costs or expenses in connection with its preparation - such as, for example, accountants' or valuers' fees - he should apply to the liquidator for his sanction, submitting an estimate of the costs in question. If there is no liquidator, a similar application should be made to the court. Unless such sanction is obtained, the costs or expenses involved will not be allowed out of the assets, except by order of the court[81].

[36.72] The court has power to dispense with the requirements as to filing a statement of affairs[82]. An application for an order to that effect must be supported by a report of the liquidator showing the special circumstances which, in his opinion, render such a course desirable[83].

[36.73] Unless the court otherwise orders, the liquidator must send, as soon as practical, to each creditor mentioned in the statement and to the contributories a

---

[77]   For the appointment of a provisional liquidator, see para **[36.84]** below.

[78]   Rules of the Superior Courts 1986, SI 1986/15, App M Form 13.

[79]   Rules of the Superior Courts 1986, SI 1986/15, Ord 74, r 24(1).

[80]   Companies Act 1963, s 224.

[81]   Rules of the Superior Courts 1986, SI 1986/15, Ord 74, r 25.

[82]   Companies Act 1963, s 224.

[83]   Rules of the Superior Courts 1986, SI 1986/15, Ord 74, r 26(1).

summary of the company's statement of affairs, including the causes of its failure, and any observations thereon which the liquidator may think fit to make[84]. Where prior to the winding-up order the company was being wound up voluntarily, the liquidator may, in his discretion, send the creditors and contributories an account of the voluntary winding up[85].

[36.74] The court may from time to time require any of the persons named in s 224(2) to attend before the court for the purpose of giving such further information in relation to the company as the court may think fit[86].

Proceedings under the winding-up order

[36.75] The order must be advertised by the petitioner once in *Iris Oifigiúil* and once in each of the newspapers in which the petition was advertised, unless the court otherwise directs[87]. It must also be served on such persons (if any) and in such manner as the court may direct[88].

[36.76] A certified copy of the order is to be left at the office of one of the Examiners of the High Court within ten days of its perfection. If this is not done, any other person interested in the winding up may take this step and be given the carriage of the winding-up proceedings by the court[89].

[36.77] A notice to proceed under the order must then be taken out and served on all the parties who appeared at the hearing of the petition[90]. On the return day fixed by this notice, a time is fixed for the next major step in the winding up: the proof of debts and the settling of the list of contributories. Directions are given by the Examiner as to the advertisements to be published for all or any of these purposes and generally as to the proceedings and the parties to attend thereon[91].

The liquidator

Appointment of the liquidator

[36.78] The court appoints a liquidator or liquidators to carry out the winding up. He is described by the title of 'the Official Liquidator'. He must, within 21 days after his appointment publish in *Iris Oifigiúil* a notice of his appointment and must deliver to the Registrar an office copy of the order appointing him[92]. If

---

84 Rules of the Superior Courts 1986, SI 1986/15, Ord 74, r 28(1).
85 Rules of the Superior Courts 1986, SI 1986/15, Ord 74, r 28(2).
86 Rules of the Superior Courts 1986, SI 1986/15, Ord 74, r 25(2).
87 Rules of the Superior Courts 1986, SI 1986/15, Ord 74, r 20.
88 Rules of the Superior Courts 1986, SI 1986/15, Ord 74, r 20.
89 Rules of the Superior Courts 1986, SI 1986/15, Ord 74, r 21.
90 Rules of the Superior Courts 1986, SI 1986/15, Ord 74, r 21.
91 Rules of the Superior Courts 1986, SI 1986/15, Ord 74, r 21.
92 Companies Act 1963, s 227.

he fails to comply with these requirements, he is liable to a fine not exceeding £250[93].

[36.79] The liquidator can be appointed by the court either without previous advertisement or notice to anyone or following the publication of an advertisement in the prescribed manner[94]. He is required to give security on his appointment, and the usual requirement is that he enters into a bond with two or more sureties in a sum approved by the Court[95]. The court may, however, authorise him to act as liquidator without giving security for such time as the court may fix[96].

[36.80] It should be noted that there is no requirement in the Acts or the Rules that the liquidator should be qualified in any manner. In practice, it is almost invariable for the liquidator to be a practising accountant and he is usually a member of one of the recognised professional institutes.

[36.81] Certain persons are, however, disqualified from acting as liquidator. Under the Principal Act, only bodies corporate were disqualified (under s 300): the categories of disqualified persons were expanded by s 300A[97], to include the following:

(1)   persons who are, or have been within 12 months of the commencement of the winding up, officers or servants of the company;

(2)   except with the leave of the court, a parent, spouse, brother, sister or child of an officer of the company;

(3)   a person who is a partner or in the employment of an officer or servant of the company;

(4)   persons disqualified by these provisions from acting as liquidator of a subsidiary or holding company of the company or of a 'sister' company.

[36.82] If a liquidator becomes disqualified as a result of the above provisions, he thereupon vacates his office and must give notice in writing within 14 days to the court that he has vacated his office for that reason. Any person who acts as a liquidator when disqualified under these provisions is guilty of an offence and liable on summary conviction to a fine not exceeding £1,000 and, for continued contravention, a daily default fine not exceeding £50 and on indictment to a fine

---

93   Companies Act 1963, s 227 as amended by the Companies (Amendment) Act 1982, s 15.
94   Rules of the Superior Courts 1986, SI 1986/15, Ord 74, rr 29, 30.
95   Rules of the Superior Courts 1986, SI 1986/15, Ord 74, r 31.
96   Rules of the Superior Courts 1986, SI 1986/15, Ord 74, r 31.
97   Inserted by the Companies Act 1990, s 146.

of £10,000 and, for continued contravention, to a daily default fine not exceeding £250. The same penalties apply where he fails to give notice of his having become disqualified. In the case of bodies corporate acting as liquidators, the fine remains as fixed by the Principal Act, ie £100.

Remuneration

[36.83] The court directs what remuneration the liquidator is to receive[98]. There is no scale of fees fixed for remuneration: the court considers the circumstances of the particular case and determines what is fair. The court is in no sense bound by the scales of fees fixed for accountancy work by professional institutions, although it may take such scales into account in determining what is fair remuneration if it thinks proper. In practice, the court will naturally seek to ensure that there is reasonable uniformity in the fixing of remuneration for accountancy work of similar types. In order to achieve this result, a practice has developed in recent times of appointing a creditor - usually the Revenue - to represent the general body of creditors in an inquiry into the liquidator's charges before the Examiner. The procedure is not dissimilar to the taxation before a taxing master of a successful litigant's costs. The Examiner then submits a report on the inquiry to the judge. The foregoing was adopted by McCarthy J, speaking for the Supreme Court in *Re Merchant Banking Ltd*[99], as a correct statement of the law. He added the following important qualification, however:

> '... The inquiry into the liquidator's charges before the examiner is one of amount and not of nature or kind ...'

It is also clear from the same judgment that the parties to the inquiry, ie the liquidator and the 'monitoring' creditor, must be afforded an opportunity of making whatever case is appropriate in relation to particular items under scrutiny.

Provisional liquidator

[36.84] The court may in certain cases appoint a provisional liquidator before any winding-up order is made. This will usually be done when the company's assets are in danger. He can be appointed without advertisement or notice to any party unless the court directs otherwise and without giving security[100].

Resignation and removal

[36.85] The liquidator may resign or be removed by the court 'on cause shown'[101]. Thus, a liquidator was removed when he insisted on acting in the

---

[98] Companies Act 1963, s 228; Rules of the Superior Courts 1986, SI 1986/15, Ord 74, r 47.
[99] [1987] ILRM 163.
[100] Rules of the Superior Courts 1986, SI 1986/15, Ord 74, r 14(1).
[101] Companies Act 1963, s 228.

shareholders' interests only, although there was no reasonable prospect of paying the debts in full and the liquidator was acting in good faith[102].

[36.86] A vacancy in the office of liquidator, however caused, is filled by the court. When the liquidator resigns or is removed, he has to deliver all books, papers, documents and accounts in his possession relating to his office to the new liquidator. He will not be released from his office until he has done so[103].

Duties of the liquidator

[36.87] The principal duties of the liquidator are:

(1)   to take possession of the company's assets and protect them;

(2)   to make out lists of the creditors and contributories;

(3)   to have disputed cases adjudicated upon by the court;

(4)   to realise the assets;

(5)   to apply the proceeds in payment of the company's debts and liabilities in the proper priority;

(6)   to distribute the surplus (if any) among the contributories and adjust their rights.

[36.88] As soon as he has been appointed, the liquidator must take into his custody or under his control all the property and choses in action to which the company is, or appears to be, entitled[104]. Should there be any interval between the making of the winding-up order and his appointment, the property during that period is in the custody of the court[105].

[36.89] The property of the company, of which the liquidator may need to have possession, includes its books and records and other documents relevant to its affairs. Some of these may be held by persons claiming a lien on them in respect of work or services they have performed for the company. (A lien is a right to retain possession of property or sell it to enforce payment of money owed by the owner.) Thus, solicitors or accountants may refuse to hand over such documents because they are owed professional fees by the company. Section 244A of the Principal Act, which was inserted by s 125 of the 1990 Act, provides that in a compulsory winding up, no person is to be entitled to withhold possession of such documents from the liquidator or to claim a lien in respect of them. However, where a mortgage, charge or pledge has been created by the document,

---

[102] *Re Rubber and Produce Investment Trust* [1915] 1 Ch 382.

[103] Rules of the Superior Courts 1986, SI 1986/15, Ord 74, r 36.

[104] Companies Act 1963, s 229.

[105] Companies Act 1963, s 229.

this provision is without prejudice to the person's rights under it, except his right to possession of the document.

[36.90] The documents to which this provision extends are widely defined and comprise

> 'any deed, instrument or other document ... or the books of account, receipts, bills, invoices or other papers of a like nature relating to the accounts or trade, dealings or business of the company ...'.

[36.91] The court may, on the liquidator's application, make an order vesting all or any part of the assets in him in his official name[106]. Unless such an order is made, the assets remain vested in the company: there is no *cessio bonorum* merely by virtue of the winding-up order.

[36.92] If an order is made vesting any property in the liquidator, he may then institute or defend in his official name any proceedings relating to that property or which it is necessary to bring or defend for the purpose of effectively winding up the company[107]. Any other proceedings are brought by him in the name of the company.

[36.93] It would appear to follow that, where a winding-up order is made, not merely the legal title but the equitable interest in the assets of the company remain vested in the company, even where the company is insolvent and the only persons who would be interested in the realisation of the company's assets would be the creditors and not the owners of the company. As Atkin LJ put it in *Re Wait*:[108]

> 'it would have been futile in a code intended for commercial men to have created an elaborate structure of rules dealing with rights of law, if at the same time it was intended to leave, subsisting with the legal rights, equitable rights inconsistent with, more extensive and coming into existence earlier than the rights so carefully set out in the various sections of the code.'

However, doubts as to the position in Ireland have arisen as a result of the decision of the Supreme Court in *Re Frederick Inns Ltd*[109]. In that case, it was held that where a company was insolvent the assets were held in trust for the benefit of its creditors even prior to any winding up: *a fortiori*, it would follow that, in the case of any insolvent company, the equitable interest in its assets would vest automatically in the creditors on a winding up. Some support for that view of the law may be derived from the decision of the House of Lords in

---

[106] Companies Act 1963, s 230.
[107] Companies Act 1963, s 230.
[108] (1927) 1 Ch 606 at 635-636.
[109] [1994] 1 ILRM 387.

Ayerst v C & K (Construction) Ltd[110]. The speech of Lord Diplock in that case, however, has been subjected to severe criticism, as indeed has the decision in *Re Frederick Inns Ltd*[111].

The committee of inspection

[36.94] The liquidator may be supervised and assisted in the conduct of the winding up by a committee of inspection composed of creditors and contributories. If the court so directs, he must summon a meeting of creditors and contributories or separate meetings of each category in order to decide whether an application should be made to the court for the appointment of a committee and who are to be its members[112]. If separate meetings of the creditors and contributories are held and come to conflicting conclusions as to whether a committee should be appointed or as to its composition, the court can resolve the dispute[113].

[36.95] There are provisions in the Principal Act as to when the committee is to meet; as to the majority required for its decisions; and as to the resignation, forfeiture of office, removal and replacement of members[114]. It has been held that the members may not purchase the assets of the company or make a profit from the winding up[115], without the sanction of the court.

Meetings of creditors and contributories

[36.96] There are provisions in the Acts and Rules for the summoning by the court and the liquidator of meetings of creditors and contributories[116]. The former are called 'Court Meetings' and the latter 'Liquidator's Meetings'. The Rules prescribe the procedure for summoning such meetings, the manner in which they are to be conducted and the proof by creditors of their entitlement to vote and contain provisions for voting by proxy[117].

Powers of the liquidator

[36.97] Certain powers are specifically conferred on the liquidator by s 231 of the Principal Act, but the list is not exhaustive. Some of the powers - principally the carrying on of the company's business, the bringing or defending of civil or

---

[110] [1976] AC 167.
[111] Fealy, *The Role of Equity in the Winding Up of a Company* 17 DULJ (1995) 18.
[112] Companies Act 1963, s 232. For the procedure see Rules of the Superior Courts 1986, SI 1986/15, Ord 74, r 51.
[113] Companies Act 1963, s 232(2); Rules of the Superior Courts 1986, SI 1986/15, Ord 74, r 51.
[114] Companies Act 1963, s 233.
[115] *Dowling v Lord Advocate* 1963 SLT 146.
[116] Companies Act 1963, ss 232 and 309.
[117] Rules of the Superior Courts 1986, SI 1986/15, Ord 74, rr 50-83 inclusive.

criminal proceedings, the employment of a solicitor, the settlement of claims and the making of calls - he can exercise only with the consent of the court or the committee of inspection. Without such consent, he can do the other things specified in the section, including 'all such other things as may be necessary for winding up the affairs of the company and distributing its assets'. Thus, the liquidator, without such consent, may:

(1)   sell any property of the company;

(2)   accept and make bills of exchange or promissory notes on the security of the assets;

(3)   prove in the bankruptcy of any contributory;

(4)   take out administration to the estate of a deceased contributory;

(5)   execute deeds, receipts and other documents.

But while the liquidator is entitled to sell any property of the company without the sanction of the court, it is the usual practice for him to apply to the court for its approval in the case of the sale of assets of any significant value. He is entitled to apply to the court for directions under s 260 of the Principal Act and this right is frequently availed of in the case of sales of the company's property. The procedure applicable where the property is being sold subject to the court's approval is dealt with in para **[36.105]** below.

[36.98] The liquidator is specifically given power by s 290 to disclaim with leave of the court any property which is unsaleable or not sufficiently saleable, because of obligations attached to it, such as land burdened with onerous covenants, shares or stocks in companies or unprofitable contracts. The disclaimer, to be effective, must be made in writing within the time prescribed by the Act and he can be required to elect whether he will disclaim or not by a person interested in the property. There are ancillary provisions as to the vesting of disclaimed property, the rescission of onerous contracts and damages for their breach.

[36.99] Section 290 expressly provides that the disclaimer is not to affect the rights and liabilities of third parties except so far as is necessary for the purpose of preserving the company and its assets from liability. This means that the right of the landlord of property to recover rent from a guarantor (or the original lessee where the lease has been assigned) is not affected by a disclaimer. This was so held by Keane J in *Tempany v Royal Liver Co*[118] in which he refused to follow the English decision of *Re Katherine et Cie*[119].

---

[118] [1984] ILRM 273. The decision in *Tempany* was followed by Murphy J in *Re GWI Ltd* (unreported, 16 November 1988).

[119] [1932] 1 Ch 70.

Position of the liquidator

[36.100] The liquidator is an agent of the company with fiduciary obligations arising from his office and with statutory obligations imposed on him by the Acts[120]. If the company has not been dissolved, he may be ordered to pay damages or compensation under s 298 of the Principal Act[121]; and if the company has been dissolved, he may be sued for breach of his statutory duties[122]. It would seem that while he may be loosely described as a 'trustee' for the company, he is not in any sense a trustee for its members or creditors[123].

Payment in of money, sales of property and declaration of dividends

[36.101] The liquidator must pay all moneys received by him into the Bank of Ireland to the account of the liquidator within seven days from their receipt and can be charged interest and disallowed his remuneration if he fails to do so[124]. He must also deposit notes, bills and other securities in the Bank as soon as they come to hand[125].

[36.102] The court may order any person who owes money to a company to pay it into such bank as the court may appoint to the account of the liquidator and all moneys and securities so paid are to be subject in all respects to the orders of the court. The Rules provide the machinery whereby this is done[126].

[36.103] The Rules provide for the signing and countersigning by the liquidator and the Examiner of cheques[127]; for the investment of moneys standing to the credit of the liquidator in their joint names[128]; and for the payment of dividends and interest into the liquidator's account[129].

[36.104] It is normal for the liquidator to be given a float account which enables him to draw cheques without the countersignature of the Examiner. He then accounts for the operation of the float at intervals prescribed by the court, to the Examiner.

[36.105] The Rules of the Superior Courts dealing with the sale of real and personal property with the approval of the court are applicable to sales of

---

[120] *Re Belfast Empire Theatre of Varieties* [1963] IR 41 at 49.
[121] See para **[36.165]** below
[122] *Smith & Sons (Norwood) Ltd v Goodman* [1936] Ch 216.
[123] *Re Belfast Empire Theatre of Varieties* [1963] IR 41 in which *Re Uniacke* (1944) ILTR 154 was not followed.
[124] Rules of the Superior Courts 1986, SI 1986/15, Ord 74, r 117.
[125] Rules of the Superior Courts 1986, SI 1986/15, Ord 74, r 118.
[126] Rules of the Superior Courts 1986, SI 1986/15, Ord 74, r 119.
[127] Rules of the Superior Courts 1986, SI 1986/15, Ord 74, r 121.
[128] Rules of the Superior Courts 1986, SI 1986/15, Ord 74, r 122.
[129] Rules of the Superior Courts 1986, SI 1986/15, Ord 74, r 123.

property belonging to a company in the course of a winding up. The conditions or contract of sale must be settled and approved by the court unless the court otherwise directs; and the court may, on a sale by public auction, fix a reserve[130].

[36.106] The court must ensure that the best price possible is realised for any property being sold; and, save where a binding contract has been entered into with its approval, it will direct the liquidator to accept a higher offer for the property even where an earlier lower offer has been recommended for acceptance by the liquidator[131].

File of proceedings

[36.107] All documents in the winding-up proceedings must be filed by the liquidator in one continuous file and kept by him as the court directs. Every contributory and creditor who has proved is entitled to examine the file free and take copies or extracts at his own expense. The file must be produced in court as required[132].

Contributories

[36.108] For the purpose of getting in the assets of the company, the liquidator must obtain payment from the 'contributories' within the meaning of the Acts of the amount, if any, uncalled on their shares in the company.

[36.109] The Principal Act provides that, in the event of the company being wound up, every present and past member is to be liable to contribute to the assets to an amount sufficient for the payment of its debts and liabilities and the costs of the winding up, and for the adjustment of the rights of the contributories between themselves[133].

[36.110] To this general principle, there are certain qualifications specified in s 207. The most important in practical terms is that which limits the liability of a member of a company limited by shares to the amount, if any, unpaid on his shares. In the case of a company limited by guarantee, it is limited to the amount which he has undertaken to contribute in the event of a winding up.

[36.111] Past members, who ceased to be members more than a year before the winding up commenced, are also exempted. Even those who were members within the year are not liable for debts contracted since they ceased to be

---

[130] Rules of the Superior Courts 1986, SI 1986/15, Ord 51, Ord 74, r 124.
[131] *Van Hool McArdle Ltd v Rohan Industrial Estates Ltd* [1980] IR 237, [1982] ILRM 340, distinguishing *Re Hibernian Transport Co Ltd* [1972] IR 190.
[132] Rules of the Superior Courts 1986, SI 1986/15, Ord 74, r 133.
[133] Companies Act 1963, s 207.

members and are not liable to contribute at all unless the present members are unable to make the contributions required from them under the Act.

[36.112] To enforce the liability of contributories, the liquidator at the time directed by the Court makes out a list of persons whom he claims to treat as contributories[134]. So far as practicable, he must observe the requirements of s 235(3) by distinguishing between persons who are contributories in their own right and as representatives of others[135]. The list is settled by the Examiner, unless it appears to the court that it will not be necessary to make calls or to adjust the rights of contributories in which case the settlement may be dispensed with[136].

[36.113] The list is made out in two parts: 'A', consisting of the present members and 'B', of the past. 'A' members are primarily liable, the 'B' members being called upon to contribute only if the 'A' members' contributions are exhausted.

[36.114] Calls are to be made on contributories to the extent of their liability for the payment of any money which the court considers necessary to satisfy the debts and liabilities of the company; and, for this purpose, debts and liabilities include estimated debts and liabilities. Calls are enforced by court order. The application for the order is made by motion on notice stating the proposed amount of the call. The procedure for making calls is provided by Rules 92 to 94[137].

Distribution of surplus assets among contributories

[36.115] Subject to the payment of the creditors and of the costs of the winding up, the assets are distributed among the contributories in accordance with their rights and interests.

[36.116] The surplus is first applied in repaying to the contributories the amounts they have paid up on their shares. Where it is more than sufficient for this purpose, the actual amount paid up is first returned to them and any balance left over is distributed among them in proportion to the nominal amount of the share capital held by each of them[138].

---

[134] Rules of the Superior Courts 1986, SI 1986/15, Ord 74, r 81. A bankrupt should be placed on the list of contributories as being liable for calls, if the bankruptcy petition has been presented before the winding-up petition (*Re Ligoniel Spinning Co Ltd* [1900] 1 IR 250). It would seem that in Ireland a fully paid up shareholder should also be placed on the list although the company is insolvent: *Re Hollyford Mining Co* (1867) IR 1 Eq 39. (But see *Re Consolidated Goldfields of New Zealand* [1953] Ch 689.)

[135] Rules of the Superior Courts 1986, SI 1986/15, Ord 74, r 86.

[136] Companies Act 1963, s 235(2); and see *Re Paragon Holdings Ltd* [1961] Ch 346.

[137] For calls generally, see Ch 17 above.

[138] *Ex parte Maude* [1870] 6 Ch App 51.

[36.117] Where the surplus is not sufficient to repay all the capital paid up, the liquidator must, if necessary, 'equalise' the amounts paid up. He does this by making calls on the contributories who have paid less than others for amounts sufficient to make all the shares equally paid up. The surplus is then distributed in proportion to the nominal amount of the share capital held by each contributory[139].

[36.118] Where, however, the articles of association provide that losses are to be borne in proportion to the amount of the capital paid up or which ought to have been paid up by the contributories, the general rule does not apply and the liquidator cannot equalise the amounts paid up by making calls[140].

[36.119] The memorandum and articles may contain other provisions modifying or excluding the general principles stated above. In construing any such provisions, it must be borne in mind that the phrase 'surplus assets' may bear different meanings according to the context in which it is used. It may mean the balance left after the creditors and the costs of the winding up have been paid; or it may mean what remains after payment of the capital paid up on all classes of shares.

The creditors

[36.120] The principle of limited liability means that the creditors' remedy is solely against the company. The usual object of a winding up by the court is to prevent the creditors from maintaining separate actions against the company and to provide machinery whereby all the creditors are paid so far as the assets of the company permit. Accordingly, the Acts and the Rules prescribe the manner in which they are to come in and prove their claims and the priority which certain classes of creditors are to enjoy.

[36.121] The debts which can be proved are specified in s 283 of the Principal Act. All debts payable on a contingency and all claims against the company, present or future, certain or contingent, and whether ascertained or sounding only in damages, are admissible to proof against the company. A just estimate must be made, as far as possible, of the value of any debts or claims which are subject to a contingency or which sound only in damages or for some other reason do not bear a certain value.

[36.122] The liquidator must reject debts barred by the provisions of the Statute of Limitations 1957 provided that the statutory period of limitation has expired before the commencement of the liquidation[141].

---

[139] *Ex parte Maude* [1870] 6 Ch App 51.
[140] *Re Kinatan (Borneo) Rubber Ltd* [1923] 1 Ch 124.
[141] *Re General Rolling Stock Co Ltd* (1872) 7 Ch App 646.

Application of the rules in bankruptcy

[36.123] Section 284 of the Principal Act provides that in the winding up of insolvent companies, the same rules are to apply as in the law of bankruptcy with regard to:

(1)   the respective rights of secured and unsecured creditors;

(2)   debts provable, and

(3)   the valuation of annuities and future and contingent liabilities.

[36.124] It should be noted that s 284 does not mean that all the bankruptcy rules apply in a winding up. Only those which deal with the three matters specified apply. In particular, the bankruptcy rules the effect of which is to increase the assets available for the bankrupt's creditors by invalidating certain transactions, do not apply[142]. The Principal Act, as we have seen, contains equivalent provisions appropriate to a winding up.

[36.125] It does mean, however, that a debt not provable in bankruptcy cannot be proved in a winding up. But claims for unliquidated damages arising from personal torts are provable.

[36.126] The application of the bankruptcy rules means that the provisions of the Bankruptcy Act 1988 (1st Schedule, Rule 17(1)), which deal with the setting off of debts, are imported into a winding up. Rule 17(1) provides that where there are mutual debts owing or there has been mutual credit given by and between the bankrupt and any other person, one debt or demand can be set off against the other, notwithstanding an act of bankruptcy prior to the debts being contracted or the credit given. Only the balance after such set off can be proved in a winding up.

[36.127] All debts may be set off under the section, but there must be 'mutuality'. Thus, a trustee cannot set off a debt owed by him personally to the company against a debt owed by the company to him as a trustee[143]. An unsecured debt may be set off against a secured debt under the section[144].

Procedure for ascertaining the creditors and proving their claims

[36.128] In order to ascertain the creditors, an advertisement is published at such time as the court directs fixing a time within which the creditors are to send in to the liquidator particulars of their claims. This advertisement also appoints a day for adjudicating on the claims[145].

---

[142] *Re Irish Attested Sales Ltd* [1962] IR 70; *Re McCairns Ltd* [1989] ILRM 501.

[143] *Re Newman, ex parte Brooke* (1876) 3 Ch D 494.

[144] *McKinnon v Armstrong* (1877) 2 App Cas 531.

[145] Rules of the Superior Courts 1986, SI 1986/15, Ord 74, r 93; App M Form 35.

[36.129] The liquidator sets out in an affidavit the debts which he thinks should be allowed without further evidence and those which should be proved[146]. At the adjudication, the Examiner decides which debts should be allowed upon the liquidator's affidavit and which creditors should come in and prove[147]. The liquidator then gives notice to the latter of the time at which they are to attend to prove their claims[148].

[36.130] The value of contingent or unliquidated claims is to be ascertained, as far as possible, according to their value at the date of the winding-up order[149]. Debts can be proved by sending particulars of the claim through the post, an affidavit not being necessary unless the liquidator and the Examiner specifically require one[150]. A creditor may come in and prove at any time before the final distribution of assets, but he cannot disturb any dividend already paid[151].

The Examiner states the results of his adjudications in certificates[152].

Preferential debts

[36.131] Certain debts set out in s 285 of the Principal Act (as subsequently amended) are given priority. Subject to this, all unsecured creditors are on an equal footing and must be paid equally. The State as such has no priority to be paid first and in full out of the assets, the existence of such a right being an aspect of the royal prerogative which did not survive the enactment of the Constitution of Saorstát Éireann[153]. Judgment creditors who have not completed execution of their judgments have no priority[154].

[36.132] Before any debts, including the preferential debts, are paid, a sum to meet the costs and expenses of the liquidation must be retained[155]. The remuneration, costs and expenses of the liquidator form part of these costs and expenses and consequently have priority over the preferential debts[156].

[36.133] Under the Rules of the Superior Courts[157], these include, not merely the remuneration of the liquidator, but also the fees and expenses properly incurred

---

[146] Rules of the Superior Courts 1986, SI 1986/15, Ord 74, r 97.
[147] Rules of the Superior Courts 1986, SI 1986/15, Ord 74, r 95.
[148] Rules of the Superior Courts 1986, SI 1986/15, Ord 74, r 95.
[149] Rules of the Superior Courts 1986, SI 1986/15, Ord 74, r 99.
[150] Rules of the Superior Courts 1986, SI 1986/15, Ord 74, r 102.
[151] *Re General Rolling Stock Co Ltd* (1872) 7 Ch App 646.
[152] Rules of the Superior Courts 1986, SI 1986/15, Ord 74, r 101.
[153] *Re Irish Employers' Mutual Insurance Association Ltd* [1955] IR 176.
[154] Companies Act 1963, s 291; and see *Re Leinster Contract Corpn* [1903] 1 IR 517.
[155] Companies Act 1963, s 285(8).
[156] *Re Redbreast Preserving Co (Ireland) Ltd* [1958] IR 234.
[157] Rules of the Superior Courts 1986, SI 1986/15, Ord 128, r 1.

in realising and getting in the assets and any 'necessary disbursements' of the liquidator.

[36.134] Problems have arisen in recent years in determining whether certain tax liabilities of the company which have arisen since the winding up should be regarded as part of the properly incurred expenses and necessary disbursements of the liquidator and thus entitled to priority over all other debts. It was held by the Supreme Court in *Re Van Hool McCardle Ltd*[158] that so to construe the rule would be to afford the taxes in question a priority which they were not afforded by the Act itself. The preferential status of tax liabilities under the Act was, the court pointed out, confined to liabilities incurred prior to the liquidation[159]. Hence, it would have been *ultra vires* the rule making authority to afford post-liquidation taxes any preferential status. Accordingly, the capital gains tax for which the company was liable as a result of the realisation by the liquidator of one of its assets could not be paid in priority to the other debts.

[36.135] The somewhat surprising consequence, as demonstrated by the subsequent decision in *Re Hibernian Transport Co Ltd v Palgrave Murphy Ltd*[160], was that interest earned by money put on deposit by the liquidator was also free of tax. It was not a necessary expense or disbursement, having regard to the decision in *Re Van Hool McCardle* and it could not claim preference as a revenue debt, having been incurred after the winding up.

[36.136] The decision in *Re Van Hool McCardle Ltd* has been strongly criticised by Ussher[161] as not taking into account the fundamental difference between debts incurred before the liquidation which must abate ratably (subject to any preferential status they may have) and debts incurred by the liquidator during the winding up which, if properly incurred, must be paid in full as part of the expenses of the liquidation. He also points out that there was no reference to a previous Supreme Court decision of *Irish Provident Association Co Ltd v Kavanagh*[162], which lays emphasis on the liquidator's rights to make payments in the nature of salvage payments during the course of a winding up.

[36.137] The effect of the decision in *Re Van Hool McCardle* was reversed by statute in s 556 of the Finance Act 1983 so far as capital gains tax was concerned. It has recently been made clear that the Revenue enjoy a more favourable position in voluntary windings up: see para **[38.46]** n 37 below.

---

[158] [1982] ILRM 340.
[159] See para **[36.140]** below.
[160] [1984] ILRM 583.
[161] Ussher, *Company Law in Ireland*, p 499-500.
[162] [1930] IR 231.

[36.138] The liquidator can ensure that the progress of the liquidation is not complicated by the existence of unascertained preferential debts. Under sub-s (14) inserted by s 285 of the 1990 Act, priority applies only to those debts which within a period of six months after advertisement by the liquidator for claims in at least two daily newspapers circulating in the district where the registered office is situate have been notified to him or have become known to him.

[36.139] The list of debts in s 285 does not provide an order of payment. Although they take priority over all other debts, they rank equally among themselves and if the assets are insufficient to pay them all, they must abate in equal proportions.

[36.140] The debts in question include:

(1)   local rates which became due and payable within 12 months prior to the 'relevant date'[163];

(2)   all assessed taxes, including income tax, corporation tax, value added tax and capital gains tax[164], not exceeding in the whole one year's assessment;

(3)   sums deductible by the company as an employer under the relevant PAYE regulations, within the period of 12 months before the relevant date;

(4)   wages and salaries (including sums due by way of commission) payable to any clerk or servant by the company for service rendered to the company during the four months prior to the relevant date;

(5)   wages payable to any workman in the employment of the company (including sums payable by way of piece or time rates) within the period of four months prior to the relevant date;

(6)   holiday remuneration;

(7)   contributions payable by the company under the Redundancy Payments Act 1967 during the 12 months prior to the commencement of the winding up or the making of the winding-up order;

(8)   damages for personal injuries due to people employed by the company.

A director of the company may be a 'clerk or servant' of the company within the meaning of (4)[165].

---

[163] In the case of a compulsory winding up, the date of the winding-up order or the appointment of a provisional liquidator; in the case of a voluntary winding up, the passing of the necessary resolution.

[164] Capital gains tax is included by virtue of the Taxes Consolidation Act 1997, s 982.

[165] *Stakelum v Canning* [1976] IR 314, in which *Beeton & Co Ltd* [1913] 2 Ch 279 was followed and *Re Newspaper Proprietors' Syndicate Ltd* [1900] 2 Ch 349 was not followed.

[36.141] The section also provides that where a person advances money to an employer for the purpose of paying wages or salaries, the lender is entitled to the same right of priority as the employee would have had. In legal terms, the persons advancing the money (such as a bank) are subrogated to the rights of the employee, ie they stand in their shoes. It may not be easy for a bank or similar lending institution to establish that an account was opened expressly with a view to funding the payment of salaries or wages, but it was held by Plowman J in *Re Rampgill Mill Ltd*[166] that a benevolent rather than a narrow construction should be given to the section and in that case he permitted subrogation where the account had been opened to enable the company to meet its commitments and they clearly included wages due to employees. A similar approach was adopted by Carroll J in *Re Station Motors Ltd*[167].

[36.142] A further statutory right of subrogation is given to the Minister of Labour under the Protection of Employees (Employers Insolvency) Act 1984. Under that Act, the Minister is empowered to make payments to employees out of the Redundancy Fund established under the Redundancy Payments Act 1967 in respect of certain debts owed by an insolvent employer (including a company in liquidation) to his employees. The debts include arrears of wages, holiday pay and awards under various modern acts dealing with a minimum notice, redundancy payments, unfair dismissal and employment equality. The Minister is given by s 10 the same right of priority as the employee would have enjoyed in respect of any of the debts.

Secured creditors

[36.143] Secured creditors are creditors who have some mortgage, charge or lien on the company's property.

[36.144] The application of the bankruptcy rules means that a secured creditor may adopt any of the following courses in a winding up:

(1) he may rely on his security and not prove in the winding up;

(2) he may realise his security and, if it is insufficient, prove for the deficiency;

(3) he may value his security and prove for the deficiency, the liquidator having the option of accepting his valuation;

(4) he may surrender his security and prove for his debt like an unsecured creditor[168].

---

[166] [1967] Ch 1138.
[167] (Unreported, 22 November 1984).
[168] Bankruptcy Act 1988, 1st Schedule r 24.

[36.145] A solicitor who holds a lien on documents of the company for his costs is a secured creditor[169]. A landlord is not a secured creditor, simply because he has a power of distress[170]. A creditor who has obtained a conditional order of garnishee, but has failed to serve it on the debtor before the winding up commences, is not a secured creditor[171].

[36.146] A person who executes a judgment against a company's lands or goods before the commencement of the winding up is a secured creditor; but under the provisions of s 291, he must have completed the execution before the winding up begins. The Principal Act obliges the sheriff, if required by the liquidator so to do, to hand over goods not actually sold; and when a judgment exceeds £20, the sheriff must retain the proceeds of sale for 14 days and if he receives notice of a winding-up order during that period must pay the proceeds, less the costs of execution, to the liquidator[172]. Anyone who buys goods from the sheriff in good faith acquires a good title to them, notwithstanding the winding-up order[173].

Leasehold property

[36.147] Where a lease to a company being wound up contains a power of re-entry, the lessor may apply to the court for liberty to re-enter and the court will allow him to do so, without his having to bring proceedings[174].

[36.148] When the liquidator takes possession, or remains in possession, of leaseholds for the purpose of more effectively realising the assets, the lessor is entitled to payment of the rent in full as part of the expenses properly incurred by the liquidator[175]. The liquidator is then responsible for any repairs or other obligations for which the lessee is liable under the lease[176]. He may disclaim the lease with the leave of the court under s 290 of the Principal Act and the lessor can then prove for any damage he has sustained. The measure of such damage is the difference between the rent which would have been paid by the company under the lease and the rent which the lessor is likely to obtain during the unexpired residue[177].

---

[169] *Re Safety Explosives Ltd* [1904] 1 Ch 226.
[170] *Re Coal Consumers' Association* (1876) 4 Ch D 625 at 629.
[171] *Re Stanhope Silkstone Colliery Co* (1879) 11 Ch D 160.
[172] Companies Act 1963, s 292.
[173] Companies Act 1963, s 291(3).
[174] *General Share and Trust Co v Wetley Brick and Pottery Co* (1882) 20 Ch D 260 at 266.
[175] *Re Oak Pits Colliery* (1882) 21 Ch D 322.
[176] *Re Silkstone & Dodworth Co* (1881) 17 Ch D 158.
[177] *Re Hide, ex p Llynvi Coal Co* [1871] 7 Ch App 28, applied by Murphy J in *Re Bank (IR) Ltd* [1985] ILRM 751.

Interest

[36.149] The interest upon debts which carry interest ceases to run from the date of the commencement of the winding up, unless the assets are sufficient to pay all the debts in full[178].

[36.150] In order to ascertain the balance for which a secured creditor can prove after realising his security, the proceeds of the security are applied in payment of the principal sum with interest down to the date of the commencement of the winding up. He may then prove for the balance of principal and interest due down to that date as an unsecured creditor[179].

Fraudulent preferences

[36.151] The law as to winding up has, as we have seen, imported some of its rules and principles from the law of bankruptcy which came first in time[180]. Among these is the concept that the fair distribution of the insolvent person's assets among his creditors should not be compromised by a selective payment by him before the axe falls to a creditor whom he for some reason favours at the expense of the others. Under s 286 of the Principal Act any act relating to its property made or done by or against a company within six months before the commencement of the winding up was rendered invalid as a 'fraudulent preference' if it qualified as a fraudulent preference in the bankruptcy of an individual. This included a conveyance, mortgage, delivery of goods, payment or execution.

[36.152] This section was replaced by s 135 of the 1990 Act, which eases somewhat the task of the liquidator in proving that there has been a fraudulent preference, but retains the basic concept of the replaced section. The references to the law of bankruptcy are dropped, but the criteria for ascertaining whether there has been such a preference are retained. These are that the company was unable to pay its debts at the commencement of the winding up and that the impugned transaction was entered into with a view to giving the creditor a preference over the other creditors.

[36.153] As we shall see shortly, this is not always easy to establish. However, in the case of a transaction with a 'connected person' entered into within two years before the winding up commenced, there is a presumption that it was made with a view to giving that person a preference over the other creditors and hence is presumed to be a fraudulent preference. The onus, in short, is on the creditor in

---

[178] *Re International Contract Co Ltd Hughes' Claim* [1872] LR 13 Eq 623.
[179] *Quartermaine's Case* [1892] 1 Ch 639.
[180] See para **[36.123]** above.

such a case to prove that the transaction was not a fraudulent preference. A 'connected person' is defined as one who at the time of the transaction was:

(1)   a director of the company;

(2)   a 'shadow director'[181];

(3)   a person connected within the meaning of s 26(1)(a) of the 1990 Act with a director, eg members of his immediate family;

(4)   a 'related company' within the meaning of s 14 of the 1990 Act, ie a holding, subsidiary or sister company[182];

(5)   a trustee of, or surety or guarantor for the debt due to, any of the foregoing.

[36.154] In any other case, the burden of proof remains, as before, on the liquidator to prove that the preference was fraudulent. It is not an easy onus to discharge: in the words of Bacon VC, in *Ex p Blackburn*[183], cited with approval by Holmes LJ in *Re Oliver*[184]:

> 'The payment must, in order to be void, be made "in favour of any creditor with a view of giving such creditor a preference over the other creditors." So that, unless it can be made clearly apparent, and to the satisfaction of the court which has to decide, that the debtor's sole motive was to prefer the creditor paid to the other creditors, the payment cannot be impeached, even though it is obviously in favour of a creditor. The act of the debtor alone is to be considered - the object and purpose for which the payment is made can alone be inquired into - and although it is perfectly legitimate, and in all cases requisite, that all the attending circumstances should be carefully investigated, yet if the act done can be properly referred to some other motive or reason than that of giving the creditor paid a preference over the other creditors, then I conceive neither the statute, nor any principle of law or policy, will justify a court of law in holding that the payment is fraudulent.'

In particular, the fact that the payment was made in response to pressure, including the threat of proceedings, will normally be taken to mean that the debtor was not unfairly favouring the creditor concerned but was simply giving way to the pressure. Nor is it enough to prove that there was an actual preference from which an intention to prefer is then, with hindsight, inferred. The liquidator must prove an intention to prefer at the time the payment was made[185]. But where there is no direct evidence of intention, there is nothing to prevent the court from

---

[181] For the meaning of this expression, see para **[27.05]** above.

[182] Ie a subsidiary of the same holding company.

[183] (1871) LR 12 Eq 358.

[184] [1914] 2 IR 356.

[185] *Re K M Kushler Ltd* [1943] Ch 248; *Re Corran Construction Co Ltd v Bank of Ireland* (unreported, 8 September 1976), HC (McWilliam J).

drawing an inference of an intention to prefer where no other possible explanation is open[186]. Where, however, the liquidator proves no more than a state of facts which is equally consistent with guilt or innocence (an expression used for convenience since there is no question of criminal liability) he will have failed to discharge the onus[187].

[36.155] The payment alleged to be a fraudulent preference may have benefited the person concerned only indirectly. This will not prevent it, however, from being a fraudulent preference. This frequently arises in guarantee cases: a director of the company may have personally guaranteed the company's overdraft and may then procure the repayment by the company of the overdraft with a view to eliminating his personal liability. In such a case, if an intention to prefer the director indirectly by the repayment of the overdraft can be inferred, this will constitute a fraudulent preference. This position, well settled by judicial decisions[188], was confirmed by statute: the provisions in the 1990 Act were applied to the preferring not merely of a creditor but 'any surety or guarantor for the debt due to such creditor'.

[36.156] Some other provisions applicable to fraudulent preferences should be noted. The fact that a transaction is found to be a fraudulent preference does not affect the rights of any person making title in good faith and for valuable consideration through or under a creditor of the company[189]. If a transaction is void as a fraudulent preference of a person whose property is mortgaged or charged to secure the company's debt, he is to be treated in the winding up as though he were a surety for the debt to the extent of his charge or interest in it[190].

[36.157] The section is for the benefit of all the creditors and cannot be invoked if the result of recovering the property comprised in the fraudulent preference would be to the benefit of a section only of the creditors[191].

Any conveyance or assignment by a company of all its property to trustees for the benefit of all its creditors is void to all intents.

Fraudulent transfer of assets

[36.158] The power to set aside a transaction as a fraudulent preference was supplemented by a power conferred by s 139 of the 1990 Act on the court to order a person to return property of the company being wound up which was disposed of in order to perpetrate a fraud on the company, its members or

---

[186] *Re K M Kushler Ltd* [1943] Ch 248.

[187] *Re K M Kushler Ltd* [1943] Ch 248.

[188] See, eg, *Station Motors Ltd* (unreported, 22 November 1984).

[189] Companies Act 1963, s 286(4).

[190] Companies Act 1963, s 287.

[191] Companies Act 1963, s 286(2).

creditors. This arises where the disposition was by way of conveyance, transfer, mortgage, security, loan 'or in any way whatsoever whether by act or omission, direct or indirect', provided the effect of the transaction was to perpetrate such a fraud. The court may make the order where it considers it just and equitable so to do and the order may be made against any person who appears to have the use, control or possession of the property or the proceeds of the sale or development thereof. Alternatively, he may be ordered to pay a sum in respect of it to the liquidator. The application may be made by the liquidator or any creditor or contributory. The court in deciding whether to make the order is to have regard to rights acquired in the property *bona fide* and for valuable consideration.

Reckless and fraudulent trading

[36.159] The liquidator may apply to the court for an order under ss 297 and 297A of the Principal Act as inserted by ss 137 and 138 of the 1990 Act for a declaration that the directors and other persons have been guilty of fraudulent or reckless trading and should be held personally liable for some or all of the company's debts and liabilities. The scope of these provisions has already been considered in Chapter 33 above.

Contribution to debts by related companies

[36.160] A frequent source of frustration for many creditors has been to find that companies in a group effectively controlled by the same person can continue trading although one of the group has collapsed, owing them unpaid debts. We have already seen that the 1990 Act makes provision for the winding up at the same time of 'related companies'[192]. Another mechanism to deal with the same problem is provided by s 140 which enables the court to order the payment by a 'related' company to the liquidator of a contribution to the whole or part of any of the debts provable in the winding up. The meaning of 'related' companies has been explained in para **[36.34]** above.

[36.161] As in the case of a joint winding-up order, the court may make the order, on the application of the liquidator, or any creditor or contributory, where it is satisfied that it is just and equitable so to do and may make the order on such terms and conditions as it thinks fit. It must have regard to:

(1)   the extent to which the related company took part in the management of the company being wound up;

(2)   the conduct of the related company towards the creditors of the company being wound up;

---

[192] See para **[36.34]** above.

(3) the effect which the order would be likely to have on the creditors of the related company.

[36.162] The order cannot be made unless the court is satisfied that the circumstances that gave rise to the winding up are attributable to the actions or omissions of the related company. It may not be made solely on the ground that the companies are related or that the creditors of the company being wound up relied on the fact of their being related.

[36.163] For the purposes of this provision, a creditor means one or more creditors to whom the company being wound up is indebted by more in aggregate than £10,000.

Property held in trust

[36.164] Property which can be identified as belonging to, or held by, the company in trust for any persons may be followed and recovered by the liquidator[193].

Misfeasance proceedings

[36.165] Section 298 of the Principal Act as substituted by s 142 of the 1990 Act provides a useful summary remedy for recovering money from the promoters, directors, managers or other officers of the company which they have misapplied or have wrongfully received or for which they are accountable to the company. It can also be used when the directors have been guilty of some negligence or misfeasance for which they are answerable to the company in damages. It should be noted that the section does not create any new offence or cause of action; it simply provides a more expeditious remedy[194].

[36.166] Misfeasance proceedings have been taken when the directors have used funds of the company for objects not sanctioned by the memorandum[195]; or have paid dividends out of capital[196]; or have made secret profits[197]; or have sold their own property to the company[198]. In all cases, it must be shown that actual pecuniary loss has been caused to the company[199].

---

[193] *Re Lang Propeller Ltd* [1926] Ch 585 at 595; *Shanahans' Stamps Auctions Ltd v Farrelly and Dawson* [1962] IR 386.
[194] *Re Irish Provident Assurance Co* [1913] 1 IR 352.
[195] *Coats v Crossland* [1904] 20 TLR 800.
[196] *Moxham v Grant* [1900] 1 QB 88.
[197] *Pearson's Case* (1877) 5 Ch D 336.
[198] *Re Cape Breton Co* (1885) 29 Ch D 795.
[199] *Re SM Barker Ltd* [1950] IR 123 at 137.

[36.167] Misfeasance proceedings are brought by motion on notice. The notice must state the nature of the declaration or order which is sought and the grounds of the application. It must be served personally, together with a copy of any report or affidavit on which it is grounded, on every person against whom an order is sought not less than seven clear days before the day named for hearing the application[200].

[36.168] Misfeasance proceedings are abated by the completion of the winding up. They are not revived if the dissolution of the company is declared void under s 310 of the Principal Act[201].

[36.169] Under s 8 of the Civil Liability Act 1961 on the death of any person, all causes of action subsisting against him survive against his estate, with certain exceptions which are not material; and consequently the estate of a deceased director can be sued in the ordinary way for any tort or breach of trust committed by him during his lifetime. But it would seem that this does not enable misfeasance proceedings to be brought against his estate[202].

Examination by the court

[36.170] The Court was empowered under s 245 of the Principal Act to examine persons who might be in possession of information or documents relevant to the company being wound up. These powers were strengthened by a new s 245 and s 245A inserted by ss 126 and 127 of the 1990 Act.

[36.171] The court may summon before it under this procedure any officer of the company or any person known or suspected to have in his possession any of the property of the company or suspected of being indebted to the company or any person whom the court may deem capable of giving information concerning the promotion, formation, trading, dealing, officers or property of the company. The power becomes exercisable at any time after the appointment of a provisional liquidator or the making of a winding-up order. The examination may be held either before the judge or an officer of the court, such as the Master or the Examiner.

[36.172] It was held by the former Supreme Court in *Re Redbreast Preserving Co (Ireland) Ltd*[203] that the court could direct such an examination to be held in private, since it did not constitute the administration of justice and hence such a procedure was not invalid having regard to Article 34.1 of the Constitution. That provision requires justice to be administered in public 'save in such special and

---

[200] Rules of the Superior Courts 1986, SI 1986/15, Ord 74, r 49.
[201] *Re Lewis & Smart Ltd* [1954] 2 All ER 19.
[202] *Re British Guardian Assurance Co Ltd* (1880) 14 Ch D 335.
[203] 91 ILTR 12.

limited cases as may be prescribed in law'. However, in *Re R Ltd*[204], Walsh J remarked:

'If the dictum of the former Supreme Court in *Re Redbreast Preserving Co Ltd* means that the constitutional requirement that justice is to be administered in public is satisfied by the public pronouncement of a decision based on evidence taken other than in public, then where that is not expressly authorised by a post-Constitution statute it is clearly incorrect and ought not to be followed.'

[36.173] Section 245, both in its original and amended form, contains no such express authorisation for the holding of the examination in private. In the result, it would clearly be unsafe to hold the examination in private, unless it is anticipated that the evidence will not be required in court proceedings but, for example, will be used solely for the benefit of the liquidator in his conduct of the winding up.

[36.174] Before the examination takes place, the court may require the person whose attendance is sought to place before it, in such form as it directs, a statement of any transactions between him and the company of a specified type or class. The person examined may also be ordered to pay the costs of the examination where the court considers this just and equitable. Where a person without reasonable cause fails to attend his examination, he is guilty of contempt of court[205]. All of these provisions were inserted for the first time by the 1990 Act. The court already had power to order the arrest of a person who refused to attend without being excused: this power was extended to cases where there are reasonable grounds for believing that a person has absconded or is about to abscond with a view to avoiding or delaying his examination. In addition, his books, documents and moveable property may be seized[206].

[36.175] The court was also given a new power by the 1990 Act where during the course of the examination it appears to the court that the person examined is indebted to the company or has in his possession or control any money, property, books or papers of the company. Formerly, it would have been necessary for the liquidator to institute independent proceedings: now the court may order the person concerned to pay the debt or hand over the property on such terms as the court directs[207].

[36.176] The section provides that none of the answers of the person shall be admissible in evidence against him in any other proceedings, civil or criminal, except proceedings for perjury in respect of any of the answers. It was held by O'Hanlon J in *Re Aluminium Fabricators Ltd*[208] that this did not prevent the

---

[204] [1988] IR 126.
[205] Companies Act 1963, s 245(4), (5) and (7).
[206] Companies Act 1963, s 245(8).
[207] Companies Act 1963, s 245A.
[208] [1984] ILRM 399.

transcript being used in proceedings under the winding-up order itself, eg an application under the fraudulent trading section.

[36.177] If it appears that any officers and members of the company have been guilty of offences in relation to the company for which they are criminally liable, the court can direct the liquidator, either of its own motion or on the application of anyone interested in the liquidation, to refer the matter to the Director of Public Prosecutions. The liquidator must then give such information and access to and facilities for inspecting and copying documents in his possession or under his control as the Director may require[209].

Offences

[36.178] The Act provides for the punishment of certain offences by officers of a company which is being wound up or is subsequently wound up. These offences, which include the falsification of books, concealment or removal of property and fraudulent practices relating to creditors are set out in ss 293, 294, 295 and 296 of the Principal Act. They are punishable on conviction on indictment by penalties ranging from penal servitude for a term not exceeding two years, a fine not exceeding £500 or both to penal servitude for five years or a fine not exceeding £10,000 or both. They are also punishable summarily, the maximum sentence being imprisonment for six months or a fine not exceeding £100 or both.

Termination of the winding up

[36.179] When the liquidator has passed his final account, he applies to the court for directions as to the application of the balance[210]. When the application, as so directed, has been vouched to the Examiner, the Examiner certifies that it has been so vouched and that the affairs of the company have been completely wound up[211]. If the company has not already been dissolved, the liquidator immediately after such certificate has become binding applies to the court for an order that the company be dissolved from the date of the order[212]. An office copy of the order is to be forwarded by the liquidator to the Registrar within 21 days from the date of the order[213].

The dissolution may within two years be declared to have been void[214]. The application for such a declaration is made to the court by motion on notice.

---

[209] Companies Act 1963, s 299 as amended by the Companies Act 1990, s 143.
[210] Rules of the Superior Courts 1986, SI 1986/15, Ord 74, r 137.
[211] Rules of the Superior Courts 1986, SI 1986/15, Ord 74, r 137, App M Form 46.
[212] Companies Act 1963, s 249(1).
[213] Companies Act 1963, s 249(2).
[214] Companies Act 1963, s 310.

Chapter 37

Protection Orders

The History of protection orders

[37.01] The belief that some companies in financial difficulties could be put back on a sound footing and so avoid a winding up with all it entails for creditors and employees alike prompted the introduction of legislation in the United States, England and (in the form of the 1990 (No 1) Act) Ireland.

[37.02] The United States legislation sought to assimilate the position of insolvent companies more closely to that of a person who goes bankrupt. The latter does not suffer the death sentence with a stay of execution which is the fate of a company in liquidation: it would seem logical that a company should have the same opportunity to being restored to financial good health. The English legislation, implementing in the main the recommendations of the Cork Committee[1], sought to build on the experience derived from cases where receivers were appointed. Very often such a step is simply the prelude to liquidation. But in England the taking over of management by an accountant with long experience of ailing businesses sometimes resulted in the successful relaunch of the company in a more streamlined form with the jettisoning of unutilised assets and the shedding of superfluous jobs. It was thought that this result could be facilitated by the intervention of the court and the staying of any proceedings against the company while the surgery went ahead.

[37.03] While our 1990 (No 1) Act was closely modelled in some respects on the English 1986 Act[2], there were also major differences. In England, to give effect to the concept that the 'administrator' appointed by the court is in essence taking on the role of a receiver, but one charged with the task of rescuing the company rather than simply protecting the debenture holder's security, the administrator takes over the management of the company to the exclusion of the directors. In Ireland, where an 'examiner' as he is called, is appointed, the directors retain their powers, unless the court otherwise orders. In England, it is seen as important that a debenture holder who wants to appoint a receiver should retain the option of an out of court receivership. To provide otherwise, it was felt, might imperil the present structures under which the banks can safely advance money to companies. Hence, the debenture holder with power to appoint a

---

[1] Cmnd 8858.

[2] Insolvency Act 1986.

receiver is in effect given a veto over the appointment of a court administrator. In Ireland, under the 1990 (No 1) Act an examiner can be appointed unless a receiver has been in office for at least three days before the application. In England, guarantors of the company's debts, such as directors, remain personally liable: in Ireland, during the period the court protection lasts (generally 70 days) no action can be taken against guarantors.

[37.04] While the professed objects of the 1990 (No 1) Act were generally regarded as laudable, some of its key provisions were strongly criticised from the outset and the manner in which it operated in practice did little to allay such anxieties.

[37.05] The legislation seriously abridged the rights of creditors, including, it should be emphasised, ordinary creditors and not merely secured creditors. That no doubt was a necessary feature of the statutory scheme, but it might have been thought that the criteria to be met before an examiner could be appointed by the court would be relatively strict. That did not prove to be the case in practice. Concern was expressed that the interests, not only of creditors but also of competitors of ailing companies, were not properly taken into account. In addition, the power of the examiner to incur further liabilities on behalf of the company during the protection period, which were then given priority over all the other liabilities of the company, could be exercised in a manner seriously detrimental to other creditors and competitors.

[37.06] The person to act as examiner was nominated by those seeking his appointment, almost invariably the company or its directors. The examiner was required to present a report to the court within a specified period in which he stated his view as to whether the company had a viable future. Since he was effectively the company's nominee, there was an understandable inclination on the part of examiners to see the company's prospects in a relatively optimistic light. There were also cases in which it was obvious that the petitioners had failed to disclose relevant facts to the court. There was, however, no provision for an independent examination of the company's affairs and prospects before the examiner was appointed. Moreover, an interim order appointing him could be made without any notice to the creditors.

[37.07] These aspects of the 1990 (No 1) Act were considered in the first Report of the Company Law Review Group. They said:

> '... we experienced some difficulty in formulating a precise statement of the public interest justification for the examinership process with its associated impairments of the rights and interests of creditors and competitors.

> Yet, within the group, and indeed in many of the submissions made to us, there is a belief that examinership, albeit in a modified form, is a useful mechanism which should be available in Irish company law. That this view was expressed

by bodies representing people whose interests have been impaired by the operation of the examinership legislation is worthy of particular note ...

It is essential, however, while allowing for consideration of the individual merits of each case, to set limits to the availability of examinership, to set parameters for the operation of the legislation and to provide checks and balances.'

The group, then went on to make a number of recommendations, most of which have now been implemented by the 1999 (No 2) Act. Among other changes, the criteria for determining whether a company has a viable future have been clarified, provision has been made for an independent assessment of its affairs and prospects before the petition is presented and the liabilities incurred by the examiner no longer enjoy a priority over secured creditors of the company.

[37.08] The Act, however, again following the recommendations, leaves unaltered two features of the 1990 (No 1) Act which have been strongly criticised, ie the continued management of the company during the protection period by the directors and the freeze on taking action against personal guarantors of the company's debts during the same period.

[37.09] The principal features of the statutory scheme under the 1990 (No 1) Act, as amended by the 1999 (No 2) Act can be summarised as follows. The effect of the appointment of the examiner by the court is to prevent the company from being wound up or its assets being seized by the creditors as long as the 'protection order' lasts. This is for a period of 70 days only which can be extended for one additional period of 30 days but no more. Prior to the 1999 (No 2) Act, the period was three months. The court can, however, defer its decision beyond these periods and the protection period is also extended until the decision. During that time, the examiner must present a report to the court, containing his proposals. If he thinks the company has a viable future, he may propose a scheme of arrangement, ie a settlement with the creditors for less than 100p in the £. It is for the court to decide whether any such scheme should be implemented: the examiner's role is an investigating and reporting one. Again the difference from the English 1986 Act should be noted: there, if the administrator can carry the creditors with him, he does not need the approval of the court.

[37.10] Unlike the scheme of arrangement under the Principal Act[3], such a scheme can be imposed on all the creditors, even though not every class of creditor has agreed to the settlement. The examiner's proposals may also extend to the reconstruction of the company, the sale of some of its assets and changes in its management. Again it is for the court to decide whether they should be

---

3   See para **[32.10]** above.

implemented. The alternative to the implementation of any proposals put forward by the examiner would normally be the winding up of the company.

Grounds for appointing an examiner

[37.11] An examiner can be appointed where three conditions are met:

(1)   it appears to the court that the company, is, or is likely to be, unable to pay its debts;

(2)   there is no winding up in being, compulsory or voluntary;

(3)   the court is satisfied that there is 'a reasonable prospect' of the survival of the company and the whole or any part of its undertaking as a going concern.

[37.12] Prior to the enactment of the 1999 (No 2) Act, an examiner could be appointed in any case where the company was unable to pay its debts and no winding up was in being. The Act also provided that, in particular, the order could be made where it was likely to facilitate the survival of the company as a going concern. Hence, it was clear that the making of the order was discretionary. (In this, it differed from the English 1986 Act under which the court had to consider that one of four stated purposes would be served before the order could be made.) Thus, it would seem that an order could have been made where, for example, the court was satisfied that the company's assets would be more effectively realised for everyone's benefit than in a winding up, even if there was no prospect of the company itself surviving.

[37.13] It was suggested in the second edition that under the 1990 (No 1) Act, the court should consider whether there was a 'real prospect' that the company would survive or that the interests of those financially interested in its future would be better served by appointing an examiner. In *Re Atlantic Magnetics Ltd (in receivership)*[4] Lardner J in the High Court said that the test to be applied when deciding whether the examiner should be appointed was whether there was 'some reasonable prospect of survival'. A different view, however, was taken by the Supreme Court: the 'reasonable prospect of survival' test was rejected and Finlay CJ, speaking for the majority, indicated that it was sufficient if there was 'some prospect of survival'.

[37.14] The 'reasonable prospect of survival' test favoured by Lardner J has now been adopted by the legislature and, in addition, is now an essential precondition to the appointment of an examiner[5]. The court, moreover, must be 'satisfied' that such a prospect exists and it would seem to follow that the usual burden of proof

---

[4]   [1993] 2 IR 561.

[5]   Companies (Amendment) (No 2) Act 1999, s 12.

in civil proceedings applies and that it must be established on the balance of probabilities that there is a reasonable prospect of the company's survival. It had also been stated in *Re Atlantic Magnetics Ltd (in receivership)* that there was no onus of proof to establish as a matter of probability that the company was capable of survival as a going concern but it is clear that this no longer represents the law.

Application for the appointment of an examiner

[37.15] The application for the appointment of an examiner is made by petition. It may be presented by any of the following:

(1)   the company;

(2)   the directors;

(3)   a creditor or contingent or prospective creditor, including an employee;

(4)   a member holding not less than one fourth of the voting shares.

The petition may be presented by all or any of these, together or separately[6]. It has been held in England that, provided a resolution is passed at a duly convened meeting of the board of directors authorising an application, it is immaterial that not all the directors were present[7].

[37.16] The 1990 (No 1) Act stated that the petition was to be supported by such evidence as the court might require. Although, as has been noted, the court had, in general, to be satisfied that there was some prospect of the company's survival before the examiner was appointed, there was no requirement for the submission of a detailed report by the proposed examiner on the company's prospects before his appointment. A period of three weeks was allowed for the preparation by the examiner of his first report dealing in detail with the company's affairs, whether it had a viable future, and, if so, the steps that should be taken to secure that future as far as possible.

[37.17] The 1999 (No 2) Act now requires[8] that the petition is to be accompanied by the report of an 'independent accountant': this report effectively replaces the first report presented by the examiner under the 1990 (No 1) Act within the 21 day period from his appointment. For that reason, as already noted, the initial protection period is reduced from three months to 70

---

[6]   Companies (Amendment) Act 1990, s 3
[7]   *Re Primlaks (UK) Ltd* (1989) BCLC 734.
[8]   Companies (Amendment) Act 1990, s 3(3A) as inserted by the Companies (Amendment) (No 2) Act 1999, s 7.

days. An 'independent accountant' is defined as the auditor of the company or a person qualified to be the auditor of the company.

[37.18] The report of the independent accountant must contain the names and addresses of the officers and 'any shadow directors' and the names of any other companies of which the directors are also directors. It must contain a statement of the affairs of the company, showing so far as is reasonably possible, particulars of the company's assets and liabilities (including contingent and prospective liabilities) as of the latest practicable date, the names and addresses of its creditors and the securities held by them respectively and the dates when they were given. It must also state whether any deficiency there may be between the company's assets and liabilities has been satisfactorily accounted for and, if it is not, whether there is evidence of a substantial disappearance of property which has not been adequately accounted for.

[37.19] The principal object of the report is, however, to inform the court whether the independent accountant's investigations indicate that the company has a viable future and what steps, including possible arrangements with its creditors, are necessary to that end. Accordingly, it must include the opinion of the independent accountant as to whether the company would have a reasonable prospect of survival as a going concern and a statement of the conditions which he considers are essential to ensure its survival. It should be noted that one of the matters to which he must have regard in this context is 'the internal management and controls of the company'. He must state his opinion as to whether proposals for a compromise or scheme of arrangement would offer a reasonable prospect of survival and whether carrying on the company's business would be likely to be more advantageous to the members as a whole and the creditors as a whole than a winding up. The report must set out his recommendations as to the course that he thinks should be taken, including, if warranted, draft proposals for a compromise or scheme of arrangement. He must also give his opinion as to whether the facts disclosed to him would warrant further enquiries with a few to proceedings under s 297 or s 297 A of the Principal Act, ie civil or criminal proceedings for fraudulent or reckless trading[9].

[37.20] Two matters which must be dealt with in the report of the independent accountant are of particular importance. First, he must give details of the extent of the funding required to enable the company to continue trading during the period of protection and the sources of that funding. Secondly, he must state his recommendations as to which liabilities incurred before the presentation of the petition should be paid. This latter provision is the result of the concern expressed in the first report of the Company Law Review Group as to the

---

[9]   See Ch 33 above.

payment by a company to which an examiner had been appointed of 'pre-petition' debts. While creditors of the company could not enforce payment of such debts following the appointment of the examiner, there was nothing to prevent the management from paying them voluntarily and, in effect, preferring some creditors to others. This might be particularly the case where the management was being pressed to pay suppliers. The group recommended that only those pre-petition debts that were referred to in the report of the independent accountant should be paid and this recommendation has been implemented by the legislation, subject to the important proviso that the court may, in specified circumstances, authorise the payment of particular pre-petition debts.

[37.21] Finally, the report is to state the opinion of the independent accountant as to whether the work of the examiner would be assisted by an order of the court appointing a creditors' committee to assist him in the exercise of his functions. It is also to set out such other matters as he thinks relevant.

[37.22] The Company Law Review Group acknowledged that circumstances might unexpectedly arise where the survival of a company as a going concern was threatened but no independent accountant's report was completed or even in course of preparation. To allow for what were thought to be the rare cases in which this might occur, the court should have the jurisdiction to make a protection order for a maximum period of ten days from the presentation of the petition to allow the independent accountant's report to be prepared. This recommendation is implemented by the 1999 (No 2) Act: the court may make such an order, placing the company concerned under its protection for a period of ten days where it is satisfied:

'(a) that, by reason of exceptional circumstances outside the control of the petitioner, the report of the independent accountant is not available in time to accompany the petition;

(b) that the petitioner could not reasonably have anticipated the circumstances referred to in paragraph (a)'.[10]

The use of the expression 'exceptional circumstances' is important. It is obviously the intention of the legislature (carrying into effect the report of the Review Group) that this jurisdiction should not be availed of as a matter of routine by companies in difficulties. In this context, it should be noted that the legislation makes it clear that the mere fact that a receiver has been appointed does not, of itself, amount to 'exceptional circumstances outside the control of the petitioner'.

---

[10] Companies (Amendment) (No 2) Act 1999, s 9.

[37.23] It should also be noted that liabilities incurred by the company during the interim period of protection permitted by this provision enjoy no priority over other creditors of the company.

[37.24] The independent accountant must supply a copy of his report to the company or any interested party, which makes a written application to him for the report. The court, however, may direct that parts of the report are to be omitted from copies supplied to the company or an interested party: in particular, it may order the omission of information the inclusion of which would be likely to prejudice the company's survival as a going concern[11].

[37.25] The petition must nominate a person to be appointed as examiner and be accompanied by the consent in writing of the nominated person to act. It must also be accompanied by any proposals for a compromise or scheme of arrangement (if such have been prepared)[12]. The court cannot give a hearing to a petition presented by a creditor until he has furnished such security for costs, as it considers reasonable[13]. As already noted, an examiner cannot be appointed if a receiver has been in office for at least three continuous days prior to the presentation of the petition.

[37.26] The petitioner must give notice of the petition in the prescribed form to the Registrar within three day of its having been presented. The Rules require the petitioner to apply to the court for directions as to the proceedings to be taken in relation to the petition[14]. The court would normally direct the petition to be advertised in two national newspapers and fix a day, generally a Monday, for the hearing of the petition.

[37.27] Until the enactment of the 1999 (No 2) Act, the creditors of the company were not entitled, as of right, to be heard by the court before the appointment of an examiner. Under the Rules the court could direct service of notice on such parties as it thought fit. In practice it has been usual for service to be directed on the company (unless it is the petitioner), all the secured creditors, a receiver, if one has been appointed, and some, at least of the ordinary creditors. Where, as is usually the case, the Revenue Commissioners were creditors, the service was also directed on them. Now the 1999 (No 2) Act provides that the court is not to make an order either appointing an examiner or dismissing a petition without having afforded each creditor of the company, who has indicated to the court his desire to be heard, an opportunity to be so heard[15]. It would seem to follow that,

11 Companies (Amendment) (No 2) Act 1999, s 11.
12 Companies (Amendment) Act 1990, s 3(4).
13 Companies (Amendment) Act 1990, s 3(5).
14 Rules of the Supreme Court (No 3) 1991, SI 147/1991.
15 Companies (Amendment) (No 2) Act 1999, s 10.

in every case, the court should now direct service of the petition on all the creditors of the company.

[37.28] On the hearing of the petition the court may:

(1)   appoint an examiner;

(2)   dismiss the petition;

(3)   adjourn the petition;

(4)   make an interim order;

(5)   make such other order, as it thinks fit.[16]

[37.29] Although the 1990 (No 1) Act did not expressly provide that the power to make an interim order extended to the appointment of an examiner on an interim basis, it seems clear that this is what was intended. The Rules provide for the making of an *ex parte* application to the court, which may treat it as the hearing of the petition, and at which an examiner may be appointed on an interim basis until the adjourned hearing of the petition. Although the 1999 (No 2) Act now provides that an order appointing an examiner cannot be made until the creditors have been given an opportunity of being heard, it is expressly provided that this is not to affect the power of the court to make an interim order. It should be noted, however, that, where an application is being made *ex parte* for the appointment of an interim examiner, the obligation remains on the petitioner to furnish the report of the independent accountant, save in the 'exceptional circumstances' already referred to, where the court may appoint an examiner for an interim period not exceeding ten days to enable the report to be prepared and submitted to the court.

[37.30] Where an examiner is appointed to a company, the court may also appoint an examiner of a 'related company'. In deciding whether to do so, the court is to have regard to whether this will facilitate the survival of the company or the related company or both as going concerns. It is now provided under the 1999 (No 2) Act that the court is not to make the order unless it is satisfied that there is a reasonable prospect of the survival of the related company, and the whole or any part of its undertaking, as a going concern[17]. 'Related company' is broadly defined so as to include holding companies and subsidiaries, companies where more than half the equity share capital is held by the other or similar control is exercised by voting power or where,

> '... the business of the companies has been so carried on that the separate business of each company, or a substantial part thereof, is not readily identifiable.'

---

[16] Companies (Amendment) Act 1990, s 3(7)

[17] Companies (Amendment) Act 1990, s 4.

[37.31] The court has power, under s 31 of the 1990 (No 1) Act, to hear the whole or any part of the proceedings in private, including the application for the appointment of an examiner. Having regard to the strict view taken by the Supreme Court as to the circumstances in which such a power can be exercised by the court in relation to companies, it would seem that the court should be satisfied that publicity would be seriously damaging to the interests of everyone financially concerned in the company, including its creditors, before making such an order[18].

The examiner

Qualification

[37.32] As is the case with the liquidator, the examiner is not required to have any professional qualifications. In practice, he will almost invariably be a qualified accountant. He is disqualified from acting if he would also be disqualified form acting as liquidator, ie if he is, or has been within the 12 months preceding the appointment, an officer or servant of the company or its auditor or has occupied a similar position in relation to an associated company or is a close relation of any of these categories. (In the last instance, however, he can so act with the leave of the court.) Partners of officers, servants and auditors are also disqualified[19].

Remuneration and expenses

[37.33] The provision as to the examiner's remuneration and expenses are also broadly similar to those applicable to a liquidator[20]. The court determines the amount of his remuneration: he is also entitled to be recouped reasonable expenses, which he has properly incurred. While he may employ such assistance as he considers appropriate, he is also allowed to make use of the company's staff and the extent to which he does so is to be taken into account in determining his remuneration and expenses.

[37.34] Section 10 of the 1990 (No 1) Act provided that:

> 'any liabilities incurred by the company during the protection period which are referred to in sub-section (2) shall be treated as expenses properly incurred ... by the examiner.

The liabilities referred to in sub-s (2) are those certified by the examiner at the time they are incurred to have been incurred in circumstances where, in the

---

18 See para **[26.64]** above.
19 See para **[36.81]** above.
20 See para **[36.83]** above.

opinion of the examiner, the survival of the company as a going concern during the protection period would otherwise be seriously prejudiced.

[37.35] This was to prove one of the most contentious features of the 1990 (No 1) Act as it operated in practice. Section 29 provided that the remuneration, costs and expenses (including the liabilities certified under s 10) were to be paid in priority to all other creditors, secured and unsecured, when a scheme of arrangement was being implemented or a winding up or receivership ensured. Since the protection period could last for four months, the extent of the liabilities incurred by an examiner could be considerable and the effect on the company's creditors correspondingly serious. (The extent to which the court was necessarily bound by a certificate of the examiner in respect of such liabilities is considered below.) The law has now been altered by s 28 of the 1999 (No 2) Act, which provides that such expenses are now to enjoy priority over ordinary creditors only and not over secured creditors.

[37.36] The limitations on the exercise of this power were explained by Murphy J in *Re Don Bluth Entertainment*[21]. There is first the requirement expressly imposed by the section that the examiner should have formed the opinion that the survival of the company as a going concern would be seriously prejudiced if such liabilities were not incurred. Secondly, it is only liabilities incurred during the protection period which may be certified: such expenses as legal fees payable in connection with the presentation of the petition were held in that case not to be certifiable. Thirdly, 'great care and professional expertise' should be exercised by the examiner in issuing certificates. Murphy J added:

'I would anticipate that an examiner from whom a certificate is sought would require the directors managing the business of the company to submit to him their proposals in relation to any particular liabilities which they proposed to incur and to satisfy him as to how the services or goods to be obtained would benefit the company, and in particular how they would contribute to the survival of the company during the protection period.'

[37.37] It is also clear from *Re Don Bluth Ltd* that, while it is possible in theory for the certificate not to be writing, since the section does not expressly so provide, a written certificate is 'an obvious and inescapable administrative necessity'.

[37.38] As already noted, the remuneration and costs of the examiner are given priority over the claims of all other creditors, secured and unsecured, and this, it has been held on two occasions by the Supreme Court, allows the examiner to have recourse, if necessary, to assets subject to a fixed charge. It has also been held more recently by the Supreme Court in *Re Springline Ltd*[22] that the words

---

[21] [1994] 3 IR 141. See also *Re Edenpark Construction Ltd* [1994] 3 IR126.
[22] [1997] 1 IR 467.

'any other claim, secured or unsecured' include the claim of a subsequently appointed liquidator to his remuneration, costs and expenses: the examiner's costs and remuneration enjoy priority over those of the liquidator.

Liability

[37.39] The examiner, like the receiver, is personally liable on any contracts entered into by him whether in the name of the company or in his own name. He is also entitled to be indemnified out of the assets of the company in respect of his personal liability[23].

Resignation

[37.40] The examiner may resign at any time and may also be removed by the court on an application by the creditors' committee, the company or any interested party[24]. If for this or any other reason, there is a vacancy in the office of examiner, it may be filled by the court[25].

Effect of the order appointing an examiner

[37.41] Where the court appoints an examiner, the company is deemed to be under the protection of the court for the period of 70 days from the date of the presentation of the petition together with any extension not exceeding 10 days which may have been granted by the court where the report of an independent accountant is not available in time[26]. The protection period will come to an end before the expiration of that period if the petition is either withdrawn or refused.

[37.42] During the protection period, the following consequences ensue:

(1) no voluntary or compulsory winding up can be initiated;

(2) no receiver can be appointed or, if appointed less than three days before the presentation of the petition, can act as such;

(3) no attachment, execution, distress or sequestration can be enforced against the company's property or effects without the consent of the examiner;

(4) no secured creditor can take any steps to realise his security without the consent of the examiner;

(5) goods of the company subject to hire purchase agreements, retention of title clauses etc may not be repossessed;

---

23 Companies (Amendment) Act 1990, s 13(6).
24 Companies (Amendment) Act 1990, s 13(1) and (2).
25 Companies (Amendment) Act 1990, s 13(2).
26 Companies (Amendment) Act 1990, s 5 as amended by the Companies (Amendment) (No 2) Act 1999, s 14.

(6)   no proceedings of any sort may be taken against a person liable for the company's debts, such as a guarantor, nor may any attachment, distress, sequestration or execution be put in force against his property in respect of the company's debts[27].

In addition, no other proceedings in relation to the company may be commenced except by leave of the court and the court may also stay any such proceedings on the application of the examiner[28].

[37.43] The provision at (6) prohibiting the enforcement of personal guarantees during the protection period is of particular significance. Directors who have given such guarantees may be strongly tempted to apply for the appointment of an examiner in order to give themselves a 70 day respite and it may not be easy for a court to refuse the order, although there are grounds for suspecting that the reasons for its presentation are not those contemplated by the legislature. The Company Law Review Group were of the view that the freezing of the guarantees during the protection period should continue and their recommendation to that effect has been accepted by the legislation in the 1999 (No 2) Act. However, the Act also gives effect to their recommendation that certain anomalous consequences that could flow from the exercise by the guarantor of rights of subrogation should be addressed and the relevant provision is considered at para **[37.76]** below.

[37.44] We have seen that the 1999 (No 2) Act preserves a central feature of the 1990 Act, ie the power of the court to appoint an examiner despite the opposition of a debenture holder entitled to appoint a receiver, except where a receiver has actually been appointed more than three days prior to the presentation of the petition. In any other case, not merely may an examiner be appointed: the court may also order a receiver who has been appointed to cease to act or to act, from a specified date, only in respect of certain specified assets. The court may also direct him to deliver all books, papers and records in his possession or control relating to the company to the examiner and to give the examiner full particulars of his dealings with the property and undertaking of the company. These provisions clearly imposed drastic limitations on the efficacy of debentures, but the Company Law Review Group were of the view that they should be retained and their recommendation was accepted by the legislature.

[37.45] The opportunity was taken, however, in the 1999 (No 2) Act to deal with a possible conflict which might arise where a receiver had been appointed within the three day period. Under s 98 of the Principal Act, a receiver appointed under a floating charge must pay preferential creditors (such as the revenue) out of

---

[27] Companies (Amendment) Act 1990, s 5(2).
[28] Companies (Amendment) Act 1990, s 5(3).

assets coming into his hands before paying over any sums due to the holder of the charge. The 1999 (No 2) Act now provides that the court may make an order that this provision in the Principal Act is not to apply where an examiner has already been appointed or, in the opinion of the court, may be appointed and the making of the order would be likely to facilitate the survival of the company as a going concern. Before such an order is made, any preferential creditor of the company must be afforded an opportunity of being heard[29].

[37.46] Where at the time the examiner is appointed, a provisional liquidator has already been appointed, the court may either appoint him or some other person to be the examiner. Again the survival of the company is the criterion which the court must apply in deciding which course to follow and, where the provisional liquidator is not appointed examiner, the court may make the same orders as in relation to a receiver, ie that he ceases to act as such, delivers all books etc and gives full particlars of his dealings to the examiner[30].

[37.47] The examiner must publish notice of his appointment and the date thereof in *Iris Oifigiúil* and two daily newspapers circulating in the district where the registered office or principal company is situated, within 21 days in the case of *Iris Oifigiúil* and three days in the case of the newspapers[31].

Hearing to consider irregularities in the company's affairs

[37.48] We have seen that the report of the independent accountant, now required by the 1999 (No 2) Act to accompany the petition, must include the opinion of the accountant as to whether any deficiency between the assets and liabilities of the company has been satisfactorily accounted for or, if not, whether there is evidence of a substantial disappearance of property that is not so adequately accounted for.

[37.49] The Act also provides that:

> 'where arising out of the presentation to it of the report of the independent accountant or otherwise, it appears to the court that there is evidence of a substantial disappearance of property of the company concerned that is not adequately accounted for, or of other serious irregularities in relation to the company's affairs having occurred, the court shall, as soon as is practicable, hold a hearing to consider that evidence[32]'

---

[29] Companies (Amendment) (No 2) Act 1999, s 17.
[30] Companies (Amendment) Act 1990, s 6(2). As to provisional liquidation, see para **[36.132]** above.
[31] Companies (Amendment) Act 1990, s 12(2).
[32] Companies (Amendment) (No 2) Act 1999, s 21.

[37.50] Where directed by the court so to do, the examiner must prepare a report setting out any matters which he considers will assist the court in considering the evidence concerned at the hearing. The report is to be supplied by him to any person mentioned in it and any interested party who makes a written application to him for the report. The court may direct the omission from the report of specified parts of it, including, in particular, information which would be likely to prejudice the survival of the company as a going concern. The report must also be furnished, in the case of banks and similar institutions, to the Minister or the Central Bank as the case may be.

[37.51] The following persons are entitled to appear to be heard at the hearing:

(1)   the examiner;

(2)   the independent accountant where the hearing is being held because of matters contained in his report;

(3)   the company;

(4)   any interested party;

(5)   any person referred to in the report of the independent accountant or a report prepared for the hearing by the examiner;

(6)   where the company is a bank or similar body, the Minister or the Central Bank, as the case may be.

[37.52] The Act provides that:

'The court may on a hearing under this section, make such order or orders as it deems fit including, where appropriate, an order for the trial of any issue relating to the matter concerned.'

[37.53] While there are no express limitations on the power of court to make such orders as it deems fit, it was presumably envisaged that, where no satisfactory explanation arises during the hearing for the disappearance of the company's property or the other irregularities under investigation, the court could order an issue to be tried as to whether any of the persons concerned in the management of the company had been guilty of reckless or fraudulent trading or had improperly diverted assets of the company for their own or other persons' benefit.

Powers and duties of the examiner

[37.54] Prior to the enactment of the 1999 (No 2) Act, the duty of the examiner was to conduct an examination of the affairs of the company and report the results to the court within a specified period. In the scheme established under the 1999 (No 2) Act, that report is effectively replaced by the report of the independent accountant which must now accompany the petition. Accordingly, the duty of the examiner, once appointed, is now:

'(a) as soon as practicable after he is appointed, [to] formulate proposals for a compromise or scheme of arrangement in relation to the company concerned

(b) without prejudice to any other provision of this Act [to] carry out such other duties as the court may direct him to carry out.[33]'

[37.55] The examiner must report to the court, within 35 days of his appointment or such longer period as the court may allow, as to whether he has been able to formulate any proposals for a compromise or scheme of arrangement. Where he is not in a position to enter into any agreement with the interested parties and any other persons concerned or to formulate proposals for a compromise or scheme of arrangement, he may apply for directions to the court within the same period and the court may make such order as it deems fit, including, if it considers it just and equitable to do so, an order for the winding up of the company.

The court's powers in relation to the approval of compromises or schemes of arrangements are considered in more detail in para **[37.72]** below.

[37.56] Save in one respect, the powers of the examiner are circumscribed by the general scheme of the Act which, as we have seen, is to keep intact the powers of the directors. They are as follows:

(1) the same powers as inspectors appointed by the court enjoy to require the production of documents (including documents relating to bank accounts) and the giving of sworn evidence by the officers of the company[34];

(2) the same powers as auditors enjoy relating to the supplying of information and co-operation by the officers of the company[35];

(3) power to convene, set the agenda for and preside at board meetings of the directors and general meetings of the company and propose resolutions and present reports at such meetings[36];

(4) the right to attend board meetings and general meetings and to be given reasonable notice of their being held[37];

(5) power to apply to the court for the determination of any question arising in the course of his office[38].

---

[33] Companies (Amendment) Act 1990, s 18 as amended by the Companies (Amendment) (No 2) Act 1999, s 22.

[34] Companies (Amendment) Act 1990, s 8. See para **[35.22]** above.

[35] Companies (Amendment) Act 1990, s 7(1). See para **[30.143]** above.

[36] Companies (Amendment) Act 1990, s 7(2).

[37] Companies (Amendment) Act 1990, s 7(3).

[38] Companies (Amendment) Act 1990, s 7(6).

In addition, where he becomes aware of acts, omissions, decisions or contracts by the company, its officers or anyone else which are likely, in his opinion, to be detrimental to the company or any interested party, he is entitled to take any steps which are necessary to 'halt, prevent or rectify' the acts etc in question[39]. It was held by the Supreme Court in *Re Holidair Ltd*[40] that the examiner was entitled, by virtue of this provision, to repudiate contracts entered into by the company prior to his appointment and this included provisions in the debenture requiring the company to apply for the consent of the debenture holder to borrowings by the company.

[37.57] The law has now been changed by the 1999 (No 2) Act which provides that the examiner may not repudiate a contract entered into by the company prior to his appointment. Special provision, however, is made for clauses restraining the company from borrowing or pledging its property without the consent of the debenture holder. Such clauses are not binding if the examiner is of the opinion that the clause, were it to be enforced, would be likely to prejudice the survival of the company as a going concern and he serves notice on the other party to the agreement containing the clause informing him or them of that opinion.

[37.58] The court may, in circumstances set out in s 9 of the 1990 (No 1) Act vest all or any of the directors' powers exclusively in the examiner on his application. The court may only make such an order where it considers it just and equitable to do so, having regard to any of the following considerations:

(1)   the fact that the company's affairs are being conducted, or are likely to be conducted, in a manner which is calculated or likely to prejudice the interests of the company or its creditors as a whole;

(2)   the expediency of curtailing or regulating the directors' powers for the purpose of preserving the assets of the company or of safeguarding the interests of the company or its creditors as a whole;

(3)   a resolution by the company or its directors that such an order should be sought;

(4)   any other matter the court thinks relevant.

Where such an order is made, the court may also order that the examiner is to have the same powers as a liquidator in a compulsory winding up.

[37.59] One consequence of such an order is that the examiner can dispose of any of the company's assets if he considers that this would facilitate the achievement of the objectives for which he was appointed. We have seen that his appointment will generally have the effect of 'freezing' any debenture but,

---

[39] Companies (Amendment) Act 1990, s 7(5).
[40] [1994] 1 ILRM 481.

unless the debenture holder consents, the examiner will be unable to dispose of assets which are subject to a floating charge. To meet this difficulty, s 11 of the 1990 Act enables the court to authorise the examiner to dispose of any such assets as if they were not subject to the security in question. In the case of a floating charge, the holder has the same priority in respect of the proceeds of sale as he had in respect of the charged property. In the case of any other security, the proceeds are to be applied towards discharging the sum secured and, if they are less than the open market value, that deficiency must be made up. There are similar provisions in respect of goods subject to hire purchase agreements, retention of title clauses etc.

[37.60] What is the status of a floating charge if a receiver has been appointed by the debenture holder before the appointment of the examiner? It might have been thought that the crystallisation of the floating charge in such circumstances would have afforded the holder of the floating charge the same security as the holder of a fixed charge during the period of the examinership. However, it was held by the Supreme Court in *Re Holidair Ltd* that the floating charge 'decrystallised' on the appointment of an examiner. Thus, in that case, it was held that a floating charge over book debts which had been converted into a fixed charge 'decrystallised' on the appointment of the examiner and that, accordingly, the examiner was entitled to make use of the book debts during the currency of the examinership.

Compromises and schemes of arrangement

[37.61] After his appointment, the examiner must, as soon as practicable, formulate proposals for a compromise or scheme of arrangement. If he is unable to do so, he must report accordingly to the court, which may then make an order terminating the protection order and, if it considers it just and equitable, winding up the company[41].

[37.62] For the purpose of formulating proposals, the examiner is empowered to convene meetings of members and creditors and may also appoint a committee of creditors. He must then report to the court on the nature of the proposals and the outcome of the meetings and the court may confirm the proposals or not as it thinks proper.

[37.63] A creditors' committee may be appointed by the examiner to assist him in the exercise of his functions (and must be appointed if the court so orders). It consists of no more than five members and must include the holders of the three largest unsecured claims who are willing to serve. The committee must be

---

41 Companies (Amendment) Act 1990, s 18 as amended by the Companies (Amendment) (No 2) Act 1999, s 22.

furnished with a copy of the proposals and may give their opinion of them to the examiner either on their own behalf or on behalf of the creditors or classes of creditors represented on the committee[42].

[37.64] The proposals for a compromise or scheme of arrangement have to specify the classes of members and creditors of the company. They must also indicate the classes whose interests will be 'impaired' by the proposals and those whose interests will not be so impaired[43]. A creditor's interests are 'impaired' within the meaning of these provisions if in effect he gets less than the amount of his claim against the company as a result of the examiner's proposals[44]. The interest of a member is 'impaired' if:

(1)   the nominal value of his shares or of a fixed dividend on the shares is reduced or

(2)   he is deprived of any of his rights as a shareholder or

(3)   his percentage interest in the total issued share capital is reduced or

(4)   he is deprived of his shareholding.

[37.65] The criteria for determining classes of members and creditors will be similar to those employed in schemes of arrangement under s 201 of the Principal Act. As we have seen, members will normally be divided into ordinary and preference shareholders and creditors into preferential, secured and unsecured creditors. But again there may be further categories to be considered.

[37.66] The proposals must provide equal treatment for each person in a particular class, unless the person concerned agrees to less favourable treatment. They must also indicate how they are to be implemented and specify any changes in the management and direction of the company which the examiner considers necessary or desirable for facilitating the survival of the company.

[37.67] The proposals as thus formulated by the examiner are then put to meetings of the different classes. They are deemed to have been accepted by members if a majority of the votes cast at the meeting are in favour. They are deemed to have been accepted by creditors if a majority representing a majority in number and value of the claims represented at the meeting are in favour[45]. So far as preferential creditors are concerned, the largest single such creditor is almost invariably the Revenue Commissioners and the acceptance by that class of a proposal could be inhibited by the legal limitations imposed on the revenue so far as the waiving of tax is concerned. To meet this difficulty, there is

---

42 Companies (Amendment) Act 1990, s 21.
43 Companies (Amendment) Act 1990, s 23(3) and (4).
44 Companies (Amendment) Act 1990, s 23(5).
45 Companies (Amendment) Act 1990, s 23(3) and (4).

provision that a State authority may accept a proposal which 'impairs' their interest, notwithstanding any other enactment[46].

[37.68] The procedure to be followed in relation to meetings of members and creditors is laid down in Ord 75A, r 18 of the Rules of the Superior Court (No 3) 1991. The members and creditors must receive proper notice of their respective meetings. Section 22(2) of the 1990 Act provides that a statement of the assets and liabilities must be attached to each copy of the proposals submitted to a meeting together with a description of the estimated financial outcome of a winding up for each class.

[37.69] Section 23(8) further provides that the notice convening the meetings must be accompanied by a statement explaining the effect of the scheme of arrangement. It must also state any material interests of the directors and the effect on them of the compromise or arrangements insofar as it is different from the effect on the like interest of other persons.

[37.70] A modification of the examiner's proposals may be put to the meeting, but may only be accepted with his consent[47].

[37.71] Where the examiner is formulating proposals for a scheme of arrangement, he is entitled to affirm or repudiate any contract, which is still to any extent unperformed by the company or the other contracting party. There are two qualifications, however: the provision does not apply where the unperformed element is payment and the affirmation or repudiation must be approved by the court. If a person suffers loss or damage as a result of the repudiation of the contract, he ranks as an unsecured creditor for the amount involved which can, if necessary, be determined by the court[48].

[37.72] The examiner must present his report on the proposals to the court within 35 days of his appointment or such longer period, not exceeding 30 days, as the court may allow[49]. After a hearing at which the company, the examiner and any creditor or member whose interests would be impaired by the proposals are entitled to be heard, the court either confirms the proposals (with or without modifications) or refuses to confirm them. The court cannot confirm the proposals unless

    (1)   they have been accepted by at least one class of creditors whose interests would be impaired by their implementation;

---

46 Companies (Amendment) Act 1990, s 23(5).
47 Companies (Amendment) Act 1990, s 23(2).
48 Companies (Amendment) Act 1990, s 20.
49 Companies (Amendment) Act 1990, s 18 as amended by the Companies (Amendment) (No 2) Act 1999, s 22.

(2) (a) they are 'fair and equitable' in relation to any class of members and any class of creditors who have not accepted them and whose interests would be impaired and

(b) they are not unfairly prejudicial to any interested party.

[37.73] The requirement in the 1990 Act that the proposals must also have been accepted by at least one class of members whose interests would be impaired has been removed by the 1999 (No 2) Act, following a recommendation to that effect by the Company Law Review Group.

[37.74] The court is also precluded from confirming the proposals if their sole or primary purpose is the avoidance of tax[50].

[37.75] At the hearing, any member or creditor whose interests would be impaired by implementation of the proposals is entitled to object to their confirmation on any one of a number of specified grounds, ie

(1) that there was some material irregularity at one of the members' or creditors' meetings;

(2) acceptance of the proposals was obtained by some improper means;

(3) the proposals were put forward for some improper purpose;

(4) the proposals unfairly prejudice the interests of the objector[51].

A person cannot, however, object if he has in fact voted for acceptance of the proposal, except on the ground that the acceptance was obtained by improper means or that, after the vote, he became aware that they were being put forward for an improper purpose[52]. If the court upholds the objection, it can make such order as it deems fit, including an order setting aside the decision of any of the meetings and order a meeting to be reconvened[53].

[37.76] The effect of the proposals on guarantees given to the creditors of the company must be carefully noted. Such personal guarantees by directors are frequently insisted on by financial institutions as a condition of their affording credit to the company. Clearly, a creditor asked to agree to a reduction of the company's indebtedness to him as part of a scheme of arrangement may wish to retain his right to enforce his guarantee against the guarantor for the full amount of his debt. Doubts as to whether the right of the creditor to enforce the guarantee may be affected by his agreeing to a compromise or a scheme of arrangement have now been removed by the 1999 (No 2) Act which provides that the liability of the guarantor is not to be affected by the fact that the debt is

---

50 Companies (Amendment) Act 1990, s 23(4).
51 Companies (Amendment) Act 1990, s 25(1).
52 Companies (Amendment) Act 1990, s 25(2).
53 Companies (Amendment) Act 1990, s 25(3).

the subject of a compromise or a scheme of arrangement which has taken effect[54].

[37.77] The 1999 (No 2) Act, also provides, however, that where the creditor proposes to enforce his rights under the guarantee, he may make an offer in writing to the guarantor to transfer to him his right to vote on the proposals. If he does so, and the guarantor accepts the offer, the guarantor is then entitled to exercise the creditor's right to vote at the relevant meeting. If the creditor does not make such an offer, he cannot subsequently enforce the guarantee against the guarantor. The making of such an offer, does not, however, prevent the creditor from objecting to the proposals at the subsequent court hearing[55].

[37.78] The criteria which should be applied by the court when it is considering whether a compromise or scheme of arrangement should be upheld were considered by Costello J, in *Re Wogan's (Drogheda) Ltd (No 2)*[56]. In that case, a secured creditor and a preferential creditor (the Revenue Commissioners) objected to a scheme under which a substantial portion of the debts owing to them were being written off. A majority in number and value of the ordinary creditors, however, who were being paid only 10% of the sums due to them under the scheme, voted to accept the scheme.

The learned High Court Judge refused to approve of the scheme on three grounds. First, he took the view that there had been an abuse of the court's process, the debt due to the Revenue Commissioners having been deliberately understated at the time of the presentation of the petition. (Section 13 of the 1999 (No 2) Act has now given express statutory emphasis to the requirement as to utmost good faith in the presentation of the petition.) Secondly, the implementation of the scheme was dependent on the granting of tax clearance certificates by the Revenue Commissioners: without such certificates, an outside investor, an investment by whom was essential to the success of the scheme, was not prepared to go ahead. The Revenue Commissioners declined to grant such certificates and Costello J held their refusal was reasonable and fatal to the viability of the scheme. Thirdly, there were certain defects in the scheme - notably the fact that the proposed investor could unilaterally withdraw from the scheme at any time - which made it uncertain whether it could in fact ever proceed, even if it were upheld.

[37.79] It is also of interest that the court in that case attached significance to the fact that the scheme did not deal in any way with the personal guarantees which

---

[54] Companies (Amendment) Act 1990, s 25A as inserted by the Companies (Amendment) (No 2) Act 1999, s 25.

[55] Companies (Amendment) Act 1990, s 25A as inserted by the Companies (Amendment) (No 2) Act 1999, s 25.

[56] (Unreported, 7 May 1992).

had been entered into by the directors. Under the doctrine of subrogation the directors could recover the amount they were required to pay on foot of the guarantees from the company itself, and Costello J was of the view that this was a fact which should have been, but was not, taken into account when the scheme was being prepared.

[37.80] If the modifications proposed to be made to a scheme already considered by the shareholders and creditors were to alter it in a fundamental manner, it would be necessary for further meetings to be held to enable them to consider the altered scheme. This was held by Hamilton P in *Re Goodman International*[57]. In that case, the petitioners were a large group of companies who controlled a significant part of the meat processing industry. A protection order was made when the group was in serious financial difficulties. (The 1990 (No 1) Act was enacted because of the crises in the industry resulting from the possible collapse of the group.) A number of banks who were secured creditors agreed to the examiner's proposals for the restructuring of the group's capital and borrowing structures and the disposal of some of the assets. Some modifications to the scheme were, however, suggested by a number of the banks. The majority of the creditors were prepared to accept the modified scheme and it was confirmed by Hamilton P, who also concluded that it was not necessary to adjourn the matter to enable further meetings to be held. He had this to say on the nature of the court's jurisdiction:

'This section appears to me to give absolute discretion to the Court in this regard. It is of course a discretion that must be exercised judicially and if the modifications suggested were to fundamentally alter the proposals which had been considered by the members and creditors of (the company), then a Court would be slow to modify the scheme without having the modifications considered by the members and creditors. I am however satisfied that the modifications considered to the scheme do not fundamentally alter the proposals'.

[37.81] If the court confirms the proposals, they are binding on everyone concerned: ie all the members or classes of members affected, all the creditors or classes of creditors affected and the company. They are also binding on anyone who is liable for the debts of the company, eg a director who is also a guarantor[58]. The court's order comes into effect on the date fixed by the order[59]. It should be noted that, while the examiner must present his proposals to the court not later than 70 days from the date of his appointment, the court may

---

[57] (Unreported, 28 January 1991).

[58] Companies (Amendment) Act 1990, s 24(5) and (6).

[59] Companies (Amendment) Act 1990, s 29(9).

defer its order confirming or refusing to confirm the proposals for such period as it thinks necessary and for that purpose may extend the protection period[60].

[37.82] The court has power to order the revocation of any confirmation on an application by the company or any interested party within 180 days after the confirmation, if the court is satisfied that it was obtained by fraud[61].

[37.83] Where the examiner is unable to secure the necessary agreement to his proposals or where the court refuses to confirm the proposals, an order for the winding up of the company can be made, if the court considers it just and equitable so to order[62]. In most cases, such a winding up will be the inevitable sequel to an abortive proposal for a scheme of arrangement.

Fraudulent or reckless trading

[37.84] The court has precisely the same powers, in the case of a company under protection, of imposing liability on the officers of the company or any other person knowingly involved where the company was guilty of fraudulent or reckless trading as the court possesses in the case of a winding up. There are also the same criminal consequences for the persons concerned[63].

Cessation of protection of company

[37.85] The company ceases to be under the protection of the court when a scheme of arrangement becomes effective or at an earlier date if the court so orders. The appointment of the examiner also terminates as from that date[64].

---

[60] Companies (Amendment) Act 1990, s 18(4).
[61] Companies (Amendment) Act 1990, s 27.
[62] Companies (Amendment) Act 1990, s 24(1).
[63] See Ch 33 above
[64] Companies (Amendment) Act 1990, s 26.

Chapter 38

Voluntary Winding up

[38.01] A company can be wound up voluntarily in the following circumstances:

(1) if the company resolves by special resolution that it should be wound up voluntarily;

(2) if the company in general meeting resolves that it cannot by reason of its liabilities continue its business and that it be wound up voluntarily;

(3) when the period, if any, fixed for the duration of the company by the articles expires, or the event, if any, occurs on the occurrence of which the articles provides that the company is to be dissolved, and the company in general meeting has passed a resolution that it be wound up voluntarily[1].

Of these, (1) and (2) are by far the most common. It should be noted that where the company is wound up voluntarily because of its inability to stay in business, the necessary resolution can be passed with a simple majority and the same applies to a winding up on the rare occasions when (3) is invoked. In any other case a three-fourths majority is required.

[38.02] There are two types of voluntary winding up: members' and creditors'. In a members' winding up, certain important matters (notably the appointment of a liquidator) remain under the control of the company. In a creditors', this control is transferred to the creditors or a committee representing them.

Commencement of a voluntary winding up

[38.03] A voluntary winding up is always begun by a resolution of the company, but as we have seen, the form of the resolution will depend on the circumstances which give rise to the winding up. The company must give notice of the passing of the resolution by advertisement in *Iris Oifigiúil* within 14 days from its being passed. If this is not done, the company and every officer in default are liable to a fine not exceeding £125. The liquidator is deemed to be an officer of the company for this purpose[2].

---

[1] Companies Act 1963, s 251.

[2] Companies Act 1963, s 252 as amended by the Companies (Amendment) Act 1982, s 15.

Declaration of solvency

[38.04] Before the resolution for a voluntary winding up is passed, the directors of the company (or where there are more than two of them, a majority of them), may make a declaration as to the solvency of the company at a meeting of the directors[3]. The importance of this declaration is that it determines whether the winding up is a members' or a creditors' winding up. If no declaration is made, the winding up proceeds as a creditors' winding up. As we shall see, there is also a procedure available to creditors under which they can apply to the court for an order that the winding up continue as a creditors' winding up, although a declaration of solvency has been made.

[38.05] Before the 1990 Act, the declaration by the directors alone was sufficient. An amendment effected by s 128 requires it to contain in addition confirmation by a suitably qualified independent person that the company is solvent. The declaration by the directors must be to the effect that, having inquired fully into the affairs of the company, they have formed the opinion that the company will be able to pay its debts within a specified period, which must be not more than 12 months from the commencement of the winding up. It must also contain a statement of the company's assets and liabilities as at the latest practicable date before the making of the declaration and in any event not more than three months before the making of the declaration. The report attached to it by the independent expert must state whether, in his opinion and according to the explanation given to him, the directors' opinion and the statement of assets and liabilities are reasonable. The expert must be a person qualified to act as auditor of the company and the statement must include a statement by him that he has given, and not withdrawn, his consent to the issue of the declaration with his report attached.

[38.06] A creditor may apply to the court, where a declaration is made, for an order that the winding up continue as a creditors' winding up. Such an application must be made within 28 days from the advertising of the resolution for winding up and the creditors applying and those creditors supporting him or them must represent at least one-fifth in number or value of all the creditors[4]. The court may make the order if it is of opinion that it is unlikely that the company will be able to pay its debts within the period specified in the declaration of solvency.

[38.07] The declaration is of no effect unless it is made within the 28 days immediately preceding the passing of the resolution and is delivered to the Registrar for registration not later than the delivery of a printed copy of the

---

[3] Companies Act 1963, s 256 as substituted by the Companies Act 1990, s 128.
[4] Companies Act 1963, s 256(3).

resolution to the Registrar as required by s 143 of the Principal Act. (Such a copy must be delivered not later than 15 days after the passing of the resolution.)

[38.08] Where a declaration is made by the directors and it is subsequently proved to the satisfaction of the court that the company is unable to pay its debts, the courts may declare any director who joined in the declaration to be personally responsible without limitation of liability for all or any part of the company's debts and liabilities. It may make such an order where it thinks proper to do so and where the director in question had no reasonable grounds for his opinion that the company would be able to pay its debts within the specified period[5]. (It would seem that here as elsewhere the legislature is contemplating an objective test[6].) Where the company's debts have not been paid within the specified period, it is to be presumed, until the contrary is proved, that the director did not have reasonable grounds for his opinion.

[38.09] This provision replaced one in the Principal Act under which a director could be fined or imprisoned for making a declaration in such circumstances. It would seem that there were few (if any) prosecutions under that provision, although there must have been many dubious declarations filed during the 25 years of its existence and the legislature may well be justified in its belief that the prospect of personal liability for its debts will be more effective in ensuring that such declarations are made in a responsible manner.

[38.10] The declaration of solvency does not affect the right of the creditors of the company to have it compulsorily wound up if in fact they can prove that it is insolvent.

The creditors' meeting

[38.11] In the case of a creditors' winding up, the company is obliged by the Acts to summon a meeting of the creditors[7]. They must also publish an advertisement giving notice of it at least once in two daily newspapers circulating in the district where the registered office or principal place of business of the company is situated. The director of the company must cause a full statement of the position of the company's affairs, a list of its creditors and the estimated amount of their claims to be laid before the meeting. They must also appoint one of their number to preside at the meeting. A maximum fine of £500 can be imposed in the event of the company or any of its directors failing to comply with these requirements[8].

---

5   Companies Act 1963, s 256(8) and (9).
6   See para **[33.14]** above.
7   Companies Act 1963, s 266(1).
8   Companies Act 1963, s 266(6) as amended by the Companies (Amendment) Act 1982, s 15.

[38.12] Should the meeting of the company at which the resolution for voluntary winding up is dealt with be adjourned and the resolution be passed at the adjourned meeting, any resolution passed at the meeting of the creditors is to have effect as if it were passed immediately after the passing of the winding up resolution[9].

Appointment of a liquidator in a creditors' winding up

[38.13] At the creditors' meeting, the creditors and the company may each nominate a person to be liquidator of the company. If different persons are appointed, the creditors' nominee is to be the liquidator. If no person is nominated by the creditors, the company may appoint the liquidator. There is a provision that in the event of different persons being nominated as liquidators, any director, member or creditor of the company may within 14 days after the creditors' nomination apply to the court for an order directing that the company's nominee be liquidator instead of or jointly with the creditors' nominee or an order appointing some person other than the creditors' nominee to be liquidator[10].

[38.14] Under s 301A of the Principal Act, inserted by s 147 of the 1990 Act, any creditor at such a meeting, who has a connection with the proposed liquidator must make the fact known to the chairman of the meeting who must in turn disclose it to the meeting. The chairman must similarly inform the meeting of any connection he may have with the proposed liquidator. A person has such a connection where he is a parent, spouse, brother, sister or child of the proposed liquidator or is a partner of, or employed by, him. Any person who fails to comply with this section is liable to a fine not exceeding £1,000 and the court may take the non-compliance into account where it is considering an application for the appointment or removal of a liquidator.

[38.15] On the appointment of a liquidator, all the powers of the directors cease, except so far as the creditors, or their committee of inspection, sanction their continuance[11].

Consent of liquidator

[38.16] The appointment of a liquidator is of no effect unless the person nominated has prior to his nomination given his consent in writing to his appointment. Unless the liquidator or his representative is present at the meeting where he is appointed, the chairman of the meeting must within seven days

---

9 Companies Act 1963, s 226(5).
10 Companies Act 1963, s 267(2).
11 Companies Act 1963, s 269(3).

notify him in writing of his appointment. A person who fails to comply with this requirement is liable to a fine not exceeding £1,000[12].

The committee of inspection

[38.17] The creditors in a creditors' winding up are given important powers which enable them to supervise the actual conduct of the liquidation. These are exercised through a body called 'the committee of inspection'. The committee is appointed by the creditors at the creditors' meeting or at a subsequent meeting and consists of not more than five members. The company may, if it wishes, appoint three additional members to the committee at the meeting when the winding-up resolution is passed or at any time subsequently in general meeting. But the creditors have a power of veto over any such appointment by the company and, if they so resolve, the persons thus appointed are disqualified from acting, unless the court otherwise directs. The court has jurisdiction to appoint other persons instead of those disqualified by the creditors' resolution. The number of members on the committee cannot in any event exceed eight[13].

Remuneration of liquidator in creditors' winding up

[38.18] The committee of inspection fixes the remuneration to be paid to the liquidator in a creditors' winding up. If there is no committee, the creditors do so. Any creditor or contributory who thinks the remuneration is excessive can apply to the court within 28 days after it has been fixed to have it fixed by the court[14].

Appointment of a liquidator in a members' voluntary winding up

[38.19] In a members' voluntary winding up, the company in general meeting appoints one or more liquidators and can fix his or their remuneration. On the appointment all the powers of the directors cease, except so far as the company in general meeting or the liquidator sanctions their continuance[15]. The passing of the special resolution that the company be wound up voluntarily is an essential preliminary to the appointing of the liquidator.

[38.20] The liquidator can be appointed at the same meeting at which the winding-up resolution is passed and this is the usual practice. It is not strictly necessary that the notice convening the meeting should expressly refer to the appointment of the liquidator, but it is obviously preferable that it should. In

---

12 Companies Act 1963, s 276A as inserted by the Companies Act 1990, s 133.
13 Companies Act 1963, s 268.
14 Companies Act 1963, s 269.
15 Companies Act 1963, s 258(2).

practice, the notice usually states that a named person will be proposed at the meeting as liquidator. If this resolution is not passed, the meeting can appoint another person. If there is any doubt as to the validity of the appointment, the court will usually appoint the person whom the meeting intended to appoint.

Powers and duties of the liquidators in a voluntary winding up

[38.21] The liquidator in a voluntary winding up may exercise all or any of the powers vested in an official liquidator in a compulsory winding up. Some of these, however, may only be exercised with the sanction of a special resolution of the company (in the case of a members' winding up) or the court, committee of inspection or creditors (in the case of a creditors' winding up). They are the powers to:

(1) pay any class of creditors in full;

(2) make compromises or arrangements with creditors or persons claiming to be creditors or having, or alleging themselves to have, claims against the company;

(3) compromise calls, liabilities to calls and debts and claims between the company and contributories or other debtors or possible debtors[16].

If there is no committee of inspection in the case of a creditors' winding up, the powers may be exercised with the sanction of the court or the creditors.

[38.22] All the other powers conferred on the liquidator in a winding up by the court can be exercised by the liquidator in a voluntary winding up without sanction. These include the power:

(1) to bring or defend actions in the name of and on behalf of the company;

(2) to carry on the business of the company so far as may be necessary for its beneficial winding up;

(3) to sell the property of the company;

(4) to execute deeds and other documents in the company's name and where necessary use its seal;

(5) to draw cheques etc in the company's name and on its behalf;

(6) to borrow money on the security of the company's assets;

(7) to do anything else that may be necessary for winding up the company[17].

---

[16] Companies Act 1963, s 276(1).
[17] Companies Act 1963, s 276(1).

[38.23] These relatively extensive powers of the liquidator could be exercised by the liquidator of an insolvent company before the calling of a creditors' meeting, which, as we have seen, can then replace the liquidator with one of their choice. To avoid the danger of a compliant nominee of the company acting to the detriment of the creditors, the 1990 Act provides that the powers can only be exercised with the sanction of the court during this period[18]. The liquidator may, however, without leave:

(1)   take into his custody or control all the company's property;

(2)   dispose of perishable goods and other goods the value of which is likely to diminish if they are not disposed of immediately;

(3)   do anything else which may be necessary to protect the company's assets.

[38.24] The liquidator must also attend the creditors' meeting and report to it on the manner in which he has exercised his powers. He must also apply to the court for directions where the company fails to call a creditors' meeting or the directors fail to lay a statement of affairs before the meeting or appoint one of their number to preside at the meeting.

[38.25] Where the liquidator fails to comply with any of these requirements of the 1990 Act he is guilty of an offence and liable on summary conviction to a fine not exceeding £1,000 or imprisonment for a term not exceeding 12 months or both and on indictment to a fine not exceeding £10,000 or imprisonment for a term not exceeding three years or both.

[38.26] It is in theory possible to appoint more than one liquidator, but this is very rarely done nowadays. Where more than one is appointed, the liquidators' powers may be exercised by such one or more of them as may be determined at the time of their appointment, or in default of such determination, by any number not less than two[19]. They cannot make a general delegation of their powers to one of their number, although they may delegate the execution of a particular document. When one of them dies, the survivor cannot act alone: a new liquidator must be appointed.

[38.27] The liquidator's duty, as in a compulsory winding up, is to get in the assets of the company, pay the creditors and adjust the rights of the contributories. He is an officer of the company.

---

[18] Companies Act 1990, s 131.
[19] Companies Act 1963, s 276(3).

Duty of liquidator where company may be insolvent

[38.28] Where a members' voluntary winding up is in progress and the liquidator at any time thinks that the company will be unable to pay its debts in full within the period specified in the declaration of solvency, he is under a statutory duty to summon a meeting of creditors to explain the position fully to them. The requirements of the Principal Act in this context were sparse and were elaborated in the 1990 Act[20].

[38.29] Where the liquidator is of this view, he must summon a meeting of the creditors for a day not later than 14 days from the day on which he forms his opinion. The creditors must be given not less than seven days' notice by post and the holding of the meeting must also be advertised in *Iris Oifigiúil* and two daily newspapers circulating in the locality where the company's principal place of business is situated at least ten days before the meeting. The creditors must also be given by the liquidator, free of charge, prior to the meeting such information as they may reasonably require as to the company's affairs.

[38.30] The liquidator must preside at the meeting and lay before it a statement in the prescribed form as to the affairs of the company, including its assets and liabilities, a list of the outstanding creditors and the estimated amount of their claims. From the day on which the meeting is held, the winding up becomes a creditors' winding up and, accordingly, the Acts take effect as though the declaration as to solvency had not been made.

[38.31] If the liquidator fails to summon the meeting, give the notices and information or publish the advertisements as required by these provisions, he is guilty of an offence and liable on summary conviction to a fine not exceeding £1,000 and on indictment to a fine not exceeding £10,000.

Meetings of the company and creditors

[38.32] The liquidator may summon general meetings of the company for the purpose of obtaining its sanction to the exercise of the powers which require such sanction. He may also summon a meeting for any other purpose as he thinks fit[21].

[38.33] In the case of a members' winding up, he must summon such a meeting at the end of the first year from the commencement of the winding up and at the end of each succeeding year, or at the first convenient date within three months from the end of the year. He must lay before the meeting an account of his acts and dealings and of the conduct of the winding up during the preceding year and

---

[20] Companies Act 1963, s 261 as substituted by the Companies Act 1990, s 129.
[21] Companies Act 1963, s 276(1).

must within seven days after the meeting send a copy of his account to the Registrar. He is liable to a fine not exceeding £250 if he fails to comply with these requirements[22]. There is a similar requirement to call a meeting of the company and of the creditors in the case of a creditors' winding up and to lay before them a similar account[23].

Remuneration of the liquidator

[38.34] In a members' voluntary winding up, the company in general meeting may fix the remuneration to be paid to the liquidator[24]. As has already been noted, in a creditors' winding up, it is determined by the committee of inspection, or, if there is no such committee, by the creditors[25].

If the remuneration is not so fixed, it may be fixed by the court, each case being considered with regard to its particular facts[26].

[38.35] Where the winding up resolution is set aside as invalid and the company is afterwards ordered to be wound up, the liquidator in the voluntary winding up is not entitled to be paid anything for his services as such. He is, however, entitled to reasonable remuneration for any work done by him which has been useful to the company for business purposes unconnected with the liquidation or which has been used by the official liquidator with full knowledge of the facts[27].

Applications to the court

[38.36] The liquidator may apply to the court under s 280 for the determination of any question arising during the course of the winding up. He may also ask the court to exercise in relation to the enforcing of calls or any other matter all or any of the powers which might be exercised by the court if the company were being wound up by the court. Such applications may also be made by any creditor or contributory of the company. The court may accede wholly or partially to the application, if satisfied that the determination of the question or the exercise of the power will be 'just and beneficial'[28].

[38.37] This power, like the corresponding power conferred on receivers by s 316, is very useful and liquidators should not hesitate to make use of it if they have any serious doubts as to how to proceed. It has been held in England that

---

22 Companies Act 1963, s 262 as amended by the Companies (Amendment) Act 1982, s 15.
23 Companies Act 1963, s 272 as amended by the Companies (Amendment) Act 1982, s 15.
24 Companies Act 1963, s 258.
25 Para **[38.18]** above.
26 *Re Amalgamated Syndicates Ltd* [1901] 2 Ch 181.
27 *Re Allison, Johnston & Foster Ltd, ex p Birkenshaw* [1904] 2 KB 327.
28 Companies Act 1963, s 280(2).

the powers conferred by the corresponding section of the 1948 Act should be liberally construed[29]. On an application under the section the court may, among other things, restrain proceedings being brought against the company. Unlike an order for the winding up of the company by the court, a voluntary winding up does not automatically prevent such proceedings being taken. The usual course is to stay the proceedings.

[38.38] An application for the examination of directors or other persons either in private or public may also be made under the section[30].

Such an application was made in *Re Comet Food Machinery Co Ltd (in liquidation)*[31]. It was, however, made by a creditor and not by the liquidator. The creditor suspected that the owners of the company had diverted assets to another company and had paid off the trade creditors of the former with a view to frustrating the execution by the creditor of any judgment it might recover in proceedings instituted by it against the company in liquidation. The application was granted by the High Court and the decision was upheld on appeal in the Supreme Court. It had been held in England in *Re Embassy Art Products*[32] that a creditor, in such circumstances, would have to demonstrate that the examination would probably result in some benefit accruing to him. The court was of the view in *Comet* that this criterion had been met, since the examination might lay the ground for an application pursuant to s 139 of the 1990 Act for the return to the liquidator of assets improperly transferred by the company.

[38.39] The liquidator may also find it necessary to apply to the court under this section in relation to calls. As we have seen, in the case of a compulsory winding up, the list of contributories and the amounts which they are required to pay are settled by the Examiner[33]. In the case of a voluntary winding up, the liquidator may settle the list himself, applying the same principles, ie distinguishing between present and past contributories and having recourse to the past contributories only when the liability of the present has been exhausted. If he is in any doubt about the amount which should be called up or the liability of any member he should apply to the court.

[38.40] The liquidator may also find it advisable to apply to the court for a direction as to whether he should carry on the business of the company. He is perfectly entitled, however, to carry on the business without the sanction of the court and his decision will not be capable of challenge if it has been arrived at in

---

[29] *Palmer's Company Law* (25th edn), Vol 3, 15.127.
[30] See para **[36.171]** above.
[31] [1999] 1 IR 485.
[32] [1988] BCLC 1.
[33] See para **[36.112]** above.

good faith and having obtained any advice which he might reasonably be expected to seek[34].

[38.41] The court may also make an order under the section annulling the resolution to wind up or staying all proceedings in the winding up[35]. This may happen, for example, where the company has come to an arrangement with its creditors. Where such an order is made, an office copy of it must be sent forthwith by the company to the Registrar for registration.

Possession of books and assets and sales by liquidator

[38.42] The liquidator is entitled upon his appointment to obtain possession of the books and records of the company and of all its assets. He should enforce this right without delay, and in the case of choses in action, ie things which can only be recovered by action and not by obtaining possession, such as book debts, he should give notice at once to the persons concerned, such as the debtors, of his appointment. If he encounters any difficulty, he should apply to the court without delay.

[38.43] In the case of books and other records and documents, the person in whose possession they are may claim a lien, ie a right to retain possession of them until he has been paid for services rendered to the company. This may arise, for example, in the case of a solicitor, and the liquidator will usually agree to pay the amount of the costs - subject to the bill being taxed, if necessary - out of the assets which come into his hands.

[38.44] The liquidator may sell all or any of the assets of the company without the sanction of the court. He should, of course, where appropriate obtain expert advice and valuations and this should always be done in the case of real or leasehold property. It is also normal to fix a reserve price in the case of such sales. The liquidator has power to execute any contracts, conveyances, etc in the name of the company.

Removal of liquidator

[38.45] The court has power under s 277 to remove a liquidator on cause shown and appoint another in his stead. The most usual ground for such an application is the possibility of a conflict of interest[36] but any misconduct on the liquidator's part will also, of course, justify the making of such an order.

---

34 *Re Great Eastern Electric Co Ltd* [1941] Ch 241.
35 Cf *Walsh v Registrar of Companies* (unreported, 26 November 1987) (Carroll J).
36 Eg *Re Charterland Goldfields Ltd* (1909) 26 TLR 132.

Costs

[38.46] Section 281 provides that all costs, charges and expenses properly incurred in the winding up, including the remuneration of the liquidator, are to be payable out of the assets of the company in priority to all other claims[37]. Solicitors frequently require payments on account of their costs as liquidation proceeds: where this is done, the liquidator should obtain from the solicitor an undertaking to refund any amount which has been paid by the liquidator but disallowed on taxation.

The costs of the liquidator have no priority over the claims of secured creditors. He will, however, be entitled to be paid any costs incurred by him in realising or preserving the security[38].

Final meeting and dissolution

[38.47] As soon as the affairs of the company are fully wound up, the liquidator must make up an account of the winding up and call a general meeting of the company and (in the case of a creditors' winding up) a meeting of the creditors for the purpose of laying the account before the meetings and giving any explanation of it which may be necessary. The account must show how the winding up has been conducted[39].

[38.48] The meeting must be called by advertisement in two daily newspapers circulating in the district where the registered office is situated. It must specify the time, place and object of the meeting and must be published at least 28 days before the meeting. The liquidator must send a copy of the account to the Registrar within a week from the date of the meetings - or where they are not held on the same date, from the date of the later meeting - together with a return to him of the holding of the meetings and of their dates. If no quorum was present, it is sufficient to state that fact. The Registrar must register the accounts and return on receipt of them, and on the expiration of three months from their registration the company is deemed to be dissolved.

[38.49] The court may on the application of the liquidator or any other person who appears to the court to be interested make an order deferring the date at which the dissolution is to take effect until such time as the court thinks fit. The person who obtains such an order must send it to the Registrar for registration

---

[37] It was held by the Supreme Court (*Burns v Hearne* (unreported, 25 July 1988), SC) that the charges included a liability to tax an interest on money placed on deposit by the liquidator, in contrast to the position under a compulsory winding up: see para **[36.134]** above.

[38] *Re Regent's Canal Ironworks Co, ex p Grissell* (1875) 3 Ch D 411.

[39] Companies Act 1963, ss 263 (members' winding up) and 273 (creditors' winding up) as amended by the Companies (Amendment) Act 1982, s 15.

within 14 days from its being made, and if he fails to do so is liable to a fine not exceeding £50.

[**38.50**] If the liquidator fails to call the general meeting of the company or meeting of creditors he is liable to a fine not exceeding £250.

[**38.51**] As in the case of a winding up by the court, the dissolution may within two years be declared to have been void[40].

Winding up under supervision

[**38.52**] The 1908 Act provided a procedure for the winding up of companies 'subject to the supervision of the court'. This enabled a voluntary winding up to continue, but under the court's supervision. An order for winding up under supervision had the same effect as a compulsory winding up order in relation to proceedings against the company: they were automatically stayed by the order. It was, however, rarely invoked in practice and both Cox and Jenkins recommended its abolition, a recommendation which was implemented by the Principal Act.

---

[40] Companies Act 1963, s 310. See para [**36.179**] above.

Index